A TEXTBOOK ON
CONTRACT

A TEXTBOOK ON

CONTRACT

Third Edition

T. Antony Downes

BLACKSTONE
PRESS LIMITED

This edition published in Great Britain 1993 by Blackstone Press Limited, 9–15 Aldine Street, London W12 8AW. Telephone 081–740 1173

© T Antony Downes, 1987

ISBN: 1 85431 285 5

First edition 1987
Second edition 1991
Third edition 1993

Typeset by Kerrypress Ltd, Luton
Printed by Ashford Colour Press, Gosport, Hampshire

Contents

For my mother

Preface

This new edition of *Textbook on Contract* retains the aims pursued in earlier editions: to make clear and accurate statements of the law, and to confront the major issues of contract law today, in a way which is comprehensible to those with no previous training in law. In so doing, it seeks to serve the needs of first-year law undergraduates, and those studying contract law as a single course in some other discipline. To that end, this edition retains the first part dealing briefly with the English legal system, including the impact of EC law. In this edition the substance of the law of contract indicates an increasing need to be aware of this impact.

It is a little under two years since I had to draft the Preface for the previous edition. That a new edition should already be required is gratifying if a little demanding (since those who assess 'research' in universities place no value on the writing of student texts, such writing must be accomplished without diminishing the research effort!). There have been fewer significant changes to be taken into account than last time, although it is quite surprising just how much there has been. My firm resolve always to throw out as much old material as there was new material to incorporate failed me at the first test, so that this edition has again grown. It had been my intention to state the law as of 1 April 1993, but it seemed important to relax that deadline in order to incorporate the final text of the Directive on unfair terms in consumer contracts, and at the very last minute it was possible to take account of the decision of the House of Lords in *Tinsley* v *Milligan*. There are no major revisions of the structure of the book this time; but it may be that the significance of the unfair contract terms Directive will be such that the next edition will have to be more substantially revised.

There are many who must be thanked for their various contributions to the writing of this book. I should like to thank all my colleagues at Reading, especially Lizzie Cooke, Jennifer James and Chris Newdick, who have patiently endured my wilder flights of fancy and brought them down to earth. I must also thank Robin Widdison at Durham, who continues to provide enormous support, and all others involved in the Law Courseware Consortium Contract Team. I should like to thank the many students who have contributed to the constant process of refining my thinking about contract, often by asking perverse questions, and refusing to accept established ideas which do not stand up to close examination. As always, the staff of Blackstone Press have been efficient, helpful and caring; on this occasion it is surely appropriate to single out Jonathan

Harris to thank him for his support over several years, and to wish him well for the future.

As always, I must thank my wife Barbara, and children Thomas and Sophie; their support outweighs all other, and their patient tolerance of my absences in the study cannot properly be compensated by simple words of gratitude.

I have dedicated this book to my mother — a small return on a large investment.

T. Antony Downes
Reading
July 1993

Table of Cases

Table of Statutes

PART I LEGAL METHOD

ONE

The legal structure

1.1 INTRODUCTION

Part I of this book is devoted to an explanation of the bare essentials of legal method. It is intended that a student taking a single course in the law of contract should have at his or her disposal an account of the workings of the legal system necessary to an understanding of the substance of the book in Parts II and III. To this end, the account concentrates on those parts of the law which operate to facilitate the activities of private individuals and to remedy grievances arising therefrom. Moreover, where possible examples have been drawn from the body of the law of contract. Nevertheless, it must be accepted that such a short account omits much detail, and much which is essential to a rounded understanding of the whole of the English legal system. Students seeking such an understanding must refer to one of the large number of specialist texts (e.g. T. Ingman, *The English Legal Process*, 4th edition, Blackstone Press, 1992).

It has been assumed in preparing this account of the English legal system that readers will have a basic knowledge of the British constitutional framework. There are three organs of government: Parliament, the executive (i.e. the Prime Minister and other Ministers), and the courts. We shall be most concerned with the workings of the courts. It is important, however, always to bear in mind that the senior organ of government is Parliament. Acts of Parliament are the highest domestic source of law, and the courts cannot disregard them. The several incidents of this superiority are usually summarised by reference to the doctrine of the sovereignty of Parliament (*2.2.2*).

1.2 TRADITIONAL CLASSIFICATIONS OF LAW

This section considers some important categories and distinctions in English law. While the relevance of these distinctions and the labels used to describe them may seem far from clear at this stage, they represent an unspoken foundation for the way we treat law. Each label is a shorthand description of a set of values and attitudes relevant to the type of law in question, and reference to the label allows lawyers to communicate without needing to rehearse every time the background against which they assume they are operating.

1.2.1 Three meanings of 'common law'

1.2.1.1 Historical: common law and equity After the Norman conquest of England local laws gave way to a general law of the country, which became known as the common law. The king's courts became the most important forum for the resolution of disputes between citizens. An action could only be brought in these courts by obtaining (purchasing) a writ. Over time the forms of such writs became fixed, and only Parliament could approve a new type of writ designed to meet a claim which could not be accommodated within the existing writs and forms of action. This rigidity in the legal system was often the cause of hardship to individual litigants, and the practice grew of petitioning the king for justice in the individual case. The petitions were dealt with by the chancellor, who in this period was a man of the church and who was regarded as the 'conscience' of the king. In due course a formal procedure for such petitions evolved, culminating in a Court of Chancery, presided over by the Lord Chancellor, applying a system of rules known as 'equity' rather than the common law of the ordinary courts.

Although the Court of Chancery was effective in remedying injustices, the existence of parallel jurisdictions brought problems and injustices of its own. Chancery developed procedures separate from, but at least as complex as, those of the common law courts. A litigant had to be sure of the classification of the rule he sought to have applied, in order to commence his action in the right court. The equity of the Chancery Court became a set of rules almost as precise as those of the common law. In the case of conflict between the two systems, the rules of equity prevailed. Parliament sought to put an end to these divisions with the Judicature Acts 1873–1875, which established a unified system of courts which were charged with applying both the common law and equity.

To the non-lawyer 'equity' is probably synonymous with the idea of natural justice. Although that was the origin of the Chancery jurisdiction, it has long since disappeared from the rules of equity. The rules of equity are just as capable today as those of the common law of producing resolutions of disputes which may be viewed as just or unjust. Indeed, since the two types of rules are now applied by the same courts, there is little significance left in the distinction. Nevertheless, in two respects it has left a legacy which still has an impact on today's courts. In the first place, while common law rules are available to plaintiffs as of right, equitable remedies are discretionary in the sense that they are subject to some general conditions of availability. For example, there is no absolute right to specific performance of a contract (see *12.2.2.3*). Secondly, the existence of parallel systems of rules, the one based on formal procedures, the other based originally on the idea of substantial justice, has allowed some judges to invoke the tension between the two systems as a source of judicial creativity in developing the law to meet new situations. For example, Lord Denning has used this device in relation to the enforceability of promises (see *6.4.3*) and in relation to contracts affected by mistake (see *7.3.3*).

1.2.1.2   Common law and statute   In another sense, the common law is the law applied by the courts developed through the system of precedent (see *2.1.2 et seq*) without reference to legislation passed by Parliament. Although statute has become the most prolific source of law in this country, this has only relatively recently been the case. Centuries ago, much of the law was applied by the courts independently of any statutory source. The constitutional fiction was that the judges merely declared what the law was, as though it was already there and merely had to be discovered. Today it is accepted that the courts *created* the law, although there is no reason to suppose they often acted arbitrarily in so doing. No doubt they acted in response to the values and needs of society, as they perceived them, in making law. This process created the body of the common law, which in this sense includes the law made by all the courts, including those of Chancery.

1.2.1.3   Common law as a 'family' of legal systems   A wider meaning still of 'common law' is as a description of a group of related legal systems. The English legal system was exported around the world wherever British influence dominated. The legal systems of the USA, and of the 'old' Commonwealth countries, are all based on the English common law. In much the same way, the legal systems of continental European countries were exported around the world. They are usually described as the civil law systems, of which the most influential has been that of France, because by producing the Code Civil Napoleon gave to France the first modern European legal system, which was copied elsewhere.

1.2.2   Criminal law, civil law and public law

1.2.2.1   Criminal law   Most people have some understanding of what criminal law is. It deals with actions, or failures to act, which are contrary to the interests of society as a whole, and for which some penalty has been prescribed. Criminal law is a species of public law, in the sense that prosecutions of those accused of committing crimes are (except rarely) brought by public officials in the name of the state. It must be remembered that a crime which is contrary to society's general interest may also cause particular loss or injury to an individual. It would then also be a civil wrong (called a 'tort'), for which the individual would be able to claim compensation. Such compensation would normally be claimed by civil action in the civil courts (*1.3.2* and *1.3.3*), but in a criminal trial the courts have power to award compensation to persons injured, payable by a person convicted at the trial (s.35, Powers of Criminal Courts Act 1973, as amended by the Criminal Justice Act 1982).

1.2.2.2   Civil law   As well as denoting the continental European family of legal systems, civil law is the title of one category of English law. In one sense civil law is all law other than criminal law. This book is mainly concerned with the law of contract, which is a small but significant part of the civil law. Other important parts are torts and property. It has been traditional to describe the law relating to public administration as part of the civil law. In part this is because it is regarded as constitutionally important that the executive is subject to control by the 'ordinary' courts, an idea described by Dicey as part of the 'rule of law' and regarded as a founding tenet of British constitutional law. Nevertheless, the courts have come to appreciate that in important respects the law applicable to public authorities requires different considerations from the law applicable to private citizens. By civil law, today we often mean English *private* law.

1.2.2.3 Public law The expression public law has existed for some time, but had little significance other than to indicate that the subject-matter in some way involved a public authority. Continental European legal systems, on the other hand, had developed the idea of public law into a separate and specialised body of rules applicable only to cases involving the administration. English law has not yet taken such a radical step, but in *O'Reilly* v *Mackman* [1982] 3 All ER 1124 the House of Lords drew a distinction between private law and public law rights. The latter can only be asserted by means of a special procedure which provides certain safeguards for the administration which do not exist in ordinary actions for private law rights. The full impact of this development in English law is still to be seen.

1.2.3 Substantive law and procedure
The distinction between substantive law and procedure is, in simple terms, the distinction between the rules applicable to the merits of a dispute and the rules governing the manner of resolution of a dispute. For those who practise law the rules of procedure are very important, but at the academic stage of legal studies the focus is on the substantive rules. It is nevertheless important to have some understanding of procedure, because procedure can affect the application of the substantive rules. In fact, the rules of procedure were in the past of great significance in shaping the substantive rules, since English law has, from the time of the need to frame one's action within the form of an existing writ (see *1.2.1.1*), proceeded from the existence of a remedy to the establishment of a right (*ubi remedium ibi ius*). It might almost be said that procedure came before substantive rights. An outline of civil procedure is given below (*1.5*).

1.3 THE COURTS

The courts are at the centre of the dispute resolution function of law, and they provide the 'due process' under which penalties may be imposed upon members of society. They are commonly thought of as 'dispensing justice', but this image must be treated with some circumspection. It is not the function of the courts merely to decide each case on the basis of what would be fair between the parties, without reference to the law and to the interests of society as a whole. As we shall see below (*2.1.2*), the decisions of the courts are regarded as reliable indicators of the meaning of rules, and of the outcome of similar disputes. They are an important element in providing a degree of certainty in the law, which is usually regarded as a necessary ingredient of a developed legal system. Whatever 'justice' means, then, it must include not only fairness but elements of certainty and predictability, as well as perhaps social utility. In any particular field, and indeed for any particular rule, the precise blend of these sometimes contradictory elements will vary.

Although the courts are subordinate to Parliament, in that they must decide disputes consistently with the will of Parliament and cannot overrule statutes, they are nevertheless of great importance in both developing and making law. This is because the courts must *interpret* statutes, and must decide all disputes, whether Parliament has provided a rule for their resolution or not. Thus, traditionally, the study of law has involved the study of the law applied by the courts, since it is in the courts that rules may be observed in their most certain form. Nevertheless, it should be remembered that many rules are rarely, if ever, the subject of litigation, and the courts must not be regarded as the sole focus of legal activity.

1.3.1 Jurisdiction over criminal trials

1.3.1.1 Magistrates' court Minor offences are only triable summarily, and this work is the main preoccupation of the magistrates' courts. It represents the great proportion of criminal trials. In addition, some crimes are triable either summarily or on indictment, so that the accused may agree to trial in the magistrates' court. In such a case, the court may refer the accused to the Crown Court for sentencing if it feels a sentence greater than it may impose is merited. For crimes triable on indictment the court holds committal proceedings (as 'examining justices') to establish whether there is a prima facie case against the accused.

1.3.1.2 Crown Court The main role of the Crown Court is to conduct trials on indictment (that is, of serious offences) once an accused has been committed for trial by the examining justices. On a 'not guilty' plea such trial takes place before a jury. The court also hears committals for sentencing from the magistrates' courts (*1.3.1.1*). It has appellate jurisdiction over appeals from the magistrates' court (*1.3.1.3*). The judges of the Crown Court are High Court judges (the most senior), circuit judges (of which there is the largest number), recorders (part-time judges appointed for a specified period) and magistrates (who must sit with one of the other three).

1.3.1.3 Appeals Appeal lies from the magistrates' court to the Crown Court, and also lies either directly, or via the Crown Court, by special procedure (known as 'case stated') to a Divisional Court of the High Court. From trial on indictment in the Crown Court appeal lies to the Court of Appeal, and then to the House of Lords, while in the case of summary trials appeal lies from the Divisional Court to the House of Lords. The organisation of the Court of Appeal and the House of Lords is dealt with in more detail in relation to civil jurisdiction below (*1.3.3.2* and *1.3.4* respectively).

1.3.2   First instance jurisdiction over civil trials

1.3.2.1   High Court   In terms of importance the High Court is the senior
first instance court for civil trials. The court consists of a small number of
senior judges and not more than 80 High Court (or 'puisne') judges. Its
jurisdiction over civil proceedings is almost unlimited, but recent changes
introduced under the Courts and Legal Services Act 1990 have moved
jurisdiction over many 'ordinary' trials to the county courts (*1.3.2.2*). The
High Court normally sits in London but on the direction of the Lord Chancellor
it may sit anywhere in England and Wales. For administrative purposes it
is split into three Divisions. Except when sitting as a Divisional Court, it is
usual for judges to sit alone.

The Queen's Bench Division is presided over by the Lord Chief Justice,
and is responsible for the greatest volume of work of the High Court. It has
general jurisdiction over civil trials, such as for breach of contract. Under its
auspices there exist two specialised courts, dealing respectively with commercial
and admiralty matters. The main advantages of the commercial court for the
business community lie in its judges who are recruited from barristers expert
in commercial law and in its simplified and relatively fast procedure.

The Chancery Division is presided over by the Lord Chancellor, but this
is only an acknowledgement of the history of Chancery, and the real head
is the Vice-Chancellor. The Division's jurisdiction reflects that of the former
Court of Chancery. It includes litigation relating to land, mortgages, trusts,
bankruptcy, administration of estates and rectification or rescission of deeds
and other written instruments.

The Family Division is presided over by the President of the Family Division,
and as the name suggests its jurisdiction embraces family law matters not heard
in the county court or magistrates' courts.

1.3.2.2   County court   The county court was established to hear at a local
level relatively minor civil litigation. There are 320 courts around the country,
and the principal judges are the circuit judges (who also sit in the Crown
Court) and district judges (formerly registrars, who are also the court
administrators). Trials are heard either in the court for the district where the
defendant lives (or has his business) or for the district where the cause of
action arose. Previous limits on county court jurisdiction were abolished by
the High Court and County Courts Jurisdiction Order 1991 (SI 1991 No.
724), made under s. 1 of the Courts and Legal Services Act 1990. The order
came into force on 1 July 1991. The new rule is based on the plaintiff having
a free choice of forum, with presumptions that claims worth less than £25,000
should be heard in a county court and that claims worth more than £50,000
should be heard in the High Court. An exception to this freedom of choice
is that personal injury claims for less than £50,000 must be commenced in
a county court. In terms of case-load the county court is much more significant
than the High Court, and is likely increasingly to be so. In part this is because
the county court also has jurisdiction over undefended matrimonial causes such
as divorce, but in part it is attributable to the fact that the court offers a

relatively inexpensive and relatively fast procedure for civil trials. In addition, the county court provides a small claims arbitration procedure (*1.5.8*).

1.3.2.3 Magistrates' court The magistrates' courts have a limited civil jurisdiction over domestic proceedings such as adoption, affiliation, care and financial provision between spouses upon desertion, etc. They also have jurisdiction over recovery of council tax and payments for water, gas and electricity.

1.3.3 Civil appeals

1.3.3.1 High Court There is a limited appellate jurisdiction in the High Court. The Chancery Division hears appeals from decisions of tax commissioners, and from decisions of the Comptroller-General of Patents, Designs and Trade Marks. A Divisional Court of the Chancery Division hears bankruptcy and land registration appeals from the county courts. A Divisional Court of the Family Division hears appeals from magistrates' courts on family matters.

1.3.3.2 Court of Appeal The principal appellate jurisdiction in civil matters (and for serious criminal offences) is the Court of Appeal. The civil division is presided over by the Master of the Rolls, and the criminal division by the Lord Chief Justice. The work is largely carried out by these two and by the Lords Justices of Appeal (up to 18 in number). High Court judges may occasionally be requested to sit in the Court of Appeal. The Court of Appeal usually sits in panels of three judges, and in the civil division there are usually two or three panels sitting at any one time.

The civil division hears appeals from the High Court and from the county courts. It may sit anywhere in England and Wales, but almost inevitably sits in London. An appeal is not a retrial. The court reads the documents in the case and listens to legal argument before coming to its decision. In the civil division all three judges may give judgment, and the appeal is decided by the majority. In the criminal division separate judgments are only given when the presiding judge rules that there is a question of law on which it would be appropriate to have more than one judgment.

1.3.4 House of Lords

The House of Lords is one of the Houses of Parliament and as such is part of the legislature. At the same time, its 'Appellate Committee' is the highest court of appeal. This apparently anomalous breach of the separation of powers is of minimal real importance, since lay peers do not participate in appeals. Since the United Kingdom joined the European Economic Community the House of Lords has not been the highest court of the legal system, but it remains the highest court of appeal since there is no *appeal* from the courts of a national legal system to the European Court of Justice (see *3.2.4*).

The House of Lords in its judicial capacity is presided over by the Lord Chancellor, and its judges are the Lords of Appeal in Ordinary (salaried life peers), of whom there may be between 7 and 11 and any peer who has held high judicial office. It mainly hears appeals from the Court of Appeal, which may only be made by leave of either the Court of Appeal or the House of Lords itself. Some appeals are made from the Divisional Court of the Queen's Bench Division in minor criminal matters, and there are a very small number of appeals direct from the High Court, by what is known as the 'leap-frog' procedure. Such an appeal may be made on a point of law of general public importance concerning either:

(a)   the interpretation of a statute or statutory instrument; or
(b)   a previous decision of a higher court binding on the High Court.

The appeal may only be made with the consent of both parties, upon certification by the trial judge and with leave of the House of Lords.

It should be noted that the Lords of Appeal in Ordinary also sit in the Judicial Committee of the Privy Council, whose prime function is to hear appeals from Her Majesty's dominions and from certain Commonwealth countries. These decisions have no formal part in the legal system of England and Wales, but not surprisingly have persuasive authority as precedents (*2.1.5.4*).

1.3.5   Tribunals
Certain types of legal dispute have been transferred from the ordinary courts to specialist jurisdictions created to deal with them, known as tribunals. The types of case heard in tribunals are minor, although they are no doubt of great importance to the litigants. Today tribunals hear far more cases than the ordinary courts. Although they are technically regarded as inferior to the courts, making them subject to the supervisory jurisdiction of the High Court (which operates by way of judicial review), they represent for many people the only point of contact with the legal system. Among the more important of these special jurisdictions are industrial tribunals, social security appeal tribunals, rent tribunals and mental health review tribunals. Composition and procedure vary from tribunal to tribunal. In a small number of tribunals legal representation is not allowed. Much more seriously, for very nearly all tribunals legal aid is not available for legal representation.

1.3.6   Supra-national authorities
The United Kingdom's membership of certain international organisations means that two supra-national 'courts' have become relevant to our legal system. Membership of the European Economic Community makes EC law applicable in this country, and the European Court of Justice is at the apex of the EC legal system. Its status and role are discussed below (*3.2.4*).

The United Kingdom also subscribes to the European Convention on Human Rights, made under the auspices of the Council of Europe (and more correctly known as the Convention for the Protection of Human Rights and Fundamental Freedoms). Aggrieved litigants in the British courts sometimes say that they will 'take the case to the European Court of Human Rights', as though entitled to a further appeal to that body. In fact, the convention is not part of English

Figure 1.1   The ordinary courts and appellate structure

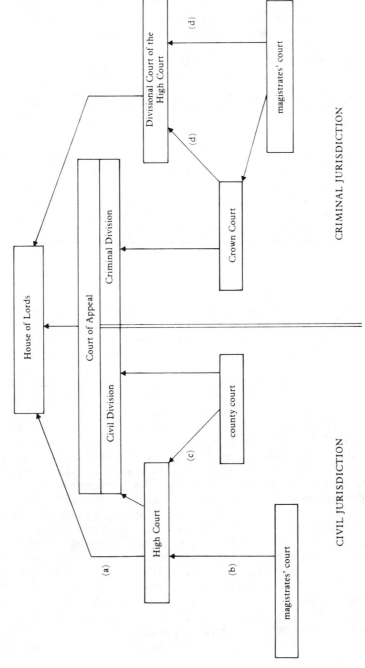

CIVIL JURISDICTION

CRIMINAL JURISDICTION

(a)   The leapfrog procedure (1.3.4).
(b)   Appeal to the Divisional Court of the Family Division in matrimonial and family matters (1.3.3.1).
(c)   Appeal to the Divisional Court of the Chancery Division on bankruptcy and land registration (1.3.3.1)
(d)   Appeal to the Divisional Court of the Queen's Bench Division, by way of case stated (1.3.1.3).

law, so that it is quite legitimate for an English court to come to a conclusion consistent with English law but inconsistent with the convention. However, a person may petition the Commission of Human Rights, which may in turn refer the case to the Court of Human Rights for decision. The member state concerned is responsible for enforcing the decision, which in the United Kingdom almost inevitably involves the need for legislation.

1.4 LEGAL PERSONNEL

1.4.1 Judges

1.4.1.1 The Lord Chancellor The Lord Chancellor is the head of the judiciary and of the court system. This position is another anomolous breach of the separation of powers, since the Lord Chancellor is also a member of the Cabinet and thus of the executive. In fact, the Lord Chancellor rarely sits in his judicial capacity, since his time is taken up by running his Department, which is responsible for the administration of justice, and by acting as Speaker of the House of Lords. He has a very influential role in the appointment of judges and in advising the government on the structure of the legal system.

1.4.1.2 Judicial appointment and tenure Senior judges, that is the presidents of the Divisions of the High Court and of the Divisions of the Court of Appeal, Lords of Appeal in Ordinary and Lords Justices of Appeal, are appointed by the Queen on the advice of the Prime Minister. They are recruited from among existing judges of the superior courts, or from barristers of 15 years' standing.

High Court ('puisne') judges, Crown and county court ('circuit') judges, and recorders are appointed by the Queen on the advice of the Lord Chancellor. The Courts and Legal Services Act 1990 introduces major changes in the appointment of judges, with the effect that for the first time solicitors may be appointed as High Court judges (an office previously reserved to barristers alone). Appointment to judicial office is no longer linked to the fact of having been a barrister for a qualifying period of years, but depends upon having enjoyed certain rights of audience (*1.4.2*) which will in future be open to solicitors as well as barristers. Moreover, all circuit judges (irrespective of which branch of the profession they are from) are eligibe for promotion to the High Court. The 1990 Act also renames county court registrars 'district judges', reflecting the fact that much of the work that they do is of a judicial nature.

Judges of the rank of puisne judge and above may not be removed from office except by address of both Houses of Parliament, thus guaranteeing their independence. They must retire at 75. These rules do not apply to the Lord Chancellor, since his appointment is political. He holds office at the Queen's pleasure, effectively putting his appointment and tenure at the disposal of the Prime Minister of the day. Circuit judges and recorders may be removed by the Lord Chancellor on the ground of incapacity or misbehaviour, and must usually retire at 72.

1.4.1.3 A critique In recent years the judiciary as an institution has come under attack. The most readable account, perhaps because of its polemic rather than academic style, is provided by Professor John Griffiths (*The Politics of the Judiciary*, 4th edn, Fontana Press, 1991). The essence of the criticism is that judges are drawn from a very narrow and unrepresentative section of society. A disproportionate number were educated at public schools and/or at the universities of Oxford and Cambridge. Those not recruited from this narrow sector usually find that the pressure to 'conform' during the early years of legal practice, in order to further their careers, has the effect of homogenising them with the standard judicial profile. Judges are then seen as establishment figures, playing a significant but unarticulated political role, without democratic accountability and not always in step with the will of the majority of British citizens.

There is no denying some of the allegations made, and evidence can be found which appears to fit the analysis (e.g. the GLC 'Fares fair' case: *Bromley LBC* v *Greater London Council* [1982] 1 All ER 129). However, the argument confuses two strands of analysis which are not necessarily causally linked. The judiciary are no different from any other part of the 'ruling class' of the United Kingdom, in which public school and Oxbridge dominate. Nor is it surprising that some cases should have a 'political' aspect. The judiciary must decide all cases coming before them, and some cases inevitably raise questions and sometimes conflicts of policy. Where the law leaves any element of discretion to the judge in either its application or its interpretation, it is equally inevitable that judges will exercise that discretion in accordance with their view of the world, which must be influenced to some degree by their upbringing and current status. It is far from clear, however, that the law often leaves blanket discretions, as opposed to those which can only be exercised within narrow confines of permissible choice; and it is far from clear that the judiciary today go out of their way to exercise this political role.

Such evidence as can be found is inconclusive, but it, and Griffiths' analysis, must be treated as a warning of an inescapable weakness in the apparent objectivity of the legal system. The weakness is caused by simple human limitations: no person can entirely escape his context and conditioning. The warning must go to the law-makers, so that unfettered discretion is not given to the judges.

1.4.2 Barristers and solicitors
The practising legal profession is divided into the two main branches of solicitors and barristers. Solicitors are by far the more numerous, there being something like five times as many solicitors as barristers. To the general public it often appears that barristers are the superior branch of the profession. In many ways that is a misleading impression. Average earnings of solicitors are higher than those of barristers, and the average age of those at the bar is under 40. The recruitment and training of new members of both branches follow similar patterns, mainly involving taking people in their early twenties with law degrees and giving them one year of vocational training followed by a period of apprenticeship before being fully qualified. It would be more correct to say,

therefore, that if there is any difference at all between the two branches, it is that barristers specialise in certain forms of legal work, while solicitors are rather more general practitioners.

The Courts and Legal Services Act 1990 introduces important changes to the previous balance between the two main branches of the legal profession. In future, solicitors may be authorised by the Law Society to exercise rights of audience and conduct litigation. One result of this change is that it will no longer be possible to argue that solicitors are unsuited for judicial office because they lack necessary courtroom experience. The Act nevertheless maintains the right of the judiciary to supervise the work of advocates in their courts. It seems unlikely that all solicitors will immediately seek to be authorised to conduct litigation, and the profession will almost certainly continue to comprise some who specialise in advocacy, and some who specialise in other kinds of legal work. It may be, however, that the titles of 'barrister' and 'solicitor' will in time come to have less significance.

In many countries the legal profession is not split as it is in this country, and from time to time calls are made for the profession in this country to be fused. Most recently, the Royal Commission on Legal Services rejected a call for fusion of the profession, on the ground that there was a need for a specialised bar. Nevertheless, the level of specialisation is not great. There is little doubt that the legal expertise of a solicitor in a specialist department of a large London firm is likely to be greater than that of a relatively young barrister, especially since the resources for research available to the solicitor may be far greater than those available to the barrister. As differences between the branches continue to be eroded, it may be that the case against fusion is getting progressively weaker.

1.4.3   Personnel in the magistrates' court

The majority of the justices of the magistrates' courts are lay magistrates. They are appointed by the Lord Chancellor, who consults a local advisory committee. They receive training over a period of a year, but its purpose is not to make them experts in the law they must apply. Rather, it is intended to familiarise them with the duties they will have to carry out. Lay magistrates usually sit in panels of three, and in legal matters are assisted by a justices' clerk who is legally trained. His main duty is to advise the magistrates on the law, but they need not follow his advice, and the clerk must take no part in the actual decision of the bench. In London and other large cities the panel of lay magistrates is sometimes replaced by a professional ('stipendiary') magistrate, who is a trained lawyer and sits alone.

1.5   OUTLINE OF CIVIL PROCEDURE

This section sketches an outline of the procedures involved in bringing legal action in the civil courts. Unless otherwise indicated, it is assumed for the purposes of examples given that the action brought is for breach of contract.

1.5.1 The decision to take action

The decision to take legal action is never lightly made. It will almost certainly involve costs, especially if the litigation is unsuccessful, in terms of lawyers' fees, and of the litigant's time, which might otherwise have been used more profitably. It may also sour a good relationship with the co-litigant more valuable in commercial terms than any damages which may be recovered. The following elements, amongst others, play an important role in the decision whether to take action.

1.5.1.1 Legal advice For most people the decision to take legal action will not be taken without seeking the advice of a lawyer, which in the first instance means consulting a solicitor. For large companies this may present no problem, but for small companies and private individuals the initial cost of legal advice may be a disincentive to legal action. For individuals, but not for companies, legal aid may be available to those without the means to bring an action, provided that their claim is certified as being worthwhile. Even then, the legal aid fund has first claim to any compensation recovered to pay legal costs not recovered from the losing party. Under recent proposals, a litigant would have to contribute a not insubstantial amount of his own capital before being considered eligible for legal aid.

1.5.1.2 Evidence A potential plaintiff must also consider whether he can muster the evidence necessary to substantiate his claim. In most contract cases there is likely to be a written document representing the main terms of the agreement, but there are difficulties as soon as terms other than those contained in the document are alleged. Equally, it may be necessary to call expert witnesses if there are issues of how a loss was caused, or what is the best financial computation of the loss suffered. The would-be plaintiff must remember that, however willing the court is to believe his story, it will demand objective evidence to substantiate the claim.

1.5.1.3 Settlement Since a party bringing legal action almost inevitably faces considerable costs, even if successful, any potential litigant must consider whether it would not be better to settle the dispute rather than allow it to go to trial. Although one would not normally expect to recover the same amount of compensation in a settlement as in legal proceedings, the difference may well be offset by the additional cost of going to trial. Moreover, the court may penalise in costs a plaintiff failing to accept a reasonable offer of settlement (*1.5.6*). Although reliable figures are difficult to achieve, it is generally believed that only a very small percentage of disputes actually result in a trial.

1.5.1.4 Limitation of actions In order to protect possible defendants from the endless threat of legal proceedings, and to avoid the difficulty of conducting trials at a time when it is no longer possible to be confident that the true facts have emerged, the law places a finite limit on the time during which legal proceedings may be begun. The rules on limitation of actions are complex and beyond the scope of this section. The normal limitation period in contract actions is six years from the date on which the cause of action accrues, which is normally the date of the breach (Limitation Act 1980).

1.5.2 Starting proceedings

1.5.2.1 By writ The usual method of starting proceedings is to issue a writ. The writ is prepared (in triplicate) on a standard form, setting out the names of the parties and a brief statement of the claim. It is issued by lodging a copy, upon payment of a fee, with the High Court in London or with a district registry. The other copies are stamped with an official seal, and one must be served on the defendant, giving him notice of the proceedings, within one year of issue. At the same time a form is delivered to the defendant, which he must return within 14 days, acknowledging service of the writ and stating whether it is intended to contest the proceedings. Even if it is intended to dispute the validity of the writ, or any other aspect of the proceedings, it is essential to return the form. The consequence of not doing so may be to allow the plaintiff immediate judgment in the case. The issue of a writ is often a catalyst to settlement of the dispute.

1.5.2.2 By originating summons In some circumstances proceedings may be commenced by originating summons. It provides, amongst other things, a relatively straightforward means of obtaining a ruling on a point of law or the meaning of a statute or legal document, such as a contract. The summons is issued in much the same way as a writ, and must be served on the defendant in the same way. It differs in that it must contain a much more specific statement of claim than a writ, since the intention is to proceed as soon as possible to a determination of the point raised.

1.5.3 Pleadings

The pleadings are the process of establishing exactly what is in dispute between the parties. The first shot is fired by the plaintiff preparing, through a barrister hired by his solicitor for this purpose, a statement of claim. It states the facts on which the plaintiff will rely, but makes no legal argument. The defendant must then respond. If the statement of claim is unclear, or if he wishes to buy time to consider his response, he may request further and better particulars. Alternatively, he may admit the plaintiff's claim and offer to settle, or file a defence. In this last case he must respond point by point to facts alleged in the claim which it is intended to contest, either denying them, in which case he must make his own statement of fact in opposition, or not admitting them, which has the effect of putting the onus on the plaintiff to prove them at trial.

1.5.4 Pre-trial procedures

1.5.4.1 Discovery The process of discovery is an important stage in preparing for trial. It involves the gathering together of all documents relevant to the litigation. Each side must do it and disclose the existence of the documents to the other side, and must then make them available for inspection. The only documents exempt from inspection are those which are in some way 'privileged', or those which are for some good reason no longer in the possession of the party in question. Privilege usually attaches to any documents which have been made in contemplation of the litigation, such as solicitor-client correspondence. If one party believes a particular relevant document to exist which has not been disclosed by the other, he may apply to the court for specific discovery.

1.5.4.2 The role of the master After the process of discovery the plaintiff must issue a summons for directions, which is the first opportunity after issue of the writ for the court to consider the substance of the claim. The summons is heard by a High Court master, an officer of the court with special responsibility for supervising procedural matters. In the county court this function is called the pre-trial review, and is carried out by the district judge. The master decides preliminary ('interlocutory') points, and is empowered to eliminate as much as possible that is not strictly relevant from the forthcoming litigation, so that the court is faced with the essence of the dispute. It is clear that at this stage there is some scope for settlement, and that some masters are more active than others in pushing the parties towards amicable resolution of their dispute.

1.5.5 The trial

1.5.5.1 Order of play Civil trials in this country are almost always heard by a single judge, sitting without a jury. In civil cases juries are only found in fraud and defamation cases. The trial proceedings are opened by counsel for the plaintiff. He will outline the facts, take the judge through the pleadings and the documentary evidence, and then introduce whatever oral evidence he requires by the examination in chief of witnesses called by his side. The first opportunity defence counsel has to take part is in cross-examination of the plaintiff's witnesses, in which he seeks to discredit evidence produced or to discover further evidence more favourable to his own client. Thereafter, the plaintiff's counsel may re-examine witnesses. At the close of the case for the plaintiff the defendant's counsel proceeds to introduce oral evidence in precisely the same way. He may preface the introduction of evidence by an opening speech outlining the defendant's case, but the practice is discouraged in the county court. Counsel for the defendant makes his main address to the court after conclusion of the evidence. Counsel for the plaintiff is then entitled to respond. Thereafter, the judge delivers a reasoned judgment. In complex trials the judge will adjourn the proceedings in order to consider his judgment.

1.5.5.2 Burden of proof The burden of proof is the responsibility lying on one of the parties to prove his claim. Since the whole adversary process of an English trial does not allow the possibility of a 'draw', there is a presumptive rule that if the party who has the burden of proof fails to satisfy it then the other party wins. In civil litigation the main burden is on the plaintiff, although under the substantive legal rules applicable to the dispute the burden on a particular issue which is part of the dispute may be reversed (see, for example, contracts in restraint of trade: *8.8.1*). The burden is satisfied by proof of what has been alleged 'on a balance of probabilities', which is taken to indicate that the burden is not particularly difficult to satisfy, and is less severe than the burden on the prosecution in criminal trials of proof 'beyond reasonable doubt'.

1.5.6 Costs

The general rule is that the costs of litigation must be met by the losing party. The rule is thought to be one of the greatest incentives to settlement. Nevertheless, until very recently it was usual to award only such costs as had been incurred after issue of the writ, and as were *necessary* to the litigation ('party and party costs'). These costs only amounted to about two-thirds of the total, and the winning party would have to pay the balance. Now, costs are to be awarded on what formerly was called the 'solicitor and own client costs' basis. As a result, recovery of all costs reasonably incurred will be allowed (Rules of the Supreme Court (Amendment) 1986, SI No 1986/632). A defendant making an offer of settlement may, if it is rejected, pay the amount offered into court. If the court awards damages below or equivalent to that amount, the plaintiff is only awarded costs up to the moment of payment into court, after which the defendant is awarded costs. This rule puts pressure on the plaintiff to settle, since to continue with the litigation may be a substantial risk.

1.5.7 Actions to recover debts

Many contract actions, especially in the county court, are brought to recover unpaid debts. There may be no dispute of facts or law. Trial procedures are essentially the same, but in debt actions they have been streamlined because the process is essentially administrative and in the interests of the creditor should be completed as soon as possible. A specially endorsed writ is issued and served, combining both writ and statement of claim. Further, the plaintiff may apply for summary judgment. The effect is to avoid usual pre-trial procedure, and to oblige the defendant to appear before a master to show that there is a defence. Failure to attend, or failure to persuade the master, results in judgment for the plaintiff. If a triable defence is shown to exist, the full trial procedure must be embarked upon.

1.5.8 County court small claims procedure

For claims less than £1,000 the county court must order an arbitration process. Its purpose is to provide a less formal and less expensive means of dispute resolution. The order may be overturned if the case is legally or factually complex, or there is a charge of fraud, or the parties agree that they want full trial in court. On the other hand, where the claim is for more than £1,000 parties may agree to submit to the arbitration procedure. The arbitration is normally conducted by the district judge, is often private and not subject to formal rules of evidence. A lawyer may be employed to make legal representations, but in order to discourage this practice the rule is that the cost of hiring a solicitor or barrister is not recoverable by the winning party. The arbitration procedure is otherwise not unlike that for civil trials.

TWO
Sources of law

2.1 CASE LAW

The most widely recognised distinguishing characteristic of the common law is that it is built out of the decisions of the courts. This section considers the mechanisms by which the decisions in individual cases come to form a system of law. An important preliminary matter is the physical source of case law.

2.1.1 The law reports
Since the law is contained in the decisions in cases, it is to be found in the published reports of those cases. Not all cases are reported. The general rule is that only those cases of the superior courts (i.e. High Court and above) which contain legal points of importance or interest are reported. Since the late nineteenth century official reports have been published by the Incorporated Council of Law Reporting. Before that time law reporting was in private hands, and was of variable quality. Most important reports pre-dating official reporting are now collected together in a reprinted series called 'English Reports'.

The official reports of High Court and Court of Appeal appear in three series: Queen's Bench (QB), Chancery (Ch) and Family (Fam). A further series reports the decisions of the House of Lords and the Judicial Committee of the Privy Council: Appeal Cases (AC). In addition there are two series of general reports, which appear weekly and well in advance of the main official series: Weekly Law Reports (WLR) and All England Reports (All ER). For purposes of legal research there are now computer-based legal data bases, which make finding the law easy and which provide a very efficient reporting service. The best known of these is LEXIS, which also reports cases otherwise unreported in published form. The courts are reluctant, however, to allow reference to this kind of report in the course of argument before them.

2.1.2 The notion of precedent
When it is said that the English common law is built out of the decisions in individual cases, what is meant is that the courts, in deciding a case, do not approach it entirely from first principles. Rather, they consider whether such a case has previously been ruled upon by the courts, and if it has then they *may* choose to decide the instant case in the same way. The decision

in the previous case is a 'precedent'. In some circumstances it is more formally correct to say that the subsequent court *must* follow the decision in the previous case, notably where the precedent was established by a court superior in the hierarchy (*2.1.5*, and see Figure 1.1) to the court now deciding the case. However, it will become apparent that the scope for avoiding any obligation to follow precedent is so great (see below, and *2.1.4*) that it is misleading to suggest that the system of precedent is in any sense mechanical.

The reason for any legal system to adopt the principle of following precedents may be explained in a number of ways. At a very simple level there is a need for certainty in the law, especially in regard to contractual and commercial matters, since those in business will rely on the law remaining constant in order to plan their activities. In more abstract terms, to be designated a *system* of law there is a requirement of order in the manner in which the rules are applied. Alternatively, by deciding cases in a certain way which is observable by others, the courts create expectations of how legal disputes will be resolved. One of the central tenets of western conceptions of justice is the protection of legitimate expectations, so that the precedent system is an essential buttress of the concept of justice. To put the same argument in constitutional terms, the rule of law in a democratic society requires that all men be treated equally by the law, and the essence of equal treatment by the courts is to treat like cases alike. These are not independent reasons. They are different ways of explaining the single, largely untested instinct that a legal regime which permitted like cases to be treated differently on an *ad hoc* basis would soon descend into chaos. Even those legal systems, such as that of France, which deny any law-making power to the judiciary and which formally prohibit the use of precedent in judicial reasoning, nevertheless admit the need for stability and certainty in the legal system created by treating like cases alike.

The central principle of the precedent doctrine, that like cases be treated alike, is the source of the considerable flexibility which nevertheless exists within a system intended to promote certainty. The crucial test is always whether one case is *like* another. In relation to the common law, a major element in legal reasoning is to establish whether sufficient analogy exists between cases for the rule or principle established in one to be transposed to the other (*2.1.4*). The courts have never formulated a fixed test of analogy, preferring to keep, through moveable criteria of analogy, the flexibility necessary to allow the law to develop as society develops.

2.1.3   *Ratio decidendi* and *obiter dictum*
The doctrine of precedent has so far been explained in terms of the potentially binding force of judicial decisions in subsequent cases. We must now be more precise about which part of a judicial decision may be binding in subsequent cases. The actual result of the case is of little relevance. It is of course binding on the parties to the dispute, so that the same matter between the same parties cannot be raised in further proceedings, except on an appeal. The result is said to be *res judicata* (a matter which has been judicially determined). The doctrine of precedent operates at the level of legal rules, so that it is the rules from previous cases which may be binding on subsequent courts. A further

distinction must still be made. In the course of reasoning towards a decision in a case judges may refer to a number of rules. Only the rule actually employed to decide the particular issue in dispute (the *ratio decidendi*) has precedent value. An incidental statement of a rule, not strictly relevant to the determination of the dispute (an *obiter dictum*), does not have precedent value, although such a statement may be very persuasive authority (see *2.1.3.2*).

2.1.3.1 *Ratio decidendi* The *ratio decidendi* (usually abbreviated to *ratio*) of a case is literally the reason for the decision. The process of common law reasoning involves mastering the techniques of identifying the *ratio* of a case. Unfortunately, these techniques are best learned through practice, and there is no simple formula guaranteed to identify the reason for each and every judicial decision. Nevertheless, some ground rules may be identified.

In approaching a recent case, on which there has been no further judicial comment, the *ratio* is very often to be found by examining the facts treated by the judge as relevant, and the judge's decision based on those facts. Take the famous case of *Roscorla v Thomas* (1842) 3 QB 234. It involved the sale of a horse and a promise, after the sale had been completed, that the horse was free from vice. The court treated as material the facts that there had been a sale, that the promise was made subsequently to the sale without any other payment being made in return for it, and that the promise was not true. The fact that the subject-matter of the sale was a horse, and the nature of the promise, were not material. The court's decision was that an action for breach of contract based on the promise must fail. The *ratio* is that an action for breach of a warranty (promise) of quality cannot be based on a promise which is not in the form of a contract, either by being a term incorporated into the main contract of sale or by being separately paid for (*6.3.3*).

It can be seen that in formulating the *ratio* of a case some of the specific facts are omitted. It is generally the case that the longer a case remains in circulation as a leading authority on a point of law the more abstract its *ratio* becomes, as it becomes less and less fact-specific. Thus, today *Roscorla v Thomas* is regarded as leading authority on the unenforceability of promises made subsequently to contracts, whatever the nature of the contract, and not only for contracts of sale.

It can be seen, therefore, that although what the judge considered to be the relevant facts may be a useful guide, it is not infallible. In the process of reasoning by analogy a subsequent court may find that a fact apparently treated as material by the judge was not really material, allowing the extension of the rule to a new line of cases. A striking example of this process may be found in Lord Denning's extension of the equitable estoppel doctrine to promises to accept payment of a lesser sum in full satisfaction of the whole debt in *Central London Property Trust v High Trees House* [1947] KB 130. The doctrine had previously applied to non-contractual modifications of certain types of contract clause, but never to price clauses. By finding that the type of clause to be modified was not a material fact Denning J (as he then was) was able to extend the doctrine to a wholly different series of situations (*6.4.3.1*). Thus, in a very real sense, once a decision has been followed by a subsequent court the *ratio* may best be regarded as what the subsequent court says it is. Until a decision has been followed, our statement of the *ratio* is really only a prediction of what subsequent courts will say is the *ratio* of the case.

2.1.3.2 *Obiter dictum* The simplest definition of an *obiter dictum* is: a judicial statement of law without precedent value. This definition does not, however, help to identify such statements. They are statements of law which do not contribute directly to the resolution of the actual dispute, and they are probably denied legal authority because, not being central to the dispute, they may not have been properly considered. Nevertheless, they may be of persuasive authority, especially when made by judges of high standing. In the *High Trees* case, since Denning J found that the equitable estoppel doctrine did not apply on the facts, his detailed exposition of how it might apply to a non-contractual variation of a price term was strictly *obiter dictum*, but it was made with the intention of being, and has been, followed by subsequent courts.

2.1.4 The art of distinguishing
We have already seen how, by progressive elimination of 'material' facts, judges may extend the scope of a *ratio* as a tool of judicial creativity (*2.1.3.1*). Another, more common, judicial technique in relation to the doctrine of precedent is that of distinguishing previous cases in order to avoid applying them to the case in hand. Sometimes the process of distinguishing involves nothing more than showing that the facts of the previous case and the case in hand are not sufficiently analogous for them to be treated as 'like cases', so that there is no reason why the same rule should apply to both. Where a judge is anxious to avoid being bound by a previous decision, the process may involve treating as material a fact not really regarded as material in the original case. Such 'fictitious' distinguishing offers considerable scope for judges to escape applying a rule which they consider would be inappropriate in the circumstances, even though they are technically bound by it. Nevertheless, the technique does not provide an unfettered discretion to ignore precedent. The appeals system and the fear that by abuse the law might be brought into disrepute operate as constraints on over-active distinguishing.

Distinguishing may alternatively involve a conscious decision that although the cases are similar on their facts, some element of policy present in the first does not apply to the second, or vice versa. Thus, if a rule is designed to implement some policy it may not be applicable to otherwise similar facts if the policy of the rule would not be forwarded by its application in the particular case. For example, the rule introduced by Denning J in the *High Trees* case (*2.1.3.1*) is often described as being intended to prevent injustice. For that reason, it was not applied by Lord Denning MR in *D & C Builders Ltd* v *Rees* [1966] 2 QB 617 on the ground that no such risk of injustice existed on the facts (*6.4.3.3*).

Finally, a judge may refuse to follow a previous decision if he believes that it would not be fair, as between the parties before him, to apply the rule in the instant case. Nevertheless, it is rare for a judge to articulate such a reason for distinguishing a case. It is more usual to disguise the case as one of fact-based or policy-based distinguishing. It would be wrong, however, to give the impression that judges in deciding cases do not consult their instinct of what is fair, just as it would be wrong to suggest that they are guided by that alone. These issues are considered in more detail below (*2.4*).

2.1.5 The hierarchy of authority

Not all previous decisions, even in like cases, are binding on subsequent courts. The original rule was that previous decisions were binding on subsequent courts of the same rank or lower. That rule is now somewhat diluted. Except in the Court of Appeal and the Divisional Courts, there is no longer an obligation to follow previous decisions of courts of the same rank, although in practice such decisions are followed unless there is good reason to depart from them. To examine the rule in detail it will be useful to consider it as it applies to each stage in the hierarchy of courts (see Figure 1.1).

2.1.5.1 The House of Lords   The House of Lords is the highest court of appeal in the English legal system, and, except in EC matters, is the senior court. One of its main functions is to ensure the consistency and proper development of the common law. Its decisions are binding on all lower courts. Until fairly recently it had regarded its decisions as also binding itself. Although such a rule led to great certainty, it suffered from the weakness that it did not allow the House of Lords to develop the law away from old precedents even when it was desirable to do so, as for example when social conditions or attitudes have changed. It could once be argued that such a change in the law in a democracy should only be made by the legislature, not by the judiciary. In recent times it has been impossible to sustain this argument because parliamentary time has been too preoccupied by party-political matters for there to be enough scope for necessary law reform. In 1966, therefore, their Lordships issued a Practice Statement ([1966] 3 All ER 77) in which they declared their intention for the future to overrule previous decisions where it appeared desirable to do so. Nevertheless, the presumption is that the House of Lords will follow its own decisions unless very good reason is shown for overruling them. The power created by the Practice Statement has only rarely been used, but it appears to have engendered, or at least coincided with the start of, a period of more active development of the law (by creative distinguishing) by the House of Lords.

2.1.5.2 The Court of Appeal   The Court of Appeal is bound by decisions of the House of Lords and by its own decisions. To the latter rule there are a number of exceptions, the most important of which were enumerated in *Young* v *Bristol Aeroplane Co. Ltd* [1944] KB 718. In that case it was held that the Court of Appeal is free to depart from its own decisions where:

(a)   there are conflicting decisions (in which case the subsequent court can choose between them);

(b)   the previous decision is inconsistent with a subsequent decision in the House of Lords;

(c)   the previous decision was made *per incuriam* (that is, was itself inconsistent with existing statute or binding authority).

It has subsequently been held that the Court of Appeal is not bound by a decision of two judges on an interlocutory matter, and that the Criminal Division is not bound by previous decisions going against the defendant, where the law had been misinterpreted or misapplied.

In recent years commentators outside the Court of Appeal, and Lord Denning MR within, have argued that the Court should not be bound by its own decisions. Lord Denning said it was not so bound in *Davis* v *Johnson* [1978] 1 All ER 841, but although a majority agreed with him in the result in that case they did not accept his sweeping proposition, preferring to adopt strictly limited further exceptions to the basic rule. In the House of Lords it was said that whatever the logic of Lord Denning's proposition it could not prevail until accepted by all the judges of the Court of Appeal. This appears to recognise that it is not for the House of Lords to determine whether the Court of Appeal should be bound by its own decisions. Rather, it is open to the Court of Appeal to issue a Practice Statement changing its previous rule, provided all the judges agree.

2.1.5.3   The High Court   The Divisional Courts of the High Court (which are appellate jurisdictions: *1.3.3.1*) are bound by decisions of the House of Lords and Court of Appeal, and by their own decisions. The trial courts of the High Court are of course bound by all decisions of courts of higher rank, but are not bound by their own previous decisions. The practice is nevertheless to follow them unless good reason exists for not doing so. Where there is a conflict between the decisions of courts of higher rank (e.g. between the House of Lords and the Court of Appeal) the court is obliged to follow the decision of its immediate superior, and to leave the resolution of any conflict to a possible appeal.

2.1.5.4   Other courts   Other trial courts (i.e. county court, Crown Court, magistrates' court) are in the same position as the trial courts of the High Court. They are bound by the decisions of courts of higher rank, but not by their own decisions.

As noted earlier (*1.3.4*), the Judicial Committee of the Privy Council, which hears Commonwealth appeals, is not part of the English legal system, so that its decisions are not binding on English courts. However, since its judges include the Lords of Appeal in Ordinary, where the foreign law is regarded as the same as English law its decisions (technically known as 'advice') are persuasive authority in English courts.

2.2 STATUTES

2.2.1 Physical sources

Just as important cases are published in the law reports, legislation is published in statute books. The full official text of statutes is published in annual volumes by HMSO. More useful to the student of law, however, are three other publications. *Halsbury's Statutes of England* is an encyclopaedia of legislation which groups statutes together under subject headings. For example, all statutes relating to contract law are published together in one volume. Annotations of amendments, repeals and other important matters are provided. Publication of the most recent edition commenced in 1985 and when complete, continuation volumes will be issued to keep the series up to date. The updating process is made easier by the official publication *Statutes in Force*, which has a loose-leaf format allowing rapid replacement of parts as amendments and repeals occur. It, too, groups statutes together under subject headings. The most useful series of annual statute books is *Current Law Statutes Annotated*, which publishes with important legislation comprehensive notes explaining its purpose, meaning and how it fits with the existing law. Statutes may also be searched on the LEXIS information retrieval system, which provides the user with an up-to-date amended version of the text.

Statutes are almost always cited by their short title and the year in which they were passed (e.g. Unfair Contract Terms Act 1977). In the past statutes were cited by regnal year and chapter number. Thus, the Law Reform (Frustrated Contracts) Act 1943 could also be cited as: 6 & 7 Geo. 6 c.40. That is, it was the fortieth statute to be passed in the parliamentary session beginning in the sixth and ending in the seventh year of the reign of King George VI. In previous times it was more normal to cite statutes by this latter form, and older statutes are still sometimes cited in this way.

2.2.2 The nature of legislation

In constitutional terms statutes are the highest domestic source of law. The doctrine of the sovereignty of Parliament means that legislation passed by Parliament overrides any other source of law, especially case law, while only Parliament itself by further legislation can override statute (*1.1*). The only limit on the scope of Parliament's sovereignty is brought about by the United Kingdom's membership of the European Economic Community, which means that sometimes Parliament must bow to the superior law-making power of the Communities' institutions (*3.4.3*).

In practical terms statutes are also, in terms of volume, the most important source of law. This was not always the case, but the twentieth century attitude to the role of government, which accepts much greater state intervention in the lives and affairs of ordinary citizens, has generated much more legislation than ever before. Today, more often than not litigation involves disputes about the interpretation and application of statutes, rather than the 'declaration' and application of rules of common law. Legislation is generated by a number of impulses. Much is the product of the programme of action put forward by a political party in its manifesto before coming to power. However, while labour law and criminal law sometimes take on a party-political aspect, much of the law studied by students, such as contract law or commercial law (sometimes described as 'lawyers' law'), is rarely of party-political significance, and the impulse for legislation comes from one of the law reform bodies, such as the Law Commission.

Statutes generally contain a very condensed presentation of very detailed rules. To employ a crude metaphor, the number of 'rules per square inch' is much greater than in a report of a judicial decision, which despite the precise language employed by the judiciary is an altogether more 'impressionistic' source of law. It is a common failing among law student beginners not to take account of the difference, and to read statutes as they would a law report, producing a very impressionistic version of the content of the statute. That approach is unacceptable. Statutes are very precisely and concisely worded. Each section must be read several times, and wrestled with until its exact meaning is clear and can be accurately summarised.

2.2.3 The legislative process

A proposal for enactment by Parliament as a statute is known as a Bill. Bills are usually drafted in the Office of Parliamentary Counsel by specialists in turning principles and policy into specific rules. They are instructed by the particular government department, acting under the responsibility of a Minister, which seeks to introduce the legislation. An exception to this procedure may occur in the case of legislation resulting from a Report of the Law Commission, in which case the Commission itself may have provided a draft Bill in an appendix to its report.

A Bill must then be introduced into one or other House of Parliament. Money Bills are introduced in the House of Commons; 'lawyers' law' Bills quite often start in the House of Lords. The *first reading* consists of no more than reading the short title to the House in order to notify members that the Bill has been proposed. At the *second reading* debate takes place on the general principles of the Bill, so that for any contentious matter this is a crucial stage. For non-contentious legislation the second reading is not particularly important. There follows the *committee stage*, when the Bill is discussed in detail, and its provisions minutely examined and where necessary amended. The discussion normally takes place in a standing committee, but the Bill may alternatively be referred to a select committee, to a joint committee drawn from both Houses, or even to a committee of the whole of the House through which it is currently passing. Next comes a *report stage* when amendments made in committee are drawn to the attention of the House, after which the Bill must pass its *third reading*.

If the Bill passes its third reading it is then ready to be introduced into the other House, where it must go through exactly the same procedures. If further amendments are made at this stage the particular changes must be referred for approval to the House which first considered the Bill. Nevertheless, in normal circumstances the spade work on a Bill is done in the House where first introduced, and passage through the other House should be less difficult. At that point, the Bill is ready to receive the *royal assent*, whereupon it becomes law, although it may not actually come into force until some later date, specified in one of the closing sections of the statute.

2.2.4 Interpretation of statutes

An inherent weakness of law is the general imprecision of language. When the language of judges is vague or ambiguous it may be a nuisance, but it is not particularly significant because subsequent courts have considerable scope for 'reinterpreting' what a judge said in order to discover the *ratio* of a case (*2.1.3.1* and *2.1.4*). Where the language of a statute is vague or ambiguous, however, it presents far greater problems. Statutes are the highest source of law, and it would be as constitutionally wrong for a judge to misapply a statute as to attempt to overrule it. Thus, one important job for the parliamentary draftsman is to produce a text which is clear and free from ambiguity, so that the judges who must apply the law may know precisely what it is. In an ideal world statutes would also be readily intelligible to the lay person, but it seems precision and clarity are not always compatible. The compromise between them is that the meaning of the statute should be clear to the ordinary citizen's legal adviser. However, despite the best efforts of the draftsmen the language of statutes is not always clear and unambiguous, and the courts have developed approaches (they are not really 'rules': see *2.2.4.4*) to interpretation.

2.2.4.1 The 'literal' rule The first and still the most important approach to statutory interpretation is to rely on the ordinary meaning of the words used. Unless there is a positive reason to think otherwise (such as a definition in the statute of the particular word for the purposes of the statute) the presumption must be that Parliament intended the word or phrase to be given its ordinary meaning. This approach only really becomes controversial when it is alleged to be the only legitimate approach to statutory interpretation, on the apparent supposition that all words and phrases have identifiable and universally agreed *ordinary meanings*. Most lawyers today accept that some words and phrases do not have ordinary meanings in this sense, either by virtue of something inherent in the word or phrase itself or by virtue of the contexts in which they are used. Thus, the word 'reasonable' is sometimes used deliberately in legislation when the intention is to leave the identification of the precise standard to be demanded to the judges. It is inherently uncertain. Equally, the word 'road' has a number of meanings, and the one intended may only be clear after consideration of the context in which the word was used, if then (*2.2.4.4*). The avoidance of such difficulties is beyond the skill of any draftsman, and there will always be times when the emphasis on precision causes some sacrifice of clarity. The 'literal rule' then becomes no more than an injunction not to distort the natural language of the statute in interpreting it when a clear and unambiguous single meaning may without doubt be taken from the words used.

2.2.4.2 The 'golden' rule The first response to the recognition that perfection in clarity and precision of meaning is unattainable by reason of the limits of language itself was a limited relaxation of strict adherence to

the literal meaning. Using this approach, a judge might depart from the natural meaning of the words used if that meaning was absurd, or perverse, so that it would be unreasonable to imagine that Parliament had intended such an interpretation. In its place the judge may put some other possible meaning *of the words used* where it seems reasonable to suppose that Parliament is more likely to have intended the second meaning. Thus, departure from the ordinary meaning is not allowed unless some other meaning may be discerned. It appears to be accepted that in determining whether the ordinary meaning is absurd or perverse the court is entitled not only to consider criteria of internal consistency (i.e. whether the ordinary meaning 'fits' with the other provisions of the statute) but may also consider the practical result of applying the ordinary meaning and whether that accords with what is taken to be the legislative intent.

2.2.4.3 The 'mischief' rule The growing acceptance of consideration of legislative intent led to a second, less restricted response to the limitations of the literal approach to interpretation. Today it is usually referred to as the 'purposive' approach. It involves interpreting the statute in the light of the mischief which the legislation was intended to prevent, or, more generally, in the light of the purpose of the legislation. It goes beyond the 'golden' rule in that it does not depend upon absurdity or perversity of the ordinary meaning. The approach depends upon being able to establish the legislative purpose, which is not always easily done, and which leads judges sometimes to speculate about the purpose of legislation (but see *2.2.4.6*). Some judges have regarded this fact as a blessing, leaving scope for 'creative interpretation' by manipulation of the supposed legislative intent. At such times it is important to remember the injunction of the 'literal' approach against distorting the natural language of the statute when a clear and unambiguous ordinary meaning may be identified. Provided it is genuinely clear and unambiguous, such an ordinary meaning is the best indication of legislative intent.

2.2.4.4 The amalgamation of approaches It should be clear from the above descriptions that there are not three rules of interpretation, each separately applicable when prescribed conditions are shown to exist. Rather, there is a spectrum of approaches to interpretation in which literal meaning, context (or 'register') and legislative intent combine in any number of different ways according to what the court thinks is appropriate in the individual case. The starting point ought always to be the natural meaning of the words used, and deviation from that standard is permitted to whatever degree is necessary according to the vagueness or ambiguity encountered. Legislative purpose appears to be relevant in two ways. It determines the context or register in the light of which a statute may be tested for ambiguity. For example, in the case of a statute whose purpose is the regulation of the use of motorised vehicles, it would be possible to exclude the meaning of 'road' as a piece of water near the shore where ships may ride at anchor, and thus to exclude any finding of ambiguity. Secondly, legislative purpose guides the search for meaning when the natural meaning has rightly been rejected.

2.2.4.5 Other aids to interpretation The most important source of interpretive aids for any statute is the statute's definition section, should it have one. The modern tendency is to include one. Its main purpose is to provide definitions of words having ordinary meanings, or which are vague, which have been used as terms of art in the statute. For example, ss.1, 12 and 14 of the Unfair Contract Terms Act 1977 contain definitions (including 'negligence', 'dealing as a consumer', 'business', etc.).

In addition to the main approaches to interpretation outlined above, there are certain presumptions about the drafting of statutes which judges sometimes resort to where the intention is not otherwise clear. Some of these presumptions are based on notions of fairness. For example, a statute is presumed not to be retrospective, and is presumed not to destroy private rights without compensation unless express words to that effect are used. Others refer to the context in which words are used to restrict the impact of the statute. The *ejusdem generis* rule restricts the meaning of general words appearing in a statute after specific words which all belong to a single class to other things of 'the same class'. Thus, under this rule the expression 'ships, boats, yachts, canoes and other means of transport' would be restricted in meaning to other means of transport *on water* and would exclude cars, trains and aeroplanes. For the most part these presumptions are no more than common sense reasoning, and provided it is remembered that a statute must always be read in its context in order to achieve a proper understanding the student need not be over concerned to learn them all.

2.2.4.6 Extrinsic aids to interpretation The approaches to interpretation considered until now have largely been based upon identifying meaning from within the text of the statute itself. Even when applying the mischief rule the first approach of the court is to seek the purpose of the statute from the text itself. Nevertheless, extrinsic (or outside) sources of information may shed light on the meaning of a statute, and in recent years courts have overcome previous reluctance to consult such sources. This process has culminated in a recent decision of the House of Lords permitting consultation, in limited circumstances, of the report in *Hansard* of statements made in Parliament at the time of the passage of the Bill in question. An important early step in admitting extrinsic evidence was to allow the courts to consider reports of bodies such as the Law Commission, which had been involved in drawing up draft Bills eventually submitted to Parliament. It is usually said that such material may be taken into account to establish the mischief which the legislation was intended to combat, but not to establish the meaning of particular words used (e.g., *A-G's Reference (No. 1 of 1988)* [1989] 2 All ER 1 at 6 *per* Lord Lowry). Nevertheless, the line between these two functions may sometimes be a fine one: in *Smith* v *Eric S Bush* [1989] 2 All ER 514 at 530 Lord Griffiths referred to a report of the Law Commission in seeking Parliament's *intention* in enacting the Unfair Contract Terms Act 1977, and it is not clear whether that intention was referable to the mischief or to the meaning. In *Pepper (Inspector of Taxes)* v *Hart* [1993] 1 All ER 42, the House of Lords allowed reference to *Hansard* 'where such material clearly discloses the mischief aimed at or the legislative intention lying behind the ambiguous or obscure words' (*per* Lord Browne-Wilkinson at 64). Their Lordships reached this conclusion whilst acknowledging counter-arguments based upon practical considerations such as extra cost and delay, and upon the constitutional significance of permitting such reference. Ultimately, the belief that consulting *Hansard* was the best means to ensure that the courts give effect to the intentions of Parliament prevailed over the counter-arguments.

2.3 DELEGATED LEGISLATION

2.3.1 Nature of delegated legislation

A major response to the increase in legislative activity, and the shortage of parliamentary time for it, has been for Parliament to delegate its legislative powers to some subordinate body, such as a Minister, local authority or public corporation. The delegation of legislative power by Parliament cannot be reviewed by the courts, since it is an exercise of the sovereignty of Parliament, but the legislation made by the subordinate body can be reviewed by the courts. Review takes place under a doctrine known as *ultra vires*. In delegating its legislative power Parliament does not give a free hand to the subordinate body, but sets out purposes for which and limits within which the legislative power may be exercised. If the court finds that in making legislation the subordinate body has gone beyond the powers granted (*ultra vires*) it will declare the legislation void. It is unusual, but not unknown, for major changes in the law to be introduced by delegated legislation. Usually the major principles are enacted by parliamentary legislation and the details filled in by delegated legislation.

2.3.2 Physical sources

The most common form of delegated legislation is called the *statutory instrument*, which is a regulation made by a Minister. They are published as they are made, and run to several bound volumes for any one year; for, just as statutes have surpassed case law in terms of the volume of law-making, so statutory instruments now far surpass statutes in volume. The LEXIS information retrieval system (*2.1.1*) allows statutes and statutory instruments to be searched simultaneously, so that the user may be sure of having all legislative texts on a particular point at his disposal.

2.4 JUSTICE, MORALITY AND PUBLIC POLICY

Although the courts are commonly thought of as 'dispensing justice', it is not their function merely to decide each case on the basis of what would be fair between the parties, without reference to the law and to the interests of society as a whole. Nevertheless, inherent in that statement is the suggestion that judicial decision-making involves consultation not only of the formal sources of law, that is case law (*2.1*), statutes (*2.2*) and delegated legislation (*2.3*), but also other less finite standards, at least in some cases. Those standards may for convenience be described as justice, morality and public policy, but the labels matter less than the general question of the extent to which judges have recourse to *values* as a source of law. In many cases the scope for a reference to values will be negligible, because the dispute between the parties falls squarely within the ambit of an established rule. But in a limited number of cases some novel element in the dispute results in the affirmation of a value, whatever decision is reached. Unless there is always a single right answer to the way in which the law should develop in response to new situations, such development will involve a choice which, except if made upon the toss of a coin, reflects a reasoning which ranks some values higher than others. All the evidence, such as dissenting judgments in the Court of Appeal and the House of Lords, suggests that it is possible for there to be legitimate difference of opinion on the more desirable way in which to develop the law, casting doubt upon 'single right answer' theories. The cases in which such choices are made are, of course, the ones which are influential in terms of precedent, and for that reason the values to which they give priority must be seen as an indirect source of law.

THREE
The impact of the
European Community

3.1 INTRODUCTION

The European Economic Community was established in 1958, with an initial membership of six countries (Belgium, France, Germany, Italy, Luxembourg and the Netherlands), who had earlier formed a more limited Coal and Steel Community. The avowed aims of the Community, set out in arts.2 and 3 of the Treaty of Rome establishing the EEC, are economic: harmonious development of economic activities, continuous and balanced expansion, accelerated raising of the standard of living. It must be acknowledged, however, that a motivating force for the establishment of the Community was the desire to increase European political stability after the Second World War, which it was thought might be achieved by means of the economic interdependence of the independent European states. European union has continued to be an important theme in Community activities since its foundation, its most recent expression being found in the Single European Act of 1986, and the current hesitant progress towards ratification of the (Maastricht) Treaty on European Union. The Community has now increased in size to 12 members (the newcomers being: Denmark, Greece, Ireland, Portugal, Spain and the United Kingdom). The United Kingdom became a member on 1 January 1973. The particular importance of the Community for students of law is that the Treaty of Rome established an entire legal system which has profound effects on the domestic law of any member state. In the now well-known words of Lord Denning MR in *H.P. Bulmer* v *J. Bollinger SA* [1974] Ch 401 at 418: 'When we come to matters with a European element, the treaty is like an incoming tide. It flows into the estuaries and up the rivers. It cannot be held back.'

3.2 COMMUNITY INSTITUTIONS

3.2.1 The Council
Primary political, legislative and executive responsibility rests in the Council, which by art.145 of the Treaty of Rome is charged with the coordination of the general economic policies of the member states (see also art.189). The Council consists of representatives from the governments of each member state. The

general Council consists of the respective Foreign Secretaries, but when the Council meets to discuss specialist matters (e.g. agriculture) it consists of the respective relevant Ministers. Although the Treaty provides for qualified majority voting on the Council, the practice since 1966 has been to require unanimity on all important matters. In relation to measures affecting the achievement of the internal market, a return to qualified majority voting is required by arts.16–19 of the Single European Act. Much of the important legislation emanating from the Community is passed by the Council acting on proposals from the Commission (*3.2.2*).

In addition to the ordinary meetings of the Council, it became customary to hold regular summit meetings of member state heads of government, which became known as the European Council. That body has now achieved official legal status (art.2, Single European Act).

3.2.2 The Commission
The everyday executive work of the Community is performed by the Commission, which combines governmental and civil service functions. It must ensure the enforcement of Community law, by monitoring and by bringing actions when necessary against individuals, or member states, or other Community institutions. It also makes proposals for legislation to the Council. It has general executive powers conferred by the Council, and is responsible for implementation of the budget. Its members are appointed by the member states, but must be independent of the governments of those states. That is, they do not serve as representatives (in the way that members of the Council treat their role), but must act always in the general Community interest, irrespective of national affiliation.

3.2.3 The Parliament
Until recently this body was more properly known as the Assembly, although it had begun to call itself the Parliament in the early years of the Community, and has now been officially accorded that title by the Single European Act. Its members are directly elected by universal suffrage, but it should not be confused with parliaments existing in member states. It has no legislative powers, and the scope for democratic control through the Parliament is severely limited. Its most important functions are its consultative role, especially in the legislative process, and its power to question the Commission and Council. Its powers backed by real force are the motion of censure, which would force the entire Commission to resign and which has never been used, the power to reject the draft budget, which has been used twice (in 1979 and 1984), and powers granted under Budget Treaties of 1970 and 1975 to amend, within a set limit, the amounts to be spent on items such as regional, social or environmental policy. As the Parliament demonstrates increasing responsibility and maturity it may be anticipated that its powers will increase, especially if further steps are taken towards European union. For example, under the Maastricht Treaty the Parliament gains a power of legislative co-decision with (or veto over) the Council of Ministers in important areas of Community activity. Equally, it

gains the power to make proposals for legislation, which was previously the exclusive prerogative of the Commission.

3.2.4 The Court of Justice

3.2.4.1 Role and structure The Court of Justice is the head of the new legal order established by the Treaty of Rome. It has responsibility for enforcement of Community law, in a judicial not executive capacity. From that responsibility have derived important roles of supervising the harmonious interpretation of the law and, perhaps inevitably for the highest court of the system, creative development of the law. The court structure in the Community is very unusual, in that for many purposes there is no appeal from the lower courts to the highest court. In some matters, such as restrictive practices cases (see *8.8.7*), the Commission acts as court of first instance, in which case the Court of Justice is an appellate court. But in many cases the national courts of the member states serve as first instance courts, in which case there is no *appeal* from the national courts to the Court of Justice, which instead exercises its supervisory function by means of interpretative references (*3.2.4.2(a)*).

There are 13 judges of the Court of Justice, one from each member state plus one additional judge from, in turn, France, Germany, Italy and the United Kingdom. Despite the appearance of national representation, it is an essential feature of the independence of the Court that the judges are themselves independent, and decide issues judicially and objectively, without reference to national interest. The judges are aided in their task by a number of Advocates-General, a position common in civil law systems but with no real equivalent in the common law. The function of the Advocate-General is to make a reasoned submission to the Court in any given case on both the law and the merits, representing no party, nor the Community institutions, but the public interest. Except when a member state is a party to proceedings before the Court, the judges usually sit in chambers of three or five judges, and cases are heard by a single chamber. Even so, the work load of the Court is now enormous, and the back-log of cases growing.

Under the Single European Act powers were taken to create a further court within the Court of Justice which would specialise in types of litigation which produce a large volume of work, such as competition cases and employment disputes involving Community employees. This Court of First Instance came into being on 25 September 1989. For the time being its jurisdiction is limited to competition and staff cases, although there has been speculation that in due course anti-dumping cases will be added. These cases place great emphasis on the appreciation of the facts. Appeal on a point of law lies to the full Court of Justice.

3.2.4.2 Jurisdiction

(a)   Under art.177 (Treaty of Rome) the national courts may, and in some circumstances must, refer matters of EC law to the Court of Justice for a preliminary ruling on interpretation. The Court of Justice does not state how the particular case should be decided, but gives a general ruling on how the law is to be interpreted. This function is particularly important in relation to EC law which directly affects individuals (see *3.3.2*).

(b)   Under arts. 169-171 (Treaty of Rome) the Court has jurisdiction over proceedings against member states, brought by the Commission or by another member state, for failure to fulfil treaty obligations.

(c)   Under art.172 (Treaty of Rome) the Court has jurisdiction over actions brought by individuals (including legal persons such as corporations) contesting the imposition of penalties. This jurisdiction is in effect an appeal from a decision of the Commission. The commonest situation of imposition of a penalty is for breach of the restrictive practices or monopoly rules of the Treaty (cf. arts.85 and 86: *8.8.7*).

(d)   Under arts.173-176 (Treaty of Rome) the Court has power to review the legality of the actions or inaction of Community institutions. In order to invoke this jurisdiction a person must be able to demonstrate a particular and specific interest affected by the alleged illegality. The Council, the Commission and the member states are assumed to have a general interest in ensuring Community legality, and so may invoke this jurisdiction without showing special interest.

(e)   In addition to the above major grounds of jurisdiction, the court has powers to hear a miscellany of cases, including claims for compensation for injury or loss caused by the wrongful act of Community institutions (art.178), and disputes between the Community institutions and their employees (art.179).

3.3   SOURCES OF COMMUNITY LAW

3.3.1   Treaty

The highest sources of EC law are treaties. The Treaty of Rome, which established the Community, is its written constitution. Two other forms of treaty are also important. From time to time changes are made to the structure established by the Treaty of Rome, and such changes can only be made by further treaties made under international law. Examples of this kind of treaty are the Accession Treaty made when a new member joins the Community, and the Single European Act (1986). Moreover, the member states sometimes wish to take a joint initiative in relation to some matter ancillary to, but not strictly part of, the main aims of the Treaty of Rome. Such initiatives are made by treaty. Important examples of these may be found in the field of conflict of laws, in which the Community has sought to create common approaches among the member states to the law applicable to contracts (Convention on Contractual Obligations), and to jurisdiction of courts and the reciprocal enforcement of member state judgments (Brussels Convention on Jurisdiction and the Enforcement of Judgments in Civil and Commercial Matters). Under United Kingdom law treaties do not become part of our law except by specific incorporation by Act of Parliament.

3.3.2   Regulations

Regulations are the main form of Community legislation, although they are, strictly speaking, subordinate legislation since they may only be made in accordance with powers created under the Treaty (arts.189–191, Treaty of Rome). They are generally binding in their entirety on all member states, and they bind both member states (where relevant) and individuals. Regulations require no national measure before they become applicable within the legal systems of the member states. The impact of EC law, and especially regulations, on national legal systems is considered in more detail below (see generally *3.4*).

3.3.3 Directives
A directive is a binding instruction issued to member states to take action themselves to achieve a stated goal. The purpose is to allow member states to determine individually, within a stipulated time-limit, what is the most appropriate way to achieve the goal consistently with their existing national structures and legislation. Normally, therefore, directives require legislative or executive implementation within each member state before becoming applicable. However, in limited circumstances they may still create direct legal rights for individuals even before national implementation (*3.4.2*).

3.3.4 Decisions
Decisions are specific rather than general acts of the Community institutions, and are binding only on those to whom addressed. They may be addressed to a member state or to an individual (including a legal person). They are usually the vehicle for executive action to implement or enforce Community law.

3.3.5 Others
In addition to the above formal sources of Community law, the Court of Justice has drawn on a wide range of sources in its creative filling of the gaps in the new Community legal order. In the first place the Court may draw on the national law of the member states, especially where principles common to all countries can be identified. Article 215 (Treaty of Rome) provides that in the exercise of its jurisdiction over claims for compensation for wrongful acts of Community institutions (under art.178) the Court shall apply 'general principles common to the laws of the member states'. In *Transocean Marine Paint Association* v *EC Commission* [1974] ECR 1063 the Court adopted as part of Community law the rule of natural justice found especially in English law that no judicial decision should be made against a person without that person being given the opportunity to be heard. In similar fashion the Court has established general principles of 'legal certainty', 'equality' and 'proportionality'.

The Court may also draw on international law, especially as a source of fundamental rights. For example, in *Rutili* v *Minister of the Interior* [1975] ECR 1219 the Court of Justice referred to the European Convention for the Protection of Human Rights and Fundamental Freedoms, made under the auspices of the Council of Europe, of which all member states are contracting parties.

3.4 IMPACT OF EC LAW ON NATIONAL LEGAL SYSTEMS

The creation of the new Community legal order raised important and difficult questions about the relationship between EC law and the domestic law of the individual member states. At issue were: whether EC law automatically became part of national law by virtue of accession to the Community; whether, although apparently a species of international law, it created rights and obligations for individuals as well as for states; and whether it was superior to national law.

3.4.1 Direct applicability

The concept of direct applicability describes the status of EC law which automatically becomes part of national legal systems. As noted above (*3.3.1*), in the United Kingdom treaties do not become part of the legal system until incorporated by Act of Parliament. Thus, the Treaty of Rome and Accession Treaty were incorporated by s.2(1) of the European Communities Act 1972. Regulations, on the other hand, are made under powers created by the Treaty of Rome, and by art.189 are directly applicable in the member states. That is, they require no further national enactment, once promulgated by the Community, to become part of the law of each member state. This construction has been confirmed more than once by the Court of Justice (e.g. in *Bussone* v *Italian Ministry of Agriculture* [1978] ECR 2429). It is generally thought that since directives require national measures of implementation they cannot be directly applicable. This does not mean, however, that they cannot have any direct effect (see *3.4.2.2*).

3.4.2 Direct effect

The concept of direct effect describes the status of Community law which creates rights for individuals which must be upheld by the national courts. Such rights may normally be enforceable against public authorities or against other individuals. In other words, EC law which is of direct effect is for most purposes indistinguishable, except in terms of source, from the domestic law of member states (but see *3.4.3*). As a general rule (but see *3.4.2.2*), to be of direct effect a provision must be directly applicable (*3.4.1*) and suitable for application to individuals. In its first decision the Court of Justice made clear that a provision may create rights for individuals without necessarily addressing individuals at all (*Van Gend en Loos* v *Nederlandse Belastingadministratie* [1963] ECR 1). It seems now that a relatively clear test of direct effect has emerged. To be suitable for application to individuals, and so to create individual rights, a provision must be clear and unambiguous, unconditional and not dependent on enactment by Community or national authorities (see *Marshall* v *Southampton and South West Hampshire Area Health Authority* [1986] 2 All ER 584).

3.4.2.1 Direct effect of Treaty provisions and regulations Since regulations are directly applicable, and Treaty provisions become part of national legal systems once incorporated, the first condition of direct effect is easily satisfied. Indeed, in respect of Treaty provisions and regulations it may be

more appropriate to reverse the presumption, and state that they are of direct effect unless failing to satisfy the second condition.

3.4.2.2   Direct effect of directives   The concept of direct effect has a slightly distorted meaning in the case of directives. Since directives are not directly applicable they fail to satisfy the first condition of direct effect. Nevertheless, the Court of Justice has held a few directives to be of direct effect, even without national implementation, in the limited sense of creating rights for individuals against a national government (*Van Duyn* v *Home Office* [1974] ECR 1337). Direct effect will only apply where the right created by the directive is clear and unambiguous, and where a deadline for action by the national government has passed without such action. Probably the best explanation of this exceptional meaning of direct effect is that a national government should not be allowed to plead its own failure to comply with a directive as ground for denying to an individual a right which would otherwise exist. It follows from this argument that this form of direct effect should be limited to the enforcement of rights against national governments, and should not extend to enforcement against other individuals, since individuals can have no control over the failure of government to act within the permitted time. Nevertheless, the Court of Justice has given the direct effect of directives a wider scope than might have been anticipated, by laying down a very broad interpretation of the 'state' (*Foster* v *British Gas plc* [1990] 3 All ER 897, ECJ, applied in [1991] 2 All ER 705, HL).

3.4.3   Supremacy of Community law
For the European Economic Community to succeed as a unified group pursuing common economic goals it is essential, amongst other things, that Community law be applied equally and consistently throughout the member states, and that policies enshrined in Community law should not be subject to distortion by 12 different national interpretations. These conditions are promoted by the doctrine of supremacy of Community law. The doctrine is nowhere stated in the Treaty of Rome, but it is implicit in the idea of a supra-national organisation pursuing common goals, and has been clearly articulated many times by the Court of Justice (e.g. in *Amministrazione delle Finanze dello Stato* v *Simmenthal SpA* [1978] ECR 629). It is apparent that the doctrine is a potential source of conflict between national law and Community law, especially where the doctrine is at odds with the prevailing constitutional arrangements within a member state.

In the United Kingdom the doctrine of supremacy of Community law is in potential conflict with the doctrine of the sovereignty of Parliament (*2.2.2*). There is no risk of conflict in the case of non-legislative sources of law, or in the case of legislative sources of law pre-dating United Kingdom membership of the Community. Section 2(1) of the European Communities Act 1972 gives legal effect in the United Kingdom to law created by or under the Treaty of Rome, and so the doctrine of sovereignty of Parliament operates in the case of common law and existing statutory rules to confirm the supremacy of Community law, since the effect of parliamentary legislation is to overrule all previous inconsistent law. It must be stressed that s.2(1) operates to confer supremacy not only on Community law existing at the time of enactment but also on Community law created subsequently. The potential for conflict exists in the case of parliamentary legislation passed subsequently to the European Communities Act, since under the sovereignty doctrine Parliament cannot bind itself for the future to abstain from any particular action. Thus, a conventional view of the British constitution says that s.2(1) of the European Communities Act is powerless to provide supremacy for Community law over subsequent United Kingdom legislation. Indeed, seemingly conscious of that fact, s.2(4) of the Act does not provide that future legislation incompatible with Community law shall be invalid, but merely seeks to ensure *interpretation* of future legislation in a manner consistent with the supremacy of Community law.

Lord Denning suggested a practical approach to be adopted by the courts in cases of potential conflict (in *Macarthys Ltd* v *Smith* [1979] 3 All ER 325). In general the presumption must be that Parliament intended to legislate in a manner consistent with its Treaty obligations, which include allowing supremacy to Community law. Mere inadvertent inconsistency with Community law, therefore, should be reinterpreted to make it consistent, or not applied. But it is open to Parliament to make the deliberate choice to go against its Treaty obligations and to legislate in a manner inconsistent with Community law. In such a case the courts would give effect to the national legislation. It is presumed, however, that Parliament would not deliberately legislate in conflict with the supremacy of Community law, signalling an intention to withdraw from the Treaty of Rome, without using express and unambiguous language to that effect.

There is some evidence from recent cases decided in the House of Lords to support this view. In *Litster* v *Forth Dry Dock & Engineering Co. Ltd* [1989] 1 All ER 1134 their Lordships followed the so-called *Von Colson* doctrine (see case 14/83 [1984] ECR 1891) in interpreting UK legislation in order to comply with an EC directive, even though on its face the UK legislation did not literally bear the meaning given. More significantly, in *Factortame Ltd* v *Secretary of State for Transport (No 2)* [1991] 1 All ER 70, ECJ and HL, the House of Lords accepted the ruling of the European Court of Justice to the effect that in appropriate circumstances an interlocutory injunction should be available against the Crown in order to prevent a breach of Community law. In the most striking example of the effect of EC membership on Parliamentary sovereignty to date, the House of Lords granted an interlocutory injunction to prevent the Government enforcing the Merchant Shipping Act 1988, which of course was an Act of Parliament passed *after* the European Communities Act 1972.

3.4.4 Community law in national courts

For students of the law of contract the significance of Community law for contract litigation (and hence for all aspects of contracting) is steadily increasing. Initially, contract litigation was largely untouched by Community law except for attempts to employ the 'Euro-defence' based upon the competition provisions of art. 85 EC to avoid obligations to perform (see *8.8.7*). Such attempts were almost universally unsuccessful. Recent directives passed in the process towards completion of the single internal market are likely to have greater impact. In particular, the Package Travel, Package Holidays and Package Tours Regulations 1992 (SI 1992/3288) implement in English law Council Directive 90/314 (OJ 1990 L158/59), and have the effect of importing particular obligations into contracts of the kind addressed by the directive (see *10.4.3.3*). In due course it is expected that the Council will approve a directive of much wider general impact defining the minimum legal obligations to be undertaken in entering into contracts for the supply of services. Already, the Council has adopted Directive 93/13 (OJ 1993 L95/29) on unfair terms in consumer contracts, which will require further changes to English law in a field already policed by the Unfair Contract Terms Act 1977 (see *10.7*). Contracting parties may be unaware of the European origin of the rules which must be applied in respect of their contracts, and indeed that is how the process of law reform by means of directives is supposed to work. However, lawyers must be aware that the European origin of the rules opens avenues of recourse for their clients which may not be available in the case of purely domestic law. This is because in the final analysis it is the text of the Community legislation which must take precedence over the national implementing measure, so that the individual's rights must be determined in the light of the Community rule. Protection of these rights may even lead to the member state being liable where it has failed to implement Community law properly.

Remedies in respect of rights created under Community law remain a matter within the scope of the national legal system (*Rewe-Zentralfinanz* v *Landwirtschaftskammer für das Saarland* (case 33/76) [1977] 1 CMLR 533), although that principle is subject to a number of important qualifications. We have already seen that the *Von Colson* doctrine of indirect effect requires national law to be interpreted in the light of and consistently with Community legislation (see *3.4.3*). The House of Lords is reluctant to accept that this should apply to legislation passed to implement EC directives (*Duke* v *GEC Reliance Ltd* [1988] AC 618), and this approach may be justified on the basis of the need to protect individuals who act legally within the scope of national law, and who cannot be expected to have taken into account Community law which was not specifically addressed to them. Further qualifications are that the remedy provided must be equally effective as the remedy for a similar breach of domestic law (*Rewe Handelsgesellschaft Nord* v *Hauptzollamt Kiel* (case 158/80) [1982] 1 CMLR 449), and that, moreover, the remedy provided must be real and effective to assert the right in question and to deter such breaches (*Harz* v *Deutsche Tradex GmbH* (case 79/83) [1986] 2 CMLR 430). The application of these principles is becoming clearer. In *Factortame Ltd* v *Secretary of State for Transport (No. 2)* [1991] 1 All ER 70, the House of Lords was required to provide a remedy where none existed (an interlocutory injunction against the Crown), demonstrating that the requirement of a real and effective remedy takes precedence over the principle of equivalence with domestic remedies. The logic of the *Factortame* decision was extended still further by the European Court of Justice in *Francovich* v *Italian State* [1992] IRLR 84, where the member state was required to compensate individuals who had suffered losses because it had failed to implement a directive under which they should have acquired rights. This last decision may be of particular significance in relation to the recent directives which will require amendments of the domestic law of contract.

PART II   THE LAW OF CONTRACT

FOUR

Introduction to the law of contract

4.1   THE NATURE OF CONTRACTUAL LIABILITY

Major legal concepts, such as 'contract', are notoriously difficult to define. All that will be attempted here is a generalisation, which admittedly is subject to exceptions and incomplete, but which it is believed gives an adequate indication of the core of the concept. Contracts are *legally enforceable agreements*. Liability for breach of contract is, therefore, liability for failure to keep to the terms of such an agreement. To say that an agreement is 'legally enforceable' is merely a shorthand way of saying that it is one to which the law gives its sanction, to be distinguished from mere social arrangements which exist outside the framework of the law and which are binding only in the sense of moral obligation or social convention. Thus, our definition of contract implies (at least) three distinct fields of legal rule relating to contracts. There must be rules relating to the formation and content of agreements, rules relating to the enforcement of agreements, and rules which distinguish those agreements which *are* legally enforceable from those which are not.

4.1.1   Essential ingredients of enforceability

The rules determining whether an agreement is to be regarded as enforceable are the subject of Chapter 6. They embrace three separate elements: intention (*6.2*), consideration (*6.3*) and form (*6.5*). Thus, an agreement will only be classed as a contract if the parties intend legal consequences to result from it, if it satisfies the requirements of consideration, and if it meets any special rules of evidence which may exist.

Of the above elements the most important is consideration, which is a distinguishing feature of the common law contract not found in civil law systems. Consideration will be defined below (*6.3.1*) as the action, inaction, or promise thereof by one party which induces the action, inaction, or promise of another. Consideration for one promise may therefore be provided by another promise, and so a contract may be constituted out of nothing more than an exchange of promises. There are good functional reasons for the enforceability of promises which have induced the reliance of another, but it has sometimes been suggested that liability upon a promise which has not yet induced another's reliance is an unnecessary feature of the law. The reason for that suggestion is that where there has been no reliance no harm will be caused by failure to keep the promise.

Despite the apparent logic of this reasoning, the law has rightly rejected it for practical reasons of evidence. That is, it may in some circumstances be extremely difficult to prove reliance on a promise. For example, if A promises to sell to B 100 tons of grain, and B agrees to buy it, but before A commences delivery or B makes any payment one of them backs out of the agreement, it might be said that no harm will be done by cancellation of the contract since neither party has done anything in reliance on it. What if, however, B has already sold the grain to C, or A has turned down the opportunity to sell the grain to D, on account of the contract? Rather than put the parties to the proof of their reliance the law assumes that promises have a tendency to induce reliance, and so liability attaches to the mere act of reciprocal promising. Contracts in which performance on both sides remains in the future are described as 'executory', and the binding nature of such agreements is an important element in the commercial value of the device of contract.

4.1.2 Agreement

The rules relating to the formation and the substance of agreements are the subjects respectively of Chapters 5 and 10. In defining contracts as being based on agreements it is implicit that we are concerned with obligations which are consensually (or voluntarily) undertaken. Moreover, it follows from the description of consideration given above (*4.1.1*) that agreements usually consist of reciprocal promises. It is important, however, to give an early warning about the limits of the notion of agreement. In the first place, not all undertakings are completely voluntary, in that the law imposes certain obligations on those who enter particular types of agreement (see *10.4.3*). Thus, the fact of entering the agreement may be voluntary, but the substance of the agreement is to some extent (e.g. undertakings as to the quality of goods sold) dictated by law.

Secondly, not all agreements are consensual if by that term we are to understand a precise symmetry between the real intentions of the parties. It was once common to speak of agreements being formed by a 'meeting of the minds' of the parties, which suggests that their *subjective* intentions must coincide. It is of course almost impossible to discover a person's real or subjective intentions, and for this reason the law regards agreements as formed by a coincidence of *objectively ascertained* intentions. That is, what each party actually intended is irrelevant if to all outward appearances the parties are in agreement. The objective test of formation of contracts, and especially the meaning of 'objectivity' in this context, are considered in detail below (*5.1.2*).

4.1.3 Enforcement

When we consider the necessity of enforcing the obligations created by those agreements which qualify as contracts it is inevitable that our attention will primarily be focused on those remedies for breach of contract which are available in the ordinary courts. Our understanding of the rules of the law of contract, including those rules relevant to enforcement, is largely derived from judicial statements. The enforcement of contractual obligations by legal proceedings is the subject of Chapter 12. It is necessary here only to summarise what

n more detail in the introduction to that chapter (*12.1*). Although
he enforcement of contractual obligations, the paradigm remedy
...each of contract is compensation for non-performance (*12.1.3*) rather
than compulsion of the performance promised in the contract (*12.1.2*). Moreover,
although in the field of criminal law the idea of 'law enforcement' involves
the imposition of penalties for non-compliance, the law of contract denies any
role to penalties in securing performance of contracts (*12.1.1*).

It is important, however, not to be misled by the concentration on judicial
remedies for breach of contract into believing that the courts are the most
important element in the enforcement of contracts. For the practising lawyer
litigation is the last resort. His first thought is towards restoring the relationship
between the parties, and thereby securing performance. Failing that, he will
seek a negotiated settlement of the dispute. In that case the legal rules may
play a part, but the terms of the settlement will probably owe less to the
legal rules than to a compromise between the parties (although it must be
recognised that such a compromise is itself a contract: see *6.3.2.2*). Even where
compromise is not possible, litigation in the ordinary courts is not the only
means of dispute resolution. The parties may agree at the time of making
the contract, or subsequently, that disputes be submitted to arbitration, which
may have advantages of cost, time and informality of procedure over the ordinary
courts (cf. Kerr (1980) JBL 164). Commercial disputes are frequently settled
in this way. At the other end of the scale, disputes involving small sums of
money are determined by arbitration under the county court small claims
procedure (see *1.5.8*). Finally, it may sometimes be more appropriate to invoke
the powers and assistance of the trading standards officer, or the Office of
Fair Trading, both of whom have regulatory powers over contracts.

4.2 CONTRACT AND TORT

English law maintains a fairly strict division between contract and tort, which
represents one of the major divisions of legal classification between obligations
voluntarily assumed and obligations imposed by law. Contractual obligations
are voluntarily assumed in that they derive from agreements which individuals
are free to make or refrain from making. Tortious obligations arise independently
of the will of those involved, and derive from standards of behaviour imposed
by law. In this section we shall be referring exclusively to the tort of negligence,
which imposes an obligation not to breach the duty of care (i.e. the duty to
behave as would a reasonable person in the circumstances) which the law says
is owed to those who may foreseeably be injured by any particular conduct
or activity. The leading case on the law of negligence is *Donoghue* v *Stevenson*
[1932] AC 562, which involved the notorious snail in the bottle of ginger beer.
The manufacturer and bottler of the ginger beer was held to owe to consumers
a duty not to allow foreign bodies to enter his product which might make
such consumers ill (see also *13.1*).

It is ironic that a marked distinction is maintained between contract and
tort, since the action for breach of contract was originally a sub-species of
an early form of action for tort (see *4.3*). The strictness of the distinction

appears to owe much to nineteenth century developments. The prevailing philosophy of the time, sometimes summarised under the epithet *'laissez-faire'*, regarded man as master of his own destiny, and believed that if given free reign man's intelligence would operate to the benefit of all. This philosophy gave rise to two specific legal notions relevant to contracts. The first, and more important, is 'freedom of contract' (*4.4*). The second was that, being based in free will, contract was the *superior* norm. That is, contractual obligations were supposedly superior to all others because of the manner of their generation. Thus, obligations which might otherwise be imposed by law would give way to obligations contractually agreed between the parties. Modern writers are deeply sceptical of this second notion. Some go so far as to talk of the 'death of contract' (cf. G. Gilmore, *The Death of Contract*, Ohio State Univ. Press, 1986), suggesting that the law is moving progressively to a system of imposed obligations even in those fields traditionally regarded as the exclusive domain of the law of contract. Reports of the death of contract are no doubt greatly exaggerated, but there is no denying that there has been a marked retreat from the high point of contractual superiority.

4.2.1 Overlap of contract and tort

That there is nothing which makes contractual obligations necessarily superior to tortious obligations appears to be a logical conclusion from the fact that there are many instances where the two may overlap. A simple example should suffice to demonstrate that the same factual situation may give rise to both contractual and tortious liability. A student (A) arranges with a haulier (B) to send his case of belongings to C college, paying in advance for the service to be provided. In the course of performance of this service the case is placed in an open truck and, as the truck goes round a sharp bend, one side comes down and the case falls off the truck into the river. A has a contract with B. There are reciprocal, voluntarily assumed obligations (A to pay: B to deliver the case). A may therefore bring an action for breach of contract against B. Alternatively, if A can prove negligence on B's part (which may not be difficult, since the assumption must be that it is not normal for a case to be lost in this way) A may sue in tort, since B will be in breach of a duty to take proper care of A's case. Thus, the same facts may give rise to an action either for breach of contract or for breach of a duty of care arising in tort.

At first sight it may seem curious to regard the contractual obligation in this situation as superior to that arising in tort, since they are identical. It is possible, however, to modify the nature of the obligation by contract, for example by inserting an exemption clause in the contract which limits or excludes B's liability (see generally *10.6*). It is the potential for the parties to stipulate the substance of the obligation which led to the belief in the superiority of contractual obligations. That potential is today seriously diminished. For example, a clause purporting to limit B's liability in the above situation would only be valid if it were reasonable (see *10.6.3.2*). Thus, absolute freedom of contract, if it ever existed, has given way to a much more limited freedom which must coexist with many rules of contract law which impose obligations on the parties.

4.2.2 Remaining significance of the division

Despite the blurring of the distinction between contract and tort which has taken place in recent years, it is easy to identify ways in which contract and tort remain separate. An obligation of positive performance some time in the future can normally only be created by contract, even if some of the substance of that obligation will be defined by legal imposition. The standard of performance required under a contract is often strict (see *10.5*), while liability for the tort of negligence depends upon the plaintiff being able to prove that the defendant acted unreasonably. Nevertheless, the blurring of the distinction between contract and tort has led to the disappearance of, or uncertainty over, differences traditionally regarded as fundamental.

4.2.2.1 Measure of loss recoverable The traditional distinction between damages for breach of contract and damages for negligence was that in the former damages for loss of profit might be recovered (see *12.3.1*), while in the latter lost profit (or pure economic loss) could not be recovered, and the plaintiff was limited to the recovery of reliance loss (the amount necessary to restore the plaintiff to his position before the tort took place). It has been accepted for some time that a plaintiff bringing an action for breach of contract may claim reliance losses rather than lost profits if he prefers (see *12.3.2.5*). Although English law has flirted with the converse rule, that a plaintiff bringing an action in tort may recover expectation loss (or 'pure economic loss'), it has now repudiated such a doctrine. The rule has important repercussions for subcontractors. In this field, at least, the notion that contract is the superior norm still prevails to some extent.

4.2.2.2 Remoteness of damage In both contract and tort damages may not be recovered for losses which are too remote, that is, which were not a reasonably foreseeable consequence of the breach of duty which has occurred. It has been traditional to assert that the test of remoteness is more strict in contract claims than it is in claims in tort, but that assertion is now clouded with doubt. In *H. Parsons (Livestock) Ltd* v *Uttley Ingham & Co. Ltd* [1978] 1 All ER 525 the members of the Court of Appeal were unable to agree whether there was any difference at all in the remoteness tests of contract and tort, or whether such difference as there was lay not between contract and tort but between expectation and reliance losses. The respective merits of these potential rules, and the policies they may be taken to represent, are discussed below (see generally *12.3.3.3*).

4.2.2.3 Limitation of actions Under the Limitation Act 1980 a standard limitation period of six years applies to claims both in contract and in tort (see *1.5.1.4*), with the exception of personal injury cases in tort when the period is three years (s.11 of the 1980 Act). Nevertheless, a distinction remains between contract and tort since the time at which the limitation period begins to run varies. In contract it begins to run at the time of breach. In tort it does not begin to run until some damage occurs, because there is no cause of action up to this time.

4.3   HISTORY OF CONTRACT LAW

The history of the law of contract is complex and contentious, and those who seek a comprehensive account must refer to specialist works (e.g. A. W. B. Simpson, *A History of the Common Law of Contract*, OUP, 1987; Simpson also wrote the historical introduction to M. P. Furmston, *Law of Contract* (Cheshire & Fifoot) 12th edn, Butterworth, 1991). The intention in this section is to provide a brief historical explanation of some elements of the law of contract, since it is an inevitable feature of the common law, based as it is in the system of precedent, that ancient doctrines sometimes return to haunt the modern law. Two periods of history are especially significant in the development of the law of contract. The first, which is examined here, covers a period of some three hundred years, ending in the early years of the seventeenth century, when the action for breach of contract first developed. The second period covers the late eighteenth and nineteenth centuries, which saw the climax of the philosophy of freedom of contract and which laid the foundations upon which our modern law is built.

At the beginning of the thirteenth century the royal courts did not hear actions relating to contracts. Of course, many transactions took place which we would today recognise as contracts, such as sales and loans, but they were left to be regulated by the many specialist or local jurisdictions which existed at the time. The first common law action for breach of contract was that of *covenant*; it was unable to develop into a general law of contract, however, because it was restricted to contracts made under seal (cf. *6.1*). A further action of *debt* was developed which applied in the case of informal agreements, and which enabled the recovery of a specific sum of money owed to the plaintiff on the fiction that the plaintiff was recovering his own money. Debt nevertheless had its limitations. It did not allow the recovery of an unliquidated sum by way of damages for failure to perform a promised action (as opposed to the mere payment of money). In addition, trial procedures for debt were open to abuse by defendants which made success in such actions something of a lottery.

When the royal courts finally sought to expand their jurisdiction by taking control over contract actions, they did not seek to develop either of the existing writs which today we recognise as contractual in nature. Rather, they turned to a more flexible writ, which was the forerunner of the modern tort of negligence, known as *trespass on the case*. The advantage of the trespass action was that the procedure was much more secure from abuse than was debt. By the end of the fourteenth century the courts would allow claims based on trespass for defective performance of an undertaking, which in the medieval latin of court pleadings was known as an *assumpsit*. Assumpsit is the real foundation of the law of contract, but it developed relatively slowly, since in the early period it was only available for defective performance of an undertaking, and was not available for non-performance. This discrepancy can be explained in terms of formal procedure, but in practical terms was clearly illogical, and it was finally removed in *Thoroughgood's Case* (1584). The remaining obstacle to the development of assumpsit as a complete contract doctrine was the action for debt, since some courts would not allow an action to recover a specific sum of money on assumpsit, but insisted on the action being brought in debt, with its associated procedural difficulties. This obstacle was removed, and the law of informal contracts brought within the unified cause of action of assumpsit, by *Slade's Case* (1602).

In the peculiar way of the common law, the establishment of a unified remedy for all types of contract action was the catalyst for the development of general principles of contract law. The most important, and yet the most baffling to scholars, was the development of the doctrine of consideration. There are broadly two schools of thought as to how consideration came into English law. The first attributes it to the doctrine of *causa* found in Roman and civil law, and which is said to have made its way into the common law via Canon law and then the Chancery court. The second attributes it to an analogous (but far from identical) requirement of the action of debt, and the requirement of detriment in the action of trespass, which were somehow transferred to the action of assumpsit to give it form. Whichever may be the true explanation, the precise mechanics of the development of the doctrine of consideration are obscure. All that may be said with confidence is that by the seventeenth century the requirement of consideration in informal contracts was in place, and the law of contract began to take on a shape which we still recognise today.

4.4 ROLE OF CONTRACT AND OF CONTRACT LAW

The central role of contract in our legal and economic systems is not accidental. If lawyers, judges and latterly Parliament have worked at refining, honing and polishing the law, and litigants continue to rely on it, it is because contract serves important purposes in society. Indeed, it appears that the device of contract is put to important uses in many diverse societies, and it would be wrong to assume that contract law as we know it is the only model, or is of universal application. It is essential to distinguish between the device of contract, which has universal qualities, and the law of contract, which is the vehicle for adapting those universal qualities to the particular needs of a given society.

4.4.1 Role of contract

All societies require a vehicle through which *planned exchanges* can be made. Societies which have moved beyond hunting and subsistence farming require methods of ordering existence so that such cooperation as is deemed necessary may take place. The role of *planning* embraces the need people have to project into the future reliable courses of action. The idea of *exchange* includes not only 'one-off' contracts but also long-term business relationships comprising perhaps many hundreds of individual contracts; it may also include interpersonal relationships and even the individual's relationship with the state. There is a relationship of mutual support between societal stability, the idea of planning and the existence of exchange. The ability to plan ahead is an important factor in creating stability, while a stable society in which it can be predicted that exchanges will take place is an essential ingredient of reliable planning.

What may seem to be an entirely theoretical description of the role of contract may be put into context by a simple example. For many readers, the only experience of contracting will be as an ultimate consumer, so that each contract made seems isolated and discrete. In that sort of situation the planning element in contracts is not self-evident. So, when one purchases a book in a shop there is no doubt that the machinery by which the purchase is executed is a contract, but there is little sense of being merely one link in a chain, since one is the last link. A moment's consideration will reveal, however, that the particular contract of sale can only be achieved within a complex matrix of other contracts. If it is a technical book it is likely to have been commissioned by a publisher from the author. Both parties derive planning benefits from such a contract. The author knows that the time spent labouring on the book will be rewarded by publication and (he hopes) the payment of royalties on sales. The publisher is able to fill a gap in the list of books he publishes, in the secure knowledge that he will have such a book to offer to booksellers after a certain period. Before the decision to go ahead with the book is made, the publisher's employees will probably have carried out some market research, and a decision will have been reached on the price at which such a book will sell. The publisher will seek to meet that price target by making contracts with printers and binders which will keep costs at the estimates made when fixing the price of the book. The printers and binders will in turn make long term contracts with their raw material suppliers, so that they too may be sure that their costs remain within estimates. Delivery services, wholesalers and retail bookshops will all be involved in the process of delivering the book to the ultimate consumer. Business men do not assume that the link between author and reader will be achieved by a catalogue of fortunate accidents: they plan every stage of the marketing of a book, and they achieve confidence in the planning by securing it with contracts. This matrix of contractual relationships, against which any particular contract must be viewed, explains why the first instinct of contract lawyers is to seek to preserve an agreement under threat, since much more is at stake when one contract fails than just the relationship between the two contracting parties.

4.4.2 Role of contract law

If the role of the device of contract is to provide for confident planning of exchanges, the role of contract law is to mould those planned exchanges to the particular society the law serves. Thus, English contract law reflects the politico-economic philosophy prevailing in this country. Theories of the law of contract, which in recent years have been a fashionable subject of academic debate, are simply the reflection of these politico-economic philosophies. Just as few claim that any single such philosophy has a monopoly of the right answers for any given society, so it is difficult to claim that any single contract theory provides all the right answers as far as the development of the law of contract is concerned. But that does not mean that contract theory is without value.

4.4.2.1 The significance of theory There are many judges and practising lawyers who would deny the existence of any theory underlying the common law of contract, or who would dismiss theory as unrelated to the real world. This attitude may be understandable, since judges and lawyers must decide individual cases on their merits in accordance with the law, and are not primarily concerned with the elaboration of theory. Nevertheless, it may also be shortsighted. The law does not stand still, but rather has its own internal dynamism. In particular, changes in the law may result from judicial reasoning by reference to values where the court perceives the need to make a choice of how the law should develop to meet a situation not previously encountered, or where the scope of a particular rule has not been precisely defined (2.4). Consistent development of the law, so that such changes 'fit' within the existing scheme of things, assumes that judges have a sense of what the scheme of things is. Thus, an understanding of the theory of contract is essential to rational choices in developing the law, and should provide the student of law with criteria by which to assess the appropriateness of choices made. A satisfactory theory must explain how the law has developed to the point it is at today, and must provide the basis for establishing how the law may develop in the future by indicating general principles capable of giving rise to specific rules. Dissatisfaction with theory in general may have been caused by the growing inability of classical theory, which until now has dominated, to account for the existing rules of the law of contract. The question remains whether there is any more satisfactory theory which can take its place.

The discussion in this section inevitably refers to the substance of the law which is described later in this book. Readers may find it beneficial to return to this section after completing their study of the substantive law.

4.4.2.2 Classical theory The roots of classical theory go back at least as far as the 18th century. In seeking to explain the somewhat adventitious development of contract law in England, 19th-century commentators borrowed from the writings of French legal theorists, who by 1804 had succeeded in embodying in the French civil code a highly individualist conception of contract. The parties were regarded as having the power and the unrestricted freedom to make the law which was to govern their relationship. This French approach, which was the product of the political liberalism of the 18th century, fell in with the economic liberalism of 19th-century England to produce an equally individualist theory of contract law in this country. Nevertheless, the realities of the process of adjudication meant that the substantive law was obliged to move away from a purely individualist or subjective approach to contract, so that the much vaunted sanctity of individual autonomy in contracting, which made contract immune from judicial interference, was much more a theoretical ideal than a rule of law.

When we talk about the classical theory of contract today (see Fried, *Contract as Promise*, 1981), we must consider a modified form of the theory which has tried to account for the way the law has developed. Nevertheless, at the core of this 'modern' classical theory is the binding nature of the promise which has been voluntarily made. The crucial element in contract, which marks it out as different from most other areas of the law of obligations, is that it is more than reactive: it is creative. It does not merely provide the means of resolving disputes which may arise when certain events happen: it provides the mechanisms whereby things can be made to happen. For early contract scholars it was a crucial observable phenomenon that without any reliance by either party the law regarded the mutual exchange of promises as, without more, sufficient to create a binding obligation (see *6.3.1.1*). Tort and restitution were obligations produced by a reaction to events; but contract produced obligation as the result of the mere *exercise of will* in the form of promise. It was not surprising, therefore, that promise became the core of the theory, since it appears to be the essential ingredient marking contract out as separate from the rest of the law of obligations.

Before we examine how classical theory fits with the law of contract described later in this book, we should examine why the mere fact of promise (or voluntary undertaking) produces obligation. A first explanation, which owes much to political liberal theory, is that there is a *moral obligation* inherent in promising which is derived from the social convention of creating expectations by one's undertaking (Fried, *op cit.*, pp. 14–17). The social convention came into being because the liberal ideal of respect for persons and property could only be achieved if reliable cooperation could be established. There is support for this idea in the rule that the measure of damages for breach of contract is the amount necessary to put the non-breaching party into the position he would have been in had the contract been performed (*12.3.1*), which is generally regarded as protecting that party's expectation under the contract. We know that this protection of expectation is restricted by rules relating to foreseeability (*12.3.3.3*) and certainty (*12.3.2.4*), but a cogent argument can be made that these doctrines are no more than necessary limits to cope with procedural problems such as the fallibility of the means of proof, and do not take away from the basic premise that the promisee's actual expectation is to be protected. A more serious objection arises out of the fact that the objectivisation of contract apparent in the formation of contracts (*5.1.2*) and in remedies for breach of contract (*12.3.3.3*) appears to be more than procedural, and seems to substitute for the actual expectation a collective appraisal of what the expectation should have been.

A second explanation of the binding nature of promise, not entirely distinct from the first, derives from the liberal economic theories of the 19th century. Here, individual autonomy is not the goal itself, but it is a pivotal tool in the achievement of the actual goal of *maximisation of wealth* to the greater good of all in society. Maximisation of wealth is achieved by market exchanges where both or all the parties involved count themselves as benefited by the exchange which has taken place. The concept of market depends upon the binding nature of bargains made in the market, so that the individual's promise is required to be binding for the market system to work. Support for this version of classical theory can be found in the existing English rules relating to exemption clauses in genuinely freely negotiated contracts (see *10.6.4*). The purpose of such devices is said by economists to be to provide a mechanism whereby the parties may allocate the risks of the enterprise between them:

if they are both wealth-maximisers they may be assumed to have allocated those risks in a mutually beneficial way. To overrule exemption clauses in such circumstances is wrong, since the effect would be to reallocate the risk away from what the parties had calculated was mutually beneficial (*10.6.4.3*). Nevertheless, classical theory is ill-equipped to account for such intervention in freedom of contract as is provided, for example, by the Unfair Contract Terms Act 1977 (*10.6.3*).

It is not surprising that classical theory provides a coherent explanation of the rules of formation of agreement (*chapter 5*). Promise is the essence of the theory. Promises create expecation, and can only do so if clear lines of communication are established. These rules do no more than set out the means whereby promises are made. Nevertheless, the fact that the rules are consistent with the theory cannot hide the fact that there is increasing doubt, even among the judiciary, about whether the existing rules really conform to what business people do in practice (see *5.1.1*).

It is perhaps surprising that classical theory should cavil at the doctrine of consideration (Fried, *op cit.*, pp. 28–39, especially at p. 35). After all, the paradigm of consideration is usually said to be the mutual exchange of promises. Perhaps the consideration doctrine is no more than a trace of the Protestant work ethic in the common law: a rule against getting something for nothing! More probably, it shows that the common law idea of contract is founded in economic rather than political liberalism: wealth maximisation results from mutual exchange, and there is no exchange involved in gratuitous promising.

Beyond the rules relating to the formation of contracts the position of classical theory is less secure. Where the law must react to events which are outside the scope of the will of the parties, or to which the parties have for whatever reason given no attention, the insistence of classical theory on the autonomy of the will of the parties is inconsistent with the rules of the law of contract as they exist today. Thus, we shall see that in relation to mistake (*chapter 7*), illegal contracts (*8.7*), implied terms (*10.4*) and frustration (*11.4*) the approach of contemporary law is to impose a solution, often on the criterion of what is reasonable in the circumstances, and to abandon the fiction of searching for and complying with the will of the parties. That is not to say that classical theory is wholly without relevance. There is no doubt that it shaped the law in a crucial period of its development, and that it draws attention to an important element in modern contract law, the binding nature of mutual promises. But it cannot be regarded as a satisfactory theory when it is unable to account for important areas of the law. Its failure in this regard probably reflects the fact that the politico-economic philosophy which inspired it is no longer the philosophy underlying our contemporary law. Nevertheless, the doctrine of binding precedent (*2.1.2*) ensures that cases decided during the period when the classical concept of contract was at its height remain influential today, so that classical theory still makes a significant contribution to existing law.

In recent years two separate perceptions have generated the belief among many commentators that classical theory is unable to explain the entirety of modern contract law. The first is that contract law is not merely a response to the exercise of will by the contracting parties. Contract law also responds to events, often by imposing an obligation generally regarded as nevertheless contractual, or by modifying an already existing obligation. In each case the reaction of the law is independent of the will of the parties. Examples of this response to events may be found in the law relating to promissory estoppel (see generally 6.4), and other areas of law.

The second perception is that the limited empirical evidence available (see Beale and Dugdale (1975) 2 Br J Law Soc 45) suggests that in practice business people do not behave in a manner consistent with the classical conception of contract. For example, only in a formal sense could their contractual undertakings be regarded as promises, or the product of an exercise of will, since they frequently had little knowledge of the detailed undertakings contained in contractual documents. Moreover, business people often did not seek to avail themselves of the full remedy available for breach of contract (damages for lost profit) where there was a mutual exchange of promises but no performance. Thus, where an order was cancelled before any work had been done most of the firms surveyed would accept the cancellation without seeking compensation. Where there had been some but not complete performance by the time of cancellation, a charge would be made, usually based on the cost of work actually done, and an allowance for profit related not to the entire contract but solely to the means of computing actual costs incurred.

4.4.2.3 Reliance-based theories   The most signfiicant post-classical theory of contract is based on the notion that obligation results from the fact of reliance (and its most eloquent exponent has been Professor Atiyah: see especially (1978) 94 LQR 193). Both the practice of business people and some of the legal doctrines noted above (especially promissory estoppel) suggest that the important factor was not the promise made, but the fact of reliance on it. Promise remains important in providing evidence of what has been undertaken, but it is not the source of obligation. Even in the field of formation of agreements where classical theory is relatively secure the analysis is sometimes improved by considering reliance as the source of obligation. This view is certainly a more rational explanation of the cases relating to what are known respectively as the 'battle of the forms' (5.3.1.3) and 'agreements to agree' (5.6.3 and 5.6.4).

In general it seems that our instinct of obligation (or its absence) lies not in the mere fact of promise, but in the quality of the reaction to the promise. Consider this well-known example: A says to B: 'Let's go out for dinner. I'll pay for the meal: you buy the wine'. B agrees, and they arrange to meet at the restaurant. A does not keep the date, preferring to go to the cinema with C. It is almost universally accepted that A's behaviour should not be regarded as a breach of contract actionable in the courts. For classical theory that conclusion presents a problem, since there appears to be no difference in moral terms between this promise and a promise of a more commercial nature (e.g., to deliver goods for payment). The social convention of keeping promises applies equally to both. Nor is there an absence of exchange: A's promise is not gratuitous, and therefore appears to meet the wealth-maximising criterion. Why then is it our first instinct that A's promise did not give rise to a contractual obligation? The answer appears to lie in the quality of our reaction to the promise, which involves weighing the extent and nature of the reliance placed upon it. Thus serious consequences are likely to result from the failure to deliver goods which have been promised in return for payment, but it is not easy to predict very serious consequences resulting from the failure to keep a dinner date. Notice, however, that our reaction is not in terms of what actually happened: it is a generalised reaction based upon what in our experience would normally be the case, or what would be reasonable in the circumstances.

It seems clear, therefore, that in some circumstances reliance may provide a better explanation of the source of contractual obligations than does classical theory. Nevertheless, it also seems that, like classical theory, reliance cannot alone account for the whole of the law of contract. In the first place, there is the problem of wholly executory contracts, which are enforceable after the mere exchange of promises. They may be less significant in real life than the place given to them in the textbooks, but there is no denying that the law does enforce contracts which exist in the absence of any reliance. Secondly, there is the problem of promissory estoppel, which although a source of obligation is only a qualified source: it does not create any new obligations where none existed previously (6.4.2.4). How can reliance be the major source of obligation when the principal reliance-based doctrine does not itself create active obligations? Finally, there is the problem of those rules of contract law which are based on criteria independent of the parties to the contract. A weakness of the reliance theory is that it is as much based in the relationship between the contracting parties as is classical theory. In respect of classical theory it was suggested that one flaw was its inability to cope with those rules of contract law which permit judicial intervention in the agreement between the parties according to what is reasonable rather than according to what is presumed to have been their intention. The same criticism applies to reliance theory, in that it is unable to account for the court's intervention in the contract on grounds of reasonableness which do not derive from the dealings between the parties but from a collective or community sense of what is right in the circumstances.

4.4.2.4 A collective theory of contract A somewhat different response to the inadequacy of classical theory has been the suggestion that contractual obligation is derived from the need to protect reasonable or legitimate expectation (e.g., Reiter and Swan, 'Contracts and the protection of reasonable expectation', in *Studies in Contract Law* (Toronto: Butterworths, 1980), pp. 1–23). This theory is similar to classical theory in seeing expectation as the essence of contract, but it goes beyond classical theory in recognising that promise is not the only means of creating expectation. Indeed, it assumes that in many circumstances society (through the courts) will regard one party's expectation as reasonably held and so deserving of protection irrespective of the will of the other party. So, some expectation will be created by promise, some by reliance, some by other means, including perhaps the protection of certain classes within society and 'fairness'. The essence of the collective approach to contract and its basis in reasonable expectation is that it endeavours to be sufficiently flexible to account for most if not all observable instances of contractual obligation.

This theory rests heavily on the roles both of the device of contract and of contract law. Contract law, it was suggested above, is the vehicle which adapts the device of contract, which is important for its facilitation of planned exchanges, to the need of a particular society. Classical contract law, therefore, reflected the use made of planned exchanges in the aggressively free enterprise society of the 19th century. It would not be surprising to find classical ideas of contract law unsatisfactory if the nature of society had itself changed. Most people accept that there has indeed been a change in the nature of society since the 19th century, from out-and-out free enterprise to mixed economy. That is, in our society today resources are allocated partly through the decisions of private individuals and companies, and partly through the decisions of government (including the courts) and State-owned enterprises. The precise balance of the mixture changes from time to time, and the 1980s saw a swing back from a more collectivist towards a more individualist approach.

In this context 'allocation of resources' involves the redistribution of wealth between the more and less powerful in society by means other than taxation and welfare legislation. Thus, the law administered by the courts does not strive only for allocative efficiency, as a free-market approach would prescribe. It also contains an element of distributive justice which cannot be explained in terms of market economics. The law, whether it is a judicial creation or the creation of Parliament, attempts to redress the balance between the weak and strong elements in society, protecting the former against the latter. On the other hand, the very idea of a *mixed* economy means that where the functions of balance and protection are not required the legal system must enable private ordering of exchange. So, the law must assess the level of intervention required according to the type of contract confronting it. It is able to do so by amending the nature of what it deems to be a reasonable expectation according to the circumstances of the case. The relevant circumstances to be consulted in evaluating what are the reasonable expectations in any given situation will include the nature of the parties, and especially their relative positions. But they will also include the nature of the subject-matter of the contract, the manner in which the contract was entered into, and relevant public policies of the society in which the contract was made. The result is that we should have general principles of the law of contract, but also specific rules tailored to particular types of contractual activity.

This theoretical breaking down of contractual activity into distinct groups, to which distinct rules may apply because of the different assumptions we make about what would be a reasonable expectation within each particular type of activity, appears to have been reflected in recent developments in the substantive law. Although there is still a common core of principles of contract law, many discrete areas of contractual activity have developed their own specialised rules. Employment contracts, contracts for the sale of goods (see 4.5), contracts made by consumers, contracts of insurance, contracts of international trade, are all examples where it is necessary to proceed from an understanding of the general law of contract to more specific rules relevant to the particular context alone. One detailed example will serve to illustrate the point. In contracts for the sale of goods there is no blanket implied term guaranteeing the quality of goods sold, but there is such an implied term where the seller is in the business of selling (s.14(1) and (2) Sale of Goods Act 1979; see *10.4.3.2*). This implied term about quality can be excluded by express words in the contract of sale where the buyer is also in business, but it is not possible to exclude the guarantee of quality in the case of a sale to a consumer (s. 6(2) and (3) Unfair Contract Terms Act 1977; see *10.6.3.5*). Thus we find that within the law relating to the sale of goods there are differing rules which apply according to the nature of the contracting parties. The rules which apply between business people exist to enforce the bargain made between them by their express promises; but the rules applicable in the case of contracts with consumers impose standards of 'fair' contractual behaviour intended to prevent the stronger party taking advantage of the weaker, and those standards reflect the collective values of society as a whole.

4.4.2.5 Conclusion If any single theory can explain the disparate elements of 20th-century contract law, it is perhaps the chameleon-like theory of protection of reasonable expectations. It has been argued that the theory rests on a circular argument, since the expectation only exists by virtue of the fact of its protection, and so the theory is no more than a self-fulfilling prophecy. This argument neglects the importance of the role of the device of contract (see *4.4.1*), which suggests that the function of confident forward planning which is facilitated by contract would continue to be used by the great majority of contracting parties whether or not contracts were legally enforceable. Equally, the mere fact that contracts are enforceable would not cause parties to contract unless the device were perceived to be socially useful. In other words, like classical theory, the theory of protection of reasonable expectations derives its sense of obligation from social convention, from the socially practised habit of contracting in order to provide for planned exchanges. The important difference between classical, promise-based, theory and the protection of reasonable expectation is that under the latter theory the content of the expectation may be dictated by something other than an individual's voluntary undertaking. Of course, in many contracts, especially those of a commercial nature, the law allows the dimension of individual autonomy to govern the expectation, and in those situations this theory may be little different from classical theory. Thus, in commercial matters the law must be servant and not master of those engaged in business. But in many other types of contract the law imposes limits on the dimension of individual autonomy in contracting, and contractual expectations are shaped by collective evaluations of what the content of obligations should be.

4.5 CONTRACT AND THE SALE OF GOODS

Contracts for the sale of goods are amongst the most common types of contract encountered. For many readers their main experience of contracting will have been in purchasing goods. For that reason, many of the hypothetical examples of contracts used in this book are based on simple sales transactions. Nevertheless, it is important to enter a note of caution about contracts for the sale of goods.

Such contracts have developed as a distinct category, to which the general principles of contract law apply, but on top of which have been grafted special rules applicable to sales transactions alone. This law was originally codified in 1893, and subsequent amendments have been consolidated in the Sale of Goods Act 1979 (SoGA 1979). A detailed study of these rules requires a separate book (e.g. P. S. Atiyah, *Sale of Goods*, 8th ed., Pitman, 1990). Particular rules applicable to the sale of goods are noted throughout the book, but it is necessary here to explain the important impact of the notion of 'property' which is central to such contracts.

4.5.1 The central role of property rights

Section 2(1) of the Sale of Goods Act 1979 defines a contract of sale of goods as a 'contract by which the seller transfers or agrees to transfer the property in goods to the buyer for a money consideration'. 'Property' here means ownership, and so the legal effect of a sales transaction is to transfer the ownership of the goods from seller to buyer. When dealing with sales contracts it is important to keep that legal effect in mind, since it has important consequences for the rest of the law. It is also important to realise that the parties' reasons for entering a sale transaction may only incidentally coincide with the legal purpose of the transaction. In litigation, however, the parties' motives will take second place to the legal purpose.

The overriding importance of the transfer of ownership is well demonstrated by the decision in *Rowland* v *Divall* [1923] 2 KB 500.

The plaintiff had bought a car from the defendant. He then resold the car to a third party. The car was repossessed by the police after a period of four months because it had been stolen by the person who had sold the car to the defendant. The plaintiff repaid the money he had received from the third party, and then claimed back the price he had paid to the defendant, on the ground of total failure of consideration (*12.4.2*). That is, he claimed that he had received nothing of what he was entitled to receive under the contract of sale.

The defendant sought to resist this claim by saying that the failure of consideration was not total, since the plaintiff had had the (potential) use of the car for four months. His defence failed, because the plaintiff was entitled under a contract of sale not merely to use of the car, but to legal ownership. Since the car was stolen, the defendant was not in a position to transfer legal ownership, and so the whole contract failed.

4.5.2 The power to transfer ownership

The general rule is that the seller can only transfer such title to goods as he himself enjoys (s.21(1) SoGA 1979). Where the seller is not the owner, therefore, he cannot transfer ownership to the buyer. Unfortunately, lawyers and judges often still refer to this rule by its latin name, so it is necessary to give it here: *nemo dat quod non habet*. The rule is subject to a number of important exceptions, which are of particular importance in the law of agency (see *15.3.4*). The operation of the rule can be demonstrated by reference to the facts of *Rowland* v *Divall* [1923] 2 KB 500 (above). The plaintiff was obliged to refund the money to the third party to whom he thought he had sold the car because he had not been able to pass the ownership of the car to that third party. The reason for his inability to pass on ownership was that he had not been owner since the defendant, who had purported to sell the car to him, was also not owner at the time of the sale. Thus, a defect early in the chain of sales (the defendant did not acquire ownership when he unwittingly bought the car from a thief) caused all the subsequent sales to be defective because ownership was not transferred by the transaction.

Of course, had one of the exceptions to the general rule applied to any one of the chain of transactions, then ownership would have been transferred even if the seller had not himself been owner, and from that point on subsequent sales would not have been defective. For example, if the thief had been a mercantile agent who was known regularly to sell cars on behalf of others, and had been in possession of the car with the consent of the owner before he misappropriated it, then the defendant would have acquired good title (s.2(1) Factors Act 1889), and the subsequent sales in the chain would have been unaffected by the early defect in title. The rule is clearly an obstacle to the free flow of goods in commerce, especially where it necessitates the unravelling of complex chains of sales, and the exceptions to the rule have been developed precisely to avoid if possible the need to unravel contracts which at the time of the transaction neither contracting party knew to be affected by a defect in title to the goods purportedly sold.

4.5.3 Void and voidable contracts and sales to third parties

The rule relating to the power to transfer ownership is further complicated by the distinction which must be made between void and voidable contracts. A void contract is no contract at all, and so a void contract can have no effect; it is as if any semblance of agreement there may be had not taken place. An agreement which is affected by 'common mistake' is, for example, void: the contract fails from the very beginning and no consequences can ensue from it (7.3.1). A voidable contract remains a valid contract until the party who has the right to complain takes steps to have it set aside. Should that party choose, as is his right, not to have the contract set aside, the contract is valid and all the usual effects of contract flow from it. An example of a voidable contract is an agreement affected by misrepresentation (9.1).

These differences of effect between void and voidable contracts have an impact on the power to transfer ownership. Since a void contract can have no effect, it is impotent to transfer ownership between the purported seller and buyer. Thus, if a contract of sale from A to B is void, a third party (C) who subsequently purports to buy the goods from B cannot obtain ownership of the goods since B is not the owner. This consequence can only be avoided if one of the exceptions to the rule about transfer of ownership applies (see 4.5.2). On the other hand, since a voidable contract is of full effect until actually set aside, it can transfer ownership between seller and buyer. Thus, if a contract of sale from A to B is merely voidable, a third party (C) who subsequently purports to buy the goods from B does obtain ownership of the goods provided the sale by B to C takes place before A takes steps to have the contract set aside. This rule is embodied in s.23 of the Sale of Goods Act 1979. A close corollary of the rule is that once third party rights have intervened in the case of a voidable contract the party who had the right to have the contract set aside loses that right (see, for example, *8.6.4* and *9.4.1.1(d)*).

FIVE
Formation of agreements

5.1 INTRODUCTION

In this chapter the final element in the definition of contracts as 'legally enforceable *agreements*' (see *4.1*) is considered. In everyday language the word 'agreement' embraces a spectrum of notions from the very precise to mere consensus of opinion. In the law of contract the requirement of certainty, and the focus in the nineteenth century (when contract law was developing) on the intentions of the individual contracting parties, have led to a very specific meaning for 'agreement'. At the most general level it can be said that an agreement is the product of an offer and an acceptance. One party (the *offeror*) makes a proposal, and if the other (the *offeree*) accepts it in its entirety then the parties have 'agreed'. However, this definition is so general that it raises more questions than it answers. At what point in time does the agreement come into existence? (For the significance of this question see *5.4.3*, below.) What happens when the offeree accepts all but a small part of what is offered (see *5.3.1.2* and *5.3.1.3*)? Where there is an apparent agreement, but a dispute as to what was agreed, whose version of the 'truth' is to be believed (see *5.1.2* and *5.6*)? Is it possible to conclude that despite the appearance of agreement none exists? If there is really an agreement, what is included in it (see *5.7*)? Finally, is it the rule that there must be an offer and an acceptance, or is it merely that there must be an agreement?

5.1.1 Offer and acceptance

At the turn of the century it was fashionable to believe, at least in legal academic circles, that every contract required the existence of an offer and an acceptance. That view is no longer so fashionable. It is probably the case that the judges never accepted what was in fact an attempt by academics to impose a restrictive framework of 'logical' rules on to an imprecise web of decisions largely dependent upon the facts of individual cases. Not many years ago Lord Denning MR suggested in *Butler Machine Tool Co.* v *Ex-cell-O Corp.* [1979] 1 All ER 965 that analysis of the existence of agreement by demonstrating offer and acceptance should be abandoned. Instead, the court should be allowed to establish the existence of agreement from an examination of the totality of the evidence available. He sought support for this view in the speech of Lord Wilberforce in *New Zealand Shipping Co. Ltd.* v *A.M. Satterthwaite & Co. Ltd*, 'The

Eurymedon' [1975] AC 154 (the facts are given at *6.3.5.4;* see also *6.3.6*). Lord Wilberforce had said:

> It is only the precise analysis of this complex of relations into the classical offer and acceptance . . . that seems to present difficulty. . . English law, having committed itself to a rather technical and schematic doctrine of contract, in application takes a practical approach, often at the cost of forcing the facts to fit uneasily into the marked slots of offer, acceptance and consideration.

Out of this acknowledgement of the limitations of offer and acceptance analysis Lord Denning tried to construct a whole new approach to the question of agreement. It seems he wished to replace what was a question of law (subject to precise and sometimes detailed rules) with a pure question of fact.

While it may be that the House of Lords accepts that analysis by way of offer and acceptance has its limitations, it has not been prepared to countenance the sweeping change proposed by Lord Denning MR. Lord Diplock considered his proposal in *Gibson* v *Manchester City Council* [1979] 1 All ER 972. He admitted that there may be certain types of contract which do not fit into the 'normal analysis of a contract as being constituted by offer and acceptance', but he made it clear that offer and acceptance were to remain the normal method of analysis. Although his statement must be regarded as a reaffirmation of orthodoxy, two significant conclusions may be drawn from it. In the first place, the House of Lords accepts that offer and acceptance are only a method of analysis: they are not a requirement of the existence of a contract. Secondly, in some circumstances offer and acceptance analysis does not apply. However, where two identified parties have consciously negotiated with each other towards agreement it will be difficult to persuade a court that anything other than analysis by offer and acceptance is relevant.

Where offer and acceptance analysis does not work very well, and may therefore in future be expected to be abandoned, is in the case of contracts or agreements which do not fall within this paradigm. Such divergence is normally attributable either to the involvement of one or more third parties in the negotiating process (see *Clarke* v *Dunraven* [1897] AC 59), or to the fact that the offer is made more generally than to a single identified offeree (see *Wilkie* v *London Passenger Transport Board* [1947] 1 All ER 258), or to the fact that the court is using the vehicle of contract to impose an obligation (see *Upton-on-Severn RDC* v *Powell* [1942] 1 All ER 220).

5.1.2 Subjectivity versus objectivity
The emphasis of nineteenth century lawyers on contract as an exercise of will by the contracting parties led to an inevitable conflict between theory, which saw contract as based on the actual intention of the individual, and practice, which required means of establishing by satisfactory evidence the contents of agreements. Not surprisingly, practical considerations prevailed, and by the second half of the nineteenth century the law had fixed on the ascertainment of agreements by objective criteria. The subjective intention of a contracting

party is largely irrelevant except in so far as it coincides with the objectively ascertained common intention of the parties.

5.1.2.1 A residual subjective element? Although the main test of agreement is now accepted as being objective, the question remains whether there is some residual subjective element in the approach taken by the courts. In *The Hannah Blumenthal* [1983] 1 All ER 34 the issue before the court was whether arbitration, provided for in the contract between the parties, had been abandoned by agreement. Any such agreement could only be inferred from the parties' failure to take active steps in regard to the matter. Lord Diplock attempted a formulation of the objective test of offer and acceptance. He said that it was necessary that 'the intention of each as it has been communicated to and understood by the other (even though that which has been communicated does not represent the actual state of mind of the communicator) should coincide'.

In *The Leonidas D* [1985] 2 All ER 796 Robert Goff LJ, giving the judgment of the court, said that Lord Diplock's formulation in *The Hannah Blumenthal* appeared to involve the requirement that the actual intentions of both parties should in fact coincide. This interpretation stems from the fact that Lord Diplock required each party's actual understanding of the other's intention to coincide with the understanding of a reasonable man. His approach called for a coincidence of actual understanding, if not of actual intention, and so imported a subjective element into the test of agreement. The Court of Appeal refused to follow Lord Diplock's formulation, preferring that of Lord Brightman in the same case. Robert Goff LJ described Lord Brightman's formulation thus:

> If one party (O) so acts that his conduct, objectively considered, constitutes an offer, and the other party (A), believing that the conduct of O represents his actual intention, accepts O's offer, then a contract will come into existence, and on those facts it will make no difference if O did not in fact intend to make an offer, or if he misunderstood A's acceptance, so that O's state of mind is in such circumstances irrelevant.

This formulation represents the orthodox approach to testing the existence of agreement. The only exception to this orthodox test is that an offeree may not rely on a reasonable interpretation of what the offeror said if he knows as a matter of fact that it is not what the offeror intended (see *7.4.2*). Only in this sense is a subjective consideration relevant.

5.1.2.2 Three meanings of objectivity Although Lord Brightman's formulation as described by Robert Goff LJ is the orthodox approach, it leaves unarticulated one important matter: the meaning of 'objectively considered'. It is possible to define three distinct meanings of objectivity (see Howarth (1984) 100 LQR 265). The meanings vary according to the standpoint of the observer. Lord Brightman's formulation probably assumes an objective consideration by a reasonable person in the place of the offeree. This too is the orthodox approach, and authority can be found for it in the judgment of Blackburn J in *Smith* v *Hughes* (1871) LR 6 QB 597. In the same case, however, Hannen J suggested that the existence of agreement should be tested from the standpoint of a reasonable person in the place of the offeror. This version of objectivity has not found favour with subsequent courts, although Lord Diplock's formulation in *The Hannah Blumenthal* [1983] 1 All ER 34 might be seen as an attempt to incorporate both offeror and offeree objectivity. Increasingly in recent years objectivity has been taken outside the parties to the agreement, and is sometimes denoted as 'fly on the wall' objectivity. In *Thake* v *Maurice* [1984] 2 All ER 513 at first instance Peter Pain J said: 'The test as to what the contract in fact was does not depend on what the plaintiffs or the defendant thought it meant, but on what the court objectively determines that the words used meant.'

Although in the Court of Appeal the more orthodox objective test of agreement was used, the first instance judgment is instructive as an example of how judges use 'fly on the wall' objectivity especially in cases where the traditional offer and acceptance analysis works only imperfectly. *Thake* v *Maurice* is a case in which it is far from clear that the parties realised they were negotiating a contract, as opposed to discussing a surgical operation, and the judgment at first instance may well fall into the category of court-imposed contractual liability. It is not surprising that judges who favour greater judicial intervention in the formation of contracts tend also to be those who advocate the 'fly on the wall' approach to objectivity, since it gives greater scope for a creative approach to interpreting the contract. There have been suggestions in speeches in the House of Lords that this approach to objectivity is appropriate in some cases, including in the speech of Lord Diplock in *Gibson* v *Manchester City Council* [1979] 1 All ER 972.

5.1.3 Conclusion

In the paradigm contracting situations of direct negotiation between identified parties an objective analysis of offer and acceptance is the normal means of testing the existence of agreement. It is not possible to give any fixed meaning to 'objective' in this statement because no fixed meaning emerges from the judicial statements. The truth of the matter is almost certainly that the courts do not wish to be tied down to a single meaning, preferring either to adopt the position of a reasonable person in the place of the offeree, or to take a 'fly on the wall' approach, according to the court's perception of the merits of the case. The fact that offer and acceptance are not a requirement of a valid contract, but only a means of analysing the existence of agreement, means that the whole of the law relating to offer and acceptance should best be regarded as resting on a small number of general principles, which are exemplified by innumerable decisions of fact in the individual cases. It is not very helpful to regard the law as consisting of a complex system of narrowly drawn rules, since the apparent predictability inherent in a system of rules can be thwarted in any case where the court chooses not to apply offer and acceptance analysis or to use a different standard of objectivity. In the sections which follow the law will be stated in terms of such general principles, and the leading cases used to demonstrate how those principles have been applied by the courts.

5.2 OFFERS AND INVITATIONS TO TREAT

5.2.1 General

The fact that the law in this field may be reduced to a small number of general principles is well demonstrated by the law relating to offers. An offer is an expression of willingness to contract on specified terms, requiring only acceptance for a binding agreement to be formed (see, for example, *Anglia Television* v *Cayton* (1989), *Independent*, 17 February 1989). It must be distinguished from all other statements made in the course of negotiations towards a contract: only an offer is capable of immediate translation into a contract by the fact of acceptance. The most common form of statement requiring to be distinguished from offers is an invitation to treat. A technical definition of invitation to treat would be restricted to statements indicating the maker's willingness to receive offers. However, the expression is commonly used to describe any negotiating statement falling short of an offer which furthers the bargaining process. Such statements may take the form of attempts to stimulate interest, requests for or the supply of information or any other stage in the sometimes lengthy progress to agreement.

Obviously, on many occasions offers and invitations to treat are easy to distinguish. On the other hand, there are times when the distinction is a fine one. While some commentators prefer to speak in terms of rules, in practice the courts look to the individual facts of each case in making the distinction. It is probably safer to proceed on the basis of the single principle that an offer must be:

(a)   sufficiently specific and comprehensive to be capable of immediate acceptance; and

(b)   made with an intention to be bound by the mere fact of acceptance.

The cases can all be seen as consistent with this principle.

5.2.2 The principle in practice

5.2.2.1 Advertisements   The cases reveal a variety of common contracting situations in which the distinction between offer and invitation to treat is not immediately obvious. The first situation is that of a newspaper advertisement. In *Partridge* v *Crittenden* [1968] 2 All ER 421

> the appellant had placed an advertisement indicating that he had certain wild birds for sale. It was an offence to offer such birds for sale. The advertisement did state a price, but gave no details about delivery or quantities available.

On appeal the appellant's conviction was quashed because the court held that the advertisement did not amount to an offer, but was merely an invitation to treat. It was scarcely sufficiently specific to amount to an offer, nor would it be reasonable to think that the appellant was willing to be bound by any and every acceptance made. In the words of Lord Parker, there was 'business sense' in treating such an advertisement as no more than an invitation to treat.

Nevertheless, it is quite possible for an advertisement to amount to an offer if the facts justify such a conclusion. In *Carlill* v *Carbolic Smoke Ball Co.* [1893] 1 QB 256 (see *5.5* generally)

> the defendants had placed an advertisement in which they promised to pay £100 to any person catching influenza after proper use of their patent remedy. The advertisement stated that £1,000 had been placed in a separate bank account in order to meet any claims made. The plaintiff had caught influenza after apparently proper use of the smoke ball.

The court treated the deposit of money as an indication of a willingness to be bound by the terms of the advertisement, thus constituting it an offer. In the case of advertisements for sale it may be rare for sufficient detail to be provided for there to be an offer. The normal situation will be that advertisements are only invitations to treat, for the reason that sellers have to be protected from the possibility of demand exceeding supply. So, in *Grainger & Sons* v *Gough* [1896] AC 325 a wine merchant's catalogue and price list was held to be no more than an invitation to treat on precisely that ground. If, however, the catalogue had stated, for example, that unlimited supplies were available then it may be that it would have been sufficiently specific to amount to an offer.

5.2.2.2 Shop displays The second typical situation is the display of goods in a shop window or on supermarket shelves. In *Fisher* v *Bell* [1961] 1 QB 394 it was held that to display a flick-knife with a price marker in a shop window did not amount to commission of the offence of offering such a knife for sale. In *Pharmaceutical Society of Great Britain* v *Boots Cash Chemists* [1953] 1 QB 401 it was held that the display of goods on shelves in a self-service store did not amount to an offer of the goods for sale, so that no contract was formed merely by the customer taking the goods off the shelf. The facts were as follows:

> there was a legal requirement that certain drugs and medicines only be sold under the supervision of a registered pharmacist. The cash desks were supervised by such a person, but it was impossible for all the shelving to be supervised. Thus it was crucial whether the sale (in other words, the moment of formation of the contract) took place at the time when the goods were taken from the shelf or at the time when the goods were presented at the cash desk and the transaction approved by the cashier under the pharmacists supervision.

The court explained its decision in terms of the inconvenience to customers of not being able to take goods from the shelves, put them in baskets, and subsequently change their minds about the purchase, which would be the situation in theory if taking the goods from the shelves amounted to acceptance of an offer. The normal situation is that the shopkeeper reserves the right to refuse to sell, and that option is exercised in each case by the cashier on his behalf when the goods are presented for payment at the cash desk. Nevertheless, it is possible to imagine a situation in which the display of goods in a shop would amount to an offer. For example, American courts have found the display of a specific number of sale items available on a first-come first-served basis to be an offer.

5.2.2.3 Requests for information In some cases a party may supply information in the course of negotiations without giving any commitment to go through to a firm agreement. In *Harvey* v *Facey* [1893] AC 552

> the appellants sent a telegram to the respondent, asking: 'Will you sell us Bumper Hall Pen? Telegraph lowest cash price, reply paid.' The respondent replied simply: 'Lowest price for Bumper Hall Pen £900.' The appellants then purported to accept this 'offer', while the respondent denied that his reply had been an offer.

The court agreed with the respondent. He had supplied the information requested, but there had been no unequivocal indication of a willingness to be bound by the mere acceptance of an offer.

5.2.3 Contracts by tender
The request for tenders is a negotiating device common in the world of major commercial contracts. A company seeking to purchase a major item or service, such as a piece of equipment or some construction work, will invite tenders from those interested in supplying the good or service sought. Such an invitation may be published generally, or in a trade journal, or circulated to companies likely to be interested. In normal circumstances the invitation for tenders is not treated as an offer, since the company issuing it may have criteria other than price which they wish to take into account in awarding the contract. In that case the tenders themselves are the first offers made (see *Spencer* v *Harding* (1870) LR 5 CP 561). On the other hand, it is always possible that a request for tenders be both specific and intended to be turned into a contract by mere acceptance, in which case it will be an offer. The usual case is where the expression 'highest bidder' or 'lowest bidder' is used, indicating a system of competitive tendering under which the person issuing the invitation to tender has declared himself willing to be bound by the most competitive tender. There are *obiter* statements to this effect in *Spencer* v *Harding* (above).

The process of competitive tendering ran into a particular difficulty in the recent case of *Harvela Investments Ltd* v *Royal Trust Co. of Canada (CI) Ltd* [1985] 2 All ER 966.

> The vendors of a plot of land sought a 'single offer' for the whole plot from each of two interested parties, promising to accept the highest offer received provided it met other conditions stipulated. Both parties submitted bids complying with the conditions, but while one merely stated a price it was prepared to pay, the other stated both a concrete sum and a referential bid (i.e. '$101,000 in excess of any other offer'). The question for the House of Lords was which of the two bids was

the higher, thus constituting the acceptance necessary for the formation of the agreement.

In one sense the referential bid was the higher offer, but such a conclusion was only possible provided only one party made such a bid. The court took the view that one of the main purposes of competitive tender bargaining is to ensure that negotiations come safely to fruition. To allow unrestricted use of referential bids was to risk such bargaining being abortive. The House of Lords therefore implied into the request for bids a stipulation that referential bids would not be accepted. In the opinion of Lord Templeman, with whom all their Lordships agreed, it was open to the vendors to initiate a process of bargaining by referential bids (which would be a form of auction) but such an interpretation would not be placed on a request for competitive tenders in the absence of express words to that effect.

5.2.4 'Negotiation management' contracts

In *Harvela Investments Ltd* v *Royal Trust Co. of Canada (CI) Ltd* [1985] 2 All ER 966 (see *5.2.3*), Lord Templeman faced a conceptual difficulty in respect of the implied stipulation against referential bids, in that there was no contract immediately apparent into which the stipulation could be implied. It could not be implied into any eventual contract to buy the land, since such a term would be too late and would only bind one party. Lord Diplock overcame the problem by describing the tendering process as being governed by a unilateral contract (see *5.5.4*) under which the competing would-be purchasers agreed to bid according to the rules laid down by the sellers, and the sellers agreed to abide by those rules and sell to the highest bidder. A fictional contract was also used in *Blackpool and Fylde Aero Club Ltd* v *Blackpool Borough Council* [1990] 3 All ER 25, CA, to provide a means of managing the tendering process, although somewhat surprisingly the court was not referred to the speech of Lord Diplock in the *Harvela Investments* case.

> The council ran an airport, and granted a single concession to operate pleasure flights from the airport. For a period of years that licence had been held by the plaintiff club. When the concession came up for renewal, the council determined to invite competitive tenders for it. Tenders were to be submitted by 12 noon on a given day. The council's letter-box was not cleared between the time of the club posting its tender and the closing time for bids, with the result that the club's tender was not considered. The club claimed that the council was in breach of a contract to consider all tenders received before the deadline.

The club's claim was upheld by the courts. There was a contract governing the conduct of the tendering process, and it was an implied term of that contract that all bids arriving before the deadline would be considered. Bingham LJ acknowledged that contracts are not lightly to be implied, but it is clear that in this case such judicial reluctance was outweighed by the opportunity to do substantive justice which the implied contract was perceived to offer. The court stressed, however, that the only contractual obligation was to *consider* the bid. The House of Lords has recently confirmed that an agreement to agree, or an agreement to negotiate, would be unenforceable for uncertainty (*Walford* v *Miles* [1992] 1 All ER 453; see *5.6.3*).

5.3 ACCEPTANCE

5.3.1 General: the 'mirror image' rule

In the standard situation of contracts consciously negotiated between identified parties, acceptance is the key element. Acceptance is what turns a specific and comprehensive offer, made with the intention to be bound, into an agreement. The general principle applying to acceptance can be stated in two parts:

(a) to constitute acceptance (and thus agreement) the offeree's expression of intention and assent must be made in response to and must exactly match the terms of the offer;

(b) the matching acceptance must be communicated to the offeror.

This principle is so well established as to need little general comment. Such difficulties as exist arise out of the application of the principle to the realities of everyday contract negotiation. In simple consumer transactions it is common enough that only one offer is made, and acceptance is straightforward. No detailed negotiation of terms is involved. Taking the example of a sale in a self-service shop (see *5.2.2.2*), the customer takes a price-marked item off the shelf and presents it to the cashier, thus making an offer to buy it for the marked price. The cashier accepts the offer on behalf of the shop, payment is instantaneous, and terms as to quality are left to be implied under the Sale of Goods Act 1979 (see *10.4*). The role of acceptance in this case is crucial but without legal difficulty. Commercial contracts, especially for non-standard goods, may be very different. Frequently more than one offer will be made before negotiations are complete, and the language of 'acceptance' may be used before a technical legal analysis would identify acceptance as having been made. Part (a) of the general principle is often referred to as the 'mirror image' rule, and its impact is examined in the following three sections.

5.3.1.1 Acceptance in response to the offer The rule that acceptance must be made in response to the offer is a close relative of the rule which defines consideration as that which induces the promise of the other party (see *6.3.1*). Thus, it will be suggested later that the decision that a claimant was not entitled to a reward when his performance of the condition was done in ignorance of the reward offer could be explained either in terms of an absence of consideration or in terms of an absence of agreement (see *6.3.1.1*: *R* v *Clarke* (1927) 40 CLR 227). That is, either the performance was not induced by the offer, or the acceptance (which in such a contract is constituted by the performance: see *5.5.2* below) was not made in response to the offer.

The rule has the slightly odd result of leaving parties who are in fact subjectively agreed on all matters without a contract if they cannot objectively be shown to have gone through the process of agreement. If two parties both make offers to each other more or less simultaneously (ie, before receiving the other's offer) then even if the offers are made in identical terms there is no contract. The offers may correspond, but there is no agreement because there is no acceptance made in response to the other's offer (*Tinn* v *Hoffman* (1873) 29 LT 271). It should be pointed out that the apparent harshness of this rule is mitigated by the fact that any small act of performance by one party may well be regarded as acceptance by conduct sufficient to seal the agreement (see *5.3.1.2*). The finding of no contract in the absence of some act of performance was explained in *Tinn* v *Hoffman* as a rule of convenience to avoid uncertainty over whether a contract had come into existence or not.

5.3.1.2 Counter-offers Each time one party alters the terms contained in the other's offer in responding to it a new offer is made. This new offer is referred to as a counter-offer. Its impact is to deny the effect of acceptance to the communication made, and to make the possibility of agreement depend upon acceptance of the counter-offer by the original offeror. The further effect of a counter-offer is to operate in the same way as a rejection to cause the original offer to lapse. So, should the original offeror find the counter-offer unacceptable it is not open to the original offeree to accept the original offer at that point, unless the original offer has been revived expressly by the original offeror. This effect is clearly demonstrated in relation to a price term in the case of *Hyde* v *Wrench* (1840) 3 Beav 334.

> A offered to sell land to B for £1,000. Two days later B replied offering £950. Clearly that was not an acceptance but a counter-offer. A rejected the counter-offer, whereupon B purported to accept the original offer.

A denied that any contract had been made, and the court found in his favour. It was not open to B to revive A's offer unless A was willing to revert to those terms.

Where the variation in terms is in relation to something less central than the price clause it is common for the reply to the offer to be described as an 'acceptance'. The truth is that in this situation also the reply is only a counter-offer. In *Jones* v *Daniel* [1894] 2 Ch 332:

> A offered £1,450 for land belonging to B. Purporting to accept the offer, B sent a document for signature to A containing terms additional to those proposed by A, relating to method of payment, proof of title and final performance.

Although there was nothing unreasonable about the terms, they could not be part of an agreement until A had assented to them. Since A did not agree, there was no contract. Thus, even where there is agreement on the major terms (eg, price and subject-matter) there may still be no contract because of failure to agree on the ancillary terms. For this reason, courts have sometimes suggested that acceptance of all essential terms is sufficient to give rise to a contract, even when no agreement has been reached in respect of non-essential terms (see *5.3.1.3*). However, in most cases the counter-offer rule prevails, because terms relating to method of payment and mode of performance are often crucial. Nevertheless, the rule can lead to difficulty where the parties are not particularly concerned about the details of the ancillary terms, and fail to notice discrepancies between the offer and the purported acceptance.

The difficulty is illustrated by *Brogden* v *Metropolitan Ry Co.* (1877) 2 App Cas 666.

> The appellants had for some time supplied coal as required to the respondents. The parties decided to enter into a more formal long-term agreement. After negotiations a draft contract was drawn up by the respondents and sent to the appellants. They made minor changes, filled in certain parts left blank expressly for that purpose, and returned it to the respondents. In technical terms the appellant's communication was a counter-offer, but the respondent's manager, being satisfied with it, merely put it in a file. He did not communicate his acceptance of the additions made. The parties then commenced performance under the agreement. Subsequently, a dispute arose in which it was questioned whether in fact any long-term contract had come into existence.

The court found that the commencement of performance by the respondents, who had ordered and taken delivery of coal consistently with the terms of the alleged agreement, was acceptance by conduct of the appellant's counter-offer.

5.3.1.3   The battle of the forms   The rule that a counter-offer may be accepted by conduct leads directly to what is known as the 'last shot' rule: where documents with varying terms shuttle between the parties, the last document to be sent before performance begins is likely to be the one which turns out to be the agreement between the parties. The sometimes unseemly scramble to be the party last to send a document containing terms before performance begins is usually referred to as the 'battle of the forms'. The battle is usually won by succeeding in firing the last shot, but that is not the only possible result. In the first place, the court may find that the negotiations between the parties never resulted in an offer being made. In that situation the acts of performance cannot, of course, amount to acceptance. The only remedy then is to call a halt to performance, if it is not complete, and order payment for what has been done on the basis of *quantum meruit* (a restitutionary remedy giving the performing party a reasonable price for work done: see *12.4.3*). Once performance has started courts are noticeably reluctant to come to such a conclusion (see *Peter Lind & Co.* v *Mersey Docks & Harbour Board* [1972] 2 Lloyd's Rep 234, and *British Steel Corp.* v *Cleveland Bridge & Engineering Co. Ltd* [1984] 1 All ER 504).

Recently, in *Butler Machine Tool Co. Ltd* v *Ex-cell-O Corp.* [1979] 1 All ER 965, Lord Denning MR suggested more radical approaches to resolving the battle of the forms, although the case was actually decided in line with the traditional rule. The facts were as follows:

The sellers offered to sell a machine to the buyers. The offer was made in a document containing certain terms, including a price variation clause, which were to 'prevail over any terms and conditions in the buyer's order'. The buyers placed an order, and their letter contained conflicting conditions, and especially had no price variation clause. At the bottom of the order was a tear-off confirmation slip expressly subject to the buyers' terms, which the sellers completed and returned. The sellers claimed to be entitled to vary the contract price, but the Court of Appeal rejected that claim.

Lord Denning said:

> In some cases, . . . the battle is won by the man who gets the blow in first. If he offers to sell at a named price on the terms and conditions stated on the back and the buyer orders the goods purporting to accept the offer on an order form with his own different terms and conditions on the back, then, if the difference is so material that it would affect the price, the buyer ought not to be allowed to take advantage of the difference unless he draws it specifically to the attention of the seller. There are yet other cases where the battle depends on the shots fired on both sides. There is a concluded contract but the forms vary. The terms and conditions of both parties are to be construed together. If they can be reconciled so as to give a harmonious result, all well and good. If differences are irreconcilable, so that they are mutually contradictory, then the conflicting terms may have to be scrapped and replaced by a reasonable implication.

This statement goes some way beyond what is generally accepted as English law. It may be correct to say that an offeror may stipulate that the contract is to be on his terms or not at all. As in the normal case, a purported acceptance would not be an acceptance at all. The court might be unwilling to treat it as a counter-offer capable of acceptance by conduct, but would seem to be likely to be equally unwilling to bind an offeree by his acceptance and yet to disallow the varying terms of that acceptance. In *Pagnan SpA* v *Feed Products Ltd* [1987] 2 Lloyd's Rep 601, however, the Court of Appeal came very close to doing precisely that. A contract was found to have come into existence once there was agreement on the essential terms, even though other terms remained to be negotiated, including those relating to important matters such as place of payment, rate of payment for permitted variations in delivery, and whether measurement was to be in short tons or metric tonnes. Lloyd LJ, giving the only judgment of the Court of Appeal, added that failure to agree in due course on the outstanding matters would not invalidate the existing contract, unless without those terms it was unworkable or void for uncertainty. This approach goes a good distance beyond the orthodox, and it remains to be seen to what extent it will be followed. It also seems that we shall have to go some way further down the road to judicial intervention in the process of contracting before the courts will construct a contract on behalf of the parties out of the conflicting terms and conditions in the various documents passing between them (see *Anglia Television* v *Cayton* (1989) *Independent*, 17 February 1989 but see, in the USA, section 2-207 of the Uniform Commercial Code).

5.3.2 Communication

The second limb of the general principle of acceptance is that for a contract to come into being acceptance must be communicated to the offeror. When the parties negotiate to a conclusion in each other's presence there is little problem. There is little danger of uncertainty as to whether agreement has been reached, although recollections may differ as to its content if it has not been recorded. The general rule is that words of acceptance must not only be spoken, they must be heard by the offeror. Thus, if words of acceptance are drowned by a loud noise they must be repeated before the contract is concluded. When the parties are not in each other's presence then communication becomes a more critical issue, especially when the agency of a third party, such as the Post Office, or of a machine, is involved. The law has developed a distinction of potentially fundamental importance between instantaneous and non-instantaneous communication. The former is treated more or less as if the parties are in each other's presence; to the latter special rules may apply.

5.3.2.1 The postal rule

The problem with contract negotiation by post is that letters may either be delayed or lost. Those are risks inherent in the use of the post, and the real question is who should bear that risk. In *Adams* v *Lindsell* (1818) 1 B & Ald 681

> the defendants offered to sell wool to the plaintiffs, asking for a reply 'in course of post'. The defendants' letter was misdirected, so that the plaintiffs' reply was delayed beyond the normal course of post, and the defendants sold the wool to someone else. Nevertheless, the plaintiffs had sent a letter of acceptance on the same day that they had received the offer, and claimed that there was an enforceable contract.

The court upheld that claim, and since this case the rule has been that where acceptance is communicated by post the contract is formed as soon as the letter is sent, without need for it ever to reach the offeror. The rule applies equally to all potential consequences, both procedural matters such as time and place of making the contract and substantive matters such as non-performance by an offeror ignorant of the fact of acceptance: *Household Fire and Carriage Accident Insurance Co. Ltd* v *Grant* (1879) 4 ExD 216.

Attempts have been made to justify the rule on all kinds of grounds. It is said that without such a rule offerees would never know whether a contract had been formed or not. It is also suggested that such a rule prevents offerees from speculating by writing an acceptance and then (if the market changes) withdrawing it by speedier means (e.g., telephone). Alternatively, it is argued that if the offeror indicates that use of the post is permissible then he should bear the risks of that system. This last explanation is borne out by *Henthorn* v *Fraser* [1892] 2 Ch 27, in which it was made clear that the postal rule is only applicable where it was reasonable in all the circumstances for the offeree to have used the post. Such would most obviously be the case where the offer had been sent by post.

The truth of the matter is almost certainly that whenever one of the risks of the use of the post materialises whatever conclusion the court reaches will be harsh on one of the parties. The postal rule is no more than a rule of convenience adopted in the interests of certainty. Offerors should know the risks inherent in use of the post, and can protect themselves if they so wish.

5.3.2.2 Avoiding the postal rule   In *Household Fire and Carriage Accident Insurance Co. Ltd* v *Grant* (1879) 4 ExD 216 there is a powerful dissent made by Bramwell LJ, who would have preferred the ordinary rule of communication to apply equally to acceptance by post. The most significant part of his judgment is where he says that the harm he perceives in the postal rule 'will be obviated only by the rule being rendered nugatory by every prudent man saying: "Your answer by post is only to bind if it reaches me."' This statement reveals an important limitation on all non-instantaneous negotiations. The offeror enjoys a legal power to stipulate the medium by which communication is to be made. The effect of this power is clearly stated by Buckley J in *Manchester Diocesan Council of Education* v *Commercial & General Investments Ltd* [1969] 3 All ER 1593. It may be summarised as follows:

(a) The offeror may stipulate that acceptance be made by a particular means.
(b) If the stipulation is entirely to the benefit of the offeror, however, and the offeree communicates by some other means, the offeror may waive the stipulation, making the acceptance effective.
(c) Moreover, where a method of acceptance is prescribed, but acceptance is not expressly limited to that method alone, then an equally efficacious method of acceptance will also be valid.

Thus, the best means of protection available to an offeror are to stipulate a particular means of acceptance. This rule was put to interesting use in *Holwell Securities Ltd* v *Hughes* [1974] 1 All ER 161.

> The defendant gave the plaintiff an option for the purchase of certain land, which was said to be exercisable by *notice in writing to* a given address within a certain period. An option is no more than an offer, and a letter accepting the offer in question was posted by the plaintiff, but failed to arrive.

The Court of Appeal upheld the trial court in saying there was no contract. The main finding was that the mere words 'notice in writing to' were sufficient to override the postal rule. These words amounted instead to a stipulation that notice must reach the offeror, thus reinstating the general principle of communication. If this interpretation of what are in fact common words in options and like offers is followed in subsequent cases, a large part of the postal exception to the general communication rule may have been swept away.

5.3.2.3 Other forms of distant dealing   Modern technology provides forms of long-distance communication other than the post. In *Entores Ltd* v *Miles Far East Corp.* [1955] 2 QB 327 the Court of Appeal decided that telex communications are instantaneous, and are therefore to be treated as if the parties were in each other's presence. The rationale of this decision was that the intended recipient of a telex message should know when it has not arrived, and so can and must ask for it to be repeated. In an *obiter dictum* in the same case Denning LJ made it clear that the same reasoning would apply to the telephone. The decision was approved by the House of Lords in *Brinkibon Ltd* v *Stahag Stahl* [1983] AC 34, although Lord Wilberforce points out (with Lord Brandon's support) that today telex machines frequently send messages out of business hours, leaving messages stored until the following day. His view was that in some cases telex communication was not instantaneous, in which case the general principle would not apply. He was not clear, on the other hand, what rule would apply.

Lord Wilberforce's comments have left the law in a state of uncertainty, and it might have been better to state clearly that when as a matter of fact communication is non-instantaneous the postal rule (or an equivalent *dispatch* rule) applies. The courts may soon have to cope with problems arising out of communication between computer systems, electronic mail and other products of the information technology revolution. Those in commerce who have to rely on such mechanisms would surely have preferred above all else a certain indication of who bears the risk.

5.3.3   Exceptions to the communication rule

5.3.3.1   Silence   The emphasis in the second limb of the general principle of acceptance on communication to the offeror has led to some difficulty in those cases where the alleged acceptance is something other than spoken or written words. Of course, it has already been shown (see *5.3.1.2: Brogden* v *Metropolitan Ry Co.* (1877) 2 App Cas 666) that in some circumstances conduct amounting to initial performance of the terms of an alleged agreement is adequate acceptance. The use of actual words of acceptance cannot, then, be said to be a prerequisite. On the other hand, the need for satisfactory evidence of agreement means that courts are reluctant to hold that a contract had been formed in the absence of communication by either word or conduct.

It is sometimes suggested that the offeror may waive the need for communication. The authority usually given is *Carlill* v *Carbolic Smoke Ball Co.* [1893] 1 QB 256 (see *5.2.2.1*). However, it will be recalled that that case involved a unilateral contract founded upon an offer made to 'the whole world'. Acceptance in such contracts is constituted by conduct amounting to performance (see generally *5.5.2*). It is probably wrong, therefore, to regard *Carlill* as a case of waiver of the need for acceptance. It is more probably simply a variant of the acceptance by conduct described above. Even if it can be regarded as a case of waiver of the need for acceptance, it is doubtful whether the principle would extend beyond unilateral contracts based on offers contained in public notices, as in the case of rewards.

In standard bilateral negotiations the offeror cannot waive the need for communication if the effect would be to take advantage of an offeree who does no more than remain silent. Some commentators would go further and say that silence is never acceptance, a rule for which *Felthouse* v *Bindley* (1862) 11 CBNS 869 is usually regarded as good authority.

> An uncle and nephew had been negotiating the sale of a horse, but there had been a disagreement over the price thought to have been agreed. The uncle wrote offering to split the difference, saying that if he heard no more he would assume that the nephew agreed. The nephew appears to have been satisfied with this arrangement, since he instructed an auctioneer to withdraw the horse in question from a sale. But that fact was not communicated to the uncle. When the auctioneer mistakenly sold the horse the uncle sued him for conversion, claiming to be the owner of the horse under a contract with his nephew.

The court did not accept his claim, stating as one of its reasons that 'the uncle had no right to impose upon the nephew a sale . . . unless he chose to comply with the condition of writing to repudiate the offer'.

Nevertheless, it is almost certainly overstating the rule to say that silence can never be acceptance. In some contexts, especially where there has been a continuing course of dealing, silence can be sufficient acceptance. If A operates a coal delivery round, and regularly delivers two bags of coal to B, either collecting the money on delivery or leaving an invoice to be paid later, without any formal order being placed, B would be unable to deny the existence of a contract for coal actually delivered. B's silence would in those circumstances be sufficient acceptance, and to avoid liability B would have had to prevent the delivery of the coal. Equally, many people rely on the automatic annual renewal of their insurance policies to ensure that the required cover starts as soon as the previous year's cover comes to an end. Yet it is not uncommon, at the crucial date, for the policy holder not to have replied to the company's proposal, which is no more than an offer needing acceptance. What the courts will not countenance is that an offeror should, without any previous course of dealing, force upon an offeree the need to reply in order to avoid the formation of a contract. In the case of 'pressure sales' to consumers the Unsolicited Goods and Services Act 1971 (as amended in 1975) makes the delivery of goods in such circumstances an unconditional gift, and the demand of payment may be a criminal offence.

5.3.3.2 Unauthorised communication Particular difficulty is caused by the case where the offeror is told of an acceptance by the offeree, but the communication is made by someone without authority to make it. In *Powell* v *Lee* (1908) 99 LT 284

> the plaintiff was an applicant for the post of headmaster of a school for which three candidates were interviewed. The managers at first determined to appoint the plaintiff, and authorised one of their number to inform another applicant that he had been unsuccessful; no instruction was given, however, to inform the plaintiff of the outcome. Nevertheless, the same member of the board of managers did inform the plaintiff that he had been appointed. Subsequently the managers reopened their decision and decided against employing the plaintiff. When informed the plaintiff claimed that the managers' decision was a breach of contract since he had already received

communication of the managers' acceptance of the offer he had made in applying for the post.

The court dismissed the plaintiff's claim on the ground that the communication to him was unauthorised.

In the light of *Powell* v *Lee* the rule must be that unauthorised communication of acceptance is inadequate to form a contract. Nevertheless, care must be taken in such cases to take into account the rule of the law of agency that where a principal creates the impression to a third party that the agent does have authority to act on his behalf the principal is bound by the agent's acts whether authorised or not (the rule is explored in more detail below: see *15.2.2*). The effect of this rule may be to limit the rule in *Powell* v *Lee* to a relatively small number of cases where there is no question of apparent authority having been conferred on the person making the unauthorised communication.

5.4 TERMINATION OF OFFERS

To be capable of acceptance an offer must not only be specific and comprehensive, and have been made with the intention of being bound (see: *5.2.1*): it must also be current. Acceptance made after an offer has ceased to be valid is ineffective to form a contract. This section examines the means by which offers terminate, other than by the offeree making a counter-offer or a rejection, which were examined earlier (see *5.3.1.2*).

5.4.1 Lapse of time
Where an offer is left open indefinitely there may come a time when the offeree can no longer accept. In *Ramsgate Victoria Hotel Co. Ltd* v *Montefiore* (1866) LR 1 Ex 109

> the defendant had applied for shares in the plaintiff company in early June 1864. Shares were allotted to him in late November 1864. The defendant refused to pay for the shares, although he had not withdrawn his application at the time when the shares were allotted.

The court found that he was not obliged to go through with the purchase of the shares. The company's response to the defendant's offer had not been made within a reasonable time (see also *Chemco Leasing SpA* v *Rediffusion* [1987] 1 FTLR 201, CA). It is not possible to give any indication of what is a reasonable time, which will be a question of fact in each case. Where the offer is expressly stipulated to be open for a limited period that is an exercise of the offeror's power to stipulate a particular mode of acceptance (see *5.3.2.2*) with which the offeree must comply (but see also *5.4.3.1*, below).

5.4.2 Death
The death of either party may terminate an offer. In the case of the death of the offeree in a proposed bilateral contract the proposition is self-evident, since the offer is peculiar to the offeree. In the case of the death of an offeror

the position is not so clear, but depends upon the subject-matter of the contract and the knowledge of the offeree. Where the contract is for the performance of a personal service by the offeror which depends upon some skill which is exclusive to the offeror then death automatically terminates the offer. Thus, an offer by a concert pianist to perform at a concert could not be accepted after the death of the pianist. In other contracts, where the subject-matter is something available in an open market, there is no difficulty about obtaining substitute performance of what had been offered. The issue is then whether the executor of the dead offeror's estate should have to arrange such substitute performance. The orthodox view is that the burden should not fall upon the executor provided notice of the death of the offeror has been given to the offeree. But where the offeree has no notice of the death of the offeror at the time when the acceptance is made then the deceased's estate will be bound. There are *obiter dicta* to this effect in *Bradbury* v *Morgan* (1862) 1 H & C 249.

5.4.3 Revocation
In negotiations towards a bilateral contract the general rule is that the offeror is at liberty to withdraw the offer at any time before acceptance (*Offord* v *Davies* (1862) 12 CBNS 748). Revocation of an offer is not effective until communicated to the offeree.

5.4.3.1 'Firm offers' It is not uncommon for an offer to be expressed as 'open' for a given period of time, which is no more than a promise not to revoke the offer before that period has elapsed. This kind of promise is sometimes called a firm offer. English law is clear that such a promise is no different from any other promise and is unenforceable unless supported by separate, valuable consideration. There is authority to this effect in *Routledge* v *Grant* (1828) 4 Bing 653.

> The defendant offered to take a lease of premises belonging to the plaintiff, at the same time promising to hold his offer open for six weeks. After only three weeks the defendant purported to revoke this offer, while at the end of the six weeks the plaintiff purported to accept it.

The court found there to be no contract. Such a promise supported by consideration would be an option contract. In the absence of consideration the offer may be withdrawn at any time even before expiry of the duration promised.

The English rule on firm offers is not accepted by most other legal systems. Even most American states, whose contract law has developed out of English law, have abandoned the rule at least in the case of firm offers made by those in business in relation to potential sales of goods (see Uniform Commercial Code section 2-205). The firm offer is a valuable tool in forward planning, especially where a firm wishes to be able to rely on prices quoted by potential subcontractors when tendering for a major contract. It might therefore be thought desirable for the English rule to be abandoned. Such a reform might be achieved simply by identifying a very small reciprocal benefit to the offeror, such as might amount to consideration under the approach adopted in *Williams v Roffey Bros & Nicholls (Contractors) Ltd* [1990] 1 All ER 512, CA (described as a 'subjective benefit' approach at *6.3.2.1* and *6.3.5*). There might, for example, be some subjective benefit to the offeror in having an identified offeree carefully considering his offer, even if it may not be converted into the objective benefit of an actual contract.

5.4.3.2 Impact of acceptance Revocation of an offer after the time of acceptance is ineffective. Indeed, since the contract is formed from the moment of acceptance, attempted revocation after that time might amount to breach by anticipatory repudiation (see *11.3.2*). In all types of negotiation, whether instantaneous or not, revocation is ineffective until actually communicated to the offeree, and until that time the offer is open to acceptance. On the other hand, to be effective a communication of revocation need not be authorised by the offeror, provided the offeree ought reasonably to believe it. In *Dickinson v Dodds* (1876) 2 ChD 463

> the defendant had offered to sell a house to the plaintiff, and had promised to leave the offer open for three days, although the plaintiff had given no consideration for the promise. The plaintiff had decided to accept the offer, but had taken no steps to communicate his decision to the defendant when he was informed by Berry, an apparently reliable person, that the defendant had been offering or agreeing to sell the property to a third party. The plaintiff then attempted to communicate his acceptance to the defendant, but was unable to do so before the property had been sold to the third party. The plaintiff claimed that there had been no effective revocation of the offer before his communication of acceptance.

The court held that the manner of communication of revocation was irrelevant provided the plaintiff knew without any doubt that the defendant no longer intended to sell the property to him by the time his purported acceptance was made.

5.4.3.3 Revocation and the postal rule The fact that the postal rule applies in the case of acceptance (see *5.3.2.1*) but does not apply in the case of revocation (see *5.4.3.2* above) means that the courts must pay close attention to the timing of communications. An acceptance posted after the posting but before the receipt of a revocation is nevertheless effective to form a contract. Just such a state of affairs arose in *Byrne & Co. v Van Tienhoven & Co.* (1880) 5 CPD 344.

> A letter of revocation of an offer was sent from Cardiff to New York on 8 October. Acceptance of the original offer was telegraphed on 11 October from New York to Cardiff, followed on 15 October by a letter of confirmation, each being sent before the letter of revocation had arrived.

The court found a contract to have come into existence before an effective revocation had been made.

5.5 UNILATERAL CONTRACTS

It was suggested at the start of this chapter that traditional offer and acceptance analysis of the formation of agreements may not always be appropriate in situations other than conscious negotiation between two identified parties. A unilateral contract is a contract where one party (the promisor) binds himself to perform a stated promise upon performance of a stated condition by the promisee, but under which the promisee gives no commitment to perform the condition but rather is left free to choose whether to perform or not. Such contracts are sometimes referred to as 'if contracts', since they take the form of the following well-known example first cited in *Great Northern Ry Co.* v *Witham* (1873) LR 9 CP 16: 'If you will go to York, I will give you £100.' This kind of bargain is outside the standard contracting situation, usually described as bilateral or synallagmatic. Unilateral contracts can be explained in terms of offer and acceptance, but sometimes only with difficulty. It was in the context of just such a contract that Lord Wilberforce commented upon the artificiality of offer and acceptance analysis in *The Eurymedon* [1975] AC 154 (see *5.1.1*).

5.5.1 Offer

Little need be added to what has already been said about offers in the context of bilateral contracts (see *5.2.1*). In unilateral contracts two essentially different offers may be made. In the first place, an offer may be made to an identified individual. In *Great Northern Ry Co.* v *Witham* (1873) LR 9 CP 16 the defendant argued that an offer in the form of a conditional promise to the plaintiff could not result in a contract because there was no reciprocity from the promisee. That argument was roundly rejected by the court, which saw such offers as a matter of everyday practice.

Alternatively, the offer may be made to the public at large, or to a particular class of persons. The classic example of such offers is the offer of a reward in return for the performance of some service, such as the apprehension of a criminal or the finding of lost property. In *Carlill* v *Carbolic Smoke Ball Co.* [1893] 1 QB 256 (the facts are given at *5.2.2.1*) the defendants sought to avoid having to pay the promised sum, although the plaintiff had caught influenza after apparently proper use of the smoke ball, by saying that there could be no contract because there would otherwise have been a unilateral contract with the whole world. Bowen LJ rejected this argument, saying:

> It is not a contract made with all the world. There is the fallacy of the argument. It is an offer made to all the world; and why should not an offer be made to all the world which is to ripen into a contract with anybody who comes forward and performs the condition? It is an offer to become liable to anyone who, before it is retracted, performs the condition, and, although the offer is made to the world, the contract is made with that limited portion of the public who come forward and perform the condition on the faith of the advertisement.

5.5.2 Acceptance and consideration

The general rule is that in unilateral contracts acceptance and consideration are constituted by the same thing, namely, performance of the condition stipulated in the offeror's promise. Thus, in *Daulia Ltd* v *Four Millbank Nominees Ltd* [1978] 2 All ER 557 Goff LJ said: '[T]he true view of a unilateral contract must in general be that the offeror is entitled to require full performance of the condition which he has imposed and short of that he is not bound.' Nevertheless, in two respects acceptance and consideration may be separated. For some purposes acceptance may be constituted by commencing performance of the stipulated condition (see below: *5.5.3* Revocation), since this will be sufficient notification to the offeror. Secondly, it may be that in some circumstances no actual acceptance need be made.

In *Carlill* v *Carbolic Smoke Ball Co.* [1893] 1 QB 256 one argument for the defendant company was that no obligation to pay had arisen because there had been no notification of acceptance. In rejecting this argument Bowen LJ at first suggested that this was simply a case of the offeror having dispensed with the need for notification, as the offeror was entitled to do since the requirement of notification exists for the benefit of the offeror. This explanation is unsatisfactory, however, since it is probably the case that notification is important for more than just the offeror because it provides the best objective evidence that agreement exists. Indeed, it is probably the case that there is no acceptance until notification. Bowen LJ goes on to give a second more satisfactory explanation. Starting from the orthodox rule on unilateral contracts that acceptance is constituted by performance of the condition in the offer, he explains that the plaintiff did accept in the conventional way by purchasing the smoke ball, using it according to the instructions, and then *claiming* upon catching influenza. To adopt the judge's example of an advertisement offering a reward for finding a lost dog, a claimant would not qualify for the reward merely by finding and identifying the dog. It would be necessary to bring the performance to the attention of the offeror, presumably by returning the dog.

It has already been noted with regard to acceptance in bilateral contracts that acceptance must be made in response to the offer made (see *5.3.1.1*). The rule is of particular application to unilateral offers made to the whole world, such as rewards.

5.5.3 Revocation

Revocation presents particular difficulty in the case of offers of unilateral contracts as a result of the rule that acceptance is constituted by performance of the condition stated in the offer. In theory it would be open to the offeror to revoke the offer at any time before completion of performance even where the offeree had gone to effort or expense in attempting performance, since the revocation would have been made before the moment of acceptance (see *5.4.3*). It has long been recognised that application of the normal rule in this situation can cause hardship and injustice, but attempts to overcome the rule have run into conceptual difficulties. It is generally accepted that it would be more desirable for the power to revoke to be lost once the offeror has notice that an offeree has unequivocally embarked upon performance. Loss of the power to revoke would not affect the rule that acceptance is only constituted by full performance of the condition in the offer. There are *dicta* to that effect from Goff LJ in *Daulia Ltd v Four Millbank Nominees Ltd* [1978] 2 All ER 557. The difficulty is in finding a conceptual explanation for such a rule.

5.5.3.1 Promissory estoppel Perhaps the most obvious explanation lies in the doctrine of promissory estoppel (see *6.4.3*), since it is not difficult to identify a representation that the offer would be held open long enough for performance to be completed and a reliance by the other party on that representation. In *Errington* v *Errington* [1952] 1 All ER 149

> a father had bought a house for his son and daughter-in-law to live in, promising that although the house and accompanying mortgage were in his name he would transfer the house to their names once they had paid off all the mortgage instalments. The father died and the son left the daughter-in-law, who continued to live in the house and to pay the instalments. The question arose of whether the daughter-in-law could be forced to surrender possession of the house.

Denning LJ said:

> The father's promise was a unilateral contract — a promise of the house in return for their act of paying the instalments. It could not be revoked by him once the couple entered on performance of the act . . . They have acted on the promise and neither the father nor his widow, his successor in title, can eject them in disregard of it.

There is a hint in the passage quoted that Denning LJ viewed the inability to revoke the promise as based on estoppel, since he referred expressly to the fact that the couple had acted on the promise.

In many cases, however, such analysis will not work, because there is no pre-existing legal relationship (see *6.4.2.1*) and because the doctrine is not to be used to found a cause of action (see *6.4.2.4*). Since *Errington* v *Errington* involved the expenditure of money on land belonging to another it may be justified on the basis of the analogous doctrine of proprietary estoppel (see *6.4.2.5*), but that places a serious limitation on the case as explaining the loss of the power to revoke.

5.5.3.2 Acceptance upon commencement An alternative explanation is to question the usual rule that in unilateral contracts acceptance and consideration are synonymous and simultaneous. The main difficulty with such a simple rule is that it has always been accepted that an offeree is entirely free whether to perform or not, and indeed free to commence performance and then stop before completion without fear of any penalty other than the loss of the opportunity to earn the promised reward. If acceptance were to be constituted by starting performance then the contract would of course be in existence from that moment. The offeree would then be obliged to complete performance or face an action for breach of contract should he fail. To tie the offeree in by such a rule would be to defeat one of the objects of the unilateral contract, which is to avoid the need for initial reciprocity inherent in the consideration doctrine as applied to bilateral contracts.

5.5.3.3 Collateral contract A third explanation rests on the identification of two contracts in such cases. The first is the main unilateral contract with acceptance and consideration furnished in the orthodox way by performance of the condition stipulated in the offer. But there is an additional collateral (or ancillary) unilateral contract. It consists of an offer to hold the offer in the main contract open long enough for performance in return for the offeree commencing the main performance immediately, or as soon as possible. Once performance begins the condition in the collateral offer has been performed so that there is an enforceable promise to hold the main offer open. There is no real conceptual difficulty over this explanation, but it is highly artificial and bears no resemblance to the manner in which unilateral offers are in fact made. Nevertheless, recent developments in respect of 'negotiation management' contracts (see *5.2.4*) may lend support to this approach to the problem.

5.5.3.4 Conclusion None of the above explanations is entirely satisfactory. The one involving least conceptual difficulty involves an undesirable resort to legal fiction. Of the other two, promissory estoppel appears best to describe what actually happens and to leave the unilateral contract device intact for the functions for which it is so useful. It seems fairly safe to predict that the courts will continue to find offers of unilateral contracts irrevocable after performance has begun, and it may be that as until now the courts will be reticent about explaining why. On the other hand, it may be that in the promissory estoppel explanation lie the seeds of the wider development of that doctrine into a principle of full liability.

5.5.4 Function of unilateral contracts
The typical unilateral contract is usually regarded as being the offer of a reward for the performance of some service (see *R* v *Clarke* (1927) 40 CLR 227), or the repeat option for the supply of goods provided in a long-term contract to deliver goods as and when ordered (see *Great Northern Ry Co.* v *Witham* (1873) LR 9 CP 16). These functions are well known and well documented, and require no further comment. In addition to these typical functions, unilateral contracts are sometimes used by the courts to manipulate the facts of situations of negotiation into binding contracts where instinct suggests that a contractual relationship exists but the facts do not lend themselves to a conventional analysis of a bilateral contract. Two relatively recent House of Lords cases will serve to illustrate the point.

The facts of *The Eurymedon* [1975] AC 154 are related elsewhere (see *6.3.5.4* and *13.6.1*). The essential point is that the court found a contract to exist between a shipper and a stevedore although the two had not dealt directly with each other, but rather each had a separate contract with the carrier in the case. Lord Wilberforce explained the existence of the contract between shipper and stevedore in the following way:

> The bill of lading brought into existence a bargain initially unilateral but capable of becoming mutual, between the shippers and the stevedore, made through the carrier as agent. This became a full contract when the stevedore performed services by discharging the goods. The performance of these services for the benefit of the shipper was the consideration for the agreement by the shipper that the stevedore should have the benefit of the exemptions and limitations contained in the bill of lading.

There is little doubt that this analysis owes more to the court's legitimate desire to avoid the doctrine of privity of contract than it does to any genuine description of the nature of the negotiations between the three parties.

The facts of *Harvela Investments Ltd* v *Royal Trust Co. of Canada* [1985] 2 All ER 966 are stated above (see *5.2.3*). The essential issue was whether in a request for single bids for the purchase of property a referential bid was permissible. Lord Templeman's speech is couched in terms of an implied stipulation by the offeror about the nature of any acceptance (see *5.3.2.2*). Lord Diplock, however, appears to believe that the decision can be explained on the basis of a 'business efficacy' implied term (see *10.4.4*), which at first sight is a little surprising since, at the time of the request for bids, by any conventional analysis no contract had come into force. Lord Diplock saw a contract into which a term might be implied in the following way:

> It was not a mere invitation to negotiate for the sale of the shares . . . Its legal nature was that of a unilateral or 'if' contract, or rather of two unilateral contracts in identical terms to one of which the vendors and Harvela were the parties as promisor and promisee respectively, while to the other the vendors were promisor and Sir Leonard was promisee.

Lord Diplock's approach is further evidence of the way the unilateral contract device can be used to 'find' a contract where by a conventional analysis none exists.

5.6   CERTAINTY OF AGREEMENTS

5.6.1   General

More complex than the issue of mere existence of agreement is the problem raised where the existence of an agreement in formal terms is not disputed, but one party alleges either that a crucial element is missing or that the terms are too vague, so that the contract is unenforceable. It is an area where there is at least potential for conflict between the relational nature of contracting and the once-and-for-all focus inherent in judicial intervention in contracts. To adopt the words of Lord Wright in *Hillas & Co. Ltd* v *Arcos Ltd* (1932) 147 LT 503, it is accepted that when 'business men make big forward contracts for future goods over a period . . . in general in such contracts it is impossible

. . . to specify in advance all the details of a complicated performance'. Parties sometimes leave trivial details to be worked out later, or in long-term contracts leave the price to be agreed from time to time, or otherwise consciously leave gaps in their agreements because the information and transaction costs of negotiating an agreed allocation of any particular risk are out of proportion to the likelihood of the risk maturing. Sometimes, as a safety-net, they put in an arbitration clause for the resolution of matters which cannot be worked out amicably between them. In nearly all cases they rely on their goodwill at the time of contracting and their mutual interest in maintaining the relationship (which almost certainly extends beyond the individual contract in question) to iron out any problems not covered by the agreement.

Problems are generated by the fact that loosely drafted contracts are not uncommonly some way down the line of performance before vagueness or lack of provision are discovered. At that point, if the matter goes to court, the judge is left with an invidious task. He is to enforce the agreement between the parties, but if they have left some matters deliberately unspecific the judge may have nothing tangible to enforce. At that stage, of course, if the matter has got as far as litigation, there is a danger that the goodwill on which the parties once relied may have evaporated. Yet, if there has been more than trifling performance by one or both parties, it is a drastic step to say that the matter is too vague for there to be any real agreement, and thus there is no contract.

The task of the court is to walk the narrow line between writing the parties' agreement for them (which has traditionally been viewed as beyond the judge's powers and an infringement of freedom of contract) and maintaining the contract by supplying 'reasonable' terms to be implied from the perceived intentions of the parties (on implied terms generally, see: *10.4*). Turning again to *Hillas & Co. Ltd v Arcos Ltd*, Lord Wright makes it clear that the role of the judge (at least where there has already been some performance) is to preserve the contract whenever possible. He said:

[T]he court is [not] to make a contract for the parties . . . except in so far as there are appropriate implications of law, as for instance, the implication of what is just and reasonable to be ascertained by the court as a matter of machinery where the contractual intention is clear but the contract is silent on some detail. Thus in contracts for future performance over a period, the parties may neither be able nor desire to specify many matters of detail . . . Save for the legal implication I have mentioned, such contracts might well be incomplete or uncertain.

As with the rest of the area of formation of agreements, much depends upon the facts of each case. There are no bright lines dividing enforceable from unenforceable agreements. Rather it is merely a question of degree coupled with the extent of the willingness of the judge to intervene to rescue the contract. The general principle can probably be stated as follows: to be enforceable as a contract an agreement must be sufficiently precise (taking into account the whole context of the negotiations) for the court to be confident that what it is enforcing complies with the parties' actual intentions (objectively ascertained, of course: see *5.1.2*) rather than any imputed to them by the court itself. The problem, ironically, is that the principle is itself vague and an invitation to the exercise of a considerable amount of judicial discretion. It is possible, however, to discern certain guidelines.

5.6.2   Agreements which are irresolvably vague or ambiguous
In *Raffles* v *Wichelhaus* (1864) 2 H & C 906

> the plaintiff had promised to sell and deliver to the defendant 125 bales of cotton at a given price 'to arrive ex *Peerless* from Bombay'. There were two ships called *Peerless*, and one left Bombay in October while the other left Bombay in December. The plaintiff's cotton was on the latter ship while (as a matter of procedurally established fact) the defendant intended to buy cotton carried on the former. At the time of contracting the existence of the two ships sailing from Bombay within a short space of each other appears not to have been known to either party.

The court was asked to enforce the 'agreement', but refused so to do. Understanding the case is not easy, since the court gave no reason for its decision. The case is cited by some as one of the last vestiges of a subjective approach to intention (see *5.1.2*). The real intentions of the parties (assuming the court had discovered their real intentions) did not coincide, so that there was never really any agreement. On the other hand, it seems likely that neither a detached bystander, nor a reasonable man in the defendant's shoes, would have had any way of knowing from the words used between the parties which of the two ships was intended. In that case there is what is sometimes referred to as a latent ambiguity, which in this case cannot be resolved by resort to any objective standard. The court can have been left with no alternative but to say that there was no contract.

A similar result can be seen in the recent case of *British Steel Corp.* v *Cleveland Bridge & Engineering Co. Ltd* [1984] 1 All ER 504.

> Work had begun on a major construction before all the elements of the contract had been agreed, although there was a confident expectation on both sides that reaching agreement would present no difficulty. Final agreement was never reached, and eventually the plaintiffs ceased performance and claimed *quantum meruit* for the work which had been done, while the other side counter-claimed damages for breach of contract.

Robert Goff J found that so much remained to be agreed that it was 'very difficult to see' how a contract had been formed. At issue were the price, delivery and applicable terms and conditions. The claim for breach of contract failed, and the plaintiffs recovered reasonable payment for the work done.

It should be noted that in both the above cases significant performance towards the purported contractual goal had taken place, but the vagueness or ambiguity was so great that no agreement could be found. Nevertheless, other cases suggest that courts are reluctant to come to such a conclusion where there has been performance, and will strive to maintain a contract whenever possible. Where there has been no performance a different attitude prevails. This rule of thumb is sometimes described as the 'threshold doctrine', and may be regarded as resting on the element of reliance present where performance has begun, but otherwise absent.

5.6.3   Where there is vagueness and no reliance
In *May & Butcher* v *R* [1934] 2 KB 17n

> an agreement had been made for the sale of surplus war equipment to the plaintiff, the price being left to be agreed between the parties. The parties were unable to agree, and the plaintiffs sought to enforce the agreement at a 'reasonable price' to be determined by the court.

The court refused. The point was not articulated as part of the reasoning, but there can be little doubt that the court's conclusion that no contract had come into existence was made much easier by the fact that no performance under the agreed terms had taken place. See also *Scammell and Nephew Ltd* v *Ouston* [1941] 1 All ER 14.

A further example of the reluctance of courts to enforce 'agreements to agree' where there has been no performance under the terms of the alleged contract arose in *Walford* v *Miles* [1992] 1 All ER 453.

> The parties, negotiating for the sale and purchase of a business, had entered into a 'lock-out agreement', the purported effect of which was to prevent the respondent would-be sellers negotiating with anyone other than the appellants. Negotiations were unsuccessful, and after a time the respondents decided to sell to a third party. The appellants then brought an action for breach of the 'lock-out agreement'.

The agreement was found to be unenforceable. According to Lord Ackner, who gave the only substantial speech in the House of Lords, the fatal weakness of the agreement was that it was indefinite in length. It was a bare agreement to negotiate, and therefore without legal force. On the other hand, had the 'lock-out agreement' stipulated a period of time during which exclusive negotiations were to take place, it would have been enforceable, because the element of uncertainty would have been removed.

There was no substantial reliance on the 'lock-out agreement'. Indeed, the only consideration provided by the appellants was a comfort letter from their bank confirming the offer of a loan to cover the purchase price. Had there been substantial reliance, the House could have reached a similar conclusion without denying any legal effect to the agreement by implying a term that the agreement could be terminated upon reasonable notice (see *11.4.2.3*).

5.6.4   Where there is vagueness but substantial reliance
It was suggested above that *British Steel Corp.* v *Cleveland Bridge & Engineering Co. Ltd* [1984] 1 All ER 504 (for the facts see *5.6.2*) is an unusual case in that there had been very substantial performance when negotiations broke down

and the plaintiffs called a halt to their performance. Normally in such cases the courts are reluctant to say that there is no contract.

For example, in *Hillas & Co. Ltd* v *Arcos Ltd* (1932) 147 LT 503

> the plaintiffs had agreed to purchase an assortment of timber from the defendants during the 1930 season. The contract also contained an option for the purchase of timber during the 1931 season on very favourable terms. The option clause gave no description of the goods to be sold. The plaintiffs made a valid exercise of the option, but the defendants had sold their entire season's production already and claimed that no contract could ensue from the option because it was too uncertain to be enforced.

The House of Lords rejected this argument, although it was forced to go to considerable lengths in implying terms in order to make sense of the agreement. However, there had already been one year's performance of the contract, and the option clause had been part of what the plaintiffs had paid for. To have found it unenforceable as too vague would have been to deprive the plaintiffs of part of their bargain, and the preferable course was to rescue the contract if at all possible. The contrary conclusion in *BSC* v *Cleveland Bridge & Engineering Co. Ltd* is probably explained by the fact that the judge clearly found the defendants largely responsible for the failure to agree. To have found a contract in the circumstances might have exposed the plaintiffs to an action for breach by the defendants, penalising the plaintiffs for something which in the judge's view was not their fault.

Even where the element left uncertain is as fundamental as the price, the courts will enforce the contract if they possibly can once performance has begun. In *Foley* v *Classique Coaches Ltd* [1934] 2 KB 1

> the parties had made an agreement for the supply of the defendants' petrol requirements, to be supplied at a price to be agreed from time to time. The contract included an arbitration clause, and was linked to a deal whereby the defendants purchased a parcel of land from the plaintiffs. Performance continued without incident for three years. The defendants argued that the requirements contract was unenforceable because the price clause was uncertain.

The Court of Appeal found that the agreement was enforceable, the defendants having to pay a 'reasonable price' for petrol supplied. What was reasonable in the circumstances might be determined if necessary by arbitration. In part it seems that it was the fact of actual performance, including the conveyance of the parcel of land, and the danger of depriving the plaintiffs of one important element of their bargain, which persuaded the court. It is interesting to note that the court did not allow the decision of the House of Lords in *May & Butcher* v *R* (5.6.3) to dissuade it. It seems that uncertainty as to price is not as a matter of law always fatal to an agreement; rather, it is a question of construction of the contract in each case. The most obvious distinguishing feature between the two cases, however, is the lack of performance in one and the substantial performance in the other.

Section 8 of the Sale of Goods Act 1979 (substantially reproducing the same section of the 1893 Act) provides:

(1) The price in a contract of sale may be fixed by the contract, or may be left to be fixed in a manner agreed by the contract, or may be determined by the course of dealing between the parties.

(2) Where the price is not determined as mentioned in subsection (1) above the buyer must pay a reasonable price.

In *May & Butcher* v *R* Lord Dunedin suggested that subsection (2) applies only where the contract is silent as to price, and does not apply where a price-fixing formula has failed to work. Such an interpretation seems to be unduly narrow. To say nothing at all about price is surely less certain than to attempt to make a flexible provision which takes into account the changing value of money through time.

This interpretation also appears to be inconsistent with the common law (a possible but unlikely and undesirable conclusion). In *Sudbrooke Trading Estate Ltd* v *Eggleton* [1982] 3 All ER 1

a lease contained an option to purchase the land in question at a price to be agreed by two valuers, one to be appointed by each party. The lessors refused to appoint a valuer and claimed that the option clause was unenforceable because the price term was uncertain.

The House of Lords refused to find the clause unenforceable. No doubt their Lordships were influenced by the fact that there had been considerable performance of the main contract and there was a danger of the lessee being deprived of an important part of its bargain had a contrary result been reached. In part the decision rests on Lord Diplock's view that if the parties have provided convenient and sensible machinery for fixing the price, which is for some reason frustrated, then the court should attempt to take the place of that machinery by identifying a price reasonable in the circumstances.

It would be strange if in the case of the sale of goods as opposed to other commercial contracts the provision of such price-fixing machinery should be an impediment to the court being able to supply a reasonable price. It seems preferable to conclude that it is ultimately a question of fact in each case whether the contract is sufficiently clear for the court to be able to enforce by reasonable implication the apparent agreement between the parties.

5.7 INCORPORATION OF TERMS

5.7.1 General
The final matter to be considered in the formation of agreements is the determination of which terms are included. The law on this issue has evolved almost entirely through litigation in respect of clauses excluding or limiting liability (see *10.6*), especially those contained in standard form contracts. Nevertheless, the principles are equally applicable to all express terms, and

are really no more than a particular application of the rules of offer and acceptance. In relation to exclusion and limitation clauses the law on incorporation of terms is less crucial than once it was because other means of control of such devices now exist (see *10.6.3*) which make it less important for a plaintiff to establish that the clause in question was not part of the agreement. Recently, however, analysis of this kind was used in *Interfoto Picture Library Ltd* v *Stiletto Visual Programmes Ltd* [1988] 1 All ER 348 to exclude a clause which purported to impose a severe penalty for late performance. It is not proposed to consider at this stage the law relating to the distinction between pre-contractual statements which are incorporated into agreements and those which are treated merely as representations inducing agreement. It is a related topic, but requires an understanding of the law relating to misrepresentation (see Chapter 9) and to terms (see Chapter 10) and will be dealt with at that point (*10.1.2*).

5.7.2 Contracts in writing and signed

When a document containing contractual terms is signed, without there being any misrepresentation, the party signing it is usually regarded as bound by the terms. Normally, therefore, no enquiry will be allowed into whether the party signing had read the document or otherwise knew what the terms said. This rule is an important buttress of contractual certainty, but its unbending application has sometimes appeared to cause hardship. In part that is because unscrupulous businessmen have exploited the rule to take advantage of others, particularly consumers. In *L'Estrange* v *Graucob Ltd* [1934] 2 KB 394

> the plaintiff had bought a cigarette vending machine from the defendants. The latter employed a standard form contract with a multiplicity of terms reproduced in very small print on poor quality paper, which the plaintiff had signed. She was held to be bound by an exclusion clause in the document.

On more than one occasion Lord Denning has suggested that in the case of particularly sweeping exclusion clauses the law ought to impose on the offeror a more positive obligation to draw the attention of the offeree to the clause in question before being prepared to hold the offeree to have had constructive notice of the clause. In *Thornton* v *Shoe Lane Parking Ltd* [1971] 1 All ER 686 he said: 'In order to give sufficient notice, it would need to be printed in red ink with a red hand pointing to it, or something equally startling.' (See also *J. Spurling Ltd* v *Bradshaw* [1956] 2 All ER 121.) Some jurisdictions have experimented with detailed regulation of print size and presentation of exclusion and similar clauses, but no such initiative has been seen in this country.

The traditionally strict approach to signed documents was, however, disregarded in *Harvey* v *Ventilatorenfabrik Oelde GmbH* (1988) 8 Tr LR 138.

> In a contract of sale there was the usual exchange of documents comprising the contract. One half of what was otherwise a duplicate set contained additional terms in German. This document was signed by the plaintiff and returned to the defendants. The question arose whether the terms in German formed part of the contract.

The Court of Appeal found that the circumstances, and especially the difference between the documents, justified the court enquiring whether the plaintiff had in fact assented to the German terms, even when he had signed the document. The court took the view that its decision was consistent with *L'Estrange* v *Graucob Ltd*, in which it had been suggested that the strict approach to signed documents would not apply where the party claiming not to be bound was misled.

5.7.3   Written terms and oral contracts

It is not uncommon for contracts to comprise some oral and some written terms, and for the actual acceptance to be made independently of any document containing written terms which are subsequently alleged to be part of the agreement. The general principle is that written terms which have not been signed by the offeree may still be incorporated into the agreement provided the offeree had reasonable notice of them before the time of accepting the offer. In *Olley* v *Marlborough Court Ltd* [1949] 1 KB 532

> a hotel sought to exclude its liability for the loss of valuable personal possessions by a guest at the hotel by reference to an exclusion notice on the back of the hotel bedroom door. The contract had been made in the entrance hall of the hotel before the offeree had any possible means of knowing about the purported exclusion of liability. The court found the notice to be ineffective.

This general principle does not apply where there is a course of dealing between the parties or where it is common knowledge that contracts are made subject to restrictive conditions.

5.7.3.1   Tickets   It has been suggested that printed notices contained in tickets are an exception to the general principle, in that they may be effective to exclude liability although not actually delivered to the purchaser until after the moment of agreement between the parties. Certainly the nineteenth century ticket cases are not easy to explain. In *Parker* v *South Eastern Ry* (1877) 2 CPD 416

> the railway company operated a left luggage office in which the plaintiff left a bag, paying the required fee and receiving in return a ticket. On the ticket were the words 'See Back', and on the back was a clause purporting to limit the company's liability in the case of luggage lost to £10. The plaintiff's bag was lost; its contents were worth more than £10.

The court found the clause on the ticket sufficient to limit the company's liability as stated.

Mellish LJ took the view that printing on a ticket would be incorporated into a contract provided a reasonable person would appreciate that there was writing containing conditions on the ticket. This view appears to neglect the issue of whether such notice as there was came too late, since it is common for the point of offer and acceptance to precede the issuing of the ticket.

Bramwell LJ may have been sensitive to this problem, since in his judgment there is a hint that the case is no more than an early example of the situation referred to above where it is common knowledge that the type of contract in question is made subject to certain conditions which are available for consultation upon request. It must be remembered that only a few years before the date of this litigation 'tickets' had been no more than bills of lading presented to the purchaser for signature, and it may be that the law had not adjusted to the new ticket issuing machines which did not give the purchaser the same degree of notice of writing on the document.

Whatever the explanation of the nineteenth century cases, there has been a quiet revolution in the law relating to conditions printed on tickets. In the first place, it is recognised that in some cases a ticket is not a contractual document at all, but only a receipt for money paid, with the result that writing on the ticket is seen much too late to be incorporated into any agreement. In *Chapelton* v *Barry UDC* [1940] 1 KB 532 a ticket issued by a deck-chair attendant was found only to be a receipt, and the exclusion clause on it was found to be ineffective. In *Thornton* v *Shoe Lane Parking Ltd* [1971] 1 All ER 686 a ticket referring to conditions displayed inside a multi-storey car park was found to be ineffective to incorporate an exclusion clause into the agreement because at the time of issue the motorist was already committed to using he car park, and so the contract between the motorist and the car park company had already been formed. Lord Denning described the nineteenth century cases as based on a fiction, and said he was not prepared to apply them in the case of a ticket issued by an automatic machine. Nor does the nineteenth century rule apply in the case of tickets issued in advance by a travel agent, where at the time the contract for travel facilities is made the particular conditions said to apply to the contract are not available for inspection (*Hollingworth* v *Southern Ferries Ltd, The Eagle* [1977] 2 Lloyd's Rep 70).

In the case of railway tickets it might still be difficult for a court to distinguish *Parker* v *South Eastern Ry*, and there is some justification for the view that reasonable people realise that such tickets are issued subject to conditions. It must be remembered that there are now statutory restrictions on the power of those who supply transport services to limit or exclude their liability (see, for example, *10.6.3.2*), so that the impact of this slightly anomalous rule is now small.

5.7.3.2   A stricter approach   In *Interfoto Picture Library Ltd* v *Stiletto Visual Programmes Ltd* [1988] 1 All ER 348 the Court of Appeal refused to regard as part of the contract a clause which was nevertheless available for inspection before the time when the contract was formed. The term in question was a form of penalty clause, which, on a contract worth a relatively small sum, would have resulted in a payment of £3,783.50 being required for a short delay in returning the photographic negatives which were the subject of the contract. The Court of Appeal regarded the clause as particularly onerous and unusual, and argued that such a clause would not be regarded as *fairly* brought to the notice of the other party 'unless it was drawn to his attention in the most explicit way'. Dillon LJ regarded himself as bound to find in this way by the reasoning of the majority in *Thornton* v *Shoe Lane Parking Ltd*. With respect to the Court of Appeal, there is no real justification for applying different rules of incorporation for different types of clause, especially when the test for which clauses are subject to the stricter rule is necessarily vague and unpredictable.

5.7.4   Course of dealing

Where the parties deal with each other on a regular basis, on standard terms and conditions, the courts will not demand that reasonable notice of those terms and conditions be available to the offeree on each and every occasion for them to be incorporated into the particular contract. Nevertheless, the party seeking to rely on a course of dealing for the incorporation of terms will have to sustain the burden of proving that the course of past conduct has been sufficiently consistent to give rise to the implication that in similar circumstances a similar contractual result will follow. In *McCutcheon* v *David MacBrayne Ltd* [1964] 1 All ER 430

> the plaintiff had previously used the defendants' ferry service for his car on several occasions. Sometimes he had been asked to sign a note containing an exclusion clause, but sometimes he had not. On the occasion in question the ferry sank, and no note had been signed. The defendants were unable to rely on the course of dealing to incorporate an exclusion clause into the contract.

The decisions in course of dealing cases turn on their particular facts. For a case where the clause was found to have been incorporated, see *PLM Trading Co. (International) Ltd* v *Georgiou* [1986] BTLC 404. The same course of conduct had been followed on four previous occasions, and that was held to be sufficient to establish a course of dealing which caused the clause to be incorporated. It was clear that on previous occasions the buyer had signed a document with the clause on it. The court did not refer to the fact that each time he may have signed after the contract was made.

5.7.5   Common knowledge

In some limited circumstances the courts may be willing to incorporate a term into a contract without actual notice and without any prior course of dealing. Except in the railway ticket cases, which may be explained under this principle (see *5.7.3.1* above), the courts will only incorporate terms in these circumstances where there is some common basis shared by the parties which justifies the presumption that the parties share a common understanding that the terms will apply. The common basis will usually be supplied by the fact that both parties belong to and are familiar with the terms of a particular trade, and indeed there may be standard conditions issued by a trade association. An example of incorporation in this form can be found in *British Crane Hire Corporation Ltd* v *Ipswich Plant Hire Ltd* [1974] 1 All ER 1059.

5.7.6 Incorporation by reference
A common way for terms to be incorporated into a contract is for a simple document, probably stating no more than the parties, the subject-matter of their agreement, and the price, to provide that the contract is governed by terms and conditions which may be found in another document. Such provision will usually be found to be sufficient notice of those terms for them to be incorporated into the contract (e.g., *Smith* v *South Wales Switchgear Co. Ltd* [1978] 1 All ER 18, 23–25, 28–30). In the light of the decision in *Interfoto Picture Library Ltd* v *Stiletto Visual Programmes Ltd* [1988] 1 All ER 348 it is presumably possible that particularly onerous or unusual clauses could not be incorporated in this way.

5.7.7 Incorporation of written terms in practice
It is convenient for the purposes of presentation to treat the various means of incorporation of terms as conceptually distinct categories. In practice, the lines between categories may be blurred, and the judge may be willing to treat a term as incorporated because an argument may be made for that conclusion under more than one head. A good example is *Circle Freight International Ltd* v *Medeast Gulf Exports Ltd* [1988] 2 Lloyd's Rep 427, 428–433. Taylor LJ found an exemption clause to have been incorporated on three distinct grounds: incorporation by reference to the standard conditions of the Institute of Freight Forwarders; a course of dealing over 11 previous transactions; and trade usage known to everybody in the particular business. The various categories considered in this section must, therefore, be seen as no more than tools available to an imaginative lawyer with which to fashion a convincing argument for the client.

SIX

Essential ingredients of enforceability

6.1 INTRODUCTION

In the introduction a contract was defined as a legally enforceable agreement (see *4.1*). We have already considered the normal means whereby agreements are reached (see Chapter 5). In due course we shall have to examine some of the pitfalls along the way to agreement (see especially Chapters 7 and 9). The detailed rules governing the mechanisms of enforcement of agreements are the subject of Chapter 12. It is an implicit assumption of the definition, however, that not all agreements are contracts. There must therefore be a body of legal rules by which it is possible to determine whether an agreement is a contract or not. The subject of this chapter is those rules by which it is determined whether any particular agreement is of the type which the courts will enforce.

It was suggested in the introduction that in its formative period English law developed by the curious means of first identifying remedies and then inductively developing the rights which gave rise to those remedies. In the case of contract the result was that once a remedy for breach of an undertaking was identified, the courts had still to develop a test for distinguishing enforceable agreements from those which the courts were unwilling to enforce (see *4.3*). The major indicator of enforceability adopted by the common law was that of mutual exchange of (at very least) promises of value. In the terminology of the law, where a promise in an agreement was given in return for something of value (including another promise), then the first promise was given for *consideration* and could be enforced by legal action.

A promise given without consideration (gratuitous promise) was unenforceable unless made under seal. This strange expression means no more than that the promise had to be contained in a document on which the promisor had fixed an impression in wax of some identifying mark, such as a crest. Until the present day, documents have been made under seal, particularly for the conveyance of land which has been sold, but the traditional wax seal has given way to a modern red sticker, and sometimes not even as much as that. Recent reform has changed the formal requirements for the making of deeds (s.1 of the Law of Property (Miscellaneous Provisions) Act 1989). Deeds no longer require a seal to be valid, and need no longer be written on parchment, although there are stricter requirements for the attestation of signatures, and the deed must be 'delivered' by the person making it (which does not require physical transfer, but merely recognition that it legally binds the deliverer). It is easy to understand how consideration became the cornerstone of the common law contract, since those seeking to make promises enforceable could avoid quite considerable formality simply by providing evidence of an exchange of things of value. On the other hand, for two reasons consideration has often been a source of heart-searching among lawyers.

In the first place, many legal systems in the world have efficient and just rules of contract law without any requirement of consideration as a pre-condition of enforceability. Secondly, some agreements which are acknowledged to satisfy the requirement of consideration are said nevertheless to be unenforceable, either because the court is unwilling to believe that the parties ever intended that they should be enforced by legal action (see 6.2 below), or because the court is not satisfied that there is adequate evidence of the alleged agreement (see 6.5 below). In consequence some commentators have suggested that the requirement of consideration should be abandoned, on the ground that the task of sorting enforceable from unenforceable agreements is already achieved by rules on intention to create legal relations and on essential formalities for certain types of contract. Others have suggested that rules on intention to create legal relations and evidential formality are themselves redundant since the consideration doctrine embraces such functions. The orthodox view remains that intention to create legal relations, consideration and in some cases evidential formality are all essential ingredients of enforceability.

6.2 INTENTION TO CREATE LEGAL RELATIONS

6.2.1 General

It is generally accepted that legal systems must have some means of identifying those agreements which, although to all outward appearances qualify as contracts, are regarded as being beyond the reach of legal remedies. Consider the following simple example: Tom is a 19-year-old student, living at home with his parents during the vacation. He has no money, and approaches his father, Dick, for an allowance. Dick says that if Tom will clean the family car once a week, do the shopping and keep the garden tidy, he will give him £15 per week. Tom agrees. Not many people would disagree with the conclusion that despite the outward appearance of agreement *and consideration* (a promise to do the various odd jobs about the house in exchange for a promise to pay an allowance) this arrangement should not be regarded as a contract, in the sense that the courts ought to be unwilling to enforce trivial family agreements. For much of the nineteenth century, the period of development of modern contract law, the underlying theory was that contracts were built upon the will of the parties. It is not surprising, therefore, that the test for identifying those contracts beyond the reach of the law was framed in terms of whether the parties intended legal relations. Nevertheless, today it is accepted that reference to the parties' intentions may be no more than a convenient short way of describing a test which is rather more complex than that. In fact, it is notoriously difficult to prove intention since there is no objective evidence which may be produced as conclusive proof. If every party seeking a legal remedy under a contract were put to the burden of establishing that both parties positively intended legal consequences to their agreement it would be a major stumbling block to the formation of valid contracts. For this reason the law has had to accept a much more restricted test of intention.

6.2.1.1 Presumed intention   The conventional view of intention to create legal relations is that agreements divide for these purposes into two general types: commercial agreements and social/domestic agreements. For each type there is a corresponding presumption. For commercial agreements the presumption is that there is an intention to create legal relations; for social/domestic agreements the presumption is that no such intention exists. One difficulty with this otherwise straightforward scheme lies in the nature of presumptions, which are technical devices of the law of evidence. A presumption may be displaced by any actual evidence to the contrary. Such a precarious status is inconsistent with the role the particular presumptions are called upon to play in relation to intention to create legal relations, which is precisely to avoid instability of contracts caused by parties finding it too easy to avoid liability by denying the relevant intention.

From the cases below it should be apparent that in this particular area the presumptions are by no means easily displaced, and indeed it may seem that they are at times impossible to displace. The true situation seems to be that presumption is not being used in its technical evidential sense here. Rather, when we say intention is presumed in relation to commercial agreements, we mean that a reasonable person in this situation would have expected legal consequences to flow from this agreement, and in the absence of some reason of policy against it the court will enforce that reasonable expectation. Equally, when we say that there is a presumption of an absence of intention to create legal relations in social/domestic agreements (like Tom and Dick's, above) we mean that the reasonable expectation is that no legal consequences would flow from the agreement. It is true that some aspects of normal presumptions are present in those in use here, notably the fact that a presumption in favour of one conclusion places the burden of proof on the party seeking to establish the opposite. In other words, any party seeking to establish that a commercial agreement was not intended to be legally binding must persuade the court that that is the case, and failure to persuade results in the opposite conclusion prevailing. The difference is that here persuading the court may be very difficult; in legal terms, the burden of proof is very high.

The truth of the matter seems to be that the rules of presumed intention and presumed absence of intention are really based on a judicial policy of unwillingness to interfere in domestic disputes. In the words of Atkin LJ in the leading case of *Balfour* v *Balfour* [1919] 2 KB 571: 'In respect of these promises each house is a domain into which the King's writ does not seek to run'.

6.2.2 Commercial dealing

It was suggested earlier (see *4.4*) that one of the main economic purposes of contracts is to stimulate exchange. It would be undesirable, therefore, for the intention to create legal relations doctrine to become a further hurdle in the way of a party seeking to enforce a commercial contract. For this reason the presumption that intention exists in such contracts is extremely difficult to displace, so that only a party with solid evidence of a contrary intention would risk litigation.

6.2.2.1 Advertising The only exception to this general rule in relation to commercial agreements operates as a protection of advertisers, who may in some circumstances be able to rely on an absence of intention to create legal relations in order to avoid being held to the exact words of advertisements. If a beer producer chooses to promote its product by claiming that it refreshes parts which other beers do not reach, it is no doubt seen by reasonable people as a joke and not as a serious claim to be elevated into a contractual promise. Nevertheless, the exception does not apply in every case. In *Carlill* v *Carbolic Smoke Ball Co.* [1893] 1 QB 256

> the company had claimed that their product when used properly was an infallible protection against influenza, and had promised to pay £100 to anyone able to show that they had contracted influenza after proper use of a smoke ball. To demonstrate the good faith of this promise the company had placed £1,000 in a special bank account.

Particularly in the light of this last fact, the court was unwilling to accept that the promise was no more than overblown advertising. A claimant who had contracted influenza was able to enforce the promise.

As is clear from this case, the exception depends very much upon the particular facts of the cases. The result is that judges may be in total agreement about the law applicable, but unable to agree upon its application to the facts. There is no better example of this problem than the case of *Esso Petroleum Co.* v *Commissioners of Customs & Excise* [1976] 1 All ER 117.

> The company had organised a promotional effort in conjunction with the 1970 World Cup whereby the purchase of four gallons of petrol entitled the purchaser to a free 'World Cup Coin'. The coins had no real value, but those collecting the coins would presumably buy Esso petrol in preference to other brands for the duration of the promotion. The Customs & Excise Commissioners sought to recover purchase tax on the coins on the ground that they had been produced for general sale.

In the House of Lords one argument was that the coins could only be for sale if there was an intention to create legal relations in respect of the transfer of the coins between garage proprietors and customers purchasing petrol. The majority felt that there was, relying on the business context and the large commercial advantage Esso expected to derive from the scheme. The minority found no intention to create legal relations, pointing to the language of the offer, the trivial value of the coins and the unlikelihood of any motorist denied a coin believing that a legal remedy was available for that grievance.

6.2.2.2 Rebutting the presumption
In a handful of noteworthy decisions, the presumption in respect of commercial agreements has been found to have been rebutted. The leading case is *Rose and Frank Co.* v *J.R. Crompton & Bros* [1925] AC 445.

> The plaintiffs were to be the defendants' agents to sell a certain kind of paper in the United States, and the document setting out the agency agreement contained a term usually referred to as the 'honourable pledge clause'. It purported to provide that the agreement was to be viewed as a definite expression of intention, but not as a formal or legal agreement subject to the jurisdiction of the courts. The parties continued their relationship for some time, and from time to time the plaintiffs would make a specific order which was met by the defendants. The defendants then suddenly announced that they would fulfil no more orders, and the plaintiffs sued to enforce the general agency agreement.

The House of Lords upheld the 'honourable pledge clause', effectively saying that in the main agency agreement there was no intention to create legal relations. The same was not true of the specific orders, which were ordinary contracts. The presumption of intention can be seen as having been rebutted by the express clause in the agreement, but there is some logical difficulty about this view since the clause could have no legal force if the agreement in which it was contained was found not to be a contract. On its face the agreement, which had been signed by both parties, was perhaps good objective evidence of intention, but there must be some doubt about that since the purpose of the clause appears to have been to avoid the impact of American laws on restrictive practices. Since it seems clear that the main agency agreement would have been regarded as a contract but for the clause it is also slightly surprising that the clause did not fall foul of the rule against ousting the jurisdiction of the courts (see *8.7.3.2*).

The question of intention to create legal relations in commercial agreements was considered again recently in *Kleinwort Benson Ltd* v *Malaysia Mining Corporation Bhd* [1989] 1 All ER 785:

> The plaintiff bank agreed to make a loan facility available to M, a wholly owned subsidiary of the defendants. In the course of negotiations the parties had not been able to agree upon any security to be given for the loan, but the defendants had provided a 'letter of comfort', containing the key sentence: 'It is our policy to ensure that the business of M is at all times in the position to meet its liabilities to you under the above arrangements'. When the tin market collapsed, M ceased trading and went into liquidation, without paying its very considerable debt to the plaintiffs. They then sued the defendants, claiming that the sentence quoted was a contractual promise, which in the event had been breached.

The Court of Appeal found that the action must fail, because there was no contractual promise made. As such the case might be regarded as consistent with the decision in *Rose & Frank Co.* v *J. R. Crompton & Bros*. However, the Court of Appeal said that the case was not to be treated as one turning upon the question of intention to create legal relations. Such a question would only arise if there was a separate agreement that the undertaking given should not be of legal effect. In the absence of such a separate agreement, the only issue was what was the proper construction of the crucial sentence. It was construed to amount only to a statement of present intention, and not to be a promise about the future conduct of the defendants, and so was said to be without contractual force. In coming to this conclusion the court noted the fact that the parties had been unable to agree upon more formal security, and that the notion of a comfort letter was known by both sides to describe a document by which the defendants gave comfort to the plaintiffs, 'by assuming, not a legal liability to ensure repayment of the liabilities of the subsidiary, but a moral responsibility only'. It might seem that there is little difference between this approach, and that followed in respect of intention to create legal relations in *Rose & Frank Co.* v *J. R. Crompton & Bros*. However, although it was said to be of no practical signficance in the outcome of this case, the Court of Appeal suggested that in its approach of relying simply on the construction of the words used, the onus of proof lay on the plaintiffs to show that it should be treated as a contractual promise. This ruling reverses the position described above in relation to legal intention in commercial contracts, and introduces a critical and difficult distinction into an already murky area of the law of contract, between separate agreements that contracts will not be legally enforceable (where the burden of proof is on the party denying legal force), and statements made without legal force (where the burden of proof is on the party asserting legal force). It is perhaps for this reason that the decision has been criticised in some quarters, because it makes it all too easy for firms to avoid legal responsibilities (see *Banque Brussels Lambert SA* v *Australian National Industries*, noted at [1991] JBL 282).

In many cases direct evidence of intention will not be available, and the courts must draw such implications as they may from the surrounding circumstances. In both *Rose and Frank Co.* v *J. R. Crompton & Bros* and *Kleinwort Benson Ltd* v *Malaysia Mining Corporation Bhd* there existed a document which on its face indicated an apparent absence of legal intention, respectively in the 'honourable pledge clause' and the designation of the document containing the relevant assurances as a 'comfort letter'. In *Orion Insurance Co. plc* v *Sphere Drake Insurance plc* [1992] 1 Lloyd's Rep 239 agreement was reached orally, and subsequently recorded in writing. The plaintiffs, who sought to prove that the agreement was not legally enforceable, argued that the oral agreement had been agreed to be no more than a matter of goodwill, although no mention of this element was to be found in the written record. The Court of Appeal nevertheless upheld the trial judge's findings of fact which led to the conclusion that there had been no intention to create legal relations. It was quite permissible to admit parol evidence (see *10.1.3*) to show an absence of such intention. Moreover, although the presumption of legal intention is said not to be easily rebutted in commercial cases, it is clear that in the Court of Appeal's view the appropriate burden of proof remains the usual civil test of balance of probabilities.

Often it seems that a decision on the question of intention to create legal relations is a cloak for a more pressing question of policy. In *Ford Motor Co.* v *AUEFW* [1969] 2 QB 303 the court was faced with the question of whether a collective bargaining agreement between management and the union was legally binding. The matter was clearly commercial, and so the burden lay on the union, which sought to deny contractual intention. The court found in the union's favour. In so doing it relied on evidence from industrial relations experts which was general rather than relevant to the particular agreement. Thus the actual intentions of the parties seem to have been less relevant than the court's view that it was desirable as a matter of policy to keep such agreements out of the courts. The matter is now governed by s.179 of the Trade Union and Labour Relations (Consolidation) Act 1992, which reverses the presumption otherwise prevailing in commercial cases.

6.2.3 Social and domestic arrangements

The law relating to intention to create legal relations is most difficult in the case of non-commercial agreements. The difficulty stems partially from identifying social and domestic arrangements and partially from the desire to be able to enforce certain agreements even if they are social or domestic in character. It was in the case already mentioned of *Balfour* v *Balfour* [1919] 2 KB 571 (see *6.2.1.1*) that Atkin LJ first clearly articulated the test based upon the intentions of the parties. The facts of that case serve as a good example.

> The husband worked overseas, and it became clear that for reasons of health his wife could no longer live where he worked. They agreed that she would return to England and he would pay her £30 per month for her living expenses. Subsequently they became estranged, and the wife sued to enforce the promise of financial support.

The court found that the promise was not legally enforceable because there had been no intention to create legal relations. There is no doubt, as subsequent cases have shown (see *Merritt* v *Merritt* [1970] 2 All ER 760), that if the maintenance agreement had been made upon breakdown of the marriage, rather than prior to breakdown when relations between the parties were entirely amicable, the agreement even though between husband and wife would have been enforceable. It is not disputed that legal relations are intended in the latter situation. It may well be that the fact of breakdown takes the agreement outside the sphere of domestic arrangements.

These cases are further examples of the way in which many potential contractual rights crystallise at the time of formation of the agreement, and cannot be affected by subsequent events. In *Balfour* v *Balfour* the only relevant intention was that existing at the time of making the agreement, and the fact that subsequently the marriage had broken down and the wife intended to enforce the agreement could not change it from being beyond the scope of the law.

6.2.3.1 Rebutting the presumption   In the case of the presumption against intention to create legal relations it is unlikely that courts would find any express statement of the parties to be conclusive, since it is here that the policy element of the doctrine is most strong. Thus, in the example of Tom and Dick it is unlikely that we would be any happier about the legal enforceability of their agreement had it contained a clause stating that it was intended to create legal relations. The policy against judicial intervention in such agreements would still prevail. Nevertheless, the courts have been willing to find social/domestic agreements enforceable in some cases. It is not always easy to see what is the evidence which caused the presumption to be rebutted.

An instructive case is *Jones* v *Padavatton* [1969] 1 WLR 328.

> The plaintiff sought to persuade her daughter to take up a new career by offering her a generous living allowance while she pursued studies to become a barrister. The plaintiff also bought a house, in which the daughter had rooms, the rest being let to tenants. Eventually, after more than one unsuccessful attempt at the examinations, mother and daughter fell out, and the mother sought to evict the daughter from the house.

The majority in the Court of Appeal found that the daughter had no right to stay in the house because there was no contract betwen her and her mother. They relied on the speech of Atkin LJ in *Balfour* v *Balfour* [1919] 2 KB 571. Salmon LJ agreed with the result of this reasoning, but preferred to base his decision on a contract under which the daughter was not entitled to expect anything further from her mother, because it could not be regarded as an open-ended promise to pay for her to live in London for as long as she failed to pass the Bar examinations. In his view there had been an intention to create legal relations. It was impossible to think that the daughter had given up her secure and lucrative career without the protection of an enforceable promise of financial support.

There is much to commend the reasoning of Salmon LJ in this case. It suggests that while families' trivial agreements are beyond the scope of the law, when families come to agreements which will have a serious impact on the lives of their members they are as entitled to the remedies of the courts as everybody else. Such a principle would seem to be inconsistent with the decision in *Balfour* v *Balfour*, however, in that it is difficult not to admit that the agreement between the Balfours had a serious impact on their lives. Nevertheless, other cases do seem to support the idea that where the subject-matter of the dispute is more than trivial the courts will be more willing to find the requisite intention for a contractual remedy to be available. In *Parker* v *Clark* [1960] 1 WLR 286

> an elderly couple agreed with another couple some years younger than them that if the younger ones would sell their home and move in with the others, sharing household expenses, then the older ones would leave a certain sum upon the death of the husband to the younger ones. The two couples later fell out, and the younger ones were asked to leave. They therefore sought damages for breach of contract.

The judge could not believe that the plaintiffs could have taken the drastic step of selling their own house without the security of a legal right to live in the home of the other couple.

6.2.3.2 Intention and reasonable expectation The major difficulty with the view that social/domestic agreements will be held enforceable where they are more than trivial and have a serious impact on the parties is that while it appears to coincide with what the courts often do, it is not entirely consistent with what the judges say they are doing. On the other hand, the orthodox language of intention appears to be based on a legal fiction, in that few if any parties turn their minds at the time of forming such agreements to the question of whether legal rights are being created. This is hardly surprising since such agreements are entered into in confident anticipation of continued good relations. It would be undesirable if the nobler feelings of parties to serious social or domestic agreements became an impediment to legal recourse in situations where their good relations have broken down. For this reason the courts must put themselves in the place of the parties at the time of the agreement and ask whether it would have been reasonable to expect legal relations to result from the agreement, in the undesirable event of amicable relations ending. In this way the 'rose tinted spectacles' of the parties at the time of making the agreement are avoided. It is not surprising therefore that the courts' willingness to find intention increases, the more serious are the promises made in the agreement.

6.3 CONSIDERATION

6.3.1 Definitions
Consideration is the principal essential ingredient of enforceability of agreements. Traditional analysis has usually considered the existence of consideration to be demonstrated by proof of a benefit and/or a detriment. In *Thomas* v *Thomas* (1842) 2 QB 851 Patteson J said:

> Consideration means something which is of some value in the eye of the law, moving from the plaintiff; it may be some detriment to the plaintiff or some benefit to the defendant, but at all events it must be moving from the plaintiff.

Modern English law has abandoned benefit/detriment analysis, preferring the definition of consideration provided by Sir Frederick Pollock (in *Principles of Contract*) to the effect that consideration is constituted by 'an act or forebearance of one party, or the promise thereof,' being 'the price for which the promise of the other is bought.' It is of course possible still to detect elements of benefit and detriment in this definition, but what is most important is the emphasis upon *exchange*. Simple benefit and detriment analysis cannot account for some of the decisions of the courts (see *6.3.2*), but it is important to be familiar with the formulation given above, in part because some of the cases still use the language of benefit and detriment but more especially because some sub-rules of the doctrine of consideration owe their existence to the traditional formulation (see *6.3.2* and *6.3.4*, below). A good example of the continuing influence of the language of benefit and detriment is the recent decision of the Court of Appeal in *Williams* v *Roffey Bros & Nicholls (Contractors) Ltd* [1990] 1 All ER 512, which has caused a thorough re-evaluation of the doctrine of consideration (see especially *6.3.5.3* and *6.3.6*). However, in analysing in a contemporary problem whether consideration exists in an agreement it would be much better to rely on the notion of exchange. The essential test is whether what is provided by the one party (be it action, inaction or merely a promise thereof) induced the action, inaction or promise of the other.

6.3.1.1 Executory and executed consideration

We have defined consideration both in terms of acts done or not done and in terms of promises. We have already seen that the great value of contract as a commercial device is that it provides for liability on an obligation even where performance on both sides remains in the future (see *4.4*). It is in this facility that the strength of contract as an instrument of planning lies. Where consideration consists only of an exchange of promises it is described as executory. The classic example is a contract for the sale of goods where the seller agrees to deliver the goods at some time in the future, and the buyer agrees to pay for them either on delivery or by some other credit arrangement. At the time of the agreement neither side has done anything towards the performance of the promises made, but the agreement still has contractual force.

Where consideration consists of an exchange of a promise for an act then it is described as executed. The classic example of such contracts, sometimes described as unilateral contracts (see *5.5*), are promises of rewards. For example, in *R* v *Clarke* (1927) 40 CLR 227

> the government of Western Australia offered a reward for information leading to the arrest of certain criminals. Clarke gave information which led to a conviction, and sued to recover the reward, although he admitted that at the time of giving the information his only motive had been to clear his own name.

He was held unable to recover. The case is usually described as being an example of the impossibility of giving assent to an offer of which one has no knowledge. Clarke, however, had seen the reward offer. The better view may therefore be that his action was not induced by the promise of reward, and therefore consideration was absent.

Executed consideration consists of a promise followed by an act. Care must be taken to distinguish the situation where an act is followed by a promise, which does not amount to consideration (see *6.3.3* 'past consideration').

6.3.2 Value, exchange and inducement

The exchange theory of consideration still requires the offering up, in exchange for a promise, of something of *value*. Mere motive in making a promise, unattached to any element of value, is not sufficient consideration. In *Thomas* v *Thomas* (1842) 2 QB 851 a dying man had expressed the wish to the executors of his will that his wife should be able to live in his house for as long as she should wish to and remained a widow. On the strength of this wish the executors promised the house to the widow.

The court was unanimous in its view that whatever the moral obligation in such a situation the mere motive of satisfying the wishes of the now dead man was not consideration.

Once something of *value* can be shown, however, the court makes no inquiry into whether the thing offered is a genuine equivalent of the promise made. At some early point in its history the doctrine of consideration might have developed as a means to police bargains between parties, requiring the exchange of things of equivalent value. As such it would have been part of the law's armour against duress and fraud (see *6.3.5*, below, and Chapter 8). In fact, the doctrine of freedom of contract and no doubt the mere practical difficulty of proving equivalence intervened to prevent such a development. There is no investigation of whether the value given in return for the promise is any real benefit to the promisor or any real detriment to the promisee, let alone of whether the promises exchanged are of equivalent value. All that is required is that actual value be given. Thus, in *Thomas* v *Thomas* the widow to whom the house was promised had in turn promised to pay £1 per annum as ground rent and to maintain the property in good and tenantable repair. This return promise was found to be of actual value, and thus to amount to sufficient consideration. This rule finds frequent expression in the provision in leases for peppercorn rents.

6.3.2.1   Benefit/detriment and value

In saying that in *Thomas* v *Thomas* (1842) 2 QB 851 there was an exchange of things of value it is possible, though not particularly revealing, to analyse that exchange in terms of benefit and detriment. Such analysis fails altogether in the case of *Chappell & Co.* v *Nestlé Co.* [1960] AC 87.

> The case involved an offer to the public of records at a very low price as a promotional scheme for a brand of chocolate. Copies of a particular dance record could be obtained for 1s 6d (7.5p) and three chocolate wrappers, whereas the normal price was 6s 6d (32.5p). Manufacture and sale of the records was breach of copyright in the song unless royalties were paid to the copyright owners, who in this case were the plaintiffs. Under a statutory scheme a copyright owner was not entitled to object if informed and paid a royalty of 6.25% of the ordinary retail selling price. The defendant gave notice, stating the ordinary retail selling price to be 1s 6d, and the plaintiffs objected.

The House of Lords took the view that whether the chocolate wrappers were part of the price paid depended upon whether they were part of the consideration for the sale of the records to the public. A minority of the House found in the promotional scheme evidence of motive but not of consideration. Lord Reid, making the leading speech for the majority, conceded that the wrappers could not be seen as either benefit or detriment in themselves: the chocolate company threw them away as soon as they arrived, and no doubt the consuming public would have thrown them away before that but for the offer. What mattered was that the company saw fit to require the delivery of the wrappers in exchange for its delivery of the record. Its motive for so doing was of no interest to the court, but the requirement of exchange demonstrated the existence of consideration.

This minimalist approach to benefit was again evident in *Williams v Roffey Bros & Nicholls (Contractors) Ltd* [1990] 1 All ER 512 (the facts are given at *6.3.5.3*). The Court of Appeal had to decide whether a variation of a contract was enforceable, despite the fact that the plaintiff had apparently given nothing in return for the promise which constituted the variation. Two members of the Court of Appeal (Glidewell and Purchas LJJ) were willing to find consideration, despite its absence on an objective analysis, in the subjective benefit to the promisor. That is, if the promisor was induced to make his promise by the promisee remaining willing to perform his side of the bargain, that was enough to make the promise binding. Russell LJ took a more radical, normative approach. The existence of consideration is to be determined in the light of the view one takes of the desirability of enforcing the promise in question. In this case, he was influenced by the commercial nature of the relationship between the parties, and the unconscionable result of not enforcing the promise. The majority reasoning in *Williams v Roffey Bros & Nicholls (Contractors) Ltd* was followed by Hirst J in *Anangel Atlas Compania Naviera SA v Ishikawajima-Harima Heavy Industries Co. Ltd (No. 2)* [1990] 2 Lloyd's Rep 544. In another case involving contract variation, the judge found that consideration was constituted by the 'practical conferment of benefit or a practical avoidance of disbenefit'. Here, despite the existing contract between the parties, the judge found the defendants to have admitted that there was a practical (or subjective) benefit to them in holding the plaintiffs to the original delivery date under the contract, in market conditions in which many clients were seeking to cancel contracts or to postpone delivery dates. By promising amendments to the contract advantageous to the plaintiffs, in return for their taking delivery on the due date, the defendants hoped to influence other clients to keep to their contracts. Consequently, the amendments were legally enforceable.

The definition of consideration in *Chappell*, and in *Williams v Roffey Bros & Nicholls (Contractors) Ltd*, may be regarded as coinciding with Sir Frederick Pollock's definition of consideration as 'the price for which the promise of the other is bought' (see *6.3.1*), provided it is realised that price here means anything of actual subjective value to the promisor. It is worth giving some attention to the test by which the courts determine whether something is of sufficient value to amount to consideration. It appears to embody elements of both law and fact. There seems to be a rule excluding mere sentiment from constituting consideration. It is also the case that the objectivisation of contract (see *5.1.2*) means that the court is the ultimate arbiter of each party's intentions. Subject to these obvious legal limitations, however, it seems that anything may be of sufficient value to amount to consideration if the party receiving it regards it at the time as a sufficient inducement to give his return promise, which is an essentially factual test. This idea of mutual inducement as the most basic kind of exchange is at the heart of the majority opinion in *Chappell*, and many of the more difficult English cases on consideration fit more comfortably with that analysis than any other.

6.3.2.2 Settlement of claims When a legal claim is settled out of court the settlement is binding on the parties by virtue of the law of contract, and if no contract can be shown to exist then the settlement is not binding. Consideration exists on the one hand in a promise not to sue, or to drop any action which has already commenced, and on the other hand in the payment of a sum of money as final settlement of the claim. Identification of consideration is less easy, however, where a true legal analysis reveals that the original claim which has been settled would without doubt have been unsuccessful. In that case, a promise not to pursue the claim in the courts is worthless.

In *Horton v Horton (No. 2)* [1961] 1 QB 215

> the husband agreed to pay the wife £30 per month maintenance, and in return she was not to bring legal action for maintenance. He did not deduct income tax from the sum paid. Some time later, when the issue of tax arose, he promised instead to pay such sum as would leave £30 after deduction of tax. When presented by the Inland Revenue authorities with a claim for tax notionally deducted by him he stopped the payments, claiming that his second promise was not supported by any fresh consideration.

If consideration existed it was in the settlement of the wife's claim for rectification of the original agreement. Rectification is a remedy aimed at making a document which does not express the actual intention of the parties into a correct version of their common intention (see *7.2.1*). In this case it seems possible that a claim for rectification would not have succeeded. Upjohn LJ held that whether it would have succeeded was irrelevant to the question of whether the settlement of the wife's claims was enforceable. Provided she believed she had some good claim, consideration was present.

This decision makes little sense in terms of an analysis of benefit and detriment, since there is scant benefit in a promise not to pursue a worthless claim. On the other hand, the promise of £30 per month free of tax induced the relinquishment of the claim (and vice versa). In that sense there was consideration. There remains a quite separate issue, unrelated to consideration, of whether the wife was being fraudulent; that is, did she genuinely believe that her claim was legally valid or at least a debatable legal point? If not, her behaviour might amount to fraud (see *9.3.1*), and it makes little difference for most purposes whether we say there is no contract on that ground or because there is no consideration (but see *4.5.3*). If her belief was genuine there is consideration arising out of inducement.

6.3.2.3 Forebearance In *Alliance Bank v Broom* (1864) 2 Dr & Sm 289

> the defendant owed an unsecured debt of £22,000 to the plaintiffs. The plaintiffs asked for security for the loan, and the defendant promised to provide as security

goods he was about to receive from a third party. When the defendant failed to fulfil this promise the plaintiff sued to obtain the title documents to the goods in question.

The promise was only enforceable if part of a valid contract supported by consideration. In such cases consideration is normally found in a promise by the creditor not to call in the debt for a certain period of time, but in this particular case no such promise was given. The court was obviously anxious nevertheless to make the promise of security enforceable, presumably because such arrangements were common and a necessary bulwark of the credit system. It found consideration to be constituted by the fact of actual forebearance from suing by the bank, even in the absence of any promised period of grace.

Without a promise not to sue (or a promise not to foreclose on the security given for a stated period), forebearance fits uneasily into an analysis of benefit and detriment, since the fact that the bank may if it chooses foreclose tomorrow means that it may suffer no detriment and the debtor derive no benefit. But there is no doubt that the bank was induced actually to forebear by the promise of security, while in turn that promise was induced by the bank's actual forebearance, which created a not unreasonable expectation on the part of the defendant that the bank would continue to forebear. The truth of the matter is that the whole arrangement was a commercial 'bargain' between parties who had been dealing amicably with each other in attempting to cope with the changing financial position of one of them. In the circumstances the court was unwilling to allow a technicality to interfere with their arrangement.

6.3.2.4   The fiction of value   Cases such as *Alliance Bank v Broom* (1864) 2 Dr & Sm 289 strain even the more flexible modern version of the doctrine of consideration to the limit, raising the suspicion that where a court is determined to make a promise enforceable it can always 'find' something of value for which the promise is exchanged. It must be remembered that the modern law of contract developed somewhat earlier than the modern law of torts, especially in relation to liability for negligent misstatements (see *9.3.2.1*) and for extra-contractual economic loss (see *4.2.2.1*). It is not surprising, therefore, that some (especially nineteenth century) courts have attempted to squeeze cases into the category of contract in order to found a liability which otherwise would be avoided.

De la Bere v Pearson [1908] 1 KB 280 appears to be just such a case.

A newspaper offered free financial advice, and the plaintiff wrote asking the name of a good stockbroker for an investment. The paper negligently gave the name of a man who was an undischarged bankrupt and who subsequently misappropriated money sent to him. At the time, in the absence of contract the paper would have escaped liability altogether.

In the judgments of the Court of Appeal little discussion is devoted to the existence of a contract, and most of that is addressed to the questions of offer and acceptance. Only Vaughan Williams LJ addressed the question of consideration, finding it on the one hand in the advice given and on the other in 'the tendency to increase the sale of the paper'. Since the plaintiff was already a reader it is impossible to say that he was induced to purchase the paper in order to obtain the financial advice. Equally, he gave nothing of value over and above what he normally paid for the paper. It seems most likely that today such a case would not be regarded as raising a contractual liability at all. It may be that there would be liability in tort for negligent misrepresentation (see *Hedley Byrne & Co. Ltd* v *Heller & Partners Ltd* [1964] AC 465; and see *9.3.2.1*).

6.3.3 Inducement: past consideration

It was suggested earlier that where it is alleged that a contract exists on the basis of an act followed by a promise the courts will not enforce such a promise (see *6.3.1*). In such cases the consideration is described as 'past', and the rule is easily explained by the theory of exchange and inducement. The rule is well illustrated by the classic case of *Roscorla* v *Thomas* (1842) 3 QB 234.

> The plaintiff had negotiated the purchase of a horse from the defendant for a given price. When the negotiations had been completed and the contract had formed, the defendant assured the plaintiff that the horse was sound and free from vice. The horse failed to match that description, and the issue was whether any enforceable warranty (i.e. promise) that the horse was sound had been given.

At the time courts were very unwilling to imply terms into contracts unless strong evidence of actual intention of the parties was available (see *10.4*). No implied warranty was found in this case; today the case might well be decided differently on this point under s.14 of the Sale of Goods Act 1979. In the absence of an implied warranty, the plaintiff's only remedy lay in the express warranty given, which could only be enforceable if of contractual force. Since no new consideration had been given subsequent to the assurance of the fitness of the horse, the express warranty could only be binding if in some way it could be brought within the original contract. The court refused to allow such an extension of the consideration through time, and indeed it can be seen that the promise that the horse was sound and not vicious was not given in exchange for, or induced by, the payment made for the horse.

This decision is consistent with the rules on incorporation of terms into contracts (see *5.7*). If this express promise had been found to be included within the contract, it is difficult to see how existing rules preventing the incorporation into contracts of clauses excluding or limiting liability might be maintained. The current position is that a clause not brought to the attention of the promisee at the time of contracting, but brought to the promisee's attention before the time of the defective performance giving rise to any claim, is not part of the contract (*Olley* v *Marlborough Court* [1949] 1 KB 532; see *5.7.3*). A promise relating to quality and an exemption clause are legally identical however functionally different, and the same rule must apply to the question of whether either type of term is part of the exchange between the parties. To put the same argument in commercial terms, the price of a horse guaranteed sound is greater than the price of a horse given without any guarantee as to quality, and for the court to have decided in any way other than it did in this case would have been to interfere in the bargain between the parties.

A note of caution must be entered about past consideration cases like *Roscorla v Thomas*. This was not a case where all the performance preceded any promise. There was a contract, followed by an additional promise. Such a promise might be classed as a variation of the contract (*6.3.5.3*). As such, until recently the result would have been the same, because contract variations were not legally binding unless supported by fresh consideration. However, as a result of the decision of the Court of Appeal in *Williams* v *Roffey Bros & Nicholls (Contractors) Ltd* [1990] 1 All ER 512, such a variation might be regarded as binding by virtue of the existing duties under the contract. If that were the case, then *Roscorla* v *Thomas* might be decided differently today, on this ground. On the other hand, a case like *Re McArdle* [1951] Ch 669 (*6.3.3.2*) would not be affected, because there was no pre-existing contract in respect of which the subsequent promise was made.

6.3.3.1 The requested performance 'exception'

The conventional view is that there is a significant exception to the past consideration rule in cases in which it can be said that there was an understanding that a good or service was to be paid for, but no express agreement had been reached as to the amount payable before the time for performance. In such cases a subsequent promise to pay a stated sum might well appear to be past consideration. On the other hand, it would be undesirable as a matter of policy for such understandings not to be enforceable, not least because many professional people such as accountants and solicitors operate on the basis that their services are to be paid for but that a fee will not be stated until after performance. This example makes it clear that it is not really an exception to the past consideration rule at all. The subsequent promise to pay is no more than quantification and evidence of an obligation to pay which had already arisen by virtue of a simple contract between the parties. As we saw in Chapter 5, s.8 of the Sale of Goods Act 1979 makes express provision for the price in contracts within its scope to be left unspecified in the contract and fixed at a subsequent date.

The earliest example of the exception is *Lampleigh* v *Braithwait* (1615) Hob 105.

Braithwait killed a man, and asked Lampleigh to intercede with the King to get him a pardon. Lampleigh did as he was asked, and was successful. Braithwait then promised him £100.

There is no doubt that Lampleigh's performance was executed before the promise was made, but the court said that the fact that the service had been requested meant that the promise was nevertheless within the consideration, i.e. the performance by Lampleigh. In other words, in making the request Braithwait must be taken impliedly to have promised to pay for the service rendered.

This explanation of *Lampleigh* v *Braithwait* was put forward in *Re Casey's Patents* [1892] 1 Ch 104 by Bowen LJ:

Even if it were true . . . that a past service cannot support a future promise, you must look at the document and see if the promise cannot receive a proper effect in some other way. Now, the fact of a past service raises an implication that at the time it was rendered it was to be paid for, and, if it was a service which was to be paid for, when you get in the subsequent document a promise to pay, that promise may be treated either as an admission which evidences or as a positive bargain which fixes the amount of that reasonable remuneration on the faith of which the service was originally rendered.

A positive bargain here might be one of two kinds. It might be the settlement of a quasi-contractual claim for the value of services rendered (*quantum meruit*: see *12.4.3.1*). Alternatively, it might be an enforceable implied agreement to agree the price in the future (see *Foley* v *Classique Coaches Ltd* [1934] 2 KB 1; and see *5.6.4*).

6.3.3.2 Distinguish commercial from domestic agreements It may be that in relation to past consideration it is also valid to make a distinction between commercial and domestic agreements, although it is doubtful whether the distinction is as clear as it is in the case of intention to create legal relations (see *6.2.1*). Nevertheless, there is some evidence that a court may be more willing to imply a promise to pay in the case of a commercial relationship than a domestic one, and that would seem to follow from the presumptions operating in the case of intention to create legal relations.

In *Re McArdle* [1951] Ch 669

> the children of a family were by their father's will entitled to a house after their mother's death. During the life of the mother one of the married children lived in the house and his wife paid for several improvements to be made. Subsequently, all the children signed a document in which they promised that the wife should be repaid £488 out of the estate for the work done.

This promise was held to be unenforceable because the work had been executed before the promise was made, so that the promise was made for past consideration. The court did not find in this domestic situation any implied promise to pay dating from before the time when the work was done. One explanation is that there had been no request by the promisors that the work be carried out, but it seems that in commercial cases an implied promise may be found even in the absence of an express request.

One example is *Re Casey's Patents* [1892] 1 Ch 104 (see *6.3.3.1* above). The owners of patent rights promised their manager a share in those rights in consideration for his previous services for them. In finding that promise enforceable and not merely supported by past consideration, Bowen LJ found evidence on which to base the implication of a promise to pay in the entirety of the circumstances without identifying an express request for the service. In *Pao On* v *Lau Yiu Long* [1979] 3 All ER 65 (another commercial case; the facts are given at *8.5*), Lord Scarman in giving the advice of the Privy

Council provided the following definition of the conditions for operation of the exception:

> The act must have been done at the promisor's request, the parties must have understood that the act was to be remunerated either by a payment or the conferment of some other benefit, and payment, or the conferment of some other benefit, must have been legally enforceable had it been promised in advance.

These conditions were held to have been met, although the necessary request was not made expressly but was inferred from another agreement between the parties in relation to the same subject-matter (see 6.3.4 below). Lord Scarman laid great stress elsewhere in his opinion upon the fact that the case involved businessmen bargaining at arm's length ([1979] 3 All ER 65 at 77), and it seems clear that in such circumstances, where the whole arrangement was couched in terms of commercial exchange, consideration might be found to exist where both request and promise were only ever implied.

6.3.3.3 Genuine exception for negotiable instruments A negotiable instrument is a document containing a promise of payment which when transferred gives the transferee for value a right to enforce the promise against the promisor free of any defences which have been available to the promisor against the transferor (see 13.4.3). A good example is a cheque. Section 27 of the Bills of Exchange Act 1882 provides that valuable consideration for a bill may be constituted by either consideration as normally defined in contract law or by 'an antecedent debt or liability'. Thus, a bank receiving a third party's cheque from a customer whose account with the bank is overdrawn is a transferee for value of the cheque, since by this section the customer's pre-existing debt to the bank is consideration for the transfer by him to the bank. This rule is a genuine exception to the past consideration rule.

6.3.4 Inducement: third party beneficiaries
We saw above (see 6.3.1) that the definition of consideration given by Patteson J in *Thomas* v *Thomas* (1842) 2 QB 851 stated that consideration must move from the plaintiff (or, as it is more usually phrased, from the promisee). In other words, a party who has not furnished consideration may not bring an action to enforce a contract. Modern authority for the rule is to be found in *Dunlop Pneumatic Tyre Co.* v *Selfridge & Co. Ltd* [1915] AC 847, although it appears to originate in *Tweddle* v *Atkinson* (1861) 1 B & S 393. In the latter case,

> after a marriage the partners' respective fathers entered into an agreement whereby each would pay a sum of money to the husband, and by the agreement the husband was to have the power to sue for the sums of money promised. After the death of his wife's father the husband sued his estate to recover the sum promised.

His action failed, one reason being that he had provided no consideration under the agreement.

Often this rule is coterminous with the quite separate rule that only a party to an agreement may bring an action on it (see generally Chapter 13, 'Privity of Contract'). Such was the case in *Tweddle* v *Atkinson*, and may have been the case in *Dunlop* v *Selfridge*, although the point was not definitively settled because the House of Lords rested its decision on the consideration rule. Nevertheless, it is technically possible, if unlikely, that a contract might exist to which a promisee was party without providing consideration, as the more probable interpretation of *Dunlop* v *Selfridge* shows.

6.3.4.1 Relevance of the rule The main modern relevance of the rule is that it restricts the contractual rights of consumers in the case of defective goods to such remedies as may be available against the seller. Normally the seller in a consumer sale is not the manufacturer, and the consumer may feel that it would be more appropriate to seek a remedy from the manufacturer than from the seller, especially where the goods purport to come with the manufacturer's guarantee. Nevertheless, since in many cases the consumer gives no consideration for whatever promises the manufacturer's guarantee contains, he cannot in those cases sue in contract if the promises are broken.

Although not involving a consumer claim the facts of *Dunlop* v *Selfridge* illustrate the way in which this rule prevents the use of contract actions which leapfrog steps in the chain of production between manufacturer and ultimate consumer.

> Dunlop sold tyres to a distributor, who in turn sold them to Selfridge. It was a condition of Dunlop's contract with the distributor that the latter would not sell them to anyone else without obtaining the purchaser's undertaking not to resell the tyres below a stated price, on pain of payment of a penalty of £5 per tyre to Dunlop. Selfridge's contract with the distributor contained provisions to that effect, but Selfridge ignored them and sold tyres below the stated price and then refused to pay the penalty.

The House of Lords held that even if the distributor had been Dunlop's agent in obtaining the undertaking from Selfridge, making Dunlop a party to the deal (see Chapter 15 generally), the fact that no consideration moved from Dunlop in return for the undertaking meant that it could not recover the penalties stipulated for. Since it had provided no consideration, Dunlop could not leapfrog the distributor to maintain an action in contract against Selfridge.

6.3.4.2 Basis of the rule A technical analysis of these cases can explain the rule by saying that a party not providing consideration is not part of the axis of inducement or mutual exchange which is central to the enforceability of agreements. Nevertheless, it is not easy to discern any policy interest making such a rule necessary. It is not suggested in these cases that the promises are gratuitous, merely that the person seeking to enforce the promise did not provide the consideration for it. Since the doctrine of privity would prevent those not parties to the agreement from enforcing any promise contained therein (see *13.2.*), there seems to be no reason for this further rule. It may be that the courts will be willing to limit it as much as possible, although as yet no English case has taken such a line.

In Australia, however, the High Court appears to have accepted such an argument in *Coulls v Bagot's Executor and Trustee Co.* (1967) 119 CLR 460.

> Coulls entered into a contract with a company under which, in return for the right to quarry on his land, the company would pay a weekly royalty to Coulls and his wife. Coulls and his wife both signed the agreement, and after Coulls' death the question arose of whether his widow was legally entitled to continue to receive the weekly royalty or whether it belonged entirely to Coulls' estate.

The court's decision against the widow turned ultimately on the fact that the mere signing of the agreement did not constitute her a party to the contract. Nevertheless, the court expressed the view that had she been a party to the agreement, and thus been a joint promisee with her husband, it would not have inquired into whether the consideration for the company's promise of a royalty was provided by them jointly or by one or the other.

6.3.5 Inducement: performance of existing duty

It has traditionally been the rule that in most circumstances the performance of an existing duty cannot be consideration for a further promise. In terms of our definition of consideration the reason is relatively clear. Where one is under a legal duty to do something already, one cannot be said to have been induced to do that something by the further promise of another. It is traditional to subdivide the rule between three different types of case:

(a)   performance of a public duty;
(b)   performance of an existing contractual duty;
(c)   performance of a duty owed to a third party.

Until recently, the rule was consistently applied in the first two categories, while the third was already established as an exception. As a result of *Williams v Roffey Bros & Nicholls (Contractors) Ltd* [1990] 1 All ER 512, the second category may also be an exception to the rule, at least in the course of a commercial relationship. For ease of exposition, the traditional divisions are maintained here.

6.3.5.1 Public duties

The leading case in the area of public duties is *Collins v Godefroy* (1831) 1 B & Ad 950. The plaintiff was promised payment in return for his undertaking to give expert evidence at a trial at which he was in any case obliged to attend to give evidence because he had been summoned by subpoena. In those circumstances the promise of payment was unenforceable because of the plaintiff's existing public duty to attend the trial. Although the principle of the case still stands, there is now a statutory exception to the rule in the case of payment of expenses to *expert* witnesses which merely reflects what had long been the practice (see s.36(4) of the Supreme Court Act 1981).

A more modern, and in view of recent industrial strife more topical, statement of the rule is given by the House of Lords in *Glasbrook Bros* v *Glamorgan CC* [1925] AC 270.

> This case involved a claim by a local authority to recover payment for the provision of police to guard a mine during a strike. The defendants argued that the police were charged with a public duty to guard the mine as part of their general duty to keep the peace, prevent crime and protect persons and property from criminal injury. However, at the time of the strike the colliery owners had insisted on a greater level of manning than the local police had deemed necessary.

The House of Lords, by a bare majority, decided that the only duty on the local authority was to provide such policing as was, in the appreciation of the police authority, necessary. The decision as to what was necessary was not open to review by the courts in a case of this kind. Provision of policing beyond what was deemed necessary was not therefore performance of an existing duty, and could amount to consideration for a promise to pay for the service provided (see also *Harris* v *Sheffield United F.C. Ltd*, [1987] 2 All ER 838).

The notion of performance of something more than the bare existing legal duty is thought by some commentators to explain the otherwise difficult case of *Ward* v *Byham* [1956] 2 All ER 318.

> The father of an illegitimate child agreed to pay the mother £1 per week to maintain the child provided the mother was able to show that the child was 'well looked after and happy' and that the child was allowed to choose for herself whether to go to live with her mother or to carry on being cared for by a neighbour of the father's, which had been the previous arrangement. The child went to live with the mother, but the father stopped the payments when the mother married.

Denning LJ treated the case as one of performance of an existing duty, because he took the view that the mother was under a legal obligation properly to look after the child. Nevertheless, he would have enforced the promise of maintenance because in his view a promise to perform an existing duty was good consideration. The majority of the Court of Appeal, however, while acknowledging that the mother did owe some existing duty, found 'ample consideration' for the promise in the mother's undertakings to keep the child happy and to allow her to choose where to live (see also *Williams* v *Williams* [1957] 1 All ER 305). These cases were relied upon by Glidewell LJ in *Williams* v *Roffey Bros & Nicholls (Contractors) Ltd* [1990] 1 All ER 512, but not by the other members of the court (Purchas LJ expressly declined to rely upon them). The view of the majority appears the more desirable, since these were public duty cases, while *Williams* v *Roffey Bros & Nicholls (Contractors) Ltd* is a contractual duty case where, as the majority indicate, other considerations apply.

6.3.5.2 Contractual duties Traditionally, the rule was that performance of an existing contractual duty could not be consideration for a further promise from the party to whom the existing duty was owed. The leading case was *Stilk* v *Myrick* (1809) 2 Camp 317:

> a crewman had contracted to work a vessel on a voyage for a fixed sum, promising to do all needed in all the emergencies of the voyage. During the voyage two men deserted. The master offered extra payment to those remaining if they would work the ship home, and then on arrival refused to pay.

The promise of extra payment was unenforceable, because desertion of crewmen was an emergency of the voyage, and there was already a duty to work the ship home in such a case, and so there was no consideration for the promise of further payment. Most commentators accept that there is a considerable element of policy in the decision: to have enforced the promise was perceived to have been to risk exposing ships' masters to blackmail by the crew when far from England. The doctrine of consideration performed the function of a rule against economic duress (see *8.5.2*).

In *Williams* v *Roffey Bros & Nicholls (Contractors) Ltd* [1990] 1 All ER 512, *Stilk* v *Myrick* was effectively overruled (Glidewell LJ preferred to describe his approach as being to 'refine and limit the application of that principle'). In a commercial setting, where it is possible to infer from all the circumstances that the parties both intended the further promises made to have legal force, the courts will give effect to that intention without being constrained by the rigid approach to the concept of consideration found in *Stilk* v *Myrick*. No single majority emerges from the three judgments in the Court of Appeal, but three stands of reasoning can be identified: (a) the policy element in *Stilk* v *Myrick*, which resulted in the consideration doctrine being applied in a very formal way, is no longer present because of the emergence of the doctrine of economic duress, which allows much more substantive appraisal of potentially unconscionable contracts (see *8.5.2*); (b) the necessary consideration in a commercial case of this kind might be constituted by a subjective benefit to the promisor, if the promisor was in fact induced to make the promise by the benefit he perceived himself to be receiving; (c) by analogy with the third category of pre-existing duty cases (performance of a duty owed to a third party may be consideration for a contract with a separate promisor: *6.3.5.4*), no further consideration is required for the modification of an existing contract provided there is sufficient evidence of an intention that the variation be legally binding. Arguments (b) and (c) are conceptually very different, but it would be wrong to make much of this, in the light of the ease with which a court may find a subjective benefit if it so requires; consequently, the two arguments are functionally very closely related.

6.3.5.3 Variation of contract To say that performance of an existing duty may not be consideration for a further promise from the person to whom that duty is owed, is simply a more technical way of stating another traditional rule: that a contract may not be varied except by means of another contract (unless the original contract provided for such unilateral variation: e.g., *Lombard Tricity Finance Ltd* v *Paton* [1989] 1 All ER 918). Problems over consideration in contract variation cases are of two kinds: either, one party wishes to provide the same performance, but to obtain something greater than was originally agreed from the other party; or, one party wishes to obtain the agreed performance from the other party, while giving something less than was agreed in return. *Williams* v *Roffey Bros & Nicholls (Contractors) Ltd* [1990] 1 All ER 512 was a case of the former kind:

> the defendants were main contractors on a building contract, and they identified that the plaintiffs, who were subcontractor carpenters on the job, were in financial difficulty and at risk of not completing the work. Had the plaintiffs failed to complete the work, the defendants would have become liable for liquidated damages (apparently not a penalty: *12.3.4.2*). The defendants therefore took the initiative to avoid the problem, by offering extra payments if the job were to be finished on time. The plaintiffs accepted that offer, and then, when the additional payments were not made as promised, quit the job and sought damages in reliance on the further promise.

The problem confronting the plaintiffs, arising out of *Stilk* v *Myrick* (1809) 2 Camp 317, was that they gave nothing in return for the promise of extra payment, except the performance they had undertaken to provide under the original contract. On the other hand, the commercial sense of the agreement was that the promise should be enforceable, and this view prevailed with the Court of Appeal. There was a real benefit to the defendants in avoiding having to pay the sums due for late completion of the main contract, and so the avoidance of the risk of breach by the subcontractors clearly induced their promise.

The problem of inability to pay the full price for the originally agreed performance (which is the mirror-image of *Williams* v *Roffey Bros & Nicholls (Contractors) Ltd*) has long troubled English courts. The problem is easily illustrated: A sells his book to B for £10, payable next Tuesday; on Tuesday B has not got £10, but offers £8 which A accepts, promising that he will not seek to recover the remaining £2 from B. In *Pinnel's Case* (1602) 5 Co Rep 117a it was held that a promise such as that made by A was unenforceable, unless B gave some new consideration for it. On the other hand, provided something was given, the court was not entitled to enquire whether what was given was equal in value to the promise made (see *6.3.2*). The rule in *Pinnel's Case* was confirmed by the House of Lords in *Foakes* v *Beer* (1884) 9 App Cas 605, although Lord Blackburn opposed the rule, arguing:

> All men of business . . . do every day recognise and act on the ground that prompt payment of a part of their demand may be more beneficial to them than it would be to insist on their rights and enforce payment of the whole. Even where the debtor is perfectly solvent, and sure to pay at the last, this is often so. Where the credit of the debtor is doubtful it must be more so.

Such reasoning is very much in sympathy with the prevailing view in the Court of Appeal in *Williams* v *Roffey Bros & Nicholls (Contractors) Ltd*, and it is difficult to justify any difference in treatment between this category of contract variation case and that encountered in *Williams v Roffey Bros & Nicholls (Contractors) Ltd*. The result is to bring the Court of Appeal into conflict with the decision of the House of Lords in *Foakes v Beer*, but the truth is that serious inroads had already been made into that decision by the doctrine of promissory estoppel (*6.4.3.1*). It remains to be seen whether it will be necessary to resort to promissory estoppel in such cases, or whether the subjective benefit approach of *Williams v Roffey Bros & Nicholls (Contractors) Ltd* will now prevail here also.

Some indication of the possible future attitude of the courts may be derived from the first instance decision in *Anangel Atlas Compania Naviera SA v Ishikawajima-Harima Heavy Industries Co. Ltd (No 2)* [1990] 2 Lloyd's Rep 526.

> Plaintiffs entered a contract to purchase a ship built by the defendants. The world shipping market fell into recession, and the plaintiffs discovered that the defendants were offering more advantageous terms to other clients. They sought and obtained the defendants' agreement that they should be accorded 'most favoured customer' status, so that in all respects, including price and terms of payment, they would be treated as favourably as any other customer. They subsequently sought to enforce this agreement, alleging that another customer had paid a lower price on more favourable payment terms. The defendants argued that the agreement was not supported by consideration.

There was no suggestion that the plaintiffs' request for more favourable terms constituted economic duress. *Foakes v Beer* is not referred to in the judgment, but the practical effect of the agreement was to allow the plaintiffs to pay less than the sum originally agreed. By enforcing this agreement in express reliance on *Williams v Roffey* and the notion of practical or subjective benefit (see *6.3.2.1*), Hirst J seems to have avoided the problem posed by *Foakes v Beer*.

6.3.5.4 Duty owed to a third party   The performance of an existing duty may be consideration for a promise by a third party who is not already a beneficiary of the duty in question. Early evidence of the exception may be found in *Scotson v Pegg* (1861) 6 H & N 295.

> A entered into a contract with B to deliver coal to C. C then said to A that if A would deliver the coal to him C would unload the coal at a fixed rate per day. C failed to keep his promise, and in response to legal action by A claimed that his promise was unsupported by consideration since A was already bound by his contract with B to deliver the coal to C.

C was nevertheless found liable, and the court expressed the view that performance of an existing contractual duty might be consideration for a separate promise by a third party. It is not clear, however, whether this was the basis of the decision or whether on account of facts not disclosed in the report A's promise to C carried an extra burden by comparison with his promise to B.

There is also a trace of the exception in *Shadwell* v *Shadwell* (1860) 9 CBNS 159, although the decision is of doubtful authority on several grounds, including a possible absence of intention to create legal relations since it was a family agreement, and little reliance should be placed on it.

Whatever the authority of the earlier cases, the exception has been confirmed by two recent decisions of the Privy Council which are generally accepted as representing English law on the matter. In *New Zealand Shipping Co. Ltd* v *A. M. Satterthwaite & Co. Ltd, The Eurymedon* [1975] AC 154 Lord Wilberforce, giving the majority opinion, said:

> An agreement to do an act which the promisor is under an existing obligation to a third party to do, may quite well amount to valid consideration and does so in the present case: the promisee obtains the benefit of a direct obligation which he can enforce. This proposition is illustrated and supported by *Scotson* v *Pegg* . . . which their Lordships consider to be good law.

In *The Eurymedon*

> the carrier of goods had by contract validly limited his liability to the shipper of the goods. It was the carrier's responsibility to procure a stevedore to unload the goods, but the court found that the stevedores enjoyed a quite independent contract with the shippers (on this aspect of the case see *13.6*). The clause in the carrier's contract with the shippers which limited their liability purported also to limit the liability of any independent contractor employed by the carrier. Even assuming the clause was part of the agreement between shipper and stevedores, the question arose of whether sufficient consideration had been given for it to be enforceable by the latter, since any duty the stevedores might owe to the shippers to unload the vessel was a duty already owed by the stevedores to the carriers.

The court ruled that a promise to perform a duty owed to the one might be consideration for a promise by the other.

6.3.5.5 The basis of the exception In *Pao On* v *Lau Yiu Long* [1979] 3 All ER 65 the Privy Council followed '*The Eurymedon*' [1975] AC 154 on the question of consideration and performance of a duty owed to a third party. The main interest of the case for current purposes lies in the discussion by Lord Scarman of the purpose of the 'pre-existing duty' rule. Although the court was not prepared to commit itself to any particular view, it appeared sympathetic to the idea that it might be based in the prevention of duress by contracting parties against those to whom they owed contractual obligations (see [1979] 3 All ER 76–8; and see *6.3.5.2*, above). It might be thought that in the case of promises by third parties the risk of such coercion would be considerably diminished, so that no such public policy need for the rule would exist in this type of case. The Privy Council, however, went further. Lord Scarman said:

> [W]here businessmen are negotiating at arm's length it is unnecessary for

the achievement of justice, and unhelpful in the development of the law, to invoke such a rule of public policy . . .. If a promise is induced by coercion of a man's will, the doctrine of duress suffices to do justice.

In fact, the *Pao On* case was an important stage in the recent development of a doctrine of economic duress (see *8.5.2*), which has made the possibility of success on a claim of duress much greater. For this reason, Lord Scarman's argument above was broad enough in scope to apply not only to pre-existing duties as consideration for third party promises but also to the pre-existing duty cases in which traditionally there has been said to be no consideration. This proposal had already been made by Denning LJ in *Williams* v *Williams* [1957] 1 All ER 305 (see *6.3.5.1*, above): 'A promise to perform an existing duty is, I think, sufficient consideration to support a promise, so long as there is nothing in the transaction which is contrary to the public interest'. The development of the modern doctrine of economic duress, and the decision of the Court of Appeal in *Williams* v *Roffey Bros & Nicholls (Contractors) Ltd* [1990] 1 All ER 512 (*6.3.5.2*) may have combined to make Denning LJ's proposal a good statement of the law.

6.3.6 Conclusions: the future of consideration

Although consideration appears to be firmly established in a central role in the English law of contract, and indeed appears to be the single element which distinguishes the common law contract from its continental civilian cousin, it would be wrong to conclude this section without acknowledging that for much of the twentieth century consideration has been under attack from various quarters. In 1937 the Law Revision Committee (see its 6th Interim Report, Cmd 5449) recommended a number of amendments to the detailed rules. Some of these proposals would have wrought a major change in our law, and could not be achieved without parliamentary intervention. For example, it was proposed that a promise in writing should be enforceable even if not supported by consideration. But other proposals have been at least partially achieved (see, for example, the pre-existing duty rule (*6.3.5.2 et seq.*); the rule that promisors in unilateral contracts should not be allowed to revoke once a promisee has started to perform (*5.5.3*); and the suggestion that where a promise is relied upon by the promisee it should be binding on the promisor — see generally *6.4* below), and these changes have been brought about by judicial development, which is testimony to the continuing internal dynamism of the common law.

In recent years Professor Atiyah has argued that there are historical grounds for saying that consideration is not the sole test used by the courts to determine whether a promise shall be enforceable, and that where justice required the courts have enforced promises on the basis of reliance by the promisee (see P.S. Atiyah, *Consideration in Contracts: A Fundamental Restatement*, Australian National University Press, 1971). Such a notion, as we shall see (*6.4.4*, below), is consistent with developments in the United States.

These criticisms made by the Law Commission and Professor Atiyah may be amongst the most eloquent, but they do not stand alone. In the first edition of this book, it was suggested that there was likely to be a gradual progression away from the technical analysis of benefit and detriment towards the more impressionistic notion of inducement, which allows the judges greater freedom to decide according to the flavour of the transaction whether agreements and promises should be treated as binding. The way forward was pointed by Lord Wilberforce in *The Eurymedon* [1975] AC 154 (see *6.3.5.4*), where he said of the transaction in dispute:

> If the choice, and the antithesis, is between a gratuitous promise, and a promise for consideration, . . . there can be little doubt which, in commercial reality, this is. The whole contract is of a commercial character, involving service on one side, rates of payment on the other, and qualifying stipulations as to both. The relations of all parties to each other are commercial relations entered into for business reasons of ultimate profit. To describe one set of promises, in this context, as gratuitous, or *nudum pactum*, seems paradoxical and is prima facie implausible. It is only the precise analysis of this complex of relations into the classical offer and acceptance, with identifiable consideration, that seems to present difficulty.

The decision in *Williams* v *Roffey Bros & Nicholls (Contractors) Ltd* [1990] 1 All ER 512 confirms the trend, and it only remains to assess just how much the foundations of the doctrine of consideration have been shaken by that case. The variety of reasons given for enforcing the promise of extra payment (*6.3.5.2*) makes it possible to identify both a narrow and a wide consequence from the decision. At the narrowest, it seems that the law relating to variation of contracts has changed, so that any post-contractual promise relating to the main agreement will be enforced, subject to proof of the necessary intention and the absence of duress. Moreover, aspects of the law relating to past consideration may consequently have changed (*6.3.3*). It also seems likely that other areas of the law of contract, where the requirement of consideration may be said to be simply 'technical', will no longer be troublesome, because the identification of a 'subjective benefit' will always be possible when the commercial context makes it implausible for the promise not to be regarded as binding. An example might be the rule that a promise to keep an offer open is only binding if it is supported by consideration (see *5.4.3.1*). On the other hand, all three judges make clear that they believe the particular context, which so influenced their reasoning, to be distinct from that of the formation of initial contracts. Consequently, there seems little scope for arguing that the result of *Williams* v *Roffey Bros & Nicholls (Contractors) Ltd* will be that the doctrine of consideration will be abandoned altogether. Indeed, it would have been astonishing if such an interpretation were to have been suggested. There is no reason to think that English law should suddenly wish to make all gratuitous promises enforceable. The restrictive comments of the judges in this important case were clearly designed to bring home the point that the doctrine of consideration remains central to mainstream contracts. Nevertheless, in *Anangel Atlas Compania Naviera* v *Ishikawajima-Harima Heavy Industries Co. Ltd (No 2)* [1990] 2 Lloyd's Rep 526 at 545 Hirst J rejected the argument that *Williams* v *Roffey Bros & Nicholls (Contractors) Ltd* 'should be read as having only a very narrow ambit', although in the context the judge does not extend the *ratio* beyond the question of contract variation.

There may, however, be wider repercussions of the decision in *Williams* v *Roffey Bros & Nicholls (Contractors) Ltd*. As was noted earlier, it may be found in time to make redundant many of the developments since the 1950s in the field of promissory estoppel, and *Anangel Atlas Compania Naviera SA* v *Ishikawajima-Harima Heavy Industries Co. Ltd (No 2)* appears to confirm this (see *6.3.5.3*). More remote still, it may cause some reassessment of the rule that mere extra cost does not entitle a party to treat a contract as frustrated (*11.4.2.3*). If in such circumstances a unilateral variation of the contract promising extra payment is enforceable, how long will it be before it is argued that unreasonable refusal to make such a unilateral variation is a ground of frustration?

It is as well to end with a note of caution about the developments which arise out of *Williams* v *Roffey Bros & Nicholls (Contractors) Ltd*. Although the tone of the preceding analysis may have been to regard those developments as a benefit, that benefit is achieved at a price. The traditional consideration rules had the virtue of simplicity, and the absence of difficult judgmental issues. The new rule invests the judges with an enormous discretion over such cases, especially in ascertaining intention and in determining whether behaviour amounted to illegitimate pressure and consequently economic duress. Before the old rules, and the occasional hard cases they engendered, are abandoned, we should be sure that the greater discretion of the new rule is in the best interests of the commercial community it must serve.

6.4 PASSIVE ENFORCEABILITY — RELIANCE AND ESTOPPEL

6.4.1 Variation of contracts

The role of consideration is not limited to the initial formation of contracts. The most secure way for any agreement between the parties to take effect is *by contract*. Agreements between contracting parties not to continue with the deal, or to change the terms of the deal, are normally unenforceable in the courts unless themselves contracts (see, for example, *The Hannah Blumenthal* [1983] 1 All ER 34), which means that consideration must be present. In practice what happens may be very different. Parties on very good terms, and who regularly contract with each other, may be willing to uphold non-contractual variations and terminations of contracts. The problem with relying on the good relationship between the parties rather than on a legally enforceable agreement is that unforeseen circumstances may intervene to sour the good relationship or to make its impact irrelevant. This is especially true where the original party is replaced by a trustee who is under a legal obligation to insist on strict legal rights, irrespective of any changes made by friendly arrangement. The classic situations of replacement by a trustee (or equivalent) are bankruptcy, receivership or death of one of the parties.

6.4.1.1 Termination As far as the termination of agreements is concerned, it is fairly easy to establish consideration in those cases where the contract

is wholly or partially executory; that is, where both parties still have some or all of their performance under the agreement left to execute. In this situation, if both parties give up their right to receive the remaining performance from the other party then there is in that fact an exchange amounting to consideration. It does not matter that the performances outstanding are disproportionate, since the rule that consideration must be sufficient but need not be adequate (see *6.3.1*) prevents examination of the equivalence of the exchange. Where one party has performed fully, however, a release of the other party requires further consideration to be binding in contract.

6.4.1.2 Variation Variation of the terms of a contract presents greater difficulty. A variation intended to be advantageous to both sides is automatically supported by consideration, since there is a mutual exchange of benefits (see *6.3.1*). Sometimes what appears at first to be a one-sided variation can nevertheless, when properly analysed, be brought within the consideration doctrine. Consider the following example. A agrees to sell to B 10 boxes of biscuits, 10 packets of tea and 10 loaves of bread for £20. Before either party has performed B asks A to substitute five jars of coffee for five of the packets of tea. A agrees, saying that the price will remain the same. Is the variation enforceable? It might seem that the variation lacks consideration, since A is to perform something other than what was first agreed while B is only to pay what was originally asked. However, if the variation is seen as a two-stage, rather than single-stage, process it is possible to discern consideration for the change made. The first stage is where B agrees not to receive five packets of tea in return for which A agrees not to receive whatever proportion of the total price is represented by the five packets. That stage represents one contract. Then A agrees to supply five jars of coffee in return for which B agrees to pay whatever balance brings the total price back to £20. This is a second contract, and the variation is thereby enforceable. The court may not consider whether a packet of tea is in fact worth the same as a jar of coffee, again because of the rule that consideration must be sufficient but need not be adequate.

Where, however, a variation benefits only one of the parties (usually at the request of that party) some consideration additional to that of the original contract has traditionally been regarded as being required for the variation to be binding. This rule has recently been modified by the decision of the Court of Appeal in *Williams* v *Roffey Bros & Nicholls (Contractors) Ltd* [1990] 1 All ER 512 (see especially *6.3.5.3*). However, it is too early to say what the impact of this decision will be, although it seems that the consequence will be to make the legal requirements of contract variation rather less demanding. Nevertheless, serious problems can arise where the good relationship between the parties obscures the need to make a variation legally binding.

6.4.2 Equitable estoppel
Towards the end of the nineteenth century the courts developed a doctrine intended to prevent injustice arising out of the kind of situation described above. One-sided variations of contract might in some circumstances be

enforceable even in the absence of consideration. The best example of the operation of the doctrine is the leading case: *Hughes* v *Metropolitan Ry Co.* (1877) 2 App Cas 439.

> Hughes was lessor of property to the railway company. The lease contained a covenant requiring the lessee to repair upon notice from the lessor. Hughes gave notice requiring repair within six months. The company responded by offering to sell back to the lessor the company's remaining interest in the property under the lease. Negotiations continued for some two months before breaking down. Hughes subsequently claimed to be entitled to the property because the company had failed to carry out the required repairs within six months of the original date of the notice requiring repair. The company claimed that there was a tacit understanding (or an implied promise) that the repairs need not be carried out if the negotiations came to a successful conclusion, and that in the meantime the period of notice would not start to run.

In the House of Lords the existence of that implied promise was not really in doubt. Nevertheless, it was unsupported by consideration and therefore arguably unenforceable. The court refused to accept that argument, and the basis of the court's decision is contained in the following now famous passage from Lord Cairns LC (2 App Cas 439 at 448):

> It is the first principle upon which all Courts of Equity proceed, that if parties who have entered into definite and distinct terms involving certain legal results . . . afterwards by their own act or with their own consent enter upon a course of negotiations which has the effect of leading one of the parties to suppose that the strict rights arising under the contract will not be enforced or will be kept in suspense or held in abeyance, the person who might otherwise have enforced those rights will not be allowed to enforce them where it would be inequitable, having regard to the dealings which have thus taken place between the parties.

Thus there is, in the name of equity, a doctrine which makes certain promises enforceable even without consideration. It remains to see precisely what are the nature and limits of the doctrine. It should be noted that in some of the cases discussed in the following sections the expression *promissory estoppel* is used rather than 'equitable estoppel' which was used at the head of this section. The change in terminology came about because of developments in the law starting in 1947. Those developments are discussed below (see *6.4.3*).

6.4.2.1 Scope of equitable estoppel Lord Cairns expressed the doctrine as applying to variations of contractual obligations. Since the decision in *Hughes* v *Metropolitan Ry Co.* (1877) 2 App Cas 439, attempts have been made both to narrow and to extend the scope of the doctrine. In *Birmingham & District Land Co.* v *LNWR Co.* (1888) 40 Ch D 268 it was argued for the appellants that the doctrine applied only to cases where penal rights in the nature of forfeiture were sought to be enforced. Forfeiture occurs where all the outstanding obligations owing to a party under a contract are lost by virtue of some failure by that party. Equity provides relief from forfeiture in limited circumstances where what might be lost would be disproportionate to a merely technical breach (see now s.146, Law of Property Act 1925 and see *12.4.3 et seq.*). There are statements in *Hughes* v *Metropolitan Ry Co.* which might have given rise to the belief that the doctrine expounded was limited to such cases, but in the *Birmingham & District Land Co.* case Bowen LJ rejected the argument. In his opinion the doctrine applied where the belief is induced that contractual rights 'will either not be enforced or will be kept in suspense or abeyance for some particular time' (40 ChD 268 at 286).

In *Durham Fancy Goods Ltd* v *Michael Jackson (Fancy Goods) Ltd* [1968] 2 QB 839 the doctrine was said to apply not only to a pre-existing contractual relationship, but to any pre-existing legal relationship which could in some circumstances give rise to liabilities and penalties. The relationship in question was statutory in nature. This first instance opinion is implicitly, but not expressly, doubted in *obiter* statements in the Court of Appeal in *Brikom Investments Ltd* v *Carr* [1979] 2 All ER 753. Roskill LJ cited with approval a passage in *The Law Relating to Estoppel by Representation* (by Spencer Bower and A.K. Turner, Butterworth, 1977), in which it is stated that *Hughes* v *Metropolitan Ry Co.* cannot be cited in support of any wider proposition than that strict rights under contracts may not be enforced in given situations.

Roskill LJ found, in fact, that the strict rights in question were not enforceable because of a collateral contract between the parties by which it was agreed for consideration that they should not be. On the other hand, Lord Denning MR took the view that the facts also supported an argument based on 'promissory' estoppel, although he was alone on this view. Roskill and Cumming-Bruce LJJ nevertheless believed that the case fell within the *Hughes* v *Metropolitan Ry Co.* principle. It may be said with confidence that the doctrine applies to variations of pre-existing contractual duties, but beyond that the scope of the doctrine is unclear, and awaits authoritative statement by the courts.

6.4.2.2   The necessary representation   The doctrine only operates where there is a clear and unequivocal representation that strict rights will not be enforced. Nevertheless, it is apparent from *Hughes* v *Metropolitan Ry Co.* (1877) 2 App Cas 439 itself that the representation need not be express, since in that case it was implied from Hughes' conduct. In *Woodhouse A.C. Israel Cocoa SA* v *Nigerian Produce Marketing Co.* [1972] AC 741 Lord Hailsham said:

> The meaning is to exclude far-fetched or strained, but still possible, interpretations, while still insisting on a sufficient precision and freedom from ambiguity to ensure that the representation will . . . be reasonably understood in the particular sense required.

It seems that what is required is that only one reasonable meaning should be apparent from the representation made.

6.4.2.3   Effect of the doctrine   It seems that the effect of the doctrine is only to suspend strict legal rights and not, at least in the first instance, to extinguish them. In *Hughes* v *Metropolitan Ry Co.* (1877) 2 App Cas 439 such a consequence was inevitable, since it was impossible in the factual context to extinguish the property owner's right to have the property repaired. All that was in issue was the date by which the lessee had to have complied with the duty to repair. Subsequent cases suggest, however, that in any situation a party making a promise not to enforce strict rights may withdraw that promise upon giving reasonable notice to the promisee.

In *Tool Metal Manufacturing Co. Ltd.* v *Tungsten Electric Co. Ltd* [1955] 1 WLR 761

> the respondents were bound to pay royalties to the appellants under an agreement made in 1938 for the import, manufacture, use and sale of hard metal alloys. They were also to pay compensation if material manufactured exceeded a stated volume. At the outbreak of the Second World War the appellants agreed to suspend the right to compensation. In 1945 the appellants claimed to have revoked that suspension, and to be entitled once more to compensation.

That claim failed, but was held by the House of Lords in this later case to be sufficient notice to the respondents of termination of the suspension of the right to compensation.

It may well be that, where strict rights are suspended in a contract calling for repeated performances over a period of time, rights accruing during the period of suspension are not enforceable, and in that sense are extinguished. Thus, in the *Tool Metal Manufacturing* case it seems to have been assumed that after termination of the suspension the appellants were not entitled to claim for compensation which would otherwise have been payable during the suspension of the right to compensation. Moreover, in the leading case of *Central London Property Trust* v *High Trees House* [1947] KB 130 (see *6.4.3.1*, below) there are *obiter dicta* of Denning J to the effect that performances falling due during the period of suspension of rights cannot be recovered once the suspension of rights has come to an end. From statements he made in *Brikom Investments Ltd* v *Carr* [1979] 2 All ER 753 at 760 it seems that Lord Denning believes that in some circumstances it may be impossible for the promisor to go back to the strict rights under the contract.

It seems unlikely that the courts will find that equitable estoppels extinguish strict rights except where the context demands it. On the other hand, the enforceability of joined promises *both* not to enforce strict rights, *and* not to withdraw that first promise, has not been tested in the courts.

6.4.2.4 Passive enforceability The major limitation on the equitable estoppel doctrine is that it cannot be used to found a cause of action; that is, it may not be used in legal proceedings brought to force someone to uphold a promise. It can only be used to prevent someone insisting on enforcement of their strict rights; hence the description 'passive enforceability'. In *Combe* v *Combe* [1951] 2 KB 215

> during divorce proceedings the husband had promised to pay the wife a certain

sum by way of maintenance. The wife gave no reciprocal promise to refrain from applying to the court for maintenance, so that (unusually) the husband's promise was not supported by consideration. The wife attempted to enforce the promise on the basis of 'promissory' estoppel, but her claim was refused by the Court of Appeal.

Denning LJ said:

> Much as I am inclined to favour the principle . . ., it is important that it should not be stretched too far lest it should be endangered. It does not create new causes of action where none existed before . . .. The doctrine of consideration is too firmly fixed to be overthrown by a side-wind. Its ill effects have been largely mitigated of late, but it still remains a cardinal necessity of the formation of a contract, although not of its modification or discharge.

Recently, in *Brikom Investments Ltd* v *Carr* [1979] 2 All ER 753, Roskill LJ has again stressed that 'it would be wrong to extend the doctrine of promissory estoppel, whatever its precise limits at the present day, to the extent of abolishing in this back-handed way the doctrine of consideration'.

This limitation is sometimes expressed in the maxim that equitable or promissory estoppel is a shield not a sword (see, for example, Birkett LJ in *Combe* v *Combe*). As an image the expression makes the point quite well, but it should not lead to the mistaken belief that the doctrine is available only to defendants and not to plaintiffs. Equitable estoppel cannot found a cause of action where none would otherwise exist, but it may be used by a plaintiff in support of a cause of action which has an independent existence. Thus, if in *Hughes* v *Metropolitan Ry Co.* (1877) 2 App Cas 439 the lessor had actually retaken possession of the property, and upon breakdown of negotiations the lessee had sued to regain possession, the lessee would still have been able to rely on equitable estoppel to defeat the lessor's defence based on the lessee's failure to repair, since the cause of action would be based not on the implied promise to defer the time for repair but on the right under the original lease to occupy the premises undisturbed for the period agreed.

6.4.2.5 Reliance The equitable estoppel doctrine is generally stated as depending upon some act of reliance by the promisee before it operates. What constitutes sufficient reliance is discussed below (see *6.4.3.4*). For the time being, it may be helpful to explain the functions of this requirement. A first function appears to be evidential. The existence of reliance tends to confirm that the promise was made and was taken seriously. A second function meets the statement by Lord Cairns LC in *Hughes* v *Metropolitan Ry Co.* (1877) 2 App Cas 439, that the doctrine applies to prevent the enforcement of strict rights where to enforce them 'would be inequitable having regard to the dealings which have thus taken place between the parties'. In other words, the fact of reliance is at least one element to be taken into account in assessing whether enforcement would in all the circumstances be inequitable.

6.4.3 Promissory estoppel

Recent developments have taken the equitable doctrine established in *Hughes* v *Metropolitan Ry Co.* (1877) 2 App Cas 439 into ground in which, some would argue, it had not been intended to operate. The doctrine originally applied to variation of terms, but it is now suggested that the doctrine applies equally to the part payment of contract debts.

6.4.3.1 The extension of the doctrine Earlier in this chapter (see *6.3.5.3*) we saw that on a traditional analysis the payment of a lesser sum, on its own, could not be consideration for a promise not to enforce payment of the whole sum. Such an agreement would fall foul of the rule that consideration cannot consist of performance of an existing duty. There is early authority to that effect in *Pinnel's Case* (1602) 5 Co Rep 117a. The rule appears to be going through a period of evolution, started by the decision of the Court of Appeal in *Williams* v *Roffey Bros & Nicholls (Contractors) Ltd* [1990] 1 All ER 512, and continued in *Anangel Atlas Compania Naviera SA* v *Ishikawajima-Harima Heavy Industries Co. Ltd (No. 2)* [1990] 2 Lloyd's Rep 526. It is possible to foresee a time when consideration will not be a substantial requirement of such agreements. Prior to this development, the courts had made a limited attack upon the rule, led by Lord Denning. In *Central London Property Trust* v *High Trees House* [1947] KB 130, Denning J suggested in an *obiter dictum* that where the conditions of promissory estoppel were satisfied a creditor could not go back on a promise not to enforce payment of the whole sum.

The case arose out of the classic situation (see *6.4.1*, above) of a variation of strict contractual terms between parties enjoying a friendly relationship.

> The tenant company was a subsidiary of the landlord company. The property in question was a block of flats over which the defendant tenant company had a 99-year lease, for which it paid a rent of £2,500 per year. At the outbreak of the Second World War many of the flats remained vacant, and the tenant company were unable to pay the full rent. The landlord company agreed to halve the rent (to £1,250 per year), and the tenant company paid that amount from then on. At the end of the war the flats were fully let. The landlord company was in receivership. The receiver believed the company was entitled to arrears of rent for the whole period of the war, but brought a test case claiming full rent from summer 1945.

Denning J, relying on *Hughes* v *Metropolitan Ry Co.*, said that as a result of the equitable doctrine 'a promise to accept a smaller sum in discharge of a larger sum, if acted upon, is binding notwithstanding the absence of consideration.' Denning J noted with some satisfaction that his interpretation of the authorities achieved that which had been recommended by the Law Revision Committee in 1937, that a creditor's promise to accept part-payment as full settlement should be binding.

6.4.3.2 The authority of the *High Trees* decision In one sense there is little that is startling about this proposition. Contractual provisions as to price and payment are only terms like any others, and it might be argued that as such they are as open to variation by the parties by whatever valid means as any other terms. Nevertheless, it had until that time been thought that there were clear authorities against the validity of post-contracting price variations unsupported by consideration. One authority we have already considered; in *Foakes* v *Beer* (1884) 9 App Cas 605 the House of Lords refused to enforce a promise not to seek interest on a debt when the promise was given without consideration (see *6.3.5.3*). *Foakes* v *Beer* was decided only seven years after *Hughes* v *Metropolitan Ry Co.*, without reference being made to the latter. Although it can be argued that estoppel must be pleaded before the court may rely on it, it seems inconceivable that counsel in the former case should have overlooked the latter.

The other major obstacle to the *High Trees* case is *Jorden* v *Money* (1854) 5 HLC 185, in which the House of Lords ruled that the common law estoppel principle (which prevents a person from going back on a statement made once it has been relied upon), applied only to misrepresentations of existing fact, and did not apply to promises of future conduct. On the other hand, this objection applies equally to *Hughes* v *Metropolitan Ry Co*. If that case is accepted as a valid exception to the *Jorden* v *Money* rule there would appear to be no reason why the *High Trees* case could not also be.

It is possible to explain away these inconsistencies by ingenious arguments, as Denning J did in the *High Trees* case itself, resorting respectively to 'the fusion of law and equity' and an absence of intention to be legally bound. The truth of the matter appears to be that as originally conceived in *Hughes* v *Metropolitan Ry Co.* equitable estoppel was not intended to apply to variations of price unsupported by consideration. Once, however, Bowen LJ had stated in *Birmingham & District Land Co.* v *LNWR Co.* (1888) 40 ChD 268 that the doctrine was not limited to forfeiture cases, but applied to all variations of contractual rights, no meaningful distinction could be made between price terms and any others. Denning J exploited this fact to the full by extending the equitable estoppel doctrine to its logical conclusion. Nevertheless, the subsequent cases are peppered with statements suggesting that the made by the *High Trees* decision is by no means firmly established in English law. Indeed, the House of Lords has not yet given its blessing to the doctrine of promissory estoppel. In both *Tool Metal Manufacturing Co. Ltd* v *Tungsten Electric Co. Ltd* [1955] 2 All ER 657 (per Lord Tucker at 674; see *6.4.2.3*) and *Woodhouse A.C. Israel Cocoa Ltd* v *Nigerian Produce Marketing* [1972] AC 741 (per Lord Hailsham at 758; see *6.4.2.2*), the House of Lords expressly reserved the question of the existence or at least the extent of the doctrine. It may now be that their Lordships will feel obliged to choose between the promissory estoppel doctrine, and the modified doctrine of consideration as applied by the Court of Appeal in *Williams* v *Roffey Bros & Nicholls (Contractors) Ltd* [1990] 1 All ER 512 (*6.3.5.2*). The advantage of the latter approach is that it is not restricted to 'defensive duties' in the way that equitable and promissory estoppel appear to be (*6.4.2.4*). On the other hand, there may be concern that approval of this approach might cause terminal injury to the general doctrine of consideration. Promissory estoppel is a more limited exception to the general rule. First blood in the battle appears to have gone to the *Williams* v *Roffey* approach, as a result of the decision of Hirst J in *Anangel Atlas Compania Naviera SA* v *Ishikawajima-Harima Heavy Industries Co. Ltd (No. 2)* [1990] 2 Lloyd's Rep 526 (see *6.3.5.3*). The case is only first instance authority, and alone cannot signify a major change in the law. Nevertheless, its effect is to allow a plaintiff to sue on a cause of action based on a promise supported by the flimsiest of consideration.

6.4.3.3 Duress against creditors It has already been suggested that a probable reason for the rule that consideration cannot be provided by the performance of an existing duty is the fear of duress by debtors against creditors (see *6.3.5.2*). The decision in *Central London Property Trust* v *High Trees House* [1947] KB 130 results in the enforcement of a promise to accept the diminished performance of an existing obligation in final settlement of a debt. The risk of such duress is thus raised. The problem was confronted in *D & C Builders* v *Rees* [1966] 2 QB 617.

> The debtors exploited the straitened circumstances of the creditors to extort a promise to accept immediate part-payment of the debt in final settlement.

Lord Denning MR (who was in a minority on this reasoning, but not in the result of the case) found for the plaintiff creditors by relying on the statement of the equitable estoppel doctrine by Lord Cairns LC in *Hughes* v *Metropolitan Ry Co.* Lord Denning said:

> The creditor is only barred from his legal rights when it would be inequitable for him to insist upon them . . .. Where there has been a true accord . . . then it is inequitable for the creditor afterwards to insist on the balance . . .. In the present case, on the facts as found by the judge, it seems to me that there was no true accord. The debtor's wife held the creditor to ransom.

In simple terms, there is nothing inequitable about not enforcing such a promise when the promise was obtained by duress. This approach matches that of Lord Scarman in *Pao On* v *Lau Yiu Long* [1979] 3 All ER 65, who said that there was no harm in allowing consideration to be constituted by performance of an existing duty provided there existed protection against duress (see *6.3.5.5*). Similar reasoning was used to justify a more liberal approach to the doctrine of consideration in *Williams* v *Roffey Bros & Nicholls (Contractors) Ltd* [1990] 1 All ER 512 (*6.3.5.2*).

6.4.3.4. Reliance defined Equitable estoppel and promissory estoppel (if they are not in fact one and the same thing) both depend upon the fact of reliance. The function of this element was explained above (see *6.4.2.6*), but it has not been defined. There are those who believe that reliance demands that the promisee must have been induced by the promise to have acted to his detriment in some way. Such a definition is suspiciously reminiscent of now outmoded definitions of consideration (see *6.3.1*), and may arise out of a confusion with proprietary estoppel (see *6.4.4*). In fact, it is not easy to see that the promisees in either *Hughes* v *Metropolitan Ry Co.* or *High Trees* acted to their detriment, other than that they acted in accordance with the subsequent promise rather than the original contract. The suspension of the strict rights under the contracts was, on the contrary, a benefit to the promisees.

In *W.J. Alan & Co. Ltd* v *El Nasr Export & Import Co.* [1972] 2 All ER 127 Lord Denning MR stated that he could find no support in the authorities for the view that there must be a detriment, and that all that was required was that the promisee must have 'conducted his affairs on the basis' of the promise so that 'it would not now be equitable to deprive him of' its benefit.

The one sense in which detriment is relevant to the doctrine is that there *would be* a detriment if the original contract were to be enforced unamended by the subsequent promise. Here, however, the sense of 'detriment' is nowhere near the same as that once used to define consideration. It does no more than contribute to the sense of justice inherent in the requirement that enforcement of the strict rights under the contract be 'inequitable' in the circumstances. Indeed, it may be that even the requirement of reliance is no more than the most likely way of demonstrating inequity, and is not in itself sufficient to trigger the doctrine. In *Société Italo-Belge pour le Commerce et l'Industrie SA* v *Palm & Vegetable Oils (Malaysia) Sdn Bhd, 'The Post Chaser'* [1982] 1 All ER 19 Robert Goff J insisted that the only requirement was that inequity be demonstrated. He said:

> But it does not follow that in every case in which the representee has acted, or failed to act, in reliance on the representation, it will be inequitable for the representee to enforce his rights, for the nature of the action, or inaction, may be insufficient to give rise to the equity, in which event a necessary requirement stated by Lord Cairns LC for the application of the doctrine would not have been fulfilled.

In this case the promisees did rely on the representation made, but the promisors withdrew the suspension of strict rights so soon afterwards, and before any real harm had been done, so that in the particular circumstances the judge found that it would not be inequitable to enforce the strict rights.

6.4.4 Proprietary estoppel

Proprietary estoppel may best be regarded as having little or nothing to do with the law of contract (in *Re Basham* [1987] 1 All ER 405 the judge described it as 'properly to be regarded as giving rise to a species of constructive trust'), but it is undoubtedly similar to the equitable estoppel doctrine, and recent developments in relation to the formal requirements for contracts for the sale of land (see *6.5.3.5*) suggest that it is destined to play a more important role. For this last reason, the general principles of the doctrine will be outlined here. It has been suggested that the distinction between promissory and proprietary estoppel is not helpful (per Scarman LJ in *Crabb* v *Arun District Council* [1975] 3 All ER 865), and that the proprietary estoppel doctrine is 'an amalgam of doubtful utility' (per Goff J in *Amalgamated Investment & Property Co. Ltd* v *Texas Commerce International Bank Ltd* [1981] 1 All ER

923 at 935). Nevertheless, the fact that under the doctrine of proprietary estoppel new rights giving rise to a cause of action may be created is sufficient to distinguish it from promissory estoppel, and to endow it with a utility not enjoyed by the other.

Proprietary estoppel gives rise to an equitable right under which a non-owner may become entitled to land. The estoppel was originally regarded as being created by expenditure on, or use of, land with the acquiescence of the owner, in the mistaken belief by the person making the expenditure or using the land that he is the owner (*Dillwyn* v *Llewelyn* (1862) 4 De G F & J 517). More recently, the doctrine has been extended to provide a remedy where the non-owner is encouraged by the true owner to believe that he has an interest in the land, or that the latter will grant the former an interest in the land in due course (*Crabb* v *Arun District Council* [1975] 3 All ER 865). In this last form it is possible to see that proprietary estoppel may allow the achievement of a legal result which could in other circumstances be achieved by contract. Where there is a contract that process will prevail, but proprietary estoppel may fill a gap in the law's remedial armoury where contract is unavailable (for example, where the formal requirements under s.2 of the Law of Property (Miscellaneous Provisions) Act 1989 are not satisfied: see *6.5.3.5*).

In *Re Basham* [1987] 1 All ER 405 the judge described the doctrine in these terms:

> Where one person (A) has acted to his detriment on the faith of a belief, which was known to and encouraged by another person (B), that he either has or is going to be given a right in or over B's property, B cannot insist on his strict legal rights if to do so would be inconsistent with A's belief.

Three ingredients of liability may be identified. In the first place there must be knowledge or encouragement of A's belief, and in practice this must amount to a representation upon which it is reasonable for A to rely, even if the representation is to be implied from conduct. The identification of such a representation raises issues which are largely the same as in the case of equitable and promissory estoppel (*6.4.2.2*). For an example of a case where such reliance would not be reasonable, see *Attorney-General of Hong Kong* v *Humphreys Estate (Queen's Gardens) Ltd* [1987] 2 All ER 387; reliance was not reasonable because the party said to have made the representation had made clear at all times that its statements were 'subject to contract', so that when no contract could be agreed, no liability based upon proprietary estoppel could be imposed. Secondly, there must be detrimental reliance. Here the requirement appears to be strict, and not as fluid as it appears to be in the case of promissory estoppel (*6.4.3.4*). Finally, it would seem that it must be possible to identify specific property about which the representation was made. In *Re Basham* this requirement was doubted, although in that case at least part of the general property in question was the deceased's cottage. In principle, it is not easy to understand how a proprietary interest can be created without reference to the subject-matter of that interest, and where the courts have purported to do so it would seem to be because they are anxious to avoid the consequences of the consideration doctrine, rather than by virtue of a rigorous application of the rule. Where the conditions for the establishment of proprietary estoppel are satisfied, the court may order the full ownership (fee simple) to be transferred to the party encouraged to believe an interest was to be granted; but where appropriate a more limited form of remedy may be granted (see *Inwards* v *Baker* [1965] 1 All ER 446: right to occupy property for life).

The doctrine of proprietary estoppel is not without difficulty. In particular it is not clear why it should create a cause of action when promissory estoppel does not, nor is it clear whether it applies only to real property (land), or whether it extends to other property. It is hard to resist the conclusion that these difficulties stem as much from the hard cases arising out of the doctrine of consideration, as they do from the proprietary estoppel doctrine itself.

6.4.5 Conclusion: the future of promissory estoppel

Despite doubts expressed about the doctrine in the House of Lords (see *6.4.3.2*, above), and fears that it may abolish in a back-handed way the doctrine of consideration (see *6.4.2.4*, above), promissory estoppel appears now to be too well established to be seriously at risk as a matter of English law. On the other hand, there is the possibility that it might become largely redundant by virtue of developments in relation to consideration (*6.3.6*), which avoid the difficulty encountered in the case of promissory estoppel of not giving rise to a new cause of action. However, even this difficulty was overcome in one Australian case: *Walton Stores (Interstate) Ltd* v *Maher* (1988) 164 CLR 387.

It was suggested in Chapter 4 that one reason for enforcing wholly executory promises, where there has been no reliance on the promises, is that reliance may in some circumstances be difficult to prove, so that it is safer to presume reliance will ensue from promising. This does not explain, however, why a promise should not be fully enforceable even in the absence of consideration *where reliance can be proved*. Since the test of intention to create legal relations is firmly established (see *6.2*), it could be used to eliminate from enforceability promises which were not meant to be relied upon. Moreover, where no commercial value exists in the arrangement the burden could be reversed so that the party seeking to enforce the promise made without consideration would have to prove that it was intended to be relied upon.

Subject to these limitations, is there any reason why promissory estoppel should not found a cause of action? The apparent logic of this position is accepted in the United States, where Section 90 of the Restatement (Second) Contracts states:

> (1) A promise which the promisor should reasonably expect to induce action or forebearance on the part of the promisee . . . and which does induce such action or forebearance is binding if injustice can be avoided only by enforcement of the promise.

6.5   UNENFORCEABILITY BY DEFECT OF 'FORM'

6.5.1 General

Where the law states that a contract is only enforceable if recorded in a particular way, the rule is described as a requirement of form. It is one of the commonest misconceptions of contract law among lay people that contracts are only enforceable if in writing. It is true that the job of the courts, and of lawyers advising clients, would be much easier if we were to insist that all contracts be put in writing. If one pauses to consider for a moment, however, it will be realised that that would mean that each time one bought a loaf of bread or a drink in a pub one would be obliged to countersign an invoice. There would be an intolerable burden on daily consumer intercourse. For that reason, the general rule is that there is no requirement that contracts be made in writing, and the parties are left to their own good sense as to whether written evidence is necessary.

In commercial dealings written evidence is almost inevitably available, but for the most part that is a matter of choice, not a matter of law. Where complex obligations of great value are undertaken on each side, so that any dispute may involve liability for very large sums of money, parties will inevitably choose to keep an accurate record of their agreement (and see *7.2* on rectification). In the seventeenth century the law required a large number of contracts to be made in writing. Today, it may generally be said that the law only insists on writing where the subject-matter or nature of the contract requires either absolutely certain evidence or some cautionary element to bring home to one of the parties the seriousness of the legal agreement being entered into. Thus, some consumer credit and hire-purchase agreements require a written contract as a means of protecting consumers (see *6.5.3*).

Requirements of form are of three types:

(a)   transactions requiring a particular kind of writing (*6.5.2*);
(b)   transactions which must be wholly in writing (*6.5.3*);
(c)   transactions which must be evidenced in writing (*6.5.4*).

6.5.2 Transactions requiring a particular kind of writing

The common law made provision for a particularly formal kind of legal writing by means of the document made under seal. The more picturesque formalities associated with such documents have now disappeared, but deeds must still be made in accordance with certain formal requirements, as set out in s.1 of the Law of Property (Miscellaneous Provisions) Act 1989. These include the requirement of properly attested signature and delivery (s.1(3)).

The most common transaction which must be made in the form of a deed is the conveyance of a legal estate in land (see ss.52 and 54 of the Law of Property Act 1925). A deed is also the means by which to make enforceable a gratuitous promise which otherwise would have no legal effect (see *6.1*). Although this form of enforceable promise is not often used for commercial transactions, for tax reasons it is particularly useful for covenants to make gifts to charity.

6.5.3   Transactions which must be wholly in writing

For some contracts it is an additional condition of enforceability, beyond the fact of consideration and intention to create legal relations, that the whole agreement be in writing. The principal types are listed below.

6.5.3.1   Bills of sale   By s.9 of the Bills of Sale Act (1878) Amendment Act 1882 a bill of sale is void unless made in a form made in accordance with that set out in the Schedule to the Act. A bill of sale is a document recording a transaction transferring title to goods to someone else, but not possession (see s.4 of the 1878 Act). The Acts of 1878 and 1882 were passed to prevent people obtaining credit on the security of goods which were in their possession but which they no longer owned.

6.5.3.2   Bills of exchange   By ss.3(1) and 17(2) of the Bills of Exchange Act 1882 a bill of exchange must be in writing. A typical example of a bill of exchange is a cheque (see *13.4.3*). By its nature, the kind of promise made in a bill of exchange can be made without being in writing; in such a case the promise might be enforceable as a simple contract, but would not benefit from the quality of negotiability which is an essential feature of a bill of exchange (see *13.4.3.1*).

6.5.3.3   Consumer credit agreements   By s.60 of the Consumer Credit Act 1974 a consumer credit agreement (as defined by s.8 of the Act) must be in a form prescribed by regulation (The Consumer Credit (Agreements) Regulations 1983, SI 1983 No.1553). Failure to comply with this form may not be fatal to such an agreement. The underlying purpose of the rule is to provide protection for consumer debtors without permitting the formal requirement to become a technical defence operating to protect suppliers from legal action by consumer plaintiffs.

6.5.3.4   Marine insurance contracts   By ss.21–24 of the Marine Insurance Act 1906 a contract of marine insurance will not be admitted in evidence unless contained in a document ('policy') signed by the insurer. This is not strictly a condition of validity of such a contract, but only of its admissibility in evidence in trial proceedings. In fact, the contract itself is regarded as formed by assent given before the policy is drawn up. Nevertheless, unlike the contracts detailed in the next sections, here the whole contract must be in writing, and inadmissibility in evidence may be an insurmountable obstacle to enforcement.

6.5.3.5   Contracts for sale etc. of land   The Law of Property (Miscellaneous Provisions) Act 1989 repealed s.40 of the Law of Property Act 1925, which required contracts for land to be evidenced in writing, and replaced it with a requirement that such contracts be made in writing incorporating all the terms. Section 2(1) of the 1989 Act provides:

A contract for the sale or other disposition of an interest in land can only be made in writing and only by incorporating all the terms which the parties have expressly agreed in one document or, where contracts are exchanged, in each.

Incorporation of the terms can be achieved by setting them out in the contract document or by reference to another document (s.2(2)). According to Judge Paul Baker QC, sitting as a judge of the High Court, in *Record* v *Bell* [1991] 4 All ER 471, where incorporation is alleged to have been achieved by reference to another document the contract of sale which both parties have signed must refer to and identify the other document for incorporation for the purposes of s. 2 to be effective. Each party must sign a document incorporating the terms, but it need not be the same document which bears both signatures, especially where there is to be an exchange of contract documents (s.2(3)). In *Record* v *Bell* the plaintiff had attached agreed supplementary terms to one contract document, but not to the other. Judge Paul Baker QC ruled that physical attachment of additional terms to the contract document was ineffective as incorporation unless they were attached to both the documents exchanged. Although the grant of an option to purchase land would fall within the scope of the section, the exercise of such an option would not, and so need not be signed by both parties (*Spiro* v *Glencrown Properties Ltd* [1991] 1 All ER 600). A purported contract made in contravention of these rules would be without effect. As a result, the former rule making enforceable an oral contract of which there was a memorandum in writing (which might record only the barest details) no longer applies.

Prior to the enactment of s.2 of the 1989 Act, a contract for the sale or other disposition of an interest in land which did not satisfy the requirement of being evidenced in writing might nevertheless be enforceable by virtue of the doctrine of part performance. That doctrine, which was said to exist in order to prevent fraud by parties who knew they had entered into a contract and merely sought to take advantage of the formal defect to get out of that bargain, is also repealed, by s. 2(8) and s.4 of the 1989 Act. The question then raised is whether any protection against such fraud now remains. The Law Commission, which proposed these changes to the law in its Report No. 164 (*Formalities for Contracts for Sale etc. of Land*), suggested that three possible means of protection remain available. Rectification, which is provided for expressly by s.2(4), would allow a contract to be amended in order to include matters agreed between the parties but which had wrongly been excluded from the written document (see *7.2.1*). A collateral contract might be available to provide for aspects of the contract not covered by the written document, although presumably such aspects could not be interests in land. An example might be a house sale, in which it had been agreed that carpets would be included in the purchase price, but where the sale of the carpets was not recorded in the contract document. That part of the sale might be regarded as a collateral contract, without doing violence to the principle established by s.2. In *Tootal Clothing Ltd* v *Guinea Properties Management Ltd* (1992) 64 P & CR 452 the Court of Appeal found, as an alternative ground for its decision, that an agreement by which a landlord undertook to contribute to the cost of shopfitting work to be carried out by the tenant was 'supplemental' to the main tenancy agreement, as designated by the parties, and was not, therefore, one of the terms which had to be recorded in writing. Perhaps more suprisingly, in *Record v Bell* [1991] 4 All ER 471 a warranty of title, given—because proper documentation from the Land Registry was not available—in order to induce exchange of contracts on the date previously anticipated, was said to be a collateral warranty not forming part of the contract of sale and not therefore required to be part of the writing provided for in s. 2 of the 1989 Act. Finally, the doctrine of proprietary estoppel is thought to provide protection from fraud, and it seems likely that this doctrine will bear the lion's share of the burden once borne by part performance. It applies in particular where one party has been encouraged by another to believe that he will be granted an interest in the property in question, and has acted to his detriment in reliance on that belief. The doctrine affords the party so relying a new cause of action to protect his interest, which might go so far as the court ordering the property to be conveyed to him. The doctrine is considered in more detail at *6.4.4*.

A further exception to s. 2 of the 1989 Act, not apparently contemplated by the Law Commission, was invoked by the Court of Appeal in *Tootal Clothing Ltd* v *Guinea Properties Management Ltd*. As noted above, the claim related to an undertaking to contribute to shopfitting work given in association with an agreement for a tenancy of commercial property. On the alternative basis that the undertaking was to be regarded as part of a single composite contract for the disposition of an interest in land, the Court of Appeal ruled that s. 2 still did not apply, because all elements relating to the disposition of an interest in land were already *executed*, while s. 2 applies only to *executory contracts*. This interpretation is not self-evident in the text of s. 2.

6.5.4 Evidence in writing: guarantee contracts

6.5.4.1 Scope of the rule Of the many contracts required to be evidenced in writing by the Statute of Frauds 1677 only two survived the repeals brought about by the Law Reform (Enforcement of Contracts) Act 1954. One was the contract of guarantee, described in the Statute of Frauds 1677 as a 'promise to answer for the debt, default or miscarriage of another person'. In other words, there is a promise by one person to meet the *liabilities* of another should that other become liable and fail to pay. This definition is important because the rule is said not to apply to contracts of indemnity. The latter are defined as promises to pay for another whether or not there is liability on that other. Here the promisor undertakes to be the principal debtor.

This distinction appears to have been introduced because of dissatisfaction with the operation of the Statute of Frauds, which would often operate to provide a technical defence for the unscrupulous. However, it is a distinction wholly lacking in substance or merit. The risks inherent in indemnity contracts are no different from those in guarantee contracts, and it would seem that there should be a requirement of evidence in writing for both or neither. For this reason the distinction has been subject to severe criticism in recent cases (cf. *Yeoman Credit Ltd* v *Latter* [1961] 1 WLR 828).

The requirement of writing for contracts of guarantee does not apply where the undertaking is only part of or incidental to a larger transaction (see *Sutton & Co.* v *Grey* [1894] 1 QB 285). Nor does it apply where the guarantee promise is given in order to protect property (see *Fitzgerald* v *Dressler* (1858) 7 CBNS 374). For example, if A wishes to purchase property from B in which C has a security interest on some debt by B, A may promise to C to meet B's debt should B fail to honour it, in order to obtain the property free from C's overriding interest. Such a promise need not be evidenced in writing. These exceptions may be explained by the argument that the requirement of writing is less strong when the surrounding circumstances of other transactions provide evidence of a kind of the promises made. Nevertheless, the policy of the law seems to have been buried in a mound of fine distinctions. It is difficult to resist the conclusion that this area of law is ripe for reform.

6.5.4.2   The evidence required   The Statute of Frauds 1677 states:

> The agreement upon which such action shall be brought or some memorandum or note thereof shall be in writing, and signed by the party to be charged therewith or some other person thereunto by him lawfully authorised.

For a recent case applying this provision, see *Elpis Maritime Co Ltd* v *Marti Chartering Co. Inc., The Maria D* [1991] 3 All ER 758. Interestingly, Lord Brandon said that provided the memorandum was signed by the party against whom it was sought to enforce the contract, it was of no relevance to enquire in what capacity, or with what intention, that party had signed it. It did not matter that it had not been signed with the intention of providing a sufficient memorandum of the contract of guarantee.

SEVEN
Mistake

7.1 INTRODUCTION

This chapter considers the impact of mistake on contracts. The single word 'mistake' may be misleading if it is taken to indicate a single coherent doctrine. It indicates no more than a loose association of doctrines often connected in no other way than that they are called into play in factual contexts in which one or both parties may in everyday language be said to have been mistaken. The rules in question straddle uneasily the line between formation of contracts and policing the fairness of bargains. In fact, it has been argued that English law really knows no independent doctrine of mistake, and that those cases in which apparent mistake has resulted in a contract being set aside involve the application to the particular situation of established rules of the law of contract, such as the rules of offer and acceptance. Such a conclusion almost certainly overstates the case, but it does at least reflect the fact that English law has only a limited doctrine of mistake. Much of what passes for mistake can be explained in terms of other rules of English law which have been dressed up in language borrowed from the civil law and arguably inappropriate to the common law conception of contract.

The reason for this civil law influence appears to be that the writing of systematic legal treatises began in France much earlier than it did in England, and at the end of the eighteenth century and the beginning of the nineteenth the writings of the celebrated French lawyer Pothier gained a certain currency in England. The transference of the notion of mistake from one legal system to the other was misguided, however, since French law at the time was committed to a much more subjective approach to the formation of contracts than ever prevailed in England. An allegation of mistake is inevitably much more serious where the test of agreement is subjective.

7.1.1 Effect of mistake
One reason for the limited doctrine of mistake in English law is that where mistake operates it usually operates to make the contract void. More precisely, the effect is that there is no contract and the law takes the view that there never has been a contract. The wider impact of this conclusion is such that the courts appear to have been unwilling to extend the mistake doctrine.

The fact that the contract is void is of fundamental importance in the case of the sale of goods. If no contract ever existed, title to the property which is the subject-matter of the sale cannot have passed between seller and buyer (see *4.5.3*). By contrast, if a sale is found to exist but must subsequently be unravelled, as for example in the case of a contract induced by misrepresentation (see generally Chapter 9), title does pass. Such a contract is described as voidable rather than void. It is the fact that title does not pass under contracts which are affected by mistake which has made mistake an attractive doctrine to plaintiffs, but left the courts uneasy about its application. The reason is that a seller who has not lost title to the goods in question is entitled to the return of the actual goods, by virtue of his rights of ownership. He may well be entitled to the return of his actual goods even where they have passed out of the hands of the original buyer into the hands of a third party who knows nothing of the dealings between seller and buyer. If the contract were merely voidable, and the buyer had disposed of the goods before the time of the seller's claim to an innocent third party, then the third party would be protected from recovery of the goods by the original seller.

Where the original buyer remains present and solvent the impact of the fact that a contract affected by mistake is void is slight, since if, for example, the original seller seeks redress then it is unlikely in most circumstances to matter whether he recovers the actual goods or their monetary equivalent. Where, however, the original buyer has disappeared, or is insolvent, the seller will seek a remedy by recovering the actual goods if entitled to do so. It is true that both the original seller and the third party into whose hands the goods have passed are 'innocent', so that it is unfortunate that either should suffer. Nevertheless, the original seller is in a better position to guard against mistake than the third party, who played no part in the deal between seller and buyer. It is somewhat harsh, therefore, that the third party should be the one of the two to suffer, as a result of the original seller retaining title to the goods because the contract was void. It is probably for this reason that the English courts have been unwilling to extend beyond narrow bounds the doctrine of mistake.

7.1.2 Types of mistake

The fact that there is no single doctrine of mistake reflects the different contexts in which mistake may be said to exist. In the first place there is the type of mistake where the parties share a common misunderstanding which is in some way material to their respective decisions to enter into the agreement, and where the true state of affairs is only discovered after objective agreement has apparently been reached (see *7.3*). In this case, if both parties regret making the contract once the true state of affairs is known then they may usually extricate themselves without reference to the courts. Problems may arise, however, where one party, although originally mistaken, is unwilling to surrender an advantage gained under the apparent contract. It need hardly be added that it is extremely difficult to prove, except by admission of the parties, the existence of mistake.

The second type of mistake exists where, despite what one or other party may assert, it is impossible to identify from what has passed between the parties objective evidence of agreement (see *7.4*). Here again, if both parties are willing to recognise that they have failed to come to any final agreement they may usually extricate themselves without recourse to the courts. Litigation is caused by one of the parties asserting that an agreement exists on terms as understood by that party. Cases fall into two categories: those where the parties are genuinely at cross-purposes (see *7.4.1*); and those where one party is aware that the other is labouring under a mistake (*7.4.2*).

Before examining these two main categories of mistake, however, it is proposed to consider two unrelated doctrines which may also be said to depend upon mistake. Both are concerned with contracts contained in documents. The first provides a remedy where there has been a simple transcription mistake in recording an oral agreement in writing (see *7.2.1*). The second may provide a remedy where a party asserts that a document containing his signature is not the document he thought he was signing (see *7.2.2*). This latter doctrine, although in one sense reflecting a mistake by the party signing, also bears some relationship to fraud (see *9.3.1*).

7.2 MISTAKES IN DOCUMENTS

7.2.1 Rectification

Rectification was defined above as providing a remedy where there has been a simple transcription mistake in recording an oral agreement in writing. The remedy is normally only available when the document said to incorporate the agreement fails to reproduce the common intentions of the parties. The operation of the doctrine is well illustrated by the leading recent case: *Joscelyne* v *Nissen* [1970] 2 QB 86.

> In order to help her father the daughter bought the house from which her father ran a car hire business. She and her husband occupied the upper floor, while her father and mother occupied the lower floor. Her mother became seriously ill, and her father could not afford the time to run his business. The daughter therefore agreed to purchase the business in return (*inter alia*) for granting to the father the right to live for the rest of his life in the lower floor of the house 'free of all rent and outgoings of every kind in any event'. At first this clause was interpreted by the daughter as meaning that she should pay all fuel bills and the cost of home help for the father. A dispute arose between father and daughter, and the latter ceased to pay the fuel bills or the home help, seemingly upon legal advice. The father sought rectification of the document containing their agreement to make explicit their original intention that such bills should be paid by the daughter.

The court was satisfied that the father's version of the agreement did reflect what had actually been agreed between the parties. Indeed, the daughter's defence sought less to deny that than to pursue a legal argument against rectification (discussed below). The contract was rectified in line with the interpretation originally placed on the contractual document by the daughter.

The most difficult obstacle confronting a plaintiff seeking rectification is to prove that the document does not truly reflect what was agreed. Courts are understandably reluctant to change the terms of a written agreement since in the great majority of cases the contractual document is the most secure evidence there is of what was agreed by the parties. In *Joscelyne* v *Nissen* the court said that 'convincing proof' would be required, indicating that by this expression they intended a high burden of proof to fall on the plaintiff.

If all the objective evidence is that the parties did agree in the terms used in the document it will not avail the plaintiff that he misunderstood the meaning of the words used. The point is well made in *Frederick Rose (London) Ltd* v *William Pim Jnr & Co* [1953] 2 QB 450.

> The plaintiffs were asked to supply 'Moroccan horsebeans known here as feveroles'. The plaintiffs did not know what feveroles were, and asked the defendants, who said they were simply horsebeans. The plaintiffs therefore entered into a contract to purchase the requisite number of horsebeans from the defendants. They then discovered that 'feveroles' referred to a particular size of horsebean, and that they had delivered the wrong size.

They sought rectification of the agreement with the defendants, but were refused by the court. The contract as written down reflected what had been agreed orally.

It was once thought that rectification would only be available where the parties had actually entered into a contract by virtue of their oral negotiations, and that rectification would not be available where the document itself represented the first point of contracting between the parties. This theory was rejected by the court in *Joscelyne* v *Nissen*, which said that firm agreement short of contract was sufficient provided the common intention of the parties continued up to the moment of recording their agreement in writing.

7.2.1.1 Rectification where mistake is not shared

There were authorities, culminating in *A. Roberts & Co. Ltd* v *Leicestershire CC* [1961] Ch 555, which suggested that where the document failed to record the intentions of only one of the parties, rectification might be available. It was sometimes suggested that the other party might choose in those circumstances between rectification and rescission; that is, the complete unravelling of the agreement. Those authorities were largely overruled by *Riverlate Properties Ltd* v *Paul* [1974] 2 All ER 656.

> A lessor had made a mistake in drafting a document containing a proposed lease, and subsequently sought to amend it in a way that would have increased the burden on the lessee.

The Court of Appeal refused to rectify the lease in those circumstances, although it was at pains to point out that the lessee did not know at the time of contracting of the lessor's mistake, still less had there been any kind of sharp practice.

The significance of these factors was made clear in *Thomas Bates & Son Ltd* v *Wyndham's (Lingerie) Ltd* [1981] 1 All ER 1077.

> Tenants had had a lease from the plaintiffs on two previous occasions, and on each

occasion an option for renewal in the lease contained a price term leaving the matter to be agreed between the parties, or to be fixed by arbitration. A further lease omitted provision for arbitration in the event of dispute over fixing the rent, a fact noted by the tenants but not drawn to the attention of the plaintiffs. The plaintiffs sought rectification of the lease after it had been executed.

The Court of Appeal dismissed the tenants' appeal against the trial judge's order for rectification. Rectification would be allowed even where the mistake was one-sided, provided the other party knew of the mistake but failed to draw it to the attention of the mistaken party; and provided there is some inequitable benefit to the party conscious of the other's mistake (not necessarily amounting to sharp practice). *Roberts* v *Leicestershire CC* was good law because it rested on precisely this principle.

7.2.2 Non est factum

The Latin phrase *non est factum* means literally: it is not my deed. As a rule of the law of contract it affords a defence to a party against whom action is brought in reliance upon a signed written agreement, where that party is able to show that he was unaware of the true meaning of the document when signing it. It is a very limited exception to the rule that a person's signature on a document irrevocably binds the person to its contents (see *5.7.2*). The rule developed at a time when adult literacy was far from commonplace (cf, *Thoroughgood's Case* (1584) 2 Co Rep 9a). The classic case of the operation of the rule is *Lewis* v *Clay* (1897) 67 LJ QB 224.

> The plaintiff asked the defendant to witness some deeds for him. He showed the defendant some papers, over which he held a piece of blotting-paper with a number of holes cut in it, his explanation being that the content of the deeds must remain private. The defendant signed in the spaces. The papers were promissory notes made out to the plaintiff, to the value of £11,000.

It was found as a fact that the defendant had not been negligent, and he was able to resist the plaintiff's action.

The advent of universal education and general adult literacy put the continued existence of the rule in doubt. The matter came before the House of Lords in *Saunders* v *Anglia Building Society* (aka *Gallie* v *Lee*) [1971] AC 1004.

> An elderly aunt intended to give her house to her nephew, so that he could use it as security for a loan, on condition that she be allowed to remain living there. A friend of the nephew, known to be assisting him to obtain a loan, asked her to sign a document, said to be relevant to the transfer of the house to the nephew. She had broken her glasses, and so signed without reading the document, which turned out to be a deed conveying the house to the friend. He then mortgaged the property, without paying either the aunt or the nephew. The aunt's plea of *non est factum* failed.

The House of Lords declined to abolish the *non est factum* rule. The narrow *ratio* of their Lordships' decision is that the difference between what the aunt signed and what she thought she was signing was not so great as to establish beyond doubt that she did not consent to it. She thought she was signing a document transferring ownership of the house, which is precisely what she signed. Thus, the *non est factum* defence is not available except in cases where 'the transaction which the document purports to effect is essentially different in substance or in kind from the transaction intended' (per Lord Wilberforce). Their Lordships did, however, consider the extent of the rule. Lord Wilberforce thought it would be rare today for a literate adult to succeed in a plea of *non est factum*. In the case of those who are illiterate, or blind, or lacking in understanding the position was less clear. According to Lord Wilberforce:

> The law ought . . . to give relief if satisfied that consent was truly lacking but will require of signers even in this class that they act responsibly and carefully according to their circumstances in putting their signature to legal documents.

That the rule has been severely restricted by the decision in *Saunders v Anglia Building Society* is confirmed by the peremptory dismissal of the defence by the Court of Appeal in *Avon Finance Co. Ltd v Bridger* [1985] 2 All ER 281. On the other hand, the doctrine is not quite dead. It was relied upon by two members of the Court of Appeal in *Lloyds Bank plc v Waterhouse* [1991] Fam Law 23, in a decision which emphasised the close links between *non est factum*, misrepresentation (chapter 9), undue influence (*8.6*) and unilateral mistake (*7.4.2*).

7.3 SHARED MISTAKE DISCOVERED AFTER AGREEMENT

The most difficult and perhaps most important type of mistake occurs where the parties share a common misunderstanding which is in some way material to their respective decisions to enter into the agreement, and where the true state of affairs is only discovered after objective agreement has apparently been reached, whereupon only one of the parties wishes to withdraw from the agreement. Such mistakes are sometimes referred to as 'common', sometimes (misleadingly) as 'mutual', and sometimes as 'mistakes nullifying consent'. The common law only rarely provided a remedy in such cases (see *7.3.1*), but it has been suggested that equity provides a more extended remedy in some circumstances (see *7.3.3*).

7.3.1 The 'common law' rule
There is no doubt that in some circumstances where both parties entered into a contract believing something to be true which was later found not to be true the contract has been declared void. It is easy to understand the temptation to attribute this fact to the shared mistake of the parties. However, the decisions of the courts suggest that the rule is more complex than that. The leading case is *Bell v Lever Bros* [1932] AC 161.

Bell and another were made executive officers of a subsidiary of Lever Bros.

Subsequently, the subsidiary was closed down and a further contract made between Lever Bros and the executive officers, terminating their appointments in return for substantial compensation. It was then discovered that the officers had engaged in private dealings in breach of their original contracts of employment. At the time of the contracts to terminate their appointments, therefore, Lever Bros could have terminated the contracts for breach, without needing to pay compensation. Lever Bros claimed that the termination contracts were void for mistake.

The House of Lords refused this claim. The leading speech for the majority is generally acknowledged to be that of Lord Atkin. The essential problem facing him was to identify what it was which had separated those cases where shared mistake had invalidated the agreements from those where it had not. One test he formulated was whether the mistake was as to the 'existence of some quality which makes the thing without that quality essentially different from the thing as it was believed to be'. A test of essential difference would leave great scope for judicial discretion in evaluating the facts in mistake cases. It appears to be inconsistent with at least one of the cases on which Lord Atkin relied: *Kennedy v Panama, New Zealand and Australian Royal Mail Co.* (1867) LR 2 QB 580.

> The plaintiff had bought shares in a company on the shared understanding with it that the company had recently won a contract from the New Zealand government for the delivery of mails. The New Zealand government failed to ratify the agreement, and so the shares were worth much less.

The court said that there was nevertheless a contract. Mere difference in quality, however severe, did not destroy the agreement. It is difficult to accept that there was no essential difference in this case. Nevertheless, in *Associated Japanese Bank (International) Ltd v Crédit du Nord SA* [1988] 3 All ER 902, the most recent judicial pronouncement on the doctrine, Steyn J at first instance regarded Lord Atkin's statement about a quality without which the thing was essentially different as forming the *ratio* of the case.

In *Bell* v *Lever Bros* Lord Atkin proposed a second test which appears to be consistent with all the cases on which he relied. He said:

> In these cases I am inclined to think that the true analysis is that there is a contract, but that the one party is not able to supply the very thing, whether goods or services, that the other party contracted to take, and, therefore, the contract is unenforceable by the one if executory, while, if executed, the other can recover back money paid on the ground of failure of the consideration.

He put it another way later, asking: 'Does the state of the new facts destroy the identity of the subject-matter as it was in the original state of facts?' Destruction of the identity of the subject-matter is usually thought to occur in the two types of case outlined below, and all the cases relied on by Lord Atkin fall into one or other category.

7.3.1.1 *Res extincta* The first category consists of cases where the parties contracted on the basis of a shared assumption that something existed when in fact *at the time of contracting* it no longer existed or indeed had never existed. These cases are sometimes referred to as examples of 'initial impossibility', as opposed to 'subsequent impossibility' which is better known as frustration (see *11.4*).

In *Couturier v Hastie* (1856) 5 HLC 673

> a cargo of corn was shipped from a Mediterranean port to England. At a time when the cargo owner believed the corn to be in transit the cargo was sold by him in London to the buyer. It later emerged that deterioration of the cargo had caused the master of the ship to dispose of the cargo (as he was authorised to do: *15.2.4.2*) in North Africa *before* the London contract was entered into. The seller claimed that the buyer should pay the agreed contract price, on the ground that the buyer had purchased the cargo and all inherent risks.

The court rejected this claim. The contract was for the specific cargo, and not just for so many tons of corn, and was void because the purported seller no longer had any corn to sell at the time when the contract was made. He could not therefore be expected to deliver the corn to the intended buyer, who in turn could not be expected to pay the price. It is noticeable that Coleridge J makes no reference in his judgment to mistake. The contract was void because as far as these parties were concerned the subject-matter had ceased to exist before the time of contracting.

A similar rationale lies behind *Galloway v Galloway* (1914) 30 TLR 531 and *Strickland v Turner* (1852) 7 Exch 208. In the former a contract made in contemplation of a non-existent marriage was held to be void. In the latter the court found void a contract for the purchase of an annuity on the life of someone who at the time of contracting was already dead. The *Associated Japanese Bank* case (above) may be regarded as a modern example of this doctrine, as Steyn J notes ([1988] 3 All ER 902, 913).

7.3.1.2 *Res sua* The second category consists of cases where one party is unable to deliver to the other that which the other has contracted to receive because the other is in fact already the owner. The classic example is *Cooper v Phibbs* (1867) LR 2 HL 149.

> Cooper agreed to lease a salmon fishery from Phibbs, both believing the fishery to belong to Phibbs. In fact, Cooper was already entitled to enjoyment of the fishery as a life tenant. That is, although not absolute owner, so that he could not dispose of the fishery, Cooper was effectively owner during his lifetime. He had no need to take the lease, and Phibbs had no power to grant it.

The court found that the contract could be set aside, but allowed Phibbs compensation for money mistakenly spent on the fishery. In *Bell v Lever Bros* [1932] AC 161 Lord Atkin relied on this decision of the House of Lords as an example of mistake operating to nullify a contract. He said expressly that the effect of such a mistake was to make the contract void, and not merely voidable. The significance of this remark will become clear below (see *7.3.3.2*). Lord Atkin did not regard *Cooper* v *Phibbs* as depending on a special equitable doctrine.

7.3.1.3 Total failure of consideration

As far as shared mistakes are concerned, the position would therefore seem to be that such mistakes only nullify contracts where one party is unable to deliver what the other party has contracted to receive, such as to amount to a total failure of consideration. This appears to be the real test used by Lord Atkin, as may be seen from the passage quoted above (see *7.3.1*). In seeking to interpret *Bell* v *Lever Bros* Denning LJ came to a very similar conclusion in *Solle* v *Butcher* [1950] 1 KB 671. He said:

> The correct interpretation . . . is that, once a contract has been made, that is to say, once the parties, whatever their inmost states of mind, have to all outward appearances agreed with sufficient certainty in the same terms on the same subject-matter, then the contract is good unless and until it is set aside for failure of some condition on which the existence of the contract depends . . . The cases where goods have perished at the time of sale, or belong to the buyer, are really contracts which are not void for mistake but are void by reason of an implied condition precedent, because the contract proceeded upon the basic assumption that it was possible of performance.

It is true that there is a subtle conceptual difference between total failure of consideration (see *12.4.2*) and failure of an implied condition precedent. It may be that Lord Denning's explanation is over-elaborate, since each party's consideration is the performance to be supplied, and each party's obligation to perform is conditional upon the other's (see *10.5.1*). Thus it is not necessary to search for any further implied condition. Nevertheless, both Lord Atkin's and Lord Denning's explanations result in only one conclusion: only a shared mistake which renders performance as originally agreed impossible will operate to make a contract void.

7.3.1.4 Mistake of quality

The above conclusion makes clear that mere mistakes of quality, however 'fundamental', do not result in the contract being void. In *Frederick Rose Ltd* v *Wm Pim Jnr & Co.* [1953] 2 QB 450 (the facts are given at *7.2.1*) Denning LJ said that even where both parties are under a mistake, and the mistake is of a fundamental character, the contract is not a nullity. The contract was for the sale and delivery of horsebeans, although both parties were under a mistake as to whether horsebeans were suitable for the plaintiff's purposes. It turned out that they were not, but the contract as agreed was capable of performance, and so was not void.

The classic case of mistake of quality is *Leaf* v *International Galleries* [1950] 2 KB 86.

The plaintiff had bought a painting believed to be by Constable, and represented so to be by the seller. When the plaintiff tried to sell the painting five years later it turned out not to be by Constable. The plaintiff therefore sought to have the original contract overturned.

His action for misrepresentation failed because of the lapse of time (see *9.4.1.1*), and in passing the Court of Appeal reiterated what must now be accepted as the established rule that no alternative remedy for mistake would be available in the case of a mistake only of quality. The fact that the mistake could be described as essential or fundamental did not change the fact that the contract as originally agreed continued to be capable of performance (and indeed had been performed). There was then no scope for the operation of the shared mistake doctrine.

7.3.2 Mistake and breach of warranty
It is important to make clear the relationship between mistake and the express undertakings of the parties. The fact that mere mistake as to quality does not result in the contract being a nullity means that the plaintiff's only remedies lie in establishing either an express term of the contract by which the promisor undertakes to guarantee that the quality in question be present or a pre-contractual representation that the desired quality is present. In these cases, absence of the desired quality will provide a remedy respectively for breach of contract or for misrepresentation. In other words, by their contract, or as a result of the pre-contractual negotiations, the parties have allocated the risk that the quality will not be present to one or the other. In this type of situation it would be inappropriate for the courts to intervene by means of the shared mistake doctrine. This principle is sometimes expressed in terms of the rule that mistake must not be the 'fault' of either party.

In the case of mistakes which go beyond mere quality, and which genuinely make performance of the contract as originally agreed impossible, it is still possible for the risk that the assumed state of facts will not materialise to be allocated to one or other party. Whether such an allocation of the risk of the relevant mistake to one or other of the parties has taken place must be determined before considering the operation of the shared mistake doctrine (*Associated Japanese Bank (International) Ltd* v *Crédit du Nord SA* [1988] 3 All ER 902). Where allocation of the risk has occurred, the fact that the contract as agreed cannot be performed amounts to breach rather than a ground on which the contract may be set aside. In *McRae* v *Commonwealth Disposals Commission* (1951) 84 CLR 377

the plaintiffs and the defendants had contracted for the recovery of a shipwrecked oil tanker, said by the defendants to be lying, still containing oil, on the Jourmaund Reef. The defendants provided a specific map reference allegedly indicating the ship's position. The plaintiffs went to considerable expense in equipping a salvage expedition and sailing to the location indicated by the reference. No tanker could be found, and it became apparent that none had ever been there. The defendants sought to resist the plaintiffs' claim for damages by arguing that the contract had proceeded upon a shared mistake which made the contract void.

Understandably, the High Court of Australia was unwilling to accept that argument, and gave compensation to the plaintiffs. The judgment of the court reads:

> [T]he Commission cannot in this case rely on any mistake as avoiding the contract, because any mistake was induced by the serious fault of their own servants, who asserted the existence of a tanker recklessly and without any reasonable ground. There was a contract, and the Commission contracted that a tanker existed in the position specified. Since there was no such tanker, there has been a breach of contract, and the plaintiffs are entitled to damages for that breach.

Although an Australian decision, the case is entirely consistent with English law, upon which, indeed, it was based. The case has sometimes been regarded as difficult, in that the measure of damages awarded did not correspond to the basis of liability alleged. The plaintiffs only recovered their lost expenses, and not their lost expected profit, which is the more normal measure for breach of contract (see *12.3.1*). It is suggested elsewhere that the case is probably best regarded as one in which the reliance loss was awarded because estimating the lost profit would have been too speculative in the circumstances (see *12.3.2.4*).

7.3.3   Shared mistake in 'equity'
There has been some dissatisfaction with the rule that shared mistakes, falling short of those which make performance of the contract as agreed impossible, do not make the contract void. Shared mistakes as to quality are often fundamental in the sense that in the absence of the mistake the parties would not have entered into the contract. Thus, a mistake over the authenticity of a painting is no doubt one which is central to the contract. It is a very narrow interpretation to say that the contract (for the sale of a specific painting) can still be performed and is therefore not void. As suggested above (see *7.1.1*), the explanation for the narrow interpretation is that any other rule would leave third party interests unduly exposed to disputes between parties to transactions over which the third party has no control. Nevertheless, this explanation raises the possibility that a remedy for shared mistake as to quality might be acceptable if it operated between the original parties to a transaction but did not operate to defeat third party interests. This effect would be achieved if the impact of mistake on the contract was to make it merely voidable rather than void (see *7.1.1*). During his long career on the bench Lord Denning sought to achieve just such a rule.

7.3.3.1   The proposed rule   Denning LJ (as he then was) first re-stated the law relating to shared mistake in *Solle* v *Butcher* [1950] 1 KB 671.

> The defendant agreed to lease a flat to the plaintiff for seven years at £250 per annum. The parties only arrived at this figure for the rent because both believed that the property was not subject to rent control under the Rent Acts. The plaintiff

subsequently discovered that the property was subject to rent control, and the rent payable would only have been £140 per annum. Nevertheless, had the defendant served necessary statutory notices the basic rent could have been increased to approximately £250 to take account of repairs and improvements to the property. The plaintiff sought to recover the overpaid rent over a two-year period, and a declaration that he was entitled to continue in occupation for the rest of the lease at an annual rent of £140. The defendant counter-claimed for the lease to be set aside for mistake.

The Court of Appeal gave the plaintiff the choice between surrendering the lease, or continuing in posession but paying the full amount of rent allowable (i.e. about £250) once the necessary statutory notices had been served.

Denning LJ began his analysis of the law of mistake by referring to the statement of the law by Lord Atkin in *Bell* v *Lever Bros* [1932] AC 161, and by accepting the orthodox interpretation of what Lord Atkin said (see *7.3.1.3*). He went on to suggest, however, that *Bell* v *Lever Bros* is not the whole law on shared mistake. He said that there was a doctrine of equity, not adverted to in the House of Lords in *Bell* v *Lever Bros*, by which a contract may be set aside on terms on the ground of shared mistake, including in circumstances where the mistake is only one of quality. Subsequent commentators have expressed surprise that such a talented House of Lords, addressed by such eminent counsel, should have failed to take account of this equitable doctrine. The most likely explanation is that the doctrine was Lord Denning's own creation. The evidence suggests that that is the case.

7.3.3.2 The evidence The argument in favour of the doctrine rests on a series of cases of which a representative sample of two will illustrate that there is little foundation in precedent for it, however desirable the doctrine may seem. Perhaps the most important case is *Cooper* v *Phibbs* (1867) LR 2 HL 149. It was suggested above (see *7.3.1.2*, where the facts are stated) that this was an example of the *res sua* principle of shared mistake, which Lord Atkin in *Bell* v *Lever Bros* treated as making the contract void. Denning LJ pointed out that Lord Westbury said that the contract was voidable, that the action was brought in the Chancery Court, where, had the contract been void at common law, that would have been the end of the matter, and that the court only set the contract aside after imposing terms on the parties. The circumstantial evidence is impressive, but can be explained consistently with Lord Atkin's interpretation of the case. The essential fact is that the plaintiff had to show that he was really the owner of the fishery in question. As life tenant he was not full legal owner, but had only an equitable interest. Before the Judicature Act 1873 such an interest would only be recognised in the Chancery Court. But the rule of mistake applied by the Chancery Court was the common law rule that a contract to acquire an interest in one's own property is void as impossible of performance. The court imposed terms because the would-be lessor had spent money on the land, and was entitled to be compensated for the improvements made, probably on the basis of some form of proprietary estoppel (see *6.4.2.5*).

The second case relied on by Denning LJ was *Huddersfield Banking Co. Ltd* v *Henry Lister & Son Ltd* [1895] 2 Ch 273.

> The bank was a secured creditor of the defendant company, its security being the business property and all fixed assets. The defendant company was in liquidation, so that a receiver held all the company's assets on trust for the creditors. The plaintiffs agreed to the sale of certain machinery, having determined that it was not fixed. It turned out that it had been improperly loosened, and so should have been treated as fixed assets and thus part of the plaintiff bank's security. The plaintiffs applied to have the agreement set aside.

The reason the bank had to apply to the Chancery Court was that the agreement was made under its auspices as supervisor of the liquidation, but the court treated the agreement not as voidable but as void. It relied on two cases (*Cooper* v *Phibbs* and *Strickland* v *Turner* (1852) 7 Exch 208 — see *7.3.1.1*) which have been analysed as examples of the application of the common law shared mistake rule. The reason why the contract was void in this case was that at the time when the agreement for the sale of the unfixed machinery was made there was no unfixed machinery to sell. There is no suggestion that an equitable doctrine of mistake was operating.

It seems, therefore, that the legal foundation for the proposed equitable doctrine of shared mistake is very insubstantial.

7.3.3.3   The future   Until Lord Denning's proposed doctrine is tested in the House of Lords it would be wrong to place too much reliance on it. On the other hand, there is Court of Appeal authority for it which is binding until overruled by the House of Lords, and the doctrine is not without merit. It is certainly much closer to the continental conception of mistake found in the writings of Pothier (see *7.1*) than the other elements of the narrow English doctrine. It has been followed in a number of subsequent cases. In *Grist* v *Bailey* [1967] Ch 532 Goff J set aside a contract for the purchase of a house believed to be subject to a protected tenancy whereas in fact it was available with vacant possession, making a difference of some £1,400 to the value of the property.

In *Magee* v *Pennine Insurance Co. Ltd* [1969] 2 QB 507 the Court of Appeal set aside a contract of settlement of an insurance claim on the ground that the parties had been mistaken about the insured's entitlement to claim as a result of material misstatements in the original insurance proposal. In this case there was a spirited dissenting judgment from Winn LJ, who found the case indistinguishable on its facts from *Bell* v *Lever Bros*. Nevertheless, the longer *Solle* v *Butcher* goes without adverse comment from the House of Lords the more established the doctrine becomes in our law. It may well be that it fills an important gap in the policing of the fairness of bargains in a way which achieves the desired balance between fairness between the parties and protection of subsequently created third party rights. This was certainly the view of Steyn J in *Associated Japanese Bank (International) Ltd* v *Crédit du Nord SA* [1988] 3 All ER 902, who would have been willing to apply the 'more flexible doctrine of mistake in equity' had he not found the contract to be void for mistake at common law.

7.4   MISTAKE PREVENTING FORMATION OF AGREEMENT

In the case of the previous category of mistakes, objective agreement was present but the mistake, if operative, deprived the agreement reached of any substance. The other significant category of mistakes consists of those mistakes which leave the identification of objective agreement impossible. For that reason they are sometimes called 'mistakes negativing consent'. In other words, the parties may believe that they have a contract, but a court is unable to determine what they have agreed. Such inability may derive either from the fact that it appears that the parties were at cross purposes, or from the fact that the court believes that one of the parties may have allowed the other to deceive himself into entering the 'agreement'. Instances of both kinds of mistake being pleaded successfully are rare, and the conclusion must be that in this area also mistake is a very narrow doctrine unlikely to afford relief.

7.4.1   Cross-purposes mistake

Mistakes of the kind where the parties are at cross-purposes are sometimes referred to as 'mutual mistakes', but the expression is best avoided because it has also been used, especially by nineteenth century courts, to describe shared or common mistakes. The essence of the problem created by cross-purpose mistakes is that although one or both parties may assert that a contract exists, each on terms favourable to himself, on an objective interpretation it is impossible to resolve the ambiguity over what was agreed, so that the only possible conclusion is that there is no contract. In fact, when stated in this way, it is clear that the rule is not peculiar to the law on mistake. It is the same rule as was examined in relation to the formation of agreements and certainty of terms (see 5.6.2). Thus, the famous old case of *Raffles* v *Wichelhaus* (1864) 2 H & C 906 is often treated as a case of cross-purposes mistake (for a full discussion see 5.6.2).

In *Scriven Bros & Co.* v *Hindley & Co.* [1913] 3 KB 564

> two lots taken from the cargo of a single ship were put up for sale by auction. Inspection would have revealed that one was hemp and one was tow, but the auction catalogue did not reveal this. The lots carried the same shipping marks, and the custom of the trade was that different cargoes would not normally have the same marks. A buyer bid for both lots, having inspected the hemp but not the tow, in the mistaken belief that both lots were hemp, thus paying well over the market price for the lot which was tow. He sought to be released from the apparent contract.

After considering the evidence the court allowed the buyer to avoid the contract. The court did not accept that the auctioneer realised the buyer's mistake at the time of the sale, but held that there had been no agreement.

7.4.1.1 The objective test The above decision may become easier to understand once it is remembered that the courts apply the objective test to the question of existence of agreement. The leading case on the meaning of objectivity, *Smith v Hughes* (1871) LR 6 QB 597 (see *5.1.2.2*), involved an allegation of cross-purposes mistake.

> The plaintiff offered to sell oats to the defendant. The defendant examined a sample, and agreed to take the whole consignment. On delivery it was discovered that the oats were 'new', and thus of no use to the defendant who required 'old' oats (that is, the previous season's oats). The defendant then refused to pay, claiming that the contract was void for mistake.

The court rejected this defence. The mere fact that one party had deluded himself into entering into a contract which was of no advantage to him did not enable the court to say that there was no contract. Symmetry between what was offered and what was accepted was apparent from an objective standpoint, and so the contract was upheld.

Applying that objective test to *Scriven Bros & Co. v Hindley & Co.* (above), a reasonable person in the position of the buyer might have been misled into believing that both lots on offer were hemp. Since it was impossible to say what should have been understood from the lots on display, the decision that there was no contract is quite justified.

7.4.1.2 A fault doctrine? It is difficult in relation to these cases to resist the inference that the courts apply a sometimes (but not always) unarticulated fault doctrine. Where a genuine situation of cross-purposes is seen to exist and one party is seen as responsible for provoking the mistake, then the court will decide in favour of the other party. In *Scriven Bros & Co. v Hindley & Co.* [1913] 3 KB 564 the auctioneer who sought to enforce the contract had provoked the mistake by producing a catalogue which was unclear and misleading. The court refused to enforce the contract, AT Lawrence J saying:

> [I]t was peculiarly the duty of the auctioneer to make it clear to the bidder . . . which lots were hemp and which lots were tow. . . . [A] contract cannot arise when the person seeking to enforce it has by his own negligence, or by that of those for whom he is responsible, caused, or contributed to cause, the mistake.

The decision to enforce the alleged contract in *Smith v Hughes* (1871) LR 6 QB 597 can be explained in similar terms. The party seeking to resist enforcement of the contract had contibuted to, or provoked, the mistake, and could not then be heard to say that there was no contract.

7.4.1.3 Refusal of specific performance in equity In some circumstances the remedy for breach of contract is the equitable remedy of specific performance (for detailed treatment see *12.2.2*). Since equitable remedies generally are not available as a matter of right, but only when the court considers it appropriate that they be granted, the courts of equity would sometimes refuse to award specific performance in circumstances in which the objective test of agreement was satisfied. In *Webster* v *Cecil* (1861) 30 Beav 62, for example,

> the objective evidence revealed a contract of sale at a price of £1,250. Since the defendant had already refused to sell at £2,000, it seemed clear that the defendant had made a careless mistake.

The court refused to grant specific performance of the contract against him because it would be inequitable to do so.

Nevertheless, it is probably the case that the principle is of limited value beyond those situations in which the contract would in any case be void under the common law. *Webster* v *Cecil* would be void under the ordinary rule (see below, *7.4.2*). In other cases it is likely that the fault doctrine described above (*7.4.1.2*) would prevent the court finding enforcement inequitable. Thus, in *Tamplin* v *James* (1880) 15 ChD 215:

> the defendant clearly misunderstood what the offer had been which he accepted. He thought he was buying an inn and adjoining gardens, a property well known to him, whereas the sale particulars were clear that the gardens were not included in the property on offer. The defendant had not bothered to examine the particulars of the sale.

At first instance Baggallay LJ granted specific performance against the defendant, saying:

> [W]here there has been no misrepresentation, and where there is no ambiguity in the terms of the contract, the defendant cannot be allowed to evade the performance of it by the simple statement that he has made a mistake. Were such to be the law the performance of a contract could rarely be enforced upon an unwilling party who was also unscrupulous.

7.4.2 Unilateral mistake

In some situations it is said that only one of the parties is mistaken. This is in fact no more than another way of saying that one party's understanding and the objectively observed agreement coincide, and the other party's understanding is out of line. In such circumstances the objectivity principle determines that there is a contract on the objectively observed terms which will be enforced by the courts. However, the courts will ignore the objectivity principle where it appears that the party whose understanding coincides with the objective agreement was aware that the other party was labouring under a mistake and failed to draw his attention to it. Indeed, the courts will go further and assume that a party is aware of the other's mistake where a reasonable person in that party's place would have been so aware. That is why in relation to *Webster* v *Cecil* (1861) 30 Beav 62 (see *7.4.1.3*) it was said that although the case is regarded as an example of equity refusing specific performance the contract would also have been void under the common law. The one party ought to have realised the other's mistake, and drawn it to his attention.

This very limited mistake doctrine applies where:

(a) one party is genuinely mistaken and the mistake is one without which that party would not have entered into the contract;
(b) that mistake ought reasonably to have been known to the other party; and
(c) the mistaken party is not in any way at fault.

Examples of all the conditions being met are rare. In *Hartog* v *Colin & Shields* [1939] 3 All ER 566

> the defendants offered to sell to the plaintiffs certain hare skins at ten pence farthing per pound. They intended to sell at the same price per piece. The trade custom was to sell by the piece, and there are about three pieces to the pound, so that the defendants' offer was at about one third of the normal price. The plaintiffs claimed to have accepted the offer, and to be entitled to damages for breach by the defendants' non-performance based on the contract price as mistakenly offered.

The court found for the defendants. Singleton J made it clear that the crucial element was for the defendant to establish that the plaintiff must have realised the mistake. In many cases the impact of the mistake will be much less clear, in which case the defendant may find it impossible to satisfy the burden of proof.

7.4.3 Mistake of identity
The situation in which unilateral mistake has most often been pleaded is that of mistake of identity. It should be made clear that nearly always such mistake as there is has been provoked by conduct of the other party amounting to fraudulent misrepresentation (see *9.3.1*). The disadvantage of misrepresentation is that its effect is to make the contract merely voidable, so that a remedy may only be sought against the person making the representation. In mistake of identity cases the usual situation is that property is acquired and immediately resold to a third party. The dishonest party (the 'rogue') then disappears, making the misrepresentation remedy worthless, and leaving the original owner trying to recover the property from the third party. If mistake can be proved the contract is void (see *7.1.1*) and the original owner will succeed. In order to avoid this conclusion Lord Denning has suggested that the effect of mistake of identity ought to be to make the contract voidable (see *Lewis* v *Averay* [1972] 1 QB 198). The suggestion has much to recommend it, but cannot as yet be regarded as good law.

7.4.3.1 General rule Applying the unilateral mistake formula (see *7.4.2*) to the particular context, where A believes himself to be contracting with B when in fact he is dealing with C then the contract will be void, provided that C is aware of A's mistake and that A is not at fault in making the mistake. In *Boulton v Jones* (1857) 27 LJ Exch 117

> the defendant sent an order for goods to the shop of Brocklehurst. The same day Brocklehurst had sold his business, including current stock, to the plaintiff. The plaintiff supplied the goods, but the defendant was unwilling to pay for them since he had ordered from Brocklehurst because he had a set-off against him.

The court found for the defendant, because it was not open to the plaintiff to substitute himself for the original offeree without first informing the offeror (in fact, by making a counter-offer). The defendant was not at fault in believing he was dealing with someone else, and the plaintiff was aware that the defendant intended to deal with his predecessor.

Where, however, the mistake is only as to an attribute of the party with whom the contract is made then the contract will not be void. The most common mistake of this kind is a mistake as to creditworthiness. In *King's Norton Metal Co. Ltd v Edridge, Merrett & Co.* (1897) 14 TLR 98

> the rogue established a bogus business called 'Hallam & Co.', using paper with an imposing letterhead which suggested that it was a well-established and thriving firm. The plaintiffs supplied goods to Hallam & Co. on credit, which were immediately sold to the defendants. The plaintiffs claimed that the contract was void for mistake and sought to recover the goods from the defendants.

The court rejected their claim. They had intended to deal with Hallam & Co., with whom they had in fact dealt. There was no ground for suggesting that the process of agreement was negatived by their mistake as to the company's ability or willingness to pay for the goods received.

7.4.3.2 Intention to deal with some other person The greatest difficulty confronting a plaintiff in mistake of identity cases is establishing the intention to deal with an identified person other than the party with whom agreement has apparently been reached. Since in most cases there has been deliberate fraud there is little problem in establishing that the other party knew of the first party's mistake. Where the parties negotiate at a distance it may be easier to establish such a mistake. In *Cundy v Lindsay* (1878) 3 App Cas 459

> the rogue set up business under the name Blenkarn at 37 Wood Street. A very respectable company called Blenkiron & Co. traded at 123 Wood Street. The rogue ordered goods from the plaintiffs, making his signature look as though it read Blenkiron. The plaintiffs sent the goods without payment to 'Blenkiron & Co.' at the rogue's address, and the rogue sold them to the defendants. The success of the plaintiff's plea of mistake, and thus their ability to recover the goods, depended upon whether they intended to deal with whichever firm traded at 37 Wood Street or they intended to deal with Blenkiron & Co.

The court of first instance took the former view, but the Court of Appeal and the House of Lords took the latter, and so the plaintiffs succeeded. It

seems a reasonable inference from the facts that the plaintiffs intended to deal
with a particular firm by name, as opposed to dealing with an address, which
would be of no great significance to them.

Where the parties negotiate in each other's presence, however, it will be
much harder to resist the inference that the allegedly mistaken party intended
to deal with the person present before him, without concern about who he
was. For example, in *Phillips* v *Brooks Ltd* [1919] 2 KB 243

> a rogue went into a jewellery shop and announced that he was Sir George Bullough,
> giving an address. He was allowed to take away a ring without paying for it after
> the plaintiff had checked that the name and address tallied.

The court was unwilling to allow the plaintiff to recover the ring from the
third party to whom it had been pledged, since in its view the contract was
not void. The plaintiff had intended to contract with the person who had been
present in the shop. His identity had not been the factor which had persuaded
the plaintiff to make the contract.

The same rationale explains *Lewis* v *Averay* [1972] 1 QB 198.

> The plaintiff had advertised his car for sale. The rogue offered to buy it. He said
> that he was the well-known actor, Richard Green, and wrote out a cheque, signing
> it 'R.A. Green'. The plaintiff was unwilling to allow him to take the car away until
> the cheque had cleared, but the rogue showed him an official pass for Pinewood
> Studios with his photograph on it in the name of 'Richard A. Green'. At that point
> the plaintiff allowed the rogue to take the car and the log-book. The rogue sold
> the car to the defendant, and his cheque proved to be worthless.

The plaintiff was unable to recover the car from the defendant. Lord Denning's
reasoning in the case has already been explained (see *7.4.3*). Megaw LJ proceeded
by a more orthodox analysis to the same conclusion. He felt that the plaintiff
had not been concerned about the identity of the person with whom he was
dealing. He had been misled by the rogue into believing that he was dealing
with a person of substance, but his mistake had not been such that he intended
to deal with anyone other than the person before him.

In *Ingram* v *Little* [1961] 1 QB 31

> two spinster sisters negotiated for the sale of their car to a rogue masquerading
> as one Hutchinson. At first they would not accept his cheque, but they later relented
> having checked the name, initials and address he had given them against a telephone
> directory entry. They then allowed him to take the car away immediately, and now
> sought to recover it from the innocent third party to whom it had been sold.

The Court of Appeal appears to have been satisfied, on rather flimsy evidence,
that the plaintiff had intended to deal with the person the rogue had pretended
to be rather than with whomever was present before her. In the light of the
very limited check on his identity made by the plaintiff the decision is a little
surprising. There have been ingenious attempts to explain it, but in *Lewis*
v *Averay* the case is treated as anomalous (even though strictly binding on

the court: see *2.1.5.2*). The case can perhaps best be explained as an example of the court's sympathy for the plaintiff outweighing its regard for strict legal principle, and on that basis should be ignored.

7.4.3.3 No fault by the mistaken party Where the plaintiff is able to establish an intention to deal with some person other than the one with whom agreement has apparently been made, he must go on to show that he was not at fault in making the mistake. In most cases this rule results in the onus falling on the plaintiff to show that he took reasonable steps to check the identity of the person with whom he was dealing. The decision in *Phillips* v *Brooks Ltd* [1919] 2 KB 243 (see *7.4.3.2*) may alternatively be explained on this ground. Merely to have checked that Sir George Bullough lived at the address given did not establish that the man in the jewellery shop was in fact Sir George Bullough. In *Ingram* v *Little* [1960] 3 All ER 332 the plaintiff had checked that the person who the rogue purported to be lived at the address given, but no more. It may be that on the particular facts of that case sufficient care had been taken by the plaintiff, but in most cases it will be necessary to conduct some more probative test of identity to avoid falling at the hurdle of being at fault in being mistaken over the identity of the other contracting party.

EIGHT
Policing the bargain

8.1 INTRODUCTION

This chapter considers those rules of the law of contract which say that in specified circumstances a contract, apparently validly made between the parties, is not to be enforced in the manner agreed. The 'policing' function embraces a wide variety of largely unrelated rules which make contracts unenforceable despite the fact that agreement, consideration and contractual intention are, by the standard objective test, all present. Although the conceptual basis for policing varies enormously, and public policy in this area has more than one meaning, certain elements in the method and effect of policing are common, and may be considered by way of introduction.

8.1.1 Methods of policing
The focus in this book will be on the policing of bargains through civil litigation in the ordinary courts between the parties to the contract. It is possible for one party to bring an action seeking a declaration that the contract is unenforceable, but the more usual course of events is for the party who believes the contract to be unenforceable not to perform his side of the agreement. An action for breach of contract is then met by a defence based on the alleged unenforceability of the agreement. Alternatively, one party may bring an action to recover money or property which has been handed over in pursuit of a contract subsequently alleged to be unenforceable.

8.1.1.1 Regulation of contractual activity
It is important to understand that other policing rules exist which do not depend upon civil litigation between the parties. In recent years government agencies have been given powers to regulate contracts. Important controls on traders exist under the Trade Descriptions Act 1968, the Weights and Measures Act 1963 and regulations made under the Fair Trading Act 1973, to name but a small number of the sources of regulatory control. Enforcement lies in the hands of trading standards departments and officers, and the Office of Fair Trading. In addition, ginger groups like the Consumers' Association can bring pressure to bear which amounts to a very effective form of policing. Nevertheless, the main aim of such regulation is not to provide a remedy for the individual litigant but to protect the general class of consumers, to which ultimately we all belong.

Sometimes no individual remedy is available under such legislation (e.g. Trade Descriptions Act 1968). On other occasions, the courts have interpreted protective legislation as giving rise to a civil remedy incidentally to criminal liability imposed (e.g. Factories Act 1961). Under s.35 of the Powers of Criminal Courts Act 1973 a criminal court may make a compensation order in favour of a victim at the same time as imposing criminal liability. Such remedies are not contractual, however, and are beyond the scope of this book.

8.1.1.2 Effects of contravention There are at least five different legal results of a contract being found to be contrary to the policing rules. Unfortunately, there is no golden rule for predicting what the consequence in any case may be. It is essential, therefore, when studying the individual rules, to note the legal consequence attached to each. In some circumstances more than one rule may be applicable, but the plaintiff's interest may be better served by one than by another because of the respective legal consequences. The five main consequences are listed below:

(a) *Contract void*: in this case the contract is treated as never having existed, and no consequences can flow from it.

(b) *Contract voidable*: the contract exists until such time as one of the parties seeks to have it overturned; until such time the contract achieves its intended effect.

(c) *Contract unenforceable by either party*: the contract has its intended legal effect, but neither party will be entitled to a remedy for its breach.

(d) *Contract unenforceable by one party*: where the policing rule is designed to protect a particular category of people the contract cannot be enforced against a member of that category, but it may be enforced by such a member against a non-member whose conduct the rule is intended to control.

(e) *Contract enforceable with changes*: in some circumstances a contract may be rescued from oblivion by careful pruning. The process is known as 'severance' and is discussed in detail below (see *8.7.6*).

8.1.2 Scope of the chapter
Many rules of contract law have a policing element, and it is beyond the scope of this chapter to address them all. Some are more appropriately considered in the context of the other rules to which they generally relate. This chapter addresses those which do not 'belong' anywhere else, namely capacity (in all its forms), duress, undue influence, illegality and the related issue of restraint of trade.

For the sake of completeness it is worth noting here other rules which may be regarded as having some kind of policing role. In the area of mistake, rectification (*7.2.1*), *non est factum* (*7.2.2*) and even the equitable doctrine of shared mistake (*7.3.3*) may be regarded as relating to the policing of bargains rather than to the rules of formation of contracts. The rules on misrepresentation also contribute to the policing of contractual fairness, particularly in relation to pre-contractual statements (see generally Chapter 9). The rules on the control of penalty clauses (*12.3.4.2*) and restricting the use of exclusion and limitation clauses (*5.7* and *10.6*) contribute to policing the fairness of remedies available for breach of contract. The same may be said of those rules which restrict the availability of equitable remedies, such as the 'clean hands' doctrine (*12.2.2.3*).

8.1.3 Basis of intervention

The sketched outline above of the scope of the policing rules reveals a level of judicial intervention in contracts which scarcely seems consistent with the classical doctrine of contracts, which sought to intervene as little as possible in agreements. Of course, nineteenth century courts did intervene on some of the grounds listed above, where it could be shown that consent was not 'real', notably fraudulent misrepresentation and undue influence. But these were limited doctrines, and do not compare with the increasing willingness of courts to intervene on grounds of public policy, irrespective of the intentions of the parties or the reality of consent.

Public policy (see *2.4*) in this field has two branches. In the first place, the courts sometimes act to protect a public interest which is regarded as superior to the interest and intentions of the parties. Thus, agreements between companies to contravene rules against price-fixing may be unenforceable, despite the deliberate intention of each party, because there is a stronger interest in preventing price-fixing, which operates for the good of the whole community. Secondly, there has emerged a relatively new public policy against the enforcement of contracts which are unfair between the parties, even where there is no wider public impact. Thus, the proliferation of special rules governing contracts made by consumers is largely inspired by a desire to protect the individual consumer against the probably large corporation with which he has to deal. Where the corporation has taken unfair advantage of its superior position the courts are increasingly willing to intervene to protect the weaker party. The emergence of this second strand of public policy is an important element in the argument of those who claim that contract law has moved beyond its origin in classical theory, and is now founded on the desire to protect reasonable expectations by imposing duties on the parties independently of their actual agreement.

8.2 CAPACITY OF INDIVIDUALS

The paradigm of contractual capacity is embodied in the living adult of sound mind, and any deviation from that state is cause to question a party's capacity to contract. Problems in relation to the capacity of individuals are generally raised in relation either to the impairment of the mental capacity of the party in question or to their age. The capacity of business organisations and of government agencies is dealt with below (see *8.3* and *8.4*, respectively).

8.2.1 Mentally disordered and drunken persons

Persons of unsound mind cannot, for the most part, enter into contracts, since they are incapable of giving any real consent to an agreement. The exception to this basic rule is that mentally disordered persons may be liable to pay for necessaries. A similar rule applies in the more common case of minors, and the rule is discussed in detail in that context (see *8.2.2.1*).

The main difficulty in this area is to know when the mental disorder is such as to impair the ability to give informed consent. Where a person has been declared a 'patient' for the purposes of Part VII of the Mental Health Act 1983 by the Court of Protection, it seems likely that such a person is absolutely incapable of entering into contracts (cf. *Re Walker* [1905] 1 Ch 160). The authorities relate to previous legislation which is now repealed, but there is no reason to think that the same rule will not apply. In other circumstances, mentally disordered persons are treated as having contractual capacity, but may be able to have a contract set aside at a later date if it can be shown that at the time of contracting the person was incapable of understanding the nature of the actions in question. The contract will only be set aside, however, if the mentally disordered person can satisfy the further condition of demonstrating that the other contracting party knew or ought to have known of the first party's incapacity at the relevant time (see *Imperial Loan Co.* v *Stone* [1892] 1 QB 599).

Imperial Loan Co. v *Stone* was confirmed as good law by the Judicial Committee of the Privy Council in *Hart* v *O'Connor* [1985] 2 All ER 880. Giving the advice of the Committee, Lord Brightman stressed that the validity of a contract entered into by a mentally disordered person who is at the time of contracting ostensibly sane is to be judged by the same standards as apply to a contract made by a person of sound mind. The fact that the contract appears 'unfair' is irrelevant except in so far as it would be relevant to a contract made by a person of sound mind. Thus, the law has to strike a balance between protecting those of limited mental capacity from exploitation, and protecting the integrity of contracts entered into without knowledge of the other party's incapacity. It seems after *Hart* v *O'Connor* that in most cases the latter interest will prevail.

Similar rules apply to contracts entered into by drunken persons, but there is a serious question of fact in each case as to whether the party's reason was sufficiently impaired to invalidate the contract. The presumption is to the contrary, and the courts are unlikely to be sympathetic to a party pleading his own excessive drinking as a reason to escape contractual liability. In the case of both drunks and those suffering from temporary periods of mental disorder, a contract confirmed during sober or lucid moments is valid. From this fact it is clear that the effect of such incapacity is to make the contract merely voidable, not void.

8.2.2 Minors
Much of the case law relating to the incapacity of minors is old, and the importance of this rule has diminished with the reduction of the age of legal majority from 21 to 18 (by s.1 of the Family Law Reform Act 1969). The rules applicable (until recently) derived from a combination of the common law and the Infants Relief Act 1874. They remain applicable to contracts made before June 1987, but thereafter the 1874 Act's provisions do not apply and the Act has been repealed (ss.1 and 4 Minors' Contracts Act 1987).

8.2.2.1 Contracts for necessaries Contracts for necessaries remain subject to the common law rules and are not affected by the Minors' Contracts Act 1987. In the case of goods the law has become complex and removed from reality. In s.3 of the Sale of Goods Act 1979, which provides in statutory form the common law rule on contracts for necessaries, the latter are defined in subs.3 as 'goods suitable to the condition in life of the minor . . . and to his actual requirements at the time of the sale . . .'. Necessaries are more than just what may be needed to keep body and soul together. The classic case is *Nash* v *Inman* [1908] 2 KB 1.

> The defendant, a student, while still a minor purchased clothing, including eleven fancy waistcoats, from the plaintiff. It was established that he already had a supply of clothing sufficient for his condition in life, and so the clothing purchased could not be regarded as necessaries.

The case illustrates the two difficulties inherent in the rule. In the first place, the court has to make invidious judgments about what is appropriate to any particular 'condition of life'. More seriously, a tradesman may well be unable to judge when confronted with a minor wishing to make a purchase whether the good in question is a necessary in the case of the particular minor before him. In cases of doubt, his wisest course would be to refuse to part with the goods except for cash. The Law Commission once suggested that the concept of necessaries should be abandoned and replaced with a more narrowly defined concept of necessities (see Working Paper No. 81). This suggestion was not pursued by the final report (Law Comm. No. 134), and is not implemented by the 1987 Act.

Contracts of employment, or of apprenticeship or for instruction are also treated as contracts for necessaries. They are binding on minors unless more burdensome than beneficial. For example, in *De Francesco* v *Barnum* (1890) 45 ChD 430

> the plaintiff brought an action for an injunction to prevent wrongful interference with his contract (under seal) with a minor who was apprenticed to him as a stage dancer. The contract provided that she was not to be paid unless actually employed by the apprentice master and that she should not accept other employment without his consent. The girl took employment with the defendant, and the plaintiff's action to restrain this interference in the contract of apprenticeship failed because the contract was invalid as unduly burdensome.

It is accepted that such contracts will contain onerous terms for minors. The rule is that such terms must not be out of proportion to the benefit accruing to the minor. Trading contracts do not fall within the class of necessaries, although it is not easy to defend their exclusion. It may rest on the belief that minors are not mature enough to judge the risks inherent in trading.

The liability of minors to pay for necessaries has generally been regarded as resting not on contract but on quasi-contract: it is payment for a benefit received. In that case, an executory contract (i.e. unperformed) for necessaries would be unenforceable against a minor. The wording of s.3 of the Sale of Goods Act 1979 is consistent with that conclusion. In the case of contracts of employment, however, the rule may be different. In *Roberts* v *Gray* [1913] 1 KB 520

> the defendant entered a contract to work for the plaintiff in what would today be called a billiards 'circus'. The defendant was still a minor. Shortly before the tour began the defendant withdrew, in breach of his contract. The plaintiff brought an action on the contract to recover expenses incurred in preparation for the tour.

The contract was found to be enforceable against the minor although still executory.

8.2.2.2 Contracts valid unless repudiated at majority

Certain contracts made by minors are voidable, but become valid when the minor attains majority unless repudiated at that time. The rules governing these contracts are unaffected by the Minors' Contracts Act 1987, and they continue to be governed by the common law rules. The most common types of contract within this category are contracts to acquire either shares in a company or an interest in land. In each case, what is acquired is an enduring benefit to which certain obligations attach. To be effective, the repudiation must be accompanied by a surrender of the interest in question (see *North Western Ry* v *McMichael* (1850) 5 Ex 114). The contract must be repudiated either before attaining majority or within a reasonable time of attaining majority, although what is a reasonable time is a question of fact in each case (see *Edwards* v *Carter* [1893] AC 360). Money actually paid is not recoverable in such a case except where there has been a total failure of consideration (see *Steinberg* v *Scala (Leeds) Ltd* [1923] 2 Ch 452).

8.2.2.3 Other contracts with minors

Contracts which are not for 'necessaries' and which are not 'voidable' are unenforceable against the minor. However, the rule exists to protect minors and not to prevent contracts, and so such contracts are enforceable at the suit of the minor (*Bruce* v *Warwick* (1815) 6 Taunt 118). It is sometimes said that specific performance is not available to a minor, but that rule was probably based on the principle of mutuality and the fact that a contract cannot be specifically enforced against a minor (*Lumley* v *Ravenscroft* [1895] 1 QB 683). The principle of mutuality has recently been explained (*12.2.2.3*) so that it no longer requires the possibility of specific performance against both parties, provided the party seeking specific performance has entirely performed his side of the contract. On that basis, a minor who has wholly executed the performance due from him ought now to be able to obtain specific performance against the other party in circumstances where the remedy would otherwise be available.

Since the repeal of s.2 of the Infants Relief Act 1874 by the Minors' Contracts Act 1987, it has become possible for the minor's immunity under such contracts to be removed by ratification of the contract by the minor upon reaching majority. Express ratification, in the absence of duress or undue influence, is likely to present few problems. It may be anticipated, however, that nice questions of fact will be raised by the question of whether ratification may be inferred from conduct.

Although these contracts are unenforceable against the minor, property may pass from the minor to the other party under them (*Chaplin* v *Leslie Frewin (Publishers) Ltd* [1965] 3 All ER 764). Moreover, the minor may not recover property or money which has passed under an unenforceable contract, except in circumstances where such recovery would be available to a person of full contractual capacity, such as total failure of consideration. Since property also passes to the minor under such contracts, in the case of contracts for goods such failure will not occur (cf. *Rowland* v *Divall* [1923] 2 KB 500). By contrast, there is the possibility of recovering property which has passed under the unenforceable contract from the other party to the minor (see *8.2.2.5*).

8.2.2.4 Misrepresentation of age   A difficult problem arises where the minor represents that he is of full age. The law's policy of protecting minors still applies, so that the contract is unenforceable. It would be undesirable, however, for the minor to take advantage of his own wrongdoing. A rule of equity therefore requires the minor to restore goods acquired. The same rule cannot provide for the repayment of money loaned. In *Leslie (R) Ltd* v *Sheill* [1914] 3 KB 607

> when still a minor the defendant had borrowed £400 from the plaintiff moneylenders, but had misrepresented that he was of the age of contractual capacity. The plaintiffs brought an action to recover the principal sum and interest.

The plaintiffs were unable to obtain restitution because that would have been equivalent to enforcing the contract and would be contrary to the Infants Relief Act 1874 (*8.2.2.1*). Where goods are acquired and sold the proceeds of sale may be recovered by a tracing remedy (see *Stocks* v *Wilson* [1913] 2 KB 235).

8.2.2.5 Restitutionary remedy against minors   Before the Minors' Contracts Act 1987 restitution was available against a minor in the case of fraud (*8.2.2.4*) or in quasi-contract for so-called 'waiver of tort' (*Bristow* v *Eastman* (1794) 1 Esp 172). These rules are preserved by s.3(2) of the 1987 Act, but are less favourable to a party seeking restitution against a minor than the new discretionary rule introduced by s.3(1). It will particularly benefit traders who supply goods to minors on credit, and who are then unable to obtain payment because the contract is unenforceable by virtue of the minor's age. Under s.3(1) the court may order the minor to return the property acquired if it is just and equitable to do so. 'Property' in this section is not defined, and so it is not clear whether it includes money obtained under such a contract. However, s.3(1) applies to property acquired or any property representing it, and if property acquired has been converted into something else it is likely to have been converted into money. If that may be recovered under the Act, it would be strange if money acquired directly cannot be. Another difficulty with the notion of property representing property acquired under the contract is where the proceeds are money, and it has been paid into a bank account from which withdrawals have been made, or where other goods have been purchased whose value is greater than merely the proceeds of the property originally acquired. No doubt the resolution of these problems will be clouded by the exercise of the court's discretion over whether to order restitution at all.

8.3 CAPACITY OF BUSINESS ORGANISATIONS

8.3.1 General

The common law rule of contractual capacity derived from a time when trade was almost entirely carried out by individuals, the exception being a small number of trading corporations created by Royal Charter. The commercial development engendered by the industrial revolution gave rise to many groups of people working together as businesses and wishing to trade as a single entity. This change in the nature of trade meant that the common law capacity rule was inadequate. The law therefore developed separate capacity rules for business organisations. The rules vary in their application according to whether the organisation in question is a corporation. That is, if the organisation has been constituted a legal entity independent of the identity of its respective members (i.e. *incorporated*), then special rules apply. These rules relate to corporate personality (*8.3.2*) and the '*ultra vires*' doctrine (*8.3.3*). If the organisation is not incorporated the rules of partnership apply (*8.3.4*).

8.3.2 Corporate personality

At common law incorporation could only be achieved by Royal Charter. In response to the need for this kind of business organisation Parliament began to provide means of incorporation, at first by special Act of Parliament, but later by compliance with formalities laid down by general Act. By far the most important form of incorporation exists under the Companies Act 1985, on which this section will concentrate. Other special forms of incorporation exist for building societies, charitable trusts and industrial and provident societies.

By the process of incorporation the company obtains separate legal personality. By s.13 of the Companies Act 1985, compliance with certain registration formalities entitles the company to a certificate of incorporation (s.13(1)), and from the date on the certificate it is a body corporate capable of exercising all the functions of an incorporated company (s.13(3) and (4)). The crucial effect of incorporation is to make a clear distinction between the members of the corporation and the corporation itself. This effect was confirmed by the House of Lords in *Salomon* v *A Salomon & Co. Ltd* [1897] AC 22.

> The appellant had converted his business into a limited company, to which he, his wife and his children were the subscribers. He sold the business to the company for more than it was really worth. One year later the company went into liquidation, and there were insufficient funds to pay unsecured creditors.

The Court of Appeal refused to treat the company as a legal personality separate from that of the appellant, but the House of Lords disagreed. Lord Macnaghten said:

> The company is at law a different person altogether from the subscribers to the memorandum; and, though it may be that after incorporation the business is precisely the same as it was before, and the same persons are managers, and the same hands receive the profits, the company is not in law the agent of the subscribers or trustee for them.

8.3.2.1 Reasons for incorporation The principal form of incorporation for business purposes is the limited company. By s.74(2)(d) of the Insolvency Act 1986, in the case of the winding-up of a company limited by shares no member need contribute to the company's debts and liabilities beyond the amount unpaid on shares held. Alternatively, if the company is limited by guarantee, by s.74(3) of the 1986 Act no contribution is required beyond the amount undertaken to be contributed by way of guarantee. Thus, a significant advantage of incorporation is to protect the members (shareholders) from the risks of operation of the business. By separating the assets of the company from those of the shareholders the latter do not face unlimited liability in the event of collapse of the company. Apart from the obvious personal advantage to the shareholder from limited liability, it operates as an incentive to trade and investment which is essential for the health of the economy. Limited liability allows entrepreneurism without exposure to excessive risk. The benefit of limited liability is only lost if the membership of the company is allowed to fall below two (s.24 CA 1985) or if the shareholder has been a party to fraudulent trading by the company (s.213 Insolvency Act 1986).

Incorporation also provides a degree of stability in the business organisation independent of changes in the membership. Thus, although the management, staff or shareholders of the organisation may change from time to time, no hiatus in the trading of the company is caused because its legal personality is unaffected by the changes.

8.3.2.2 Lifting the veil of incorporation It is traditional to describe the separation between the personality of the company and that of its members as the 'veil of incorporation'. It is also traditional to list certain exceptions to the separate personality principle under which the courts are said to 'lift the veil' of incorporation, although some commentators believe that the so-called exceptions are not in fact all properly regarded as exceptional, and that instances of lifting the veil are in fact rare (see, for example, Mayson, French and Ryan, *Company Law*, 10th ed., Blackstone Press, 1993–4, para. 5.2.2). There is no doubt that in the circumstances detailed below the courts are obliged to consider the attitudes or conduct of the individuals behind the company. The precise nature of this consideration need not concern us.

(a) *Illegality or fraud.* The courts will not allow corporate personality to be a cloak for fraud or illegality. In *Gilford Motor Co. Ltd* v *Horne* [1933] Ch 935 the defendant had formed a company with the intention of avoiding the consequences of a restrictive covenant he had entered into in his personal capacity.

The Court of Appeal enforced the covenant against the defendant and against the company. Lord Hanworth MR described the company as 'a device, a stratagem, . . . a cloak or a sham', and clearly felt it necessary to lift the corporate veil to prevent the defendant's fraud.

(b) *Ascertaining actions or intentions.* The corporation is an abstract legal personality. The law often attributes consequences to actions or intentions, and corporations are incapable without human intervention of either. In such cases the court must look beyond the legal entity to the individuals who control the company's actions and intentions. In *H.L. Bolton (Engineering) Co. Ltd v T.J. Graham & Sons Ltd* [1957] 1 QB 159 Denning LJ said that the state of mind of a company is to be found by examining the state of mind of its managers. In the case of negligence liability, the fault of the manager is the personal fault of the company. In the case of criminal liability, the guilty mind of the directors or managers makes the company itself guilty. While this is to go behind the corporate personality it does not disregard it, since it is the company which is made liable. It should be noted, however, that in *R v McDonnell* [1966] 1 All ER 193 Nield J ruled that the accused could not be guilty of conspiracy with two companies when he was director of both and the only person responsible for their actions, so that in effect he had 'conspired' with himself.

(c) *Compliance with formalities.* Legal personality is only created when certain formal requirements have been met. It is not surprising, therefore, that the Companies Act 1985 imposes personal liability for failure to meet the requirements. The formalities concerned are: allowing the number of members to fall below two (s.24 CA 1985); failure to comply with share capital rules (s.117 CA 1985); carrying on business without using the company's name (s.349 CA 1985).

8.3.2.3 Groups of companies An increasingly common phenomenon is the organisation of companies in groups, with subsidiaries wholly or partially owned by a parent company. Although these companies often operate as a single economic unit the approach of English law is to treat them as separate legal entities, with the parent company protected by the veil of incorporation surrounding the subsidiaries. The group will only be treated as a single legal entity if the operations of parent and subsidiary are so integrated that the subsidiary has no real independence. There is a well-known and useful six-part test of independence provided by Atkinson LJ in *Smith, Stone & Knight Ltd v Birmingham Corporation* [1939] 4 All ER 116. The effect of not lifting the corporate veil in the case of a group of companies may sometimes be to allow the parent company to run a risky venture through a subsidiary and, if it fails, to escape having to pay the creditors. For example, in *Multinational Gas & Petrochemical Co. v Multinational Gas & Petrochemical Services Ltd* [1983] 2 All ER 563 three international oil companies formed the plaintiff company to operate a joint venture to transport, store and sell liquified gas. For tax reasons the same three companies formed the defendant company to provide management services and business and financial advice for the plaintiff company and to act as its agent. The plaintiff company went into liquidation, allegedly as a result of a highly speculative venture entered into on the negligently given advice of the defendant company, and as a result of the negligence of the three oil companies in failing to realise the inherent risks of the venture. The liquidator sought to bring an action against the defendant company and against the three international oil companies who were the plaintiff company's shareholders. The question arose whether the latter were proper parties to the action.

The Court of Appeal held that the oil companies were not proper parties to the action on the ground that the decisions and acts of the shareholders were to be treated as the acts of the company itself. The plaintiff company could not complain about what were in law its own acts. There are reforms proposed under the EC programme of harmonisation of company law for the treatment of groups of companies (see especially the 7th and 9th Directives), but for the time being the law must be regarded as depending upon the basic *Salomon* principle.

8.3.3   Contractual capacity of incorporated companies

The Companies Act 1989 introduced an amendment to s.35(1) of the Companies Act 1985 which came into force in February 1991. Under the old law, a company lacked the capacity to enter into contracts which were inconsistent with its *objects* as set out in its memorandum of association. Such a contract was said to be *ultra vires* the company. Originally, third parties contracting with the company were deemed to know what the objects clause said, and so were not able to enforce such *ultra vires* contracts. Protection of third parties was introduced in 1972, but it was thought not to go far enough, particularly because it only applied where the third party acted in good faith (which was extremely difficult to define); and it appeared only to apply to decisions made by all the directors together, which in large and medium-sized companies would only occur in respect of major transactions. The 1989 Act maintains the *ultra vires* rule within the company (that is, in respect of relations between the directors and the shareholders) but removes its effect in respect of relations between the company and third parties. Although the third party must still deal in good faith with the company, this requirement will not be breached by the mere knowledge that the transaction is beyond the powers of the company. Moreover, the new wording of s.35 of the Companies Act 1985 ('an act done by a company' as opposed to 'any transaction decided on by the directors') appears to suggest that protection will be available to third parties in respect of decisions in which not all directors participated. In summary, as far as the law of contract is concerned, the *ultra vires* doctrine of company law is unlikely to present problems in the future.

8.3.4 Partnership

Where a business organisation has not gone through the process of incorporation it is usually referred to as a partnership. Its essential characteristic is that it has no legal existence separate from that of its members. Thus the business is in fact carried on by the partners. The members are bound by contracts made by the business under the ordinary rules of the law of agency as principals and agents of each other (see generally Chapter 15). For example, in *Cox v Hickman* (1860) 8 HLC 268

> a trader assigned property to trustees (who represented the trader's business creditors), so that the trustees could supervise his trading and thus ensure that the creditors would be paid out of the profits. The question arose whether there was a partnership between the trader and his creditors.

The House of Lords found that there was no partnership, and one reason for this finding was that the creditors were not bound as principals by contracts made by the trader; that is, the relationship of agency was not present. The only concession to the existence of the business as an entity is that the name of the firm may be used in documents and instruments as a collective description of the members, and under RSC Ord. 81, r.1 legal action may be brought by or against the partnership in the name of the firm, and judgments may be enforced against the firm's property. It was once a major advantage of partnerships that they were not subject to the *ultra vires* rule, but that rule is now of very limited impact (see *8.3.3.2*).

Of fundamental importance is that the liability of the partners, except in the case of limited partnerships (of which there are very few), is unlimited. The contractual liability of partners is joint (*Kendall v Hamilton* (1879) 4 App Cas 504). That is, each partner is liable on the contract for the entire obligation in a single action, so that release of one partner from the obligation operates to release all the others, and an unsatisfied judgment against one partner prevents further action to recover the loss from other partners. Although this rule may cause hardship, the ability to bring an action against the partners under the firm's name enables a plaintiff to make sure that all the partners are 'in court' in the one action brought. Moreover, s.3 of the Civil Liability (Contribution) Act 1978 abolishes the rule that action against one person who is jointly liable prevents further action against others, who are jointly liable with the first, to recover losses not satisfied by the first action. By s.1 of the 1978 Act a partner held liable may recover contribution from the other partners.

8.4 CAPACITY OF THE CROWN AND PUBLIC AUTHORITIES

It has sometimes been said that the Crown and other public authorities lack contractual capacity. In part this view was caused by confusion between the absence of liability in civil suits on the part of the Crown and the more general rule on contractual capacity. The Crown's immunity from suit, however, did not derive from any lack of capacity. It resulted from a constitutional fiction whereby the personal immunity of the sovereign was extended to the Crown as a political entity responsible for the government of the country. Crown immunity in this extended sense was effectively ended, except in the case of action by Crown servants, by the Crown Proceedings Act 1947.

The Crown and other public authorities lack capacity to make contracts which limit their future choices of political action. Thus, the government cannot contract not to take any decision which may subsequently become necessary. The only difficulty of this rule is in drawing the line between ordinary commercial contracts made by the Crown and those unduly fettering future action. The decision to buy helicopters from one company may effectively mean that the government cannot buy helicopters from any other company for some time to come! Such a contract would nevertheless be within the Crown's contractual capacity. The type of contract outside its capacity is demonstrated by *Rederiaktiebolaget Amphitrite* v *R* [1921] 3 KB 500.

> The British legation in Stockholm promised the owners of a ship that if it sailed to England with a certain cargo it would be allowed free passage. In the event free passage was not given.

Rowlatt J said that such a promise was unenforceable because the Crown lacked the capacity to bind itself in that way.

8.5 DURESS

8.5.1 The limited early doctrine

The common law always accepted that some forms of coercion in the making of contracts resulted in the victim of the coercion being afforded a remedy. Either the contract would be set aside, or money paid could be recovered. However, the forms of coercion recognised as having such an effect were very limited. There was no doubt that duress to the person had such an effect, whether it took the form of threatened or actual violence (*Barton* v *Armstrong* [1976] AC 104) or a threat of imprisonment (*Williams* v *Bayley* (1886) LR 1 HL 200), although the latter rule only arose after the intervention of equity. As such the doctrine was of little significance, since the number of cases of duress to the person has always been small.

It was once thought that duress to goods would not result in any ensuing contract being set aside (*Skeate* v *Beale* (1840) 11 A & E 983). However, rather inconsistently, money paid under duress of goods could be recovered (*Maskell* v *Horner* [1915] 3 KB 106). In recent years the duress to goods rule has been roundly condemned by commentators. At the same time, the courts, led by Lord Denning, have paid far greater attention to the requirement of fairness in bargaining. Thus, in *D & C Builders* v *Rees* [1966] 1 QB 617 (see *6.4.3.3*) Lord Denning MR refused to apply the promissory estoppel doctrine to enforce a promise to accept a payment in final settlement of a debt, on the express ground that the promise had been extracted by undue pressure and intimidation. The result of these developments has been the emergence of a new and potentially more significant doctrine of economic duress.

8.5.2 Economic duress

The idea that mere economic duress might be a ground upon which a contract could be set aside was first canvassed by Kerr J in *Occidental Worldwide Investment Corp.* v *Skibs A/S Avanti, The Siboen and The Sibotre* [1976] 1 Lloyd's Rep 293. The typical situation raising the possibility of action for economic duress is where one party threatens breach of contract unless the contract is renegotiated, and the other agrees rather than face disastrous consequences as a result of breach. The area is fraught with difficulty, however, since companies who deal with each other on a regular basis will often agree quite voluntarily to renegotiate a contract, and such agreements are the essence of the level of cooperation necessary in the business world. It would be unfortunate if they were threatened by the new doctrine. On the other hand, changes to the law relating to consideration, particularly in the area of variation of commercial contracts (see *Williams* v *Roffey Bros & Nicholls (Contractors) Ltd* [1990] 1 All ER 512; *6.3.2 et seq.*), are likely to make the need for such a doctrine all the greater. In the past, contract changes achieved by oppression could be resisted on the formal ground of absence of consideration. It will now be necessary to provide substantive controls over the problem. The modern development of the law relating to economic duress was reaffirmed by its application by the House of Lords in *Dimskal Shipping Co. SA* v *ITXF, The Evia Luck* [1991] 4 All ER 871.

8.5.2.1 Establishing economic duress In *The Siboen and The Sibotre* [1976] 1 Lloyd's Rep 293 Kerr J identified two questions central to the determination of the existence of economic duress. Did the victim protest at the time or shortly thereafter? Did the victim regard whatever settlement was reached as closing the transaction in question, or did he seek to reopen it? The application of these tests is well demonstrated by *North Ocean Shipping Co. Ltd* v *Hyundai Construction Co. Ltd, The Atlantic Baron* [1979] QB 705.

> The defendants threatened to breach a ship construction contract unless the plaintiffs agreed to pay 10 per cent on top of the contract price. Consideration for this agreement was furnished by the defendants agreeing to provide an additional letter of credit as security of performance. The plaintiffs agreed to the deal because if the ship had not been available they would have lost a very valuable charter. Eight months after delivery of the ship the plaintiffs attempted to recover the overpayment.

The court ruled that the defendants' demand would have amounted to economic duress making the contract voidable, but the failure to protest or reopen the issue for such a long time amounted to constructive affirmation of the contract. The plaintiff was no longer entitled to a remedy based on duress.

The tests proposed by Kerr J in *The Siboen and The Sibotre* and applied by Mocatta J in *The Atlantic Baron* reflect a cautious expansion of the duress doctrine by the courts. The victim of alleged duress is still left with a difficult choice when deciding what course to follow. To sit back and fail to perform, relying on the duress as a defence to any action by the other party, runs the risk of being interpreted as affirmation of the contract. On the other hand, if the danger perceived by the victim is sufficient to persuade him to enter the contract despite its disadvantageous terms, it will also very likely be the case that the victim will not want to risk causing the other party to abandon performance by making an ill-timed protest. It seems that the courts will have to accept that the economic duress itself will prevent anything but mild protest until performance is complete. At that time the victim will have to take almost immediate action to avoid constructive affirmation of the contract. For a good example of a case where the doctrine was successfully invoked, see *Atlas Express Ltd* v *Kafco (Importers & Distributors) Ltd* [1989] 1 All ER 641.

8.5.2.2 The basis of the doctrine The economic duress doctrine was first approved by the judges of the House of Lords in a Privy Council case: *Pao On* v *Lau Yiu Long* [1979] 3 All ER 65 (see *6.3.5.5*).

> The plaintiffs agreed to sell a building which was under construction to the defendants. The transaction was to be achieved by an exchange of shares. In order to provide security for the plaintiffs, it was agreed that they would receive 60 per cent of the shares in the defendants' company for a year at a price of $1 per share, and sell them back to the defendants at $2.50 per share. Because the shares were to be sold at a fixed price there was a possibility that if the value of the shares were to go up it would result in a windfall profit to the defendants. Realising this, the plaintiffs threatened to breach the contract unless the security arrangement were cancelled and replaced by an indemnity contract, which would provide the same protection for the plaintiffs without creating the possibility of the windfall profit. Fearing delays, and a loss of confidence in their company if the deal were not completed, the defendants agreed to the plaintiffs' demands. In fact the shares lost value so that the plaintiffs' profit was less than anticipated, and they sued on the indemnity contract.

Lord Scarman, giving the advice of the Privy Council, said that there was nothing wrong in principle in recognising economic duress as a factor making contracts voidable. The essence of the rule, he said, was that 'there must be a coercion of will such that there was no true consent . . . it must be shown that the contract entered into was not a voluntary act'. It was essential to distinguish between mere commercial pressure, which is an everyday incident of the hard-nosed bargaining which goes on in the business world, and duress. Where the line is to be drawn is a queston of fact in each case, but factors to be taken into account include: whether the victim protested; whether any alternative course was open to the victim, such as an adequate legal remedy; whether the victim was independently advised; and whether after entering the contract the victim took steps to avoid it. In the present case the defendants coolly analysed the options and took a commercial decision that the risk to their company of non-performance was greater than the risk of the need to pay an indemnity. This did not constitute duress.

The decision in *Pao On* v *Lau Yiu Long* is not without critics. It perpetuates the theory adopted in earlier duress cases that the doctrine only operates to avoid contracts where there was no true consent. It has been cogently argued that the situation of duress is not one in which consent is absent. On the contrary, duress involves positively and consciously choosing between two evils (cf. Atiyah, (1982) 98 LQR 197). There is no doubt that the decision is intentional and in that sense the consent is voluntary. In the criminal law the House of Lords has been clear in saying that the defence of duress does not depend upon the absence of a voluntary act, but rather depends upon intentional submission in the face of no other practical alternative (*Lynch v DPP for Northern Ireland* [1975] AC 653). So, in the law of contract, duress would provide good reason for the court to intervene, presumably on the ground of the public policy of fairness between the parties (see *8.1.3*). Duress would not, however, negate the existence of consent. This reasoning is borne out by the fact that duress has always been regarded as making a contract merely voidable, and not void (*Whelpdale's Case* (1605) 5 Co Rep 119a), as is confirmed by the recent economic duress cases.

In *Universe Tankships Inc. of Monrovia v International Transport Workers' Federation, The Universe Sentinel* [1983] 1 AC 366 Lords Diplock and Scarman admitted that duress in contract law does not involve the destruction of will but intentional submission to the inevitable. Although they came to differing conclusions on the facts they were also agreed that duress consists of two ingredients. There must be coercion or compulsion of the will, and that must be brought about by pressure which the law regards as illegitimate.

Their formulation of the economic duress test is subject to the same criticism as can be made of *Pao On v Lau Yiu Long*, that the tests proposed are vague and provide little guidance to those contemplating litigation or attempting to advise clients. It is far from clear where the line between legitimate and illegitimate pressure is to be drawn. Nor is it clear how much resistance the victim of duress must show or how unrealistic any alternative courses of action must be. These issues were not tested in *The Universe Sentinel*, since the union involved conceded that there had been compulsion, and the issue of the legitimacy of the pressure exerted hinged upon the interpretation of the Trade Union and Labour Relations Act 1974. Similarly, in *Dimskal Shipping Co SA v ITWF, The Evia Luck* [1991] 4 All ER 871 the decision turned upon whether conduct, regarded by statute as legitimate in the country where it occurred (Sweden), was legitimate for the purposes of the English law of contract. These cases probably cannot be regarded as useful guides to the general law of contract, since they are set against the very particular context of trade disputes. For the doctrine of economic duress to become a significant weapon in policing the fairness of contractual bargaining the limits of its applicability must be more clearly defined by the courts. For the moment it seems that a commercial concern engaged in apparently arm's-length bargaining will find it very difficult to satisfy all the conditions of the doctrine's operation.

8.6 UNDUE INFLUENCE

8.6.1 General: the requirement of 'domination'

Undue influence is an equitable doctrine which provides relief from contracts entered into under improper pressure not amounting to duress. The courts will only intervene where there is some relationship between the parties which has been exploited and abused to gain an unfair advantage. It is clear that the basis of the court's intervention is the public policy of fairness in contract bargaining (*Goldsworthy* v *Brickell*, [1987] 2 All ER 853, 856 per Nourse LJ; see *8.1.3*). The manner in which the relationship is exploited may be either domination of one party by the other or abuse of a particular duty of confidence owed by one party to the other, usually by virtue of some office e.g. by a solicitor to his client. In *Goldsworthy* v *Brickell* the Court of Appeal rejected the argument that, as a result of the decision of the House of Lords in *National Westminster Bank Ltd* v *Morgan* [1985] 1 All ER 821, the doctrine of undue influence required at all times domination of one party by the other. Domination was no more than one form of undue influence, which could equally well be established by showing abuse of a relationship of confidence falling short of domination. Indeed, according to Nourse LJ, the party seeking to have the contract set aside does not have to prove dishonesty or conscious abuse. On the other hand, it is a requirement in any allegation of undue influence whether based on actual undue influence or on a presumption thereof, that the transaction be to the manifest disadvantage of the plaintiff (*Bank of Credit and Commerce International SA* v *Aboody* [1990] 1 QB 923). The same case also stands as authority for the proposition that there must be a causal relationship between the undue influence and the manifest disadvantage. In this case, the Court of Appeal (having decided the case on other grounds) indicated that it would not have given the relief sought, because it was persuaded that the complainant would have entered into the transactions in any event.

Abuse of the duty of confidence is today the more common type of undue influence, and is likely to remain so as the distinction between duress and undue influence by domination becomes increasingly blurred. This blurring is caused partly by the fact that in the case of domination, as in the case of duress, no special relationship of confidence need be shown in order to succeed. Thus, in *Morley* v *Loughnan* [1893] 1 Ch 736 action was brought by executors to recover £140,000 paid by the deceased to a member of a religious sect. Wright J, finding for the plaintiffs, said that there was no need to show a special relationship between deceased and defendant, because 'the defendant took possession, so to speak, of the whole life of the deceased, and the gifts were . . . the effect of that influence and domination'. Many of the domination cases involve dubious spiritual advisers (cf. *Allcard* v *Skinner* (1887) 36 ChD 145; see *8.6.4*). It would be wrong to think that the line of domination cases has come to an end while religious cults continue to attract those whose hearts rule their heads.

8.6.2 Abuse of duty of confidence

Abuse of a duty of confidence as a form of undue influence depends upon the existence of such a duty, and the duty only arises in the course of a special relationship as defined by law, such as parent and child, solicitor and client, doctor and patient. There is apparently no exhaustive list of such special relationships, but relations between husband and wife are expressly excluded (*Midland Bank plc* v *Shephard* [1988] 3 All ER 17). On the other hand, a husband may exercise actual undue influence over the wife (and, presumably, vice versa), and, it has been suggested, may be the agent of a third party such as a bank in procuring a particular transaction by means of undue influence (authority for both propositions can be found in *Bank of Credit & Commerce International SA* v *Aboody* [1990] 1 QB 923). A third party would similarly be affected if it had notice that the transaction it sought to enforce had been procured by undue influence (*Avon Finance Co. Ltd* v *Bridger* [1985] 2 All ER 281). These two lines of argument were considered in *Barclays Bank plc* v *O'Brien* [1992] 4 All ER 983, and the agency approach to depriving creditor banks of security in husband and wife cases was rejected as artificial. Nevertheless, the Court of Appeal was unanimous in the belief that married women as a class required some form of protection against husbands and financial institutions which combined to persuade such women to put their own interests at risk in guaranteeing the debts of their husbands. Scott LJ found that security given in such circumstances would be unenforceable by the creditor

> if (i) the relationship between the debtor and the surety and the consequent likelihood of influence and reliance was known to the creditor; and (ii) the surety's consent to the transaction was procured by undue influence or material misrepresentation on the part of the debtor or the surety lacked an adequate understanding of the nature and effect of the transaction; and (iii) the creditor, whether by leaving it to the debtor to deal with the surety or otherwise, had failed to take reasonable steps to try and ensure that the surety entered into the transaction with an adequate understanding of the nature and effect of the transaction and that surety's consent to the transaction was a true and informed one.

It must be questioned whether today it is appropriate to develop a rule which protects married women, but does not apply equally to married men.

Part of the difficulty in this area is that there are some half-way relationships where it is a question of fact in each case whether a special relationship of confidence exists. In the recent leading case on undue influence, *National Westminster Bank Ltd* v *Morgan* [1985] 1 All ER 821 the facts were as follows:

> the husband and wife jointly owned their home, and the husband was unable to meet the mortgage repayments. He arranged refinancing of the house purchase with the bank, in exchange for a charge over the house to the bank. The bank manager called at the house for the wife to execute the charge, without providing for her to be independently legally advised. The wife insisted that the charge should not extend to her husband's business liabilities, since she had no faith in his business ventures, and she was incorrectly but not fraudulently informed that the charge did not cover such liability. Their financial problems continued, although the husband's business was not in debt to the bank. Then the husband died, and the bank obtained an order for possession of the house against the wife, who appealed against that decision.

Lord Scarman suggested that the relationship between bank and customer may be one of confidence, but that in the particular situation the bank 'had not crossed the line' into the realm of confidence. Where the relationship between bank and customer is the ordinary commercial one, and not a special relationship of confidence, it must be remembered that the bank will still owe an ordinary duty of care to give accurate advice which may be the basis of liability towards a customer (see *Cornish* v *Midland Bank Ltd* [1985] 3 All ER 513).

Tate v *Williamson* (1866) LR 2 ChApp 55 serves as a good example of this kind of undue influence outside the difficult area of husband and wife cases.

> An improvident student consulted his cousin about selling part of his estate in order to raise money to pay his college bill. The cousin offered to purchase it for £7,000, and the deal went through at that price. The cousin had had the estate valued at £20,000, but did not disclose that fact before the sale went through. Excessive drinking led to the student's death a year later, and his executor sought to have the contract of sale set aside.

The court found in the executor's favour. There had been a confidential relationship once the request for advice had been made, and failure to make a full disclosure of all material facts was a breach of that confidence amounting to undue influence. The court made it clear that the reason for the court's intervention was not the mere existence of a special relationship but the abuse thereof. The same point was stressed by Lord Scarman in *National Westminster Bank Ltd* v *Morgan*. The respondent had argued that upon establishment of a confidential relationship there would be a presumption of undue influence. The House of Lords in fact found there to be no special relationship, but Lord Scarman said that had there been one that fact alone was not a ground upon which a contract could be set aside. There must also be a transaction 'which is to the manifest disadvantage of the person influenced'.

Where a special relationship exists *and* one party to it has obtained a particularly advantageous contract apparently at the expense of the other, then undue influence will be presumed. The presumption may only be rebutted by showing that the person to whom the duty of confidence was owed was in a position to make a free and unfettered judgment. Often this will be established by showing that that person had access to independent advice of a relevant kind and availed himself of it. The mere existence of independent advice may not be enough, however; in *Tate* v *Williamson* the student had access to independent solicitors, but without disclosure of the valuation their advice was not enough to rebut the presumption of undue influence.

8.6.3 A wider doctrine

In *Lloyds Bank Ltd* v *Bundy* [1975] QB 326 Lord Denning MR attempted to show that undue influence was not really an independent doctrine but merely part of a broad power of equity to intervene where there has been an abuse of unequal bargaining power between the parties.

> The case involved financial advice given to an old man by a bank in connection with the mortgaging to the bank by the old man of his farm as security for a business venture of his son's.

The majority in the Court of Appeal did not agree with Lord Denning's analysis, but found for the old man on the basis of a conventional analysis of undue influence. They found that the particular relationship between the bank and its customer did give rise to a duty of confidentiality, largely because the relationship had been built up over a number of years and the old man clearly relied on the advice he received.

In *National Westminster Bank Ltd v Morgan* [1985] 1 All ER 821 Lord Scarman referred with approval to the conventional analysis provided by Sir Eric Sachs. Lord Denning's analysis received a very lukewarm reception from their Lordships, and for the moment it would clearly be unsafe to rely on it. Nevertheless, some of the older cases cited by Lord Denning (e.g. *Fry* v *Lane* (1888) 40 ChD 312) have always been uneasily explained by conventional analyses, while his very inventive judgment was able to make sense of what has not previously been a particularly coherent area of the law. It may be that there is scope for a single principle as the basis for policing the fairness of bargains. The point is considered further in the conclusion to this chapter.

8.6.4 Effect of undue influence
Contracts affected by undue influence are voidable, not void. As with duress, the doctrine does not go to the reality of consent: it is concerned with the protection of victims of improper behaviour. In *National Westminster Bank Ltd* v *Morgan* [1985] 1 All ER 821 Lord Scarman said that undue influence did not rest on 'a vague "public policy"', but it is hard to resist the conclusion that it is an example of the second head of public policy (see *8.1.3*) which demands fairness between the parties, especially during the bargaining process.

Since a contract tainted by undue influence is voidable the victim must bring an action for rescission to avoid it, and property passes under it. The remedy of rescission may be lost in two ways. The victim may be held to have affirmed the contract in some way once the undue influence has ceased. In particular, failure to act within a fairly short time of it ceasing may be interpreted as constructive affirmation. In *Allcard* v *Skinner* (1887) 36 ChD 145

> the plaintiff, under the influence of her spiritual adviser, joined an order called the 'Sisters of the Poor', to which her spiritual adviser was confessor. During the eight years she was a member the plaintiff gave some £7,000 to the defendant, who was head of the order. Six years after leaving the order she sought to recover the balance of that sum remaining unspent (about £1,700).

The gift to the defendant was found to have been made under undue influence, because the plaintiff had not been independently advised. The plaintiff was, nevertheless, unable to recover the balance of her money because she had allowed six years to elapse before claiming, during which time she had been unaffected by the influence of her former adviser and when independent advice was presumably available to her. Further, where third party rights have intervened (e.g. by resale of property which passed under the contract) rescission cannot be obtained because the property cannot be returned. But, the third party acquiring the property must do so without knowledge of the undue influence, or else the second transaction will be equally tainted and also capable of being overturned (*Bridgeman* v *Green* (1757) Wilm 58).

8.7 ILLEGALITY

The courts will not enforce contracts which are tainted with illegality. The notion of illegality covers a wide spectrum of factors which have been said at one time or another to deprive contracts of legal force. The factors have little in common other than that they are for the most part within the compass of the first category of public policy (see *8.1.3*) where the public interest prevails over whatever may be the intentions of the parties. Since the general public interest is the predominant concern, illegality is an exception to the normal pleading rules. The court is not obliged to wait for one or other party to raise the matter, but may raise the issue of illegality of its own motion (*Northwestern Salt Co. Ltd* v *Electrolytic Alkali Co. Ltd* [1914] AC 461). Commentators have always had difficulty in classifying the separate heads of illegality. The courts have not sought a conceptual basis for intervention, but have simply stepped in whenever there was a reason of public policy to do so. It has sometimes been suggested that the types of illegality may be broken down according to their effect, some contracts being illegal and void, others being merely void and yet others not being void but only 'unenforceable'. These categories reflect a more complex situation, which is that the effect of illegality varies according to the nature and gravity of the illegality in question, and so is dependent upon the facts in each case (see *8.7.4–8.7.6*). The recent attitude of the courts is well summarised by the following passage from the judgment of Bingham LJ in *Saunders* v *Edwards* [1987] 2 All ER 651, 665–6:

> Where issues of illegality are raised, the courts have (as it seems to me) to steer a middle course between two unacceptable positions. On the one hand it is unacceptable that any court of law should aid or lend its authority to a party seeking to pursue or enforce an object or agreement which the law prohibits. On the other hand, it is unacceptable that the court should, on the first indication of unlawfulness affecting any aspect of a transaction, draw up its skirts and refuse all assistance to the plaintiff, no matter how serious his loss or how disproportionate his loss to the unlawfulness of his conduct.
> . . . on the whole the courts have tended to adopt a pragmatic approach to these problems, seeking where possible to see that genuine wrongs are righted so long as the court does not thereby promote or countenance a nefarious object or bargain which it is bound to condemn.

Very recently in *Tinsley* v *Milligan* [1993] 3 All ER 65 at 75 the House of Lords condemned any approach to illegality of contracts which suggests that the courts simply have a discretion as to whether to grant or refuse relief, but the truth remains that the factual situations giving rise to judicial intervention on the ground of illegality are so varied that they defy conceptual classification. Some traditional categories may be used for ease of exposition, but it should be remembered at all times that the categories are only descriptive, and few if any legal consequences derive from them. It should also be noted that contracts in restraint of trade are usually treated as a type of illegal contract. They are treated under a separate heading in this chapter partly to ease the organisation of material, but also because the public policy issues therein are not restricted to those of the first category (see *8.8.1*).

8.7.1 Statutory illegality

The rule against illegal contracts is a common law doctrine, but the courts have had to adapt it to prohibitory rules contained in statutes, which in the twentieth century have had a major impact on our legal system. The only issue in relation to such rules is to determine their precise effect on the contract.

Sometimes the statute expressly prohibits the type of contract in question, in which case it is clear that the contract cannot be enforced, whatever the state of mind of the parties when they entered into it. In *Re Mahmoud and Ispahani* [1921] 2 KB 716

> the statute prohibited unlicensed dealing in linseed oil. The defendant misrepresented to the plaintiff that he had a licence, but subsequently refused to accept delivery. Despite the plaintiff's innocence, the contract could not be enforced.

Sometimes, however, the illegality is not so overwhelming as to prevent enforcement by an innocent party. In *Archbolds (Freightage) Ltd* v *Spanglett Ltd* [1961] 1 QB 374

> the defendants agreed to carry a cargo of whisky to London for the plaintiffs, who were unaware that the defendants did not have the required licence. The whisky was stolen.

The plaintiffs were allowed to sue on the contract for the defendants' loss of the goods en route. The contract itself was not illegal, and the plaintiffs were not party to the illegal performance.

Some statutes are interpreted by the courts as being intended to regulate the activities of a particular class of persons, in which case only the party belonging to that class is disbarred from enforcing the contract. In *Bloxsome* v *Williams* (1824) 3 B & C 232

> the defendant sold a horse to the plaintiff, giving a warranty as to its age and fitness. The sale contravened Sunday trading laws, and the defendant sought to resist an action for breach of warranty by pleading the illegality of the contract.

He was unsuccessful. The Sunday trading laws were not aimed at all persons making contracts, but at *traders*.

Finally, in some cases the penalty provided for by the statute is thought to be sufficient sanction for the prohibition in question, so that the contract may be enforced by both innocent and guilty parties (see *St John Shipping Corp.* v *Joseph Rank Ltd* [1957] 1 QB 267).

8.7.2   Gambling contracts

A gambling contract is a contract under which two persons mutually agree
that upon the determination of some uncertain, and normally future, event
one shall pay to the other, the winner, a sum of money or other stake (*Carlill
v Carbolic Smoke Ball Co.* [1892] 2 QB 484 at 490). A contract will be treated
in the same way if its purpose is gambling even if the parties have dressed
the contract in the guise of a sale (*Brogden* v *Marriot* (1836) 3 Bing NC 88).
Gambling includes 'gaming' (betting on the outcome of games, including
horseracing) and other wagers, and the two are sometimes treated differently.
There is little good reason of policy why they should be.

At common law such contracts were valid, but a series of statutes have very
largely reversed that rule. Since the unenforceability in this area extends also
to securities (*8.7.2.2*) and loans (*8.7.2.3*) detailed treatment must be left to
practitioners' works (cf. *Chitty on Contracts* 26th ed. (1989), Vol.II, Chapter
8). Below is a brief summary of the law.

8.7.2.1   Gaming Act 1845   Section 18 of the Gaming Act 1845 states:

> All contracts or agreements, whether by parole or in writing, by way of
> gaming or wagering shall be null and void; and no suit shall be brought
> or maintained in any Court of Law or Equity for recovering any sum of
> money or valuable thing alleged to be won upon any wager, or which shall
> have been deposited in the hands of any person to abide the event on which
> any wager shall have been made.

The effect of this section is threefold. In the first place recovery on the
basis of a gambling contract is impossible. Secondly, collateral contracts
associated with gambling contracts are also unenforceable. Thus a contract
to pay gambling debts in return for not being posted as a defaulter, although
not itself a gambling contract, is unenforceable since any suit would be brought
to recover a sum alleged to have been won on a wager (*Hill* v *William Hill
(Park Lane) Ltd* [1949] AC 530. Finally, money deposited with a stakeholder
cannot be recovered as winnings, although the section has been interpreted
as allowing a party to recover his own deposit before it has been paid over
to the winner (*Diggle* v *Higgs* (1872) 2 ExD 422).

8.7.2.2   Securities   Sometimes a winner receives a security, such as a cheque,
in payment. Such a security has been unenforceable in the case of gaming
winnings since the passing of the Gaming Act 1710. This rule caused hardship
in the case of negotiable instruments (see *13.4.3*) given as security since they
might subsequently be given in payment to a third party, who would be deprived
of their value for no good reason. Relief was provided by the Gaming Act
1835, which said that such securities were to be deemed to be given for illegal
consideration. The result was that a third party receiving the negotiable
instrument would be able to enforce it if able to show that consideration had
been given for it without notice of the illegality. In the case of securities given
for non-gaming winnings, after the Gaming Act 1845 a similar rule applies,

but the burden of proof in this case is on the person making the instrument to show that no value has been given (*Lilley* v *Rankin* (1887) 56 LJQB 248).

The Gaming Act 1968 legalised some forms of gaming, and by s.16 cheques which are not post-dated, and which are given in exchange only for the face value of the cheque in order to be able to take part (e.g. a cheque to purchase chips) are enforceable by the holder of an appropriate licence under the Act.

8.7.2.3 Loans Loans made in connection with gambling contracts are also irrecoverable, although the court may be faced with a difficult question of fact as to whether the loan is for gambling or merely for the general use of the gambler. Under s.1 of the Gaming Act 1892 a loan to pay off gambling debts is irrecoverable if paid directly to the winner by the lender, as is a loan paid to the loser and specifically earmarked for gambling debts (*Macdonald* v *Green* [1951] 1 KB 594). But where the money is paid to the loser who retains control over how it shall be spent then the transaction does not have a sufficient link with the illegal gambling contract, and so the money is recoverable (*Re O'Shea* [1911] 2 KB 981).

It is probably also the case that a loan made to finance future gambling contracts is irrecoverable. That would seem to be the case for an earmarked loan by virtue of s.1 of the 1892 Act. In the case of non-earmarked loans there is authority in *Carlton Hall Club Ltd* v *Laurence* [1929] 2 KB 153 to the effect that these too are unenforceable, by virtue of the Gaming Acts of 1710 and 1835. However, the decision has been almost universally criticised and the authority is unreliable. The 1968 Gaming Act imposes further restrictions on the giving of credit for the purposes of gaming.

8.7.3. Public policy under the common law
As a discretionary tool in the hands of judges public policy has been used and abused, and its strength and weakness can be measured by the quality of those who apply it. It is traditional for judges to deprecate resort to public policy (cf. Burrough J in *Richardson* v *Mellish* (1824) 2 Bing 229 at 252), and to point to the adverse effect on freedom of contract of allowing public policy arguments to prevail (cf. Jessel MR in *Printing & Numerical Registering Co.* v *Sampson* (1875) LR 19 Eq 462 at 465). Nevertheless, the different heads of public policy under which courts have declared contracts to be unenforceable are numerous, and despite judicial statements there is no reason to think that they may not increase still further. Listed below are the more common heads of public policy so far identified. The policies are described without favourable or critical comment!

8.7.3.1 Contracts to commit crimes or civil wrongs A contract to commit a crime is self-evidently illegal (see *Bigos* v *Boustead* [1951] 1 All ER 92: contract contrary to exchange control regulations). Contracts to defraud the revenue are also illegal (see *Alexander* v *Rayson* [1936] 1 KB 169: contract designed to make the value of property seem less to the rating authority). A contract which envisages the commission of a civil wrong which is not also criminal is nevertheless tainted by illegality (*Clay* v *Yates* (1856) 1 H & N

73: contract to publish a libel). Contracts of indemnity for unlawful acts may also belong to this category, and are equally unenforceable (*Gray v Barr* [1971] 2 QB 554: insurance claim refused because the loss followed directly upon threatening violence with a gun).

8.7.3.2 Contracts prejudicial to the administration of justice Contracts are illegal by which a party promises to give false evidence (*R v Andrews* [1973] QB 422) or promises to withdraw a prosecution (*Keir v Leeman* (1846) 6 QB 308). Under s.5(1) of the Criminal Law Act 1967, however, it is no longer an offence to withhold information which might secure a conviction if it is withheld in return for reparation for loss caused by the offence. It may be, therefore, that such a contract is no longer unenforceable.

Contracts which oust the jurisdiction of the courts are illegal. However, arbitration clauses in contracts are enforceable (*Scott v Avery* (1855) 5 HLC 811), provided no attempt is made to oust the supervisory role of the courts. Maintenance agreements between husband and wife in which one party agrees not to apply to the court for maintenance have been held to be contrary to public policy (*Hyman v Hyman* [1929] AC 601), but the impact of that decision is considerably reduced by legislation (s.34 Matrimonial Causes Act 1973).

8.7.3.3 Contracts prejudicial to the family Contracts of marriage brokage, by which one party is to procure the marriage of another for a fee, are illegal (*Hermann v Charlesworth* [1905] 2 KB 123). So are agreements restraining marriage (*Baker v White* (1690) 2 Vern 215). A separation agreement between parties currently cohabiting or prior to marriage is invalid (*Cartwright v Cartwright* (1853) 3 De GM & G 982), but where the agreement is made after or immediately before separation it is valid. There are statutory prohibitions on relinquishing the obligations of a parent (e.g. s.2(9), Children Act 1989).

8.7.3.4 Contracts prejudicial to (sexual) morality It is sometimes said that contracts contrary to public morals are unenforceable. The rule is probably limited to sexual morality. Thus, a promise of payment in order to induce a woman to become one's mistress is unenforceable (*Benyon v Nettlefold* (1850) 3 Mac & G 94). There is no reason to think the same is not true where the sexual roles are reversed. Contracts ancillary to immoral purposes are equally affected (*Pearce v Brooks* (1866) LR 1 Ex 213: contract of hire of a carriage for the known purpose of prostitution). It should be noted that attitudes to sexual morality change, and the law is less severe than once it was on unmarried cohabitees whose relationship is stable.

8.7.3.5 Contracts prejudicial to foreign relations Contracts which involve doing illegal acts in foreign friendly countries are unenforceable (*Regazzoni v Sethia (1944) Ltd* [1958] AC 301), as would be a contract hostile to such a country's interests to be performed elsewhere. In a similar vein, trading with an enemy is illegal (*Potts v Bell* (1800) 8 Term Rep 548; Trading with the Enemy Act 1939). In *Lemenda Trading Co. v African Middle East Petroleum Co. Ltd* [1988] 1 All ER 513, Phillips J suggested that an English court should not enforce a contract governed by English law which would be contrary to English public policy, where the same public policy applies in the country of performance, making the contract unenforceable there.

8.7.3.6 Public corruption Contracts which further corruption in public life are illegal. The rule is most commonly applied in the case of sales of public offices or honours. For example, in *Parkinson* v *College of Ambulance Ltd* [1925] 2 KB 1

> the plaintiff was encouraged to believe that if he were to make a substantial donation to a certain charity the officers of the charity would be able to get him a knighthood. The sum of £3,000 was agreed and paid, but no knighthood was forthcoming.

The plaintiff sued to recover the amount paid, but was unable to succeed because the contract was found to be illegal (see also the Honours (Prevention of Abuses) Act 1925). It is clear from *Lemenda Trading Co. Ltd* v *African Middle East Petroleum Co. Ltd* [1988] 1 All ER 513 (*8.7.3.5*) that illegality of this kind does not rest on the fact that the party promising to exercise influence in return for payment occupies a public office.

8.7.4 General effect of illegality
The effect of illegality varies according to the gravity with which the illegality is viewed by the court. For examples of this eminently sensible principle one need only reconsider the cases on statutory illegality (see *8.7.1*). The general principle that illegal contracts are unenforceable may be traced back to *Holman* v *Johnson* (1775) 1 Cowp 34, and the primacy of this long-standing authority was very recently reaffirmed by Lord Goff (with whom Lord Browne-Wilkinson agreed on this point) in *Tinsley* v *Milligan* [1993] 3 All ER 65 at 72 and 79.

The defence of illegality does not exist for the benefit of the defendant, but exists for the benefit of society as a whole and rests on public policy. Consequently, if plaintiff and defendant were to reverse roles the defence might still apply. In particular, a plaintiff will not succeed if his claim is based on an illegal contract, or if the illegality of the contract must be pleaded to support the claim. Equally, a plaintiff will not succeed if to do so would result in him benefitting from his own illegal contract. It is sometimes said that these particular aspects of the rule must not be seen as exhaustive in stating the effect of illegality, and the overriding public policy element may result in the courts refusing relief to a plaintiff where illegality is disclosed even if there is no direct reliance on an illegal contract nor any benefit from the plaintiff's wrongdoing. It was in this sense, in a case not relating to a claim in contract, that Hutchison J in *Thackwell* v *Barclays Bank plc* [1986] 1 All ER 676 employed what has been described as the 'public conscience test'; he accepted counsel's argument that in circumstances where there was no technical bar to plaintiff's action the nature of the illegality might nevertheless be such that no court would be willing to assist the plaintiff, for fear of appearing to assist or encourage criminal acts. In a series of subsequent cases in the Court of Appeal the notion of a 'public conscience test' was very considerably developed, and eventually its meaning distorted, so that ultimately in *Howard* v *Shirlstar Container Transport Ltd* [1990] 3 All ER 366 a plaintiff was permitted to benefit from his own illegal acts, and to rely upon an illegal contract in making his claim. In this case, therefore, the public conscience test, rather than providing a further residual ground upon which the plaintiff's action might be refused, became an argument to overturn the general principle of public policy against enforcement of illegal contracts, because of what the court deemed to be an absence of affront to the public conscience on the particular facts.

This development has been roundly condemned by the House of Lords in *Tinsley* v *Milligan* [1993] 3 All ER 65. Although Lord Goff was in the minority in respect of the final outcome of the appeal, Lord Browne-Wilkinson who gave the principal speech for the majority agreed with his trenchant criticisms of the Court of Appeal's development of the law. Lord Goff said:

> This development has been allowed to occur without addressing the questions (1) whether the test is consistent with earlier authority, (2) if it was not so consistent, whether such a development could take place consistently with the doctrine of precedent as applied in the Court of Appeal, or (3) whether the resulting change in the law, if permissible, was desirable.

He went on to make clear that in his view it would not be appropriate for the House of Lords, to whom it was technically possible to make such a development in the law since there was no House of Lords authority directly on the matter, to adopt such a rule. He declined to express an opinion on the question whether the original and residual version of the public conscience test expounded in *Thackwell* v *Barclays Bank plc* was good law; such a residual rule certainly appears to be consistent with the public policy articulated by Lord Mansfield in *Holman* v *Johnson*. Lord Goff would have allowed the appeal in *Tinsley* v *Milligan*; in fact it was overruled on grounds referred to immediately below.

A plaintiff may succeed if his claim does not require any reliance on the illegal contract, provided always that the residual principle of affront to the public conscience does not apply. This may occur where the claim made is not contractual at all (e.g., *Saunders* v *Edwards* [1987] 2 All ER 651; claim in tort for fraud giving rise to a contract which was tainted with illegality); or where the illegality does not affect the contract upon which the claim was based, but some related transaction (e.g., *Euro-Diam Ltd* v *Bathurst* [1988] 2 All ER 23: claim on a contract of insurance in respect of goods stolen in the course of a transaction tainted with illegality); or where the defendant does not have to plead the illegality but is merely asserting a property right (*per* Lord Browne-Wilkinson in *Tinsley* v *Milligan*: claim to have an equal share in property, despite the house having been put in only one name as a device to contribute to a fraud on the Department of Social Security; see further 8.7.5.4). Sometimes, in order to ensure that 'genuine wrongs are righted' the courts will go so far as to allow recovery on a collateral contract, thereby avoiding by a fiction the problem of allowing a claim founded upon an illegal contract. In *Strongman (1945) Ltd* v *Sincock* [1955] 2 QB 525 a builder was informed by his client that the client would obtain the necessary licences, which the client then failed to do. A contract to build without a licence was absolutely prohibited by statute.

The Court of Appeal nevertheless found an enforceable collateral contract to obtain the licences, of which the client was found to be liable for breach. The limit on this doctrine is that a remedy under a collateral contract must not be the equivalent of enforcing the illegal contract. This difficulty might have been avoided in *Re Mahmoud and Ispahani* [1921] 2 KB 716, which on its facts is not easy to distinguish from *Strongman* v *Sincock*, by bringing an action for misrepresentation, for which a different measure of loss would apply (see *9.4.2.4*). This (fictitious) kind of enforceable collateral contract must be kept separate from other transactions collateral to illegal contracts. For example, security given in respect of payment for or performance of an illegal contract is tainted by the illegality of the main transaction (*Fisher* v *Bridges* (1854) 3 E & B 642). Finally, where one party is not involved in the illegal intention, as for example in the case of a class-protecting statute (cf. *Bloxsome* v *Williams* (1824) 3 B & C 232; see *8.7.1*), that party may enforce the contract or recover under a restitutionary remedy.

8.7.5 Recovery of money or property
The general rule stated in *Holman* v *Johnson* (1775) 1 Cowp 341 applies equally to actions brought to recover money or property passing as a result of an illegal contract as it does to enforcement of the contract itself. Thus, where the parties are equally guilty even a restitutionary remedy is barred. Nevertheless, the rule may be avoided in a number of situations where either the parties are not regarded as being equally guilty, or the illegality need not be pleaded in order to obtain the remedy.

8.7.5.1 Where one party withdraws from the illegal transaction Restitution may be available where one party withdraws before the illegal purpose is carried into effect. In *Taylor* v *Bowers* (1876) 1 QBD 291 Mellish LJ suggested that withdrawal is allowed at any time before completion, and the decision in that case is only really consistent with that interpretation. However, in *Kearley* v *Thomson* (1890) 24 QBD 742 it was suggested that restitution would be denied once performance of the illegal purpose had started, irrespective of whether it was ever completed. The latter rule appears to be more consistent with the public policy requirements inherent in the control of illegal contracts. For similar reasons, the withdrawal from the transaction must be voluntary. In *Bigos* v *Boustead* [1951] 1 All ER 92 restitution was refused because the plaintiff had only 'withdrawn' from the transaction after the illegal purpose had been frustrated by the duplicity of the other party.

8.7.5.2 Class-protecting statutes In some cases a statute is intended to protect one class of contracting party against exploitive behaviour by another. The Rent Act 1977, s.125, provides for recovery of a premium paid to secure a lease. Before the 1977 Act the courts had held that such a premium was recoverable under the common law. The parties were not equally guilty because the rule against payment of a premium was intended to protect lessees (*Gray* v *Southouse* [1949] 2 All ER 1019).

8.7.5.3 Fraud, duress or undue influence Where one party is induced to enter into an illegal contract by fraud, duress or undue influence that party is clearly not equally guilty as the other. While it would be undesirable in such circumstances to enforce the contract, some remedy may be provided by permitting the victim to recover money or property passed as a result of the contract. In *Hughes* v *Liverpool Victoria Legal Friendly Society* [1916] 2 KB 482

> the plaintiff was fraudulently induced to take out a policy of insurance on the life of someone in which she had no insurable interest. She was able to recover the premiums paid.

The suggestion that recovery in such cases depends on the fraud of the defendant rather than the innocence of the plaintiff (cf. *Harse* v *Pearl Life Assurance Co.* [1904] 1 KB 558) is difficult to reconcile with the basis of this right to recovery, which is that the parties are not equally guilty. Insurance companies might take proper care in such cases if a negligent misrepresentation (*9.3.2*) by their agent, inducing an innocent party to enter a contract, were also to entitle that party to recover premiums paid.

8.7.5.4 Proprietary remedy not relying on the illegal contract Restitution will be allowed where the defendant is merely asserting a property right, and need not rely on the fact that the contract is illegal. In the case of the sale of goods it is established that property passes despite the illegality (*Singh* v *Ali* [1960] AC 167). Therefore, a proprietary remedy would not be available in a sales case, since there would be no property right to assert (see *4.5*). However, where something less than full title is passed, as in the case of a lease, bailment or pledge, there may be scope for restitution. Nevertheless, if, in order to assert that property has not passed to the other party, it is necessary to plead the illegality of the transaction under which physical possession was transferred, then no remedy is available (*Taylor* v *Chester* (1869) LR 4 QB 309).

A common form of bailment is the hire-purchase agreement. In *Bowmakers Ltd* v *Barnet Instruments Ltd* [1945] KB 65

> goods were delivered to the defendants under an illegal hire-purchase agreement. The defendants had failed to make payments and had sold some of the goods. The plaintiffs sued for damages for conversion; that is, they sued to recover the value of the goods, asserting their property right.

The court allowed this claim. In the case of the goods which had been sold their right to them could be asserted without reference to the terms of the contract, by virtue of the common law of bailments. However, the decision has been criticised for also allowing recovery for the goods retained by the defendants, since any right to their value, resulting from the failure to make the payments, must have depended on the terms of the contract, on which the court was not entitled to rely. In *Tinsley* v *Milligan* [1993] 3 All ER 65 Lord Browne-Wilkinson, speaking for the majority in the House of Lords, took the view that an action brought to assert a joint interest in a house, which had been put into the name of only one of the parties in order to assist in a fraud against the Department of Social Security, did not involve any reliance on an illegal contract, but was simply an action to enforce a property right in the form of a trust. He did not believe that the fact that the property right asserted was in the form of an equitable rather than legal interest had any impact on the case. Lord Goff, for the minority, took the view that an equitable property right could not be used in this way to avoid the consequences of the illegal contracts rule, because of the distinct maxim of equity that he who comes to equity must come with clean hands. Lord Browne-Wilkinson accepted that at some time in the past an equitable property right might have had to be treated differently, but was persuaded that the fusion of law and equity (see *1.2.1.1*) allowed the plaintiff to avoid the consequences of the illegal contracts rule by relying on a property right whether legal or equitable.

8.7.6 Severance

In some circumstances illegal contracts remain enforceable by both parties provided changes are made by removing the offending parts. The rule is especially relevant in the case of contracts in restraint of trade (see *8.8* below).

Severance is only allowed if it is consistent with the public policy which made the contract containing the offending part illegal. If the whole contract is tainted by the illegality severance cannot save it. In *Napier* v *National Business Agency* [1951] 2 All ER 264 a contract of employment contained provisions on pay and expenses which were clearly designed to defraud the Inland Revenue. The plaintiff was not allowed to enforce it to recover his salary by severing the part relating to the payment of expenses.

The illegal portion of the contract must be capable of being verbally and grammatically separated from the rest. This principle is usually called the 'blue pencil test'. In *Goldsoll* v *Goldman* [1915] 1 Ch 292

> The plaintiffs were dealers in imitation jewellery, and entered into an agreement with the defendant, a competitor, to the effect that the defendant would no longer compete with them in any capacity, either in his own right or as agent or employee of others, for a period of two years. The clause purported to cover 'the county of London, England, Scotland, Ireland, Wales, or any part of the United Kingdom of Great Britain and Ireland and the Isle of Man or France, the United States of America, Russia or Spain, or within twenty-five miles of Potsdamerstrasse, Berlin, or St Stefans Kirche, Vienna'.

The Court of Appeal was willing to enforce the contract but for the unreasonable geographical extent of the restraint, and did so after severing the words from 'or France' to the end of the clause.

The illegal part of the contract must not be the main subject-matter, since its severance would totally unbalance the agreement, making it essentially different from the original bargain. In *Bennett* v *Bennett* [1952] 1 KB 249

> husband and wife separated, and the wife commenced divorce proceedings in which she applied for a maintenance order against her husband. Before the trial she entered into an agreement with the husband by which he undertook to pay her an annuity and to convey property to her, in return for which she promised not to pursue any claim for maintenance in the courts. The husband did not keep his side of the bargain.

The promise not to seek maintenance was illegal (*8.7.3.2*), so that the whole of the consideration to be furnished by the wife failed. Even where the illegal part is not the main subject-matter of the contract, the courts will not sever it and enforce the rest if to do so would alter entirely the scope and intention of the agreement. This rule appears to be the most satisfactory explanation of *Attwood* v *Lamont* [1920] 3 KB 571, which is otherwise not easily distinguished from *Goldsoll* v *Goldman*. In the former case

> the respondent was the owner of a department store which carried out tailoring and general outfitting. The appellant was employed as a cutter in the tailoring department, and his contract of employment contained a clause restraining him from working at any time in the future within 10 miles of the store in the 'business of a tailor, dressmaker, general draper, milliner, hatter, haberdasher, gentlemen's, ladies' or children's outfitter'. The restraint was found to be too wide, since the appellant's only significant skill was as a tailor, and the question arose whether the other functions on the list might be severed.

The Court of Appeal found that the rest of the clause could not be severed, and that this was a covenant 'which must stand or fall in its unaltered form'. Whether in any particular case the scope and intention of an agreement will be so altered by severance is a question of fact. Consequently, the application of the principle will vary from case to case. Nevertheless, in *Carney* v *Herbert* [1985] 1 All ER 438 the Privy Council identified two limits on its impact. In the first place, the significance of the illegal term or terms in relation to the whole of the transaction is to be judged not at the time of contracting, but at the time of trial. Consequently, the fact that a party would not have been willing to enter the contract but for the illegal term may be irrelevant. Secondly, where the parties enter into a lawful contract, and there is an illegal ancillary provision which exists solely for the benefit of the plaintiff, which the plaintiff may waive without prejudicing the substance of his claim, the court will normally permit the provision to be severed, providing there will be no overriding affront to the public conscience.

8.8   CONTRACTS IN RESTRAINT OF TRADE

Unlike the elements of the illegality doctrine previously dealt with, contracts in restraint of trade require reference to both types of public policy (see *8.1.3*). Such contracts may be subject to the intervention of the court on the ground either of protecting the general public interest or of maintaining fairness between the parties. Moreover, the illegality doctrine causes the public interest to be brought into conflict with the countervailing interest in freedom of contract. In the case of restraint of trade the intervention takes place precisely to protect the public interest in freedom of contract. Contracts in restraint of trade are contracts whereby one or both parties agree to limit their individual freedom to contract. The common law will not tolerate such limitations if the public interest in free competition is adversely affected or if the limitation is unfair between the parties.

8.8.1   General principles
During the nineteenth century the restraint of trade doctrine barely existed. Unless the agreement imposed a total restraint the view was that no harm would be done, and that freedom of contract was the more important policy to pursue (*Printing & Numerical Registering Co.* v *Sampson* (1875) LR 19 Eq 462). This attitude neglected, or at least lagged behind the progress of industrialisation and commercial agglomeration which had taken place. However, in *Nordenfelt* v *Maxim Nordenfelt* [1894] AC 535 the House of Lords restated the restraint of trade rule, and its decision in that case is the foundation of the modern law.

> The case concerned a restraint upon the seller of an ammunition and arms manufacturing company, which prevented him engaging in such business anywhere in the world for 25 years.

The leading speech is that of Lord Macnaghten. His statement of the law may be summarised as follows. There is an initial presumption that contracts in restraint of trade are void. The courts may of their own motion refuse to enforce such a contract (see *8.7*). The presumption may only be rebutted by showing special justifying circumstances. Whether the circumstances alleged to justify the restraint do so is a question of law for the court. For a restraint to be justified it must be reasonable both in the interests of the parties and in the public interest. Generally, the burden of proof in relation to what is reasonable between the parties rests on the party seeking to enforce the contract. If that burden is sustained the party resisting enforcement has the burden of showing that the restraint is contrary to the public interest.

It has been argued that the presumption that such contracts are void is inconsistent with the fact that the burden of proof in relation to the public interest rests on the party resisting enforcement. In *Attwood* v *Lamont* [1920] 3 KB 571 it was suggested that the more accurate presumption might be that such contracts were valid until proved otherwise. That suggestion had been firmly rejected, however, by the House of Lords in *Mason* v *Provident Clothing*

and Supply Co. Ltd [1913] AC 724. The conclusion must therefore be that
of the two streams of public policy in relation to contracts in restraint of trade,
fairness between the parties is predominant, since once that has been established
the presumption switches to one of validity. In *Schroeder Music Publishing Co.
Ltd v Macaulay* [1974] 3 All ER 616 at 623 Lord Diplock went so far as
to suggest that fairness between the parties is the only concern of the doctrine.
It is submitted that his view must be open to considerable doubt.

8.8.1.1   Reasonable between the parties   What is reasonable between the
parties must be determined in each case individually. However, the decision
of the House of Lords in *Herbert Morris Ltd v Saxelby* [1916] AC 688 provided
guidance on how the issue was determined. In that case

> the defendant was employed as engineer by the plaintiffs, a leading manufacturer
> of hoisting machinery. His contract of employment contained a seven-year restraint
> on carrying on a wide range of related trades anywhere in the United Kingdom
> should he leave the plaintiffs' employment. The plaintiffs sought to enforce the
> clause.

They failed. Their Lordships identified two different types of contract in restraint
of trade in which different policy considerations apply. In the sale of a business
restraints are permitted which seek to preserve the value of the 'goodwill' of
the business by preventing the vendor setting up in competition with the
purchaser. In contracts of employment it would not normally be reasonable
to prevent a former employee from working in any capacity for a competitor,
but restraints to prevent the loss of trade secrets or the poaching of customers
to whom the employee had access are permitted. In each case, the identification
of a legitimate interest to be protected is only the first stage in the process
of justification. It must also be shown that the duration and geographical extent
of the restraint are not out of proportion to the interest identified. It was
suggested in *Allied Dunbar (Frank Weisinger) Ltd v Weisinger* [1988] IRLR
61 that it was not appropriate to import the doctrine of proportionality into
the field of restraint of trade. It is respectfully submitted that the point is
largely semantic: in assessing reasonableness by weighing the severity of the
restraint against the need to protect legitimate interests, the test is inevitably
one of proportion.

While at first sight it may seem difficult to imagine how any restraint can
be reasonable to the party upon whom it is imposed, it is essential to consider
the whole contract in its economic context. In many cases the contract as a
whole might not have been made, or at least the person accepting the restraints
might not have succeeded in obtaining such favourable terms, but for the
restrictive terms. It is acknowledged, therefore, in *Esso Petroleum Co. Ltd v
Harper's Garage (Stourport) Ltd* [1968] AC 269 that what is fair between the
parties can only be assessed in the light of the consideration paid. To give
a simple example, if in the sale of a business the vendor seeks to place a high
value on the goodwill of the business then the purchaser will be entitled to
restraints to ensure that the vendor cannot subsequently undermine that value

by competing for his former customers. Such restraints might not be permitted at all if in the sale no value was allocated to the goodwill.

8.8.1.2 Reasonable in the public interest It has sometimes been suggested that no contract reasonable between the parties can be unreasonable in the public interest. Lord Diplock is a recent advocate of that view (in *Schroeder Music Publishing Co. Ltd v Macaulay* [1974] 3 All ER 616; see *8.8.1*), although the impact of his statement may be limited by interpreting what he said as meaning no more than that in contracts of employment of individuals (and analogous transactions) it is rare that a restraint will have any perceptible effect on the competitive structure of the market as a whole. It is certainly the case that there are *dicta* contradicting the wider view in the House of Lords decision in *Esso Petroleum Co. Ltd v Harper's Garage (Stourport) Ltd* [1968] AC 269. The public interest is an important consideration especially in those cases falling outside the employment contract and sale of business type of restraint identified in *Herbert Morris Ltd v Saxelby* [1916] AC 688. When two companies, as a result of arm's-length bargaining, agree not to compete with each other one may assume that both think that the contract is reasonable. In such a case it is the public which is likely to suffer, and control by the courts in its interest is essential.

8.8.2 Employment contracts

Restraints in employment contracts are usually only subject to attack in so far as they purport to operate after the period of employment has terminated. During employment the employer is entitled to control the activities of the employee, unless the nature of the restraint is to stifle rather than utilise the employee's skills. In this respect there may be an analogy between contracts of employment and restraints on those who engage in professional sport or in popular entertainment (see *8.8.6*).

The common legitimate interests which may be protected are trade secrets and clients or customers to whom the employee may have had access during his employment. The restraint must not go beyond the scope of the type of activity carried on by the particular employee. In *Home Counties Dairies Ltd v Skilton* [1970] 1 WLR 526

> a milk roundsman agreed not to sell milk or dairy produce to his former employer's customers. The restraint was only found reasonable upon an interpretation of 'dairy produce' limiting it to the kind of products with which he had dealt during the course of his employment.

In *Mason v Provident Clothing & Supply Co. Ltd* [1913] AC 724

> the constraint purported to prevent the employee entering into a similar business within 25 miles of London. His employment had been in a small shop in Islington, and for that reason the restraint was too wide to be reasonable.

As noted above, it is rare that a restraint in such a contract will be contrary to the public interest, although this was the basis of the somewhat anomalous decision in *Wyatt* v *Kreglinger and Fernau* [1933] 1 KB 793. Nevertheless, it is possible that in the case of a person eminent in their field, such as a surgeon or scientist, the public interest might be adversely affected in a perceptible way. In *Oswald Hickson Collier & Co.* v *Carter-Ruck* [1984] 2 All ER 15 Lord Denning MR (with whom the other members of the Court of Appeal agreed) suggested that it would not be in the public interest for a solicitor to be restrained from acting for his client, especially in view of the fiduciary relationship between them. However, in *Deacons* v *Bridge* [1984] 2 All ER 19 the Privy Council refused to recognise this as a general rule, and this view was followed in respect of a doctor in general practice within the National Health Service by the Court of Appeal in *Kerr* v *Morris* [1986] 3 All ER 217. These later decisions do not seem to detract from the proposition that a restraint upon a particularly expert specialist in a given field may be contrary to the public interest.

8.8.3   Sale of a business
In the case of sale of a business, equality of bargaining power is more likely to exist between the parties, and so fairness between the parties might be thought to be a less crucial and the public interest a more prominent concern. The classic case is *Nordenfelt* v *Maxim Nordenfelt* [1894] AC 535. The House of Lords identified the goodwill of the business as the interest entitled to protection. Lord Macnaghten stressed that the public have 'an interest in every person's carrying on his trade freely', and that restraints which are fair between the parties must not be 'injurious to the public'. It is slightly surprising that there appear to be no cases of this kind where the public interest has been found to be the reason for the contract being void. Courts have usually referred to the public interest as an important factor to be considered, but have not matched their words with action. It may be that courts have not been sufficiently vigilant in this area since the changes supposedly wrought by the decision in *Nordenfelt's* case.

8.8.4   Cartels
Cartels are agreements between supposedly competing undertakings at the same level in the commercial chain. They are sometimes known as horizontal agreements. At least at the time of contracting it must be assumed that the parties believe they are beneficial to them both, and there is little chance of an inequality of bargaining power being exploited. On the other hand, where cartels consist of agreements not to compete, the conventional economic wisdom (and current political judgment) is that the public may well be harmed if competition is unnaturally impaired. The reluctance of the courts to interfere with freedom of contract led in the past to the Privy Council suggesting that cartels are not injurious to the public (*Attorney-General of Australia* v *Adelaide Steamship Co.* [1913] AC 781). The reluctance of the courts to take necessary measures against these harmful agreements led to intervention by Parliament. Cartels are now largely controlled under statutory regulations administered

by a special court (cf. Restrictive Trade Practices Act 1976 and the Competition
Act 1980). The study of those rules is beyond the scope of this book.

8.8.5   Exclusive dealing

Exclusive dealing agreements are agreements between undertakings at different
stages in the commercial chain which provide for a closer tie between the
undertakings than a mere contract of supply. They are sometimes known as
vertical agreements. They may well have advantages for both parties in terms
of forward planning, but where one party is a retailer and the other a
manufacturer the security of supply for the retailer may be provided at too
high a price. The leading case is *Esso Petroleum Co. Ltd* v *Harper's Garage
(Stourport) Ltd* [1968] AC 269.

> The parties made a contract, known as a solus agreement, under which the garage
> owners agreed to purchase petrol only from the company. In the case of one garage
> the tie was to last for just under five years, and in return the garage owners received
> a discount on the price of petrol supplied to them. In the case of a second garage
> the tie was to last for 21-years, and in return the garage owners received a mortgage
> loan of £7,000.

The House of Lords made it clear that there is no overall ban on such contracts.
An investigation must be made in every case into whether there is a legitimate
interest to be protected, and if so whether the restraints imposed are reasonable
to protect the interests in question. On the particular facts their Lordships
found the shorter restraint to be reasonable, but the 21-year restraint was
unreasonable and unenforceable.

There are *dicta* in the *Esso* case suggesting that an agreement for these kinds
of restraint if contained in a lease would always be considered valid. It was
apparently feared that to say otherwise might cause unnecessary interference
in the law of real property relating to restrictive covenants. That opinion has
been questioned by subsequent commentators. An attempt to avoid the restraint
of trade doctrine by means of a series of leases was thwarted in *Alec Lobb
(Garages) Ltd* v *Total Oil (GB) Ltd* [1985] 1 All ER 303. The first instance
decision in this case was overturned by the Court of Appeal, but on the ground
that the restraint in question was in fact reasonable. The applicability of the
doctrine of restraint of trade to leases was therefore upheld.

8.8.6   Restraints on professional sportsmen and entertainers

In some circumstances restraints are imposed to ensure that a person provides
services only for one recipient. Such contracts are common in the world of
professional sport and entertainment. The individual who is restricted may
not have a contract of employment with the beneficiary of the restriction, but
is nevertheless unable to supply his services to anybody else. This category
includes those agreements where employers agree to regulate employment in
a particular sector, and especially agree not to employ those who have previously
worked for other parties to the agreement. Such agreements may be equivalent
in effect to the restraints contained in contracts of employment (see *8.8.2*),

and for that reason they are within the restraint of trade doctrine. In *Greig* v *Insole* [1978] 1 WLR 302

> the organisers of international and English county cricket sought to exclude from their matches players who participated in games promoted by a private cricketing 'circus' established in a battle over television rights. The plaintiff, who until this time had been captain of the England team, successfully challenged the ban imposed on the ground that it interfered with freedom of employment.

The most striking cases are those where the bodies responsible for the organisation of professional sport impose a rule upon their members intended to prevent large clubs poaching the best players from small clubs. Often such rules are claimed to be justified in the interests of the sport-watching public. The employees of the clubs can find that they are unable to make the best commercial exploitation of their skills. The cases make it clear that such rules are in restraint of trade and thus invalid (cf. *Eastham* v *Newcastle United Football Club Ltd* [1964] Ch 413). It should be noted that trade unions are exempt from this rule under the Trade Union and Labour Relations Act 1974, s.2(5).

In *Schroeder Music Publishing Co. Ltd* v *Macaulay* [1974] 3 All ER 616

> an unknown songwriter entered into a contract with a music publisher. The contract was renewable up to a period of 10 years, and terminable at the option of the music publisher, who had copyright in all compositions, but not at the option of the songwriter. The publisher was not obliged to publish any songs.

The songwriter sought to escape the confines of the contract after achieving considerable popular success, and was permitted to do so on the ground (*inter alia*) that the restrictions removed all incentive to creativity.

8.8.7 The impact of EC law

Further restrictions on the making of contracts in restraint of trade derive from the United Kingdoms's membership of the EC. The Treaty of Rome and all law made under it becomes part of English law by virtue of the European Communities Act 1972 (see *3.4.1*). Article 85 of the Treaty and reg. 17 are designed to control contracts in restraint of trade in so far as they prevent the realisation of the aims of the common market by hindering trade between member states. Some EC law only operates at the level of governments, but where provisions are of 'direct effect' they create rights in individuals which may be protected and enforced by direct legal action in the national courts (see *3.4.2*). By the decision of the European Court of Justice in *Belgische Radio en Televisie* v *S.V.S.A.B.A.M.* [1974] ECR 51 art. 85 is of direct effect. Thus, agreements which infringe art. 85 may not only be subject to investigation and possible fines imposed by the EC Commission, they may also be unenforceable by legal action by the parties in the English courts even before the Commission has ruled against them.

Under art. 85(2) such agreements are void. It is possible (under art. 85(3)) to gain exemption from the operation of this rule, but such exemptions may only be granted by the Commission, and not by the national courts of the member states. Until an exemption is given the agreement remains unenforceable, however harmless it may appear (*Brasserie de Haecht* v *Wilkin (No.2)* [1973] CMLR 287). In *Chemidus Wavin Ltd* v *TERI* [1978] 3 CMLR 514 the Court of Appeal found that in appropriate circumstances an offending clause might be severed, and the untainted remainder of the contract enforced by a national court. It should also be noted that the House of Lords has indicated that art. 85 may be a source of the tort of breach of statutory duty, compensatable in damages where any person can show loss occasioned by its breach (*Garden Cottage Foods* v *Milk Marketing Board* [1983] 2 All ER 770).

Although art. 85 regulates agreements affecting trade between member states, it should not be thought that a purely domestic agreement cannot have such effect. In *Brasserie de Haecht* v *Wilkin (No.1)* [1968] CMLR 26 the European Court of Justice was asked whether a brewery solus agreement affected trade between member states. It answered in the affirmative, on the ground that, where the agreement was a small part of a large network of similar agreements such that most bars in the country were tied in a similar manner to breweries established in that country, then the opportunities for imports to that country by foreign brewers were so minimal that it was correct to regard trade between member states as affected. Thus, an agreement in restraint of trade need not relate directly to imports or exports to fall foul of the EC regulations. It will become increasingly important for all British contract lawyers to be familiar with those regulations.

8.8.8 Remedies where the restraint is valid

Where a valid restraint of trade clause is sought to be enforced, the party for whose benefit the clause was included will usually be more concerned to prevent breach of the clause than to recover damages. Indeed, since restraints which are reasonable are often quite short in duration, he will require immediate protection; by the time the matter comes to a full trial the period of restraint may be close to expiry. Such immediate protection may be provided by the grant of an interlocutory (or interim) injunction, and in *Lawrence David Ltd* v *Ashton* [1991] 1 All ER 385 the Court of Appeal ruled that the test to be applied in respect of an application for an interlocutory injunction was the usual test set out in *American Cynamid Co.* v *Ethicon Ltd* [1975] 1 All ER 504. According to that test such an injunction would only be granted where: (a) there was a serious issue to be tried; (b) damages at the time of full trial would not be an adequate remedy; and (c) the balance of convenience was in favour of granting it. In *Lansing Linde Ltd* v *Kerr* [1991] 1 All ER 418 the Court of Appeal held that in respect of the first part of the test, where the full hearing would only be held at or about the time of the expiry of the period of restraint, an interlocutory injunction would only be granted where not only was there a serious issue to be tried but the plaintiff was more likely than not to succeed at the full trial. Once the case for an injunction is made out, the plaintiff will normally be granted an injunction covering the whole scope of the restraint clause, and the fact that the injunction will be ineffective to win back a client 'poached' in breach of the clause is irrelevant (see *John Michael Design plc* v *Cooke* [1987] 2 All ER 332).

8.9 CONCLUSION: UNCONSCIONABILITY

This chapter has considered a number of doctrines under which the courts intervene in agreements without regard to the objectively ascertainable common intention of the parties. The intervention can usually be traced to one of two types of public policy: either the protection of public interest or the protection of parties defined by law as 'weaker', in the interest of fairness between the parties. Some doctrines, such as illegality (*8.7*) rest almost entirely on the former. Others, such as duress (*8.5*) and undue influence (*8.6*), rest almost entirely on the latter. Some doctrines, such as restraint of trade (*8.8*), straddle the two streams of public policy. However, the courts have not attempted a systematic analysis of whether there is a common factor underlying the public policy of fairness between the parties. The various bases of policing are usually presented as a rag-bag of unrelated aspects of anti-social behaviour.

As noted earlier (*8.6.3*), in *Lloyd's Bank Ltd* v *Bundy* [1975] QB 326 Lord Denning MR attempted to make sense of many of these disparate doctrines by suggesting that they were merely examples of a broader principle he called 'inequality of bargaining power'. As yet this novel idea in English law has not found favour with many other judges. Nevertheless, there have been indications from some judges and from commentators to suggest that there may be a place in English law for a doctrine of abuse of unequal bargaining power. In *Lloyd's Bank* v *Bundy* the inequality between the large corporate bank and the unadvised and aged Mr Bundy was plain to see. The capacity rules relating to individuals (8.2), duress and undue influence may also be seen as examples of situations where there is a danger of abuse of an unequal bargaining power. In *Schroeder Music Publishing Co. Ltd* v *Macaulay* [1974] 3 All ER 616 (*8.8.1*) Lord Diplock used the idea of inequality of bargaining power to assess what he considered to be fair between the parties. A similar principle seems to underlie the legislation making special provision for the position of consumers which has been passed in recent years. For example, the test of reasonableness of an exclusion clause, set out in Schedule 2 to the Unfair Contract Terms Act 1977 (see *10.6.3.7*), includes a reference to 'the strength of the bargaining positions of the parties relative to each other'.

Lord Denning was careful in *Lloyd's Bank Ltd* v *Bundy* to avoid defining unequal bargaining power only in terms of the obvious disparity between commercial enterprises and individual consumers. He defined it as existing whenever a party's bargaining power is 'grievously impaired by reason of his own needs or desires, or by his own ignorance or infirmity'. In this sense even economic duress against a large corporation would fall under the inequality of bargaining power principle. A weak bargaining position might be caused by other commercial commitments. In order to succeed, however, the corporation would also have to show abuse of that position by exertion of *undue* pressure on the part of the other contracting party. It has been suggested that Lord Denning's proposed doctrine exposes a risk that any contract, resulting from bargaining in which one party had the upper hand, might be overturned by the courts. That would be a source of great commercial uncertainty. The risk ought not to materialise provided it is remembered that the doctrine depends not on the existence of inequality of bargaining power but on its abuse. That fact may not have been sufficiently clearly articulated by Lord Denning in his judgment.

Something very like a doctrine of abuse of unequal bargaining power already exists in Section 2-302 of the American Uniform Commercial Code, which reads:

> (1) If the court as a matter of law finds the contract or any clause of the contract to have been unconscionable at the time it was made the court may refuse to enforce the contract, or it may enforce the remainder of the contract without the unconscionable clause, or it may so limit the application of any unconscionable clause as to avoid any unconscionable result.

The code itself does not define 'unconscionable', but the commentary published with it says that the section is aimed at preventing 'oppression and unfair surprise' and is not intended to disturb normal allocations of risk resulting from disparities in bargaining power. It is a question to be determined by the court in each case whether the behaviour of one party has crossed the line between the free play of market forces and oppression. The relevance of bargaining power in the doctrine is that what may in some circumstances amount to oppression will be regarded between parties of more equal bargaining power as legitimate negotiating tactics.

Despite Lord Denning's efforts English law is some way from achieving a similar doctrine (see *National Westminster Bank Ltd* v *Morgan* [1985] 1 All ER 821 at 830: cf. *8.6.3*). It is unlikely to make progress until there is some change in the courts' attitude to the extent to which intervention by the courts in the interest of fairness between the parties is desirable.

NINE

Misrepresentation

9.1 INTRODUCTION

Misrepresentation comprises the law relating to contracts entered into on the basis of a false statement made during the course of contractual negotiations. A contract made as the result of a misleading representation is, subject to the limitations described in this chapter, voidable at the instance of the person to whom the misrepresentation was made (the representee). That person may also be able to recover compensation for loss sustained. Once the essential conditions for recovery for misrepresentation have been established (9.2), the combination of remedies available (9.4) depends upon the nature of the misrepresentation in question, whether fraudulent, negligent or innocent (9.3). The law applicable is a complex blend of common law, equity and statute.

Although misrepresentation is a separate body of law, requiring individual treatment, it should be noted that it enjoys close relations with and indeed sometimes overlaps several other important areas of contract law. When confronted with a problem which at first sight seems to raise issues of misrepresentation it is important to consider whether any other doctrine is also relevant, and especially to consider whether another doctrine might provide a better remedy for the victim.

In the first place, since misrepresentation relates to misleading statements made in the course of contractual negotiations, it is possible for such a statement to take on even greater significance, and by operation of the rules of offer and acceptance and incorporation of terms (see generally Chapter 5) to become an express term of the contract (see 9.2.4 and 10.1.2). The consequences of being a term are explained below (9.2.4), but the most obvious is that the falsity of the statement will inevitably result in a breach of the contract, giving rise to remedies quite different from those available for misrepresentation (see generally Chapter 12).

In addition, the circumstances giving rise to a claim of misrepresentation may also substantiate a claim of mistake (Chapter 7). For example, to state incorrectly that a piece of furniture is a genuine antique is a misrepresentation, however innocent, and may also give rise to relief in equity for common mistake (7.3.3). Equally, to enter a contract masquerading as some other person is a fraudulent misrepresentation, while it may also give rise to relief on grounds of a (unilateral) mistake of identity (7.4.3). The advantage of mistake over misrepresentation in many situations (but not in the equitable common mistake doctrine) is that if established it makes the contract void, and not merely voidable (*7.1.1*), so that the party seeking relief may be able to recover property even after it has passed into the hands of third parties.

Finally, misrepresentation must be seen as a further arm of the several doctrines designed to 'police the bargain' (see generally Chapter 8). In providing remedies for fraudulent and negligent misrepresentation, it makes a considerable contribution to policing contractual fairness. On the other hand, when considering action to be taken in the event of discovering a misleading pre-contractual statement, it is important to remember regulatory legislation intended to police such behaviour. In the case of the Trade Descriptions Act 1968 and the Property Misdescriptions Act 1991 the making of false statements is an offence, but there is no complementary civil liability incurred (although the law of misrepresentation as described in this chapter may well apply). In the case of the Package Travel, Package Holidays and Package Tours Regulations 1992 (SI 1992 No 3288) there is no civil liability arising out of the main regulations relating to false and misleading statements, but reg. 4 provides that organisers or retailers must compensate consumers for loss resulting from the supply of misleading information.

9.2   ACTIONABLE REPRESENTATIONS

For an action for misrepresentation to succeed there must have been an unambiguous, false statement of existing fact which induced the plaintiff to make the contract.

9.2.1   Representation of fact

9.2.1.1   Unambiguous, false statement   The requirement of a false statement in misrepresentation has received a quite strict interpretation. The general rule is that mere silence is not actionable, even if it amounts to concealment of a true state of affairs not apparent to the other contracting party (see *9.2.2*). Nevertheless, the courts may be willing to find the existence of a representation from conduct, without the need for words (*Curtis v Chemical Cleaning & Dyeing Co. Ltd* [1951] 1 KB 805 at 808: the facts are given at *10.6.2.3*). The critical requirement, other than the obvious one that the representation be false, is that it be unambiguous. A party making a representation which on a reasonable construction is true will not be liable for misrepresentation simply because the representee has put some other construction on it which is not true. In *McInerny v Lloyd's Bank Ltd* [1974] 1 Lloyd's Rep. 246

> the purchaser of a business defaulted on the contract, causing loss to the plaintiff seller. The seller claimed to have been induced to enter the contract by a statement in a telex sent at the purchaser's request to the seller by the defendant bank. The statement in question was an opinion expressed to the purchaser about whether

the seller would be likely to find the financing arrangements acceptable, and could not reasonably be construed as advising the seller to agree to the deal proposed.

The Court of Appeal ruled that the bank was not liable for an unreasonable interpretation put on its statement by the plaintiff seller. Thus, conduct will only give rise to an action for misrepresentation if the meaning attached to the conduct by the plaintiff is a reasonable conclusion to be drawn from the defendant's actions.

9.2.1.2 Representation of intention A representation as to the future is not a representation of existing fact, and is therefore not actionable. Thus, a person may state an intention to follow a certain course of conduct in the future. It is not misrepresentation if he is prevented from following that course of conduct, or if circumstances change so that he changes his mind about that intention, although in the latter case there may be an obligation to disclose the change of mind (see *9.2.2.2*). Nevertheless, if at the time of stating the intention the person did not in fact have any such intention then that would be treated as misrepresentation, since a present intention is a fact which can be falsely described. For example, in *Edgington* v *Fitzmaurice* (1885) 24 ChD 459

> the directors of a company offered debentures for sale, saying that the purpose of the issue of debentures was to raise money for alterations and additions to premises, and for other purposes implying an expansion of its business. In fact, the money was needed to meet the company's liabilities.

Bowen LJ noted that a representation as to the future would normally not form the basis of an action for misrepresentation, but had no hesitation in finding that where the state of a man's mind can be ascertained it is 'as much a fact as the state of his digestion'. As a result, a misstatement of the state of a man's mind is an actionable misrepresentation, and the directors in the case in question were found liable.

9.2.1.3 Statement of opinion A statement of opinion is not normally treated as a statement of fact. For example, in *Bisset* v *Wilkinson* [1927] AC 177

> the appellant sold land to the respondent, having told him that in his opinion if properly worked the land would carry 2,000 sheep. The appellant had not worked the land himself as a sheep farmer, and the statement was no more than an honest estimate, made without particular expertise, of the capacity of the land. The fact that the land did not have such a capacity did not make the appellant's statement a misrepresentation.

The Judicial Committee of the Privy Council pointed out in *Bisset* v *Wilkinson* that, where a reasonable man with the state of knowledge of the appellant could not have held the same opinion as was stated, then the fact that the statement was made in the form of an opinion would not have protected the appellant from an action for misrepresentation. This is because in stating an opinion there is an implicit representation that facts exist which are a reasonable ground for the opinion. Where in fact there is no reasonable ground for an opinion, and especially where the party stating the opinion has exclusive access to the relevant facts, then such a statement amounts to a misrepresentation. So, in *Smith v Land & House Property Corp.* (1884) 28 ChD 7

> the vendor described the tenant of property sold as 'a most desirable tenant', which was far from being the case. It was argued on the vendor's behalf that his statement had been no more than an expression of opinion.

This argument was rejected by Bowen LJ, who said that a statement of opinion by one who knows the facts best is often a statement of fact because there is an implicit assertion that facts are known which justify the opinion.

It may be that the rule that statements of opinion are not normally representations of fact may be no more than a particular application of the rule relating to the effect of misrepresentation that it is not actionable unless made with the intention that it be relied upon by the representee (*9.2.3.3*). Thus, it is common practice to preface a remark by saying, 'It is only my opinion', when it is intended that no reliance should be placed upon it. In some circumstances a statement will be made which can only be an opinion, in that conclusive proof of its truth is unavailable at the time of making the statement. Nevertheless, the courts will impose liability for misrepresentation if it was made negligently, by an apparent 'expert', and with the intention that it be relied upon (see *Esso Petroleum Co. Ltd v Mardon* [1976] 2 All ER 5; *9.3.2.1*).

9.2.1.4 Representation of law A misstatement of law will not found an action for misrepresentation. The point is acknowledged in passing in *Solle v Butcher* [1950] 1 KB 671 at 703, although the case is more relevant as an example of the fact that it is rare for a person to make a simple representation of general law. A representation of law is abstract and made without reference to particular facts (e.g. 'rent control does not apply to premises which have been substantially altered so that they are in effect new premises'). More common is for the representation to combine law and facts, so that it is a statement of the effect of the law in a given situation (e.g. 'the alterations done to these premises have made them new premises in the eyes of the law, so that rent control will not apply'). Such a statement, if false, is often described as a misrepresentation of private rights, and is actionable.

9.2.2 Silence

In most situations mere silence does not amount to an unambiguous, false representation, and therefore will not give rise to an action for misrepresentation. The general rule is usually said to be that there is no duty to disclose facts which if known might affect the other party's decision to enter the contract (*Keates v Lord Cadogan* (1851) 10 CB 591). The rule reflects the attitude of classical contract law that the parties must look after their own interests in making contracts. It may also be justified by saying that a general duty of disclosure would be too vague, since it would be impossible to specify precisely what should be disclosed. Nevertheless, the general rule is subject to certain exceptions.

9.2.2.1 Half-truths It is a misrepresentation to make statements which are true, but which do not reveal the whole facts, and so are misleading. Thus, to describe property which is the subject of negotiations for sale as fully let, without disclosing that the tenants had given notice to quit, is a misrepresentation (*Dimmock* v *Hallett* (1866) LR 2 Ch App 21).

9.2.2.2 Change of circumstances Where a truthful statement is made which is rendered misleading by a change of circumstances there is a duty to correct what has become a false impression. The classic example is *With* v *O'Flanagan* [1936] Ch 575.

> The defendant wished to sell his medical practice, and gave information to the plaintiff about the income to be derived from the practice which was true at the time it was given. The defendant then fell ill, and the income from the practice fell away almost to nothing. The sale took place five months after the original information had been given, and without the defendant disclosing that the income had fallen dramatically. On discovering the state of the practice the plaintiff sought rescission of the contract of sale.

He was successful. He was entitled to continue to believe the statement made until the time of the sale or until it was corrected, so that failure to correct it amounted to a misrepresentation.

It is less clear whether a change of circumstances causing a person to amend an opinion voiced in the course of negotiations imposes a duty to disclose the change of opinion. It might be thought that since in some circumstances an opinion is treated as a statement of fact (*9.2.1.3*), in those same circumstances at least there would be a duty of disclosure where the opinion changed. Indeed, an argument could be made for extending the duty further, since one category of opinions treated as statements of fact is those where there are no reasonable grounds for the opinion held. A change of circumstances would bring a once honestly held opinion into that category, and would appear to justify a duty of disclosure. The same argument appears to apply to statements of intention when the intention changes but is not disclosed before the time of contracting. However, despite some authority to the contrary (*Traill* v *Baring* (1864) 4 DJ & S 318), recent authority suggests that there is no duty to disclose a change of intention. In *Wales* v *Wadham* [1977] 2 All ER 125

> the plaintiff and the defendant, formerly husband and wife, agreed in the course of divorce proceedings that the plaintiff would pay to the defendant £13,000 from his share of the sale of their house in return for her promise not to seek a maintenance award. The defendant had stated several times that she would not remarry. By the

time of this agreement she had changed that intention, but did not reveal the fact to the plaintiff, who subsequently claimed that he would not have entered into the agreement had he known she was to remarry. His action for rescission failed.

9.2.2.3 Active concealment Where non-disclosure goes beyond merely remaining silent, and involves active steps taken to conceal a defect, it may amount to misrepresentation. In *Horsfall* v *Thomas* (1862) 1 H & C 90

the seller of a gun disguised a serious defect in its manufacture by inserting a metal 'plug'. The buyer did not examine the gun before entering into the contract. The gun exploded almost immediately upon its first use.

The concealment of the defect would have amounted to fraud, but for the fact that the gun had not been examined (see *9.2.3.2*).

9.2.2.4 Fiduciary or confidential relationship A fiduciary relationship is a relationship of special confidence between certain classes of people, imposing particular duties of care on those to whom confidence is entrusted. Typical examples of such relationships are solicitor and client, agent and principal (*15.4.1*) and partnership (*8.3.4*). In such a relationship there is a duty of disclosure of all material facts. There is a close relationship between this duty of disclosure and the doctrine of undue influence, as can be seen from the case of *Tate* v *Williamson* (1866) LR 2 ChApp 55 (see *8.6.2*).

9.2.2.5 Contracts *uberrimae fidei* Certain types of contract impose a duty to disclose irrespective of the nature of the relationship between the parties. They are called contracts *uberrimae fidei* (of utmost good faith), and the most common example is the contract of insurance. The insured is under a duty to disclose all material facts at the time of making the contract of insurance, and failure to disclose such facts entitles the insurer to refuse to pay when a claim is made. The rule may be explained as necessary to enable the insurer to make a proper assessment of the risk it is to underwrite. It leaves a person seeking insurance in a difficult position as far as identifying what facts are material and must be disclosed. The test is that facts must be disclosed which a reasonable or prudent insurer might treat as material (*Lambert* v *Co-operative Insurance Society Ltd* [1975] 2 Lloyd's Rep 485). On this test it has been held that a spouse's conviction for handling stolen goods is material to a contract of insurance of valuables (*Lambert* v *CIS Ltd*, above), and that a conviction for theft was material to a contract of fire insurance (*Woolcott* v *Sun Alliance & London Insurance Ltd* [1978] 1 All ER 1253).

Family settlements are also contracts *uberrimae fidei* (*Gordon* v *Gordon* (1816-19) 3 Swan 400). Certain contracts, such as contracts of suretyship, for the sale of land or for the sale of shares, are sometimes treated as being *uberrimae fidei*. The correct view is that they are not, but in each case there may be a limited duty of disclosure greater than that applying to ordinary contracts.

9.2.3 Inducing the contract
For the representation to be said to have induced the contract, four conditions must be satisfied.

9.2.3.1 Material A representation only induces a contract if it is material. It must represent a fact which would cause a reasonable person, considering entering the contract, to decide positively in favour of so doing. In many circumstances the requirement of materiality may be something of a formality, serving only to exclude trivial misstatements from actionability, or to enable the court to infer actual inducement (9.2.3.4). Thus, where a statement is made with the intention of inducing a contract (9.2.3.3), and was such as would influence a reasonable person to agree (that is, was *material*), it is not difficult to infer actual inducement (*Smith* v *Chadwick* (1884) 9 App Cas 187 at 196). Alternatively, if a representee does not act unreasonably in actually being induced to contract, it may be assumed that the representation was material.

9.2.3.2 Known to the representee It need scarcely be stated that a representation cannot be said to have induced a contract unless it was known to the representee. Thus, in *Horsfall* v *Thomas* (1862) 1 H & C 90 active concealment was held to be a misrepresentation, but the plaintiff's failure to inspect the thing in question (a gun) meant that the misrepresentation never came to his attention, and so did not induce the contract. Consistently with the general law of agency (see Chapter 15), a representation made to an agent is 'known' to the principal, whether actual knowledge exists or not (e.g., *Strover* v *Harrington* [1988] 1 All ER 769). In addition, a representation made by one party to another, which induces a third party to enter a contract, is actionable by the third party provided the first party knew or ought to have been aware that the representation would be likely to be communicated to the third party (*Yianni* v *Edwin Evans & Sons* [1981] 3 All ER 593).

9.2.3.3 Intended to be acted upon To be actionable, a misrepresentation must be intended to be acted upon. For example, in *Peek* v *Gurney* (1873) LR 6 HL 377

> the promoters of a company issued a prospectus which contained material misstatements. The intention had been to induce people to apply for the allotment of shares on formation of the company. The plaintiffs claimed to have been induced by the statements in the prospectus to purchase shares on the market.

They were unable to recover their losses, since there had been no intention on the part of those issuing the prospectus that it should be relied upon by those dealing in the shares subsequently to the original allotment. As noted above (9.2.1.3), the qualification of a statement as merely an opinion is often taken to indicate that it is not intended that the statement be relied upon.

9.2.3.4 Actually acted upon To establish that the representation induced the contract it may not be enough merely to show that it was made and known and material, and that the representee entered the contract. It is open to the representor to attempt to prove that the representee did not rely on the misstatement in deciding to enter the contract, but was persuaded by some other factor. Thus, if the representee chooses to test the truth of the statement made by making his own investigations, then he is held to rely on his own judgment and not upon the misrepresentation. For example, in *Attwood* v *Small* (1838) 6 Cl & Fin 232

> the plaintiffs sought to rescind a contract for the purchase of a mine, citing in evidence false statements made by the defendant seller about the mine's potential. However, the plaintiffs had sought to verify the seller's claims by appointing their own agent to examine the mine, and the agent had reported in similar terms.

The court found that the contract should stand, since the plaintiffs had relied on their own expert and not on the word of the seller. The fact that they had failed to discover the truth did not make the seller liable.

The mere fact that the representee fails to avail himself of an opportunity to discover the truth, for example by inspection of goods or property, does not prevent reliance on the misrepresentation. In *Redgrave* v *Hurd* (1881) 20 ChD 1

> an elderly solicitor wished to sell his house and a share in his practice. He told a prospective younger partner that the income of the practice was about £300 a year, showing him ledgers covering some £200 a year and stating that the balance was made up by income not shown in the ledgers, but derived from other work represented by a bundle of papers he had. The prospective partner did not examine the bundle of papers; had he done so he would have discovered that the income they represented was minimal.

At first instance it was held that failure to take the opportunity of inspecting the papers indicated that there had been no reliance on the misstatement. On appeal that finding was unanimously overturned. This decision, while remaining unchallenged, must now be read in the light of the developing law on negligent misrepresentation and the application thereto of the doctrine of contributory negligence (see *9.3.2.3*).

A representation will be found to have induced the contract even if it is not the only factor to have contributed to the decision to enter the contract. In *Edgington* v *Fitzmaurice* (1885) 24 ChD 459 (above, *9.2.1.2*) the representee entered the contract partly as a result of misrepresentations made, and partly as a result of his own mistake in thinking that the benefits of the contract were greater than was really the case. He was nevertheless entitled to rescission of the contract.

9.2.4 Representations which become terms
As noted above (*9.1*), a misrepresentation may in some circumstances become a term of the contract, giving rise to a possible right to terminate the contract,

and to damages, for breach. At one time it was particularly important to attempt to establish that a representation had become a term of the contract, because unless fraud could be established (9.3.1) the remedies available for misrepresentation compared very unfavourably with the remedies for breach. It has become less important since the development of more adequate remedies for negligent misrepresentation (9.3.2). Moreover, it is no longer the case that the fact that a representation has become a term extinguishes the right to rescission for misrepresentation (s.1 Misrepresentation Act 1967). Nevertheless, it will still be important to be able to determine whether a representation has become a term of the contract. In the first place, damages and rescission for negligent misrepresentation are to some extent discretionary (9.4.2.3), while damages for breach are available as of right. Further, a different measure of loss applies to misrepresentation from that applying to breach (9.4.2.4). A skilful lawyer may be able to manipulate these distinctions to his client's advantage. Detailed consideration of the circumstances in which representations become terms may be found below (10.1.2).

9.3 CATEGORIES OF MISREPRESENTATION

The remedies available for misrepresentation depend upon the nature of the misrepresentation. Important changes regarding the categories of misrepresentation and the consequent remedies occurred in the law as a result of the Misrepresentation Act 1967. It is now necessary, before it is possible to say what remedies are available, to determine whether the representor was fraudulent, negligent or innocent in making the false statement which induced the contract. In this section the elements of each type of misrepresentation are considered, while the next section (9.4) considers the elements of the various available remedies.

9.3.1 Fraudulent misrepresentation
Fraud was defined by the House of Lords in Derry v Peek (1889) 14 AppCas 337 as constituted by a false statement, made knowingly, or without belief in its truth, or recklessly, careless whether it be true or false. It must be understood that mere lack of care does not amount to recklessness, so that ordinary negligence does not amount to fraud. Lord Herschell, who provided the above definition, went on to say that, in order to constitute fraud, recklessness must amount to an absence of belief in the truth of the statement made. At one time the distinction was crucial, since proof of fraud was essential to establish a right to damages. Today, a right to damages also exists in the case of negligent misrepresentation (9.4.2.2), but the distinction is still important in some cases, since proof of fraud may permit a greater measure of recovery (9.4.2.4), and bars the court's discretion to award damages in lieu of rescission (9.4.2.3).

9.3.1.1 Remedies Fraud provides the strongest combination of remedies for misrepresentation. Rescission and damages are available, and it is generally accepted that in the case of fraud the courts will compensate all loss which

is a direct result of the misrepresentation (*Doyle* v *Olby (Ironmongers)* [1969] 2 All ER 119).

9.3.1.2   A note of caution   It is suggested above that there are still advantages, in terms of the remedies available, to a representee who can establish the existence of fraud, rather than mere negligence. Against those advantages must be weighed the fact that the courts regard fraud as a very serious allegation, and may demand more than the usual civil burden of proof from the party seeking to demonstrate its existence, and may penalise in costs a party failing to make out his case. On the other hand, the remedies for negligent misrepresentation are often as good as those for fraud, and under s.2(1) of the Misrepresentation Act 1967 the burden of proof falls partially on the representor (*9.3.2.2*). In those circumstances, bringing an action for fraud is not something which should be lightly undertaken.

9.3.2   Negligent misrepresentation
Misrepresentations which were made without due care, but were not reckless in the sense of being fraudulent (*9.3.1*), were once treated as innocent misrepresentations. As a result, although rescission was available, no damages could be recovered. It was a rule which was regarded by many lawyers and commentators as unsatisfactory, and led to sometimes artificial interpretations to the effect that a representation had been incorporated in a contract, in order to allow the recovery of damages for what would then be breach. Eventually the rule changed, but as a result of almost simultaneous, parallel common law and statutory developments, the law relating to negligent misrepresentation has become unnecessarily complicated.

9.3.2.1   Negligent misstatement at common law   In *Hedley Byrne & Co. Ltd* v *Heller & Partners Ltd* [1964] AC 465 the House of Lords extended the common law tort of negligence to the field of negligent statements which cause loss.

> The plaintiffs had been asked for credit by a company, and had sought advice on the financial standing of the company from its bankers, the defendants. The defendants, who had known the purpose of the plaintiffs' request, had carelessly said that the company was financially sound.

The House of Lords said that the defendants owed a duty of care to the plaintiffs, but that since in the particular case the advice had been given expressly 'without responsibility' there was no liability.

At common law, therefore, liability arises where there is a duty of care to do all that is reasonable to ensure that the statement made is correct. The House of Lords said that the duty exists where there is a 'special relationship' between the parties, although their Lordships were not clear what constituted a special relationship. It seems certain at least that particular types of adviser, commonly regarded as professional (such as solicitors, barristers, accountants, surveyors, etc.), have a special relationship with their clients and so owe the duty of care to those to whom they give advice. Common law negligent misstatement has recently been subject to very thorough scrutiny as part of the radical review of the law of negligence carried out by the House of Lords. In *Caparo Industries plc* v *Dickman* [1990] 1 All ER 568 their Lordships reaffirmed that liability for negligent misstatement may be imposed, but were most anxious to make clear that it would only be imposed where there is a close degree of interrelationship between the party making the statement and the party subsequently complaining. In particular, those making statements do not owe a duty of accuracy to the whole world, or to anyone who may happen to have the statement communicated to them. Lord Oliver said:

> The necessary relationship between the maker of a statement or giver of advice (the adviser) and the recipient who acts in reliance on it (the advisee) may typically be held to exist where (1) the advice is required for a purpose, whether particularly specified or generally described, which is made known, either actually or inferentially, to the adviser when the advice is given, (2) the adviser knows, either actually or inferentially, that his advice will be communicated to the advisee either specifically or as a member of an ascertainable class, in order that it should be used by the advisee for that purpose, (3) it is known, either actually or inferentially, that the advice so communicated is likely to be acted on by the advisee for that purpose without independent inquiry and (4) it is so acted on by the advisee to his detriment.

The House of Lords clearly intended to place a restrictive interpretation on the doctrine, and that lead has been followed in subsequent cases (e.g., *McNaughton (James) Papers Group Ltd* v *Hicks Anderson & Co.* [1991] 1 All ER 134; in *Morgan Crucible Co. plc* v *Hill Samuel Bank Ltd* [1991] 1 All ER 148 a duty was found to exist, but the Court of Appeal expressly relied upon the strict test outlined above).

It seems that the English courts may be willing to find a special relationship wherever the person giving advice holds himself out as possessing some expertise or special skill, and knows that the other party will rely on the advice given, irrespective of whether he is in fact a 'professional' adviser. In *Esso Petroleum Co. Ltd* v *Mardon* [1976] 2 All ER 5 the Court of Appeal found the duty of care to exist in the following circumstances:

> a salesman for the oil company made a representation about the petrol sales potential of a garage to a prospective tenant. The salesman was experienced and knew much more about the business than did the tenant, and the tenant relied on his judgment.

The common law negligent misstatement doctrine is not limited to representations which result in a contract between representor and representee (*Hedley Byrne & Co. Ltd* v *Heller & Partners Ltd*). On the other hand, it does apply to representations which induce a contract between representor and representee (*Esso Petroleum Co. Ltd* v *Mardon*). The burden of proving the existence of the duty of care and its breach rests on the representee.

9.3.2.2 Section 2(1) of the Misrepresentation Act 1967 Section 2(1) of the Misrepresentation Act 1967 provides:

Where a person has entered into a contract after a misrepresentation has been made to him by another party thereto and as a result thereof he has suffered loss, then, if the person making the misrepresentation would be liable to damages in respect thereof had the misrepresentation been made fraudulently, that person shall be so liable notwithstanding that the misrepresentation was not made fraudulently, unless he proves that he had reasonable ground to believe and did believe up to the time the contract was made that the facts represented were true.

The statutory right to damages for negligent misrepresentation is in one sense wider than that existing at common law, since it does not depend upon the existence of any kind of special relationship. In another sense, however, it is narrower, since it only applies where the representee has been induced to enter a contract with the representor by the misrepresentation. Thus, a case like *Hedley Byrne & Co. Ltd* v *Heller & Partners Ltd* [1964] AC 465 (above, *9.3.2.1*) does not fall within the ambit of the section, since the negligent misstatement did not result in a contract between the party giving the advice and the party seeking it. It is potentially narrow in another sense, in that it may not apply to the exceptional cases of representation by silence (*9.2.2 et seq.*), on the ground that such a misrepresentation is not 'made' within the terms of s.2(1). There is an *obiter* statement to that effect in *Banque Financière de la Cité SA* v *Westgate Insurance Co. Ltd* [1989] 2 All ER 952, 1004, CA, although such an approach appears unduly literal and may be inconsistent with the general purpose of s.2(1).

Where the representation does fall within the ambit of the section it is likely that the representee will choose to base his action on s.2(1) of the 1967 Act, rather than the common law, since the burden of proof is reversed as regards negligence. Once the plaintiff has established the existence of a false statement which induced him to enter the contract, it is for the defendant to show that in making the representation 'he had reasonable ground to believe and did believe up to the time the contract was made that the facts represented were true'. This reversal of the burden of proof is a considerable advantage to the plaintiff. In cases in which it is not clear whether the representor was reasonable or not, at common law the plaintiff's claim will fail; but under s.2(1) of the 1967 Act in the same circumstances the plaintiff's claim will succeed (see *1.5.5.2*; cf. *Howard Marine & Dredging Co. Ltd* v *A. Ogden & Sons (Excavations) Ltd* [1978] QB 574).

Section 2(1) of the Misrepresentation Act 1967 is rather clumsily drafted, being based on what has been described as the 'fiction of fraud' (Atiyah and Treitel, (1967) 30 MLR 369). Liability is said to exist where it would exist had the misrepresentation been made fraudulently, even though in the particular case it was not. It is far from clear why this formulation was used. It may be that it was intended to indicate that the same measure of damages as for fraud should apply (see *9.4.2.4*). It is not thought that it is intended to import any of the other special rules applying to fraud (see *9.4.2.1* and *9.3.1*).

9.3.2.3 Contributory negligence

Now that damages for negligent misrepresentation may be awarded, the question arises whether the representee's own negligence, which has contributed to his decision to enter the contract, operates to reduce proportionately the liability of the representor. Such is the effect for the general tort of negligence of s.1(1) of the Law Reform (Contributory Negligence) Act 1945. That provision has been held not to apply to liability in contract (*AB Marintrans* v *Comet Shipping Co. Ltd* [1985] 3 All ER 442; see *12.3.3.1*), but common law liability for negligent misstatement is clearly tortious (*9.3.2.1*), and the fiction of fraud in s.2(1) of the 1967 Act suggests that that liability is more akin to tortious than contractual liability (*9.3.2.2*).

Older authorities suggest that contributory negligence has no effect in the case of misrepresentation (*Redgrave* v *Hurd* (1881) 20 ChD 1; *9.2.3.4*). Those cases, however, pre-date the establishment of a separate category of negligent misrepresentation. It would not be surprising for the courts to have been unwilling to apply the contributory negligence doctrine to claims for damages for fraud. Equally, as far as rescission for innocent misrepresentation is concerned, until 1945 contributory negligence would have provided a complete defence, so that the courts may have been unwilling to find contributory negligence unless it could be said that the misrepresentation had had no role in inducing the contract (see *Attwood* v *Small* (1838) 6 Cl & Fin 232; *9.2.3.4*). Today, there seems to be no reason why s.1(1) of the Law Reform (Contributory Negligence) Act 1945 should not apply to claims for damages for negligent misrepresentation. This much was confirmed, as a matter of principle, by the judgment of Sir Donald Nicholls, V-C in *Gran Gelato Ltd* v *Richcliff (Group) Ltd* [1992] 1 All ER 865. Sir Donald Nicholls, V-C said:

> It would be very odd if contributory negligence were available as a defence to a claim for damages based on a breach of a duty to take care in and about the making of a particular representation, but not available to a claim for damages under the 1967 Act in respect of the same representation.

In applying this principle, however, he decided not to make any reduction in the damages awarded, on the ground that the defendants intended that the plaintiffs should act in reliance on the misrepresentation, so that they cannot complain when liability is imposed precisely because the plaintiffs did act in the way the defendants intended. The judge suggests that his approach is supported by the decision in *Redgrave* v *Hurd*, but we have already seen that the relevance of that decision to the issue of damages for negligent misrepresentation is questionable. In fact, it has already been suggested (see *9.2.3.3*) that a misrepresentation will not be taken to have induced the contract unless it was intended to be acted upon. Accordingly, this limitation on the application of contributory negligence appears inevitably to apply whenever liability can be established!

9.3.3 Innocent misrepresentation

An innocent misrepresentation must today be regarded as a false statement which was made neither fraudulently nor negligently. In fact, as a result of the wording of s.2(1) of the Misrepresentation Act 1967, the representee must not only have believed the statement, but must be able to *prove* that he had reasonable grounds for believing it (*9.3.2.2*). The victim of an innocent misrepresentation is entitled to rescission of the contract (*9.4.1*), and to an indemnity intended to help restore the parties to the position before the contract was made (*9.4.3*). There is no right to damages for innocent misrepresentation, but the court has a discretion to award damages in lieu of rescission provided the right to rescission has not been lost (*9.4.2.3*).

9.4 REMEDIES

In this section it is intended to consider the general and common features of the various remedies. In addition to the positive remedies of rescission (*9.4.1*), damages (*9.4.2*) and indemnity (*9.4.3*), it is important to remember that misrepresentation affords a defence to an action for breach of contract brought by the representor. This defence may be subject to the same limitations as the right to rescind (*9.4.1.1*).

9.4.1 Rescission

Rescission is available for all classes of misrepresentation. The effect of misrepresentation is to make a contract voidable, not void (see *4.5.3*), and an action for rescission is an action to have the contract set aside, restoring the parties to the position they were in before the contract was made. In theory, rescission may be effected without recourse to legal action, but in practice a party is likely to prefer to have the backing of a court order, especially where it is intended to recover property. The essential requirement of rescission, apart from satisfying the conditions of liability (*9.2*), is that notice be given to the other party. Where it is impossible to trace the other party the requirement of giving notice may be waived, provided all necessary steps have been taken to recover the goods. For example, in *Car and Universal Finance Co. Ltd* v *Caldwell* [1961] 1 QB 525

> the owner of a car had been fraudulently persuaded to sell it to a rogue, who resold it to the finance company and then disappeared with the proceeds. Once aware of the true facts the owner notified the police and the Automobile Association, and asked for their help in recovering the car. These actions were found to have been enough to rescind the contract, and since they preceded the sale to the finance company the latter did not acquire good title to the car.

The rule may be explained in terms of the injustice of denying rescission simply because a rogue perpetrated a deliberate fraud and then absconded, so that notice could not be given. On the other hand, allowing rescission in those circumstances may cause hardship to a third party who has innocently acquired goods, if, as here, it is found that the rescission occurred before the third party acquired them.

9.4.1.1 Loss of the right to rescind The right to rescind may be lost in five ways:

(a) The right to rescind is lost if the contract is affirmed by the representee after discovering the true state of affairs (*Long* v *Lloyd* [1958] 2 All ER 402). Affirmation is an indication to the representor that it is intended to continue with the contract, despite the misrepresentation. It may be made by express words or by conduct. In *Long* v *Lloyd*

> the plaintiff purchased a lorry which had falsely been represented to be in good condition. On its first journey several serious faults were discovered; they were drawn to the attention of the seller who offered to pay half the cost of repairs. On a second journey the lorry broke down again, revealing more serious faults.

The plaintiff was held not to be able to rescind the contract. The first journey did not constitute affirmation, since the buyer was entitled to a 'test drive' to check the accuracy of the representation. The second journey, however, was made in the knowledge that the vehicle when sold was not in good condition, and was affirmation of the contract.

(b) In some cases the right to rescind is lost through lapse of time. In *Leaf* v *International Galleries* [1950] 2 KB 86 (*7.3.1.4*)

> a painting was sold having been misrepresented as being by Constable. Five years later the misrepresentation was discovered, and the purchaser sought to rescind the contract of sale. His action failed because of the lapse of time since the sale.

The misrepresentation in this case was innocent (which at the time embraced both negligent and wholly innocent misrepresentation). It is generally accepted that this rule would not apply to fraudulent misrepresentation, although it might provide some evidence of affirmation. Nevertheless, it would not be strong evidence since affirmation depends upon discovery of the truth.

(c) The right to rescind is lost if *restitutio in integrum* is no longer possible; that is, if it is no longer possible to restore the parties to their position before the contract was made. Such will be the case where the nature of the subject-matter has been changed (*Clarke* v *Dickson* (1858) EB & E 145), or it has declined in value. For example, a contract for the purchase of a bottle of wine, induced by a misrepresentation about its quality, cannot be rescinded once the wine has been opened and drunk. Nevertheless, although a limited form of rescission was available at common law for fraud, it is essentially an equitable remedy, and the Chancery Court did not allow minor imperfections in the restoration of the original position to stand in the way of the remedy. For example, in *Armstrong* v *Jackson* [1917] 2 KB 822 a major depreciation in value of shares sold under a misrepresentation did not bar rescission, since it was possible to return the shares. In ordering rescission the court may impose terms, for example to account for profits and to allow for deterioration, in order to do what has been described as 'what is practically just' (Lord Blackburn in *Erlanger* v *New Sombrero Phosphate Co.* (1878) 3 AppCas 1218 at 1278). The court is much more likely to be willing to overlook imperfections in the process of restoring the original positions in the case of fraudulent than in the case of negligent or innocent misrepresentations (Lord Wright in *Spence* v *Crawford* [1939] 3 All ER 271 at 288).

(d) The right to rescind is lost if third party rights intervene (see *4.5.3*). Since a contract affected by misrepresentation is only voidable, not void, a person acquiring goods under such a contract may pass good title at any time before rescission to an innocent third party purchaser who has no notice of the misrepresentation (s.23 Sale of Goods Act 1979; and see *7.1.1*).

(e) In the case of negligent and innocent misrepresentation the right to rescind may be lost by the court's exercise of its discretion to award damages in lieu of rescission under s.2(2) of the Misrepresentation Act 1967 (*9.4.2.3*).

9.4.2 Damages

9.4.2.1 At common law The original common law position was that damages were only available for fraudulent misrepresentation, by way of a tortious action for deceit (*9.3.1*). An innocent misrepresentation, which included negligent misstatement, might be rescinded in equity, but gave rise to no common law right to damages. Instead, as part of the process of rescission an indemnity might be awarded (see *9.4.3*). It is still the case that a wholly innocent misrepresentation gives no general right to damages (but see *9.4.2.3*). However, the development of the tort of negligence (see *4.2*) eventually gave rise to an action for negligent misstatement which exists in tandem with the statutory right to damages for negligent misrepresentation (see below and *9.3.2*). Subject to s.2(2) of the Misrepresentation Act 1967 (*9.4.2.3*), the right to damages is additional to the right to rescission. Provided there is no double recovery a representee is entitled to rescission and damages. On the other hand, the Court of Appeal has recently reaffirmed that where a party goes ahead with a contract with knowledge of the misrepresentation, thereby losing the right to rescind (*9.4.1.1(a)*), the right to damages remains (*Production Technology Consultants Ltd* v *Bartlett* [1988] 1 EGLR 182).

9.4.2.2 Section 2(1) of the Misrepresentation Act 1967 Section 2(1) of the Misrepresentation Act 1967 created a statutory liability for negligent misrepresentation, providing a remedy in damages as well as the existing right to rescission (*9.3.2*). The liability is distinct from the recently established common law liability for negligent misstatement. In general there are advantages in pursuing the statutory remedy, but in some circumstances the common law right to damages may offer the only chance of compensation (*9.3.2.2*).

9.4.2.3 Damages in lieu of rescission Section 2(2) of the Misrepresentation Act 1967 provides:

Where a person has entered into a contract after a misrepresentation has been made to him otherwise than fraudulently, and he would be entitled, by reason of the misrepresentation, to rescind the contract, then, if it is claimed, in any proceedings arising out of the contract, that the contract ought to be or has been rescinded, the court or arbitrator may declare the contract subsisting and award damages in lieu of rescission, if of the opinion that it would be equitable to do so, having regard to the nature of the misrepresentation and the loss that would be caused by it if the contract were upheld, as well as to the loss that rescission would cause to the other party.

The aim of this provision is to prevent the use of the remedy of rescission, which has the very serious consequence of unravelling the contract, in the case of trivial misrepresentations for which compensation would be an adequate remedy. It should be noted that s.2(2) does not apply to fraudulent misrepresentation, since the law never treats fraud as trivial. The remedy is entirely within the discretion of the court, neither party having the right to insist upon its application. In exercising that discretion the court must weigh how serious was the misrepresentation, whether the representee will suffer greatly if not allowed to rescind, and whether the representor would suffer unduly if rescission were allowed. An example of the kind of situation covered by the section might be an innocent misrepresentation, inaccurate by only one year, of the age of a secondhand cooker. Assuming the misrepresentation was sufficiently material to have induced the sale, it might be thought that the remedy of rescission would be unduly harsh in those circumstances; but for s.2(2) it would be the only remedy available.

When the right to rescission has been lost (*9.4.1.1*), the discretion to award damages in lieu of rescission does not apply, since s.2(2) appears only to apply when there is a continuing right to rescission. The rule is perhaps to be regretted. Where the right to rescission is lost because *restitutio in integrum* is no longer possible, or third party rights have intervened, no remedy at all is available in the case of innocent misrepresentation, and it might have been preferable to allow the award of damages in lieu of rescission in those circumstances also.

9.4.2.4 Measure of damages Since the action for fraudulent misrepresentation (*9.3.1*) is the tortious action for deceit, the measure of damages is the usual tortious measure of out-of-pocket loss, rather than the contractual measure of expectation loss (cf. *12.3.1*). Thus, the representee is to be put into the position he would have been in had the representation not been made (*Peek* v *Derry* (1887) 37 ChD 541). The sum payable is usually calculated by reference to the difference between the amount actually paid and the real value of the thing in question (cf. *Smith Kline & French Laboratories Ltd* v *Long* [1988] 3 All ER 887). So, if as a result of a misrepresentation £2,500 was paid for a car really worth only £1,500, damages would be assessed at £1,000. In the case of fraud the courts are usually willing to award damages for all loss, including consequential loss such as expenses incurred as a result of entering the contract (*Doyle* v *Olby* (*Ironmongers*) *Ltd* [1969] 2 QB 158). In *East* v *Maurer* [1991] 2 All ER 733 the Court of Appeal found the *Doyle* v *Olby* (*Ironmongers*) *Ltd* formula of 'all the actual damage directly flowing from the fraudulent inducement' to include lost profits (which are more normally associated with a claim in contract). However, the profit which might have been achieved was assessed not on the basis that the representation could be regarded as a contractual promise to achieve a certain result, but only on the basis of the potential for profit had the representation been true. Damages on the latter basis were lower than on the former, presumably reflecting the element of uncertainty involved.

For negligent misrepresentation, s.2(1) of the Misrepresentation Act 1967 does not make clear the measure of damages applicable. However, since the section is based on what is known as 'the fiction of fraud' (*9.3.2.2*), it seems the statutory right to damages, as the common law right (*9.3.2.1*), is based in tort, and so the tortious (out-of-pocket) measure applies. The case law on this point has not been wholly uniform in its approach. Occasionally the courts have allowed recovery of expectation loss, but the weight of authority now seems to favour out-of-pocket loss only. Certainly, it would not seem appropriate to allow the 'fiction of fraud' to permit recovery of lost profit by analogy with *East* v *Maurer* (above). This reasoning is reflected in the decision of the Court of Appeal in *Royscott Trust Ltd* v *Rogerson* [1991] 3 All ER 294, although *East* v *Maurer* had not been reported at the time of the hearing in the case, and is not referred to. The Court of Appeal dismissed earlier conflicting authorities as wrongly decided, and concluded that it was now clear that the tortious measure of damages must be applied. However, the Court would not go against the express literal words of the statute (the 'fiction of fraud') in order to apply the general test of foreseeability for negligence, and instead allowed the more generous test in fraud (cf *Doyle* v *Olby*) to govern. To allow the *East* v *Maurer* principle of recovery of lost profits in fraud cases to apply here, by analogy with this reasoning, would not only contradict the express finding of the Court of Appeal in this case to the effect that the tortious measure of damages applies under s.2(1) of the 1967 Act; it would also be contrary to recent judicial unease about the recovery of expectation losses in tort.

It may be that the measure of damages awarded in lieu of rescission is more restricted than either the out-of-pocket or lost expectation measures. The inference from s.2(3) of the 1967 Act is that it is anticipated that damages under s.2(2) will be lower than damages under s.2(1), since the former are to be taken into account in assessing the latter. However, if the purpose of the damages is to compensate for the loss of the right to rescind, then it would seem that that loss is best measured by the difference between the contract price paid (which cannot now be recovered) and the actual value of the thing, which is the tortious measure of damages. G.H. Treitel (*Law of Contract* 7th ed., Stevens, 1987 at p.279) suggests that the limit on such damages then might be that consequential loss would be available under s.2(1), but not available under s.2(2).

9.4.3 Indemnity

As was noted earlier (*9.4.2.1*), there is no general right to damages for a wholly
innocent misrepresentation (*9.3.3*). Instead, where rescission is available it may
be possible to recover an indemnity, which falls short of any measure of damages.
An indemnity provides compensation for expenditure occurring as a result of
'obligations which have been created by the contract into which' the representee
has been induced to enter (Bowen LJ in *Newbigging* v *Adam* (1886) 34 ChD
582 at 593). The difference between indemnity and damages may be
demonstrated by reference to the facts of *Whittington* v *Seal-Hayne* (1900)
82 LT 49.

> The plaintiffs were induced to take a lease of a farm, intending to use it for poultry,
> by an innocent misrepresentation that the water supply was healthy. It proved not
> to be, and a farm manager became ill and the poultry died. They were ordered
> by the local council to renew the drains, and they lost profits and spent money
> on medical care, rent, rates, outbuildings and other business expenses. They sought
> to recover an 'indemnity' for all these costs.

They were able to recover compensation for rent, rates and renewing the drains,
since these were obligations created by the fact of taking the lease. But they
could not recover the other expenses; they were items of damages, but did
not qualify for an indemnity. They were expenses resulting from operating
a poultry farm, and there was no *obligation* to run a poultry farm *created* by
the contract.

9.4.4 Exclusion clauses

It is possible, within the limits allowed by law, to exclude or limit the normal
liability arising for breach of contract by means of an express clause in the
agreement. Such a clause operates to exclude or limit liability for a pre-
contractual statement which has been incorporated in the contract as a term
(*9.2.4*). Exclusions of this kind are treated elsewhere (*10.6*). It is also possible,
in some circumstances, to exclude liability for pre-contractual misrepresentations
which are not incorporated into the contract, by means of an express term
in the contract which was allegedly induced by the misrepresentation. In many
respects such exclusions are subject to the same constraints as exclusions of
contractual liability. For example, the clause will be interpreted restrictively,
and will only apply if it covers the representation in question (*10.6.2.2*). Some
particular rules apply in the case of misrepresentation.

In the first place, the law will not accept the exclusion of liability for one's
own fraud (*S. Pearson & Son Ltd* v *Dublin Corp.* [1907] AC 351), although
it is possible to exclude liability for the fraud of employees and others.

Secondly, s.3 of the Misrepresentation Act 1967 (as amended by s.8 of the
Unfair Contract Terms Act 1977) provides as follows:

> If a contract contains a term which would exclude or restrict —
>   (a) any liability to which a party to a contract may be subject by reason
> of any misrepresentation made by him before the contract was made; or

(b)   any remedy available to another party to the contract by reason of such a misrepresentation,
that term shall be of no effect except in so far as it satisfies the requirement of reasonableness as stated in s.11(1) of the Unfair Contract Terms Act 1977; and it is for those claiming that the term satisfies that requirement to show that it does.

It should be noted that this section applies to both negligent and innocent misrepresentations. Its effect is to raise a presumption that the exclusion clause is invalid. The clause will only be upheld if the party seeking to rely on it to avoid liability can satisfy the burden of proving that, at the time of contracting, it was reasonable, having regard to the circumstances within the contemplation of the parties (s.11(1) of the Unfair Contract Terms Act 1977). The operation of the reasonableness test is considered in more detail in relation to clauses excluding contractual liability (10.6.3.7). It may be possible to avoid the impact of the Unfair Contract Terms Act 1977 on clauses excluding liability for misrepresentation by careful drafting. Many house sale contracts contain a clause which does no more than define what are the terms of the contract, and asserts that no representations have been made which are not represented by the written terms. The effect may be to prevent a party bringing an action in reliance on a misrepresentation not expressly incorporated in the written agreement. It was suggested in *McGrath v Shah* (1987) 57 P & CR 452 that such a clause does not fall within the scope of s.3 of the Misrepresentation Act 1967. Since the purpose of such a clause is to avoid liability for misrepresentations, such a strict interpretation is perhaps to be regretted.

TEN

The substance of the contract

The essence of a bilateral contract is the existence of obligations owed by each contracting party to the other. Most disputes about contracts, and in turn most litigation, are not concerned with whether a contract has come into existence, but involve questions relating to the performance of the obligations created by the contract. Has a relevant pre-contractual statement become one of the 'promises' of the contract? Are the parties subject to obligations other than those expressed in the terms of their agreement? What standard of performance is demanded? What are the consequences of breach of the terms of the contract? Is it possible to avoid the consequences of breach? All these questions relate to the heart and substance of the contract, and are the subject of this chapter.

10.1 INCORPORATION OF TERMS

10.1.1 General

In a contract dispute it is usually much more important to know which terms have been incorporated into a contract, of which the existence is unquestioned, than it is to determine whether a contract exists at all. Nevertheless, the rules on incorporation of terms are no more than a particular application of the general principles of formation of contract, and are treated in detail in that context (5.7). So, just as a contract is only formed by an acceptance which exactly matches the terms offered (5.3.1), a term is only incorporated into the contract if it is offered by one party before the contract comes into existence and accepted by the other.

Where the terms are included in a contractual document which has been signed by the party against whom enforcement is sought, there is little scope to argue that the terms are not incorporated in the agreement (5.7.2). Where there are written terms which are alleged to have been incorporated into the agreement, it is a question of whether the offeree had reasonable notice of the terms before the time of accepting the offer (5.7.3). A third situation, where there are (often oral) pre-contractual representations which are alleged to have been incorporated into the agreement, remains to be considered below (10.1.2). Here the issue is not whether there was notice of the potential term before the time of contracting, but whether the representation was intended to raise an expectation guaranteed by the contract.

10.1.2 Representations which become terms

One legal effect of pre-contractual representations which prove to be untrue
has already been examined (Chapter 9). It was noted there that there are
sometimes advantages for the plaintiff, particularly in terms of remedies, if
the representation becomes a term of the contract (*9.2.4*). The test of whether
a representation has become a term is very imprecise. It depends upon whether,
from an objective viewpoint (*5.1.2.2*), the statement was made with the intention
that its truth be guaranteed by the contract; that is, that inaccuracy of the
statement would result in automatic breach of the contract (*Heilbut, Symons
& Co.* v *Buckleton* [1913] AC 30).

10.1.2.1 Incorporation as a term of the agreement   Although the
existence of the intention necessary for a representation to be incorporated
into the contract is regarded as a question of fact, some guiding principles
emerge from examination of the cases. In the first place, the more significant
the representation made the more likely it is to be treated as a term. In *Bannerman*
v *White* (1861) 10 CBNS 844

> the defendant asked whether sulphur had been used in the production of hops he
> was considering buying, stating that he was not interested in buying them if it had.
> He was assured that it had not. The hops were found to contain sulphur, and the
> defendant claimed to be entitled to reject them because it was a term of the contract
> that they should not.

His argument prevailed. Without the false statement there would have been
no contract, so that the statement was not merely a pre-contractual inducement
but was rather a description of the subject-matter of the sale, and was thus
a term.

Where the person making the statement is in a better position to know the
facts, or holds himself out as being, the courts may also be more willing to
treat the statement as a term of the contract. A party may hold himself out
as having special knowledge by suggesting that there is no need to check the
accuracy of the statement made (*Schawel* v *Reade* [1913] 2 IR 64). The relevance
of special knowledge is well illustrated by contrasting two cases in which material
facts about secondhand cars were falsely stated. In *Oscar Chess Ltd* v *Williams*
[1957] 1 All ER 325

> a private seller represented his car to be a 1948 Morris. It was in fact a 1939 version
> of the same model, worth substantially less. The statement of the car's age was
> held not to be a term.

In *Dick Bentley Productions Ltd* v *Harold Smith (Motors) Ltd* [1965] 2 All ER
65

> a car dealer represented a car to have an engine which had done only 20,000 miles,
> when in fact it had done five times that much.

That statement was treated as a term. The apparent distinction between the cases is the status of the person making the representation. A private seller did not have the special knowledge which indicated an intention that the statement be treated as a contractual term, but a car dealer did. This distinction led Lord Denning MR to suggest in *Dick Bentley Productions Ltd* v *Harold Smith (Motors) Ltd* that the presence of fault was the basis of the test of incorporation. It may be that in some cases fault is relevant in the sense that a person with special knowledge is held to the higher standard of contractual damages (lost expectation: *12.3.1*) by the courts because he *ought to have known better*; but it is wrong to suggest that fault is the only test, or that it is often articulated as the basis of the court's decision.

Finally, where the agreement between the parties has been reduced to writing soon after the representation was made, and the representation is not part of the writing, then there is a not unnatural presumption that the representation was not intended to be part of the contract (*Heilbut, Symons & Co.* v *Buckleton* [1913] AC 30).

10.1.2.2 Incorporation in a collateral contract In some circumstances there may be a legal reason why a representation cannot be incorporated in the major contract, for example as a result of the parol evidence rule (*10.1.3*) or the requirement of writing in respect of contracts relating to land (*6.5.3.5*). It may nevertheless, in some cases, be possible to overcome that technical disability by means of a device known as the collateral contract, which is an oral contract existing in parallel with, and sharing the subject-matter of, the major contract. For example, in *City and Westminster Properties (1934) Ltd* v *Mudd* [1959] Ch 129

> a representation was made that a landlord would not enforce a covenant in a lease preventing the tenant from residing on the premises of a shop. The tenant would not have entered into the contract without that assurance.

The assurance could not become part of the major contract because of the parol evidence rule, but the court found that it was incorporated in a separate collateral contract.

In *Heilbut, Symons & Co.* v *Buckleton* [1913] AC 30 the House of Lords said that the courts should not be quick to find such collateral contracts, and that there must be clear evidence of an intention that the representations made were intended to be of contractual force. Despite these strictures, the courts have found the collateral contract a useful device for achieving what they believe to be a just result. If anything its use has become more frequent. This trend was acknowledged by Lord Denning MR in *Esso Petroleum Co. Ltd* v *Mardon* [1976] 2 All ER 5. The Court of Appeal, in addition to finding a negligent misstatement (*9.3.2.1*), found that the apparently expert estimate of the annual petrol turnover of the garage included a collateral warranty that the estimate was sound and could be relied upon.

10.1.2.3 Conclusion In the case of incorporation in the major contract, and in the case of collateral contracts, it is difficult to give any certain rule which may confidently be used to predict which representations will be incorporated and which will not. It is hard to resist the conclusion that the courts enjoy the element of discretion which the current vague rules provide, and would not like to see them replaced by anything more certain. The basic test of contractual intention allows the court to pick and choose those representations which are to have contractual status without reference to identifiable criteria. Predictability suffers as a consequence of this rule, but it may be a price we are willing to pay for the element of fairness it may import.

10.1.3 The parol evidence rule

The parol evidence rule states that extrinsic evidence, and especially oral evidence, may not be admitted to add, delete or vary the terms of a contract which has been put into writing (e.g. *Henderson* v *Arthur* [1907] 1 KB 10). A related rule prevents use of extrinsic evidence to prove the meaning of words used in a written contract (see *10.2*). The rule only applied to express terms, and did not operate to prevent the implication of terms into the contract (*10.4*). Nor did it operate to prevent proof by extrinsic evidence of such defects in the contract as mistake (Chapter 7) and misrepresentation (Chapter 9). In disallowing any terms other than those recorded in writing the rule contributed greatly to contractual certainty, but it often did so at the expense of apparent justice, since it was often clear that further terms had been agreed, but had not been included in the writing. For this reason, the courts have developed a series of exceptions to the rule, to the extent that it can no longer be said that the general rule is that extrinsic evidence is inadmissible to prove further terms. The most important exceptions are considered below.

10.1.3.1 Rectification Rectification is an equitable remedy which allows a document to be revised where there has been a transcription mistake in recording in writing a previous oral agreement (*7.2.1*). The doctrine could not apply without there being an exception to the parol evidence rule, since extrinsic evidence must be introduced to prove the content of the original oral agreement.

10.1.3.2 Collateral contract The courts have been willing to allow the use of collateral contracts (cf. *10.1.2.2*) to step round the parol evidence rule. In theory such a contract will only be found to exist if the promise it is alleged to contain is independent of the subject-matter of the major contract (*Mann* v *Nunn* (1874) 30 LT 526). Equally, a collateral contract is supposed not to contradict the terms of the major contract (*Henderson* v *Arthur* [1907] 1 KB 10). Nevertheless, it is far from certain that courts will apply these limitations strictly. In *City and Westminster Properties (1934) Ltd* v *Mudd* [1959] Ch 129 (see *10.1.2.2*) the court found a collateral contract to exist which allowed the tenant to reside on premises let despite the fact that the major contract contained a covenant against residence.

10.1.3.3 Writing not the whole agreement A further exception to the parol evidence rule exists where the court finds that the writing which exists was not intended to include the whole of the agreement between the parties. In *J. Evans & Son (Portsmouth) Ltd* v *Andrea Merzario Ltd* [1976] 2 All ER 930

> the parties had been doing business together for some time. The plaintiffs shipped goods on trailers with the defendants, the trailers always being stored below decks on the ship. The defendants wanted to change to container transport, and the plaintiffs would only agree to the change provided the containers were also shipped below decks. The defendants gave an oral assurance to that effect. The written contract purported to allow the defendants complete freedom in the handling and transportation of the goods. One container was stored on deck, and while in transit fell into the sea.

The Court of Appeal had no doubt that there had been a breach of contract. Roskill LJ, referring to an argument based on collateral warranty, said:

> That phrase is normally only applicable where the original promise was external to the main contract, the main contract being a contract in writing, so that usually parol evidence cannot be given to contradict the terms of the written contract . . .. But that doctrine, as it seems to me, has little or no application where one is not concerned with a contract in writing (with respect, I cannot accept counsel for the defendants' argument that there was here a contract in writing) but with a contract which, as I think, was partly oral, partly in writing and partly by conduct. In such a case the court does not require to have recourse to lawyers' devices such as collateral oral warranty in order to seek to adduce evidence which would not otherwise be admissible. The court is entitled to look at and should look at all the evidence from start to finish in order to see what the bargain was that was struck between the parties.

It may be possible to avoid the kind of argument which prevailed in the above case by inserting what is known as a 'merger clause' in the written agreement. Such a clause states that the document is intended and agreed to contain the entirety of the contract between the parties. In those circumstances it would be difficult to conclude that the contract was partly in writing and partly oral. These clauses are commonly used, for example, to avoid liability for pre-contractual representations made in the course of negotiations for the sale of a house, and have been said not to fall within the scope of control of s.3 of the Misrepresentation Act 1967 over exclusion clauses (*McGrath* v *Shah* (1987) 57 P & CR 452; *9.4.4*). Whether they might be subject to s.3(2)(b)(ii) of the Unfair Contract Terms Act 1977 (*10.6.3.4*) has not been tested.

10.1.3.4 Reform The collateral warranty device, and the device of finding that the document is not intended to embody the entire agreement, both make such substantial inroads into the parol evidence rule that it may be doubted whether much of it remains to be preserved. It seems that there is ample scope for a court which wishes to avoid the rule to do so. In a recent report (Law Com. No. 154) the Law Commission decided that there was no need for legislation to abolish the rule since its effect was already widely understood to be minimal.

10.2 INTERPRETATION

Just as statutes inevitably require interpretation by the courts to overcome the inherent inability of language to capture a single meaning representing the intention of Parliament (*2.2.4*), so for similar reasons the parties' contract may also require interpretation before it can be enforced. Since the modern rules of interpretation are based on the law of the nineteenth century, which in turn was based on a theory of contractual liability created by the will of the parties (*4.4*), the basic rule is that the court must find the intention of the parties. Nevertheless, with certain exceptions, the courts are limited in the search for intention to consideration of the contract document alone. In *Lovell & Christmas Ltd* v *Wall* (1911) 104 LT 85 Cozens-Hardy MR said

> If there is one principle more clearly established than another in English law it is surely this: It is for the court to construe a written document. It is irrelevant and improper to ask what the parties, prior to the execution of the instrument, intended or understood . . .. [U]nless the case can be brought within some or one of these exceptions, it is the duty of the court, which is presumed to understand the English language, to construe the document according to the ordinary grammatical meaning of the words used therein, and without reference to anything which has previously passed between the parties to it.

The rule may be regarded as a branch of, or closely related to, the parol evidence rule (*10.1.3*). The reason for not allowing recourse to the negotiations to establish intention was explained in *Prenn* v *Simmonds* [1971] 3 All ER 237. Lord Wilberforce said that 'such evidence is unhelpful' because only when the contract is finally made is there a consensus, and until that time the parties' respective intentions may change, or be refined. There can be no guarantee, therefore, that an intention appearing during negotiations has remained constant until the time of contracting. In those circumstances it is thought safer to rely on the words of the document alone.

10.2.1 Exceptions
The exceptions which permit recourse to extrinsic evidence are limited to situations in which it can be shown objectively that there is a word or expression which has a special meaning, in which case extrinsic evidence is admissible to prove the special meaning. In *Lovell & Christmas Ltd* v *Wall* Cozens-Hardy MR said:

> If a document is in a foreign language, you may have an interpreter. If it contains technical terms an expert may explain them. If, according to

the custom of a trade or the usage of the market, a word has acquired a secondary meaning, evidence may be given to prove it.

For the first two examples given, it is possible to tell from the document itself that extrinsic evidence is needed to elucidate a special meaning. For the third example, it would be possible to take evidence from an independent expert witness that a word used in the contract did have a special trade or market meaning.

A further exception was said to exist in *The Karen Oltmann* [1976] 2 Lloyd's Rep 708. Kerr J said that, where the parties have 'in effect given their own dictionary meaning' to words used, extrinsic evidence is admissible to prove that meaning. At first sight it might seem that independent objective evidence of such a special meaning adopted by the parties could not be had, so that the exception goes beyond what had previously been allowed. However, the exception only applies where the 'contract contains words which, in their context, are fairly capable of bearing more than one meaning'. Thus, the need for interpretative help must be discernible from the document itself before extrinsic evidence of this kind will be admitted. It does not seem that the courts are willing to take the further step of admitting extrinsic evidence to establish the existence of ambiguity.

10.2.2 A residual standard for interpretation

It is sometimes said that courts should interpret documents so that the contract is given effect rather than rendered void. This rule is based on the presumption that the parties must have intended some effect from their contract when entering it, so that if two meanings are possible and one would deprive the contract of any effect the other is to be preferred. The presumption may be useful where an ambiguity cannot be resolved by reference to other evidence, but its operation should be limited to that situation. It is only a presumption, and it should not be allowed to override evidence of some other intention.

10.3 EXPRESS TERMS

10.3.1 Introduction

The primary obligations of a contract are those which determine the performance obligations of the parties (see Lord Diplock in *Photo Production Ltd* v *Securicor Transport Ltd* [1980] 1 All ER 556). The main primary obligations are created by the express terms of the contract, but it is rare for all such obligations to be articulated by the parties. Many are left to be implied as the need arises (*10.4*). In most circumstances failure to perform a primary obligation is breach of the contract (but see Discharge by Frustration, *11.4*), giving rise to a secondary obligation to pay compensation, unless the case falls within the limited category of situations in which specific performance is available (see generally, Chapter 12). The consequences of breach by one party for the other party's performance obligations depend largely upon the nature of the obligation breached (see below, *passim*), and upon whether the parties' performance obligations are 'concurrent conditions' (see *10.5.1*). What amounts to failure to perform is considered below (*10.5.2* and *10.5.3*).

Express terms fall into three categories: conditions, warranties and innominate (or intermediate) terms. The most common meaning (cf. *10.3.2.1*) of *condition* is: a major term of the contract, breach of which entitles the non-breaching party to treat the contract as having come to an end. A *warranty* is a minor term of the contract, breach of which entitles the non-breaching party to damages, but not to treat the contract as ended. An *innominate term* is a term which defies rigid classification, but may be major or minor depending upon the results of breach.

10.3.2 Conditions

10.3.2.1 Three meanings of condition In ordinary language a condition is a stipulation of something which must be fulfilled before further action will take place or results will be achieved. The law has attributed more specific meanings to the word, and it is important to distinguish between these meanings.

A *condition precedent* is a stipulation of a state of affairs which must be achieved before any contractual liability, or possibly any further contractual liability, will be incurred. In some circumstances the parties agree that a contract shall come into existence between them upon the occurrence of some event which is uncertain, but remain free to withdraw from that agreement until the event occurs (*Pym* v *Campbell* (1856) 6 E & B 370). More usually, however, the main contractual obligations do not come into force until the condition is satisfied, but the parties are contractually bound not to withdraw from the conditional agreement (*Smith* v *Butler* [1900] 1 QB 694). In these circumstances the parties may be under an obligation not to impede the occurrence of the condition (*Mackay* v *Dick* (1881) 6 App Cas 251). Sometimes there may even be an obligation to use reasonable efforts to cause the event upon which the contract is conditioned to occur, and failure to use such efforts is a breach (*Hargreaves Transport Ltd* v *Lynch* [1969] 1 All ER 455).

A *condition subsequent* is a stipulation of a state of affairs which will cause existing contractual obligations to terminate (*Head* v *Tattersall* (1871) LR 7 Ex 7). A modern example of such a condition might be a provision in a long-term supply agreement that the contract should terminate when the price of the goods in question reaches a stated amount.

Conditions precedent and subsequent, which are sometimes collectively called 'contingent' conditions, impose no positive obligation to ensure absolutely that the condition does (or does not) materialise. They must both be distinguished from *promissory conditions*, under which one party undertakes that a certain result will be achieved, and guarantees that undertaking by his promise. Failure to achieve the promised result is a breach. Thus, a promissory condition is the type of condition which is used to express a primary obligation of the contract. Where the word 'condition' is used without qualification it is almost certainly being used in the sense of a promissory condition, and it is that sense which is the subject-matter of the rest of this section.

10.3.2.2 Identifying promissory conditions Breach of a promissory condition entitles the non-breaching party to treat the contract as having been brought to an end (*10.3.2.3*). For this reason, not all the terms of the contract are classed as conditions. The parties rarely intend that breach of relatively unimportant terms should cause the entire agreement to collapse. Equally, the courts will not lightly class terms as conditions since such terms are a source of instability in contracts.

The starting point for identifying promissory conditions is the intention of the parties. Generally, description of a term as a condition, or as entitling a party to terminate the contract upon breach, will result in the court following the parties' own classification (e.g., *Lombard North Central plc* v *Butterworth* [1987] 1 All ER 267; the point is very carefully considered by Mustill LJ at pp. 271-2). Nevertheless, the courts may be unwilling to accept the parties' classification if it would produce a remedy for breach out of proportion to its result. In *L. Schuler AG* v *Wickman Machine Tools Sales Ltd* [1973] 2 All ER 39 the House of Lords refused to treat as a condition a term which began: 'It shall be a condition of this agreement that . . .'. The clause provided for weekly visits over a four and a half year period to six named firms (some 1,400 visits in total). The court did not believe that a single failure to make one of the visits would entitle the other party to bring the contract to an end. Lord Reid said:

> We must remember that we are seeking to discover intention as disclosed by the contract as a whole. Use of the word 'condition' is an indication — even a strong indication — of such an intention but it is by no means conclusive. The fact that a particular construction leads to a very unreasonable result must be a relevant consideration. The more unreasonable the result the more unlikely it is that the parties can have intended it . . ..

Diplock LJ suggested in *Hong Kong Fir Shipping Co. Ltd* v *Kawasaki Kisen Kaisha Ltd* [1962] 1 All ER 474 that a condition exists only in the case of a term 'where every breach . . . must give rise to an event which will deprive the party not in default of substantially the whole of the benefit which it was intended that he should obtain from the contract'. That definition of a condition was rejected by Megaw LJ in the Court of Appeal in *Bunge Corporation* v *Tradax Export SA* [1981] 2 All ER 513, and his view was affirmed by the House of Lords. It is too strict a test to say that *every* breach must deprive the other party of substantially the whole benefit for a term to qualify as a condition. Nevertheless, the formulation does give a good indication of the nature of terms which are conditions. They are those terms which contain the main obligations, and which are central to the existence of the contract. The determination whether or not a clause is a condition may require the court to make a 'value judgment about the commercial significance of the term in question' (per Kerr LJ in *State Trading Corporation of India Ltd* v *Golodetz Ltd* [1989] 2 Lloyd's Rep 277, approved by Lord Ackner in *Compagnie Commerciale Sucres et Denrées* v *C. Czarnikow Ltd* [1990] 3 All ER 641, 650). In *Bunge Corporation* v *Tradax Export SA* Lord Wilberforce expressly approved the *dictum* of Roskill LJ in *The Hansa Nord* [1975] 3 All ER 739 to the effect that the courts should not be too ready to interpret contractual clauses as conditions.

Certain terms which are in common use in commercial contracts have acquired, by custom and the operation of the doctrine of precedent, definitive classification as conditions. The main explanation for this is the requirement of commercial certainty. Businessmen need to know what the effect of a contractual term is, and more particularly need to know what the effect of breach will be. When words have been interpreted in a certain way by the courts, therefore, it is generally desirable that that interpretation be consistently maintained. It is particularly true of time conditions (see *United Scientific Holdings Ltd* v *Burnley Borough Council* [1978] AC 904). For example, in *The Mihalis Angelos* [1971] 1 QB 164

> a charterparty stated that the vessel was 'expected ready to load' on 1 July 1965 at Haiphong. The charterers purported to cancel the charter because their cargo was unavailable after the American bombing of the railway line to Haiphong. Such cancellation was not allowed under the terms of the contract. However, unknown to the charterers when they cancelled, at the time of entering the contract the owners had no reason to believe the ship would be ready to load on the date stated.

The phrase 'expected ready to load' was said to be a condition breach of which entitled the charterers to treat the contract as repudiated irrespective of the consequences of the breach. The point was forcefully made for time clauses generally by Megaw LJ in the Court of Appeal in *Bunge Corporation* v *Tradax Export SA*:

> I think it can fairly be said that in mercantile contracts stipulations as to time not only may be, but usually are, to be treated as being 'of the essence of the contract', even though this is not expressly stated in the words of the contract. It would follow that in a mercantile contract it cannot be predicated that, for time to be of the essence, any and every breach of the term as to time must necessarily cause the innocent party to be deprived of substantially the whole benefit which it was intended that he should have.

This approach to time clauses was recently confirmed by the House of Lords in *Compagnie Commerciale Sucres et Denrées* v *C. Czarnikow Ltd* [1990] 3 All ER 641, in which Lord Ackner cited with approval Lord Wilberforce's statement in *Bunge Corporation* v *Tradax Export SA* that time clauses in mercantile contracts should 'usually' be treated as conditions.

It should also be noted that in some circumstances, even where the original contract makes no stipulation about the time for performance, time may be made of the essence by the service of a notice to complete. In *British & Commonwealth Holdings plc* v *Quadrex Holdings Inc.* [1989] 3 All ER 492, 504 Browne-Wilkinson V-C ruled that ' . . . three requirements have to be satisfied if time for completion is to be made of the essence by the service of a notice, viz (1) the giver of the notice (the innocent party) has to be ready, willing and able to complete, (2) the other party (the guilty party) has to have been guilty of unreasonable delay before a notice to complete can be served and (3) the notice when served must limit a reasonable period within which completion is to take place'.

10.3.2.3 The effect of breach of condition Breach of condition allows the non-breaching party to treat the contract as repudiated, thus excusing any further performance on his part (*Photo Production Ltd* v *Securicor Transport Ltd* [1980] 1 All ER 556). This rule applies only to dependent conditions (see *10.5.1*). Two important points require clarification. In the first place, the slightly cumbersome expression 'allows the non-breaching party to treat the contract as repudiated', is the most accurate description of the effect of such breach. It is sometimes said that such breach discharges or terminates the contract, but neither expression is accurate since the primary obligations do not automatically come to an end, and since even if the primary obligations cease, secondary obligations under the contract exist after breach (*Photo Production Ltd* v *Securicor Transport Ltd*). It is sometimes said that such breach entitles the non-breaching party to rescind the contract, and this usage appears to have been approved by some members of the House of Lords (e.g. Lord Roskill in the *Photo Production* case, and Lord Diplock in *Gill & Duffus SA* v *Berger & Co. Inc.* [1984] 1 All ER 438). Nevertheless, this meaning of rescind is very different from the original meaning, applied in the context of misrepresentation (*9.4.1*), under which a contract is unravelled to its very beginning. Its use has been attacked several times by Lord Wilberforce (in *Johnson* v *Agnew* [1980] AC 367, and in *Photo Production*). To avoid confusion it is better to restrict the notion of rescission to misrepresentation, and in the case of breach of condition to use the more cumbersome formulation used above.

Secondly, the non-breaching party *may* treat the contract as repudiated: he is not obliged to. Thus, upon discovering a breach of condition the non-breaching party must choose (or 'elect') between regarding the contract as ended, terminating his own obligation to perform (see *Gill & Duffus SA* v *Berger & Co. Inc.* [1984] 1 All ER 438, 447), and affirming the contract, which obliges the other party to continue to perform remaining obligations under the contract and equally obliges the non-breaching party to continue to perform. In either case, the breach will cause the secondary obligation to pay damages in compensation to accrue. In either case, also, the non-breaching party's election is irrevocable (*10.3.2.4*). It is crucially important to appreciate that if, after a breach of condition, the non-breaching party affirms the contract, effectively the 'slate is wiped clean' as far as future performance is concerned. Consequently, defective or non-performance by the party electing to affirm the contract in turn becomes breach (e.g. *Motor Oil Hellas (Corinth) Refineries SA* v *Shipping Corporation of India, The 'Kanchenjunga'* [1990] 1 Lloyd's Rep 391, HL). It may even be a breach of condition entitling the other party, who was originally at fault, to treat the contract as at an end. Until such time as the non-breaching party elects to treat the contract as repudiated, it must be regarded as subsisting. In many cases, the election will be evidenced by the non-breaching party's failure to perform its side of the contract; such behaviour cannot constitute breach, as long as there has been no affirmation, because of the first breach by the other party. In the rare event of simultaneous breaches by each party, no such election can be inferred, and there will be no effect upon the parties' mutual obligations until one accepts the other's repudiatory breach (*State Trading Corporation of India* v *Golodetz Ltd* [1989] 2 Lloyd's Rep 277).

10.3.2.4 Loss of the right to treat the contract as repudiated The right to treat the contract as repudiated may be lost by election (sometimes called 'waiver'), by estoppel, and by operation of s.11(4) of the Sale of Goods Act 1979. It is not lost by mere lapse of time.

The doctrines of election and estoppel are closely related, but significant differences between them exist. The doctrine of election was described by May LJ in the Court of Appeal in *Peyman* v *Lanjani* [1984] 3 All ER 703 at 729:

> The choice becomes irrevocable even though, if and when the first person seeks to change his mind, the second cannot show that he has altered his position in any way. This being so, I do not think that a party to a contract can realistically or sensibly be held to have made this irrevocable choice between rescission and affirmation unless he has actual knowledge not only of the facts of the serious breach of the contract by the other party which is the precondition of his right to choose, but also of the fact that in the circumstances which exist he does have that right to make that choice which the law gives him.

Thus, a party only loses the right to treat the contract as repudiated if he elects to affirm the contract in full knowledge of the right to treat it as repudiated. However, in those conditions the election is binding without the other party needing to prove any reliance on the election.

It was pointed out in *Clough* v *London and North Western Ry Co.* (1871) LR 7 Ex 26 that while a party has not made an election, and is still deliberating what to do, the right to treat the contract as repudiated may be lost by estoppel if the position of the breaching party is in the meantime affected. In *Peyman* v *Lanjani* May LJ adopted the following passage from the Australian case *Coastal Estates Pty Ltd* v *Melevende* [1965] VR 433 at 443:

> If the defrauded party does not know that he has a legal right to rescind, he is not bound by acts which on the face of them are referable only to an intention to affirm the contract, unless those acts are 'adverse' to the opposite party, i.e., unless they involve something to the other party's prejudice or detriment . . .. This is a form of estoppel, for the other party has in such a case acted upon a representation, made by the defrauded party's conduct, that the latter is going on with the contract.

The application of these principles is well illustrated by the facts of *Peyman* v *Lanjani*.

The defendant entered into an agreement for the assignment to him of a lease which was expressed to be non-assignable without the consent of the landlord. The landlord's consent was obtained by deception. The plaintiff then agreed to purchase the lease from the defendant, and again an attempt was made to obtain the landlord's consent by deception, although the plaintiff was not a party to this. On discovering the deception the plaintiff consulted the solicitor acting for both parties, who urged him to proceed with the purchase. The plaintiff therefore paid the first £10,000 of the purchase price. A month later the plaintiff consulted new solicitors, who advised him of his right to terminate the agreement on account of the defect in the defendant's title caused by the original deception.

The Court of Appeal found that the plaintiff had not lost the right to treat the contract as repudiated. The payment of £10,000 was not an irrevocable election, because it had been made before the plaintiff was aware of the full facts, including that he had a right to treat the agreement as at an end. Nor did it give rise to an estoppel preventing the plaintiff from treating the contract as repudiated, most particularly because there was no detriment to the defendant.

Under s.11(4) of the Sale of Goods Act 1979 a contract may not be treated as repudiated once the buyer has accepted the goods or part of them. Under ss.34(1) and 35(1) of the 1979 Act acceptance occurs either by express indication to the seller, or, provided there has been reasonable opportunity to examine the goods, by any act inconsistent with the seller's ownership, or by lapse of reasonable time without indicating the intention to reject. This rule is similar to election in that it does not depend upon detrimental reliance by the seller; but unlike election and like estoppel it may operate without the buyer actually knowing of the right to treat the contract as repudiated.

Except as described above in the case of the sale of goods, the right to treat the contract as repudiated is not lost by mere lapse of time. The contrary view is canvassed in *Antaios Compañía Naviera SA* v *Salen Rederierna AB* [1983] 3 All ER 777, aff'd on other grounds [1984] 3 All ER 229, but the argument there that there is an implied term that notice of withdrawal must be given within a reasonable time relates to the particular context of a charterparty, and should not necessarily be regarded as being of any wider application. Nevertheless, in a limited number of circumstances lapse of time might result in prejudice to the breaching party, or might be regarded as evidence of an intention to continue with the contract, in which case the right to treat the contract as repudiated would be lost (per Fenton Atkinson LJ in *Allen* v *Robles* [1969] 3 All ER 154).

10.3.3 Warranties

A warranty is a term of a contract containing a minor primary obligation. Breach of such a term gives rise to a secondary obligation to pay damages, but does not entitle the non-breaching party to treat the contract as repudiated. The distinction between conditions and warranties is traditionally demonstrated by contrasting two cases with similar facts. In *Poussard* v *Spiers* (1876) 1 QBD 410 a singer, hired to perform during the entire run of an operetta, did not arrive until after one week of the run, when a substitute had been taken on.

The court found that the singer's obligation to appear as from the first night was a condition, the breach of which entitled the show's producer to dispense with her services. In *Bettini* v *Gye* (1876) 1 QBD 183

a singer, hired to perform during an entire season, had agreed to arrive six days in advance for rehearsals, but was three days late.

The court did not believe that the clause relating to rehearsals was so central to the main purpose of the contract that it was a condition. The singer's breach, therefore, did not allow the contract to be treated as repudiated, but only allowed recovery of damages for whatever loss had been suffered.

In the past the courts maintained that the distinction between condition and warranty was to be made without considering the actual results of breach, and was to be determined on the basis of the relative importance of the term in the context of the contract as a whole. Today, it is still the case that where the parties have expressly designated a term to be merely a warranty, or where the term is classed as a warranty by statute (*10.4.5*), the consequences of the actual breach ought not to be taken into account. But where there is no express classification of the term by either of these means it seems unlikely that the court would class a term as a warranty without, under the innominate term doctrine (below, *10.3.4.2*), first considering the result of the breach.

10.3.4 Innominate or intermediate terms

In *Hong Kong Fir Shipping Co. Ltd* v *Kawasaki Kisen Kaisha Ltd* [1962] 1 All ER 474

Clause 1 of a contract for the charter of a vessel for a period of two years described the vessel as 'being in every way fitted for ordinary cargo service'. When delivered to the charterers the vessel was unseaworthy, because her engines were old. On her first voyage under the charter she needed repairs, and it was 18 weeks before she was properly seaworthy. The question for the court was whether the breach of clause 1 entitled the charterers to treat the contract as repudiated, or only entitled them to damages.

Diplock LJ said:

There are, however, many contractual undertakings of a more complex character which cannot be categorised as being 'conditions' or 'warranties' . . . .. Of such undertakings all that can be predicated is that some breaches will, and others will not, give rise to an event which will deprive the party not in default of substantially the whole benefit which it was intended that he should obtain from the contract; and the legal consequences of the breach of such an undertaking, unless provided for expressly in the contract, depend on the nature of the event to which the breach gives rise and do not follow automatically from a prior classification of the undertaking as a 'condition' or a 'warranty'.

Such terms were christened 'innominate' (there being no technical name for them) or 'intermediate' (since they lay somewhere between conditions and warranties in terms of relative importance).

10.3.4.1 Identifying innominate terms The analysis proposed by Diplock LJ was immediately welcomed by the courts (cf. Lord Wilberforce in *Reardon Smith Line* v *Hansen-Tangen* [1976] 3 All ER 570 at 576). Nevertheless, more recently there has been some reaction against the uncertainty the doctrine can introduce into commercial contracts. In *Bunge Corporation* v *Tradax Export SA* [1981] 2 All ER 513

> Buyers agreed to purchase 15,000 tons of soyabean meal from the sellers. The contract provided for three shipments of 5,000 tons, one of which was to be made during June 1975. Under the contract the buyers were to provide a vessel at a nominated port, and were to give 15 days' notice of expected readiness of the vessel. For shipment in June, therefore, notice had to be given by 13 June. Notice was in fact given on 17 June.

The Court of Appeal and House of Lords both found the delay in giving notice to be a repudiatory breach of the contract. Lord Wilberforce said that certain contractual terms, especially those agreed by the parties to give rise upon any breach to a right to treat the contract as repudiated, were not amenable to treatment as innominate terms. He said that the contrary proposition would be 'commercially most undesirable . . . .. It would fatally remove from a vital provision in the contract that certainty which is the most indispensable quality of mercantile contracts'.

The identification of innominate terms then becomes a process of elimination, in the sense that all terms which are not so important that breach will always entitle the non-breaching party to treat the contract as repudiated (conditions), and which equally are not so unimportant that their breach would never entitle the non-breaching party to treat the contract as repudiated (warranties), are innominate or intermediate terms. In practice, the essential distinction to be made is between conditions and innominate terms (discussed above at *10.3.2.2*), since, except in the case of terms expressly designated as warranties, there will be no point in finding a term to be a warranty before considering the result of breach.

10.3.4.2 The effect of breach of an innominate term The essential flexibility, or fatal uncertainty, of innominate terms stems from the fact that it is not possible to predict before the time of the breach what the legal effect of breach of such a term will be. Thus, where the result of the breach is substantially to deprive the non-breaching party of the benefit he was intended to obtain under the contract the term will be treated as a condition (*10.3.2.3*), so that the non-breaching party is entitled to treat the contract as repudiated, subject to the usual limits on that right (*10.3.2.4*). Where, however, the result of the breach is to cause loss to the non-breaching party, without substantially depriving him of the benefit he was intended to obtain under the contract, then the term will be treated as a warranty (*10.3.3*), so that the breach gives rise to a secondary obligation to pay compensation for the loss caused, but gives no right to treat the contract as repudiated. The doctrine that the remedy available for breach depends upon the actual result of the breach was explained by Upjohn LJ in *Hong Kong Fir Shipping Co. Ltd* [1962] 1 All ER 474 in respect of a seaworthiness clause in a charterparty:

> Why is this basic and underlying condition of seaworthiness not, in fact, treated as a condition? It is for the simple reason that the seaworthiness clause is breached by the slightest failure to be fitted 'in every way' for service. Thus . . . if a nail is missing from one of the timbers of a wooden vessel, or if proper medical supplies or two anchors are not on board at the time of sailing, the owners are in breach of the seaworthiness stipulation. It is contrary to common sense to suppose that, in such circumstances, the parties contemplated that the charterer should at once be entitled to treat the contract as at an end for such trifling breaches.

The innominate term is a focal point of the tension which always exists in the law of contract between the sometimes conflicting interests of certainty and fairness. The decision in *Bunge Corporation* v *Tradax Export SA* [1981] 2 All ER 513 may have signalled a move away from excessive flexibility in favour of certainty, but it seems unlikely that the courts will be willing to institute a rigid binary classification of conditions and warranties. It is for the parties, if they value certainty so highly, to ensure by careful drafting of their contracts that the consequences of breach of every term are clearly stated, avoiding the possibility (save in exceptional cases: see *10.3.2.2*) of the court treating a term as innominate.

10.4 IMPLIED TERMS

10.4.1 Introduction

In many contracts, although the main primary obligations are contained in express terms, the parties do not express all the primary obligations, or do not provide for every eventuality. The courts use the device of the implied term to fill the gaps in the parties' contract. To take a simple example, when a student goes into a shop to buy a new textbook, the bookseller and the student do not discuss or express any terms relating to the quality of the book to be sold. Nevertheless, if the book proved to have been bound with an important section missing the student would be appalled to hear that he had no remedy against the bookseller. On the contrary, it is understood that what is being sold must be a book which is in the state a book of that description would normally be in, and fit for the purposes to which such a book would normally be put. That understanding is incorporated into the contract by means of an implied term (in the particular case, a term derived from statute: s.14(2)(b) Sale of Goods Act 1979 — see *10.4.3.2*).

The device of implying terms into contracts to fill out gaps in the express terms has existed since at least the early nineteenth century (cf. *Hutton* v *Warren* (1836) 1 M & W 466). It is something of an embarrassment to the classical theory of contract, which attributes the source of all contractual obligations to the expression of the will of the parties. At first it was maintained that the implication of terms was only ever an exercise of construction of the facts to seek the parties' intentions. In other words, implied terms were consistent with classical theory since they merely filled gaps where the parties' will had operated but had not been expressed. It is no longer possible to accept that terms are only implied when the parties had intended such terms but have simply failed to express them. It is true that some terms are implied as 'one-off' terms which seem inevitably to have been intended to supplement the express terms of the contract (*10.4.2*). It is equally clear, however, that some terms are implied irrespective of the intentions of the parties (*10.4.3*). In the example above of the sale of a book, the obligation to meet a certain quality standard is said to derive from an implied term, but it may not be certain that the bookseller intended such a term. Indeed, it may be more honest simply to state that in that situation a positive obligation of the law of contract is imposed on the seller, whatever his intentions (cf. Stephenson LJ in *Mears* v *Safecar Security Ltd* [1982] 2 All ER 865). The notion of an *imposed* obligation is all the more persuasive because in our example it may be impossible for the seller to exclude liability for the obligation (*10.6.3.5*).

In practice, in many cases the courts do not distinguish between terms implied as fact and terms implied in law, and some categories of implied term, which once might have been regarded as implied as fact, are probably now treated as types of imposed obligation (*10.4.4*). This development has taken on greater significance since the Privy Council asserted in *Tai Hing Cotton Mill Ltd* v *Liu Chong Bank Ltd* [1985] 2 All ER 947 at 957 that the law should not seek to develop tortious duties where the parties are in a contractual relationship (although in this same decision Lord Scarman doubted whether implied terms of the contract were properly to be regarded as 'imposed' obligations). The Privy Council's view on the relationship between contracts and tortious duties was adopted for English law by the Court of Appeal in *Johnstone* v *Bloomsbury Health Authority* [1991] 2 All ER 293. Whatever the conceptual basis of implied terms of this type (and no doubt the prevailing political philosophy of the 1980s discouraged courts from wishing to appear to regulate market-based transactions by imposing terms), in practice the courts are inevitably drawn into ensuring that contracts of a recognisable and frequently occurring type conform to general expectations of what obligations such contracts should contain. It is important to realise, however, that while the courts today may be more willing to imply terms than once they were, there are important limits on the implied term device. In the first place, the greater the number of gaps in an alleged contract the more reluctant the court may be to 'write the parties' contract' for them (cf. Lord Wright in *Hillas & Co. Ltd* v *Arcos Ltd* (1932) 147 LT 503: *5.6.1*). Secondly, and perhaps paradoxically, where the parties'

contract consists of a detailed set of written terms the courts may be unwilling
to add to those terms by implication, except in so far as the law generally
imposes obligations in the type of situation in question (*Shell UK Ltd v Lostock
Garage Ltd* [1977] 1 All ER 481). This raises the question of the relationship
between express and implied terms. An implied term cannot co-exist with an
express term which flatly contradicts it; but where the exact scope of an express
term leaves some latitude in its application it may be narrowed or widened
by an implied term (*per* Browne-Wilkinson V-C in *Johnstone v Bloomsbury
HA* [1991] 2 All ER 293 at 304–5).

10.4.2 Terms implied as fact
Terms are implied as fact on the basis of an intention imputed to the parties
from their actual circumstances. Thus, there is no question of imposing a legal
obligation irrespective of the parties' intentions. Such a term will only be implied
if the contract would be incomplete without it. In the words of Lord Cross
in *Liverpool City Council v Irwin* [1976] 2 All ER 39:

> What the court is being in effect asked to do is to rectify a particular —
> often a very detailed — contract by inserting in it a term which the parties
> have not expressed. Here it is not enough for the court to say that the
> suggested term is a reasonable one the presence of which would make the
> contract a better or fairer one; it must be able to say that the insertion
> of the term is necessary.

In the Court of Appeal Lord Denning MR had suggested that such a term
might be implied where it was just and reasonable in the circumstances. His
suggestion was rejected by the House of Lords, although their Lordships applied
a similar test to the separate category of terms implied in law (*10.4.3.1*).

The classic test for the implication of a term as fact is found in *Shirlaw
v Southern Foundries Ltd* [1939] 2 KB 206. MacKinnon LJ said:

> Prima facie that which in any contract is left to be implied and need not
> be expressed is something so obvious that it goes without saying; so that,
> if, while the parties were making their bargain, an officious bystander were
> to suggest some express provision for it in their agreement, they would
> testily suppress him with a common 'Oh, of course!'.

The nature of those terms which may be implied as fact is very varied, although
in practice the number of terms so implied is relatively few. Any term which
although not expressed is obviously necessary to make the contract work may
be implied, and it is impossible to give any guidelines on what is or is not
likely to be accepted by the courts. On the other hand, it must be recognised
that the so-called 'officious bystander' test stated above imposes a very strict
standard for the imposition of terms (cf. Lord Wilberforce in *Liverpool City
Council v Irwin*). Attempts to have terms implied on this basis often fail on
the simple ground that while one of the parties would clearly have assented

to the term if it had been proposed, the same cannot unquestionably be said of the other party.

10.4.3 Terms implied in law

Terms implied in law do not depend upon any intention imputed to the parties. They consist of legal obligations generally imposed on one of the parties in a common contractual relationship, without reference to the particular circumstances (except perhaps to determine whether a contrary intention has been expressed). Some such legal obligations are imposed by the courts; many, although originally imposed by the courts, have now been given statutory force.

10.4.3.1 Obligations imposed by the courts Lord Denning MR described the process of implication of terms in law in *Shell UK Ltd* v *Lostock Garages Ltd* [1977] 1 All ER 481. He said that it occurs in all common contractual relationships, such as seller and buyer, master and servant, landlord and tenant, and so on. He went on:

> In such relationships the problem is not solved by asking: what did the parties intend? Or, would they have unhesitatingly agreed to it, if asked? It is to be solved by asking: has the law already defined the obligation or the extent of it? If so, let it be followed. If not, look to see what would be reasonable in the general run of such cases . . . and then say what the obligation shall be.

The basis for the implication of terms in this way appears to be the desire to regulate certain common types of contract. It is done so that one party does not take unfair advantage of another, and so that adequate protection is given to both parties even when, as is often the case with such common contracts, little time is spent on detailed negotiation of the terms. Thus, the common contracts have taken on a standard content, by implication of terms in law. As is apparent from the passage quoted from Lord Denning MR above, in the case of terms implied in law, the finding of a term in one case may be binding in terms of precedent in subsequent cases. Such would be inconceivable in the case of terms implied in fact.

The leading case on legal obligations imposed on a contracting party by the courts is *Liverpool City Council* v *Irwin* [1976] 2 All ER 39.

> The Council let flats and maisonettes in a tower block to tenants. The lifts and rubbish chutes of the tower block constantly broke down. The tenancy agreement imposed certain obligations on tenants, but was silent about the obligations of the Council for maintaining the building. The appellants withheld their rent in protest at the Council's failure to maintain the building properly. The Council brought an action to obtain possession of the appellants' maisonette, and the appellants counter-claimed for breach of an implied obligation to keep the block in proper repair.

As was noted earlier (*10.4.2*), the House of Lords was unwilling to imply a term as fact into the particular agreement. But their Lordships were willing to imply, as a necessary incident of all tenancy agreements in which the tenants are granted the use in common of stairways, corridors, lifts etc., an obligation on the landlord 'to take reasonable care to keep in reasonable repair and usability' the common parts (per Lord Wilberforce).

According to Lord Cross, the test to be applied in deciding whether to imply such a term generally in all contracts of a particular type is 'whether in the general run of such cases the term in question would be one which it would be reasonable to insert'. Lord Wilberforce suggested that the test was one of necessity, but the term which he implied was not absolutely necessary, although the tenancy agreements would have been unreasonable without it. Lord Cross' test was followed in *Shell UK Ltd* v *Lostock Garages Ltd* (above), as appeared logical since the distinction between necessary on the particular facts and reasonable in a particular category of contracts seemed to embody the distinction between terms implied in fact and terms implied in law. However, recent authority suggests that Lord Wilberforce's test of necessity has prevailed. Lord Scarman in *Tai Hing Cotton Mill Ltd* v *Liu Hong Bank Ltd* [1985] 2 All ER 947 at 955 PC, and Lord Bridge in *Scally* v *Southern Health and Social Services Board* [1991] 4 All ER 563 at 571, both refer to terms which are a 'necessary incident' of a ('definable category of': *per* Lord Bridge) contractual relationship. Despite what may be seen as an unfortunate parallelism of language, it seems that 'necessary on the facts' and 'necessary incident of a definable category of contractutal relationship' must have different meanings. The notion of 'necessary incident' draws upon a much wider set of criteria to determine its meaning, and it must be supposed that ultimately terms implied in law on the basis of being a necessary incident of such contracts are founded upon reasonable expection (see further: Phang, 'Implied Terms in English Law' [1993] JBL 242).

10.4.3.2 Obligations imposed by statute Certain obligations once imposed by the courts have now been given statutory force. Most important among these are terms relating to quality in the case of sale or supply of goods, and those relating to the standard of care in contracts for services. For example, s.14(2) of the Sale of Goods Act 1979 provides:

Where the seller sells goods in the course of a business, there is an implied condition that the goods supplied under the contract are of merchantable quality, except that there is no such condition —
(a)   as regards defects specifically drawn to the buyer's attention before the contract is made; or
(b)   if the buyer examines the goods before the contract is made, as regards defects which that examination ought to reveal.

It should be noted that the statute does not impose the obligation to supply goods of merchantable quality on all sellers: only those who sell in the course of a business are within the scope of the section. 'Merchantable quality' is defined by s.14(6); the standard requires that the goods be fit for the purpose for which such goods are usually bought, having regard to all the circumstances, including the price. Thus, a secondhand car bought from a dealer must be merchantable, but need not be in the mint condition which would be expected of a brand new car of the same make. Under s.14(3) of the Sale of Goods Act 1979, where the buyer makes known to the seller a particular (as opposed to the usual) purpose for buying the goods in question, there is a further implied condition that the goods be fit for that particular purpose. Similar implied conditions apply to contracts for the supply of goods other than by way of sale (e.g. goods to be incorporated into building work being done) under s.4 of the Supply of Goods and Services Act 1982.

Contracts for the supply of services were until recently the domain of the common law as far as implied terms governing standards of performance were concerned (cf. *Lister* v *Romford Ice and Cold Storage Co Ltd* [1957] AC 555). Such contracts have now also been regulated by statute. Under s.13 of the Supply of Goods and Services Act 1982 there is an implied term that the supplier of services will carry out the service with reasonable care and skill. It should be noted that this standard is different from that applying to the sale or supply of goods. In the case of the latter the obligation to meet the required standard is absolute, and it will not be a defence to an action for breach of the implied term of, for example, merchantable quality, that the seller did his best to supply goods of that quality. In the case of the supply of services, however, the desired result need not be achieved provided reasonable care and skill was used in attempting to achieve it. The exact scope of the obligation of reasonable care and skill depends upon the obligations expressly undertaken by contract. In *Wilson* v *Best Travel Ltd* [1993] 1 All ER 353

> the defendant tour operator advertised a holiday in Greece in its brochure, which indicated that the tour operator inspected all accommodation offered as part of package holidays. The plaintiff was seriously injured in a fall against a glass door which met Greek but not British safety standards.

Phillips J rejected the notion that there was a general duty to provide 'safe' accommodation to be implied into every package holiday contract. But where the contract included the service of inspection of properties offered in the brochure, such inspection must be carried out with reasonable care and skill with a view to matters of safety, amongst other things. In this case the judge found the duty to have been satisfied. It seems, however, that the judge was willing to contemplate that no such duty would have arisen if the contract had not expressly indicated that such inspection would take place. It should be noted that obligations of suppliers of package holidays are affected and largely increased by the Package Travel etc. Regulations 1992 (see below: *10.4.3.3*).

As a conseqence of this difference between strict obligations and obligations of reasonable care, it may be necessary to distinguish between contracts for goods and contracts for services. The test is very much one of impression, and the courts have not given clear guidance on the matter. Broadly, it may be said that if the main purpose of the contract is to convey title to goods, and any service element is incidental to the main purpose, then the contract will be treated as relating to the sale of goods, and even the service element may be regarded as subject to a strict obligation. On the other hand, where the predominant element is service the contract will not be one of sale, although under the 1982 Act strict liability will nevertheless apply to any goods supplied. Between these two relatively straightforward possibilities lie a multitude of less clear situations for which little guidance is available. One possibility is that in some cases the service and goods elements must be severed, and liability adjusted accordingly.

10.4.3.3 Increasing significance of statutory duties Regulation of contracts belonging to definable categories, and which occur frequently, by means of statutory imposition of terms, appears to be an increasing phenomenon. Although Parliament only rarely finds time for the kind of law reform such legislation requires, there is no doubt that the particular policy of consumer protection is more likely to be accommodated within the Parliamentary timetable than more arcane matters, not least because electors take an interest in it. There is a further source of law reform the importance of which must not be overlooked. As part of the programme of harmonisation of the law of member states in order to ensure that there is a single market for goods and services, the European Community is addressing the question of the content of typical contracts throughout the member states. So, for example, the United Kingdom Package Travel, Package Holidays and Package Tours Regulations 1992 (SI 1992 3288) are based upon Council Directive 90/314/EC [1990] OJ L158/59, and the purpose of the directive is to standardize the law relating to package holidays and the contracts governing them in all member states. It should be noted that law reform of this kind, which implements EC directives in the field of consumer protection, does not require Parliamentary legislation by virtue of s.2(2) of the European Communities Act 1972, which allows such implementation to be effected by Order in Council contained in a statutory instrument. Further, more general reform of the law relating to implied terms is anticipated as a result of a proposed directive on contracts for the supply of services, although at the present time there is no agreement within the Community institutions on the drafting of the directive. These European initiatives must also be seen in the light of the Council Directive on unfair terms in consumer contracts (Directive 93/13/EC [1993] OJ L95/29: see further *10.7*).

10.4.4 Blurring the categories
Although two distinct categories of implied terms (as fact and in law) are now recognised by high authority (cf. *Liverpool City Council* v *Irwin* [1976] 2 All ER 39), it may be that the categories are not as distinct as the courts make out. For example, in *Wilson* v *Best Travel Ltd* [1993] 1 All ER 353 Phillips J expressed agreement with the judge in an unreported case who had found implication of a particular term 'neither necessary nor obvious nor reasonable', without discrimination as to what was the proper test for implying a term in the circumstances. Two particular types of implied term appear to embody elements of both categories.

The earliest forms of implied term were those implied by custom. Thus, in *Hutton* v *Warren* (1836) 1 M & W 466

> the court implied a term into an agricultural lease that upon quitting tenants were entitled to an allowance for seed and labour, on the basis of a custom which was said to be incorporated into all such contracts unless altered by them.

It was once thought that such terms were incorporated by virtue of what it might be assumed in all the circumstances must have been the intention of the parties, treating them as a species of term implied as fact. Today, the incorporation of customary terms, especially those in general use in a particular trade, may owe more to the courts' desire to regulate the content of contracts by encouraging the use of standardised terms. Such an approach would be more closely akin to that of terms implied in law. For example, in *British Crane Hire Corporation Ltd* v *Ipswich Plant Hire Ltd* [1974] 1 All ER 1059

> the Court of Appeal ruled that the contract was subject to terms not seen by the offeree before the time of contracting, but which were a version of the 'Contractors' Plant Association' terms which were customarily used in the particular trade, and with which both parties would have been familiar. The term in question related to liability for the cost of recovering a crane if it got bogged down in soft ground.

It is doubtful whether it would have satisfied the strict test for implication of terms as fact (*10.4.2*).

A fruitful source of implied terms has been the so-called 'business efficacy' rule first articulated in *The Moorcock* (1889) 14 PD 64.

> The plaintiffs had agreed with the defendants that the plaintiffs' ship should load and unload at the defendants' wharf on the Thames. Both parties knew that the ship would settle on the river bed at low tide, but the defendants had not expressly guaranteed the good condition of the river bed. The ship was damaged while at the wharf by settling on hard ground rather than on mud. The question was whether there was an implied term in the contract that the river bed was suitable for allowing the plaintiffs' ship to settle on it when at the wharf.

The court found such a term to exist. Bowen LJ said:

> An implied warranty, or as it is called a covenant in law, as distinguished from an express contract or express warranty, really is in every instance founded upon the presumed intention of the parties and upon reason. It is the implication which the law draws from what must obviously have been the intention of the parties, an implication which the law draws with the object of giving efficacy to the transaction.

These 'business efficacy' implied terms have always been regarded as examples of terms implied as fact, and the references to what is necessary to make the transaction work, and to presumed intention, support that idea (see *10.4.2*). But Bowen LJ said that such terms are also based on 'reason', which is the test normally associated with terms implied in law, and has specifically been rejected in the case of terms implied as fact (cf. *Liverpool City Council* v *Irwin* [1976] 2 All ER 39).

10.4.5 Classification of implied terms

Just as express terms may be classified according to their relative importance (*10.3.1*), so some implied terms are more important than others. Thus, the Sale of Goods Act 1979 always specifies whether the term to be implied is a condition or a warranty. For example, there is an implied *condition* that goods sold in the course of a business will be of merchantable quality (s.14(2)), so that breach of that term entitles the buyer to reject the goods and treat the contract as repudiated (s.11(3)). There is also an implied *warranty* that goods are free from any charge or encumbrance not disclosed to the buyer before the contract was made (s.12(2)(a)). Breach of that term only allows a remedy in damages. On the other hand, s.13 of the Supply of Goods and Services Act 1982, which imposes an obligation of reasonable care and skill in the supply of services, refers only to an 'implied term'. It must be assumed that the statutory intention was for this term to be treated by the courts as innominate.

Except in the case of statutory implied terms, there is no reason for prior classification of implied terms, since the terms are not known to the parties until the time of litigation. There is, therefore, no requirement of certainty or predictability of the effect of breach of such terms, since being implied they cannot be relied upon in the course of a party's planning. The court is free simply to indicate, when specifying the precise scope of the term to be implied in any given case, whether the term is a condition or a warranty. It seems likely that in practice the courts will only do so after considering the consequences of the breach which has been found to have occurred (see generally *10.3.4*).

10.5 SCOPE OF THE PERFORMANCE OBLIGATION

This section examines the standard of performance expected under a contract, and the impact on the other party of failure to achieve that standard. The basic rule is that performance must exactly match that which it was undertaken to perform in the contract, and any deviation from that standard is breach. If the term is classed as a condition, or the breach relates to an innominate term and goes to the root of the contract, the non-breaching party is entitled to cease performance of his obligations under the contract (*10.3.2.3* and *10.3.4.2*). *Arcos Ltd* v *E. A. Ronaasen & Son* [1933] AC 470 is a good example of the strict rule in operation.

> The sellers agreed to supply barrel staves, described in the contract as being half an inch thick, to the buyer. Many of the staves turned out to be one sixteenth of an inch thicker than described.

The buyer was entitled to reject the staves, although there was no suggestion they were not suitable for the purpose for which they were intended. There was an implied condition that the goods should correspond with the contract description (cf. s.13 Sale of Goods Act 1979); breach of the condition entitled the buyer to treat the contract as repudiated.

Nevertheless, the strict rule is subject to a number of exceptions. We have already encountered a major exception in that, if a term is classed as a warranty (*10.3.3*), or is classed as an innominate term and the result of breach is not particularly serious (*10.3.4*), the law does not allow the non-breaching party to treat the contract as repudiated, but only allows a remedy of damages to compensate any loss. It must be noted, however, that this exception operates to mitigate the effect of breach rather than to lower the standard of performance demanded. That is, any failure of performance to match the contractual undertaking, however slight, is still breach; but in such cases breach does not risk bringing the contract to an end. A somewhat different modification of the strict rule exists where the obligation is not to achieve a *result* (often called *strict liability*) but is only to exercise *reasonable care and skill*. Such an obligation exists under s.13 of the Supply of Goods and Services Act 1982 (*10.4.3.2*), and at comon law has long been regarded as the appropriate standard for professional people such as doctors and lawyers, whose work makes it impossible to guarantee a result. Nevertheless, any deviation from the defined standard of reasonable care would amount to breach. In *Arcos Ltd* v *E. A. Ronaasen & Son* it was suggested that deviation from the contractual undertaking would need to be 'microscopic' before the court would be willing to overlook it. Further exceptions to the strict rule are considered below.

10.5.1 Independent or concurrent conditions

Promissory conditions are of three types (per Lord Mansfield in *Kingston* v *Preston* (1773) 2 Doug KB 689). They may be independent, in which case breach by one party does not entitle the other to cease performance of his obligations under the contract. Independent conditions are rare in modern contracts. Alternatively, performance of one may be a condition precedent of the other, so that one party is not obliged to perform until the other has performed his obligation under the contract. Finally they may be concurrent, in the sense that the performance obligations are more or less simultaneous, and it is not certain which party is obliged to act first. In this case, a party must be ready and willing to perform his obligations in order to be able to maintain an action against the other party for breach. The latter two categories may both be described as dependent conditions. Of these, concurrent conditions are the more common. Whether conditions are dependent or independent is to be determined by construction of the contract.

The law is very unwilling to treat conditions as independent, since to do so removes an important security under the contract from the party to whom the obligation expressed in the condition is owed. That is, if the parties' obligations to perform are concurrent, each has an important lever he can use to ensure the other's performance, since each may withhold his own performance until the other party is ready and willing to perform. Where a condition is classed as independent it changes the effect of breach (although not affecting the standard of performance), so that the non-breaching party must continue to perform his obligations under the contract. Thus, to class a condition as independent has much the same effect as classing a term as a warranty (*10.3.3*). When it was stated earlier that the effect of breach of condition was to entitle the non-breaching party to treat the contract as repudiated (*10.3.2.3*), it was assumed that the condition was a dependent condition.

Possibly the only relevant modern example of an independent condition is the landlord's covenant to repair premises, which is said to be independent of the tenant's obligation to pay the rent (*Taylor* v *Webb* [1937] 2 KB 283). As a result, the tenant may not withhold payment of rent in order to force the landlord to perform his obligation to repair. An example of the more normal situation of dependent concurrent conditions is afforded by the main primary obligations of the contract of sale, as expressed in s.28 of the Sale of Goods Act 1979:

> Unless otherwise agreed, delivery of the goods and payment of the price are concurrent conditions, that is to say, the seller must be ready and willing to give possession of the goods to the buyer in exchange for the price and the buyer must be ready and willing to pay the price in exchange for possession of the goods.

10.5.2 Entire or divisible obligations

Some contracts involve very simple exchanges. A consumer sale for cash in a shop, for example, involves the exchange of money for goods, with possibly no other terms than an implied condition of quality. In such a contract it is easy to see, assuming that the conditions are concurrent (*10.5.1*), that the whole of each party's side of the bargain is the necessary condition for the performance of the other side. Any breach would destroy the commercial point of the exchange, and so would entitle the non-breaching party to treat the contract as repudiated.

Many contracts, however, do not involve such simple exchanges. Sales on credit terms of industrial machines, long-term requirements contracts, construction contracts, among many others, all involve complex sets of obligations on both contracting parties. This complexity gave rise to the standard form, and the difficulties it creates in the formation of contracts (*5.3.1.3*). In some such cases it is still true that any breach would destroy the commercial point of the exchange, so that the whole of each party's side of the bargain is the necessary condition for the performance of the other. In that case the obligations are described as 'entire'. In many complex commercial contracts, however, it is possible to see that breach of an important term may not destroy the whole commercial point of the exchange. The obligations in such a contract are described as 'divisible' (or 'severable'), and the result is that breach of such an obligation does not entitle the non-breaching party to treat the whole contract as having been repudiated. It will entitle him to damages, and may entitle him not to perform an obligation which was dependent upon the obligation breached.

10.5.2.1 Divisible obligations A simple example of a contract consisting of divisible obligations is a contract for sale and delivery of goods in instalments. In *Regent OHG Aisenstadt v Francesco of Jermyn Street* [1981] 3 All ER 327

> the contract called for the supply of clothing in a number of instalments. After delivery of several instalments which were accepted, one instalment was defective, being of the wrong quantity. The buyers claimed to be entitled to treat the whole contract as repudiated on the basis of breach in respect of the single instalment.

Mustill J rejected that argument. The contract was divisible, and a breach in respect of one instalment did not entitle the non-breaching party to treat the whole contract as repudiated. The judge did not say, as seemingly he should have, that the breach did, however, entitle the buyers to reject the whole instalment affected by the short delivery (cf. *Jackson v Rotax Motor and Cycle Co.* [1910] 2 KB 937). These examples were governed by the predecessor of s.31(2) of the Sale of Goods Act 1979 (an identical provision), but they demonstrate how the common law rule operates. It provides a further exception to the basic requirement of strict compliance with the contractual undertaking, again by mitigating the consequences of breach rather than by lowering the expected standard of performance (cf. *10.5* and *10.5.1*).

10.5.2.2 Entire obligations The classic example of an entire obligation is *Cutter v Powell* (1795) 6 Term Rep 320.

> A sailor was hired as mate for the voyage from Jamaica to England. He was to be paid a lump sum on completion of the voyage, and it appears that the payment was considerably in excess of the normal amount for such a voyage. Before reaching England he died, and his widow sued to recover a reasonable sum as payment relative to the period of the sailor's service before his death.

The court refused her claim. Lord Kenyon CJ regarded the contract as 'a kind of insurance', with the result that the sailor's entitlement was 'all or nothing'. Moreover, the court was unwilling to allow the remedy of *quantum meruit* under an implied contract where there was an express contract governing relations between the parties. Ashhurst J said

> This is a written contract, and it speaks for itself. And as it is entire, and as the defendant's promise depends upon a condition precedent to be performed by the other party, the condition must be performed before the other party is entitled to receive anything under it.

The result of failure to perform an entire obligation other than perfectly may be to deprive the party in breach of any payment for whatever performance there has been. For this reason the courts are often unwilling to find that the obligations under a contract are entire. Nevertheless, certain types of contract are usually found to consist of entire obligations, especially lump sum contracts for domestic building or other similar services (e.g. *Bolton v Mahadeva* [1972] 2 All ER 1322: lump sum contract to install central heating in a private house).

An advantage of the entire obligations rule in such cases is that it gives the consumer a useful means of ensuring that work is completed, since until it is completed no payment is due (see *10.5.3.1*).

10.5.2.3 Entire and divisible obligations in the same contract Although the courts sometimes refer to entire or divisible *contracts*, it is important to note that it is *obligations* which are either entire or divisible, and not the contracts themselves. A contract may well consist of both entire and divisible obligations. For example, the seller's obligation to deliver may be divisible as regards minor shortfalls in quantity, but entire as far as serious defects of quality are concerned. Thus, it seems that if a high proportion of the garments in *Regent OHG Aisenstadt* v *Francesco of Jermyn Street* [1981] 3 All ER 327 had been below the stated quality, but this was only discovered after acceptance of some instalments, the buyers would nevertheless have been entitled to treat the whole contract as repudiated (cf. *R. A. Munro & Co. Ltd* v *Meyer* [1930] 2 KB 312). Equally, although *Cutter* v *Powell* (1795) 6 Term Rep 320 is the classic example of an entire obligation, the court's reflections on the nature of entire contracts did not suggest that every minor breach of the deceased's duties as a mate during the voyage would have entitled the employer to deny him any payment for his services (per Somervell LJ in *Hoenig* v *Isaacs* [1952] 2 All ER 176).

10.5.3 Avoiding the 'entire obligation' rule
Apart from the obvious means of avoiding the 'entire obligation' rule, by classing the obligations in question as divisible (*10.5.2.1*), two other means exist of preventing the party in breach from being denied any payment where his performance, although not exactly matching his contractual undertaking, has nevertheless bestowed a substantial benefit on the non-breaching party.

10.5.3.1 Acceptance of the benefit by the non-breaching party The party in breach of an entire contract may be entitled to reasonable payment for the value of his actual performance if the non-breaching party accepts such performance as has been given and determines to keep whatever benefit he may have derived from it. 'Acceptance' in this sense does not mean an indication that the non-breaching party will not treat the contract as repudiated (which is the sense in s.11(4) of the Sale of Goods Act 1979: see *10.3.2.4*). It means simply that the non-breaching party, while regarding the breach of the entire obligation as bringing the original contract to an end, wishes to keep a benefit conferred, and is willing to pay the 'going rate' for it.

The rule is explained in *Sumpter* v *Hedges* [1898] 1 QB 673.

The plaintiff builder had contracted to build two houses on the defendant's land for a lump sum of £565. After completion of just over half the work, the builder abandoned the project. He had in fact received some payment, but not all of what his work was worth. The defendant completed the building work, using materials left on the site by the plaintiff.

At first instance the plaintiff was awarded the value of the materials used by the defendant to complete the building, but was awarded nothing for the work done but not finished. The first instance judgment was upheld on appeal. Collins LJ said:

> There are cases in which, though the plaintiff has abandoned the performance of a contract, it is possible for him to raise the inference of a new contract to pay for the work done on a *quantum meruit* from the defendant's having taken the benefit of that work, but, in order that that may be done, the circumstances must be such as to give an option to the defendant to take or not to take the benefit of the work done.

Such payment depends, then, upon finding a new, implied contract, and such a contract will not be found where the non-breaching party has no real choice about whether to accept the benefit or not. In the case of a half-finished building erected on the non-breaching party's own land there is no choice of whether to accept the benefit; the building cannot be knocked down and 'returned' to the builder in any meaningful way. The builder could not recover for his part-performance. On the other hand, building materials not incorporated into the unfinished building could have been returned, so that a positive choice had been made to keep them, and so the builder was entitled to payment of their reasonable value.

It has been suggested that the fact that payment for an accepted benefit depends upon the availability to the beneficiary of a real choice of whether to accept it, has made this rule too strict (Law Commission Report No. 121 (1983)). A case such as *Bolton v Mahadeva* [1972] 2 All ER 1322 (*10.5.2.2*) is a striking modern example.

> The plaintiff had agreed to install central heating for a lump sum of £560. It proved to be defective, but the plaintiff would not put it right, which would have cost a further £174. The plaintiff was not allowed any payment for the work done, although he had conferred a net benefit on the defendant of £386.

Nevertheless, as was pointed out in a note of dissent in the Law Commission's Report, the main value of classing an obligation as entire is that it places in the hands of the other party powerful means of ensuring proper performance of the obligation, namely, the refusal of payment. Were that to be removed, it might do harm to the interests of a significant number of people who, incidentally, are among the least likely to be willing to resort to litigation; that is, since most complex construction contracts are now designed for performance in stages, with interim payments, and so are divisible, most contracts involving entire obligations will be between small builders and domestic consumers. Entire obligations, which may once have been thought to have been oppressive to the less powerful in society (cf. *Cutter v Powell* (1795) 6 Term Rep 320), may now serve a useful purpose in consumer protection. The recommendation in the Law Commission's Report, which would have reversed cases like *Bolton v Mahadeva*, has not yet been implemented.

10.5.3.2 Substantial performance The rigours of the 'entire obligation' rule may also be avoided by means of the doctrine of substantial performance. Where performance is incomplete or defective, but the extent of the failure to match the contractual undertaking is trivial by comparison with the primary obligations which have been satisfactorily performed, then the court may be prepared to find that there has been substantial performance. The result is to prevent the non-breaching party from treating the contract as repudiated, although he will still be entitled to damages, or a set-off against the contract price, for any loss caused by what remains a breach of the contract.

In *Hoenig* v *Isaacs* [1952] 2 All ER 176

> the plaintiff had agreed to decorate and furnish the defendant's flat for a lump sum of £750. Some progress payments were made, but upon completion of the work £350 was outstanding. The defendant claimed that the plaintiff could not recover this amount since this was an entire contract (sic) and the plaintiff was in breach in that some of his workmanship was defective. It was found as a fact that some of the work was defective, but that it would cost in total no more than £56 to put it right.

It is not surprising, in those circumstances, that the Court of Appeal was unwilling to find that the plaintiff was not entitled to further payment. A very minor breach would have resulted in a large windfall for the defendant. Instead, the court said that the plaintiff had substantially performed the contract. The result was not to overlook the plaintiff's breach, but to limit the consequences of that breach to the creation of a secondary obligation to pay damages. It was not found to excuse the defendant's further performance. Although this doctrine plays a useful role in mitigating the effects of the 'entire obligation' rule, it should be realised that it is limited to minor failures to match the contractual undertaking. In *Bolton* v *Mahadeva* [1972] 2 All ER 1322, for example, the breach was far too serious to fall within the substantial performance rule.

It will be seen that there is much similarity between the doctrine of substantial performance and the category of innominate terms, the consequences of breach of which depend upon how serious the breach was (*10.3.4*). This similarity is by no means coincidental. In *Hoenig* v *Isaacs* Somervell LJ traced the origin of the substantial performance doctrine to the judgment of Lord Mansfield in *Boon* v *Eyre* (1779) 1 H Bl 273n. In *The Hansa Nord* [1975] 3 All ER 739 Lord Denning MR traced the origin of the innominate term to the same source.

10.6 EXCLUSION OR LIMITATION OF LIABILITY

10.6.1 Introduction
Clauses which purport to exclude or to limit liability for breach of contract are the most common form of what may be referred to generally as 'exemption' or 'exception' clauses. It is important to note, however, that exemption clauses come in many different forms (see *10.6.1.3*). The applicable rules remain

generally the same. Exemption clauses are an important feature of modern contracts, and in recent years have been the focus of much judicial, legislative and academic attention. A detailed study of such clauses would require an entire book (see, for example, Richard Lawson's *Exclusion Clauses*, 3rd edn, Longman, 1990). This section examines the reasons for, and the mechanisms of, control of exemption clauses.

10.6.1.1 Function and purpose   Since classical contract law saw contractual liability as something created by the operation of the will of the parties, rather than as liability imposed by law, it was inevitable that the classical law should accept the power of the parties to modify as they saw fit the nature of the liability created. Thus, while the usual result of the breach of a promise which had been duly incorporated in a valid contract was, at the very least, to create a secondary obligation to pay damages in compensation of any loss suffered, it was open to the parties to agree to contractual 'promises' which did not have this usual result. The more common means of modifying the usual liability were to exclude any obligation to pay compensation, or to limit the amount of compensation payable.

It should not be thought that exemption clauses are necessarily bad, or that the classical law was excessively naive in allowing parties to abdicate all responsibility for their promises. The classical law *assumed* (in a way which today most lawyers would challenge) that all parties to contractual negotiations would be bargaining freely, would be best placed to know their own interests, and would only agree to such terms if some, not necessarily immediately apparent, benefit would accrue from so doing.

These assumptions remain valid where the parties do in fact deal with each other on an equal footing. In that situation, typified by the commercial contract, the exemption clause is an important device for allocating the risks of the contract between the parties. Imagine a contract for the supply of machinery which depends upon the availability of raw materials from abroad. Both parties know that there is a slight risk that the usual, low-cost supplier will be slow to supply because of the unstable political conditions in its country. Alternative supplies are available at much higher cost. The seller of the machinery may quote two prices: let us say £2,500 for a guaranteed delivery date, by using the high-cost raw materials; and let us say £1,500 using the low-cost raw materials, but subject to an exclusion of liability for late delivery. The buyer may then choose which contract he prefers, knowing that the seller will not agree to bear the risk of late delivery if the cheaper contract is chosen. There is no reason for the law to interfere with this kind of use of exemption clauses, and indeed to do so would be to undermine the economic basis of the parties' agreement.

Nevertheless, it is generally accepted today that there are situations in which exemption clauses are not freely negotiated, at which point the law may seek to interfere. These situations usually involve standard form contracts. Such contracts are entered into on the basis of a standard set of contractual terms contained in a document drawn up by one of the parties. Standard form contracts are not necessarily bad. They represent the reaction of lawyers to the increase in contractual activity engendered by the industrial revolution. Just as goods were mass produced, so too it became much more convenient to use 'mass produced' contracts, since the circumstances of one sale were normally very similar to another, and so the costs of individual drafting could be avoided. It became normal practice to include one or more exemption clauses in such standardised contracts.

Sometimes the inclusion of these clauses reflected the practice of a particular trade in the allocation of risks between buyers and sellers, and so was entirely legitimate. The problem of standard form contracts, however, is that they may present little choice to the party who has not drawn up the document. If he wants the product he may have to accept the terms; if the terms are unacceptable, he will have to resign himself to not obtaining the product. For this reason they are sometimes called 'adhesion contracts'. Thus, standard form contracts may be used to *impose* an exclusion or limitation of liability which has not been negotiated, and for which the person whose normal contractual rights are diminished has received no alternative benefit. The imposition of such exemption clauses may be particularly harmful in consumer contracts, where the disequilibrium between the bargaining positions of the parties may be substantial, and where the consumer may have no alternative but to accept the terms if such exemptions are commonplace throughout the particular industry, as is often the case.

10.6.1.2 Judicial attitudes to exemption clauses Judicial attitudes to exemption clauses have hardened over the last hundred years. It is still the case that individually negotiated contracts which contain exemption clauses are generally assumed not to be harmful. The attitude to standard form contracts may be summarised by reference to the speech of Lord Diplock in the House of Lords in *Schroeder Music Publishing Co. Ltd* v *Macaulay* [1974] 3 All ER 616. Standard form contracts which are used for convenience to express common commercial agreements, and which do so in terms normal to such contracts, are presumed to be fair and reasonable. Standard form contracts in consumer transactions, and in other situations in which one party is said to have no alternative but to contract on the terms offered if he is to contract at all, are not presumed to be fair and reasonable. Rather, they are viewed as the product of the superior bargaining position of one of the parties. The courts often suspect that that superior bargaining position is being exploited to the cost of the other party, and for that reason will do everything in their power to avoid the consequences of such clauses.

It is sometimes suggested that the judicial attitude to exemption clauses in this last category is over-simplistic (cf. Trebilcock in *Studies in Contract Law* (B. Reiter & J. Swan (eds), Butterworth, 1981) at p.481). The assertion that consumers have no alternative but to contract on such terms has been challenged, and it has been suggested that consumers do get (an admittedly non-negotiated) benefit from such contracts in the form of lower prices than would prevail if each contract had to be individually negotiated. Nevertheless, there is growing evidence (e.g. in Lawson, op. cit. at p. 86) that such clauses are used in consumer contracts precisely in order to frighten off complainants, even when there is little or no prospect of the clause being upheld in a court of law. In these circumstances it seems likely that, whatever the economists may say about the reasonableness and utility of exemption clauses in all types of contract, judicial attitudes will remain unsympathetic to their use in consumer contracts. That position has been reinforced by legislation (see *10.6.3*).

10.6.1.3 Types of exemption clause It would be impossible, and fruitless, to catalogue every known type of exemption clause. The wit and invention of contracts' draftsmen have been fuelled by the courts' attempts to control such clauses into the regular discovery of new and ingenious forms, to which subsequently the courts have to react. Most common are the total exclusion of liability for part at least of what would otherwise be included in the contractual undertaking (e.g. implied terms of quality, but see *10.6.3.5*), and the limitation of liability to a particular sum (e.g. the price payable under the contract). Other common forms are those which limit the remedy available, either by imposing a short time-limit during which claims for breach must be made or by imposing onerous conditions on obtaining the remedy (such as payment of costs of transport of defective goods to and from the supplier's place of business). More difficult to control are clauses which, rather than exempting liability for breach, purport to modify the performance obligation, so that no breach occurs (cf. *10.6.3.4*).

10.6.2 Devices avoiding the impact of exemption clauses
The common law provides no rule or doctrine whereby an exemption clause may simply be declared void on the ground that it is unfair or unreasonable (*Photo Production Ltd* v *Securicor Transport Ltd* [1980] 1 All ER 556; see *10.6.4.3*). For many years, therefore, the courts' hostility to such clauses found expression in the application, often in strict or strained terms, of devices of the general law of contracts to the particular problem of exemption clauses. The more common of such devices are described below. In theory, such devices would still be applicable despite the enactment of statutory controls on certain exemption clauses; in practice, it seems likely that the courts will relinquish resort to these devices in favour of the more direct means of control where they are available.

10.6.2.1 Incorporation The rules governing the incorporation of written terms into agreements have already been examined (*5.7*). As was noted there, the law on incorporation had developed almost exclusively through judicial attempts to avoid the impact of exemption clauses. Any clause which has not reasonably been brought to the notice of the offeree before the time of acceptance of the offer (and thus the making of the contract) will not be incorporated into the contract (*5.7.3*). By means of this rule the courts have been able to eliminate from contracts terms which were printed in receipts or invoices and which had not come to the attention of the party in question when entering the agreement.

10.6.2.2 Strict interpretation As a general rule, the courts will apply strict rules of construction in relation to exemption clauses. A party seeking to avoid liability must be able to prove the common intention of the parties by clear words, since the courts will otherwise assume that the normal incidents of contractual liability were intended. This strict interpretation takes several forms.

In the first place, the courts will not imply any exemption greater than that contained in the words used. So, in *Andrews Bros (Bournemouth) Ltd* v *Singer & Co. Ltd* [1934] 1 KB 17

> the plaintiffs contracted to purchase 'new' cars from the defendant company. The contract contained a clause excluding 'all conditions, warranties and liabilities implied by common law, statute or otherwise'. One of the cars was found to have done a substantial mileage at the time of the delivery to the plaintiffs.

The exclusion clause did not protect the defendants. It excluded implied terms, while the requirement that the cars be 'new' was an express term of the contract.

Secondly, the courts operate what is known as the *contra proferentem* rule. Where the meaning of an exemption clause is ambiguous the courts will adopt the meaning which is unfavourable to the party seeking to escape liability by virtue of the clause (the *proferens*). In *Beck & Co.* v *Szymanowski & Co.* [1924] AC 43

> the contract provided that goods delivered were deemed to be in satisfactory condition unless complaint was made within 14 days of receiving them. The clause was ineffective to exclude liability for short delivery (i.e. for goods not delivered) even though complaint was made more than 14 days after receiving the goods.

Although this rule rests on the existence of ambiguity in the meaning of the exemption clause, the courts have been resourceful in finding such ambiguity when it has suited them to be able to cut down the impact of a clause. A modern example of this approach may be found in *Morley* v *United Friendly Insurance* (1993) *The Times*, 8 February 1993, CA. An insurance policy excluded claims resulting from 'wilful exposure to needless peril'. The Court of Appeal found that an intentional and risky act did not fall within the scope of the clause where the risk was modest, and the party affected did not have time to assess the peril involved.

Thirdly, in what is a particular and common example of the operation of the *contra proferentem* rule, the courts are often unwilling to extend the scope of a contractual exemption of liability to other liabilities, so that the plaintiff may have an alternative remedy in tort. The classic example of this rule of construction is *White* v *John Warwick & Co. Ltd* [1953] 2 All ER 1021.

> The plaintiff was injured when the saddle on a bicycle hired from the defendants tipped and he fell on the road. The contract of hire exempted the defendants from liability for any personal injuries to the hirers of bicycles. Without the clause, the plaintiff might have succeeded against the defendants either for breach of contract or for the defendants' negligence.

The Court of Appeal ruled that the exemption clause was only effective to exclude liability in contract, so that the plaintiff's action in tort succeeded despite the clause. Although this is a rule of construction, and so each case must be treated on its particular facts, some common threads emerge. Generally, to exclude liability for negligence as well as liability for breach of contract express words (probably including 'negligence') must be used. Where, however, the only potential liability which could arise would be for negligence the courts will usually interpret the exemption clause as covering such liability. For example, in *Alderslade* v *Hendon Laundry Ltd* [1945] KB 189

> the plaintiff sent items to the laundry which were not returned. The contract contained a clause restricting recovery for lost items to 20 times the laundering charge.

Since the laundry's only liability for lost items lay in negligence the limitation clause was redundant unless applicable to such liability, and so the court found that the defendant was able to rely on the clause.

Finally, out of the strict interpretation approach has emerged the 'repugnancy' or 'total non-performance' rule, which is closely related to the main common law means of controlling exclusion clauses (see *10.6.4.3*). The courts will be very unwilling to construe an exemption clause as depriving a main undertaking of the contract of any legal value by making it unenforceable (see *J. Evans & Son (Portsmouth) Ltd* v *Andrea Merzario Ltd* [1976] 2 All ER 930). For example, in *Sze Hai Tong Bank Ltd* v *Rambler Cycle Co. Ltd* [1959] AC 576

> the respondents had contracted to deliver a consignment of bicycles to Singapore, to be delivered to sub-purchasers on production of correct documentation. The carriers released the consignment to the original buyers (rather than to the sub-purchasers) without production of proper documentation, with the effect that the sellers were not paid. The sellers' contract with the carriers provided that the carriers' responsibility was to be deemed to 'cease absolutely' once the goods were discharged from the ship. The carriers (or rather their indemnifiers, the appellants in the action) argued that the effect of this clause was to exclude liability for the wrongful release of the bicycles to the original buyers.

The Privy Council would not accept that argument. For the Privy Council Lord Denning said:

> There is . . . an implied limitation on the clause, which cuts down the extreme width of it: and, as a matter of construction, their Lordships decline to attribute to it the unreasonable effect contended for. But their Lordships go further. If such an extreme width were given to the exemption clause, it would run counter to the main object and intent of the contract . . ..
> It would defeat this object entirely if the shipping company was at liberty, at its own will and pleasure, to deliver the goods to somebody else, to someone not entitled at all, without being liable for the consequences. The clause must therefore be limited and modified to the extent necessary to enable effect to be given to the main object and intent of the contract.

The rationale of this approach is clear: it is disingenuous to promise by contract a particular performance while in the same breath (or perhaps under it) disclaiming any liability should you simply prefer not to keep your promise. Nevertheless, this approach is only a rule of *construction*, and there can be no doubt that by carefully chosen words such an effect could be achieved (see *10.6.4.3*).

10.6.2.3 Fraud or misrepresentation A party will be unable to rely on an exemption clause if he has induced the other party to enter the contract by misrepresenting, fraudulently or otherwise (see *9.2* and *9.3*), the meaning and effect of the clause. In *Curtis* v *Chemical Cleaning and Dyeing Co.* [1951] 1 KB 805

> the defendants sought to rely on a clause exempting liability 'for any damage, however arising', which had been represented to the plaintiff only to exclude liability for particular risks, such as the beads and sequins on a dress. The Court of Appeal held that the defendants could not rely on the clause to avoid liability for a stain which appeared on the dress during cleaning, since that was damage of a type not listed in its representation to the plaintiff.

10.6.3 The Unfair Contract Terms Act 1977
The enactment of the Unfair Contract Terms Act 1977 (UCTA 1977) introduced a major change in the means of control of exemption clauses. The power to override exemption clauses found to be unreasonable was introduced in the case of implied terms in the sale of goods by the Supply of Goods (Implied Terms) Act 1973 (see now s.55 of the Sale of Goods Act 1979). The Unfair Contract Terms Act, however, introduced similar and more extensive controls to a wide range of categories of contract, so that, for contracts within the scope of the Act, the courts for the first time had a general and direct means of control of the use of exemption clauses. Further changes to this statutory régime of control of exemption clauses appear inevitable after adoption by the Council of Ministers of Directive 93/13/EC on unfair terms in consumer contracts, which must in theory be implemented in the UK no later than 31 December 1994, and which will apply to contracts concluded after that date (see further *10.7*).

10.6.3.1 Scope of the Act The Act applies (subject to certain exceptions) in the case of both contract and tort to 'business liability', which means liability for things done or to be done in the course of a business, and liability arising from the occupation of business premises (s.1(3) UCTA 1977). 'Business' is given a broad definition by the Act (s.14 UCTA 1977), so that it embraces not only the normal meaning of commercial activity but also the professions, government departments and local or public authorities. The intention appears to have been to exclude from the general scope of the Act by this expression only private, occasional contracts. For example, if Jones, a university lecturer, agrees to paint Smith's house for £350 during Jones' summer holidays, but insists that he cannot accept responsibility for any damage done to Smith's garden during the job, such a clause would fall outside the scope of the Act. If, on the other hand, Evans, another university lecturer, regularly sets up a stall in the market on Saturdays where, for a fee, he gives jewellery valuations, he is likely to be regarded as in 'business' as a valuer, and any exclusion of liability he might desire in relation to the accuracy of his valuations would be subject to the provisions of the Act.

In the case of sale and hire-purchase the Act applies irrespective of whether the liability arises in the course of a business (s.6(4) UCTA 1977), although this exception is not as major as it may appear (see below *10.6.3.5*).

It must be stressed that the Act does not provide a general power to strike out *any* term which the court considers to be unreasonable or unfair. Its main targets are exemption clauses; that is, clauses excluding or limiting liability, clauses making the enforcement of liability subject to onerous conditions, clauses restricting the right to a remedy, and clauses restricting or excluding rules of evidence or procedure (s.13(1) UCTA 1977; see also *10.6.1.3*). A recent example of a clause which restricted the remedy and procedural rules may be found in *Gill (Stewart) Ltd* v *Horatio Myer & Co Ltd* [1992] 2 All ER 257. The clause purported to prevent the buyer from withholding payment by reason of a set-off claimed in respect of breach of contract by the supplier. It was claimed on behalf of the supplier that the reference in s.13(1) to restrictions of remedies and rules of procedure only brought such clauses within the scope of the Act where they achieved indirectly an exclusion or limitation of liability which, if expressly stipulated, would be subject to control under the Act; whereas in this case the restriction on the right of set-off did not exclude or limit the liability of the supplier, but only required the buyer to prosecute his claim in separate legal proceedings. This argument was unanimously rejected by the Court of Appeal. The Act also applies to clauses which purport to modify the expected contractual obligation, rather than to exempt liability for breach (*10.6.3.4*). It does not apply to arbitration clauses (s.13(2) UCTA 1977).

Certain important categories of contracts are excluded from the scope of the major provisions of the Act. Schedule 1(1) excludes from ss.2–4 and s.7 contracts of insurance, contracts relating to interests in land, contracts relating to intellectual property, contracts relating to companies (whether or not incorporated) and contracts relating to securities. Schedule 1(2) excludes contracts of marine salvage, charterparties and contracts of carriage of goods by sea from the same provisions other than s.2(1), except where the provisions operate in favour of a person dealing as a consumer. Employment contracts are excluded by Schedule 1(4) on similar terms. Finally, under s.26 UCTA 1977 the Act does not apply to international supply contracts as defined in that section.

10.6.3.2 Liability for negligence 'Negligence' is defined by the Act as breach of an obligation to take reasonable care or to exercise reasonable skill arising out of the express or implied terms of a contract, or existing as a common law duty (i.e. in tort), or arising out of the Occupiers' Liability Act 1957. As far as the law of contract is concerned, it should be remembered that many obligations arising out of contracts are strict. That is to say, the standard of performance demanded is not merely to take reasonable care or to exercise reasonable skill in attempting to achieve the purpose of the contract. Rather, the party performing can only avoid breach by actually achieving that purpose. Exemption clauses relating to such contractual terms are not subject to the controls applying to clauses which purport to exclude or limit liability for 'negligence' contained in s.2 of the Act (but see *10.6.3.3*). Nevertheless, some contractual obligations are not strict. Where the achievement of the result is dependent to some appreciable extent on factors beyond the control of the person providing the service it would be nonsensical to *guarantee* that the result will be achieved (*10.5*). Thus a lawyer cannot guarantee that his client will escape conviction when prosecuted; he can only undertake to use reasonable skill in seeking to prevent conviction. Breach of such obligations is what is meant by 'negligence' liability in the context of contracts, and exemption clauses relating to such liability are governed by s.2 UCTA 1977.

Section 2(1) of the 1977 Act provides:

A person cannot by reference to any contract term or to a notice given to persons generally or to particular persons exclude or restrict his liability for death or personal injury resulting from negligence.

It should be noted that the section applies to more than exemption clauses contained in contracts. It would apply, for example, to a notice erected by the owner of land at an entrance to that land through which members of the public pass. Section 2(1) imposes an absolute ban on all exclusions and limitations of liability for death or personal injury caused by negligence.

Under s.2(2) UCTA 1977 liability for other loss or damage (i.e. not death or personal injury) resulting from negligence may be excluded provided the contract term or notice satisfies the requirement of reasonableness (see *10.6.3.7*).

In *Smith* v *Eric S. Bush* [1989] 2 All ER 514 the House of Lords had to consider the situation where a notice to the plaintiff purported not to have excluded liability for negligence, but rather to have prevented any obligation to the plaintiff ever arising. The Court of Appeal had accepted the argument that the words used prevented any obligation arising, and so did not fall subject to the 1977 Act, which only applied where an acknowledged liability was avoided. The House of Lords refused to accept this argument. Lord Jauncey pointed to s.13(1), which expressly states that s.2 applies to exclusions and restrictions of the relevant obligations, as well as liability. Lord Griffiths found support in the judgment of Slade LJ in *Phillips Products Ltd* v *Hyland* [1987] 2 All ER 620 (*10.6.3.4*). Lord Templeman said, robustly:

This construction would not give effect to the manifest intention of the Act, but would emasculate the Act. The construction would provide no control over standard form exclusion clauses which individual members of the public are obliged to accept.

This approach, which submits clauses which purport to define the extent of negligence obligations to the reasonableness test in the same way as clauses which exclude or limit liability are subject to it, is sometimes objected to on the ground that it makes it impossible for a professional person (for example) to impose any qualification on the obligations undertaken in the course of performance of a contract without falling within the scope of control exercised under the Act. However, this objection misses the point that such a duty-defining clause, although subject to control, would be permitted if shown to be reasonable (provided the result of any alleged negligence was not death or personal injury).

Sometimes manufacturers (and possibly distributors) of consumer goods issue a 'guarantee' of goods sold by the retailer to the consumer. Often the guarantee purports to limit or even exclude the liability of the party issuing it for negligence which leads to the goods being defective. Such an exemption may take effect as a non-contractual notice, or may constitute a separate contract between manufacturer and consumer (although not a contract of sale). The danger of such guarantees is that, while they may offer an easier remedy for trivial defects than can be had by taking the goods back to the seller, such advantage is often gained by the sacrifice of more important rights in the case of serious loss such as might result from a defect causing personal injury. For this reason purported exemptions contained in guarantees are of no effect (s.5 UCTA 1977). The section does not apply to exemptions contained in contracts of sale, which are provided for elsewhere (see *10.6.3.5*).

10.6.3.3 Exemption of liability in contract In the case of contractual obligations other than obligations to take reasonable care and to exercise reasonable skill (see above, *10.6.3.2*), the 1977 Act only applies to exemption clauses in contracts (except contracts for the sale or supply of goods, see *10.6.3.5*) where one party deals as consumer or on the other party's written standard terms of business (s.3(1) UCTA 1977). Both of these qualifying conditions require some explanation.

A party *deals as consumer* if he does not make (or hold himself out as making) the contract in the course of a business while the other party does, and, in the case of a contract for goods, the goods are of a type ordinarily supplied for private use or consumption (s.12(1) UCTA 1977). The mere fact that a party is a business (e.g. a partnership or a corporation) will not necessarily mean its contracts are made in the course of business unless the subject-matter is integral or necessarily incidental to the business in question (*Peter Symmons & Co.* v *Cook* (1981) 131 NLJ 758). For example, a manufacturing company which bought Christmas gifts for its staff would seem to be dealing as a consumer in those sale transactions. In *R & B Customs Brokers Co Ltd* v *United Dominions Trust Ltd* [1988] 1 All ER 847, it was held that a transaction would be made in the course of a business where it was integral to the nature of the business or, if only incidental to the carrying on of the relevant business, where there was a degree of regularity in entering into such transactions.

Written standard terms of business is nowhere defined in the Act. Many contracts are in standard form, and the section is clearly intended to apply to such contracts. It is not clear, however, how much 'individualisation' of such standard forms is permitted before the section ceases to apply. For example, many standard forms leave blanks in the clauses relating to quantity and to price which must be filled in for each particular contract. Presumably such forms are still within the meaning of the section. Less clear, however, is whether a standard form in which the original offeree had deleted certain terms and then sent it back (as a counter-offer), and which had then been accepted by the original offeror, would still be within the meaning of the section. As yet the courts have given no guidance on these questions.

Where a party deals as consumer, or on the other's standard terms, that other may not exclude or limit his liability for breach of contract by means of a term in the contract except in so far as the term satisfies the requirement of reasonableness (s.3(2)(a) UCTA 1977). The 'reasonableness' test is considered below (*10.6.3.7*). This section applies to the strict liability in contract described above (*10.6.3.2*). Subject to the difficulties inherent in the concept of 'reasonableness' the scope of the section is clear, and requires no further comment.

10.6.3.4 Terms which modify expected contractual obligations In general, exemption clauses operate to exclude or limit liability for breach. However, careful drafting of a contract may result in the performance obligation being such that a performance which might normally be regarded as defective does not amount to breach. In this case it is said that the term defines the performance obligation, rather than simply exempting liability for breach. Indeed, some commentators (notably Yates, op.cit., passim) argue that in most circumstances exemption clauses should be read in the context of the whole agreement, rather than as separate from the rest of the agreement, so that most so-called exemption clauses are obligation-defining rather than liability-exempting. There is some support for this approach in the speech of Lord Diplock in *Photo Production Ltd* v *Securicor Transport Ltd* [1980] 1 All ER 556.

The approach assumes that where the parties have defined the obligations in a particular way there is no reason to exert the kind of control thought to be desirable where one party seeks to exempt liability. The difficulty with this assumption is that it appears to fail to take account of the fact that many contracts are perceived as being standardised, so that there is a general expectation, independent of any particular contract, of the content of such contracts. To vary the terms from those generally expected may be just as undesirable as to exclude liability, if the effect is to deprive one party of what was reasonably expected under the contract. It is only if contracts are exclusively the product of the will of the parties, rather than constructed from common intention and certain obligations imposed by law, that it would be reasonable to suggest that the proper expectation of the content of a contract can be determined by an examination of its particular terms and nothing else. Modern contract theory does not generally accept such a proposition. The orthodox approach then is to treat exemption clauses generally as separate from the rest of the contract, and therefore not as defining the obligations, and that approach is taken by UCTA 1977. The orthodox approach was also adopted by the Court of Appeal in *Phillips Products Ltd* v *Hyland* [1987] 2 All ER 620 (see also *Smith* v *Eric S. Bush* [1989] 2 All ER 514; *10.6.3.2*). Slade LJ said:

> In our judgment, in considering whether there has been any breach of any obligation . . . the court has to leave out of account, at this stage, the contract term which is relied on by the defence as defeating the plaintiffs' claim for breach of such obligation or duty . . ..

In addition, the 1977 Act attempts to restrict the use of unreasonable obligation-defining clauses. By s.3(2)(b) UCTA 1977 a party may not claim:

(i)   to be entitled to render a performance substantially different from that reasonably expected from him; or

(ii) to be entitled to render no performance at all, except in so far as the term on which he bases such a claim satisfies the requirement of reasonableness

These provisions only apply in the case of contracts where one party deals as consumer or on the other's written standard terms (s.3(1) UCTA 1977; see *10.6.3.3*). Section 3(2)(b)(ii) is something of a red-herring. If one party is defined by the contract as being under no obligations at all, the contract must surely fail for want of consideration (*6.3.2*). Where the absence of obligation affects only part of the contract it can be dealt with under s.3(2)(b)(i).

Section 3(2)(b)(i) assumes that it is possible to identify a performance which is reasonably to be expected. This assumption might be realised in two ways. In the first place, the contract might be of a recognised and standardised type. For example, a contract for the provision of domestic decorating services is rarely negotiated in detail. In particular, it is unlikely that the parties will discuss measures to be taken to protect existing decoration which is not to be replaced. Rather, the customer will assume that the decorator will take reasonable care to avoid damage to existing decorations, and such a term would normally be implied in law (cf. s.13 Supply of Goods and Services Act 1982). If the decorator's order form, which was signed by the customer, included a term making protection of existing decorations the responsibility of the customer, such a term would have defined the contractual obligations in a way other than would generally have been expected. Section 3(2)(b)(i) does not say that it is not permitted to redefine the contractual obligations in such a way; it merely says that it is not permitted unless reasonable. This test might be satisfied relatively easily in such a case by showing that the customer was fully aware of the effect of the clause, and possibly by showing that the price charged was lower than would be charged where the decorator had to look after such precautions.

Alternatively, there may be a conflict between the apparent main purpose of the contract and the performance one party is entitled to tender under the terms contained in the fine print of the agreement. For example, in *Anglo-Continental Holidays Ltd* v *Typaldos Lines (London) Ltd* [1967] 2 Lloyd's Rep 61 the plaintiffs made particular holiday arrangements through a travel agent. The contract contained a clause stating that 'Steamers, sailing dates, rates and itineraries are subject to change without notice.' The Court of Appeal refused to allow the defendants to rely on the clause to escape liability for breach of contract when the original arrangements were changed unilaterally.

Russell LJ pointed out, however, that the clause was not an exemption clause but a clause defining the contractual liability. In his view 'the propounder of that clause cannot be enabled thereby to alter the substance of the arrangement'. Under s.3(2)(b)(i) of the 1977 Act, assuming the qualifying conditions of s.3(1) were met, the issue would have been whether the clause was unreasonable in allowing changes to be made unilaterally from what had apparently been agreed under the main provisions of the contract.

10.6.3.5 Sale or supply of goods The Act contains special provisions, additional to those in s.3, which apply to clauses purporting to exempt liability for breach of the terms implied by statute into contracts for the sale or supply of goods (see *10.4.3.2*). Section 6 applies to implied terms in the sale of goods. It should be noted that this section applies to all liability, and not merely to that incurred in the course of a business (s.6(4) UCTA 1977). However, the important implied terms of quality in s.14 of the Sale of Goods Act 1979 (SoGA 1979) only arise in the case of sales made in the course of a business. The implied condition that the seller has or will have the right to sell the goods (s.12 SoGA 1979) cannot in any circumstances be excluded by reference to a contract term (s.6(1)(a) UCTA 1977). It should be noted, however, that the parties may define the seller's obligation in a more limited way, so that he is obliged only to transfer such title as he has (s.12(3)–(5) SoGA 1979).

In the case of the other implied terms (that is, ss.13–15 of the Sale of Goods Act 1979, covering sale by description, merchantable quality, fitness for purpose and sale by sample), s.6 UCTA 1977 applies differently according to whether or not one of the parties *deals as consumer*. The meaning of this expression has already been explained above (see *10.6.3.3*). Where one party deals as consumer liability for breach of these implied terms cannot be exempted (s.6(2)(a) UCTA 1977). Where the party seeking to enforce liability is not a consumer, liability for breach of the implied terms may be exempted, but only in so far as the exemption clause satisfies the requirement of reasonableness (s.6(3) UCTA 1977).

The Supply of Goods and Services Act 1982 implies terms similar to those of the Sale of Goods Act 1979 into contracts for the supply of goods; that is, contracts under which title to goods passes but not by way of sale (e.g. a building contract under which goods are to be incorporated as part of the work into the finished structure). Attempted exemptions of liability for breach of these implied terms are governed by s.7 UCTA 1977. As far as terms relating to correspondence with description or sample, quality and fitness for purpose are concerned, the same distinction is made between contracts where one party deals as consumer and other contracts, with the same consequences, as for the Sale of Goods Act implied terms (s.7(2) and (3) UCTA 1977). Attempted exemptions of the implied condition of right to transfer title may not be excluded in any circumstances (s.7(3A) UCTA 1977; cf. s.17(2) Supply of Goods and Services Act 1982).

10.6.3.6 Special provisions An indemnity clause in a contract is a clause under which one party agrees to indemnify the other for any liability incurred. Such a clause may have the same effect as an exemption clause, and in any case often transfers liability away from the party who would normally be liable. Such a clause is only effective against a person who deals as consumer in so far as it satisfies the requirement of reasonableness (s.4 UCTA 1977). On the other hand, a transfer of liability between potential defendants, neither of which deals as a consumer, is apparently a form of duty-defining clause which is not subject to control under the Act at all, on the basis that it leaves the plaintiff's right to a remedy untouched (*Thompson* v *T. Lohan (Plant Hire) Ltd* [1987] 2 All ER 631).

Section 10 UCTA 1977 is intended to prevent the evasion of the provisions of the Act by means of a secondary contract. Since the main provisions of the Act are concerned with terms in contracts which exclude or restrict liability arising under those contracts, it was feared that the purpose of the Act might be thwarted by imposing such exclusions and restrictions by means of separate contracts. Section 10 attempts to close that loophole. A typical situation addressed by this provision would be where a maintenance contract, entered into in connection with the purchase of goods, purports to exclude or restrict rights arising under the purchase contract. In *Tudor Grange Holdings Ltd* v *Citibank NA* [1991] 4 All ER 1 Browne-Wilkinson V-C held that s.10 only applies to 'attempts to evade the Act's provisions by the introduction of such an exemption clause *into a contract with a third party*' (emphasis added). Consequently, in terms of the situation described above, s.10 would apply where the maintenance service contract, which provides the vehicle for the exemption clause, is entered into with a party other than the supplier of the goods; it does not apply where the supplier is also the principal party to the maintenance agreement. It must therefore be asked whether this interpretation of s.10 leaves a loophole in cases where the secondary contract which exempts liability is entered into by both parties to the original contract. It is submitted that it does not, because the other provisions of the Act are drafted sufficiently widely to catch terms in secondary contracts between the original parties which purport to exempt liability under the original contract. That is, the Act does not presuppose or require that the foundation of liability and any purported exemption be contained in a single contract for its provisions to apply.

The careful construction of s.10 UCTA 1977 by Browne-Wilkinson V-C in *Tudor Grange Holdings Ltd* v *Citibank NA* arose out of a challenge to a settlement of a claim. The plaintiffs claimed breach of contract by the bank, and argued that the bank's defence, based on a contractual settlement of the claim, was ineffective because the settlement was unreasonable under s.10 UCTA 1977. Since the contract settling the claim was between the original parties to the banking contract, s.10 did not apply, as we have already seen. Moreover, Browne-Wilkinson V-C saw the possibility of compromises or settlements being challenged under the Act as most undesirable as a matter of policy, and he would interpret the Act as not extending to such transactions, relying upon what he took to be Parliament's intention and the mischief aimed at by the Act.

10.6.3.7 The 'reasonableness' test The requirement of reasonableness imposed by the Act is highly, and arguably unnecessarily, complex. It is important to realise at the outset that there are three separate tests, each applicable to different situations.

In the first place, under s.11(4) UCTA 1977 there is a special test applicable to limitation clauses (i.e. clauses restricting liability to a specified sum of money). In such cases the court must have particular regard to whether the person seeking to limit his liability could expect to have resources available to meet such liability should it arise, and to the extent to which it was possible for him to have obtained insurance cover for such liability.

Under s.11(2) UCTA 1977, in the case of exemptions of implied terms in the sale or supply of goods (ss.6 and 7 UCTA 1977; see *10.6.3.5*), the court is referred to a set of guidelines on reasonableness, set out in sch. 2. Among the factors to be taken into account are: the relative strengths of the bargaining positions of the parties; whether in agreeing to the exemption a party received an inducement (e.g. a lower price); whether any condition for the enforcement of liability (e.g. claiming within seven days of performance) could practicably be complied with; and, whether the goods were specially made at the request of the buyer.

Finally, under s.11(1) UCTA 1977, in relation to general exemption clauses in contracts, the test is whether the term is a fair and reasonable one to have been included in the light of circumstances known (or which ought to have been) to the parties at the time of contracting.

In each case, the burden of proof in respect of reasonableness lies on the party seeking to rely on the exemption clause (s.11(5) UCTA 1977). Since the tests in subsections (2) and (4) are special applications of the general test in subsection (1), the crucial time at which the reasonableness of the clause must be considered is in each case the time of contracting. In other words, the courts may not take into account subsequent events, and in particular the actual effect of breach, in determining whether the exemption clause was reasonable. Nevertheless, it seems likely that the courts will be able to have regard to the effect of the breach if they wish. Under s.11(1) UCTA 1977 they may consider circumstances which should have been in the contemplation of the parties at the time of contracting. If a particularly serious breach has occurred, a court could hold that the parties should have realised the possibility of such a serious breach, and then find that it was unreasonable at the time of contracting to exclude liability for such consequences. Equally, the list of factors to be considered in assessing reasonableness contained in Schedule 2 to the Act in theory only applies to exemptions of liability for implied terms in the sale and supply of goods. It seems likely, however, that tacitly at least the courts will regard these guidelines as the best available version of the test of reasonableness for all cases, as was acknowledged by Slade LJ in *Phillips*

Products Ltd v *Hyland* [1987] 2 All ER 620 (and see *Gill (Stewart) Ltd* v *Horatio Myer & Co Ltd* [1992] 2 All ER 257 at 262 *per* Stuart-Smith LJ). Where an exemption clause falls to be considered under several overlapping provisions of the Act (e.g., ss.3 and 7) the courts will apply the sch. 2 criteria generally, rather than differentiate between the applicable provisions (*Stag Line Ltd* v *Tyne Shiprepair Group Ltd* [1984] 2 Lloyd's Rep 211).

Reported instances of the application of the reasonableness test remain rare. In part this may be attributable to the fact that such decisions are of little value except in the particular case, and are therefore of little appeal to the editors of law reports. The question of whether an exemption clause is reasonable is in many ways like (although not in fact) the exercise of a judicial discretion (per Lord Bridge in *George Mitchell (Chesterhall) Ltd* v *Finney Lock Seeds Ltd* [1983] 1 All ER 108). That is, it involves a large element of fact marshalled by a few legal rules, so that 'there will sometimes be room for a legitimate difference of judicial opinion as to what the answer should be, where it will be impossible to say that one view is demonstrably wrong and the other demonstrably right'.

There are two consequences of the significant role of the factual elements in the test. In the House of Lords in the *Finney Lock Seeds* case Lord Bridge said that when asked to review a decision on the reasonableness of an exemption clause 'the appellate court should treat the original decision with the utmost respect and refrain from interference with it unless satisfied that it proceeded on some erroneous principle or was plainly and obviously wrong'. The reason for such restraint is that first instance judges, who actually hear the witnesses, are generally thought to be much better placed to appreciate the factual elements of a case than those in appellate courts. Lord Bridge was speaking in the context of a term falling within s.55(3) of the Sale of Goods Act 1979, but intended his remarks to apply equally to s.11(1) UCTA 1977. They were followed by the Court of Appeal in a case falling within s.11(1) of the 1977 Act in *Phillips Products Ltd* v *Hyland*. In the latter case the Court of Appeal went on to say that such decisions should not be regarded as of precedent value. Slade LJ, speaking for the whole court, said:

> The question for the court is not a general question whether or not condition 8 is valid or invalid in the case of any and every contract of hire entered into between a hirer and a plant owner who uses the relevant CPA conditions. The question was and is whether the exclusion of Hamstead's liability for negligence satisfied the requirement of reasonableness imposed by the Act, in relation to this particular contract . . . . It is important therefore that our conclusion on the particular facts of this case should not be treated as a binding precedent in other cases where similar clauses fall to be considered but the evidence of surrounding circumstances may be very different.

The significance of this denial of precedent value for judicial decisions on the reasonableness of exemption clauses soon became apparent when the same clause was treated quite differently (in a different fact situation by a differently constituted Court of Appeal) in *Thompson* v *T. Lohan (Plant Hire) Ltd* [1987] 2 All ER 631.

Nevertheless, in *Smith* v *Eric S. Bush* [1989] 2 All ER 514 the House of Lords appears deliberately to have attempted to set down a general rule on the unacceptability of exclusions of liability by professional surveyors towards private house buyers. In confronting the question of reasonableness Lord Templeman and Lord Griffiths both considered 'the general pattern of house purchases' and the impact of their finding on other transactions of the same type, while limiting their 'ruling' to domestic house purchases and reserving their position on exclusions of liability in respect of surveys of commercial property.

Bearing in mind these constraints, it will suffice to give but one example of the operation of a reasonableness test. In *George Mitchell (Chesterhall) Ltd* v *Finney Lock Seeds Ltd*

> the defendants had supplied cabbage seed for £192. The cabbages did not grow properly, causing lost production to the value of £63,000. The contract purported to limit liability for defective seeds to the amount of the contract price. The contract did not fall under UCTA 1977 because it was entered into before 1 February 1978, but it was subject to the reasonableness test applicable under s.55(3) of the Sale of Goods Act 1979, which for these purposes was essentially similar to the UCTA 1977 test.

In the Court of Appeal, in finding the clause to be unreasonable, Kerr LJ reasoned as follows:

> The balance of fairness and reasonableness appears to me to be overwhelmingly on the side of the plaintiffs . . .. Farmers do not, and cannot be expected to, insure against this kind of disaster; but suppliers of seeds can . . .. I am not persuaded that liability for rare events of this kind cannot be adequately insured against. Nor am I persuaded that the cost of such cover would add significantly to the cost of seed. Further, although the present exemption clause has been in existence for many decades, the evidence shows that it was never negotiated. In effect, it was simply imposed by the suppliers, and no seed can in practice be bought otherwise than subject to its terms. To limit the supplier's liability to the price of the seed in all cases, as against the magnitude of the losses which farmers can incur in rare disasters of this kind, appears to me to be a grossly disproportionate and unreasonable allocation of the respective risks.

10.6.3.8 The effect and scope of a finding of unreasonableness Each substantive provision of the 1971 Act which subjects an exemption clause to the requirement of reasonableness is drafted in such a way as to make clear that, if the requirement of reasonableness is not met, the clause may not be relied upon to exclude or restrict a liability which would otherwise arise under the contract. So, the simple effect of a finding of unreasonableness is to cause the contract to be applied and interpreted without reference to the offending element. Difficulties may arise in respect of this 'simple' consequence where the exemption clause is in a composite form, relating to several different possible breaches of the contract in question, or purporting to exclude or restrict liability, remedies or procedural rights in more than one way. In such a case the question arises whether a failure to satisfy the requirement of reasonableness in respect of one particular dimension of the clause will cause the whole clause to fail, or whether an offending element may be severed from the remainder of the clause, where that remainder does satisfy the requirement of reasonableness. The question was confronted directly in *Gill (Stewart) Ltd* v *Horatio Myer & Co Ltd* [1992] 2 All ER 257.

The relevant clause purported to prevent the buyer withholding payment of any amount due to the supplier 'by reason of any payment credit set off counterclaim allegation of incorrect or defective Goods or for any other reason whatsoever which the Customer may allege excuses him from performing his obligations'. The plaintiffs claimed the final instalment due under the contract which the defendants had withheld because of a counterclaim in respect of an alleged breach. The plaintiffs therefore sought to rely upon the set off and counterclaim element in the exemption clause to show that withholding the sum due was not allowed under the contract even if the alleged breach by the plaintiffs could be established. The defendants argued that the element in the exemption clause relating to payments and credits was unreasonable, so that the whole clause failed.

Lord Donaldson MR (with whom Balcombe LJ agreed) appears to have been willing to believe that a clause preventing a right of set off might be reasonable, but was unwilling to believe that it might be reasonable to prevent withholding payment where the plaintiffs owed the defendants money as a result of pre-existing payments or credits. The question therefore was whether the unreasonable part relating to payments and credits could be severed from the remainder of the clause. The court was unanimous that it could not: Lord Donaldson relied upon the wording of s.11(1), which states that the requirement of reasonableness 'is that the *term* shall have been a fair and reasonable one' (emphasis added). Stuart-Smith LJ (with whom Balcombe LJ and Lord Donaldson agreed) relied upon the fact that the assessment of whether the clause is reasonable is to be made in the light of circumstances known to the parties at the time of contracting. He pointed out that it is impossible to know at the time of contracting which part of a composite and potentially severable exemption clause will be relied upon at some indeterminate time in the future, so that unless the entire clause is the subject of scrutiny and stands and falls as a whole, the reasonableness test cannot be applied as laid down by the Act. The decision is criticised by Brown and Chandler ((1993) 109 LQR 41: their suggestion that the contract was 'negotiated freely' appears to run counter to Lord Donaldson's description of the contract as being on the other's written standard terms of business) who rightly suggest that the response of contract draftsmen to the decision must be to separate composite or omnibus exemption clauses into their distinct parts, so that the unreasonableness of a single part does not render ineffective parts which on their own would not be regarded as unreasonable.

10.6.4 Contracts to which the 1977 Act does not apply

10.6.4.1 Scope Although the Unfair Contract Terms Act 1977 introduced a general power of direct control of the use of exemption clauses in a wide range of categories of contract, there remain contracts which do not fall within the scope of the Act. Such contracts are subject to the control, such as it is, of the common law. Contracts not falling within the scope of the Act fall into three broad categories.

The first category consists of international supply contracts, and of those contracts which are expressly exempted wholly or partially from the scope of the Act by the provisions of Schedule 1 UCTA 1977 (see generally *10.6.3.1*).

The second category consists of contracts which, although potentially within the scope of the Act, do not fall within either of the qualifying conditions of s.3(1) UCTA 1977 (i.e. dealing as consumer or on the other's written standard terms of business; see *10.6.3.3*), and which do not contain statutory implied terms relating to the sale or supply of goods (see *10.6.3.5*). The relevance of this latter condition is that the Act applies to purported contractual exemptions of liability for the statutory implied terms whether or not the conditions of s.3(1) are met.

The third category consists of contracts, other than contracts for the sale of goods, not made in the course of a business (s.1(3) UCTA 1977; see *10.6.3.1*). The reason for the exception in the case of sale of goods is that the Act applies to purported contractual exemptions of liability for the statutory implied terms relating to the sale of goods whether or not the contract was made in the course of a business (see *10.6.3.5*).

10.6.4.2 Fundamental breach In the 1950s there developed out of the strict interpretation approach to exemption clauses (see *10.6.2.2*) a doctrine suggesting that *as a matter of law* the courts would not allow an exemption clause to exclude or limit liability for a breach which deprived the non-breaching party of the main performance owing to him under the contract. Sometimes it was said that there were certain 'fundamental terms', liability for breach of which could never be exempted. Alternatively, it was said that certain types of breach were 'fundamental' in that they were so serious that liability for them could not be exempted. The authority for such a rule, or rules, was never very clearly explained, and such interference with the intentions of the parties as expressed in their contract was out of character for the common law.

In *Suisse Atlantique Société d'Armement Maritime SA v NV Rotterdamsche Kolen Centrale* [1967] 1 AC 361 the House of Lords attempted to put an end to this alleged rule of law.

The case involved the charter of a ship for two years' consecutive voyages between the United States and Europe. The owners were to be paid according to the number of voyages made. Eight round-trips were made in all, and the owners alleged that but for breach of the terms of the contract relating to loading and unloading a further six trips could have been made. The charterers said that the owners' damages were limited by a clause fixing compensation for delay to $1,000 per day. The owners claimed not to be bound by that clause because the charterers had committed a fundamental breach of the contract.

Viscount Dilhorne said:

> In my view, it is not right to say that the law prohibits and nullifies a clause exempting or limiting liability for a fundamental breach or breach of a fundamental term. Such a rule of law would involve a restriction on freedom of contract and in the older cases I can find no trace of it.

There can be little doubt that the other judges in the House of Lords agreed with this statement, and intended their remarks to be consistent with it. Nevertheless, their attempt to bury the fundamental breach doctrine was not entirely successful. In the first place, their remarks were strictly *obiter*, since it was found that the clause in question was not an exemption clause at all but a liquidated damages clause (see *12.3.4.1*). Moreover, several passages in their Lordships' speeches suggested that there might be a residual rule of law applicable in the case of fundamental breach, especially where the non-breaching party elected to treat the contract as repudiated. Lord Wilberforce said that it might be correct to say that there is a rule of law against the application of exemption clauses the effect of which is to deprive one party's stipulations of all contractual force, reducing the contract to 'a mere declaration of intent'. And Lord Reid suggested that an election to treat a contract as repudiated caused the whole contract to cease to exist, including the exclusion clause, so that it would be ineffective to exclude loss. Out of these fragments the Court of Appeal, led by Lord Denning MR, contrived to revive the doctrine of fundamental breach, at least in the case where the effect of breach was so serious that the non-breaching party had no real alternative but to elect to treat the contract as repudiated (see *Harbutts' 'Plasticene' Ltd v Wayne Tank and Pump Co. Ltd* [1970] 1 QB 447).

10.6.4.3 The rule of construction The House of Lords was given a further opportunity to clarify the law in *Photo Production Ltd v Securicor Transport Ltd* [1980] 1 All ER 556. This time there could be no doubt that the issue of the effect of fundamental breach on an exemption clause was squarely raised.

Under the contract in question Securicor were to make patrol visits at night and at weekends to the premises of Photo Production. The contract contained a clause exempting Securicor from liability for the acts of its employees unless they could have been prevented by due diligence on the part of Securicor; and exempting it from liability for loss caused by fire unless the loss was solely attributable to the negligence of a Securicor employee acting within the course of his employment. One night the duty patrolman deliberately started a fire, and although it was not found that his intention was to destroy the factory, his action caused a loss of £615,000.

The House of Lords overruled *Harbutts' 'Plasticene' Ltd* v *Wayne Tank and Pump Co. Ltd* [1970] 1 QB 447. It said that the question of whether an exemption clause applied in the case of a very serious or 'fundamental' breach was no more than a question of the proper construction of the particular clause. It found that in this case the clause was drafted in such terms that liability was in fact excluded.

The last vestiges of the fundamental breach rule of law were demolished by a careful analysis of the effect of a breach of condition or a serious breach of an innominate term, since the House of Lords (per Lord Diplock) took the view that the latter and fundamental breach were one and the same thing. As we have already seen (*10.3.1* and *10.3.2.3*), the effect of such breach is to give the non-breaching party the option of treating the contract as repudiated, so that there is no longer any need to perform the primary obligations. But the contract itself does not come to an end. The secondary obligations (e.g. to pay damages for loss caused by breach) remain in existence, as would any exemption clause. The Court of Appeal (and perhaps Lord Reid in *Suisse Atlantique*) had confused the ending of the primary obligations with the ending of all obligations.

The Unfair Contract Terms Act 1977 did not apply in the *Photo Production* case, but had been passed by the time the case reached the House of Lords. Lord Wilberforce indicated what he believed should be the policy of the common law towards exemption clauses after the passing of the Act, saying:

> It is significant that Parliament refrained from legislating over the whole field of contract. After this Act, in commercial matters generally, when the parties are not of unequal bargaining power, and when risks are normally borne by insurance, not only is the case for judicial intervention undemonstrated, but there is everything to be said, and this seems to have been Parliament's intention, for leaving the parties free to apportion the risks as they think fit and for respecting their decisions.

The position at common law seems to be, therefore, that the only control over the use of exemption clauses duly incorporated into the contract is to determine whether as a matter of construction they apply to the breach in question. There is little doubt that in the past the courts were willing to find ambiguity and difficulty simply in order to have a means of eliminating oppressive exemption clauses. It now seems that since oppressive clauses may be dealt with under the Act, there is no reason for the rule of strict construction which has already been acknowledged to exist (*10.6.2.2*) to stray beyond merely seeking the ordinary meaning of the words used. There are indications that the House of Lords has recognised that strict construction should not be 'strained construction' (per Lord Wilberforce in *Ailsa Craig Fishing Co. Ltd* v *Malvern Fishing Co. Ltd* [1983] 1 All ER 101; approved by Lord Bridge in *George Mitchell (Chesterhall) Ltd* v *Finney Lock Seeds Ltd* [1983] 1 All ER 108).

10.7 EC DIRECTIVE ON UNFAIR TERMS IN CONSUMER CONTRACTS

In April 1993 the EC Council of Ministers adopted Directive 93/13 on unfair terms in consumer contracts (OJ 1993 L95/29). Although such a Directive had been discussed over a 20 year period, it was the re-emphasis on completion of the internal market embodied in the Single European Act which acted as the catalyst to progress on and ultimate adoption of the Directive. The position of the United Kingdom was to welcome the proposal, while maintaining a certain scepticism about whether the measure was truly needed for the completion of the internal market. The preamble to the Directive points, however, to divergences between the protective consumer legislation in the various member states, and voices the fear that lack of awareness of the law in other countries may deter consumers from entering into transactions directly with suppliers outside their own country. It also points to general Community programmes for a consumer protection and information policy, which provides a basis for harmonisation of consumer protection laws at a Community level. The Directive includes within its scope some matters already covered by the Unfair Contract Terms Act 1977, but in some respects the Act is wider than the Directive, whilst in others it is the Directive which is the more sweeping. United Kingdom compliance with the terms of the Directive is certain to require changes to our law.

10.7.1 The scope of the Directive

According to art.1(1) the purpose of the Directive is to harmonise the law relating to 'unfair terms in contracts concluded between a seller or supplier and a consumer'. What constitutes an 'unfair term' is laid down in art.3, and is considered in more detail below (*10.7.2.2*). It is important to stress that the scope of the Directive extends beyond exemption clauses as defined in *10.6.1.3* and *10.6.3.1*. Terms may be unfair because they result in an imbalance in the contract to the detriment of the consumer party, for example by allowing the non-consumer unilaterally to vary the terms of the contract without good reason. 'Seller or supplier' is defined by art.2(c) as 'any natural or legal person who, in contracts covered by this Directive, is acting for purposes relating to his trade, business or profession, whether publicly owned or privately owned'. This expression seems to be wider than the equivalent in UCTA 1977 of acting 'in the course of a business', and may mean that contracts are caught by the Directive which fall outside s.1(3) UCTA (*10.6.3.1*). It should certainly not be assumed that the same interpretation will apply, and it may be that this is one of several matters which will have to be referred to the European Court of Justice before a definitive interpretation can be established. 'Consumer' is defined by art.2(b) as 'any natural person who, in contracts covered by this Directive, is acting for purposes which are outside his trade, business or profession'. This definition would exlude from the protection provided by the terms of the Directive a company entering into contracts not essential to its business, which under the terms of UCTA 1977 may apparently be treated as a consumer (see *10.6.3.3*).

The Directive excludes from its scope terms defining the main subject matter of the contract and questions relating to the adequacy of the contract price in relation to the performance to be provided by the other party (art.4(2)). These elements are central to the idea of freedom of contract, which is espoused by all member states, so that it was unacceptable that there should be any attempt to regulate the content of these terms. However, the general requirement of 'plain intelligible language' (art.5) does apply to such terms. Also excluded from the scope of the Directive are 'mandatory statutory or regulatory provisions' (art.1(2)), the assumption being that if member states have by legislative act given approval to particular contract terms they cannot by definition be deemed unfair (Preamble, recital 13). An example might be terms derived from international conventions, such as the Warsaw Convention limitations on liability towards passengers in aircraft; the Preamble also envisages that 'default' obligations such as s.14(2) of the Sale of Goods Act 1979 (implied condition that goods sold be of merchantable quality: *10.4.3.2*) would be excluded.

Article 10 of the Directive requires member states to implement it in their national law by 31 December 1994, and the national law so implementing the directive will apply to contracts made after that date.

10.7.2   Substantive obligations under the Directive

10.7.2.1   Plain intelligible language   Under art.5 terms offered to the consumer in writing, whether they constitute all the terms of the contract or only some of them, 'must always be drafted in plain, intelligible language'. As noted above, this requirement extends to terms defining the main subject matter of the contract and price terms, which are otherwise outside the scope of the Directive. The meaning of 'plain intelligible language' is nowhere defined, and the real value of this requirement may be doubted. The principal reason is that there is no real sanction for not using such language, except that where there is doubt 'the interpretation most favourable to the consumer shall prevail'. This rule is similar to the existing rule in English law of *contra proferentem* interpretation of exemption clauses (*10.6.2.2*), although under the Directive it applies to all terms. No doubt it would have been difficult to provide for any more effective sanction, since the principal sanction for the main substantive obligation under the Directive is to make unfair terms unenforceable against the consumer. Such a measure could not apply to any term falling foul of the plain language test, since it might render the contract meaningless. Nevertheless, since the only sanction is to be found in the contruction of the language of the doubtful term, it is perhaps overstating the case to say that terms *must* be in plain language: the obligation cannot be effectively enforced. Article 5 amounts to no more than a legislative exhortation to plain language.

10.7.2.2   Contracts in which unfair terms may be found   The control of unfair terms only applies to contractual terms which have not been negotiated individually (art.3(1)). Of course, it is most often the case that consumer contracts are in such form, but this qualifying condition goes a step beyond s.3 UCTA 1977, which applies where either one party is a consumer or where the contract is on one party's written standard terms of business. Under the Directive the control mechanism only applies where both conditions are satisfied. Article 3(1) attempts to avoid the problem of defining what is a standard form contract by the expression 'term . . . not . . . individually negotiated', although it may be doubted whether the attempt is wholly successful. Article 3(2) provides a presumptive test of when a term is not individually negotiated, that is to say

> where it has been drafted in advance and the consumer has therefore not been able to influence the substance of the term, particularly in the context of a pre-formulated standard contract.

As may be seen, the qualifying description 'standard' has not in the end been avoided, and it reappears further down the paragraph. Where a term is in a 'standard' form (which is not further defined) the seller or supplier may attempt to rebut the presumption that it was not individually negotiated, but naturally the burden of proof in such a matter rests on that party. In one respect, however, the Directive achieves a clarification which is missing in UCTA 1977, in that it is expressly provided that a contact may as a whole be treated as a pre-formulated standard form despite the fact that 'certain aspects of a term or one specific term have been individually negotiated'. The intention is clear: the fact that the consumer has been able to influence the content of the contract in a minor way does not prevent the remainder of the contract not so influenced from being treated as not individually negotiated and so potentially containing unfair terms. A literal interpretation of the Directive appears to imply that up to but no more than a single term may be so influenced, before the qualification of 'not individually negotiated' is lost, but it should be remembered that European Community law as applied by the European Court of Justice does not often restrict itself to the literal interpretation, preferring to interpret legislation in the light of its purpose. Since the purpose is to provide a means of policing contracts over which consumers have had no significant influence, it seems likely that negotiation of more than one term will not exclude the application of the Directive's rules, provided the consumer's influence on the content of the contract is insignificant. Where the consumer has had an influence on the content of a term through individual negotiation it is assumed that the term will not be unfair, so that art.3 is only to be applied to the rest of the contract. Although the logic of this provision may be understood, it is possible to imagine individual negotiation itself being affected by the inequality of bargaining power between parties where one is a consumer, so that it may be a false assumption to believe that individual negotiation is a fail-safe guard against unfairness.

10.7.2.3 Unfair terms Article 3(1) provides:

> A contractual term which has not been individually negotiated shall be regarded as unfair if, contrary to the requirement of good faith, it causes a significant imbalance in the parties' rights and obligations arising under the contract, to the detriment of the consumer.

This provision is the key to the control mechanism adopted by the Directive. It defines as unfair terms which cause a significant imbalance between the parties to the detriment of the consumer (but does not apply to terms defining the main subject matter of the contract or to price terms—art.4(2): see 10.7.1). It appears that the notion of 'detriment to the consumer' is unlikely to cause great difficulty; it is subordinate to the notion of 'significant imbalance', and its only purpose is to indicate for whose benefit the control is to be exercised. In the unlikely event of an imbalance *in favour* of the consumer art.3 would not apply.

The key notion, therefore, is a 'significant imbalance in the parties' rights and obligations arising under the contract' which is in some way contrary to the 'requirement of good faith'. These are vague and ill-defined criteria, and art.3(1) does not make clear the relationship between them. Paragraph 16 of the Preamble to the Directive defines compliance with the requirement of good faith as being satisfied by dealing equitably and fairly with the consumer, whose legitimate interests must be taken into account. However, the drafting of art.3(1) does not make clear whether the requirement of lack of good faith is additional to the condition of imbalance between the parties, or whether imbalance is to be regarded in itself as evidence of a lack of good faith. Neither the Preamble nor art.3 provides clear guidance on this matter or on what constitutes a significant imbalance. Consequently, identification of the criteria for compliance with the terms of the Directive is a process of deduction from what is termed (in art.3(3)) an 'indicative and non-exhaustive list of the terms which may be regarded as unfair' contained in the Annex to the Directive. That list is too long (17 items) to reproduce here, but it is possible to indicate its main themes. As must be expected, it includes terms which are plainly within the scope of UCTA 1977, such as terms excluding or limiting liability for death or personal injury of a consumer (para.(a)), and terms excluding or limiting the rights of (and remedies available to) consumers in the event of a breach (paras.(b) and (q)). Other items on the list appear well beyond the reach of UCTA, such as terms enabling a seller or supplier to terminate a contract of indeterminate duration without reasonable notice, except where there are serious grounds for so doing (para.(g)), and terms enabling the seller or supplier to alter the terms of the contract unilaterally without a valid reason which is specified in the contract (para.(j)). Such terms have not been subject to control under UCTA 1977 until now, although it might be argued that in some circumstances they might be classed as terms which modify expected contractual obligations and so are subject to the requirement of reasonableness under s.3(2)(b)(i) (see 10.6.3.4). The Annex also addresses terms which under present English law would be dealt with under the law relating to deposits and pre-payments, or penalty clauses (paras.(d), (e) and (f)), and in so doing goes beyond the terms of our present law. From this list it appears possible to deduce that imbalance and lack of good faith are distinct elements in the test. For example, a power to alter terms unilaterally constitutes an imbalance in the rights and obligations of the parties: but that in itself is not deemed to be unfair. There must also be no valid reason specified in the contract for such unilateral alteration, and it appears to be the absence of valid reason which constitutes the lack of good faith. Nevertheless, although the two-part mechanics of the test appear to be clearly established, the list also demonstrates the extent to which both imbalance and lack of good faith will always be questions of fact in each particular case which leave a very considerable element of discretion to the courts. This assessment is to be carried out, according to art.4(1), by

> taking into account the nature of the goods or services for which the contract was concluded and by referring, at the time of conclusion of the contract, to all the circumstances attending the conclusion of the contract and to all the other terms of the contract or of another contract on which it is dependent.

Despite the rather clumsy drafting, it must be assumed that the reference to 'the time of conclusion of the contract' is intended to prevent the assessment of fairness taking into account events occurring after the time when the contract was made, which would be consistent with the assessment of reasonableness under UCTA 1977. It should not be seen as implying that challenges to the fairness of terms must be made immediately upon conclusion of the contract if they are to be successful.

10.7.3   Effect and enforcement of the Directive's provisions
Two distinct issues arise: the measures which may be taken against unfair terms where they are identified; and the measures which must be taken by the United Kingdom to incorporate the Directive into our law.

10.7.3.1   The consequences of a term being unfair
It has already been noted that although the Directive requires written contract terms to be drafted in plain, intelligible language, failure to achieve this standard does not appear to result in the term being regarded as 'unfair', so that the consequences of unfairness addressed here do not apply to breach of art.5, for which the only sanction appears to be interpretation most favourable to the consumer (see *10.7.2.1*). Where under art.3 a term is found to be unfair the term 'shall . . . not be binding on the consumer', but the remainder of the contract 'shall continue to bind the parties upon those terms if it is capable of continuing in existence without the unfair terms' (art.6(1)). This appears to imply that where a term contains an unfair element the whole term is affected, and the contract must be read without the whole term. We have already seen that a similar approach has been taken to exemption clauses under UCTA 1977 (*10.6.3.8*). Whether such an approach is appropriate here, where the range of terms within the scope of the Directive is much broader, is open to question. Since it must surely be desirable to preserve as many contracts as possible, and since taking out whole terms increases the risk that the commercial balance of the contract will be upset, or that the contract will become too vague to be enforceable, there is a case for saying that unfair elements should be severable from the remainder of a term which is not otherwise unfair, in order to increase the chances of the underlying contract surviving. There is limited support for

the idea that under the Directive terms may be subdivided and severed in art.3(2), para.2, which refers to the possibility that certain aspects of a term have been individually negotiated, and that fact not preventing application of the Directive's provisions to the rest of the contract.

10.7.3.2 Regulation of unfair terms other than by litigation between the parties Member states are required by art.7(1) to ensure that 'adequate and effective means exist to prevent the continued use of unfair terms in contracts concluded with consumers'. The Preamble assumes that this obligation will be met by member states maintaining a regulatory or administrative system under which the use of such terms can be challenged by a mechanism other than civil litigation in respect of a contract to which a consumer is a party. Such systems already exist in France (*loi du 10 janvier 1978 D.1978 Lég.86, Ch.IV*). No further guidance on the nature of such a regulatory procedure is provided by the Directive, except to say that it must include a mechanism whereby a person or an organisation having a legitimate interest under national law in protecting consumers (the Consumers Association? the National Consumer Council?) may take action before the courts or the competent administrative body to determine 'whether contractual terms drawn up for general use are unfair' (art.7(2)). Such action might be taken against a major public utility in respect of its standard form contract, or jointly against a group of independent sellers or suppliers who habitually use a standard form contract drawn up by a trade association. It amounts to the introduction of a public interest class action in the interests of consumer protection.

10.7.3.3 United Kingdom compliance with the Directive It has already been observed that the Directive is both narrower and wider than existing provisions of English law (and, for that matter, of Scots law). Where English law maintains higher standards of protection they may be retained under the terms of art.8. So, for example, in the case of consumer contracts, exclusion of liability in respect of the implied conditions of quality in the Sale of Goods Act 1979 is completely outlawed by s.6(2) UCTA 1977, without reference to criteria of unfairness or good faith, and without any requirement that the relevant term be included in a contract which was not individually negotiated. It would seem, therefore, that in this respect the protection of the consumer under English law is stricter than that provided by the Directive, where the consumer's rights depend upon rather more qualifying conditions being satisfied. The higher standard under English law is allowed to remain by art.8. In other respects English law does not provide as high a standard of protection, and it is accepted in the Department of Trade and Industry that legislation is required to bring English law into line with the Directive. It has not yet been decided what form such legislation will take. Under s.2(2) and (4) of the European Communities Act 1972 such legislation, even if it amends UCTA 1977, may be made by Order in Council, although the usual practice when amending Parliamentary legislation is to proceed by way of further Act of Parliament. If that route is taken it seems most unlikely that the United Kingdom will be able to meet the deadline for compliance (although it will not be alone in that regard). The consequences of failure to implement on time are rather unpredictable, and the principles to be applied are set out at *3.4.4*. If the Directive is not implemented on time it would not apply to contracts where the seller or supplier could not in some way be regarded as part of the state. On the other hand, where a consumer suffers a loss as a direct result of the government's failure to implement the Directive, that loss may be recoverable from the state rather than from the other contracting party.

ELEVEN
Discharge of the contract

The discharge of a contract is the process whereby the primary obligations (i.e. the obligations to perform: see *10.3.1*) under a contract which is validly formed come to an end. In many circumstances the secondary obligation to pay damages in compensation of loss also ends (e.g. discharge by frustration: see *11.4.5*), but that is not always the consequence of discharge. In the case of discharge by breach a secondary obligation to pay damages for loss caused continues (*11.3.1*).

It is important to maintain a distinction between the discharge of valid contracts and the processes by which invalid contracts are terminated. A contract may be invalid because it is affected by mistake (Chapter 7), by misrepresentation (Chapter 9), by incapacity (*8.2–8.4*), by duress (*8.5*), by undue influence (*8.6*), or by illegality (including restraint of trade: *8.7–8.8*). In many circumstances no legal process is necessary to effect the termination of an invalid contract. Since a void contract gives rise to no obligation to perform, it is sufficient for the party asserting its invalidity to do nothing, and plead the invalidity as a defence to an action for breach (*8.1.1*). Where a contract is voidable (e.g. misrepresentation), so that the contract remains valid until brought to an end by the party empowered by law to do so, the process of termination is known as 'rescission' (see also *10.3.2.3*).

Discharge of a contract may result from performance (*11.1*), agreement (*11.2*), breach (*11.3*) or frustration (*11.4*). In the case of performance, agreement and breach, this chapter will only summarise and collect together rules which have been addressed in detail earlier in the book.

11.1 DISCHARGE BY PERFORMANCE

A contract is discharged by the satisfactory performance by both parties of all the primary obligations, express and implied, created by the contract.

11.1.1 Standard of performance

Contractual obligations require one of two standards of performance. The general rule is that the performance obligation is strict, and that any deviation from performance of the exact contractual undertaking is breach (see *10.5 et seq.*). This is sometimes called the 'perfect tender' rule. Where such an obligation exists there is no real exception to it, other than for what may be regarded as 'microscopic' deviations, but the effect of breach may be mitigated in the case of minor imperfections. In some circumstances, however, the contract imposes only what is sometimes called 'negligence' liability; that is, the performance required is only the exercise of reasonable care and reasonable skill, and there is no obligation to achieve a stated result (see *10.5*).

11.1.2 Tender of performance
A party tenders performance when he attempts to perform his primary obligations under the contract by offering the stipulated performance to the other party. Where the performance obligation requires the party actually to do something (e.g. to deliver goods) the tender of performance may be the best way for a party to show that he is ready and willing to perform, in order to be able to treat the other party's non-performance as a repudiation of the contract (see *10.5.1*). In this sense, it is the tender of performance which discharges that party's obligation.

Where the performance obligation requires the party merely to pay for something done by the other party, tender of payment relieves him of some obligations, but it does not discharge the debt. He remains obliged to pay the contract debt, and must remain ready and willing to pay to avoid repudiating the contract. This is best demonstrated by payment of the money into court. The effect is to limit his liability to the contract debt and nothing else. Thus, once the other party has refused proper payment he cannot recover interest on the original sum, and will be liable for the debtor's legal costs (RSC Ord. 22, r.1; RSC Ord. 18, r.6: see also *Dixon* v *Clark* (1848) 5 CB 365, 377). The payment obligation is a strict obligation, so that in theory the exact amount must be made available unconditonally and in legal tender (*Betterbee* v *Davis* (1811) 3 Camp 70). For those reasons payment by cheque, unless otherwise agreed, is only a conditional payment which does not discharge the debt until the cheque has been cleared. It seems likely that today, given the general access to bank accounts and automatic transfers of money, the courts will be willing to imply agreements for means of payment other than physical delivery of cash in most circumstances.

11.1.3 Time obligations
In commercial contracts the normal rule is that stipulations as to time of performance are crucial ('time is of the essence'), so that breach entitles the other party to treat the contract as repudiated (see *10.3.2.2*). In other contracts time clauses are not regarded as crucial unless expressed to be so by the parties. In the absence of express agreement, the equitable rule prevails over the strict approach of the common law (cf. s.41 of the Law of Property Act 1925), so that failure to abide by a time clause does not entitle the other party to treat the contract as repudiated. These rules are considered at length in *United Scientific Holdings Ltd* v *Burnley Borough Council* [1978] AC 904.

11.2 DISCHARGE BY AGREEMENT

A contract may be discharged by agreement between the parties. Where the discharge occurs with the free consent of both parties and without subsequent change of heart, there is no need for any particular form of agreement. The parties may simply abandon performance. In practice, however, in order to guard against a change of heart by the other party, it will be desirable to adopt some form of legally binding agreement to discharge the contract.

11.2.1 The requirement of consideration
In addition to demonstrating the existence of an agreement to discharge future obligations (cf. *The Hannah Blumenthal* [1983] 1 All ER 34; discussed at *5.1.2.1*), the parties must also demonstrate that it is legally enforceable. The best way of so doing will be to establish the existence of a second contract to discharge the first, which will require the existence of consideration (see *6.4.1*). The detailed rules of the consideration doctrine are considered above (*6.3*). Where both parties have performance obligations remaining under the contract, mutual abandonment of those obligations is enough to satisfy the requirement of consideration, so that such discharge is legally enforceable (*6.4.1.1*). However, where one party's obligations are executed and so only the other party needs to be discharged from further performance, the requirement of consideration may not be satisfied by mere abandonment of the contract.

This difficulty may be avoided in one of three ways. There may be a *release* of the party whose obligations remain to be performed. A release is only legally enforceable if made in a document under seal (see *6.1*). Alternatively, there may be *accord and satisfaction*, which is the rather archaic way of describing a separate agreement supported by new consideration. Traditionally, the essential rule was that the 'satisfaction' (consideration) must not be a lesser form of what was due under the contract (*Pinnel's Case* (1602) 5 Co. Rep. 117a; see *6.4.3.1*). However, the requirement of consideration in contract variations has apparently been substantially modified by the decision of the Court of Appeal in *Williams* v *Roffey Bros & Nicholls (Contractors) Ltd* [1990] 1 All ER 512. The identification of consideration being constituted by a subjective benefit to the promisor allowed the promisee to recover under an extra promise in the varied contract without supplying anything extra under the contract in return (see further *6.3 et seq.*) Finally, insofar as these changes to the doctrine of consideration have not made it redundant, an agreement for discharge of the contract may be binding by virtue of equitable or promissory estoppel (see generally *6.4.2* and *6.4.3*).

11.2.2 Variation and waiver
The performance obligations under a contract may be terminated by either variation or waiver. *Variation* (see *6.4.1* for detailed treatment) is the term used to describe the change of contractual terms by means of an independent contract. Potential changes include the termination of all performance obligations. In some circumstances the change may be made not by variation but by *rescission and replacement*, which is the total discharge of the original

contract followed by the substitution of a new contract between the parties (cf. *Morris* v *Baron & Co.* [1918] AC 1). In either case the requirements of a separate contract, including especially the existence of consideration, must be satisfied.

Waiver is the change of contractual terms without recourse to an independent contract, so that a variation which is ineffective because not all the conditions of a separate contract are satisfied may still take effect as a waiver. Since the development of the promissory estoppel doctrine (*6.4.3*), waiver has become indistinguishable from promissory and equitable estoppel (*6.4.2*), and it may be that it would be better if use of the term were dropped to avoid confusion. It will be recalled that the effect of equitable estoppel is said to be only to suspend contractual rights and not to terminate them (*6.4.2.3*). It might be thought, then, that it has no relevance to the discharge of contracts. Nevertheless, since it may cause instalment obligations to fall into permanent abeyance (*6.4.2.3*), and since it appears to apply to the payment of part of a debt in final settlement of the full amount (*6.4.3.1*), at least in these limited senses a contract may be discharged by waiver.

11.2.3 Self-terminating contracts
A contract may also be discharged by the realisation of a condition subsequent (*10.3.2.1*) stipulated by the parties. The condition may be an event beyond the control of either of the parties (e.g. attainment of a certain point on a cost-of-living index), or may be entirely within the control of one of the parties (e.g. giving and serving a stipulated period of notice). Indeed, where the contract on its face has no provision for termination then, in the absence of any indication of an intention that the contract be perpetual, the courts will imply a term that the contract be terminable upon reasonable notice (cf. *Staffordshire Area Health Authority* v *South Staffordshire Waterworks Co.* [1978] 3 All ER 769).

11.3 DISCHARGE BY BREACH

11.3.1 Legal effect of breach
The legal effect of breach has already been discussed in detail in the context of Chapter 10 ('The Substance of the Contract'; see especially *10.3* and *10.5*). It is intended here only to summarise those rules.

11.3.1.1 General rule In the case of a contract consisting of dependent conditions, breach of a promissory condition precedent or of a concurrent condition entitles the non-breaching party to treat the contract as repudiated (*10.5.1*). The effect of treating the contract as repudiated is to discharge any obligations under the contract which have not yet been performed. Similar results ensue from the breach of an entire obligation in a contract (*10.5.2*). For these purposes a condition may be defined as any term expressed by the parties to have such effect, or interpreted by the court as intended to have such effect ('conditions' properly so called; see *10.3.2.2*). The definition must also include innominate terms breach of which has had serious consequences, since the effect of such breach is the same as that of a breach of condition

(10.3.4.2). It must be remembered that such breach does not automatically discharge the contract: the non-breaching party may elect whether to proceed with the contract or to treat it as repudiated *(10.3.2.3)*, provided the right to treat the contract as repudiated has not been lost *(10.3.2.4)*. It must also be remembered that discharge of the remaining performance obligations under the contract does not discharge the secondary obligation to pay damages for any loss caused *(10.3.2.3)*, and does not discharge any exemption clauses validly incorporated into the contract *(10.6.4.3)*.

11.3.1.2 Exceptions to the breach of dependent condition rule The non-breaching party is not entitled to treat the contract as repudiated, and hence the primary obligations under the contract are not discharged, where the breach relates to an independent condition *(10.5.1)* or to a warranty *(10.3.3)*, or where the term is innominate and the results of the breach are not serious *(10.3.4.2)*.

11.3.1.3 Exceptions to the entire obligation rule Where the non-breaching party accepts a benefit conferred by the defective performance of the party in breach of an entire contract, the contract will still be discharged if the non-breaching party elects to treat it as repudiated, but a new contract to pay a reasonable price for the benefit accepted will be implied *(10.5.3.1)*. Moreover, the non-breaching party may be unable to treat an entire contract as repudiated if the breach is so minimal that it is possible to say that there has been substantial performance. In that case the contract is not discharged, but a secondary obligation to pay damages nevertheless accrues *(10.5.3.2)*.

11.3.2 Breach by anticipatory repudiation
It has been assumed so far that breach is constituted by either non-performance or defective (including late) performance once the time for performance stipulated in the contract has arrived. Where one party indicates in advance of the time for performance, either expressly or by conduct, an intention not to perform, or to perform in a manner inconsistent with the contractual undertaking, special rules apply; or, at least, the usual rules apply somewhat differently to this particular situation. Such an indication is sometimes called 'anticipatory breach', but should more properly be referred to as 'breach by anticipatory repudiation', since it is the announcement of intention rather than the non-performance which is in advance of the stipulated time.

The doctrine is well illustrated by the early leading case of *Hochster v De La Tour* (1853) 2 E & B 678.

> The defendant had engaged the plaintiff to start work for him in two months' time as a courier for travel through Europe. One month later the defendant wrote saying that he no longer required the plaintiff's services. The plaintiff immediately commenced an action for breach of contract, to which the defendant argued that the plaintiff was not entitled to a remedy unless he could show that on the due date for commencement of performance of his services he was ready and willing to perform his side of the contract (cf. *10.5.1*).

The court rejected that argument, saying that the plaintiff was free to choose whether to await the time for performance, in which case he must then be ready and willing to perform, or to treat the contract as immediately repudiated, in which case the concurrent condition was discharged. The main justification given for the rule was that it was better for both parties that the plaintiff should avoid the wasteful expenditure of preparing for a performance which he had already been told would not be accepted.

It is clear that the court took the view that the right to an immediate remedy was based on the fact of repudiation, and not on any notional 'acceleration' of the contract date for performance. Lord Campbell CJ explained this finding on the basis of an implied term that between the time of contracting and the due date for performance neither party would 'do anything to the prejudice of the other inconsistent with' the contractual relationship which had been created. This rule is confirmed by subsequent cases. For example, even where performance is contingent upon a condition which may never materialise, anticipatory repudiation entitles the other party to an immediate remedy (cf. *Frost* v *Knight* (1872) LR 7 Exch 111). Nevertheless, if it is clear beyond doubt that the contingency cannot materialise, so that the repudiation cannot be said to deprive the other party of any reasonably expected performance, no remedy will be available (*The Mihalis Angelos* [1970] 3 All ER 125).

11.3.2.1 Limits on the right of election The non-repudiating party's right of election upon receiving notice of the other's intention not to continue with the contract is not completely without limit. In the first place it seems that an element of the distinction which for ease may be described as that between conditions and warranties (*10.3.1*) also applies to anticipatory repudiations. In *Decro-Wall International SA* v *Practitioners in Marketing Ltd* [1971] 2 All ER 216

> the question arose whether late payment on a particular instalment, which it was known was likely to be repeated in the future, entitled the other party to treat the whole contract as repudiated. The plaintiff argued that a single late payment which was likely to be repeated amounted to an anticipatory repudiation of the whole agreement.

The Court of Appeal accepted that the late payment was breach, and that there was every likelihood of that breach being repeated in the future, but did not accept that the plaintiff was thereby discharged from further performance under the contract. The term in question was not sufficiently serious for a repudiation in relation to it to be treated as bringing the whole contract to an end.

Conversely, there is some limit on the power of the non-repudiating party to elect to affirm the contract. In *White & Carter (Councils) Ltd* v *McGregor* [1962] AC 413

> the appellants had agreed with the respondents to advertise the respondents' business on litter bins to be supplied to local authorities. On the same day the respondents

repudiated the agreement, but the appellants went ahead and performed their side of the contract for the full three years agreed.

It was held that they were entitled to do so (despite the absence of mitigation; see also *12.2.1.1*), but Lord Reid said that the general power to affirm the contract could not be exercised by a person who had no legitimate interest, financial or otherwise, in performing the contract rather than claiming damages. This statement was followed in *The Alaskan Trader* [1984] 1 All ER 129.

11.3.2.2 The risk of over-reaction A party faced with what he thinks is an anticipatory repudiation must take careful stock before acting. In the first place, his election will be irrevocable (see *10.3.2.4*). More seriously, if he is mistaken in thinking that the other party has repudiated the contract his own purported election to accept the discharge of his obligations may amount itself to an anticipatory repudiation (cf. *Federal Commerce and Navigation Ltd v Molena Alpha Inc.* [1979] AC 757). Some doubt was cast on this proposition by the House of Lords in *Woodar Investment Development Ltd* v *Wimpey Construction (UK) Ltd* [1980] 1 All ER 571. Lord Wilberforce said that a party's mistake as to his rights, in the absence of bad faith, would not lead the court to regard a purported termination of the contract as a repudiation. With respect to their Lordships, the other party may be unable to tell whether an apparent repudiation stems from a mistake as to rights or from a simple decision not to proceed with the contract. *Woodar Investment* is thus a source of considerable uncertainty in the law, and may best be regarded as limited to the situation in which the question is whether the conditions of an express termination clause have been met, when the other party would usually be able to determine the reason for the termination. Where the purported termination is for an alleged breach of condition (or its equivalent) the risk should remain with the party making the election. To remove some of the uncertainty from that risk English law would do well to imitate the provision of the American Uniform Commercial Code which enables a party who has reasonable ground for insecurity with respect to the other's performance to demand an assurance of the performance due, and if it is not forthcoming then to treat the contract as repudiated (UCC Section 2–609).

11.3.2.3 The risk of affirmation A further reason for taking careful stock when faced with an election whether to accept the repudiation or to affirm the contract is that affirmation leaves the non-repudiating party exposed to all the normal risks he would bear under the contract. In the first place, an election to affirm the contract maintains alive all the obligations of both contracting parties. Consequently, the affirming party may subsequently become liable for breach of contract if he fails to comply with all the terms. The point is well illustrated by *Fercometal SARL* v *Mediterranean Shipping Co. SA* [1988] 2 All ER 742.

Charterers of a ship gave notice of cancellation of the contract which was not in accordance with the terms of the charterparty, and amounted to a repudiation. The shipowners did not accept the repudiation, but instead gave notice of readiness to load. This notice complied with the terms of the charterparty, and constituted an affirmation, but was false, and so in turn constituted breach. The charterers consequently rejected the notice, and gave further notice of cancellation which on this occasion complied with the terms of the charterparty. The shipowners sued the charterers.

The House of Lords rejected this claim. Once the contract was treated as being still in force, it was 'kept alive for the benefit of both parties', and the party affirming could not both keep it alive and seek to justify his own non-performance by reference to the earlier repudiation.

Secondly, an affirmed contract may subsequently be discharged by frustration (see *11.4*). In *Avery* v *Bowden* (1855) 5 E & B 714

> the master of a ship had been told in advance of the last possible date for loading that there was no cargo available, which may have amounted to a repudiation. He elected to affirm the contract, and remained in port hoping that a cargo would eventually be provided. Before the last possible date for performance of the contract it was frustrated by the outbreak of the Crimean War, thus depriving the shipowners of a remedy they might have had if the repudiation had been accepted.

11.3.2.4 Other remedies for anticipatory repudiation Breach by anticipatory repudiation also presents some difficulty in relation to the remedy of damages. Those difficulties are considered below, in relation to mitigation (*12.3.3.4*) and the time for assessment of damages (*12.3.2.9*).

11.4 DISCHARGE BY FRUSTRATION

11.4.1 Introduction
It has already been stated that, in general, the performance obligation in contracts is strict (*10.5*): the promisor guarantees to achieve a stipulated result, and any failure to achieve that result is breach. Such a rule would cause injustice if, through no fault of either party, the promisor were prevented from performing and yet was held to be liable for the breach. Of course, where the performance obligation is to do no more than to exercise reasonable care and skill, the fact that the stipulated result is not achieved because of some extraneous factor will not matter, provided the promisor has exercised such care and skill. But where the performance obligation is strict the promisor must overcome extraneous interference in his performance unless the law provides some doctrine of excuse. In English law a doctrine of excuse is provided by the law relating to frustration. It provides residual rules governing intervening events whose effect on further performance of the contract is so emphatic that the contract is automatically brought to an end. In addition, the parties may themselves provide in their contract that it will terminate upon some contingency, or at least that the parties will not be liable for loss arising out of an incident which is beyond the control of the parties. Such clauses are usually referred to as *force majeure* clauses, and are usually enforced by the courts (e.g., *J. Lauritzen*

AS v *Wijsmuller BV* [1990] 1 Lloyd's Rep 1). It is possible that if such a clause were to allow a party to escape a liability which would otherwise usually be regarded as falling on him under the contract, the clause might be subject to control under the Unfair Contract Terms Act 1977 (see *10.6.3.4*).

11.4.1.1 History Until the middle of the nineteenth century English law had no general doctrine of excuse of contractual performance. The leading case was *Paradine* v *Jane* (1647) Aleyn 26.

> To an action of debt for rent due on certain land the defendant had argued by way of defence that he had been deprived of possession of the land by the action of an enemy army. The defence failed; the defendant had promised to pay rent, and if he sought to be excused in particular circumstances he should have made provision for them in his contract.

It need hardly be said that this reasoning was somewhat unrealistic, for if contracts were to contain express provision for every possible eventuality which might interfere in the contractual performance they would become very long documents indeed!

The important change in the law came in *Taylor* v *Caldwell* (1863) 3 B & S 826.

> The defendants had agreed to allow the plaintiffs to use their hall for four concerts for a fee of £100 for each day. After the contract was made but before the day of the first concert the hall was destroyed by fire, causing the plaintiffs a loss since they were without a venue for the concerts, for which preparations were well advanced. The plaintiffs sought to recover their loss from the defendants, who pleaded the accidental destruction of the hall as an excuse for their non-performance. The contract contained no express provision for such an eventuality.

The court found for the defendants. The principle of cases like *Paradine* v *Jane* was said to be limited to 'positive and absolute' contracts, which were contracts in which one party had guaranteed his performance irrespective of all risks. Not all contracts were of that type. Blackburn J said:

> Where, from the nature of the contract, it appears that the parties must from the beginning have known that it could not be fulfilled unless when the time for fulfilment of the contract arrived some particular specified thing continued to exist, so that, when entering into the contract, they must have contemplated such existence as the foundation of what was to be done; there, in the absence of any express or implied warranty that the thing shall exist, the contract is not to be construed as a positive contract, but as subject to an implied condition that the parties shall be excused in case, before breach, performance becomes impossible from the perishing of the thing without default of the contractor.

From this carefully guarded statement of law has grown a general doctrine of excuse. The 'absolute contracts principle' has become very much the exception, although it is possible for the parties to create an absolute contract by specifying that all the risks of performance are to fall on a named party (see *11.4.3*).

11.4.1.2 Legal nature of the frustration doctrine In *Taylor* v *Caldwell* (1863) 3 B & S 826 Blackburn J based his finding that performance had been excused upon an implied term of the contract between the parties that the concert hall should continue in existence until the time for performance. It is not particularly surprising that he chose to base his reasoning on an implied term since at that time the courts were adamant that it was not their role to interfere in the contracts of the parties (*4.4.2*). Reasoning based on an implied term enabled the court rather to say that it was doing no more than enforcing what was the true agreement, including such terms which were so obvious that they had not been expressed (see *10.4.2*). The implied term basis for the frustration doctrine continued well into this century (e.g. *F A Tamplin SS Co. Ltd* v *Anglo-Mexican Petroleum Products Co. Ltd* [1916] 2 AC 397 per Lord Loreburn). There is no doubt that at that time what was intended was a term implied as fact (see *10.4.2*) between the parties.

As the frustration doctrine developed, however, and the courts were willing to apply the doctrine of excuse to an increasingly wide range of circumstances, the notion of it resting on a term implied as fact between the parties became something of a fiction. This was acknowledged by the House of Lords in *Davis Contractors Ltd* v *Fareham UDC* [1956] AC 696. Both Lords Reid and Radcliffe pointed out that in many circumstances in which it was admitted that the frustration doctrine should apply the test for the implication of a term as fact would not be satisfied. Thus, when asked whether in given circumstances the contract would be discharged the parties would not reply 'Oh, of course' (*Shirlaw* v *Southern Foundries Ltd* [1939] 2 KB 206: *10.4.2*); rather, they would be likely to consider whether the risk was one which had been or ought to be allocated between them by their contract. The modern view of the frustration doctrine is generally regarded as expressed in the speech of Lord Radcliffe, who said:

> [P]erhaps it would be simpler to say at the outset that frustration occurs whenever the law recognises that, without default of either party, a contractual obligation has become incapable of being performed because the circumstances in which performance is called for would render it a thing radically different from that which was undertaken by the contract . . . .. But, even so, it is not hardship or inconvenience or material loss itself which calls the principle of frustration into play. There must be as well such a change in the significance of the obligation that the thing undertaken would, if performed, be a different thing from that contracted for.

Lord Radcliffe was anxious to make the point that, although in many cases it made no difference whether the legal basis was said to be an implied term or the application of an objective rule of contract law independent of the parties' intention, in some circumstances it might. If in implying a term the parties' intention were the guiding factor, in many circumstances the court would be unable to agree to the discharge of further performance since cases of this kind arise precisely when the parties have no intention because they have not addressed their minds to the issue. In Lord Radcliffe's view there was good authority that actual intention was not relevant (cf. *Hirji Mulji* v *Cheong Yue SS Co.* [1926] AC 497). Today, Lord Radcliffe's concern is less important, because the law of implied terms has also been modernised, so that the courts now recognise a power to imply in law terms which are reasonable in contracts of a particular type (*10.4.3.1*). Such terms are no more than obligations imposed on the parties independently of intention, and there may be little difference between Lord Radcliffe's proposed basis for the frustration doctrine and a basis of a term implied in law. In either case the difficulty of the absence of actual intention on the part of the parties is overcome.

11.4.2 Examples of frustrating events

It is usually said that the question of whether an event frustrates the contract is a question of law. That may be a confusing statement. In the first place, it draws attention away from what is really inevitable, that in every case it is largely dependent upon the relevant facts whether or not a contract is frustrated. The question of law is whether the relevant facts make the performance demanded 'radically different' from that which was undertaken (*Davis Contractors* v *Fareham UDC* [1956] AC 696; see *11.4.1.2*). It may also be confusing in that, since such cases are not heard by a jury but by a judge sitting alone, it might be thought that the distinction between law and fact is of little consequence. It is relevant, however, to whether an appellate court will be willing to overturn the finding of a first instance judge, or of an arbitrator. Nevertheless, it is crucial to realise that most frustration cases involve sometimes complex issues of fact which relate to the central question of whether the contractual performance required has been so changed by circumstances beyond the control of the parties that one party should be excused from that performance. It is, therefore, almost impossible to provide a comprehensive list of the circumstances in which a contract will be found to be frustrated. All that may be attempted is to outline some common categories of frustrating event.

11.4.2.1 Impossibility

Subject to any express allocation of the risk (*11.4.3*), the most straightforward examples of frustrating events are those where performance of the contractual undertaking has become impossible. In some cases the impossibility is due to physical causes, as in the leading case of *Taylor* v *Caldwell* (1863) 3 B & S 826, where the destruction of the concert hall made performance impossible (*11.4.1.1*). Similar to the physical destruction of something which is essential to performance of the contract is the death or illness of one of the parties in a personal contract. Some contracts, such as contracts for the sale of goods, do not require that the performance be made by any particular person, so that death or illness does not prevent actual performance. But certain contracts, especially those for the performance of some skilled service, demand performance by a stipulated person, who is usually one of the parties to the contract. In such a case it is clear that death of that party makes performance of the contract impossible (*Stubbs v Holywell Ry Co.* (1867) LR 2 Ex 311). It may also be the case that a temporary illness will frustrate the contract if the contract calls for performance on a particular day on which day the other party is unable to perform. In *Robinson v Davison* (1871) LR 6 Ex 269

> the defendant's wife had been engaged to play the piano at a concert but was unable to play on the particular day through illness. The defendant was able to plead his wife's illness as a defence to an action for breach of contract.

A prolonged illness would frustrate a normal contract of employment (*Notcutt v Universal Equipment Co. (London) Ltd* [1986] 3 All ER 582).

In some cases performance remains physically possible but the contract is still frustrated, in that since the time of contracting there has been a change in the law which makes further performance of the contract illegal. The most obvious instance of such illegality is where there has been subsequent legislation (*Denny, Mott & Dickson v James B Fraser & Co. Ltd* [1944] AC 265). Where the illegality exists before the time of contracting there is no scope for the operation of the doctrine of frustration, and the case falls to be determined according to the rules relating to illegal contracts (*8.7*). Nevertheless, in the case of the outbreak of war a potential existing illegality intervenes to frustrate certain contracts. It is against the law to trade with the enemy (Trading with the Enemy Act 1939). If at the time of contracting the other party is not 'the enemy' such a contract is not, of course, illegal; but it may become so by subsequent declaration of war. If war is declared before the time for performance the contract will be frustrated (*Fibrosa Spolka Akcyjna v Fairbairn Lawson Combe Barbour Ltd* [1943] AC 32).

Greater problems are caused when the impossibility is only temporary. For example, although it is clear that incapacitating illness on the single day for performance of the contract amounts to frustration (see *Robinson v Davison*, above), it is less easy to state with certainty the effect of prolonged illness on a contract of employment which may call for performance over a period of months or years. It is clear that such illness will excuse the employee's performance for the period of the illness, and it may give the employer the possibility of terminating the employment contract upon notice. Whether it will immediately frustrate the contract, however, will depend upon the particular circumstances. Unless the nature of the incapacity, or the anticipated duration of the illness in relation to the contractual period of employment, suggest that any performance which may subsequently be rendered will be radically different from that which was undertaken, the contract will not be frustrated (*Marshall v Harland & Wolff Ltd* [1972] 2 All ER 715). Similar considerations arise where performance of a contract is prevented by a strike, whether it be by the workforce of one or other of the parties or by that of a third party. For example, in *Pioneer Shipping Ltd v BTP Tioxide Ltd* [1982] AC 724

> a charterparty for six or seven voyages to be made during a nine-month period was reduced to half that number of voyages by a strike at the port where the ship

was to be loaded. The contract was held to be frustrated because the performance actually possible bore no relation to the performance contracted for.

11.4.2.2 Unavailability In some circumstances contractual performance is prevented because something essential to performance is unavailable. Performance is not strictly impossible, because the thing still exists, but for reasons beyond the control of the parties it may not be put to the use which they had intended. Common examples of frustration of this kind arise in shipping contracts. Thus, where a ship has been requisitioned for the remaining period of its charter so that it will be unavailable to the charterer, the contract is frustrated (*Bank Line Ltd* v *Arthur Capel & Co.* [1919] AC 435).

Here again, however, the more difficult problems in determining the existence of frustration arise in cases where the unavailability is only temporary. In *Jackson* v *Union Marine Insurance Co. Ltd* (1874) LR 10 CP 125

> a ship was chartered to proceed with all possible dispatch from Liverpool to Newport, and there to load a cargo to be shipped to San Francisco. The ship ran aground one day out of Liverpool, and was not ready to load until eight months later. The contract had imposed no particular time-limit for performance.

The court found that there was an implied term that the ship should arrive in Newport in time for completion of the contract within a reasonable time, so that the contract was frustrated by such a long delay. However, where the charter of the ship is expressed to run for a given length of time temporary unavailability will only frustrate the contract if it takes up a disproportionate amount of the whole contract period. It must be remembered that the court is supposed to decide the issue of frustration without taking account of developments after the frustrating event. No doubt in many cases the courts allow themselves a little surreptitious hindsight, but they must sometimes decide before the period of the contract has come to an end. For example, in *F.A. Tamplin SS Co. Ltd* v *Anglo-Mexican Petroleum Products Co. Ltd* [1916] 2 AC 397

> the court had to determine whether the requisition of a ship in February 1915, which was under charter until December 1917, frustrated the contract.

The court said that it did not, no doubt in the belief that the war which had occasioned the requisition would be over in time to allow a substantial period of the charter to be used as intended. With hindsight it is easy to see that the court was unduly optimistic!

A rather different problem of unavailability occurs where in, for example, a contract of sale the seller's anticipated source of supply fails. Where that source of supply is in no way a condition of the contract, but merely represents the seller's planned means of meeting his obligations, the contract will not be frustrated by failure of that source (*Blackburn Bobbin Co. Ltd* v *T.W. Allen & Sons Ltd* [1918] 2 KB 467). The reason is that unless otherwise agreed the risk of failure of a source of supply lies with the seller, who is expected to arrange alternative supplies if his planned supply is unavailable. There is no reason why the buyer should know of or be affected by the seller's planned mode of performance. Where the seller is concerned about sources of supply, and wishes to commit himself only in so far as he believes he has available sources, he may make the source of supply a condition of the contract. For example, in *Howell* v *Coupland* (1876) 1 QBD 258

> the seller specified that the crop to be sold was to be grown on specified land. The crop on that particular land failed, and the contract was frustrated.

It would, indeed, have been breach of contract to supply from any other source, although the buyer might have agreed to a contract variation if the seller had proposed it. The matter is, however, more complicated, where the contract envisages two possible sources of supply, of which one is destroyed, but only after contract performance has been allocated to it, and the other source will be exhausted by other contracts. In such circumstances, in the absence of a *force majeure* clause, it may be that the party's choice of which contract to allocate to the source which was destroyed will operate to prevent the contract from being frustrated (*J. Lauritzen AS* v *Wijsmuller BV* [1990] 1 Lloyd's Rep 1; *11.4.4*).

11.4.2.3 Impracticability Impracticability is the term used to describe circumstances in which contractual performance would impose a burden on one party quite different from that contemplated at the time of contracting, without rendering performance actually impossible. In the United States the Uniform Commercial Code has adopted a standard of impracticability rather than impossibility for all cases (UCC Section 2-615), with the express intention of replacing the absolute test of impossibility with a test of what is 'commercially impossible'. In other words, where performance under the contract is theoretically possible but commercially out of the question the contract would be frustrated. English law has largely been unwilling to accept that impracticability frustrates the contract, although there are indications that some extreme forms of impracticability might. The cases on unavailability are an example of this ambivalence. In *Jackson* v *Union Marine Insurance Co. Ltd* (1874) LR 10 CP 125 (above, *11.4.2.2*) the contract could ultimately have been performed, but the contract was nevertheless held to be frustrated. In *Blackburn Bobbin Co. Ltd* v *T.W. Allen & Sons Ltd* [1918] 2 KB 467, however, the court was unwilling to find the contract frustrated despite the fact that not only had the seller's anticipated supply failed, but it was effectively impossible to get supplies of the kind of timber required.

The leading authority on impracticability in English law is *Davis Contractors Ltd* v *Fareham UDC* [1956] AC 696.

> The appellants agreed to build 78 houses for the council over a period of eight months for a fixed price. A shortage of skilled labour caused the work to take a further 14 months. The appellants argued that the contract had been frustrated by

the delay, and that they were therefore entitled to payment on the basis of *quantum meruit* (*12.4.3*), rather than the agreed price.

The House of Lords found that the contract was not frustrated. As has already been noted (*11.4.1.2*), Lord Radcliffe said: '[I]t is not hardship, or inconvenience, or material loss itself which calls the principle of frustration into play.' It is now accepted that the fact that performance of the contract will cost more than was originally anticipated is not, of itself, enough to frustrate the contract. This principle was demonstrated by cases arising out of the closure of the Suez Canal, after the Anglo-French invasion in 1956. In *The Eugenia* [1964] 1 All ER 161 (see also *Tsakiroglou & Co. Ltd v Noblee Thorl GmbH* [1962] AC 93)

> a charterparty provided for a voyage from Genoa via the Black Sea to India. The contract did not expressly provide, but both parties assumed, that the voyage would be made through the Suez Canal. The charterers claimed that the contract was frustrated by the closure of the canal.

The Court of Appeal said that the contract was not frustrated. Its reasoning, however, suggests that some degrees of impracticability falling short of impossibility would frustrate the contract. Although the ship was actually trapped in the canal, the case was argued on the basis that it would have been possible not to enter the canal and to complete the voyage by going the long way round via the Cape of Good Hope. The court might simply have said that since performance was not impossible the contract must stand. Instead Lord Denning MR compared the total length in days of the voyage via Suez (108 days) with the length via the Cape (138 days), and found that the latter was not entirely disproportionate to the former. Lord Denning said that the fact that performance was more onerous or more expensive was not enough to frustrate the contract, but that it would be frustrated where it would be 'positively unjust to hold the parties bound'. From this reasoning it may be implied that Lord Denning did not believe impossibility to be the only test of frustration.

A party who is concerned that the cost of performance may in some circumstances prove greater than anticipated may protect himself by making express provision in the contract that performance in a particular way is a condition of the contract. Thus, in a case like *The Eugenia*, if the contract had stipulated that performance was to be via the Suez Canal, closure of the canal would have made performance impossible, rather than impracticable, and the contract would have been frustrated.

The issue of whether a contract is frustrated by impracticability is of particular importance during a period of severe inflation, such as was experienced by most western economies during the mid-1970s after the oil crisis. It is possible to view the increased cost of performance resulting from inflation as making the contractual performance something radically different from that which was originally undertaken. The law appears to exclude frustration in most cases while admitting the possibility that a small number of cases might be so severely affected as to qualify. In *British Movietonews Ltd* v *London & District Cinemas Ltd* [1952] AC 166 Viscount Simon said:

> The parties to an executory contract are often faced, in the course of carrying it out, with a turn of events which they did not at all anticipate — a wholly abnormal rise or fall in prices, a sudden depreciation of currency, an unexpected obstacle to execution, or the like. Yet this does not in itself affect the bargain they have made. If, on the other hand, a consideration of the terms of the contract, in the light of the circumstances existing when the contract was made, shows that they never agreed to be bound in a fundamentally different situation which has now unexpectedly emerged, the contract ceases to bind at that point . . ..

One problem of finding a contract to be frustrated by inflation is that the remedy of discharging the parties from further performance may be as harsh on the other party as the extra cost of performance was on the party alleging that the contract has been frustrated. A more sensible remedy might be to preserve the contract at a reasonable price in the new circumstances (cf. Downes, (1985) 101 LQR 98), but English law enjoys no such power. It is noticeable, however, that in one of the few cases in which the courts have found a contract to be terminated in circumstances of severe inflation the statutory background to the litigation enabled the court to insist upon the renegotiation of a reasonable price (*Staffordshire Area Health Authority* v *South Staffordshire Waterworks Co.* [1978] 3 All ER 769). The contract in question had run without any change in the price since 1927, so that the price payable was far below the cost of performance or the going rate for such a service. The Court of Appeal was unanimous in finding that the contract had come to an end. The majority took the view that a power to terminate upon reasonable notice should be implied into the contract, which on its face was valid in perpetuity. Lord Denning MR, however, said that the contract should cease to bind because the present circumstances were 'outside the realm' of the speculations of the parties at the time of contracting. He appeared to believe that the case fell within the exceptional category of cases referred to by Viscount Simon in *British Movietonews Ltd* v *London & District Cinemas Ltd*. Lord Denning's reasoning was followed by a majority of the Court of Appeal in *Pole Properties Ltd* v *Feinberg* (1982) 43 P & CR 121.

11.4.2.4 Frustration of the common venture In some circumstances performance of the contract may still be possible, but it has lost all its purpose for one of the parties. Such contracts may be held to be frustrated. The classic examples of this problem are the 'coronation' cases, in which a series of contracts became devoid of purpose when the celebrations connected with the coronation of King Edward VII were cancelled because of the King's illness. In *Krell* v *Henry* [1903] 2 KB 740 the plaintiff sued the defendant for the balance due on a contract for the hire of rooms from which to view the coronation processions, which had been cancelled.

The Court of Appeal found that the contract was frustrated, although Vaughan

Williams LJ laid considerable emphasis upon the fact that it was known to both parties that the subject of the contract was not merely the hire of a room, but was the provision of a view of the coronation procession. In *Herne Bay Steam Boat Co.* v *Hutton* [1903] 2 KB 683, however, the Court of Appeal reached a different conclusion.

> The contract was for the hire of a boat to observe the King's review of the Navy and for a day's cruise round the fleet.

The distinction between the cases appears to be that in the latter case the particular purpose was not the subject of the contract; that is, the contract was not intended by the parties to stand or fall upon whether the naval review took place. The distinction is also sometimes explained in terms of the fact that part of the purpose in the latter case (the cruise round the fleet) was not frustrated (per Stirling LJ). The approach of the Court of Appeal in the *Herne Bay* case appears to be consistent with the approach of the courts to impracticability (above, *11.4.2.3*), and so *Krell* v *Henry* appears to be something of an exceptional case. A modern example of this problem can be found in *Amalgamated Investment & Property Co. Ltd* v *John Walker & Sons Ltd* [1976] 3 All ER 509.

> A contract for the purchase of property in order to develop it was not frustrated despite the fact that development was more or less impossible because the property had become subject to a form of preservation order.

11.4.2.5 Contracts concerning land It has been a matter of doubt over many years whether the doctrine of frustration applies to contracts relating to interests in land. These doubts were expressed by the House of Lords in the case of a lease of which the purpose would clearly be frustrated for a period, but in all probability not for very long by comparison with the full 99 years of the lease (*Cricklewood Property and Investment Trust Ltd* v *Leighton's Investment Trust Ltd* [1945] AC 221). The particular lease was found not to have been frustrated, but the House of Lords was divided in its reasoning. For two of their Lordships the doctrine was potentially applicable but would rarely apply, since in most cases the frustration of purpose would be of short duration relative to the period of the lease. But for two of their Lordships the doctrine could never apply, since the 'purpose' of a lease was no part of the contract, of which the object was merely to convey an estate in land from one party to another. That object would always be capable of achievement.

The matter was recently reconsidered by the House of Lords in *National Carriers Ltd* v *Panalpina (Northern) Ltd* [1981] AC 675.

> A 10-year lease of a warehouse was deprived of its purpose for a period of 20 months by the closure of the only street allowing access by lorries. It was claimed that the lease had been frustrated.

The House of Lords rejected that claim on the ground that after the disruption there would still be some three years of the lease to run. A majority of their

Lordships, however, accepted that in 'rare' circumstances a lease might be frustrated. Such occasions would be very infrequent for two reasons. In the first place, since many leases run for terms of several years it is unlikely that a potentially frustrating event would take a sufficiently significant 'bite' out of the full term for actual frustration to occur. Further, the kind of major disaster which might frustrate even a long-term lease is usually provided for by express term of the contract (see *11.4.3*).

It appears to be implicit in the reasoning in *Amalgamated Investment & Property Co. Ltd* v *John Walker & Sons Ltd* [1976] 3 All ER 509 (above, *11.4.2.4*) that the doctrine of frustration may apply to contracts for the sale of land. Nevertheless, it seems that instances will again be rare, both because of the limited view of frustration of purpose taken in that case, and because conveyancers take great care to avoid such problems by express provision and by keeping to a minimum the period between making the contract and performance, which is constituted by conveying the legal estate.

11.4.3   Foreseeability and risk allocation

When circumstances intervene to frustrate a contract it may be said that a potential risk of the contract has materialised. Thus, when one enters into a contract to hire a concert hall in several months' time there is a risk that the concert hall will be destroyed in the meantime. The court must then decide whether that risk was to be borne by one or other of the parties (see also *11.4.5*). Thus, the mere fact that performance turns out to be impossible will not result in the contract being frustrated where one party took upon himself an obligation to perform in all the circumstances (see *Eurico SpA* v *Philipp Brothers* [1987] 2 Lloyd's Rep 215). In the absence of very clear express provision, the courts may be faced with difficult questions of construction of the contract to determine what was undertaken.Where one party is anxious not to have to bear a particular risk he may insert an express term in the contract, assuming the other party agrees, allocating the risk to the other party. For example, where a manufacturer is anxious not to bear the risk of increased costs of performance in a long-term supply contract he may provide that the price to be paid is to vary in proportion to some suitable index, such as an index of raw material costs. Equally, the contract may require one party to obtain an import or export licence. If the licence is refused by the authorities, it is then a question of construction whether the contract was frustrated or whether the party who failed to obtain it is liable for breach (see *Pagnan SpA* v *Tradax Ocean Transportation SA* [1987] 3 All ER 565). Where the contract contains an express provision for the particular event which is alleged to have frustrated the contract the courts will not intervene. The only limit on this rule is that as a matter of construction of the express terms of the contract a court may hold that the provision in question was not intended to apply to a supervening event of the gravity which actually occurred (cf. *Metropolitan Water Board* v *Dick Kerr & Co. Ltd* [1918] AC 119).

11.4.3.1   Unforeseen and unprovided for events

It follows from the above that frustration applies only to contracts affected by events which have not been foreseen, in the sense that they have not been expressly provided for in the contract. In the law generally, however, the notion of foreseeability embraces not only things which have been provided for, but also those which a reasonable person would have foreseen even if the particular parties did not foresee them (cf. the test for remoteness of damage: *12.3.3.3*). This idea has been extended in some cases to the doctrine of frustration, so that it is said that not only does frustration not apply to contracts in which the parties have made express provision, but it also does not apply to contracts in which the parties *could have made* express provision, in the sense that the risk was foreseeable. In *Davis Contractors Ltd v Fareham UDC* [1956] AC 696 Lord Radcliffe treated the foreseeability of the risk as one of the main reasons for finding the contract not to have been frustrated. In such circumstances it is presumed that failure to allocate the foreseeable risk is evidence of an intention that the risk be allocated to lie where it falls 'naturally'. Thus, in the case of a manufacturer's long-term contract to supply goods, in the absence of indexation of the price the risk of increased cost of performance falls naturally on the manufacturer, since the contract is for a fixed price.

Nevertheless, it must be doubted whether the fact that the risk is foreseeable will in every case exclude the operation of the doctrine of frustration. In the first place, many risks are 'foreseeable' without the probability of their occurrence being so great that the parties ought to provide for them (see *11.4.3.2*). It is possible that at any time a piece of space junk will drop out of the sky and land on one's head, but one does not plan one's contracts around that remote eventuality. Moreover, in some cases it has been held that the fact that the parties actually foresaw a particular risk but made no express provision for it did not prevent the frustration doctrine intervening to prevent the risk lying where it fell naturally. In *The Eugenia* [1964] 1 All ER 161 (the facts are given at *11.4.2.3*) Lord Denning MR said:

> It has frequently been said that the doctrine of frustration only applies when the new situation is 'unforeseen' or 'unexpected' or 'uncontemplated', as if that were an essential feature. But it is not so. It is not so much that it is 'unexpected', but rather that the parties have made no provision for it in their contract. The point about it, however, is this: If the parties did not foresee anything of the kind happening, you can readily infer that they have made no provision for it. Whereas, if they did foresee it, you would expect them to make provision for it. But cases have occurred where the parties have foreseen the danger ahead, and yet made no provision for it in the contract . . . see *W.J. Tatem Ltd v Gamboa* [1939] 1 KB 132.

In this case, the parties knew of the danger that the Suez Canal might be closed but, unable to agree on what provision should be put in the contract, had agreed to 'leave the problem to the lawyers' should it materialise. If an actually foreseen but unprovided for risk may constitute a frustrating event, the same must be true of a risk which was foreseeable but not actually foreseen.

11.4.3.2 Foreseeability as an aid to construction It seems unlikely, in the light of *The Eugenia*, that there is a rule of law that frustration cannot apply where the risk was foreseeable. The same would appear to be true even where the more qualified test of 'reasonably foreseeable' risk is used. In any case, that test is too vague to provide proper guidance. Nevertheless, there is no denying the relevance of foreseeability to the question of allocation of risk. The courts are entitled to assess the degree of foreseeability of a risk in determining whether the parties intended the risk to lie where it falls naturally. The greater the probability of the risk materialising, the more likely it is that the parties did intend the inherent risk allocation of their contract. On the other hand, where the degree of probability is close to zero, the difficulty of determining the nature of the risk and of agreeing on its allocation may outweigh the likelihood of the risk maturing. As in *The Eugenia*, the parties may prefer to leave the matter to be sorted out later. In those circumstances a presumption of allocation of the risk based on foreseeability would defeat the intentions of the parties, and it would be preferable to find the contract frustrated.

11.4.4 Fault
The doctrine of frustration only applies where the supervening event is beyond the control of the parties. It goes without saying that where performance has become impossible because of one party's breach that party cannot claim that the contract is frustrated, and the other party will almost certainly be entitled to treat the contract as repudiated (*10.5*) and to claim damages for any loss caused (*12.3.1*). The law goes further, however, and says that even in the absence of breach of contract a party may not rely on the frustration of the contract when the supervening event results from some positive action of that party.

The leading authority is *Maritime National Fish Ltd v Ocean Trawlers Ltd* [1935] AC 524, a decision of the Privy Council on appeal from Canada.

> Fishing boats using 'otter trawls' required a licence from the Minister of Fisheries. The appellants wished to operate five such boats, one of which was chartered from the respondents. They duly applied for five licences, but were only granted three. They were invited by the Minister to nominate the boats to which the licences would apply, and did not nominate the boat chartered from the respondents. They then claimed that the charter of that boat was frustrated.

Their claim was rejected. If they had wanted they could have had one of their three licences apply to the boat in question, so that it was their choice rather than the action of the Minister which deprived the charter of the boat of its purpose. The supervening event was not beyond their control, and so did not frustrate the contract. It might be assumed that if the appellants had chartered all their boats, so that two charters would have been without purpose whichever boats were nominated, then the court might have been more willing to find that the two had been frustrated. However, in *J. Lauritzen AS v Wijsmuller BV* [1990] 1 Lloyd's Rep 1 the Court of Appeal took a very strict line, and indicated that any act of choice by one of the parties would prevent the supervening event from being beyond that party's control, and so prevent the contract being frustrated. Once the impossibility of performance was attributable to the decision of one of the parties, whether or not amounting to breach of contract or negligence, it would be self-induced, and so not frustration.

It follows from that analysis that a negligent act which results in impossibility of performance may not frustrate the contract. In *Taylor* v *Caldwell* (1863) 3 B & S 826 Blackburn J clearly believed that if the destruction of the concert hall had been caused by the negligence of the owners then they could not have been excused. In many cases, however, the issue may be decided simply on the basis of the burden of proof, since a party alleging that a contract is not frustrated because the impossibility is caused by the default of the other party must prove that default (*Joseph Constantine SS Line Ltd* v *Imperial Smelting Corp. Ltd* [1942] AC 154). In this case

> the appellants chartered a ship to the respondents, with the intention that the ship should proceed to Australia to load. Before the ship could sail its boiler exploded, causing such a delay that there could be no doubt that the contract was discharged. The reason for the explosion was never discovered, although the respondents suspected that the appellants had been negligent and sought to argue that the frustration doctrine should not apply unless the appellants could prove that they had not been negligent.

The House of Lords rejected this argument. On the contrary, the burden of proving a negligent breach of the contract lay on the respondents, and in the absence of proof the contract was discharged by frustration. Although the House of Lords did not commit itself to any firm view on whether a negligent act could frustrate a contract, Viscount Simon suggested that some minor forms of negligence might certainly be overlooked, but his statements were *obiter* and must be read in the light of the judgments of the Court of Appeal in *J. Lauritzen AS* v *Wijsmuller BV* [1990] 1 Lloyd's Rep 1.

In *J. Lauritzen AS* v *Wijsmuller BV*

> the defendants agreed to transport the plaintiffs' oil rig on one of two named barges. By an internal management decision, not communicated to the plaintiffs, the defendants allocated the task to the *Super Servant Two*, and allocated other tasks to the sister vessel. The *Super Servant Two* then sank, and the defendants claimed that the contract was frustrated, while the plaintiffs claimed that the contract was still physically capable of being performed but for the defendants' choice of vessel.

As noted above, the Court of Appeal found that the loss of the vessel was within the control of the defendants, even if it was neither breach nor negligence. It was also suggested that the fact of the defendants' choice would prevent the contract being frustrated. The court does not appear to have considered whether that would be the case where the choice between the modes of performance lay entirely with the defendants, and the choice was made and communicated to the plaintiffs before the time of the allegedly frustrating event.

In the event, the court also ruled that an express *force majeure* clause would avail the defendants, provided the barge was not lost through their negligence.

11.4.5 Legal effect of frustration

The legal effect of frustration is to bring the contract to an end automatically, irrespective of the wishes of the parties (*Hirji Mulji* v *Cheong Yue SS Co.* [1926] AC 497). In this respect discharge by frustration is significantly different from discharge by breach, where the party adversely affected may elect whether or not to treat the contract as repudiated (*10.3.2.3*). In the *Hirji Mulji* case

> a ship the subject of a charterparty was requisitioned, but the owners asked the charterers if they were willing to wait a little longer, because they believed the ship would soon be released. The charterers agreed, but when release eventually came, later than anticipated, they refused to take the vessel. The owners argued that the charterers had elected to affirm the contract, despite the potentially frustrating event.

The House of Lords held that there was no scope for such an election. If the event were sufficiently serious to frustrate the contract the effect was automatic discharge of all further obligations.

11.4.5.1 Financial implications of the common law rule   The original common law rule was that frustration caused all primary obligations (to perform), and secondary obligations (to pay damages) which had not accrued, to terminate as from the time of the frustrating event, while obligations which had matured before the time of the frustrating event remained to be performed. Under this rule the distribution of loss resulting from frustration might appear quite arbitrary.

Where the contract called for full performance on one side before payment by the other, the result of frustration was to leave the party who had partially performed before the time of the frustrating event without any payment for the work done. In *Appleby* v *Myers* (1867) LR 2 CP 651

> the plaintiffs had contracted to install and maintain all machinery in the defendant's factory, payment to be made upon completion. Before the task of installation had been completed the factory and machinery were destroyed by fire. The contract was frustrated.

Because the payment obligation was not due to be performed by the time of the frustrating event the plaintiffs were not entitled to any payment for the work done. In this case the defendants received no lasting benefit from the plaintiffs' performance, since the machinery was destroyed, but the same would apply where a lasting benefit was conferred. In *Cutter* v *Powell* (1795) 6 Term Rep 320 (see *10.5.2.2*) the contract was frustrated by the seaman's death before completion of the voyage. His services before death were a benefit to his employer, but his estate was still unable to recover any payment since the contract provided for payment only on completion.

Where the contract provided for a payment (not necessarily full payment) in advance of performance, the original rule was that money paid could not be recovered in the event of frustration, and if not actually paid would remain payable despite the frustration (*Chandler* v *Webster* [1904] 1 KB 493). This case was overruled by the House of Lords in *Fibrosa Spolka Akcyjna* v *Fairbairn Lawson Combe Barber Ltd* [1943] AC 32.

> The appellants ordered machinery from the respondents to be delivered to the appellants' factory in Poland. The appellants paid £1,000 in advance under the contract. The contract was frustrated by the German invasion of Poland, and the appellants sought the return of the £1,000. The respondents resisted their request because they had already expended large sums in partial performance of the contract.

The appellants were successful in recovering their prepayment. There had been a total failure of consideration in the sense that the appellants had received none of the performance they had contracted for, and on that basis they were entitled to a restitutionary remedy to recover the money paid. The problem with this analysis was that in remedying the hardship which had previously fallen on the party making the prepayment, the House of Lords imposed as great a hardship on the party to whom payment had been made. It was very likely that the contract had provided for prepayment as a form of insurance against precisely the kind of risk which materialised. The court had interfered in the allocation of risk agreed between the parties, depriving the manufacturers of that insurance.

The common law rule on the effect of frustration was regarded as unsatisfactory, and so changes were made by the Law Reform (Frustrated Contracts) Act 1943 (LR(FC)A 1943). Nevertheless, it is still important to understand the common law background, and to remember that the Act has no impact on the issue of whether a contract has been frustrated.

11.4.5.2 Money paid or payable in advance Where the contract provides that all or part of the price shall be payable in advance, then by s.1(2) LR(FC)A 1943 money actually paid is recoverable, and money payable but not paid by the time of the frustrating event need not be paid. It is not necessary to demonstrate a total failure of consideration for this rule to operate. Section 1(2) is, however, subject to an important proviso intended to meet the objection to the *Fibrosa* case noted above. Where the person entitled to prepayment under the contract has incurred expenses directly related to the performance of the contract before the frustrating event occurs, he is entitled to retain or recover payment of such sum as the court believes is just in the circumstances. The court's discretion is limited in two ways. The sum may not exceed the total amount payable in advance under the contract. If the parties are to be assumed to have agreed to prepayment as insurance for the party who has the substantial performance obligation, their estimate of the necessary insurance cover should be adhered to. Further, the sum may not exceed the value of the actual expenses incurred. The need for such provision is unclear, since it seems unlikely that a court should find it just to allow retention or recovery of a sum greater than the actual expenses incurred. The limitation appears to be intended to prevent the prepayment being regarded as automatically forfeit upon frustration, and may also be intended to prevent recovery of any allowance for profit as opposed to actual cost of performance, although in practice the distinction may be hard to draw (cf. s.1(4) LR(FC)A 1943).

One factor likely to affect the court's assessment of what is just in the circumstances is whether the expenses incurred may be recovered in some other way. For example, in the *Fibrosa* case, it may be that the machinery was not so peculiar to the appellants' needs that it could not be sold to an alternative buyer. Such a sale would 'mitigate' the loss caused by frustration (cf. *12.3.3.4*), and so the expenses would not be allowed to be retained or recovered out of the prepayment. It has been suggested that it might in many circumstances be 'just' to divide the loss between the parties, allowing retention or recovery of half of the expenses incurred. Where the prepayment is a genuine form of insurance for one of the parties, freely negotiated between the parties, such an approach would seem to be undue interference in the parties' contract.

11.4.5.3 Performance conferring a valuable benefit Where no prepayment is provided for under the contract there is no entitlement to compensation for expenses incurred in performance of a contract which has been frustrated. However, by s.1(3) LR(FC)A 1943 if performance confers a valuable benefit on the other party before the frustrating event occurs the court may award the performing party such sum as it considers just in the circumstances. The sum may not exceed the value of the benefit conferred. In assessing what would be just the court must consider expenses incurred by the party receiving the benefit (including any prepayment covered by s.1(2)), and must also consider the effect of the frustrating event on the benefit received.

The operation of s.1(3) was considered in *BP Exploration Co. (Libya) Ltd v Hunt (No.2)* [1979] 1 WLR 783. The important judgment is that of Robert Goff J at first instance, which was subsequently affirmed by the House of Lords ([1983] 2 AC 352).

> The case arose out of a contract between the concessionaire of a potential oil field in Libya and the oil company who were to do the prospecting and development of the field. Four years after oil production began the contract was frustrated by the Libyan government's nationalisation of the plaintiff oil company's interest in the oil field. The oil company sought a just sum from the defendant concessionaire for benefits allegedly conferred by its performance under the contract before the time of nationalisation.

Robert Goff J said:

> First, it has to be shown that the defendant has, by reason of something done by the plaintiff in, or for the purpose of, the performance of the contract, obtained a valuable benefit (other than a payment of money [to which s.1(2) applies]) before the time of discharge. That benefit has to be identified, and valued, and such value forms the upper limit of the award. Secondly, the court may award to the plaintiff such sum, not greater than the value

of such benefit, as it considers just having regard to all the circumstances of the case . . . .

A key matter not entirely clear under s.1(3) is whether the destruction of the benefit by the frustrating event, as in *Appleby* v *Myers* (1867) LR 2 CP 651 (above, *11.4.5.1*), is relevant to the valuation of the benefit or to the assessment of the just sum. Robert Goff J said that the true construction of the Act was that destruction of the benefit was relevant to its valuation, although he appeared to be out of sympathy with this rule. In a case like *Appleby* v *Myers*, therefore, under the Act no just sum could be awarded, since the effect of the frustrating event was to reduce the value of the benefit, which is the 'upper limit of the award', to nil. It can be argued, however, that such is not the true construction of the Act, since s.1(3) speaks of a valuable benefit obtained 'before the time of discharge', which suggests that the valuation is to be made on the basis of circumstances existing immediately prior to the frustrating event. Moreover, s.1(3)(b) provides that the effect of the frustrating event on the benefit is to be considered in assessing what 'the court considers just'. As Treitel points out (*Law of Contract*, 6th edn, Stevens, 1983, at p.690), this alternative reading of the section leaves a wider discretion to the court without eliminating the possibility of following the narrower construction in appropriate circumstances. The court might award no sum at all if in its view that was what was just; but in other circumstances it would be able to award a just sum if justified. By linking destruction of the benefit to the setting of the upper limit to any award, rather than to the discretion to fix the sum payable, Robert Goff J perhaps unduly restricted that discretion.

11.4.5.4 Excepted contracts   The Law Reform (Frustrated Contracts) Act 1943 does not apply to all contracts. It does not apply where the parties have made express provision for the consequences of frustration (s.2(3)). Nor does it apply to wholly performed contractual obligations which may be severed from those which are affected by the frustrating event (s.2(4)). Certain types of contract for the carriage of goods by sea (s.2(5)(a)), and contracts of insurance (s.2(5)(b)), are excepted from the scope of the Act, since such contracts are themselves largely concerned with the allocation of risk, and it was not intended that the courts should interfere with such allocations. Finally, contracts for the sale of specific goods which are frustrated by the goods perishing are outside the terms of the Act (s.2(5)(c)). The confusing wording of this final exception appears to reflect excessive caution on the part of the draftsman (see P. S. Atiyah, *Sale of Goods*, 8th edn, Pitman, 1990, at pp. 333–337).

TWELVE
Enforcement of contractual obligations

12.1 THE NOTION OF ENFORCEMENT

The definition of contracts as 'legally enforceable agreements' (*4.1*) assumes that there exist mechanisms for the enforcement of those agreements which are identified by the law as creating legal obligations of performance. The mechanisms of enforcement of contractual obligations are the subject of this chapter. In fact, very few contractual obligations are 'enforced', in the sense of compelling actual performance (*12.1.2*), or in the sense of deterring non-performance by the threat and imposition of penalties (*12.1.1*). Although compulsion and penalty probably represent the popular notion of enforcement, the basic legal means of enforcement of contractual obligations is by compensation for loss caused (*12.1.3*). It is enforcement in the sense that the party who should have performed but did not may be compelled to pay the extra cost of obtaining substitute performance.

12.1.1 Penalties for breach of contractual obligations

English law has always denied any role for punishment in the enforcement of contracts. Although theorists have at times attributed the binding force of contractual undertakings to the moral obligation to keep one's promises, the law does not seek to punish promise-breakers, just as it is not directly concerned to enforce morality. Punishment is regarded as an instrument of social control, so that the law punishes criminals, and may in limited circumstances award punitive (or 'exemplary') damages against those who are particularly callous or deliberate in the commission of torts (*Cassell & Co. Ltd* v *Broome* [1972] AC 1027). There is little scope for social control in English contract law, however; the focus is rather on enabling private transactions, and in the last resort on remedying grievances. For these reasons there is no penalty for breach of contract (*Perera* v *Vandiyar* [1953] 1 All ER 1109). Where breach occurs but no loss is sustained, in most circumstances only nominal damages will be awarded (*Surrey CC* v *Bredero Homes Ltd* [1992] 3 All ER 302; but see *13.3.1.1* and *13.3.1.2*). Similarly, the courts will not enforce contractual clauses purporting to impose penalties for non-performance (*12.3.4.2*).

12.1.2 Compelling actual performance

The political and economic liberalism which were the foundations upon which nineteenth century contract law was built (*4.4*) were inconsistent with the idea of compelling a person to perform his contract against his will in circumstances in which suitable equivalent alternative performance is available. In the case of contracts for goods or services in which there is an available market the non-breaching party can obtain substitute performance. The price the party in breach must pay for not being compelled to perform against his will is whatever is the extra cost of obtaining that substitute performance. For example, if A promises to cut B's hedge on Tuesday for £5, but then arranges to cut C's lawn on the same day for £10, making performance of his contract with B impossible, there is undoubtedly a breach of contract. A will not be punished, nor will he be forced to revoke the contract with C in order to perform his contract with B. B must find someone else to cut his hedge, and if the market price for the services of a hedge-cutter is higher than £5 then A must pay the difference. The contract has been enforced only in the sense that at the end of the day B will have received the promised contractual performance at the cost to him agreed in his contract with A.

This result can be justified in terms both of the relationship between the parties and of economic efficiency. B probably is not very happy to accept A's services, since he believes A to be unreliable; equally, it may be impossible to force A to perform at his best if his performance is given against his will. Substitute performance is probably more acceptable to both. Alternatively, if A is to pay B's extra costs, B will be no worse off by allowing A not to perform, while A may be better off if B's extra cost is less than the extra profit A will make on his contract with C. That is, if B's substitute performance costs £7, then A must pay B £2 for B to be no worse off. A makes an extra profit, by contracting with C for £5, so that after paying off B he will be £3 better off. For one party to be better off while no party is worse off is, in economic terms, an efficient result. This simple example assumes that B incurred no costs in finding substitute performance.

It is only where substitute performance is irrelevant or inadequate that the law will compel actual performance. Substitute performance is irrelevant where the contractual obligation which is unperformed is to pay the price (see *12.2.1*), since compulsion of payment of the price is no different from compulsion to pay damages for the cost of substitute performance. Substitute performance is inadequate where the promised contractual performance is in some way unique, or at least exceedingly rare, so that substitution is impossible. For example, a contract to sell the Mona Lisa is a contract for a unique item, and if breached the buyer could obtain no substitute. In such circumstances damages are inappropriate, and the court will compel actual performance (*12.2.2*). Substitute performance may also be inadequate where the contractual undertaking is in the form of a promise to refrain from some activity. If A pays £50 to B, his neighbour, in return for B's promise to refrain from making loud noises during the period while A is revising for an examination, then calculating A's loss should B disturb his work may be impossible. A needs to be able actually to prevent the disturbance occurring. Again, in such circumstances damages are inappropriate, and the court will compel actual performance (*12.2.3*).

12.1.3 Compensation

Except in those cases where substitute performance is irrelevant or inadequate the method of enforcement of contractual obligations is by compensation for losses caused by their breach. The plaintiff may have suffered loss in any of three broad areas of interest, and the interest to be compensated determines the measure of damages payable. The *expectation* interest refers to whatever is necessary to put the plaintiff into the position he would have been in had the contract been performed. Compensation for lost profit is compensation of an expectation interest, as is payment of damages for the cost of substitute performance. The *reliance* interest refers to whatever is necessary to put the plaintiff into the position he was in before the contract was made. Compensation for expenditure made towards performance of the contract is compensation of a reliance interest. Compensation for physical injury caused by breach of contract is also often referred to as compensation of a reliance interest, in that damages are intended to restore the victim to the uninjured state, rather than to achieve an expected gain. This reliance interest is the same as the standard measure of damages for tort. Finally, the *restitutionary* interest refers to the restoration to the plaintiff of a benefit conferred on the defendant to which the latter is not entitled. Compensation for work done in anticipation of entering a contract which in fact never materialises is compensation of a restitutionary interest, as is the return of an advance payment under a contract which is void for mistake, or discharged by frustration.

12.2 SPECIFIC RELIEF

Specific relief is the general name for those remedies for breach of contract which compel actual performance rather than merely compensating loss caused by breach. Compulsion of performance may take the form of an action for an agreed sum, or an action for specific performance, or an action for an injunction.

12.2.1 Action for an agreed sum

The most common form of action for an agreed sum is an action for the price brought to obtain payment for contractual obligations which have already been performed. It is an action for a debt, rather than an action for damages. There are many advantages of such an action, since the amount claimed is known from the beginning ('a liquidated sum'), so that many difficulties relating to actions for damages — notably, remoteness of damage (*12.3.3.3*) and mitigation (*12.3.3.4*) — are avoided. In addition, because the issues at trial are frequently uncomplicated, there is a streamlined procedure for actions for unpaid debts (*1.5.7*). In most cases the only difficulties, if there are any, are questions of fact and problems of enforcement. Questions of fact arise where the defence offered is that the obligation to pay has been discharged by a defective performance by the plaintiff (*10.3.2.3* and *10.5.1*). Enforcement problems arise where the defendant has not paid because he lacks the means to pay. Greater difficulties arise where the party in breach will not allow the other to complete performance, which has the effect of preventing the latter bringing an action for the price, and imposing a duty to mitigate the loss.

12.2.1.1 Breach by anticipatory repudiation

In *White & Carter (Councils) Ltd* v *McGregor* [1962] AC 413 the respondents had announced before the appellants began performance that they did not wish to continue with the contract. The appellants nevertheless elected to affirm the contract (which they were held to be entitled to do: see *11.3.2.1* where the facts are given), and continued their performance, claiming thereby to be entitled to the price. In the particular case they were able to perform without the need for the other party's cooperation, so that there was nothing to prevent them performing despite the respondents' protestations that performance was pointless. Under a clause in the contract the appellants were entitled to the full price if the respondents were late on any payment instalment. The House of Lords upheld the appellants' claim despite the absence of any attempt to minimise the loss (see *12.3.3.4*). No obligation to mitigate exists in the case of an action for an agreed sum. This particular decision may have been justified on the ground either that in the particular circumstances mitigation was in any case impossible, or that the loss would have been very difficult to quantify as damages. Nevertheless, it raised the possibility that a party might be able to elect to continue performance without such good reason. If the performance remained unwanted by the other party then the cost of performance would be wasted. For this reason, the right to elect to affirm the contract is limited to those cases where the party wishing to affirm has a legitimate interest in so doing (*11.3.2.1*).

12.2.1.2 Sale of goods

A particular problem may arise in the sale of goods when legal performance, which is constituted by the passsing of property, is separated from the physical delivery of the goods, which may take place at a later date. For example, A sells his cow 'Rose' to B for £500, promising to deliver her to B's farm five days later. Since this is a contract for the sale of specific goods, property passes immediately to B (s.18, r. 1, Sale of Goods Act 1979), with the result that A has performed everything necessary to bring an action for the price (s.49(1) Sale of Goods Act 1979). If B informs A before the time for delivery that he no longer wishes to have Rose, it seems that A may still claim the price, obliging B to take on the responsibility of disposing of the cow. If B is a dealer then he may well be better able to dispose of her than A is, in which case this rule is justified. But in a similar case in which A is a dealer and B is only a consumer, it makes little sense to leave disposal of the unwanted good to the party less likely to be able to sell it without difficulty. Here again, the action for the price appears to be inconsistent with the obligation for the plaintiff to mitigate the loss which exists in the case of an action for damages.

12.2.2 Specific performance

An order of specific performance is a court order compelling actual performance of the substantive primary obligations under the contract (i.e. the obligations to perform rather than those merely to pay the price: see *12.2.1*). The court ensures compliance with its order by deterring non-compliance with threats of punitive measures against the person to whom the order is addressed. These measures include committal to prison for contempt of court, sequestration of property and fines. At common law the only remedy for breach of contract was by way of damages to compensate loss caused, and specific performance was made available by way of exception by the Chancery Court. It remains an exceptional remedy even after the amalgamation of law and equity (*1.2.1.1*), in that damages are available as of right upon breach if loss can be proved, while the availability of specific performance is subject to a number of conditions, including that damages be an inadequate remedy.

12.2.2.1 Inadequacy of damages The principle whereby damages may compensate the non-breaching party's cost of obtaining substitute performance has already been explained (*12.1.2*). In such circumstances damages may be said to be an adequate remedy, and it is for this reason that in the ordinary run of cases specific performance will not be awarded. Nevertheless, it is open to a party to demonstrate that for some reason damages would be an inadequate remedy. It is impossible to list every eventuality allowing specific performance, but the more common situations in which the remedy will be available can be identified.

The most obvious case is where substitute performance is unavailable. Thus, where goods are in some way unique no substitute for them will satisfy the buyer, and in such circumstances specific performance is the better remedy (cf. s.52 Sale of Goods Act 1979). The example of a valuable painting has already been suggested (*12.1.2*); another example of a unique good might be a family heirloom. Perhaps more significantly, it appears that the courts may be willing to accept a commercial definition of the unavailability of substitute goods. In such circumstances rarity in absolute terms may not be necessary if within the relevant time limits of the particular contract substitute performance cannot be obtained. In *Sky Petroleum Ltd* v *VIP Petroleum Ltd* [1974] 1 All ER 954

> the plaintiffs had contracted to purchase all their requirements of petrol and diesel fuel from the defendants. During a period of world-wide shortages of petroleum products the defendants purported to terminate the contract, leaving the plaintiffs with no realistic prospect of obtaining alternative supplies. The plaintiffs sought an injunction to prevent termination of the contract.

Goulding J accepted that by granting an injunction he would be specifically enforcing the contract, and that petrol and diesel fuel were not of themselves unique. Nevertheless, he granted the injunction because in the particular circumstances damages were an inadequate remedy since 'for all practical purposes' substitute performance would not be available in time to prevent the plaintiff going out of business.

Contracts for the sale of land merit separate attention. As a matter of law all land is unique, so that specific performance is available upon breach of a contract for the sale of land. This rule does not vary according to the facts of each case, so that even a modest house of a kind which may be several times duplicated in a single development is subject to the remedy. The rule extends not only to purchasers of land, but also to vendors. It is not clear that the purchaser's obligations to pay the purchase price and to take conveyance of land are in every case unique, and it seems likely that the extension of specific performance to actions brought by the vendor is based in the principle of mutuality (*12.2.2.3*).

Specific performance may also be granted when the quantification of damages is difficult for some reason, and especially where there is a risk that the plaintiff will not be properly compensated if he is restricted to the remedy of damages. In this latter sense, it may be awarded simply because the defendant is unlikely to be able to come up with the money to pay damages (*Evans Marshall & Co. Ltd v Bertola SA* [1973] 1 All ER 992). It will also be available where for technical reasons damages would only be nominal, so that the sole means of protecting the plaintiff's expectation is by compelling performance. In *Beswick v Beswick* [1968] AC 58

> a contract between uncle and nephew provided for the sale of the uncle's business to the nephew in return for payment of a pension to the uncle which was to continue after the uncle's death as payment to his widow. After the uncle's death the nephew ceased making the payments. The widow was unable to sue in her own right because of the doctrine of privity of contract (*13.3.2.1*), but she sued as administratrix of her husband's estate.

The difficulty was that the estate had suffered no loss from what was admitted to be breach of the contract, since her husband's interest, and so the estate's, ceased upon her husband's death. Nor could the estate recover damages on behalf of someone not a party to the contract (*13.3.1.1*). Nevertheless, the House of Lords was able to avoid the obvious injustice of allowing the nephew to get away with the breach by awarding specific performance of the contract.

12.2.2.2 Contracts not specifically enforceable Certain contracts which might otherwise satisfy the tests for the availability of specific performance cannot be enforced in this way because of the nature of the obligations undertaken.

It was once thought that contracts requiring considerable supervision of performance would never qualify for specific performance. For example, in *Ryan v Mutual Tontine Westminster Chambers Association* [1893] 1 Ch 116

> a lease contained a term by which the landlords undertook to provide a resident porter in constant attendance at a block of flats. The man appointed held other employment, and so was often absent from the flats.

The court refused specific performance of this term of the lease because it would require a level of supervision beyond that which the court was able to provide. This principle has been invoked in a number of different situations, including building contracts. Nevertheless, it may well be that the unavailability of specific performance on this ground can always be avoided by careful drafting. The decision in *Ryan* v *Mutual Tontine Westminster Chambers Association* was effectively distinguished in the similar case of *Posner* v *Scott-Lewis* [1986] 3 All ER 513 on the ground that in the particular circumstances what was necessary to comply with the contract could easily be defined, and did not require excessive supervision. Thus, it is not that the court lacks the power to ensure that the terms of the contract are properly being carried into effect; rather, the difficulty usually stems from the fact that the contract does not state sufficiently precisely the performance intended by the parties. Vagueness in an alleged contract does not necessarily make it unenforceable through the remedy of damages (but see *5.6.2*) but may prevent the court supervising its performance. Thus, building contracts can be specifically enforced providing 'the particulars of the work are so far definitely ascertained that the Court can sufficiently see what is the exact nature of the work . . .' (per Romer LJ in *Wolverhampton Corp.* v *Emmons* [1901] 1 KB 515).

More clearly excepted from the scope of the remedy of specific performance are contracts of personal service. The reason is usually said to be that it would be an infringement of liberty to oblige one party to work personally for the other (*De Francesco* v *Barnum* (1890) 45 ChD 430: facts given at *8.2.2.3*). This principle is so strong that the courts will not allow it to be avoided by the use of an injunction preventing the defendant from working for any other person. Such an injunction will only be granted if there is an express term of the contract preventing the party in question from taking up specified alternative employment; a blanket prohibition on alternative employment will not be enforced. For example, in *Lumley* v *Wagner* (1852) 1 De GM & G 604

> the plaintiff engaged the defendant to sing at his theatre, and the contract contained an express clause forbidding the defendant from singing anywhere else for the period of the contract. The defendant then entered another contract to sing elsewhere, and refused to perform under her contract with the plaintiff.

Specific performance was not available to the plaintiff because the contract was for personal service, but the express negative covenant could be enforced by injunction. It may also be that the courts will not enforce a term which effectively prevents the defendant from carrying out a particular type of work other than for one employer. So, in *Page One Records Ltd* v *Britton* [1967] 3 All ER 822

> *The Troggs*, a pop group, appointed the plaintiffs as their sole agent and manager for a period of five years. The contract contained an express negative covenant against working for any other music management during that period.

The court refused to enforce this covenant by means of an injunction because such a group could not work at all without a manager, and so an injunction would have had the same effect as an order of specific performance of the management contract. The reverse proposition is also true: an employer will not be forced to employ a particular person against his will. However, in exceptional circumstances this rule may not apply (*Hill* v *C.A. Parsons & Co. Ltd* [1972] 1 Ch 305). Further, a person dismissed may be entitled to reinstatement (see ss.69–71 Employment Protection (Consolidation) Act 1978).

12.2.2.3 Equitable limits: discretion, mutuality and volunteers Specific performance is an equitable remedy. This fact is significant in that equitable remedies are not available as of right, unlike the common law remedy of damages. Even where the plaintiff can demonstrate that his claim satisfies the conditions of availability of the remedy outlined above, the court has a discretion to refuse specific performance. Of course, the discretion is not entirely arbitrary. The principles of equity have developed as rules very similar to those of the common law (*1.2.1.1*). The extent of the discretion is that if the case falls within certain loosely defined categories the court may refuse to award specific performance if in the circumstances it believes that would be the right thing to do. In the first place, the court may consider the conduct of the plaintiff, and if he has not behaved entirely properly may refuse specific performance. The remedy has been refused where the plaintiff sought to take advantage of an obvious mistake by the defendant (*Webster* v *Cecil* (1861) 30 Beav 62; see *7.4.1.3*), and where the plaintiff rushed the defendant into signing the contract before he had had a proper chance to consider its terms (*Walters* v *Morgan* (1861) 3 DF & J 718). This principle is sometimes colourfully stated in the terms that 'he who comes to equity must come with clean hands'. The remedy may also be refused where it would be unfair to the defendant. It was refused in *Shell UK Ltd* v *Lostock Garage Ltd* [1977] 1 All ER 481 on the ground that the plaintiffs had granted discounts to all garages in the area other than the defendants', so that it had become impossible for the latter to compete. Evidence of unfairness may be found in undue hardship which would be caused to the defendant by specific performance (*Denne* v *Light* (1857) DM & G 774).

Specific performance may also be refused where there is no mutuality of remedy between the parties. It was once thought that this requirement meant that specific performance would not be available if at the time of contracting it could not also have been available to the other party. There was little sense in such a strict rule, and there were a number of exceptions to it. The rule has now been clarified by the Court of Appeal in *Price* v *Strange* [1978] Ch 337.

The defendant promised to grant a lease to the plaintiff in return for the latter's promise to do some internal and external repairs. The plaintiff's promise could not be specifically enforced. By the time of the trial the internal repairs had been completed, and the plaintiff had wrongfully been prevented from doing the external repairs by the defendant, who had done them herself.

The court said that the crucial time at which mutuality must be tested is the time of the trial. At that point the plaintiff must have performed all his obligations, or his obligations must themselves be capable of specific performance, or non-performance of those obligations must be adequately compensable by an award of damages (*12.2.2.1*). The purpose of the rule is to protect a defendant from the risk of being obliged to perform the actual contractual undertakings only to find that he will be inadequately compensated for the plaintiff's own non-performance. As such, it may be no more than a particular application of the undue hardship principle. In *Price* v *Strange* the plaintiff's contractual undertakings were not capable of specific performance, but by the time of the trial they had all been performed, so that there was no risk of hardship to the defendant in granting specific performance.

It is a general principle of equity that it will not 'assist a volunteer'. That is, equitable rules and remedies will not be applied in the case of a person who has not given real consideration for a promise. Thus, a promise which is binding under the common law because it was made under seal (*6.1*) or was given for a nominal and symbolic consideration such as a peppercorn (*6.3.2*) cannot be specifically enforced (*Re Parkin* [1892] 3 Ch 510).

12.2.2.4   Damages in lieu of specific performance   By s.50 of the Supreme Court Act 1981 the High Court is empowered to award damages in lieu of specific performance. In the majority of cases the plaintiff will be unlikely to invite the court to exercise its power, since it is possible to claim damages and specific performance at the same time. However, damages in lieu of specific performance may be awarded in circumstances in which common law damages would not be, although instances are likely to be rare. Where such damages are awarded they are to be assessed in the same way as common law damages for breach of contract (*Johnson* v *Agnew* [1980] AC 367).

12.2.3   Injunction

An injunction is a court order restraining the defendant from a specified activity. Its use extends far beyond the law of contract, but in this context it may be used to prevent the breach of a negative stipulation in the contract. The example given earlier of such a stipulation was a promise in the form of a contract not to make loud noises during the period when the promisee was revising for an exam (*12.1.2*). Such a promise may be enforced by means of an injunction.

The requirement that damages be shown to be inadequate before specific relief will be granted does not apply strictly to ordinary injunctions. Nevertheless, the courts will not in most circumstances allow the plaintiff to exploit this difference to achieve by injunction what cannot be achieved by specific performance. We have already seen how this principle applies in the case of contracts of employment (*12.2.2.2*). In other contracts the courts will be unwilling to enforce by injunction an express term which does no more than broadly prohibit breach of the positive stipulations in the contract, if the contract would not otherwise qualify for specific performance. Thus, injunctions are limited to specific restraints. Normally the activity to be restrained will be stipulated expressly in the contract, and the courts will be unwilling to imply a negative stipulation from the positive terms of the agreement. Such implication will occur, however, where the circumstances justify it. For example, where an exclusive dealing agreement is found not to be in restraint of trade (*8.8.5*), the court may imply a negative term preventing conduct which is inconsistent with the purpose of such a contract (*Evans Marshall & Co. v Bertola SA* [1973] 1 All ER 992). Nevertheless, it is usual for such contracts to contain explicit negative stipulations.

Ordinary (or prohibitory) injunctions are granted to prevent future breach of contract. If the plaintiff wishes to compel the defendant to remedy an injury caused by a breach which has already occurred he must obtain a mandatory injunction. The effect of such an injunction is to compel the defendant to undo work which has been done in breach of a negative stipulation in the contract. For example, a mandatory injunction might be granted to compel the defendant to cut down trees which had been planted in breach of a covenant not to restrict the plaintiff's view (cf. *Wakeham* v *Wood* (1982) 43 P & CR 40). Mandatory injunctions are subject to the same rules as specific performance. Damages must be an inadequate remedy, and grant of the injunction must not cause undue hardship to the defendant. This latter requirement may be waived where the breach was deliberately and knowingly committed (*Wakeham* v *Wood*).

12.3 DAMAGES FOR BREACH OF CONTRACT

12.3.1 The basic rule
In *Photo Production Ltd* v *Securicor Transport Ltd* [1980] 1 All ER 556 (see *10.3.1*) Lord Diplock said:

> Every failure to perform a primary obligation is a breach of contract. The secondary obligation on the part of the contract-breaker to which it gives rise by implication of the common law is to pay monetary compensation to the other party for the loss sustained by him in consequence of the breach . . ..

In some circumstances breach may also give the non-breaching party the option of bringing the outstanding primary obligations to a premature end (see *10.3* and *10.5*). In this section we shall consider the rules applicable to the secondary obligation to pay compensation for loss caused which arises whenever there is a breach of contract.

The basic rule of recovery of compensation in the case of breach of contract is that the non-breaching party is to be put into the position he would have been in had the contract been performed as agreed (*Robinson v Harman* (1848) 1 Ex 850; and see *Surrey CC* v *Bredero Homes Ltd* [1992] 3 All ER 302). This general measure of loss was described above as compensating the plaintiff's expectation interest (*12.1.3*). Lost expectation may comprise a loss of a profit which would have been made but for the breach. For example, if A bought machinery from B with the intention of making goods and selling them at a profit to C, then B's failure to deliver the machines will result in A losing the profit to be made on the sale of the goods. Subject to certain limitations (see *12.3.3*), quantification of such a loss should not present great difficulty. Lost expectation may also occur without any intention to profit from the contract, and in those circumstances quantification of the loss is more difficult. It may be measured either by reference to the diminished value to the plaintiff (*12.3.2.1* and *12.3.2.2*), or by reference to the cost of achieving the agreed performance (*12.3.2.3*).

In some cases the plaintiff may prefer (*12.3.2.5*), or may be obliged (*12.3.2.4*), to recover compensation for his reliance interest (*12.1.3*), such as out-of-pocket expenses arising out of his performance of the contract, and other expenses which it was intended would be recovered if the contract had been performed. There is no reason why both lost profit and out-of-pocket expenses should not be recovered provided there is no double compensation (*12.3.2.6*).

12.3.2 Quantification of loss

12.3.2.1 The market price rule The best example of the measurement of expectation loss in terms of difference in value is the process of assessment of damages for the seller's breach by non-delivery of a contract for the sale of goods: the market price rule. Where the goods are freely available upon demand there is no difficulty in identifying a 'market' and the price at which goods may be bought or sold. But it seems that the definition of what constitutes a market may be much more limited. In *Shearson Lehman Hutton Inc.* v *Maclaine Watson & Co. Ltd (No. 2)* [1990] 3 All ER 723 Webster J said in respect of a buyer's breach that a market would exist where: either (a) if the seller actually offers the goods for sale, there is one actual buyer on that day at a fair price; or (b) if there is no actual offer for sale, there are sufficient traders potentially in touch with each other to evidence a market in which the actual or notional seller could if he wished sell the goods. The market price of the goods (which represents their real value) is then said to be: either (a) the 'fair price' obtained by the actual sale; or (b) in the absence of an actual sale, a fair price for the total quantity of goods sold on the market on the relevant date, or such price as might be negotiated 'within a few days with persons who were members of the market on that day and who could not be taken into account as potential buyers on the day in question only because of difficulties of communication'. These principles would apply *mutatis mutandis* in the case of seller's breach. The law assumes that the buyer will mitigate his loss (see *12.3.3.4*) by immediately going to the market and buying similar goods from another source. The buyer will then only suffer a loss if he has to pay more for the substitute goods on the open market than he had originally contracted to pay. His damages will, therefore, be assessed by subtracting the contract price from the market price at the time of breach (s.51(3) Sale of Goods Act 1979). Where the buyer had anticipated making a profit on the transaction by reselling the goods at a price higher than the market price his damages are nevertheless restricted to the difference between market price and contract price, since he would have been able to make the resale and thus the profit by obtaining substitute goods on the market (*Williams* v *Reynolds* (1865) 6 B & S 495).

The converse of this measure of expectation loss applies to the buyer's breach by non-acceptance of a contract for the sale of goods. Where there is an available market it is assumed that the seller will immediately be able to sell the goods to a substitute buyer, so that he will only suffer a loss if the market price is below the price he had originally contracted to receive. His damages will, therefore, be assessed by subtracting the market price at the time of the breach from the contract price (s.50(3) Sale of Goods Act 1979).

In the case of the seller's remedy the market price rule will often result in no loss being revealed, for the reason that standard items are sold at standard prices, so that there will be no difference between market price and contract price. For example, if A has three sacks of coal to sell, and contracts to sell them at the standard (market) price of £4 per sack to B, then if B later wrongfully refuses to accept the coal, A will almost certainly be able to sell them to C at the same price. B will assert that he is entitled to benefit from A's mitigation of the loss (see *12.3.3.4*) so that no damages are payable, while A will assert that he has lost the profit on the sale to B since he would have been able to sell another three bags of coal to C. The expectation loss claimed by A is usually referred to as created by 'lost volume'. The claim will succeed in cases where supply is greater than demand. That is, if A has unlimited access to supplies of coal then it is true that he could have made sales to both B and C, so that there is genuinely one sale lost, and A should recover the profit he would have made on that sale (*W.L. Thompson Ltd* v *R. Robinson (Gunmakers) Ltd* [1955] 1 All ER 154: the case involved the sale of a new car). Where, however, demand is greater than supply the claim will not succeed. That is, if the three sacks of coal were A's last three available sacks, and no further supplies were obtainable, A could not have made sales to both B and C, and the sale to C was genuinely a substitute for the sale to B. In that case there was no lost profit (*Charter* v *Sullivan* [1957] 2 QB 117; also a new car sale). These rules do not apply in the case of unique goods, since in that case there is no scope for a substitute sale (*Lazenby Garages Ltd* v *Wright* [1976] 2 All ER 770; the good in question was a secondhand car, but there is scope for doubting whether every secondhand car is 'unique').

12.3.2.2 Alternative measures of difference in value The market price rule will not be used as the measure of loss where either there is no available market or in the circumstances the non-breaching party is not expected to avail himself of the market to mitigate his loss.

There may be no available market for a number of reasons, and it will be a question of fact in each case whether a market exists. A good example of absence of a market is where goods are specially manufactured to the order of the buyer, so that it is very unlikely that a different buyer would have ordered precisely the same goods. Another is where there is a serious disequilibrium between supply and demand. Thus, in ascertaining a seller's loss there may be no market price if supply so far outstrips demand that the seller cannot reasonably make an alternative sale. Equally, in ascertaining a buyer's loss there may be no market price if demand so outstrips supply that the buyer cannot reasonably make an alternative purchase. Where there is no market the basic principle is that the market price rule formula (*12.3.2.1*) should continue to be used, but the court must put in the place of the market price in the formula its own estimation of the actual value of the goods in question. Such estimations will sometimes be highly speculative, but the court may have some evidence available from actual contracts of resale of the goods. In some circumstances, where measurement of the expectation loss is so uncertain the plaintiff may prefer to claim his reliance losses (*12.3.2.5*).

A plaintiff buyer will not be expected to avail himself of the market to mitigate his loss when he is obliged to keep the goods despite the breach, which will occur when the breach relates only to a warranty (see *10.3.3*), or is a minor breach of an innominate term (see *10.3.4.2*), or where the breach once entitled the buyer to reject the goods but that right has been lost (see *10.3.2.4*). The buyer will still seek to be compensated for his lost expectation, which in this case will be represented by the difference in value of the goods as warranted in the contract and as actually delivered. Here again, the estimation of values may be somewhat speculative, although where there is a market the warranted value will be taken to be the same as the market price. Where goods intended for income-generation (e.g. manufacturing machinery) are delivered late the lost expectation will be the profits lost during the period when the machinery should have been in operation (see further *12.3.2.6*).

12.3.2.3 Cost of cure   In a contract for the sale of goods the seller's failure to deliver may be cured by the buyer obtaining substitute goods on the market. In that case difference in value, as measured by the market price rule (*12.3.2.1*), and cost of cure are one and the same thing. In some contracts, however, the measure of cost of cure may be very different from the measure of difference in value. Building contracts are often a source of such problems. The standard measure of loss caused by defective or incomplete workmanship is the cost of cure, since the only way the plaintiff can achieve his expectation under the contract is if the work is put right or completed (*Mertens* v *Home Freeholds Co.* [1921] 2 KB 526). This will particularly be the case where the work is to be done on land owned by the plaintiff.

Difficulty arises when the cost of cure is disproportionate to the difference in value, when the defendant may assert that only the lower amount be recoverable. For example, in a famous American case

> the plaintiffs had inserted an express clause in the contract that a particular make of piping be used in the plumbing work during the construction of a house. A different make of piping of identical quality was in fact used.

The court refused to allow damages on the basis of cost of cure, and allowed only the difference in value, which was purely nominal (*Jacob & Youngs* v *Kent* (1921) 230 NY 239). It seems likely that an English court would have come to the same conclusion. However, if the plaintiff has expressly stipulated for a particular kind of benefit he will not be deprived of the cost of cure simply because what he has chosen does not add any greater value than something much less costly to provide. For example, in *Radford* v *De Froberville* [1978] 1 All ER 33

> the defendant had contracted to build a wall on her land to mark the boundary, but failed to perform. The plaintiff was entitled to the cost of building a wall on his own land to mark the same boundary, and it was irrelevant that a less costly structure such as a fence would have done the job equally well.

It appears that the cost of cure will be awarded, however disproportionate to the enhancement of value thereby, if it can be shown that the necessary work has been or will be carried out (*Tito* v *Waddell (No. 2)* [1977] 3 All ER 129 at 313-9). Even then, it seems likely that the court would refuse a very expensive cost of cure if the difference in value was trivial (as in *Jacob & Youngs* v *Kent*), perhaps on the basis that refusal to accept what has been provided is failure to mitigate the loss (cf. *Payzu* v *Saunders* [1919] 2 KB 581; *12.3.3.4*).

It is important to realise, however, that cost of cure will only be awarded where such a remedy is appropriate to the liability assumed by the defendant. In *Watts* v *Morrow* [1991] 4 All ER 937

> the plaintiff purchaser of a house brought an action against a surveyor for breach of a contract to exercise care and skill in preparing a report on the house purchased. Defects were found which were not revealed by the defendant's report. The difference in value between what the plaintiff paid, and what the house would have been worth had the defects been known, was put at £15,000. The plaintiff paid nearly £34,000 to remedy the defects, and sought the larger sum in damages for breach of contract.

In the Court of Appeal, Ralph Gibson LJ (at 950; Bingham LJ and Sir Stephen Brown P agreed) said that to award damages for the cost of cure would amount to compensating the plaintiff for breach of a warranty by the defendant that the condition of the house was correctly described by the surveyor. No such warranty was given in a case such as this. Relying on the judgment of Denning LJ in *Philips* v *Ward* [1956] 1 All ER 874, the judge said that compensation was limited to the amount which would 'put the plaintiff into as good a position as if the contract for the survey had been properly fulfilled'. Had the survey been properly carried out, either the plaintiff would not have bought at all (in which case there would have been no loss), or he would have bought at the lower value (so that the difference in value was the proper measure of the loss). Where no particular benefit to the plaintiff can be identified in the defendant's contractual undertakings, cost of cure will not be allowed if it exceeds the diminution in value.

12.3.2.4 Expectation loss uncertain There can be no doubt that the measurement of expectation loss may be an uncertain process, especially in cases where it must be assessed by reference to difference in value and where the assumed value of the market price is unavailable as a guide. Nevertheless, as a general principle damages for lost expectation may always be recovered, subject to the various limitations considered below (see *12.3.3*). The fact that measurement of the loss is difficult or speculative will not prevent the court attempting such measurement and awarding damages accordingly. In *Simpson v London and North Western Ry Co.* (1876) 1 QBD 274

> the plaintiff sent specimens for exhibition at a trade show by rail, clearly indicating the date by which they must arrive. They arrived after that date, and the plaintiff claimed damages for loss of the profits he would have made had he been able to exhibit his specimens.

He was entitled to succeed, despite the speculative nature of his loss. The court will attempt to put some value on an expectation even when what is lost is no more than an opportunity to take the risk of making a profit, rather than a certain loss of a speculative profit. For example, in *Chaplin* v *Hicks* [1911] 2 KB 786

> the plaintiff was denied the opportunity to take part in a beauty contest by the defendant's breach of contract. She was able to recover damages for that lost opportunity, although there was no certainty that she would have won the contest. In those circumstances the loss was said to be less than the value of the prize, and depended upon the chances of her winning.

In some cases, however, the estimation of the lost expectation may be so speculative that the courts will refuse to award damages on the standard basis, and will instead only compensate the plaintiff's out-of-pocket expenses of attempting to perform the contract. The classic example of this principle is the Australian case of *McRae* v *Commonwealth Disposals Commission* (1951) 84 CLR 377 (see also *7.3.2*).

> The plaintiffs and defendants had contracted for the recovery of a shipwrecked oil tanker, said by the defendants to be lying at a specified place. The plaintiffs mounted an expedition to salvage the tanker, but no tanker could be found and it became apparent that none had ever been there. The plaintiffs claimed lost profit as the measure of their lost expectation resulting from the defendant's breach.

The court said that such recovery would be too speculative, since no details had been given at the time of contracting about the size of the tanker, or whether it still held its cargo of oil, and it could not be known whether the salvage operation would have been successful. Instead, the court awarded the plaintiffs' reliance loss, that is, the wasted cost of mounting the salvage expedition. They also recovered the price they had paid under the contract (the restitutionary interest: see *12.4.2*). It is sometimes said that the distinction between *McRae* and *Chaplin* v *Hicks* is that in the latter the plaintiff would have made a profit had the chance materialised, while in the former the plaintiff could not demonstrate that any profit would have been made. This distinction is highly artificial, and it may well be that today a case like *Chaplin* v *Hicks* would be decided by awarding the reliance interest because the expectation loss is too speculative to quantify.

12.3.2.5 Plaintiff's option to claim reliance loss

In some circumstances the plaintiff may prefer to claim his reliance loss rather than the expectation loss. Within certain limits it is now accepted that such a choice is available to the plaintiff. The essence of the limits is that such a claim must not result in the compensation of a loss which is not the result of the defendant's breach.

One reason for claiming the reliance loss would be if it was impossible to say with any accuracy what the profit under the contract would have been. In *Anglia Television Ltd* v *Reed* [1971] 3 All ER 690 the Court of Appeal said that a plaintiff who has not suffered any loss of profits, or who cannot prove what the profits would have been, is entitled to claim as an alternative the expenditure wasted as a result of the breach. This rule mirrors the decision in *McRae* v *Commonwealth Disposals Commission* (1951) 84 CLR 377 (*12.3.2.4*), where the reliance loss measure was imposed by the court rather than selected by the plaintiff.

> In this case the plaintiff television company had been forced to abandon its project to make a film when the lead actor withdrew from the project in breach of contract. The company was able to recover for wasted expenditure, including expenditure incurred before the contract with the actor had been made.

Loss caused by such wasted expenditure was recoverable provided that 'it was such as would reasonably be in the contemplation of the parties as likely to be wasted if the contract was broken' (see *12.3.3.3*).

A somewhat different reason for claiming the reliance loss may be that the contract was what is sometimes called a 'bad bargain', under which the plaintiff would not have made a profit had the contract been performed. The courts will be extremely wary of such claims. There is a danger that the plaintiff may be attempting to put himself into a better position after the breach than he would have been in had the contract been performed as agreed, since in some such cases the plaintiff might not even have recovered his expenses. This difficulty is well illustrated by *C & P Haulage* v *Middleton* [1983] 3 All ER 94.

> The plaintiff was entitled under a series of six-month contracts to the use of a garage for the purposes of his business. He had spent some money on equipping the garage for his needs, but under the contracts the equipment installed became the property of the garage owner once the plaintiff's use of the garage ceased. Ten weeks before the end of one of the six-month contracts the garage owner ordered the plaintiff out of the garage in breach of contract. The local planning authority allowed the plaintiff to use his own garage for more than 10 weeks, with the result that he saved the weekly rental on the garage as a result of the breach. His profits were, therefore, greater than if the contract had not been breached. He brought an action to recover the costs of equipping the garage from which he had been ejected.

The Court of Appeal rejected that claim on the ground that the cost of the equipment would have been lost had the contract been performed as agreed, and lawfully terminated at the end of a six-month period. The loss did not, therefore, result from the breach, but from the nature of the contract itself, and so was not to be compensated.

Nevertheless, the Court of Appeal in *C & P Haulage* v *Middleton* did not rule out the possibility of a claim for reliance loss succeeding simply because it cannot be shown that the contract would have been profitable. The very specific test of the recoverability of reliance loss must be whether the actual loss which is claimed results from expenditure wasted as a result of the breach which it was intended would be recovered out of the income produced by performance of the contract. Put in rather simplified terms, provided the contract would have resulted in the plaintiff breaking even on the venture, wasted expenditure is recoverable. It is irrelevant to such a claim that the plaintiff would not have made a net profit. Where the plaintiff would not have broken even had the contract been performed, reliance loss claimed would have to be reduced by the amount of expenditure the plaintiff would have failed to recover out of income produced by performance. An important limit on this rule, however, is that where the defendant alleges that the plaintiff would not have recovered all his expenditure in this way the defendant has the burden of proving that allegation (*CCC Films (London) Ltd* v *Impact Quadrant Films Ltd* [1984] 3 All ER 298).

12.3.2.6 Avoiding double compensation In *Anglia Television Ltd* v *Reed* [1971] 3 All ER 690 Lord Denning MR said that a plaintiff may elect whether to claim for loss of profits or for wasted expenditure, but that he cannot claim for both. That statement, although capable of rational explanation, may be misleading. Lord Denning did not indicate whether he was speaking of gross or net profits. It is true that a plaintiff may not claim both the reliance loss of wasted expenditure and the gross profit expected under the contract, since the plaintiff would expect to recover expenditure out of such gross profit, and to award both would be double compensation of the reliance loss (*Cullinane* v *British 'Rema' Manufacturing Co. Ltd* [1954] 1 QB 292). But if it is advantageous to the plaintiff to divide his claim between expenditure on performance and the lost net profit, there seems to be no good reason why he should not do so, since the net profit is calculated by deducting expenditure from the gross profit (cf. *Hydraulic Engineering Co. Ltd* v *McHaffie, Goslett & Co.* (1878) 4 QBD 670, where such a claim was allowed). To award only net profit and the expenditure wasted would involve no double compensation.

12.3.2.7 Effect of tax on quantification Where the plaintiff's claim is for lost gross profit under a contract the court must take into account the effect of tax liability before making its award. Where damages awarded in judicial proceedings for breach of contract are not subject to taxation, while profits earned through the agreed performance of the contract would have been, the latter liability for tax must be accounted for. The court must not award more than the net amount which the plaintiff would have been able to keep as a result of performance of the contract, after tax had been deducted from the gross income. This principle is best demonstrated by the decision of the House of Lords in *British Transport Commission* v *Gourley* [1956] AC 185.

> The case involved an action in tort for loss of earnings resulting from personal injury, but the reasoning applies equally to actions for breach of contract. The plaintiff suffered gross loss of earnings of nearly £38,000, which, had he received it as income, would have been reduced by liability for tax to under £7,000.

The court awarded only the lower sum, since damages for loss of earnings are not taxable, while income is. This rule does not apply to loss of a capital asset, since there is no general liability for tax on the acquisition of such a thing. Nor does it apply to many claims for lost profit, since damages for lost commercial profits are themselves taxable as income.

12.3.2.8 Consequential loss The courts sometimes speak of the award of damages for 'consequential loss' resulting from the breach of the contract. The phrase has no very precise meaning, but it usually indicates loss which does not result directly from the breach, but which is still an inevitable consequence of the breach. For example, in a contract for the sale of an animal feed hopper, if the ventilation of the hopper is defective there is a breach of the contract. The loss directly resulting is that the hopper is not worth as much as the hopper promised in the contract would have been worth, and that loss may be compensated by award of damages for difference in value (assuming the hopper was not, or could not be, rejected: *12.3.2.2*) or for cost of cure (*12.3.2.3*). Where, in addition, the farmer's livestock become ill through eating animal feed which was mouldy because the ventilation in the hopper was defective, so that the herd had to be destroyed, there is a *consequential* loss of the value of the herd resulting from the breach. In such a case the difference in value and cost of cure may be minimal, but the consequential loss very great.

To describe the loss as consequential is, however, of little significance except to find a convenient label for a loss which purists do not regard as strictly belonging to either the expectation or reliance categories. What must be remembered is that such loss raises particular questions of causation (did the loss actually result from the breach which occurred? see *12.3.3.1*), and of remoteness of damage (was this consequence of the breach within the contemplation of the parties at the time of contracting, so that the defendant in promising to perform can be taken to have promised not to cause such loss? see *12.3.3.3*).

12.3.2.9 Time for assessment of loss The basic rule is that damages are to be assessed at the time of breach, which usually occurs at the time when performance became due. For example, the buyer's damages for the seller's non-delivery in a contract for the sale of goods are to be assessed according to the market price for the goods (*12.3.2.1*) at the time when the goods ought to have been delivered (s.51(3) Sale of Goods Act 1979). This rule is based on the obligation on the plaintiff to mitigate his loss (*12.3.3.4*), and assumes that he will do so by taking immediate action. The basic rule is, however, only a presumptive rule, and it is now clear that where it would be reasonable for the plaintiff to do something other than to take immediate steps to mitigate the loss the court will postpone the time for assessment of damages until whatever date is more appropriate. In particular, the courts appear to be anxious to prevent rigid adherence to the breach-date assessment rule causing contracts to be abandoned which might with a little patience on the part of the non-breaching party have been saved. That is, the non-breaching party may be allowed time to seek confirmation that no performance will be forthcoming, or that defective performance will be cured, before being expected to mitigate the loss. In *Johnson* v *Agnew* [1980] AC 367

> the vendors agreed to sell a house and land to the purchaser, but the purchaser failed to complete the transaction on the day appointed. The vendors then obtained an order for specific performance, but it was not drawn up for some five months, by which time specific performance had become impossible. The vendors sought discharge of the order for specific performance, and to recover damages in its place.

The House of Lords found for the vendors, and said that damages were to be assessed at the date when specific performance became impossible. Lord Wilberforce said:

> In cases where a breach of a contract for sale has occurred, and the innocent party reasonably continues to try to have the contract completed, it would to me appear more logical and just rather than tie him to the date of the original breach, to assess damages as at the date when (otherwise than by his default) the contract is lost.

In *Janred Properties Ltd* v *Ente Nazionale Italiano per il Turismo* [1989] 2 All ER 444 Nourse LJ suggested that Lord Wilberforce's words must be understood in the context of the special facts of the case, and should not be taken as a statement of general principle in respect of reasonable attempts to secure actual performance. There appears to be no good reason to urge such a limitation on his statement of principle.

In some cases it may be impossible at the time of performance for the non-breaching party to discover that a breach has occurred. For example, it is breach of a contract of sale of goods to deliver goods which are defective, but the breach may remain undetected if the defect does not immediately manifest itself (e.g. a car with a latent fault which will inevitably cause it to breakdown after 1,500 miles of driving). In such a case the damages will be assessed at the time when the breach could first reasonably have been discovered (*East Ham Corp.* v *Bernard Sunley & Sons Ltd* [1966] AC 406).

Since the breach-date assessment rule is based on the assumption that a reasonable plaintiff will take immediate steps to mitigate his loss, where it is reasonable for the plaintiff to take no such steps damages will not be assessed until such time as it ceases so to be reasonable. In *Radford* v *De Froberville* [1978] 1 All ER 33 (see *12.3.2.3*) it was suggested that when at first it seems probable that the defendant will make good his default, damages will be assessed at the time when that probability ceases to exist, since the duty to take steps of mitigation arises at that point. In some circumstances it may be reasonable to take no action in mitigation right up to the time of trial. In *Wroth* v *Tyler* [1974] Ch 30

> the defendants had repudiated a contract for the purchase of a house, and in the particular circumstances the plaintiffs could not reasonably have done anything to mitigate the loss by purchasing a different house.

When damages were awarded in lieu of specific performance (*12.2.2.4*) they were assessed at the time of the hearing.

Where there is a breach by anticipatory repudiation (*11.3.2*), establishing the time for assessment of damages is more complex. Where the non-breaching party elects to affirm the contract despite the repudiation, damages fall to be assessed according to the principles discussed so far in this section. There is no duty to mitigate the loss until the time for performance. Where, however, the non-breaching party accepts the repudiation the breach-date assessment rule is subject to the crucial proviso that the duty to mitigate in such a case arises upon acceptance of the repudiation (*12.3.3.4*). Damages will then be assessed not at the time for performance stipulated in the contract, but at the time when the plaintiff could reasonably have arranged an alternative contract (*Garnac Grain Co. Inc.* v *Faure & Fairclough Ltd* [1968] AC 1130).

12.3.3 Limits on the assessment of damages

12.3.3.1 Causation and contributory negligence Damages will not be awarded to compensate loss which was not caused by the breach. We have already encountered an example of this principle in operation in the case of *C & P Haulage* v *Middleton* [1983] 3 All ER 94 (*12.3.2.5*). The user of a garage claimed his wasted expenditure in equipping the garage when the garage owner wrongfully terminated his contract to use the premises. The court rejected the claim, because 10 weeks later the owner could have rightfully terminated the contract, whereupon the equipment would in any case have become the property of the garage owner. The loss by wasted expenditure was not caused by the breach of contract, therefore, but by the nature of the contract, which in this respect was inherently disadvantageous to the plaintiff. That fact alone did not give rise to a right to compensation. On the other hand, the fact that the contractual provision is inadequate to provide a perfect solution to a given problem does not deprive the non-breaching party of compensation sufficient to achieve the imperfect solution, provided that is some real benefit. In *Dean* v *Ainley* [1987] 3 All ER 748

> the purchaser of a house stipulated for repairs to be carried out to prevent leaks from a patio to a cellar below. The repairs were not carried out. It became apparent that had they been carried out, they would only have excluded 70% of the water

penetration, since 30% was due to a problem which could not be prevented by the repairs provided for by the contract.

The purchaser was nevertheless entitled to recover the cost of the work which should have been carried out. In all cases the question whether the loss was caused by the breach will largely be a question of fact, on which it is difficult to give any guidance. In the majority of cases causation is not a difficult issue; greater difficulty arises from the question whether loss, which admittedly results from the breach, is too remote to be compensated (*12.3.3.3*).

Causation may sometimes present difficulty when it appears that the loss was caused partly by the breach and partly by some other factor. The general rule is that where breach can be shown to be an actual cause of the loss the fact that there is another contributing cause is irrelevant. The breach will entitle the non-breaching party to damages. For example, in *Wroth* v *Tyler* [1974] Ch 30 (*12.3.2.9*) the plaintiff's loss was caused partially by the defendant's breach of contract and partially by the fact that the plaintiff lacked the financial resources to take active steps to mitigate the loss. The loss was nevertheless recoverable.

Where the loss is caused by both the breach and a contributing factor which results from the fault of the non-breaching party the situation is more complex. In the law of torts, where injury is caused by the negligence of the defendant and by the contributory negligence of the plaintiff, the damages payable by the defendant to compensate the plaintiff will be reduced proportionately to the amount by which the latter's contribution was a cause of the injury (Law Reform (Contributory Negligence) Act 1945). The question is whether the provisions of that Act apply equally to the law of contract. In *AB Marintrans* v *Comet Shipping Co. Ltd* [1985] 3 All ER 442

> a ship was chartered for a voyage from New Zealand to West Africa. The cargo was badly stowed, and the ship had to return to port for the cargo to be restowed. The charterers made deductions from the hire payable and claimed further compensation to account for the delays and extra costs involved. The owners claimed that the loss was partly attributable to the fault of the charterers, and argued that compensation recoverable should be reduced proportionately in accordance with the terms of the 1945 Act.

Neill LJ (sitting as a single judge in the Commercial Court) found that on its true construction the 1945 Act did not apply to actions for breach of contract. Although only a first instance judgment this decision might be thought to be of considerable authority, but it was not followed in *Forsikringsaktieselskapet Vesta* v *Butcher* [1986] 2 All ER 488, which was itself affirmed by the Court of Appeal ([1988] 3 All ER 43). In the latter case

> the plaintiffs were insurers of a fish farm. They had effected reinsurance of 90 per cent of the risk through the defendant brokers. It was a condition of the contract of reinsurance that the farm be under a 24-hour watch. The owners of the farm informed the plaintiffs that it was impossible to comply with the condition, and the plaintiffs in turn informed the defendants. The defendants took no action, and

the plaintiffs failed to follow up their first telephone call. The farm lost 100,000 fish, and the reinsurers denied liability because of the absence of a 24-hour watch. The plaintiffs brought an action against the defendants for breach of contract, alleging negligence. The defendants pleaded the plaintiffs' contributory negligence in failing to follow up the first telephone call as a defence to this claim.

Hobhouse J did not accept that the contributory negligence doctrine had no application to actions for breach of contract. He preferred to divide claims for breach of contract into three categories, to at least one of which it did apply. Many claims for breach of contract depend upon contractual terms imposing a strict standard of performance on the defendant (*10.5*). In the case of such terms there is no scope for the operation of the contributory negligence rule. Such a rule was canvassed by the Law Commissions Working Paper No. 114, but it would appear to be an undesirable development in the law, since it would undermine the advantage which the strict liability rule gives to those who lack the bargaining power to negotiate for the level of contractual protection which it affords. In these cases the present rule seems the more acceptable: contributory negligence is only a defence to an action based on a contract term imposing strict liability if it amounts to a *novus actus* intervening in the chain of causation between the alleged breach and the loss sustained. The notion of strict liability is that the promisor must overcome difficulties (falling short of *novus actus*) in performing in accordance with the undertaking given. Where the contract terms impose only an obligation to exercise reasonable care and skill, which may be classed as a 'negligence standard' (cf. *10.5*), but there is no duty of care existing independently of the contract, it is a matter of debate whether such claims are subject to the contributory negligence rule. Neill LJ appeared to treat *AB Marintrans* v *Comet Shipping Co. Ltd* as a case of this kind, and said the Act did not apply, although the claim may have belonged to the first category. In *De Meza & Stuart* v *Apple Van Straten, Shena and Stone* [1974] 1 Lloyd's Rep 508 at first instance the 1945 Act was said to apply to such a case, but the matter was left open by the Court of Appeal. Some contracts impose a duty of care the breach of which would in any case amount to an independent tort. The *Butcher* case belonged to this category, and the judge found no difficulty in holding that the 1945 Act did apply to such a claim. As Neill LJ remarked in the *AB Marintrans* case, there is 'great force in the contention that the same rule should apply to claims whether they are based in contract or tort where the act complained of involves the breach of a duty of care'. In *Forsikringsaktieselskapet Vesta* v *Butcher* [1986] 2 All ER 43 in the Court of Appeal Neill LJ accepted that this might be achieved under the analysis offered by Hobhouse J at first instance, although he continued to have doubts about whether the wording of s.4 of the 1945 Act was capable of such an interpretation. This objection might be met by a very minor amendment of the 1945 Act to include a definition of negligence as contained in s.1(1) of the Unfair Contract Terms Act 1977, which covers 'any obligation, arising from the express or implied terms of a contract, to take reasonable care or exercise reasonable skill in the performance of the contract'.

Where the factor contributing to causation of the loss, in addition to the breach by the defendant, is the act of a third party or parties, whether that act will excuse the breaching party from the obligation to pay damages is largely a question of whether the contract has been frustrated (see *11.4*). The court is likely to be especially concerned to know whether the intervening act was so foreseeable that steps could have been taken to avoid it. For example, in *The Eugenia* [1964] 1 All ER 161 (see *11.4.2.3*)

> the charterers of a vessel breached their contract by taking the vessel into the Suez canal at a time when it was a 'dangerous' zone. The effect of that breach was made many times worse by the act of a third party in closing the canal. Nevertheless, the charterers were not excused the obligation to pay compensation for their breach.

12.3.3.2 Uncertainty   There is no rule preventing the award of damages merely because the quantification of the loss suffered is uncertain. At worst, the court may award a lower level of compensation than the uncertain amount claimed by the plaintiff (*12.3.2.4*). Nevertheless, it should be remembered that other rules may also operate to exclude the award of damages where quantification would be uncertain. For example, the restrictions on recovery of damages for non-pecuniary loss (*12.3.3.6*) result in part from the fact that such losses are notoriously difficult to quantify. Moreover, the remoteness of damage rule (*12.3.3.3*) may also operate to prevent the award of uncertain damages, since in many cases remote losses will also be uncertain in their extent.

12.3.3.3 Remoteness of damage   In *Hadley* v *Baxendale* (1854) 9 Exch 341 Alderson B said:

> Where two parties have made a contract which one of them has broken, the damages which the other party ought to receive in respect of such breach of contract should be such as may fairly and reasonably be considered either arising naturally, i.e., according to the usual course of things, from such breach, of contract itself, or such as may reasonably be supposed to have been in the contemplation of both parties, at the time they made the contract, as the probable result of the breach of it.

This rule, which is the test of the remoteness of damage, is intended to ensure that the defendant was aware when making the contract that he must avoid causing the kind of loss which occurred. The rule is concerned with the allocations of the risks of the contract between the parties, and is designed to prevent the defendant having to compensate a loss attendant upon a risk which was not his to bear.

The test of remoteness of damage established in *Hadley* v *Baxendale* is frequently described as consisting of two rules, or a single rule with two limbs (*Victoria Laundry (Windsor) Ltd* v *Newman Industries Ltd* [1949] 2 KB 528). Under the first limb, damages may be recovered for loss arising 'according to the usual course of things' from the breach of contract. The intention of this rule is to identify those losses which *must inevitably* have been within the contemplation of the parties as likely to result in the event of breach of contract. The likelihood of such losses is a reasonable deduction from the nature of the contract, and the defendant cannot simply assert that he did not know of that risk to avoid having to compensate such loss. Under the second limb, damages may also be recovered which result from special circumstances, provided the defendant knows of those circumstances. In *Hadley* v *Baxendale* Alderson B said:

> Now, if the special circumstances under which the contract was actually made were communicated by the plaintiffs to the defendants, and thus known to both parties, the damages resulting from the breach of such a contract, which they would reasonably contemplate, would be the amount of injury which would ordinarily follow from a breach of contract under these special circumstances . . ..

It is almost certain that Alderson B did not intend to establish two rules of remoteness of damage. Rather, there is a single test which requires greater knowledge on the part of the defendant as the degree of likelihood of the particular loss resulting from the breach diminishes (*The Heron II* [1969] 1 AC 350 at 385). Usual loss and loss resulting from special circumstances are no more than the polar positions of that test, and there are intermediate positions where the loss is only recoverable if the defendant has some knowledge, but without requiring communication by the plaintiff of the precise loss at risk (cf. Neill LJ in *Lips Maritime Corporation* v *President of India*, [1987] 1 All ER 957 at 968).

The operation of the rule is well illustrated by the decision of the Court of Appeal in *Victoria Laundry (Windsor) Ltd* v *Newman Industries Ltd*.

> The defendant engineering company contracted to sell a boiler to the plaintiff laundry company. It was known that the boiler was required for immediate use in connection with the plaintiffs' business, but not known that the plaintiffs had recently won a very profitable dyeing contract. The boiler was delivered late.

The plaintiffs were not entitled to recover for the loss of profit on this particular dyeing contract, since they had not informed the defendants of its existence or its favourable terms, but that did not mean that they could not recover damages for general lost profit from the expansion of their business intended as a result of purchasing the boiler. Once the defendants knew that the boiler was intended for immediate use they should have been able to work out for themselves that late delivery was likely to lead to loss of business. Had the defendants not known the boiler was intended for immediate use, however, the court might have found that even damages for loss of business were too remote. *Hadley* v *Baxendale* involved

> a claim for lost business because a mill was lying idle while the shaft was away being repaired, and was late being returned. The claim was rejected as too remote

precisely because the defendants did not know that the shaft was immediately necessary for the plaintiff's business.

It can be seen, therefore, that it is not possible to divide losses into two simple categories of those arising in the usual course of things and those arising out of special circumstances. Rather, there is a single rule that as the likelihood of the loss occurring diminishes the degree of knowledge on the part of the defendant must increase for the loss to be recoverable in damages.

It remains to determine what must be the likelihood of a loss resulting from breach for the plaintiff not to have needed to spell the matter out to the defendant at the time of contracting. In *Victoria Laundry (Windsor) Ltd v Newman Industries Ltd* Asquith LJ impliedly suggested that the test was the same as the test of foreseeability in the tort of negligence, since he said that the plaintiff may recover 'such part of the loss actually resulting as was at the time of the contract reasonably foreseeable as liable to result from the breach'. This formulation was called into question, however, by the House of Lords in *The Heron II*. Lord Reid said that the plaintiff may only recover 'loss arising naturally', or 'in the usual course of things' (echoing Alderson B in *Hadley* v *Baxendale*); and may not recover loss which, although a real possibility, was only likely to occur 'in a small minority of cases'. He went on to stress that the test of remoteness in contract is more strict than the test of remoteness in tort, for the reason that the communication of special circumstances is irrelevant to many torts, but in contract allows the defendant to modify his contract or his performance according to the known risks of the contract. The remoteness test must therefore encourage such communication.

In *H. Parsons (Livestock) Ltd* v *Uttley Ingham & Co. Ltd* [1978] 1 All ER 525 the Court of Appeal was faced with the task of making sense of the very vague tests of remoteness which were available.

> The contract was for the sale of an animal feed hopper. The ventilation of the hopper was defective, amounting to breach of the contract. The farmer's livestock became ill through eating animal feed which was mouldy because the ventilation was defective, so that the herd had to be destroyed. The particular illness and its consequence would have been considered an unlikely result of the breach in question at the time when the contract was made. The farmer claimed the loss of the value of the herd.

Lord Denning MR found for the plaintiff. He found the various formulations of the test of remoteness confusing and 'a sea of semantic exercises'. He accepted that sometimes the test is more strict than at others, but rather than distinguishing between contract and tort he distinguished between claims for economic loss (such as lost profit) and claims for physical loss (as in this case). To the latter type of claim the less strict test of remoteness applied. Provided some physical injury might be envisaged its precise nature was irrelevant. Scarman LJ (with whom Orr LJ agreed) also found for the plaintiff, but not on the same ground. He rejected Lord Denning's distinction between economic and physical loss, and ultimately decided that the remoteness tests in contract and tort were the same. This reasoning must be doubted, however, in view of Lord Reid's clear statement in *The Heron II* that the test in contract is more strict than the test in tort.

The law on remoteness of damage is thus unclear, and may require an authoritative statement by the House of Lords to settle it. In favour of Lord Reid's approach is the argument that contracts enable the parties to allocate risks between themselves, and that such allocation will only work if the parties have proper information about the risks involved. The strict remoteness test in contract would encourage the provision of such information, since unless it was provided the loss would not be recoverable. In favour of Lord Denning's approach is that it prevents the result of the case depending upon the artificial classification of the claim as either contractual or tortious. It also imposes a stricter test on those claims which are inherently speculative (lost profits), while allowing a more lenient test for claims where the loss is more readily measured (physical loss). Such differentiation may, however, be more appropriate under some other rule (cf. *12.3.2.4*). In favour of the approach adopted by Scarman LJ is that it is the most simple to apply.

12.3.3.4 Mitigation   The plaintiff may not recover damages for losses which could have been avoided. In *British Westinghouse Electric and Manufacturing Co. Ltd* v *Underground Electric Railways Co. of London Ltd* [1912] AC 673 Viscount Haldane LC said:

> The fundamental basis is . . . compensation for pecuniary loss naturally flowing from the breach; but this first principle is qualified by a second, which imposes on a plaintiff the duty of taking all reasonable steps to mitigate the loss consequent upon the breach, and debars him from claiming in respect of any part of the damage which is due to his neglect to take such steps . . ..
> [T]his second principle does not impose on the plaintiff an obligation to take any step which a reasonable and prudent man would not ordinarily take in the course of his business.

The rule is sometimes expressed in terms of a duty on the plaintiff to mitigate the loss, but the only duty owed by the plaintiff is to himself, in that he will not receive compensation for loss which could have been avoided by reasonable steps. The rule is central to many other aspects of the law relating to damages. For example, we have already seen how the market price rule for quantification of difference-in-value damages is based on an assumption of immediate mitigation of loss (*12.3.2.1*).

The mitigation principle embraces three separate means of avoiding loss. In the first place, the plaintiff must not by unreasonable action on his part increase the loss resulting from the breach. In *Banco de Portugal* v *Waterlow* [1932] AC 452

> the defendant's breach resulted in large numbers of forged banknotes circulating in Portugal. The plaintiffs undertook to honour the face value of all such notes, although they were able to detect the forgeries.

The plaintiffs' action increased the loss resulting from the breach, but was held to be reasonable because to have done otherwise would have caused a crisis of confidence in the paper currency.

Secondly, loss will not be recovered if it could be avoided by taking reasonable steps. The market price rule for quantifying difference-in-value damages embodies this form of mitigation. Where there is a market it is reasonable for the plaintiff to seek substitute performance via the market, and loss greater than that represented by the market price formula cannot be recovered. What is reasonable will very largely depend upon the facts of individual cases. In some circumstances it may be reasonable to accept the performance offered by the defendant even when that performance amounts to breach of the original contract. If it remains the best substitute performance available then it will be unreasonable not to go to that source (*Payzu* v *Saunders* [1919] 2 KB 581). What is reasonable may also depend upon the circumstances of the plaintiff. In *Wroth* v *Tyler* [1974] Ch 30 the plaintiff was unable to mitigate because he lacked the financial resources to make a substitute purchase. His failure to mitigate was not unreasonable in the circumstances.

Finally, loss cannot be recovered if, in acting to protect his own interests, the plaintiff in fact succeeds in making a much more advantageous contract, which avoids losses which might otherwise have been sustained. In the *British Westinghouse* case

> the appellants were to supply electricity turbines to the respondents' specification. The turbines never met that specification, and after a time were replaced by turbines of a different manufacture. These turbines were much more efficient to run, so that the savings over the original turbines were such that the replacement machines paid for themselves in a short time.

The respondents claimed damages for the cost of replacing the original turbines, but the House of Lords refused that claim. The respondents had rightly mitigated their loss, and had been so successful that most of the losses had been eliminated. The respondents were not entitled to anything more than the compensation already received for the period of time when the original turbines were running inefficiently.

The converse of the above principle is that if the plaintiff takes steps to mitigate the loss which at the time are reasonable it is irrelevant that in fact the steps taken were not the best way of reducing the loss (*Gebruder Metel Mann GmbH & Co.* v *NBR (London) Ltd* [1984] 1 Lloyd's Rep 614). Indeed, even if the steps taken result in increasing the loss sustained, if the steps were at the time those which a reasonable and prudent man might have taken in the course of his business then the extra loss will also be recoverable.

The mitigation principle applies to breach by anticipatory repudiation (*11.3.2*) as it applies to ordinary breach, but in some instances the effect of its application is rather different. Where the non-breaching party accepts the repudiation, loss sustained is subject to the mitigation principle from the moment of acceptance. Thus, where the plaintiff misses an opportunity to mitigate, the loss will be assessed at the date of the missed opportunity rather than at the date for performance (*12.3.2.9*). Where the non-breaching party affirms the contract, the rule that the loss must not be increased by taking unreasonable steps is reflected in the rule that a party may not affirm the contract and continue performance in the face of a repudiation unless he has a legitimate interest in so doing (*11.3.2.1* and *12.2.1.1*). However, where the contract is affirmed, the obligation to take steps to reduce the loss which will be sustained when the time for performance comes only arises at the time for performance. This rule is conceptually logical, in that the mitigation principle expects the plaintiff to take steps to reduce the loss resulting from breach. If the contract is affirmed there will be no breach until non-performance on the due date, and until then both breach and loss are only potential, so that there is no scope for the mitigation principle to apply. Nevertheless, this rule seems rather wasteful, since it allows the plaintiff to take no action even when it is clear that performance will not take place and it is also clear that some of the loss is avoidable. Avoiding such waste may be preferable to the conceptual purity of the existing rule.

12.3.3.5 Defendant's performance options Where the contract permits the defendant to choose between two or more methods of performing, it will be assumed for the purposes of assessing damages that the defendant would have chosen the method least onerous to himself and least profitable to the plaintiff. There are *obiter* statements to that effect in *Abrahams* v *Reiach* [1922] 1 KB 477. In that case

> the defendant publishers had agreed to publish a series of articles by the plaintiff, first in a magazine and then in book form. The form, price, date of publication and print run of the book were left to the defendants' discretion. They failed to publish the book, and the question arose of the quantification of the plaintiff's damages.

The Court of Appeal held that this was not a case where it was enough simply to award damages on the basis of the less costly of alternative methods of performance (e.g., the decision of the majority in *Dean* v *Ainley* [1987] 3 All ER 748), since the discretion was so wide that any number of options were open to the defendants. Damages were assessed, therefore, on the basis of the least unfavourable to the defendant of those approaches which reflected reasonable business practice in the circumstances. If, however, before the breach the defendant had committed himself to a particular method of performing, then that method will be used in assessing damages, even if the contract would have permitted a method under which the plaintiff's loss by breach would have been less.

12.3.3.6 Non-pecuniary loss It was once thought that damages could not be recovered for losses which did not affect a pecuniary interest of the plaintiff. For example, in addition to financial loss a plaintiff might suffer disappointment, hurt feelings or discomfort as a result of breach, but damages for such non-pecuniary losses were not recoverable. That view is no longer tenable, but it is still true that the courts are reluctant to award damages for non-pecuniary loss in many cases. This reluctance may be explained in part by the difficulty of quantification of such losses, by the fear of unfounded claims (since such feelings are hard to prove or disprove), and by the fear of double compensation (in that disappointment etc. may be adequately compensated by an award of damages for any pecuniary interest injured by the breach). In *Hayes* v *James & Charles Dodd* [1990] 2 All ER 815 the Court of Appeal refused to allow recovery for anguish and vexation in a commercial contract. Staughton LJ was very robust in dismissing such a claim. In his view the reason for disallowing the claim was not merely a question of remoteness of damage, but one of policy. The policy was to limit recovery for mental distress to categories of contract in which it was a central obligation to provide comfort or pleasure or the relief of discomfort.

Where the contract is specifically intended to confer a benefit other than a pecuniary gain the courts will be more willing to award compensation for such loss caused by breach. For example, in *Jarvis* v *Swans Tours Ltd* [1973] 1 All ER 71

> the plaintiff booked a winter holiday which the defendants promised in their brochure would be like a 'houseparty', with special entertainments, and proper facilities for skiing. The skiing facilities were in fact inadequate, the entertainments were far from special, and in the second week the 'houseparty' consisted of the plaintiff alone.

The Court of Appeal held that he was entitled to recover not merely the cost of the holiday, but a similar amount again as general damages for the disappointment suffered and the loss of the entertainment he should have had. Lord Denning MR pointed out that he had entered the contract not merely to purchase the travel facilities and the board and lodging, but in order to enjoy himself, and he was entitled to compensation for the loss of that part of his expectation. A similar rationale appears to underlie those cases where the court awards damages on the basis of cost of cure, even when the difference in value is small relative to that cost, in order to meet the plaintiff's particular expectation (cf. *Radford* v *De Froberville* [1978] 1 All ER 33: *12.3.2.3*). In *Watts* v *Morrow* [1991] 4 All ER 937 the Court of Appeal, placing considerable reliance on the decision in *Hayes* v *James & Charles Dodd* (above), declined to give more than a very narrow scope to the category of contracts 'to provide peace of mind or freedom from distress', and refused to regard a surveyor as having any such contractual obligation towards the purchaser of a house for whom he had prepared a report.

Where the non-pecuniary loss is not related to an expectation actually built into the contract the courts may nevertheless be willing to compensate it. In *Hobbs* v *London & South Western Ry* (1875) LR 10 QB 111

> the plaintiff and his family were taken to the wrong station by the railway company, necessitating a walk of several miles on a wet night. He recovered damages for that inconvenience.

However, had he mitigated his loss by hiring a cab (which, assuming one could be found, would have been reasonable) his expenditure would have been recoverable. Thus, although the loss was in fact non-pecuniary it might just as well have been very specifically quantifiable in financial terms. It is where the loss bears no relation to a financial loss that the courts will not award damages. In *Addis* v *Gramophone Co.* [1909] AC 488 it was held that a plaintiff wrongfully dismissed in a particularly abrupt way could not recover damages for injury to his reputation by the manner of his dismissal. Reputation of this kind is not a financial interest. Lord Loreburn went on to suggest that damages were not recoverable for the increased difficulty of obtaining alternative employment. That suggestion must be doubted, however, since in general the law will allow damages for lost opportunity (*12.3.2.4*), and loss of this kind is sufficiently similar for it to be difficult to justify any distinction being made. It may be that the rigours of *Addis* v *Gramophone Co.* are in any case being eroded (cf. *Cox* v *Philips Industries Ltd* [1976] 3 All ER 161).

12.3.3.7 Non-payment of money The commonest remedy for non-payment of money, and at one time the only remedy, was the action for an agreed sum (*12.2.1*). It has long been the common law rule that interest is not payable on such debts, and in its now limited form that rule was recently affirmed by the House of Lords in *President of India* v *La Pintada Cia Navegacion SA* [1984] 2 All ER 773. As a result, a plaintiff could not recover compensation for late payment of a debt, since the common law also ruled that damages for loss caused by non-payment were to be measured by the amount outstanding, making no allowance for any consequential loss (*London, Chatham and Dover Ry Co.* v *South Eastern Ry Co.* [1893] AC 429). The rule only applies to a consequential loss in the form of interest on the sum due. It does not apply to an exchange loss resulting from late payment (*President of India* v *Lips Maritime Corporation* [1987] 3 All ER 110). The position resulting from these rules was unsatisfactory, as was acknowledged by the House of Lords in the *President of India* case. Substantial reforms have been made in recent years, although there is still reason for some dissatisfaction.

For some time now the courts have had a statutory discretion to award interest on judgments in actions for an agreed sum. The current rule is contained in s.35A of the Supreme Court Act 1981, as amended by the Administration of Justice Act 1982. The discretion applies both where the court has given judgment and where the debt is paid after proceedings have been commenced but before judgment. There remains a loophole in these provisions, however, since interest is still not payable on debts which are paid late but before the commencement of proceedings. In the *President of India* case the House of Lords refused to close that loophole, although accepting that the law was unsatisfactory, since Parliament had so recently considered the matter and left it unchanged. The common law can close the loophole to some extent, however. In the first place, the parties may expressly provide in their contract for the payment of interest upon late payment of an agreed sum. Alternatively, the court may be willing to imply a term into the agreement for the payment of interest (*Minter (F.G.) & Welsh Health Technical Services Organization* (1980) 13 BLR 1: see generally *10.4*). Finally, in *Wadsworth* v *Lydall* [1981] 2 All

ER 401 the Court of Appeal ruled that the unavailability of damages for non-payment of money applied only in the case of general damages. Where the plaintiff had actually communicated to the defendant at the time of contracting information about a specific loss which would result from the non-payment of the particular debt then damages would be available. In this case

> the plaintiff was the vendor of land who intended to use £10,000 to be paid by the purchaser before a stipulated date as down-payment on the acquisition of other land. The defendant purchaser was aware of this intention, but only paid £7,200 by the stipulated date, so that the plaintiff had to borrow the balance for the down-payment. The plaintiff sought as damages the interest payable on the sum borrowed to enable the down-payment to be made, and was held to be entitled to recover such damages.

The decision turns on the two limbs of the remoteness of damage test in *Hadley v Baxendale* (1854) 9 Exch 341 (*12.3.3.3*). Unless the defendant knows or has reason to know that the plaintiff will suffer a particular loss by the non-payment of money, no damages will be recoverable. 'Reason to know' may be inferred from the terms of the contract, and the surrounding circumstances, including facts of which other people doing similar business may have been aware (*Lips Maritime Corporation* v *President of India*, [1987] 1 All ER 957 at 968, reversed on other grounds [1987] 3 All ER 110 sub nom. *President of India* v *Lips Maritime Corporation*).

12.3.4 Contractual provisions as to damages

As in many other areas of contract law, the nineteenth century view that contractual obligations were founded in the will of the parties resulted in the rule that the common law provisions as to the award of damages might be displaced by express agreement. The prima facie rule is that if the parties provide in their contract for the amount of damages to be paid upon breach, that term of the contract will be enforced to the exclusion of whatever might be the common law measure of damages. Such clauses are common in commercial contracts, especially to deal with delay in performance. There are advantages for both parties in the use of such clauses. The non-breaching party is spared the effort and possible expense of proving his loss, so that a claim for compensation will be relatively straightforward. The party who must perform has clear notice of the extent of his risk upon non-performance. The courts have nevertheless been unwilling to allow unfettered use of these clauses. There is a danger that where the damages payable are set too high the clause will have a punitive effect, which would be contrary to the essential purpose of enforcement of contractual obligations (see *12.1.1*). Further, there is a danger that disadvantageous terms as to damages might be forced by the stronger party on the other, rather than freely negotiated. The distinction between clauses which will be enforced and those which will not is expressed as a distinction between *liquidated damages clauses* (enforceable) and *penalty clauses* (unenforceable). For no very good reason, the rule against penalties is said only to apply to payments required to be made upon breach of the contract

(*Export Credits Guarantee Department* v *Universal Oil Products Co.* [1983] 2 All ER 205). Consequently, an equally punitive measure, such as a reduction in the price payable, which bore no relation to the loss actually sustained, would not be caught by the rule. Such a result is illogical, and the Court of Appeal did not allow this rule to prevent it classing as a penalty, and then refusing to enforce, a clause which upon breach required the defaulting party to retransfer property (shares) acquired under the contract to the vendor, without proper adjustment for amounts already paid towards purchase of the shares (*Jobson* v *Johnson* [1989] 1 All ER 621; *Export Credits Guarantee Department* v *Universal Oil Products* appears not to have been cited to the court).

12.3.4.1 Liquidated damages clauses The essence of a liquidated damages clause is that it should be a genuine attempt to pre-estimate the loss which will be suffered by breach (*Dunlop Pneumatic Tyre Co. Ltd* v *New Garage and Motor Co. Ltd* [1915] AC 79). Once that definition is established, however, it must be said that the identification of liquidated damages clauses is rather a process of elimination; that is, the clause will be enforced by the courts unless it falls foul of the rule against penalties (*12.3.4.2*). It must be stressed that the court is concerned with the impact of the clause rather than the form in which the parties have incorporated it into their contract. In *Cellulose Acetate Silk Co. Ltd* v *Widness Foundry (1925) Ltd* [1933] AC 20

> the contract contained a term providing for damages for late performance to be paid 'by way of penalty' at a rate of £20 per week. In fact the amount stipulated was by no means excessively greater than the loss actually sustained.

The House of Lords ignored its designation as a penalty and enforced the clause.

One function of a liquidated damages clause may be to keep the compensation payable upon breach below the amount of the loss actually sustained. For the party who must perform the advantage of knowing the precise extent of the risk of non-performance usually lies in knowing that the risk is limited. For example, in *Cellulose Acetate Silk Co. Ltd* v *Widness Foundry (1925) Ltd* damages payable under the clause amounted to £600, while the actual loss was £5,850. It was the non-breaching party who sought to avoid the clause on the ground that it was a 'penalty'. Cases of this kind raise the question whether liquidated damages clauses are a class of exemption clause, subject to the panoply of controls now existing over such clauses (see generally *10.6*). In *Suisse Atlantique Société d'Armement Maritime SA* v *NV Rotterdamsche Kolen Centrale* [1967] 1 AC 361 it was suggested that such a clause was not a limitation clause, since it fixed the amount payable irrespective of loss, so that the sum would be payable even if the loss were less than the amount stipulated. A limitation clause simply puts a ceiling on the loss recoverable, and if the loss is below that amount only the actual loss is recoverable. On the other hand, it would seem that a clause fixing damages at an amount below the lowest possible loss which can be envisaged at the time of contracting is a form of limitation clause. It may be that the area of overlap between limitation clauses and liquidated damages clauses requires further examination, and perhaps reform (see *12.3.4.3*).

12.3.4.2 The rule against penalties In *Dunlop Pneumatic Tyre Co. Ltd v New Garage and Motor Co. Ltd* [1915] AC 79 Lord Dunedin listed four tests of the distinction between liquidated damages and penalty clauses. The continuing authority of these tests was endorsed by the Privy Council in *Philips Hong Kong Ltd* v *A-G of Hong Kong*, *The Times* 15 February 1993. The tests are not exhaustive. They are only guidelines for the test of construction of the contract which the court must apply in the light of the circumstances at the time of making the contract.

The principal test is that the clause will be a penalty if the sum payable is 'extravagant and unconscionable' by comparison with the greatest loss which might be caused by the breach. In many cases this rule will be simple to apply. In *Philips Hong Kong Ltd* v *A-G of Hong Kong* (above) it was held that comparisons must be made in respect of reasonably likely eventualities, and it would not be adequate proof that a clause amounts to a penalty to show a serious disparity between amounts recoverable and loss actually sustained in wholly unlikely, hypothetical situations. One difficulty is to know whether the amount which the stipulated sum must not unconscionably exceed is the total loss to the non-breaching party, or the possibly lower sum of what would be recoverable as damages at common law. For example, the clause may provide for the recovery of damages which would otherwise be too remote (12.3.3.3). In *Robophone Facilities Ltd* v *Blank* [1966] 3 All ER 128 Diplock LJ suggested that it would be wrong to allow the penalty clause rule to be used to prevent a plaintiff contracting to be compensated for his entire loss rather than merely that which would be recoverable under the common law rules. His suggestion seems to be eminently sensible in the case of loss not otherwise recoverable because it would be too remote, since the clause would in any case amount to notice of a special loss. It must be doubted, however, whether it would be desirable to allow a plaintiff to contract out of the duty to mitigate (*12.3.3.4*). In *Lombard North Central plc* v *Butterworth* [1987] 1 All ER 267 the Court of Appeal ruled that a clause in an equipment leasing contract, which made a party defaulting on payment obligations immediately liable for all payments under the terms of the contract, would be a penalty clause unless the time of payment obligations were a condition of the contract (which normally they would not be) so that breach amounted to repudiation. Provision in the contract making the term a condition was not found to amount to a penalty (and presumably it would be subject to the rule in *Export Credits Guarantee Department* v *Universal Oil Products* [1983] 2 All ER 205: *12.3.4*)

Where the breach consists in not paying a sum of money, and the amount payable under the clause upon breach is greater than the sum owed, then the clause is said to be a penalty. This rule must, however, be read in the light of recent changes in the law relating to damages for non-payment of money (*12.3.3.7*), and it must be assumed now that only if the amount payable exceeds amounts recoverable under those rules will the clause be regarded as a penalty.

Where the contract provides for the same amount to be payable as damages in the event of several different types of breach, it is presumed that the clause is a penalty. The rationale of this presumption is simply that it is unlikely that each type of breach will result in exactly the same degree of loss, so that the clause does not represent a genuine attempt to pre-estimate the loss. On this basis, the presumption may be rebutted by showing that in all the circumstances the amount payable was a genuine pre-estimate of the loss resulting from each type of breach.

Finally, Lord Dunedin pointed out that the fact that the loss is difficult or impossible to pre-estimate does not of itself turn every liquidated damages clause into a penalty. In the *Dunlop* case itself

> the contract contained detailed provisions which might have resulted in a series of different breaches for which precise quantification of the loss in any given case might have been very difficult. The House of Lords upheld a clause making £5 payable upon each breach.

One of the main values of liquidated damages clauses is that they enable a precise figure to be put on the risk of breach, and the court should only intervene in such an agreement between the parties where it appears one is taking unfair advantage of the other.

12.3.4.3 Effect of classification as a penalty Until recently it was largely assumed that classification of a term as a penalty resulted in the clause being wholly unenforceable, and the non-breaching party being left to rely on his ordinary remedy in damages at common law. In *Jobson* v *Johnson* [1989] 1 All ER 621 the Court of Appeal ruled that the effect was for the court, in the exercise of its equitable jurisdiction against penalties, only to enforce the penal clause to an extent commensurate with the actual loss sustained by the non-breaching party (see [1989] 1 All ER 621, 633 per Nicholls LJ). Of course, in many cases the distinction is of no relevance, for the quantification of damages payable would be the same in each case. But in *Jobson* v *Johnson* the Court of Appeal relied on the exact nature of this equitable jurisdiction to impose complex terms on the plaintiff's right to a remedy, involving an election between alternative modes of proceeding, which went way beyond the mere recovery of damages.

12.3.4.4 Proposals for reform It can be argued that the law which distinguishes between liquidated damages and penalty clauses is unsatisfactory. Sometimes it seems that the distinction is merely used to justify the court's decision about whether a particular clause should be enforced, and does not enable the parties to predict whether an agreed damages clause will be enforceable. Equally, it may strike down a clause intended as an incentive to performance even when the clause has been freely negotiated between the parties. A better approach might be to follow the example of the Unfair Contract Terms Act 1977 (see generally *10.6.3*), and to treat contracts differently according to whether they are freely negotiated or the clause has been imposed, by virtue of a standard form or the superior bargaining position of one of the parties. In the former case there seems no good reason to disallow a penalty clause, since it must be assumed that the party subject to its terms must have had good reason to agree to it. In the latter case both penalty clauses and unreasonably low liquidated damages clauses might be disallowed. There is some evidence of a willingness to adopt such an approach in the advice of the Privy Council in *Philips Hong Kong Ltd* v *A-G Hong Kong, The Times,* 15 February 1993. Lord Woolf stressed the importance of not interfering with the freedom of parties to stipulate for themselves the damages recoverable upon breach, 'especially in commercial contracts'. On the other hand, he appeared to contemplate that courts should be more willing to interfere where the contract does not involve 'two parties who should be well capable of protecting their respective commercial interests'. Rather, where 'one of the parties . . . is able to dominate the other as to the choice of the terms of the contract' the courts should be more vigilant in ensuring that damages recoverable under a contract clause are not extravagant.

12.4 DEPOSITS, PREPAYMENTS AND RELIEF FROM FORFEITURE

Closely related to the rule against penalty clauses and the rules governing restitution of sums paid under contracts (*12.5 et seq.*) are those rules which govern claims to recover various forms of advance payment made in respect of a contract. The law in this area, like the law relating to penalty clauses, is not always logically defensible, and the different rules for different categories of payment set out below would benefit from a thorough revision, and from intergration with a revised set of rules on penalty clauses.

12.4.1 Deposits
Money paid in advance which is expressly designated as a deposit is not normally recoverable in the event of breach of the contract. Authority for this rule is well established; in *Howe* v *Smith* (1884) 27 ChD 89 the element of penalty embodied in the rule was invoked as a desirable incentive to performance. More recently, in *Damon Compañía Naviera SA* v *Hapag-Lloyd International SA* [1985] 1 All ER 475 the Court of Appeal, confirming the rule, found also that if the deposit remained unpaid at the time of the breach the non-breaching party was entitled to bring an action to recover payment. Although the rule against recovery of deposits may be the equivalent to the enforcement of penalty clauses, in that the amount of the deposit may far exceed the actual loss to the party entitled to retain it, it had been thought (subject only to an *obiter* statement of Denning LJ in *Stockloser* v *Johnson* [1954] 1 All ER 630 at 638) that the rule against penalties and the equitable jurisdiction to allow relief from forfeiture could not apply. The only exception appeared to be s.49(2) of the Law of Property Act 1925, which provides that in contracts for the sale or exchange of interests in land the court may, if it thinks fit, order the repayment of any deposit. However, in *Workers Trust and Merchant Bank* v *Dojap Investments* [1993] 2 All ER 370 the Privy Council imposed an important

limitation on the general principle. Lord Browne-Wilkinson accepted that a deposit is not normally recoverable because it is given in earnest of performance. Nevertheless, he went on to say that 'it is not possible for the parties to attach the incidents of a deposit to the payment of a sum of money unless such sum is reasonable as earnest money'. In the particular case, a deposit of 25 per cent had been demanded when the prevailing local rate was 10 per cent. The Privy Council advised that the deposit was unreasonable, and that the deposit should be repaid subject to a set off for any loss actually sustained.

12.4.2 Prepayments not expressed to be deposits
Where part of the contract price has been paid in advance, without that payment being expressed to be in the nature of a deposit, the payment may be recovered upon termination of the contract, subject to any set-off there may be for performance rendered before the time of discharge (*Dies* v *British & International Mining & Finance Corporation Ltd* [1939] 1 KB 724; and see more recently *Rover International Ltd* v *Cannon Film Sales Ltd (No. 3)* [1989] 3 All ER 423). It is therefore important to be able to distinguish between deposits (above) and mere prepayments, although *Dies* v *British & International Mining & Finance Corporation Ltd* is also authority for the proposition that in the event of doubt the prepayment rule will prevail.

The availability of a set-off against recovery of such prepayment raises, in extreme cases, the possibility that no recovery will ultimately be allowed, because the prepayment is wholly consumed by performance before the time of discharge for which payment remains due. This was the case in the important decision of the House of Lords in *Hyundai Heavy Industries Co.* v *Papadopolous* [1980] 2 All ER 29. The seller was able to recover an instalment of the price due in July, even though it proceeded to exercise an option to cancel the whole contract only two months later. The apparent reason for this perhaps surprising decision is that the instalment due related to work already done, rather than to work to be done in the future after the date of cancellation. On the basis of this reasoning, it should be possible to distinguish the case by careful analysis where the prepayment relates at least in part to future as opposed to past work.

12.4.3 Relief from forfeiture
Except in the case of deposits (*12.4.1*), where breach results in the breaching party losing the benefit of all payments or rights under the contract in a manner which is disproportionate to the actual breach or the loss caused by it, the law may provide relief from forfeiture. That is, Draconian consequences provided for by the contract may be set aside. Such relief is closely related to the rule against penalties, although the technical requirements for its application are very different. In two instances relief from forfeiture is available upon a statutory basis; apart from these, there is an equitable jurisdiction in the court to provide relief from forfeiture in some circumstances, but the courts take a very restrictive view of their powers in this area. Consequently, there are considerable advantages in being able to characterise a clause as amounting to a penalty, rather than

merely leading to forfeiture, since relief of some kind is then immediately available (cf. *Jobson* v *Johnson* [1989] 1 All ER 621: *12.3.4*).

12.4.3.1 Section 49(2) of the Law of Property Act 1925   Under s.49(2) of the Law of Property Act 1925, which (by s.49(3)) applies to sale or exchange of any interest in land:

> Where the court refuses to grant specific performance of a contract, or in any action for the return of a deposit, the court may, if it thinks fit, order the repayment of any deposit.

Courts have differed over the breadth of discretion afforded to them by this provision, but for a relatively recent example of its application, in which the view taken was that repayment of the deposit should be ordered whenever that would be the fairest solution between the parties, see *Universal Corporation* v *Five Ways Properties Ltd* [1979] 1 All ER 552.

12.4.3.2 The Consumer Credit Act 1974   As an express piece of consumer protection legislation, the Consumer Credit Act 1974 contains specific provisions which are akin to measures for the relief from forfeiture, especially in relation to contract terms which purport to make the purchaser/debtor liable for all payments under the agreement in the event of early termination of the contract (e.g., s.100(1) and (2)). This legislation only applies to 'regulated agreements', and detailed consideration of its application is beyond the scope of this book.

12.4.3.3 Relief from forfeiture in equity   Beyond the statutory provisions described above, there is a restricted equitable jurisdiction to relieve a defaulting party from the consequences of a contract term which purports to entitle the other to count as forfeit payments or other rights. Although there appears to be no functional difference between a deposit (as described in *12.4.3.1*) and an express clause allowing forfeiture of prepayments, it must be stressed that this jurisdiction does not extend to deposits as such. Equally, in the absence of express provision for forfeiture, the rules on prepayments explained above (*12.4.3.2*) will apply: forfeiture of such payments will not be implied. The modern foundation for this equitable jurisdiction is *Stockloser* v *Johnson* [1954] 1 All ER 630. The Court of Appeal ruled that a clause providing for forfeiture of prepayments would not be enforced if it was penal, and if to enforce it would be oppressive and unconscionable. The relief provided will usually be the allowance of more time in which to make an overdue payment, although sometimes the repayment of sums paid may be ordered. However, the House of Lords has subsequently ruled that the power to provide relief from forfeiture may only be exercised in relation to possessory or proprietary rights (*Scandinavian Trading Tanker Co. AB* v *Flota Petrolera Ecuatoriana* [1983] 2 All ER 763). It seems that this restriction is based on a policy of limiting the scope of relief from forfeiture, largely for reasons of commercial certainty. The ruling leads to fine distinctions between types of contract where the commercial purpose of the contract and the real effect of the forfeiture clause are more or less identical: e.g., *Sport International Bussum BV* v *Inter- Footwear Ltd* [1984] 2 All ER 321 (House of Lords refused relief in the case of a mere contractual licence to use trade-mark rights) and *BICC plc* v *Burndy Corporation* [1985] 1 All ER 417 (Court of Appeal allowed relief in the case of assignment of a patent right). Such fine distinctions are difficult to justify.

12.5 RESTITUTION

12.5.1 Introduction
It remains to consider two remedies which do not strictly fall within the scope of enforcement of the contractual obligations. Restitutionary remedies do not provide a response to one party's failure to satisfy the other party's expectation under the contract. Rather, they seek to restore money paid or the value of a benefit conferred in circumstances in which no contract exists, or in which there is no longer any obligation to perform under an admitted contract. Thus, their availability is not solely dependent upon the existence of a breach of contract, although where there has been breach the non-breaching party may have to decide whether an action for his expectation loss or a restitutionary remedy would provide a better level of compensation. It should be noted that the law of restitution covers a much broader field than just the fringes of the law of contract, and in its entirety is a field of study all of its own.

12.5.2 Total failure of consideration
A party may recover money paid in anticipation of a contractual performance which the other party has failed to provide where there has been a total failure of consideration, even in the absence of breach. Performance may be impossible because the contract has been frustrated (*11.4*), or because unknown to the parties the subject-matter of the contract had been destroyed before the time of contracting (*7.3.1*). In each case the promisee may recover money paid in advance despite the fact that the failure of performance does not amount to breach. Indeed, most claims for total failure of consideration do not arise out of breach by the other party. In the event of breach the normal reaction will be to claim damages for lost expectation, but the restitutionary remedy is available as an alternative (see *12.5.2.3*). Special rules apply where there is no performance because the contract is illegal (see *8.7.5*). The special rules only apply, however, between the parties to the agreement which is tainted with illegality. In *Lipkin Gorman* v *Karpnale Ltd* [1992] 4 All ER 512 the House of Lords had to deal with a claim to recover money stolen from the plaintiffs and then paid to the defendants in good faith but under a contract which was void under s.18 of the Gaming Act 1845 (see *8.7.2.1*). In restating the modern law of restitution Lords Goff and Templeman agreed that the essential question was whether the defendants had been unjustly enriched. That in turn depended upon whether, irrespective of their good faith in receiving the money, the defendants had given good consideration for it. It was found that they could not have given valuable consideration, because the contract was void. The mere fact of honouring gaming debts did not amount to providing consideration; as a matter of law it was no more than a gift from the gambling club to the client.

Consequently, the unjust enrichment was established, and the restitutionary claim succeeded, subject only to the defence of change of position, recognised as a general defence to restitutionary claims by the House of Lords in this case.

12.5.2.1 Relationship to consideration as 'promise' It will be recalled that in relation to the formation of contracts 'consideration' was described as constituted not merely by an exchange of performances, but also by an exchange of promises. It might be thought, therefore, that where it is possible to show agreement there can never be a failure of consideration. However, where 'consideration' is used in the technical sense of giving rise to a restitutionary remedy upon total failure, it must be understood as referring to *performance* of whatever was promised in the agreement. In *Fibrosa Spolka Akcyjna* v *Fairbairn Lawson Combe Barbour Ltd* [1943] AC 32 (see *11.4.5.1*) Viscount Simon LC explained:

> [I]n the law relating to the formation of contract, the promise to do a thing may often be the consideration; but, when one is considering the law of failure of consideration and of the quasi-contractual right to recover money on that ground, it is, generally speaking, not the promise which is referred to as the consideration, but the performance of the promise. The money was paid to secure performance and, if performance fails, the inducement which brought about the payment is not fulfilled. If this were not so, there could never be any recovery of money, for failure of consideration, by the payer of the money in return for a promise of future performance.

The *Fibrosa* case is a classic example of the operation of the doctrine.

> The seller was prevented from completing performance of a contract by the outbreak of war, since the buyer was in enemy occupied territory. The buyer had paid part of the price in advance, and since it had received none of the promised performance it was entitled to repayment of that money because there had been a total failure of consideration.

For a further, more modern example, relying on this explanation of total failure of consideration, see *Rover International Ltd* v *Cannon Film Sales Ltd (No. 3)* [1989] 3 All ER 423.

12.5.2.2 Partial failure of performance The general rule is that where the promisee has received some of the performance to which he was entitled under the contract, so that the failure is only partial, he is not able to recover money paid in advance (*Whincup* v *Hughes* (1871) LR 6 CP 78). The explanation of this rule is usually said to be that it is impossible to apportion the consideration between the performed and unperformed parts of the contract. For this reason, where performance is divisible (*10.5.2.1*), so that the money paid can easily be split *pro rata* among the several parts, recovery of part of the money for partial failure of consideration will be allowed (*Ebrahim Dawood Ltd* v *Heath (Est. 1927) Ltd* [1961] 2 Lloyd's Rep 512).

It may also be possible for a promisee to convert a partial failure of consideration into a total failure of consideration by returning any benefit he has received by such performance as has taken place. He may particularly wish to do so if of the opinion that a restitutionary remedy would be preferable to a claim for damages (*12.4.2.3*). In some circumstances, of course, restoration of the benefit will be impossible. Where building work has been done on the promisee's land, but not completed, the promisee cannot return the work done (cf *Sumpter* v *Hedges* [1898] 1 QB 673: *10.5.3.1*). If, however, it is impossible to return the performance received for some reason connected with the other party's breach there will be no obstacle to recovery of payment on the basis of total failure of consideration.

In some circumstances restoration of any performance received will not convert partial into total failure of consideration, because the promisee has had the benefit of use between the time of performance and the time of its return (*Hunt* v *Silk* (1804) 5 East 449). This rule may sometimes appear to conflict with cases in the sale of goods, where the courts will find total failure of consideration even when the good in question has been in the possession of and used by the promisee over a substantial period of time. The reason is that in the sale of goods the essential performance is the provision of good title to the thing sold, and the courts take the view that use of the good in question is irrelevant to the contract of sale (*Rowland* v *Divall* [1923] 2 KB 500). This rule makes good sense in the case of a dealer, who purchases to resell and who must therefore have title, but does not seem right in the case of a consumer, who purchases in order to use the good in question.

12.5.2.3 Restitution versus damages Where the total failure of consideration is due to breach by the other party, the promisee will normally claim damages for loss of expectation, since he will probably wish to recover the cost of mitigating his loss by resort to the market, and he may wish to recover damages for lost profits. If the contract was an advantageous one, then the expectation measure of damages will almost certainly be more attractive than recovering money paid. If, however, the plaintiff had made a bad bargain, so that he would have made a loss on the contract had it been performed, he may be glad of the opportunity provided by the total failure of consideration to retrieve intact the investment he made.

12.5.3 *Quantum meruit*

Quantum meruit is a remedy under which a party who has provided a benefit and who for some reason cannot obtain payment under a contract may recover the reasonable value of the benefit provided. It may apply where there is no contract, or where the contractual provisions as to remuneration are inapplicable.

12.5.3.1 *Quantum meruit* in the absence of contract Where one party confers a benefit on another with the intention on both sides that that benefit will be paid for, then, in the absence of any contract between the parties, the former will be able to recover reasonable remuneration from the latter under the restitutionary remedy of *quantum meruit*. A recent example of the operation of this rule is *British Steel Corp.* v *Cleveland Bridge & Engineering Co. Ltd* [1984] 3 All ER 504 (see *5.6.2*).

> Work had begun on a major construction before all the elements of the contract had been agreed. Both sides confidently expected to reach agreement without difficulty. Final agreement was never reached. The plaintiffs ceased performance and claimed a *quantum meruit* for the work they had done. Their claim succeeded.

Remuneration on the basis of *quantum meruit* may also be recoverable where performance is rendered under a contract which, unknown to both parties, is void. In *Craven-Ellis* v *Canons Ltd* [1936] 2 KB 403

> the plaintiff had worked as managing director of a company without being appointed in the legally proper manner. His contract was therefore void, but he was able to recover the reasonable value of his work.

Similar rules apply in the case of work done by companies under contracts which are void because at the time the contract was made the company had not been incorporated, and so had no legal existence (*Rover International Ltd* v *Cannon Film Sales Ltd (No. 3)* [1989] 3 All ER 423).

12.5.3.2 *Quantum meruit* despite the contract   Where there is a contract between the parties it is fundamental to the law of contract that payment is to be determined according to the terms of the contract. The courts must not interfere with the parties' agreement. However, in limited circumstances that general rule is displaced and the court will allow a *quantum meruit* remedy despite the existence of a contract.

In the first place, where the contract fails to provide for the payment to be made, a reasonable price is payable. This rule has now been embodied in statute (s.8 Sale of Goods Act 1979; s.15 Supply of Goods and Services Act 1982). It is submitted that the same applies where the contract provides a price-fixing mechanism which for some unforeseen reason fails to work (see *5.6.4*).

In an entire contract partial performance does not entitle the party who breaches by abandoning performance before completion to any payment under the contract (see *10.5.3.1*). Where, however, the non-breaching party voluntarily accepts a benefit conferred by partial performance before the contract has been abandoned, the party who has breached may recover the reasonable value of the benefit conferred. Conversely, where the non-breaching party confers a benefit on the other party before the latter's breach, the former may recover the value of that benefit under a *quantum meruit* rather than bringing an action for damages (*Slowey* v *Lodder* (1901) 20 NZLR 331, affirmed by the Privy Council at [1904] AC 442). By so doing, the non-breaching party may be able to avoid the consequences of having made a bad bargain.

THIRTEEN
Privity of contract

13.1   CONTRACTS, THIRD PARTY BENEFICIARIES AND PRIVITY

The examination of the law of contract in Part II assumed almost always that the type of contract under consideration involved two parties who were each to perform a stipulated obligation towards the other. From that assumption it followed that the enforcement of the obligations promised in the contract was a principal concern of the contracting parties themselves, and the question whether any other person may be entitled to enforce performance of the contract did not arise. This concentration on the effect of bilateral contracts between the contracting parties is inevitable, since that is the area in which most contractual disputes arise. Nevertheless, it is easy to imagine situations in which one party has stipulated in the contract that performance be made towards some other person, and examples of this type of contract have been noted in passing (see *6.3.5.4* and *12.2.2.1*). Part III considers the rules of the law of contract, and related rules, applicable to contracts which stipulate a benefit for a third party.

This type of contract may most easily be described in terms of a triangular relationship. The contract is negotiated and made

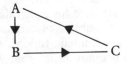

between A and B, but B stipulates that A's performance should be made to C (the third party). The questions which arise are whether C may enforce A's promise to perform to his benefit; and, alternatively, whether B may enforce A's promise. Related problems arise when B purports to stipulate not for a benefit to accrue to C from A's performance, but for C to perform B's obligations under the contract.

The general principle is that only the parties to the contract are bound by or are entitled to a remedy for enforcement of the obligations under the contract (*13.2*). This rule is known as the doctrine of privity of contract. The effect of the doctrine may be demonstrated by reference to a classic case from the law of torts. In *Donoghue v Stevenson* [1932] AC 562

the appellant and a friend went into a café, where the friend ordered a bottle of
ginger beer for the appellant. The drink came in an opaque bottle. Part of the contents
was poured out and the appellant consumed it. When the rest was poured out a
partly decomposed snail was found. The appellant suffered nervous shock and illness,
and wished to recover compensation on that account.

She chose to proceed against the manufacturer of the ginger beer, and therefore
had to claim in tort because there was no contract between her and the
manufacturer. Had she wished to proceed against the café owner she would
still have had to claim in tort, despite the fact that there was clearly a contract
between the café owner and her friend which equally clearly stipulated for
the benefit of the contract to pass to the appellant. Part of that benefit would
include the statutory implied term of merchantable quality, which had been
breached (see *10.4.3.2*).

In other words, there was no difficulty in finding by way of implication
from the facts of the case that the café owner's contract with the friend included
an undertaking to supply merchantable ginger beer to the appellant, but the
doctrine of privity of contract was a bar to the success of an action in contract
by the appellant. It might also have been possible to find a stipulation regarding
quality in the contract between the café owner and the manufacturer, intended
to benefit the former's customers generally, but the privity doctrine would
make such an exercise pointless. The unavailability of an action in contract
against either manufacturer or retailer led to the development, in *Donoghue*
v *Stevenson*, of the modern tort of negligence, under which the plaintiff may
recover compensation for loss suffered as a result of breach of a duty of care
owed to him by the defendant.

13.2 PRIVITY: THE BASIC RULE

The doctrine of privity of contract states that a person may not enforce a
contractual promise, even when the promise was expressly made in his favour,
if he is not a party to the contract. It is also the rule that a person who is
not a party to a contract may not have his rights diminished by that contract.
Both aspects of the doctrine are subject to certain exceptions, although the
exceptions to the latter rule are limited. Indeed, the rationale of the latter
rule is easy to understand, since any other rule would be an infringement
of individual liberty. The former rule, however, is less readily explained (but
see *13.2.3*). It was confirmed in English law in the early nineteenth century
(cf. *Price* v *Easton* (1833) 4 B & Ad 433). Modern authority for the rule is
found in the decision of the House of Lords in *Dunlop Pneumatic Tyre Co.
Ltd* v *Selfridge & Co. Ltd* [1915] AC 847.

> The appellants had sold tyres to a distributor on terms that he would not resell
> them at a price lower than the appellants' list price, and on terms that if sold to
> a trade buyer the distributor would obtain a similar undertaking from that buyer.
> The distributor resold some tyres to the respondents who gave the required
> undertaking, agreeing to pay £5 liquidated damages to the appellants for each tyre

sold in breach of that undertaking. The respondents sold tyres below the list price, and the appellants sued to recover the agreed damages.

In a much quoted passage, Viscount Haldane LC said:

> My Lords, in the Law of England certain principles are fundamental. One is that only a person who is a party to a contract can sue on it. Our law knows nothing of a *jus quaesitum tertio* arising by way of contract. Such a right may be conferred by way of property, as, for example, under a trust, but it cannot be conferred on a stranger to a contract as a right to enforce the contract *in personam*. A second principle is that if a person with whom a contract not under seal has been made is to be able to enforce it consideration must have been given by him to the promisor or to some other person at the promisor's request.

Viscount Haldane's statement of the privity doctrine is usually regarded as comprising two elements, one relating to the agreement component of a contract and the other relating to the consideration component. This division may be helpful in analysing cases which raise a question of privity, but it seems unlikely that it has much real impact on the outcome of such cases.

13.2.1 The agreement component

It will not normally be difficult to establish whether a person was a party to the agreement in question. It is a simple question of fact whether the person took part as a principal in the negotiations which resulted in agreement. Occasional difficulty may arise when a beneficiary under the contract has signed the contractual document, and it is disputed whether he signed as a party to the agreement or merely as someone interested under the agreement (cf. *Coulls* v *Bagot's Executor & Trustee Co.* (1967) 119 CLR 460: *6.3.4.2*).

This element of the privity doctrine may be avoided by the collateral contract device. In *Shanklin Pier Ltd* v *Detel Products Ltd* [1951] 2 KB 854

> the plaintiffs had hired a firm to paint their pier, and on the strength of a representation made by the defendants had instructed the firm to use the defendants' paint. The paint did not last anywhere near as long as the defendants had represented, but the contract for the purchase of the paint was between the firm of painters and the defendants, and so could not afford the plaintiffs a remedy.

The court nevertheless found there to be a collateral contract between the plaintiffs and the defendants to the effect that the paint would last for seven years. It is important to note, however, that the requirement that the party seeking to enforce the promise be a party to the consideration is still present. In this case the plaintiffs had furnished consideration for the defendants' undertaking by instructing the firm of painters to use the defendants' paint.

342

Privity of contract

13.2.2 The consideration component
The rule that consideration must move from the promisee has already been considered (see *6.3.4*). It appears to originate in the early privity case of *Tweddle v Atkinson* (1861) 1 B & S 393, and appears to have been the *ratio* of the decision of the House of Lords in *Dunlop Pneumatic Tyre Co. Ltd v Selfridge & Co. Ltd* [1915] AC 847 (above).

13.2.3 Critique of the rule
The reasons for the privity doctrine are not clear. It has sometimes been suggested that it rests on a principle of mutuality (cf. *12.2.2.3*), to the effect that it would be unfair to allow a person to sue on a contract who cannot be sued by the other party (cf. *Tweddle v Atkinson* (1861) 1 B & S 393). It is also sometimes suggested that it would be undesirable to allow third party rights to be created by contract, since that would restrict the freedom of the parties subsequently to amend or rescind their agreement (cf. *Re Schebsman* [1944] Ch 83: *13.5.1*). Alternatively, it is suggested that third party beneficiaries are frequently gratuitous recipients of the benefit in their favour, and so the rule is closely related to the doctrine of consideration. Each of these explanations is open to objection, either on the ground that provided the contract is freely negotiated there is no particular reason why contracting parties should not undertake obligations which lack mutuality or which restrict their future freedom to act, or on the ground that the explanation does not account for the full extent of the rule.

Whatever the explanation of the rule may be, it is far from universally popular, and it is not found in many other legal systems, including some closely related to our own. The civil law has always provided for the enforceability of stipulations to the benefit of non-parties, and many United States jurisdictions also so provide. In this country, in *Dunlop Pneumatic Tyre Co. Ltd v Selfridge & Co. Ltd* [1915] AC 847 Lord Dunedin, who felt compelled to agree with Viscount Haldane in finding against the appellants, said:

> I confess that this case is to my mind apt to nip any budding affection which one might have had for the doctrine of consideration. For the effect of that doctrine in the present case is to make it possible for a person to snap his fingers at a bargain deliberately made, a bargain not in itself unfair, and which the person seeking to enforce it has a legitimate interest to enforce.

Similar sentiments were expressed by Lord Scarman in *Woodar Investment Development Ltd v Wimpey Construction (UK) Ltd* [1980] 1 All ER 571. Indeed, in 1937 the Law Revision Committee in its 6th Interim Report (Cmd 5449) recommended that stipulations for third party benefits in contracts be enforceable by the third party. A similar call for reform is made in the Law Commission's Consultation Paper No. 121: *Privity of Contract: Contracts for the Benefit of Third Parties* (1991), although we must await the final report before commenting on the proposals. Despite Lord Scarman's view in the *Woodar Investment* case that it was open to the House of Lords to reconsider the privity doctrine, it may be that it is too firmly established in English law to be abolished other than by statute. Equally, it may be that the doctrine is not perceived to cause very much harm, since determined parties may overcome its effect, so that there is no pressing claim for the necessary Parliamentary time for statutory reform.

13.3   THE EFFECT OF THE PRIVITY DOCTRINE

13.3.1   Effect between the contracting parties

It is important to remember that the privity doctrine does not make a contract providing for a third party benefit a nullity. The contract is valid between the contracting parties, and the usual remedies are available. It may, therefore, be possible for the contract to be enforced by action by the promisee even if the third party beneficiary cannot himself enforce the contract (see *13.3.2.1*).

13.3.1.1   Promisee's action for damages   The difficulty with an action for damages in relation to breach of a contract providing for a third party benefit is that the promisee may usually only recover damages for his own loss. If the performance to be provided by the other party was intended entirely for the benefit of the third party the law takes the view that there is no loss to the promisee resulting from the breach, so that damages will be purely nominal (*Beswick* v *Beswick* [1968] AC 58). Of course, if the promisee were to receive some benefit from the other party's performance in addition to the benefit intended for the third party, then that loss would be recoverable under the normal rules (see *12.3*), but he would still be unable to recover for the third party's loss. If the promisee were to be under a legal obligation to compensate the third party in the event of non-performance by the other contracting party (e.g. as a result of a contract between promisee and third party), then that obligation would amount to a real loss to the promisee, and substantial damages would be recoverable on that account. It is open to question whether payment to the third party by the promisee on the strength of a perceived *moral* obligation to provide compensation would also be a recoverable loss.

In recent years it has been suggested that the promisee should in any case be able to recover damages for the loss suffered by the third party. If the third party were then able to compel the promisee to hand over the damages recovered (see *13.3.2.2*), such a remedy would effectively side-step the privity doctrine. Such a claim by the promisee appears to have been allowed by the Court of Appeal in *Jackson* v *Horizon Holidays Ltd* [1975] 3 All ER 92.

> The plaintiff had booked a package holiday for himself and his family. The holiday originally booked was unavailable, and the substitute holiday fell well short of the standard promised. The plaintiff brought an action for breach of contract. The defendant holiday company admitted liability, but challenged the trial judge's award of damages of £1,100, which was just less than the full cost of the holiday.

In the Court of Appeal the award was upheld. Lord Denning MR said that the award was excessive as compensation of the plaintiff's loss alone, but was a correct assessment of the aggregate loss of the whole family. The plaintiff was entitled to recover damages for loss suffered by the family members on whose behalf he had entered into the contract. The other members of the court, although upholding the award, did not openly state that it represented compensation for loss suffered by the other members of the family as well as by the plaintiff.

Lord Denning MR regarded *Jackson* v *Horizon Holidays Ltd* as an example of a general principle allowing the promisee to recover damages on behalf of third party beneficiaries. This view was disapproved in *Woodar Investment Development Ltd* v *Wimpey Construction (UK) Ltd* [1980] 1 All ER 571.

> The plaintiffs agreed to sell some land to the defendants for £850,000. It was a term of the contract that the defendant should pay £150,000 of the price to a third party. The defendants failed to go ahead with the purchase, and the plaintiffs claimed damages for what they said was a repudiatory breach.

The House of Lords found that the defendants had not repudiated the contract, but went on to discuss the privity issue. While not entirely satisfied with the privity doctrine (see *13.2.3*), they denied the existence of a general principle allowing the promisee to recover damages for loss suffered by the third party beneficiary. They did not, however, overrule the actual decision in *Jackson* v *Horizon Holidays Ltd*. Lord Wilberforce thought that the decision probably belonged to a special category of cases calling for special treatment, where one party contracts for a benefit to be shared equally among a group. Transactions which possibly fall within this special category are 'contracting for family holidays, ordering meals in restaurants for a party, hiring a taxi for a group'.

13.3.1.2 Specific performance In *Beswick* v *Beswick* [1968] AC 58 the fact that the loss suffered by the promisee was negligible, so that damages would be purely nominal, was said to be good reason for awarding the discretionary remedy of specific performance (for the facts of this case see *12.2.2.1*).

This remedy is undoubtedly the best suited to achieving the promisee's original contractual intention of conferring a benefit on the third party, but it is not without limitations. In the first place, as a general remedy specific performance is subject to restrictions (see *12.2.2.3*) which do not exist in the case of damages. Moreover, in *Beswick* v *Beswick* it was a happy coincidence that the widow had been appointed administratrix of the husband's estate, since she then had no problem of persuading the promisee to bring the action for specific performance. Since it appears that the third party cannot compel the promisee to act (*13.3.2.2*), the remedy of specific performance will only be available when it suits the promisee to enforce the contract.

13.3.1.3 Enforcement of negative undertakings Where the contractual term breached is in the form of a negative undertaking (a promise to refrain from doing something) the obvious remedy is an injunction (*12.2.3*), which is a form of specific relief similar to specific performance designed to prevent actions rather than to enforce performance. It would appear to be consistent with the reasoning in *Beswick v Beswick* [1968] AC 58 if an injunction were to be available to a promisee in appropriate circumstances in the same way that specific performance was in that case. Where the negative undertaking is a promise not to sue the third party the correct procedure is not to seek an injunction, but to ask the court to stay the proceedings which have been brought in contravention of the promise. The same reasoning should still apply. However, in *Gore v Van Der Lann* [1967] 2 QB 31 the Court of Appeal said that, even where there was a definite promise not to sue the third party, the promisee would only be granted a stay of proceedings if he had a sufficient interest in the enforcement of the promise. Such an interest would only arise if, for example, the promisee's failure to enforce the promise would result in him incurring a legal liability to the third party. This decision is somewhat narrower in scope than the corresponding decision in *Beswick v Beswick*.

In the subsequent case of *Snelling v John G. Snelling Ltd* [1973] 1 QB 87 the requirement of sufficient interest appears to have been ignored by the court.

> Three brothers each loaned money to the family company, and subsequently agreed among themselves not to seek to recover such loans should any of them resign from the company. The plaintiff resigned and brought an action against the company to recover money loaned to it. The other brothers applied to be joined as defendants to the action, and then counterclaimed for a declaration that the plaintiff was not entitled to recover the sums in question.

In theory, the plaintiff should have succeeded against the company, since the company could not enforce the stipulation made on its behalf. On the other hand, the brothers were entitled to succeed on their counterclaim. Ormrod J resolved this apparent impasse by staying the proceedings, since in reality the plaintiff had lost his action. The two brothers were under no legal liability to the company should the third fail to keep his promise to refrain from recovering the money owing to him, so that it is not easy to see what was the sufficient interest which they had in seeking enforcement of the promise. Nevertheless, the decision is more in keeping with the reasoning which prevailed in *Beswick v Beswick*, and for that reason it may be followed in the future.

13.3.1.4 Restitution Where the promisor's failure to perform to the benefit of the third party is total it may be possible for the promisee to obtain a restitutionary remedy against him (see *12.4*). Such a remedy would not avail the third party as a means of enforcement of the promise.

13.3.2 Effect between third party and contracting parties

13.3.2.1 Remedies against the promisor The essence of the privity doctrine is that the third party cannot enforce the contractual term providing for a benefit to be conferred on him (*13.2*). Unless, therefore, the third party can show that the case falls within one of the evasions of (*13.4*), or exceptions to (*13.5*), the privity doctrine, no remedy is available to him against the promisor.

13.3.2.2   Relations with the promisee   The third party's relations with the promisee are most likely to be an issue where after the time of contracting the promisee changes his mind about his intention to confer a benefit on the third party. The result of such a change of mind might be either a refusal to bring an action against the promisor for specific performance or, if damages were recoverable on behalf of the third party, a refusal to hand over the sum recovered. Lord Denning MR believed that the third party could prevent both such refusals. In the Court of Appeal in *Beswick* v *Beswick* [1966] Ch 538 he suggested that the third party could compel the promisee to bring the action by starting proceedings himself and joining the promisee as co-defendant. This procedure was rejected by the majority in the Court of Appeal, however, and their view is the more orthodox. In *Jackson* v *Horizon Holidays Ltd* [1975] 3 All ER 92 Lord Denning suggested that when the plaintiff recovered damages on behalf of the third party beneficiaries under the contract he held them as money had and received for the use of the third parties, who in theory could therefore recover them from him by legal action if he refused to hand them over. Subject to the proviso that such damages appear rarely to be recoverable (*13.3.1.1*), Lord Denning's suggestion would seem to be correct.

13.4   MEANS OF CIRCUMVENTING THE PRIVITY DOCTRINE

The appellant in *Donoghue* v *Stevenson* [1932] AC 562 (*13.1*) was able to avoid the effect of the privity doctrine by framing her action in tort. It is by no means always possible to avoid the doctrine in this way, since it depends upon being able to prove negligence and in any case may not result in the award of compensation for expectation loss (see *4.2.2.1*). Although English law flirted with the idea of permitting evasion of the privity doctrine by means of the tort of negligence (in the House of Lords' decision in *Junior Books Ltd* v *Veitchi Co Ltd* [1983] 1 AC 520), that development was rapidly abandoned, and Lord Brandon's dissenting speech has become the restored orthodoxy. In a line of cases culminating in the decision of the House of Lords in *D & F Estates Ltd* v *Church Commissioners for England* [1989] AC 177, it has become clear that the existence of a contract between the defendant and a third party (as in a subcontractor/main contractor relationship) will usually make the court unwilling to find that the defendant is also liable in tort in an independent obligation to the plaintiff (e.g., the building owner). In any case, where such a tortious obligation is shown to exist, it will not allow the recovery of pure economic loss such as the diminished value of work done, and recovery will normally be restricted to loss resulting from physical damage. Some further exceptions to the privity doctrine exist within the law of contract, and are considered below (see *13.5*). These exceptions are, however, of relatively limited impact. More significant inroads into the privity doctrine are made by the devices considered in this section, which although related to contract are independent legal concepts. In each case the device enables a benefit to be conferred on a third party who was not apparently a party to the making of the contract.

13.4.1 Assignment and agency
The law of assignment is considered in detail in Chapter 14, and the law of agency in Chapter 15. Each makes an important contribution to the commercial world. Although not strictly exceptions to the privity doctrine, they are contrary to the spirit of that rule, and have been developed to meet the practical needs of those in business, for whom the privity doctrine is unduly restricting.

13.4.2 Trusts
The trust is a device developed by the Court of Chancery long before the Judicature Act 1875 (see *1.2.1.1*). It allows a party to pass property to a second party, while stipulating that the second party must hold the property for the benefit of a third. That stipulation is enforceable by the third party. In terms of the triangular relationship outlined above (*13.1*), A (the trustee) receives property from B over which B has declared a trust in favour of C (the beneficiary or *cestui que trust*). C is then able to enforce the terms of the trust to prevent A dealing with the property other than in a manner which is to C's benefit.

The trust device was not recognised by the common law before the Judicature Act 1875. Although the relationship between the party declaring the trust (B) and the trustee (A) is not necessarily contractual, where it is, the device is inconsistent with the privity doctrine. The Court of Chancery had developed the trust in response to issues of property and conscience arising out of such cases. Chancery took the view that a properly constituted trust had the effect of actually transferring and splitting the ownership of the property in question. The legal owner (i.e. under the common law rules) was the trustee. But the effect of constitution of the trust was to make the third party the beneficial owner of the property. To allow the third party to enforce the trust was not, therefore, to allow the enforcement of a contractual right to acquire the property. The property belonged to the third party from the moment of constitution of the trust, and enforcement of the trust by him was necessary to prevent improper interference with his right, which was similar in nature to a property right. In turn, the trustee could not as a matter of good conscience interfere with that right. The right of the beneficial owner could only be lost by virtue of the acquisition of the trust property by a bona fide purchaser for value who had no notice, actual or constructive, of the trust over the property (*Pilcher v Rawlins* (1872) 7 Ch App 259).

There are four requirements of a properly constituted trust (*Halsbury's Laws of England*, 4th edn., Butterworth, 1984). There must be property which is capable of being subjected to a trust. Property includes not only land and goods but also rights, such as a right under a contract, which are known as *choses in action*. There must be a declaration of, or disposition on, trust by a competent person which demonstrates a certain intention that a trust be created. There must also be certainty of property and of object; that is, it must be possible to determine the property to which the trust attaches and the purposes for which the trust was created. Finally, the declaration or disposition must comply with any statutory requirements regarding evidence.

The most significant aspect of the trust as an exception to the privity doctrine arises where one party declares himself to be a trustee on behalf of a third party of a right to performance owed to him by the other contracting party. That is, in terms of the triangular relationship outlined above (*13.1*), where B declares *himself* to be trustee on behalf of C of the performance due to him under the contract from A. This situation is considered below (see *13.5.1*).

13.4.3 Negotiable instruments
The negotiable instrument is a device originally developed by the law merchant to overcome the privity doctrine and certain commercial disadvantages inherent in the device of assignment. In the case of assignment the assignee of a contractual right is at the very least inadequately protected unless notice of the assignment is given to the original debtor each time the right is assigned (see *14.2.1.2* and *14.3.2.2*). Moreover, the assignee takes the right which has been assigned 'subject to equities' (*14.4.1*), which means that any defences enjoyed by the original debtor against the assignor are equally valid against the assignee. Thus, an assigned right may not be worth its face value if the original debtor is entitled to a set-off against the assignor. For example, returning to the triangular relationship outlined above (*13.1*), if B agrees to sell goods to A for £100, but the goods delivered are reduced in value to £80 by a breach of warranty of quality, the fact that B has assigned to C the right to recover payment from A will not entitle C to recover any more than the £80 which B could have recovered in his own right.

If, however, A's obligation to pay is recorded in a document ('instrument') which is recognised by the law as 'negotiable', then B may transfer the right to recover the amount recorded in the instrument to C by simple delivery (i.e. by handing it over), or perhaps by indorsement and delivery (e.g. by signing it and then handing it over). There is no need to give notice of the transfer to the original debtor (A), and it may be transferred several times before the debt which it represents is collected from A. Moreover, the particular advantage of the negotiable instrument is that the transferee(s) do not take 'subject to equities' *provided* they receive the instrument for value and without notice of any defect in title which may have arisen before they became 'holder in due course' of the instrument. Common forms of negotiable instrument are bills of exchange (of which the most familiar example is the cheque) and promissory notes (of which the most familiar example is the bank note). These are now regulated by the Bills of Exchange Act 1882. It would be pointless to list all other forms of negotiable instrument, but they include certain forms of bond and share certificates.

13.4.3.1 The requirements of negotiability It is sometimes said that there are four requirements of negotiability:

(a) that the right expressed in the instrument is to be transferable upon delivery (with indorsement where necessary);
(b) that the holder of the instrument for the time being has the right to collect payment from the original debtor;
(c) that the holder for the time being, if taking for value and without notice, does not take subject to equities; and

(d)   that the instrument is of a type recognised by the law as negotiable.

However, the first three elements are not requirements but statements of the legal effect of the recognition that the instrument is negotiable. There is really only one requirement of negotiability, which is that the instrument is one which it can be shown is recognised by commercial custom, and hence by the law, to be negotiable (*Crouch* v *Credit Foncier of England Ltd* (1873) LR 8 QB 374). It is still quite possible for new instruments to acquire the quality of negotiability by development of a new commercial custom; the category is not restricted to customs developed in the distant past (*Goodwin* v *Robarts* (1875) LR 10 Exch 337). On the other hand, the mere fact that an instrument falls within a category of instruments generally regarded as negotiable does not prevent a particular instrument from being denied negotiability by express words (s.8(1) Bills of Exchange Act 1882).

13.4.3.2   The position of holder in due course   Negotiable instruments provide a means of circumventing the privity doctrine because the original contract debt is enforceable not only by the other contracting party, but by any other person for the time being holding the instrument who has been constituted holder in due course. The position of the holder in due course is strengthened still further by the fact that if the party primarily liable on the instrument fails to pay he may if necessary bring an action against all previous signatories of the instrument (s.38(2) Bills of Exchange Act 1882).

A party is holder in due course if he receives the instrument for value and in good faith, provided it is complete and regular on its face (s.29(1) Bills of Exchange Act 1882), and is in a deliverable state (s.31(3), (4)). The requirement that the transfer be made for value is considerably more relaxed than the requirement of consideration in contracts generally. In the first place, provided value has been given at some time the holder for the time being is deemed to have given value (s.27(2) of the 1882 Act). Moreover, negotiable instruments are an exception to the general rule against past consideration (s.27(1)(b); cf. *6.3.3.3*). The requirement of good faith is the same as that in other parts of the law: the transferee must not have acquired the instrument by fraud, duress, undue influence or other unacceptable behaviour, nor must he have acquired it in the knowledge that it was already tainted with such defects before it came into his hands (cf. s.30(2) of the 1882 Act). The requirement that the instrument be complete and regular on its face poses little difficulty. It covers such defects as omission on the instrument of a payee or the amount payable. The requirement that the instrument be in a deliverable state is more complex. It relates to the need in certain circumstances for the instrument to be indorsed for the delivery to be effective. An instrument made payable to the bearer (a 'bearer bill') does not require indorsement in order to be negotiated, and so is always in a deliverable state. But an instrument made payable to a named person, or to a named person 'or order' (an 'order bill'), cannot be negotiated unless indorsed, and the fact of indorsement puts the bill in a deliverable state. Transfer of an order bill without indorsement would remove one of the essential characteristics of negotiability, that the holder acquires the instrument free from equities.

13.5 EXCEPTIONS TO THE PRIVITY DOCTRINE

We have already considered devices, some of which may have had their origin
in contract but all of which must now be regarded as conceptually independent,
which may be used to circumvent the privity doctrine (*13.4*). In this section
we shall consider genuine exceptions to the privity doctrine.

13.5.1 Trust of rights created by contract

We saw above (*13.4.2*) that the concept of privity is restricted to contracts,
and does not extend to trusts. A trust may attach to property of any kind,
including a *chose in action*, which is a form of intangible property such as
a right to enforce an obligation. It follows from that definition that a right
under a contract is a chose in action, and thus may be subject to a trust.
The possibility is raised, therefore, that the promisee under a contract might
declare himself trustee of the benefit of the promise in question on behalf
of a third party, and by that means avoid the privity doctrine. This device
was used successfully during the nineteenth century (cf. *Lloyd's* v *Harper* (1880)
16 ChD 290), and its existence as a means of avoiding the privity doctrine
was acknowledged by Viscount Haldane LC in *Dunlop Pneumatic Tyre Co.
Ltd* v *Selfridge & Co. Ltd* [1915] AC 847 in the passage previously quoted
(*13.2*).

13.5.1.1 Effect of a trust of a contractual right Where a trust of a
contractual right is found to have been created the principal effect is to permit
the third party to enforce the benefit. For example, in *Les Affréteurs Réunis
SA* v *Leopold Walford (London) Ltd* [1919] AC 801

> a charterparty between shipowner and charterer provided that the shipowner would
> pay a commission of 3 per cent to the broker who had negotiated the contract for
> the parties. When the shipowner failed to pay, the broker brought an action to
> recover the commission, although he was not a party to the contract.

The House of Lords accepted that it was the practice of the shipping trade
in such cases for the charterer to sue to enforce the promise of commission
as trustee for the broker. Since the shipowners were willing to allow the case
to be treated as having been brought upon such an action, the broker succeeded
in recovering the commission.

The third party's action to enforce the contract should normally be brought
in the name of the trustee, but as *Les Affréteurs Réunis SA* v *Leopold Walford
(London) Ltd* shows, the promisor may waive that requirement, in which case
the third party may bring the action in his own name. If the trustee is unwilling
to cooperate in bringing an action to enforce the promise, the third party may
start proceedings in his own name and join the trustee as co-defendant
(*Vandepitte* v *Preferred Accident Insurance Corp. of NY* [1933] AC 70 at 79).

A further effect of the creation of a trust of a contractual right is to prevent
the contracting parties from varying or rescinding the contract, since to do
so would be an improper interference with the beneficiary's rights. An intention

to reserve the right to vary in the future if so desired has been regarded as evidence contradicting the alleged intention to create a trust (*Re Schebsman* [1944] Ch 83).

13.5.1.2 Limits of the trust exception Despite the apparent utility of the trust device as a means for avoiding the privity doctrine it has fallen into disuse. The reason is to be found in the requirements for the constitution of a trust (*13.4.2*), and especially in the requirement that there be a certain intention on the part of the person allegedly declaring the trust that a trust be created (*Vandepitte* v *Preferred Accident Insurance Corp. of NY* [1933] AC 70). The usual difficulty is that at the time of making the contract, and indeed at all times until the particular problem arises, the promisee has not thought at all about how the third party was to enforce the benefit to be conferred. In the *Vandepitte* case (a Privy Council case)

> the plaintiff's action against an insurance company depended upon whether the insured held the promised cover under a policy of motor insurance on trust for his daughter who was a minor. Under the law of British Columbia the father was civilly liable for the torts of his minor children, so that it was almost inconceivable that he should feel it necessary to hold the benefit of insurance on his daughter's behalf since the person most likely to be sued was himself. On that ground the court found there to be no trust.

Although the *Vandepitte* case is not strictly binding in English law, since then the English courts have been unwilling to imply an intention to create a trust. In *Re Schebsman* [1944] Ch 83 Du Parcq LJ said: '[U]nless an intention to create a trust is clearly to be collected from the language used and the circumstances of the case, I think that the Court ought not to be astute to discover indications of such an intention.' In practice, unless there is an express declaration of the intention to create a trust it seems that the device of a trust of a contractual right will fail.

13.5.2 Insurance
In principle the privity doctrine applies to contracts of insurance, but there are several statutory exceptions to the doctrine in the case of common contracts which provide for benefits to be payable to third parties. For example, under s.148(7) of the Road Traffic Act 1988 an injured third party may recover compensation from the insurance company once he has obtained judgment against the insured. Equally, under s.11 of the Married Women's Property Act 1882 a spouse has an enforceable right to recover sums due on a policy of life insurance taken out by the other spouse on his or her own life.

13.5.3 Contracts relating to land
Under a doctrine peculiar to land law, founded in the old case of *Tulk* v *Moxhay* (1848) 2 Ph 774, it is possible for the vendor of land to attach to it restrictive covenants which 'run with the land' and regulate its future use. Such covenants

are enforceable by adjacent landowners, and bind all subsequent purchasers. Thus, the restrictive covenant is a means not only of conferring enforceable rights on a person who is not a party to the contract; it may also, even more unusually, impose a burden on a person who is not a party to the contract. It was suggested in *Lord Strathcona Steamship Co.* v *Dominion Coal Co. Ltd* [1926] AC 108 (a Privy Council case) that the restrictive covenant rule also applied to contracts which did not concern land, but in *Port Line Ltd* v *Ben Line Steamers Ltd* [1958] 2 QB 146 that case was said to be wrongly decided. The point was recently reconsidered in *Law Debenture Trust Corp plc* v *Ural Caspian Oil Corp Ltd* [1993] 2 All ER 355. As the matter arose in preliminary proceedings, Hoffman J (as he was at the start of the trial) eventually did not have to decide between the two points of view. He noted, however, that the *Lord Strathcona* principle had been found to have continuing validity by Browne-Wilkinson J in *Swiss Bank Corp* v *Lloyds Bank Ltd* [1979] 2 All ER 853. Hoffman J was willing to proceed on the basis that this statement was correct (despite obviously entertaining serious doubts about it), because in this case it would not in any event give rise to the remedy sought by the plaintiffs. The plaintiffs effectively sought specific performance of the covenants in the original contract, the burden of which they claimed had passed to the defendants in this action. The *Lord Strathcona* case and numerous other authorities made clear that the principle if applicable would give rise to no more than an injunction to ensure compliance with a negative covenant. Hoffman J says specifically: 'One thing is beyond doubt: (the principle) does not provide a panacea for outflanking the doctrine of privity of contract.'

Section 56(1) of the Law of Property Act 1925 provides:

A person may take an immediate or other interest in land or other property, or the benefit of any condition, right of entry, covenant or agreement over or respecting land or other property, although he may not be named as a party to the conveyance or other instrument.

The precise scope of this provision has always been something of a mystery. Section 205(1)(xx) of the Law of Property Act 1925 defines 'property' as including 'any thing in action' and any interest in 'personal property', and that raised the possibility that s.56(1) was a statutory repeal of the privity doctrine in the case of written contracts, since a right under a contract is a thing (or chose) in action. That view was put forward by the majority in the Court of Appeal in *Beswick* v *Beswick* [1966] Ch 538, with the result that they found that the widow third party beneficiary was entitled to bring an action in her own name (for the facts of this case see *12.2.2.1*). On this point the decision was overruled by the House of Lords ([1968] AC 58) who, although not clear on the scope of the section, agreed that the usual meaning of 'property' found in s.205(1)(xx) did not apply in this section. It is probably the case that s.56(1) applies only to land, but in any case since *Beswick* v *Beswick* it is clear that it does not import any general exception to the privity doctrine.

13.5.4 Carriage of goods by sea

It is common in commercial transactions for one party (the shipper) to enter into a contract with another (the carrier) for goods to be taken and delivered to a third party (the consignee). The doctrine of privity of contract would prevent the consignee suing the carrier for damage caused to the goods in transit, since the consignee was not a party to the contract. In the nineteenth century Parliament attempted to solve this problem by attaching the right to sue the carrier (originating in the shipper as a party to the contract of carriage) to the ownership in the goods, so that when the consignee became owner of the goods he acquired the right to sue the carrier for damage in transit (see the Bills of Lading Act 1855). In recent years the complex nature of commercial transactions has exposed weaknesses in the solution brought by the 1855 Act, especially where the consignee is for some reason regarded by law as exposed to any risk of loss in respect of the goods, but has not acquired ownership (e.g. *Leigh and Sullivan* v *Aliakmon Shipping Co.* [1986] AC 785). By the Carriage of Goods by Sea Act 1992 Parliament has attempted to remedy the situation. The 1855 Act is repealed, and under the new legislation the right to sue the carrier passes from shipper to consignee or lawful holder of a bill of lading (as defined by ss.2, 5) by operation of law, and independently of the passing of ownership. Commercial necessity is the justification for this statutory exception to the doctrine of privity of contract.

13.6 PROTECTION OF THIRD PARTIES BY EXEMPTION CLAUSE

An exemption clause is a clause which purports to exclude or to limit liability for breach of contract. We have already examined the law relating to exemption clauses in two-party contract situations (*10.6*). Some commercial transactions, especially those involving international trade and shipping, cannot easily be analysed in terms of the traditional bilateral contract. Since in the commercial field the attitude of the English courts has always been that contract law must be the servant, and not the master, of the needs and practices of those engaged in business (see *4.4*), the law must accommodate those needs and practices as best it can without over-insisting on the purity of the conceptual framework. It was precisely in the context of an attempt to protect a third party by means of an exemption clause that Lord Wilberforce made his now well-known statement about the occasional difficulty of 'forcing the facts to fit uneasily into the marked slots of offer, acceptance and consideration' (in *New Zealand Shipping Co. Ltd* v *A.M. Satterthwaite & Co. Ltd (The Eurymedon)* [1975] AC 154: see *5.1.1*). It is on the basis of the needs and practices of the business community that an exception to the privity doctrine, which allows the protection of third parties by means of an exemption clause, has been allowed to develop. It should be noted, however, that where an exemption clause is found to be capable of protecting a third party the clause remains subject to all the usual controls (see generally *10.6*). In particular, it seems unlikely that the courts would be willing to allow a doctrine which applies to freely negotiated business contracts to be extended into the realm of consumer contracts.

13.6.1   The development of the doctrine
In *Elder, Dempster & Co.* v *Paterson, Zochonis & Co. Ltd* [1924] AC 522

shipowners, who were not parties to a contract between the shippers of goods and the charterers of the vessel, which was evidenced by a bill of lading, claimed nevertheless to be protected by an exemption clause contained therein.

The House of Lords upheld that claim. No reasons for the decision were given, other than that such a decision was consistent with the commercial realities of the situation, and that the alternative proposition, that the charterer was protected by the clause but the shipowner was not, was 'absurd'. The difficulty of this decision was that it was clearly inconsistent with the privity doctrine, but did not explain how the doctrine had been avoided.

A very similar situation arose for consideration by the House of Lords in *Scruttons Ltd* v *Midland Silicones Ltd* [1962] AC 446. It was apparent that such purported extensions of exemption clauses to third parties, and especially to stevedores employed to load and unload cargoes, were commonplace in the commercial world, and that the particular action was regarded as a test case. The majority of the House of Lords confirmed that commercial contracts were not as a category exempt from the requirement in the general law of contract of privity between parties of whom one seeks to enforce a contractual term against the other. It was accepted that the privity doctrine might be avoided by means of a separate contract between the third party and the shipper of the goods, and that such a contract might arise by implication or by way of agency (see Chapter 15), but their Lordships would not find such a contract on either ground unless the strict requirements of contract were met. In particular, Lord Reid said:

> I can see a possibility of success of the agency argument if (first) the bill of lading makes it clear that the stevedore is intended to be protected by the provisions in it which limit liability, (secondly) that the bill of lading makes it clear that the carrier, in addition to contracting for these provisions on his own behalf, is also contracting as agent for the stevedore that these provisions should apply to the stevedore, (thirdly) the carrier has authority from the stevedore to do that, or perhaps later ratification by the stevedore would suffice, and (fourthly) that any difficulties about consideration moving from the stevedore were overcome.

In the particular case there was nothing in the bill of lading to suggest that the exemption clause was intended to benefit the stevedores, and both the agency and implied contract arguments failed.

Nevertheless, the statement by Lord Reid provided a glimmer of hope to the business community, who appeared to find it commercially necessary that protection of this kind be afforded to third parties involved in the performance of their contracts. As a result, attempts were made to draft contractual exemption clauses which would meet the requirements set out by Lord Reid. One such clause fell to be considered by the Privy Council in *New Zealand Shipping*

Co. Ltd v *A.M. Satterthwaite & Co. Ltd (The Eurymedon)* [1975] AC 154.
The clause was unusually complex, and is too long to be set out here, but
it was established without difficulty that it satisfied the first three requirements
of the agency argument put forward by Lord Reid. The issue was whether
there was any consideration for the contract between the stevedores and the
shippers arranged through the agency of the carriers. The stevedores were
already under a duty by virtue of their contract with the carriers to unload
the cargo with due care, and the performance of that duty could also be
consideration for the separate contract exempting the stevedores from liability
to the shippers (see *6.3.5.4*).

One reason why it was relatively easy in this case to find that the carriers
were acting as duly authorised agents (cf. *15.2.1*) for the stevedores was that
the carriers and stevedores were part of the same group of companies. It has
been suggested (cf. *The Suleyman Stalskiy* [1976] 2 Lloyd's Rep 609) that where
there is no previous relationship between the stevedore and the carrier the
agency argument would not prevail over the privity doctrine. That suggestion
was disapproved by Lord Wilberforce in a further Privy Council case on this
point (*The New York Star* [1980] 3 All ER 257). He thought that the *Eurymedon*
principle should be regarded as of general application, and should not depend
upon fine distinctions based upon the nature of the relationship between carrier
and stevedore. This reasoning appears to be correct. If it is the practice of
the commercial world, when exemptions from liability are included in contracts,
to seek to extend the benefit of such protection to third parties necessary to
the performance of the contract, then there is no undue surprise to the other
party if the first claims also to contract as agent for such a third party, irrespective
of whether there is any other relationship between them.

13.6.2 Legal nature of the third party's contract

Although it was possible in *The Eurymedon* [1975] AC 154 to find a contract
between the shippers and the stevedores by virtue of the doctrine of agency,
there was some difficulty about describing that contract as bilateral, since at
the time when the carrier made the principal contract with the shipper the
intended stevedore might be unaware of the actual contract envisaged (this
would not affect the carrier's authority to act for the stevedore, which would
have been given in general terms). The Privy Council overcame the difficulty
by finding that the principal contract resulted in the shipper making an offer
in the form of a unilateral contract whereby it would exempt from liability
anybody undertaking to unload the cargo. That unilateral contract 'ripened'
into a full bilateral contract when the stevedore commenced performance (see
5.5.4).

FOURTEEN
Assignment

14.1 INTRODUCTION

Assignment is a device which enables one party to transfer the benefit of a performance which he has contracted to receive to another person in such a way that the assignee (to whom the benefit is transferred) may enforce performance. It should be noted that in this situation the original contract does not stipulate that the benefit of performance should go to a third party. In terms of the triangular relationship outlined at the start of Chapter 13, a bilateral contract is made between A and B. After the contract was made B (the assignor) assigns the right to enforce the contract (a form of intangible personal property known as a *chose in action*) to C (the assignee), who then has a direct right of action against A (the debtor). It should also be noted that an involuntary assignment by operation of law may occur upon death or bankruptcy. This chapter is concerned with voluntary assignments.

Except for assignments involving the Crown, which need not concern us, the common law made no provision for the assignment of choses in action. A direct right of action against the debtor could only be conferred on a third party by granting a power of attorney or by a 'novation', both of which procedures had their disadvantages. The problem with the power of attorney was that it might be revoked by the original creditor, or upon his death, so that it could not guarantee the third party's independent right of action. Novation involves the rescission of the original contract between debtor and creditor, and the substitution in its place of a new contract between debtor and third party, and thus requires both fresh consideration on the part of the third party and the consent of the debtor.

Dissatisfaction with the common law provisions as to the transfer of choses in action led to the development in equity of a doctrine of assignment. The effect of the doctrine was to permit a right of action to be conferred on a third party, but the means whereby that was achieved varied according to the nature of the chose in action. If the right was one which before the Judicature Acts 1873–75 could only be enforced in the Chancery Court (an 'equitable chose'), the assignee could bring the action in his own name and need not involve the assignor since there was no risk of conflict with the common law courts. If, however, the right was one which could be enforced in the common law courts (a 'legal chose'), the assignee had to bring the action in the name of the assignor, in order to avoid the risk of the common law courts granting to the assignor a remedy different from the solution reached by the Chancery Court. In other words, by bringing the action in the name of the assignor all the parties were within the jurisdiction of the court, and their competing interests and claims could all be adjudicated upon at the same time. If the assignor was unwilling to allow his name to be used the Court of Chancery would compel him.

The Judicature Acts 1873–75 established a unified system of courts charged with applying both the common law and equity (*1.2.1.1*), and as a result assignments became enforceable in all courts, and the distinction between legal and equitable choses became blurred. Section 25(6) of the Judicature Act 1873 introduced a new form of statutory assignment. As we shall see (*14.3*), however, equitable assignment is still important since an assignment which fails to satisfy the statutory provision may still take effect in equity (*William Brandt's Sons & Co. v Dunlop Rubber Co. Ltd* [1905] AC 454).

14.2   STATUTORY ASSIGNMENTS

14.2.1   Section 136 of the Law of Property Act 1925
Section 25(6) of the Judicature Act 1873 has been replaced by s.136(1) of the Law of Property Act 1925, which provides:

> Any absolute assignment by writing under the hand of the assignor (not purporting to be by way of charge only) of any debt or other legal thing in action, of which express notice in writing has been given to the debtor, trustee or other person from whom the assignor would have been able to claim such debt or thing in action, is effectual in law (subject to equities having priority over the right of the assignee) to pass and transfer from the date of such notice—
>
> (a)   the legal right to such debt or thing in action;
> (b)   all legal and other remedies for the same; and
> (c)   the power to give a good discharge for the same without the concurrence of the assignor.

The effect of this provision is to enable the assignor to transfer the chose in action to the assignee without requiring the consent of the debtor, and in turn to enable the assignee in his own name to enforce the chose in action against the debtor without joining the assignor to the proceedings. Other statutes have provided for the legal assignability of particular debts and rights (e.g. Policies of Assurance Act 1867 and Companies Act 1985). In this section we shall only consider the requirements of general assignments.

14.2.2   Legal requirements

14.2.2.1   Absolute assignment   An absolute assignment makes clear to the debtor to whom he should pay the debt which he owes. It is usually defined by stating what it is not.

Assignment of part of a debt is not an absolute assignment (*Forster* v *Baker* [1910] 2 KB 636), since the subdivision of the debt creates the risk of the debtor being faced by actions for enforcement by more than one person. Where, on the other hand, what is assigned is the balance of the debt after part has been paid off then the assignment is absolute, since the debtor will be faced with only one potential action for enforcement (*Harding* v *Harding* (1886) 17 QBD 442).

Assignment by way of charge is not an absolute assignment, as s.136 indicates, since it only gives a right to be paid out of an identified fund, rather than transferring the whole fund to the assignee. In many cases assignments by way of charge are also conditional assignments, which again are not absolute. For example, in *Durham Bros* v *Robertson* [1898] 1 QB 765

> a firm of builders borrowed money from the plaintiffs and as security assigned to the plaintiffs the sum of £1,080 owing to the builders under a contract with the defendant. The assignment was to last 'until the money with added interest be repaid'.

Although the assignment was reasonable between assignor and assignee, it left the defendant debtor in a difficult position since he had no access to the information upon which the condition governing to which party he was supposed to pay the money depended. It is still possible to make an absolute assignment which is subject to a condition, provided that realisation of the condition does not merely cause the assignment to cease (the situation in *Durham Bros* v *Robertson*), but imposes a duty on the assignee to *reassign* the debt to the assignor (*Tancred* v *Delagoa Bay and East Africa Ry* (1889) 23 QBD 239). In that case the position of the debtor is always protected, since once the debt is assigned to the assignee he is absolutely entitled to it, and the debtor may safely pay the money to him until such time as he receives actual notice of any reassignment.

14.2.2.2 Express notice Section 136 requires that notice in writing be given to the debtor for there to be a valid statutory assignment. However, notice need not be given by the assignor, the notice is valid provided it actually reaches the debtor before such time as the assignee commences any action upon the debt, and takes effect from the time it reaches him (*Holt* v *Heatherfield Trust Ltd* [1942] 2 KB 1).

14.2.2.3 Debt or other legal thing in action Section 136 states that a statutory assignment may be made of 'any debt or other legal thing in action'. A debt is a definite sum of money due under some legal obligation, and especially for our purposes due under a contract. It might be thought that 'other legal things in action' would correspond to the former category of legal choses (*14.1*), but it has been interpreted as meaning debts or rights not assignable at common law but regarded as assignable in equity, and so also includes equitable choses (*Torkington* v *Magee* [1902] 2 KB 427 at 430).

14.2.2.4 Other requirements Section 136 requires the assignment to be in writing and signed by the assignor.

There is no requirement of consideration for a statutory assignment to be valid between assignor and assignee, or for the assignee to be able to maintain an action in his own name against the debtor (*Re Westerton* [1919] 2 Ch 104).

14.3 EQUITABLE ASSIGNMENTS

14.3.1 Introduction

An assignment which fails to satisfy the statutory requirements may still take effect as an equitable assignment (*William Brandt's Sons & Co.* v *Dunlop Rubber Co. Ltd* [1905] AC 454). The requirements of validity of equitable assignments are in some respects different from those for statutory assignments (see *14.3.2*). In addition, the status of the assignee in the case of an equitable assignment is less strong in that in some circumstances he may not be able to bring an action without also involving the assignor in the proceedings. That status still depends upon the distinction which existed before the Judicature Act 1873 between equitable choses and legal choses (*14.1*).

In the case of the assignment of an equitable chose the assignee may bring an action against the debtor in his own name except in those cases where the assignor has some remaining interest in the debt. For example, in the case of an assignment which is not absolute, but is made by way of charge against a fund, the assignee must join the assignor to the proceedings so that all interested parties are within the jurisdiction of the court and will be bound by its decision. This procedure is essential because an assignment by way of charge only gives a right to recover a certain sum out of a greater amount, with the balance remaining as a debt owed to the assignor (*14.2.2.1*).

In the case of the assignment of a legal chose the assignee today brings the action against the debtor in his own name, but must always join the assignor to the proceedings, either as plaintiff if he is a willing participant or as defendant if not (if, for example, he disputes the validity of the assignment).

14.3.2 Legal requirements

14.3.2.1 Consideration The question whether consideration is required for an equitable assignment to be valid is not without difficulty. If, however, the first principles relating to consideration in the general law of contract are kept in mind (see *6.3*), it is possible to make sense of the cases. By way of introduction it should be pointed out that consideration is only an issue between the assignor and the assignee. It is not open to the debtor to impugn the validity of the assignment on the ground of want of consideration; his only concern is to know to which person to pay the debt alleged to be the subject of an assignment.

It is accepted without question that it is legally possible to make a gift (i.e. a gratuitous transfer) of personal property which is tangible (a chose in possession, e.g. a book). It is also recognised that it is not legally possible to make an enforceable promise to make a gift of a book at some point in the future, unless that promise is in the form of a contract, and so supported by consideration. A chose in action is a form of personal property which is intangible. It is equally capable of being the subject of a present gratuitous transfer, but a promise of a future transfer is unenforceable unless in the form of a contract and so supported by consideration. The basic principle, then, is that the question whether an equitable assignment requires consideration depends upon whether it is effective as a present gift of the chose in action (i.e. the assignment has been completed), or is only effective as a promise of a future gift (i.e. the assignment is incomplete). Only in the latter case is there a requirement of consideration.

In some cases the application of this principle is straightforward. Where there is an express agreement to make an assignment at some point in the future then it is only valid if supported by consideration (*Re McArdle* [1951] Ch 669). Moreover, it is impossible to assign property which does not currently exist. For example, an expectation of receiving a sum of money by way of damages in a court case is an expectation of 'future property', in that until judgment is made the property does not exist. An assignment of such future property can only take effect as an agreement to assign whatever interest accrues under the expectation once it has accrued (*Glegg* v *Bromley* [1912] 3 KB 474). Therefore, an assignment of future property also requires consideration (*Tailby* v *Official Receiver* (1888) 13 App Cas 523). The same would also be true of an assignment of money to be earned under a contract which, at the time of the assignment, had not been made (*E. Pfeiffer Weinkellerei-Weineinkauf GmbH & Co.* v *Arbuthnot Factors Ltd* [1988] 1 WLR 150).

In other cases where there is no express future element in the assignment it is more difficult to determine whether consideration is required. A gratuitous equitable assignment will only be invalid if the assignment has not been completed; that is, if the assignor has not done everything in his power to effect the transfer to the assignee (*Fortescue* v *Barnett* (1834) 3 My & K 36). How much the assignor must do before the assignment is complete varies according to whether the subject-matter of the assignment is an equitable or a legal chose (see *14.1*). Where the assignment is of an equitable chose the only requirements are that the assignor express an unequivocal intention that the right belong to the assignee (*Voyle* v *Hughes* (1854) 2 Sm & G 18), and that the assignment be evidenced in writing (see below, *14.3.2.2*).

In the case of the assignment of a legal chose it is not possible to be so definite about the requirements of a completed assignment. It has been argued in an Australian case (*Olsson* v *Dyson* (1969) 120 CLR 365) that any assignment not in the statutory form is incomplete, since the assignor could always have used the statutory form. On that argument consideration is always required for an equitable assignment of a legal chose, but it is not thought that the argument would prevail in the English courts, since it is accepted that it was not the intention in enacting the statutory form of assignment to diminish the scope of equitable assignment. The only advice which can be given is that the question whether an assignment of a legal chose is complete will depend upon the nature of the chose in action to be assigned and the nature of the particular assignment made. For example, the assignment of a right to enforce payment under a contract would not be complete if the amount due was not

yet a sum certain because it remained to be computed. Equally, an assignment
of a sum certain which was conditional upon an uncertain event (e.g. 'when
you have completed your education to my satisfaction') would not be complete
because further action was required by the assignor (approving the level of
education achieved).

14.3.2.2 Others   An equitable assignment of a legal chose is not required
to be evidenced in writing unless the transaction by which the chose is created
(e.g. a contract) expressly so stipulates. Any disposition, including an assignment,
of an equitable interest or chose must be evidenced in writing and signed
by the person making the disposition, who for these purposes is the assignor
(s.53(1)(c) Law of Property Act 1925).

There is no requirement for the validity of an equitable assignment of the
giving of notice to the debtor. For several reasons, however, it will be advisable
for the assignee to give such notice. Until notice is received the debtor may
pay the assignor and be discharged of the debt (*Stocks* v *Dobson* (1853) 4 De
GM & G 11). Giving notice may prevent further equities interfering with
the assignee's rights (*14.4.1*) and will be relevant to any issue of priority (*14.4.2*).

14.4   LIMITS ON ASSIGNMENT

14.4.1   Subject to equities

The assignee takes the chose in action 'subject to equities': that is, he cannot
recover more from the debtor than the assignor himself might have recovered.
Thus, defences available to the debtor against the assignor are, for the most
part, equally valid against the assignee. For this reason, the assignee must
be careful to ascertain the true value of the chose in action, including any
equities against it, if he is to take it in payment for his own contractual
performance. It should be noted that the expression 'equities' does not merely
include equitable rights; any defence, legal or equitable, will avail the debtor
against the assignee (e.g. mistake, misrepresentation or breach).

The precise scope of the rule depends upon whether the defence arises out
of the transaction which is the subject-matter of the assignment. Where that
is the case, the defence is valid against the assignee whether notice of the
assignment was given to the debtor before or after the defence accrued. For
example, in *Young* v *Kitchin* (1878) 3 ExD 127 the debtor was able to set
off his claim for damages for non-performance under his contract with the
assignor against the assignee's action for the contract price. One, rather
anomolous, exception to this rule arose in *Stoddart* v *Union Trust Ltd* [1912]
1 KB 181 when the debtor was not allowed to set off a claim for damages
for fraud by the assignor against the assignee's action. The explanation given
was that the fraud was personal to the assignor, but the result was that the
assignee was better off than the assignor would have been, which appears to
be detrimental to the interests of the debtor. It is thought that if the debtor
had sought to rescind the contract rather than merely claim damages then
that defence would have prevailed against the assignee.

Where the defence arises out of an independent transaction it is only valid against the assignee in so far as it has already accrued by the time the debtor is given notice of the assignment. For example, in *Roxburghe* v *Cox* (1881) 17 ChD 520

> a sum of money in a bank account (which in legal terms is no more than a debt owed by the banker to the account holder) was assigned to the assignee. The assignor was, at the time of the assignment, indebted to the bank to the tune of some £647, and that indebtedness was set off against the claim by the assignee for the money in the account. Notice of the assignment was given to the bank the day after it was made; if the assignor had incurred any further indebtedness to the bank after that time it could not have been set off against the assignee's claim.

14.4.2 Priorities

Difficulty may arise when more than one assignment is made of the same chose in action. It will not arise if the chose in action is sufficient to satisfy the several assignees' claims upon it, but where it is insufficient there is an issue of priority among the assignees. The rule is that priority is determined according to the order of first giving notice to the debtor (*Dearle* v *Hall* (1823) 3 Russ 1), so that it is possible for an assignment which was second in time to take priority over the previous assignment if the second assignee was first to give notice. Knowledge of the previous assignment on the part of the second assignee at the time of the second assignment would prevent the possibility of such priority arising. Knowledge of the previous assignment on the part of the second assignee at the time of giving notice would not prevent priority being given to the second assignment (*E. Pfeiffer Weinkellerei-Weineinkauf GmbH & Co.* v *Arbuthnot Factors Ltd* [1988] 1 WLR 150). The reason for the rule is that it is necessary to protect the debtor, and that the first assignee cannot complain if he has delayed in giving notice. The nature of the notice which must be given is irrelevant provided it can be proved, but for that reason it is advisable that notice be given in writing. Where more than one person is responsible for the chose in action, such as where assignment is made of an interest under a trust fund administered by several trustees, it is advisable to give notice to all trustees since notice may lapse if the notified trustee dies or is replaced (*Re Phillips' Trust* [1903] 1 Ch 183).

14.4.3 Non-assignable rights

14.4.3.1 In general The law provides that certain rights may not be assigned. The most obvious example is where the contract which creates the right in question contains an express provision against assignment (*United Dominions Trust Ltd* v *Parkway Motors* [1955] 2 All ER 557). Some rights may not be assigned for reasons of public policy. For example, social security benefits (s.87 Social Security Act 1975) and maintenance payable upon marital breakdown (*Re Robinson* (1884) 27 ChD 160) may not be assigned. Since such payments are intended to prevent their recipients from being without financial means of support it is understandable that the law should seek to prevent them being assigned away. A further archaic and anomolous example is that the salary of public officers paid out of national funds may not be assigned (*Wells* v *Foster* (1841) 8 M & W 149). Some rights may not be assigned because the contract which creates them is of a personal nature, or is a relationship of confidence, or is founded on particular qualities or attributes of one of the parties. For example, the benefit of a policy of motor insurance may not be assigned with the sale of a car, since that assignment might impose an entirely different risk on the insurance company (*Peters* v *General Accident and Life Assurance Corp. Ltd* [1937] 4 All ER 628).

14.4.3.2 Assignment of a bare right of action A bare right of action may not be assigned; that is, while it is permissible to assign the benefit of a contract which remains to be performed, it is not permitted to assign the unqualified right to sue for breach of contract after the contract has been breached. The origin of this rule lies in the old torts and crimes of 'maintenance and champerty', which prevented speculation on the result of litigation by purchasing an interest therein. The contract rule has survived despite the abolition of the torts and crimes by s.14(2) of the Criminal Law Act 1967.

The assignment will not be considered to be of a *bare* right of action where the assignee has a legitimate interest in enforcing the right in question (*Trendtex Trading Corp.* v *Credit Suisse* [1982] AC 679). For example, the assignment to the purchaser of land of the right to sue for damage done to that land by the vendor's tenants is valid (*Ellis* v *Torrington* [1920] 1 KB 399). Equally valid is the assignment, to the person who has provided finance for the transaction creating the right assigned, of the right to sue for breach where the assignment was made as a form of security for the credit facility made available (*Trendtex Trading Corp.* v *Credit Suisse* [1982] AC 679 at 696–697, 703). In this particular case there was said to be no legitimate interest in pursuing the claim since the assignment had been made with the intention of the assignee reselling the right assigned for profit.

14.4.4 Bankruptcy and liquidation
Some assignments will be unenforceable in the event of the bankruptcy of an individual assignor or the liquidation of a company assignor. These rules operate as an exception to the general rule that a trustee in bankruptcy or a liquidator is equally bound by transactions as was the individual or company before the bankruptcy or liquidation. Under s.344 of the Insolvency Act 1986 a general assignment of existing or future book debts must be registered as a bill of sale, or else it will be unenforceable against the trustee in bankruptcy, if the assignor was engaged in trade or business. Under ss.395 to 398 of the Companies Act 1985 (as amended by the Companies Act 1989), any assignment by way of charge over the book debts of a company must be registered as a charge on the company. If the charge is not registered it is void as against the liquidator.

14.5   ASSIGNMENT OF THE BURDEN OF THE CONTRACT

The general rule is that the assignment of the burden of a contract is invalid unless made with the consent of the promisee/creditor (*Robson* v *Drummond* (1831) 2 B & Ad 303). Certain apparent exceptions to this rule exist, but they are not true exceptions in that they depend upon independent legal concepts and not upon the law relating to assignment.

The promisor under a contract may subcontract the actual performance of the undertakings in the contract to another person, provided the contract does not depend upon any personal skill or quality of the main contractor (*Griffith* v *Tower Publishing Co. Ltd* [1897] 1 Ch 21). So, it would not be possible for a portrait painter to subcontract his obligation to paint a particular person to a third party. Where a permitted subcontract has been made, however, the original main contracting party remains principally liable on the contract and is the person entitled to sue on the contract (*Davies* v *Collins* [1945] 1 All ER 247).

Just as the common law has always allowed the transfer of the benefit of a contract by 'novation' (see *14.1*), the burden of a contract may also be transferred in this way. Novation involves the rescission by consent of both parties of the original contract, and the substitution of a new contract between the original promisee and the new promisor. At that point the original promisor's interest in the transaction ceases. The new contract must meet all the usual requirements of contract, and especially the requirement of consideration.

FIFTEEN
Agency

15.1 INTRODUCTION

Agency is the legal device by which one person (the *agent*: 'A') may act on behalf of another (the *principal*: 'P') in the formation of a contract between that other and a third party. The doctrine in its standard form is not really an exception to the privity doctrine, since there is no contractual relationship between the agent and the third party. Thus the agent does not stipulate for a benefit to be conferred on his principal: rather, the principal is himself a party to the contract with the third party. Nevertheless, agency may sometimes be used as a means of avoiding the impact of the privity doctrine (e.g. see *13.6.1*).

Agency is an essential ingredient of modern commercial life. A simple example is provided by the case of a contract made by a limited company. We have already seen that a limited company has a legal 'personality', so that it enjoys the capacity to enter into contracts (*8.3*). Nevertheless, companies are inanimate, and they cannot make contracts without the intervention of human beings. A company's contracts are negotiated on its behalf by its agents employed for that purpose. In today's developed and industrialised societies the specialisation of labour has resulted in the growth of all kinds of specialist agents (also known as brokers or factors) who act as intermediaries in the negotiation of commercial transactions.

Agency may be analysed in terms of three separate relationships. The first and most important is the relationship between P and A (see *15.2* and *15.4*). That relationship consists of a power invested by the law in A to create or amend relationships between P and third parties (see generally Dowrick, (1954) 17 MLR 24). That power is invested when the law determines that A has been given authority by P. In normal circumstances that authority will have been created by a contract between P and A (*15.2.1*), but there are circumstances in which the existence of authority is entirely a matter of objective ascertainment, when the relationships of agency must be regarded not as consensually created but imposed by law (see *15.2.2–15.2.4*). The second relationship is the goal of the agency which has been created: the contract between P and the third party (*15.3*). The final relationship is the potential relationship between A and the third party (*15.5*). It is only of any significance where the normal course of agency has not been followed.

A final word of caution must be entered about technical and non-technical uses of the term 'agent'. In the legal sense an agent is someone who does not act on his own account, but only as a legal representative of another person. In ordinary usage the term 'agent' may be used to describe someone who buys and sells on his own account (i.e. as principal). For example, a retailer who specialises in stocking goods made by a particular manufacturer may be described as 'agent for . . .'. He is very unlikely to be an agent in the legal sense. What matters is not the term used but whether on a proper analysis the legal relationships of agency, especially the relationship of authority, have been created. It is equally irrelevant whether there is some other legal relationship between P and A. An agent may be an employee, an independent contractor, a partner, or any other person in whom the power of representation has been invested by authority from P.

15.2   FORMATION OF THE RELATIONSHIPS OF AGENCY

15.2.1   Agency by agreement
Where agency is created by agreement between P and A it invests actual authority in A, and this is so whether the agreement is express or implied. Such agreements normally take the form of a contract, but contract is not an essential requirement of such agency. It is always open to the agent to act gratuitously, and if he does this will not affect the relationship between P and the third party. It does affect the relationship between P and A. In the absence of consideration A will be under no obligation to act for P. But where he does so act and incurs losses or expenses in the process he will be able to recover them from P, since the right to an indemnity in this way arises independently of any contract between the parties (*Brook's Wharf and Bull Wharf Ltd* v *Goodman Bros* [1937] 1 KB 534). Where a gratuitous agent does act, he may be found to owe a duty of due care and skill to his principal (see further *15.4.1.2*).

15.2.1.1   Agent's powers expressly granted   In the case of an express grant of authority the extent of the authority granted depends upon the construction of the agreement. Where the agency relationship is created in a deed (i.e. a written document complying with the provisions of s.1 of the Law of Property (Miscellaneous Provisions) Act 1989), the courts apply very strict rules of construction. For example, where the deed gives authority to do specified acts but is phrased in general terms the authority will be construed as restricted to the minimum necessary to achieve the goals in question. In *Jacobs* v *Morris* [1902] 1 Ch 816

an Australian principal authorised his English agent to buy goods and to write bills of exchange etc. 'in connection with his business'. This authority was held not to extend to the agent's borrowing money on the strength of bills of exchange, so that the principal was not liable for the debt when the agent had taken the money for his own use.

Nevertheless, it is possible to create by deed a general authority to act on behalf of P under the powers contained in s.10 of the Powers of Attorney Act 1971.

Where the agency relationship is created orally, or in writing not in the form of a deed, the usual rules of construction of the general law of contract apply (see *10.2*). The court must establish the extent of authority by inference from the words used and the surrounding circumstances, and if P has not expressed himself clearly he must accept the consequences of any actions of A which are consistent with a reasonable interpretation of the authority given. In *Ireland v Livingston* (1872) LR 5 HL 395

> P asked A to arrange shipment of a cargo of sugar. A arranged for 80 per cent of the cargo to be shipped on one vessel, and it must be assumed he intended to send the balance on another vessel. P claimed to be entitled to reject the part-cargo.

The House of Lords rejected that claim. His instructions to A had not made explicit that he required shipment of the cargo in a single instalment, and A's behaviour was reasonable in the light of the instructions given. Nevertheless, where communication is possible (which today is the usual case), A may be under an implied obligation to seek clarification from P if the latter's instructions are ambiguous (*European Asian Bank AG v Punjab & Sind Bank (No. 2)* [1983] 3 All ER 508).

15.2.1.2 Agent's powers implied When we speak of implied authority it is not intended to refer to agency which is imposed by law (see *15.2.2–15.2.4*; in particular, it is important to distinguish implied actual authority from ostensible authority, since the two are not necessarily co-extensive: *per* Parker LJ in *Industrie Chimiche Italia Centrale v Alexander G. Tsavliris & Sons Maritime Co., 'The Choko Star'* [1990] 1 Lloyd's Rep 516 at 524). Rather, it is agency created by actual authority which upon consideration of all the circumstances may be inferred to have been given to A by P. The best example of such implied authority is where express authority has been given for a particular purpose or purposes, and the court finds an implied authority to do everything necessary to achieve those purposes (*Howard v Baillie* (1796) 2 H Bl 618). For example, it is now accepted that a lawyer has authority to bind his client to any agreed compromise of litigation in which the client is engaged (*Waugh v H.B. Clifford & Sons* [1982] 1 Ch 374).

Authority may also be implied from a particular trade usage. For example, in *Howard v Sheward* (1866) LR 2 CP 148

> an agent who had sold a horse for a horse dealer was found to have had authority to give a warranty of quality in respect of the horse which bound the principal horse dealer when the horse failed to match the warranty.

The effect of this authority implied from trade usage may be to grant to A greater authority than P intended. To counter that effect P may expressly withdraw the authority usually pertaining in the circumstances. Such withdrawal of usual authority may be ineffective, however, where the third party is aware that A acts for P but unaware of the limitation of A's authority by comparison with that usual in the trade. Thus, the usual authority may be restored by virtue of the doctrine of agency by estoppel (see *15.2.2*). That doctrine only applies where the third party knows that A acts for a principal (*15.2.2.2*). This point appears to have been overlooked in *Watteau* v *Fenwick* [1893] 1 QB 346, in which an undisclosed principal was found to be bound by the acts of his agent done under a usual authority which had been expressly withdrawn.

> The defendants owned an hotel which was managed by their agent, one Humble. The defendants' ownership was in no way apparent, Humble's name appearing over the door as licensee. Humble had been forbidden to buy cigars on credit. The plaintiff, unaware of the existence of the defendants or of their instruction to their agent, sold cigars on credit to Humble. They were cigars of a kind usually supplied to such an establishment. The plaintiff was found to be entitled to recover the price of the cigars from the defendants.

The case is perhaps best regarded as wrongly decided, but may possibly be explained on the ground that of the two innocent parties (principal and third party) P was better placed to prevent the loss, and so he should bear it. He would then be able to pursue his remedy against A for exceeding his authority.

15.2.2   Agency by estoppel
Agency may be created by estoppel (and so imposed by law rather than created by the will of the parties) where A has 'apparent' or 'ostensible' authority. In other words, if P creates the impression that A has authority to act in the way in which he is acting, then P will be unable to deny that authority in order to avoid liability on a contract with a third party apparently made by A on P's behalf.

15.2.2.1   The extent of authority   The existence of agency by estoppel will always be a question largely dependent upon the interpretation of the facts of the individual case. It embraces two quite different situations. The first is the rare occurrence where P allows A to appear to have his authority when in fact he has none. For example, in *Freeman & Lockyer* v *Buckhurst Park Properties (Mangal) Ltd* [1964] 2 QB 480

> the defendant company was empowered by its articles of association to appoint a managing director. Although never officially appointed to this post, A acted in this capacity with the knowledge and consent of the other directors. A employed the plaintiffs to do certain work for the company, which then sought to avoid having to pay for the work on the ground that A did not have authority to make such a contract on the company's behalf.

The court found that A did not have actual authority, but there was an agency by estoppel since the other directors on behalf of the company had allowed the plaintiffs to gain the impression that A was empowered to act as managing director.

The more normal situation of agency by estoppel occurs where P fails to make known to the third party a limitation (in scope or time) imposed on A's admitted authority. For example, in *Watteau* v *Fenwick* [1893] 1 QB 346 (above, *15.2.1.2*) there was no doubt that A had actual authority (even if the agency had not been disclosed); the difficulty in that case arose from the fact that the third party had no way of knowing that the authority was in any way limited.

15.2.2.2 Requirements of estoppel In *Rama Corp.* v *Proved Tin and General Investments Ltd* [1952] 2 QB 147 at 149 Slade J said:

> Ostensible or apparent authority . . . is merely a form of estoppel, indeed, it has been termed agency by estoppel, and you cannot call in aid an estoppel unless you have three ingredients: (i) a representation, (ii) a reliance on the representation and (iii) an alteration of your position resulting from such a reliance.

There must first, therefore, be a representation made to the third party. As in the general law of contract (see *6.4.2.2*), the representation may be express or implied from conduct. An estoppel will not arise out of the mere silence of the supposed principal, unless there are circumstances giving rise to a duty to speak (*Arctic Shipping Co. Ltd* v *Mobilia AB, The 'Tatra'* [1990] 2 Lloyd's Rep 51). In this context representations by conduct are particularly relevant. It is crucially important that the representation is attributable to P, and is not merely an impression from A's own conduct, since only the former is sufficient evidence on which to base an estoppel (*A-G for Ceylon* v *Silva* [1953] AC 461). This requirement may raise difficulties when the principal is a company. Clearly the company itself cannot make a representation, but a duly authorised person may make a representation on behalf of the company. So, in *Freeman & Lockyer* v *Buckhurst Park Properties (Mangal) Ltd* [1964] 2 QB 480 the *acting* managing director was found to be agent by estoppel on the strength of a representation by conduct made by the other directors, whom Diplock LJ found to have *actual* authority to make such representations. This analysis raises the question whether a person with actual authority to make representations can bind the company by an agency by estoppel on the strength of a representation made about his own authority as granted by the company (i.e. where representation and subsequent contract are made by one and the same person). Such a possibility was ruled out by the House of Lords in *Armagas Ltd* v *Mundogas SA* [1986] 2 All ER 385. However, in *The Raffaella* [1985] 2 Lloyd's Rep 36

> the plaintiff entered a contract to purchase a cargo of cement from the seller. The plaintiff became concerned about serious delays in performance, and obtained a letter of guarantee signed by the documentary credit manager of the defendant bank which was financing the seller's acquisition of the cement to fulfil the contract. When delivered the cement was in very poor condition, and the plaintiff sought to enforce

the guarantee. The defendant bank denied liability on the ground that the manager was unauthorised to give such an undertaking.

The bank was found to be liable because its agent, the manager, had been allowed to act without reference to higher authority, and so to create the impression that he needed no further authorisation for the undertaking he gave. Browne-Wilkinson LJ expressed the view that a binding estoppel would be created in those circumstances, although they come close to undermining the rule that the representation must not derive from the conduct of the agent. A similar result was reached by the Court of Appeal in *United Bank of Kuwait* v *Hammond* [1988] 3 All ER 418; a solicitor with actual authority to represent himself as such gave undertakings which in the circumstances appeared to have been given in the ordinary course of business of the firm of solicitors for which he worked. The undertakings were found to have been given with ostensible authority.

Secondly, there must be some reliance by the third party on the representation made. Thus, if it can be shown that the third party knew when entering the contract that A lacked the requisite authority, whatever impression P's conduct might have given, then the contract will not bind P (*Overbrooke Estates Ltd* v *Glencombe Properties Ltd* [1974] 3 All ER 511). There may be difficult issues of fact, and the inferences to be drawn therefrom, where the circumstances of making the contract between A and the third party lead to the allegation that the third party ought to have known that A lacked authority.

Finally, there must be detriment to, or alteration of position by, the third party as a result of his reliance on the representation. It will be recalled that in relation to equitable and promissory estoppel there is some dispute as to the precise degree of reliance required, whether detriment or alteration of position (see *6.4.3.4*). A similar dispute exists in the case of agency by estoppel. Since agency by estoppel results in the creation of new rights, and so is more akin to proprietary estoppel than to equitable or promissory estoppel (cf. *6.4.2.4*), it may be that the more stringent requirement of actual detriment, which undoubtedly exists in the case of proprietary estoppel, applies in this case also (cf. *6.4.2.5*; this proposition is not accepted by Gatehouse J in *Arctic Shipping Co. Ltd* v *Mobilia AB, The 'Tatra'* [1990] 2 Lloyd's Rep 51 at 59).

15.2.3 Agency of cohabitants

It is necessary to treat the agency of cohabitants as a separate category of agency since judicial imprecision has made it impossible to determine whether this is a form of implied agency (*15.2.1.2*), or agency by estoppel (*15.2.2*), or agency of necessity (*15.2.4*). It depends upon three crucial factors, of which the first is cohabitation in a household (*Debenham* v *Mellon* (1880) 6 App Cas 24). Cases have involved wives (*Phillipson* v *Hayter* (1870) LR 6 CP 38) and mistresses (*Blades* v *Free* (1829) 9 B & C 167), so that it is conclusively established that this form of agency is not merely an incident of marriage. It must be assumed today that the principle applies equally to male cohabitants of female (and other male?) breadwinners.

The principle enables the cohabitant to obtain 'necessaries' on credit, to be paid for, by virtue of agency, by the cohabitee as principal. We have already encountered the concept of necessaries in relation to minors' contracts (*8.2.2.1*), and the criticisms made there apply equally in this context. The standard definition provided in *Phillipson* v *Hayter* (1870) LR 6 CP 38 at 42 (things 'suitable to the style in which the husband chooses to live, in so far as the articles fall fairly within the domestic department which is ordinarily confined to the management of the wife') is dated and offensive. It may be that if the principle is to be retained at all it would be better, as has been proposed for minors' contracts, to rely on a narrower class of goods and services defined as 'necessities'.

This form of agency is said to be a presumption which may be rebutted where the alleged principal is able to produce contrary evidence (*Debenham* v *Mellon*). Suitable evidence would be that the tradesman had been warned that the cohabitant did not have authority to contract on P's credit (*Etherington* v *Parrot* (1703) 1 Salk 118), that the cohabitant was adequately supplied with the things in question, or that the cohabitant had been expressly forbidden to make such contracts (*Debenham* v *Mellon*). These last two grounds of rebuttal suggest that agency of cohabitation depends upon a form of implied authority, since, being addressed to the agent rather than to the third party, they would not be sufficient to prevent the raising of an estoppel.

15.2.4   Agency of necessity

Agency of necessity is an umbrella expression under which two quite distinct types of case may be found (per Lord Diplock in *China Pacific SA* v *Food Corp. of India* [1982] AC 939 at 958). The first type of case raises the central issue of agency of whether A is acting with P's authority. The question is: does a person have authority in some circumstances (which for the time being may be described as emergencies) to bind a principal contractually to third parties, despite the absence of any formal agency arrangement, and despite the absence of circumstances giving rise to agency by estoppel (*15.2.2*)? The second type of case arises in similar circumstances of necessary emergency action, but raises no issue of agency. The only question is: is a person who acted to preserve another's endangered property entitled to an indemnity for the cost to him of so acting? There is no issue of agency since there is no question of a principal allegedly being bound to a third party.

15.2.4.1   Restitutionary claims   The second type of case is really a form of restitutionary claim, and indeed is well known in civil law countries whose law has directly descended from Roman law. English law has refused to recognise any general right of recovery in such circumstances (*Falcke* v *Scottish Imperial Insurance Co.* (1886) 34 ChD 234), although there is a statutory exception in the case of bills of exchange (ss.65, 68 Bills of Exchange Act 1882). In the light of this attitude of English law it is not surprising that attempts have been made to cloak such claims in the guise of the admitted triangular relationship of a true agency of necessity, not least because many of the arguments of fairness which apply in the latter situation appear valid for the former also.

Nevertheless, such claims belong to the law of restitution (cf. Birks, (1971) 24 CLP 110) and have no place in the law of agency.

15.2.4.2 True agency of necessity The first type of case, that is, true agency of necessity, originated in the needs and practices of the shipping business. It was essential for the best interests of all concerned that the ship's master be empowered to react to all the emergencies of the voyage without incurring personal liability. So, for example, the sale of the cargo in *Couturier* v *Hastie* (1856) 5 HLC 673, which resulted in a second sale being void for total failure of consideration or initial impossibility (see *7.3.1.1*), was made by virtue of the master's authority as agent of necessity. From these beginnings the doctrine has expanded in two different dimensions. In the first place, it has been applied in cases not involving the carriage of goods by sea. Secondly, it has been applied not only to extend where necessary an existing authority (which might be no more than an example of implied authority: *15.2.1.2*), but also to create an authority to act to bind P where no authority previously existed.

Despite this expansion, the requirements for the creation of an agency of necessity are sufficiently strict to suggest that it can only ever remain a limited doctrine. In particular, such agency will not be created unless A was unable to obtain express instructions from P before the time when it became necessary to act (*Prager* v *Blatspiel, Stamp and Heacock Ltd* [1924] 1 KB 566). Modern methods of telecommunication may make this a particularly severe requirement. In addition, A must have acted in good faith in P's interest in a manner reasonable in the circumstances (*Prager* v *Blatspiel, Stamp and Heacock Ltd*). Finally, there must be circumstances of emergency or necessity, although it is not easy to define quite what that entails. It seems it is intended to be judged on commercial criteria (*Australasian Steam Navigation Co.* v *Morse* (1872) LR 4 PC 222).

15.2.5 Agency by ratification of the agent's unauthorised acts
It has long been established that the relationships of agency may be created by subsequent ratification of an agent's unauthorised acts, and, provided A purported to act for P rather than for himself, the effect is the same as where A acts within an express actual authority (*Wilson* v *Tumman* (1843) 6 Man & G 236). In this situation, again, the want of express authority may be complete, in that A had no previous authority to act on P's behalf, or may result from A going beyond a limited existing authority conferred by P. The precise nature of such agency is unclear. Except in the standard case of agency by agreement it is possible to say that the agency is imposed by law either as a result of estoppel (*15.2.2*) or implication of law (*15.2.3* and *15.2.4*). Agency by ratification is apparently consensual, but it is unusual in English law to be able to create liability by consent for acts which have already occurred.

For an apparent ratification to bind P there must have been some real choice available whether to adopt the acts of A or not (*Forman & Co. Pty Ltd* v *The Liddesdale* [1900] AC 190). Where A acts beyond his authority and his actions are not ratified by P he will incur a personal liability towards the third party (see *15.5.2.5*).

15.2.5.1 Requirements of ratification   A third party will not be bound to P unless at the time of contracting A appeared to be acting on P's behalf, and not on his own account. For example, in *Keighley, Maxsted & Co.* v *Durant* [1901] AC 240

> A was authorised by the appellants to purchase corn at a certain price. A bought corn above the price authorised, which would have been beyond his authority, but he bought in his own name. The appellants purported to ratify the transaction, but then failed to take delivery of the corn. They resisted the respondent's action for breach of contract by claiming not to be parties to the contract since they were not entitled to ratify an agreement which had not purported to be made in their name.

This defence succeeded. It is not a requirement, however, that A must intend to act for P. P may still ratify if A's intention when claiming to contract for P was in fact fraudulently to take the benefit for himself (*Re Tiedemann and Ledermann Frères* [1899] 2 QB 66).

A third party will not be bound to P unless, at the time the contract was made with A, P was in existence and capable of being ascertained. For example, in *Kelner* v *Baxter* (1866) LR 2 CP 174

> the promoters of a new company made a contract on its behalf with a third party at a time before the company had come into existence. The company once formed purported to ratify the contract, but then went into liquidation, and the promoters themselves were sued on the contract. They argued that they had contracted as agents, and that liability on the contract had passed to the company by ratification.

This defence failed because the company's ratification was invalid since the company had not been in existence at the time of the contract in question. In the case of companies which are not in existence, the personal liability of the party claiming to contract on behalf of the company is now imposed by Statute. Section 36C(1) of the Companies Act 1985 (as amended by the Companies Act 1989) provides:

> A contract which purports to be made by or on behalf of a company at a time when the company has not been formed has effect, subject to any agreement to the contrary, as one made with the person purporting to act for the company or as agent for it, and he is personally liable on the contract accordingly.

Where the agent purports to act on behalf of a company which is only subsequently purchased 'off the shelf', the agent's action may be ratified by the company provided at the time of the agent's action the company in fact existed, albeit under another name (*Oshkosh B' Gosh Inc.* v *Dan Marbel Inc. Ltd* [1989] BCLC 507).

Finally, a third party will not be bound to P unless, at the time the contract was made with A, P was competent to make the contract, and unless, at the time when P purports to ratify, P could then do the act in question. The first rule is straightforward. If at the time A makes the contract P lacks contractual capacity he cannot later ratify it (*Firth* v *Staines* [1897] 2 QB 70). The second rule exists to prevent P taking advantage of A's unauthorised acts to achieve something which he has left it too late to achieve himself. The rule is of particular application to insurance contracts, and prevents P ratifying a contract of insurance taken out by A in excess of his authority once the risk insured against has occurred, since he could not then himself take out insurance (*Grover & Grover* v *Mathews* [1910] 2 KB 401; there is a statutory exception in s.86 Marine Insurance Act 1906).

15.2.5.2 Effect of ratification The effect of ratification, as the rule that P must be competent at the time the contract was made between A and the third party suggests, is to make P liable on the contract retroactively from the time it was first made (*Boston Deep Sea Fishing & Ice Co. Ltd* v *Farnham* [1957] 3 All ER 204). This rule may have difficult consequences for a third party who wishes to revoke an offer which has been accepted by A but which has not been ratified by P. Where the third party has been informed that the contract is subject to ratification by P he may withdraw at any time before ratification (*Watson* v *Davies* [1931] 1 Ch 455). But where the third party does not know of the need for ratification there is some imbalance between the parties since the third party is bound while P is free to choose whether to ratify or not (*Bolton Partners* v *Lambert* (1889) 41 ChD 295). There is no great hardship in this rule, however, since P is under an obligation to make his choice within a reasonable time (*Metropolitan Asylums Board Managers* v *Kingham & Sons* (1890) 6 TLR 217). Moreover, where he is unaware of the need for ratification the third party must believe he is bound by the fact of A's acceptance, so that revocation of the offer would not be open to him. Should P fail to ratify, the third party will not be left without a remedy, since A will in any case be personally liable (*15.5.2.5*).

15.2.5.3 Acts which cannot be ratified If A's acts are void they may not be rescued by ratification by P. This rule operated previously to prevent the ratification by shareholders of acts done by the directors which are *ultra vires* the company (*Ashbury Railway Carriage & Iron Co. Ltd* v *Riche* (1875) LR 7 HL 653). It must be noted, however, that the rule is of no consequence for those who contract with a company through the agency of a director acting beyond his authority as set out in the company's memorandum: s.35(1) Companies Act 1985 (as amended by the Companies Act 1989) (see *8.3.3*). As a result of this provision, the availability of ratification is of no concern to the third party. The *ultra vires* rule remains of consequence only for relations between the company (i.e., the shareholders) and the directors. By s. 35(3) of the Companies Act 1985 (as amended), action which goes beyond the company's capacity may be ratified by the shareholders by special resolution.

15.3 RELATIONSHIP BETWEEN PRINCIPAL AND THIRD PARTY

The relationship between principal and third party is the central relationship and goal of agency. Its effect varies according to whether the existence of P was disclosed to the third party by A at the time of making the contract.

15.3.1 Disclosed principal

The paradigm of agency, and its preponderant manner of expression, is the contract made by an agent acting within an express or implied actual authority on behalf of a disclosed principal. Where all those conditions are met there is a binding agreement between P and the third party which results in a bilateral contract between those two and allows A to drop out of the relationship (*15.2.1*). Equally, where P is disclosed but A acts outside any possible authority existing at the time of making the contract, then there can be no contract between P and the third party unless A's acts are subsequently ratified by P (*15.2.5*).

The exceptions to the general principle that A's authorised contract with the third party on behalf of a disclosed P allows A to drop out of the relationship are listed by Wright J in *Montgomerie* v *United Kingdom Mutual SS Association* [1891] 1 QB 370 at 371-2. The effect of these exceptions is to create a personal liability on the part of A (discussed below at *15.5.1*). The most important exception (apart from the rules applicable in the case of an undisclosed principal: *15.3.2*) is where there is express contractual provision that A should be liable. There may also be an irresistible inference that A contracted to incur personal liability if he signed a written contract without qualifying that signature by words showing that he signed only on behalf of P, especially where there is no other reference to P in the contractual document (*Parker* v *Winlow* (1857) 7 E & B 942). Other exceptions exist (see *15.5.1.4*) in the case of contracts by deed, negotiable instruments, and contracts for foreign principals, but these are now all of limited impact, and need no further mention.

15.3.1.1 Election where agent is also liable? The important question where the agent has incurred a personal liability is what effect that has on the liability of P to the third party. One effect which has been canvassed in the cases is that the third party has an election between enforcing the liability of P or that of A, with the usual consequence of election that once made it is binding on the third party who may not subsequently reverse the choice made (*Debenham's Ltd* v *Perkins* (1925) 133 LT 252). The difficulty is to know when an election has been made. It depends upon some unequivocal act committing the third party to a single course of action. Thus, obtaining judgment against either P or A will clearly suffice (*Priestly* v *Fernie* (1865) 3 H & C 977: see *15.3.2.2*).

The doctrine of the third party's election between liability of A and that of P almost certainly originates from the law relating to undisclosed principals (see *15.3.2.2*). There is no question in that situation that the third party might have understood the contract to have been made with both A and P, since the existence of P is unknown at the time of contracting. But where P's existence is disclosed and yet A has contracted for a personal liability, it might seem that the natural inference is that A and P contracted to be jointly and severally liable, with the result that judgment against the one would not be a bar to proceedings against the other unless the debt had actually been satisfied. In that case, to hold the third party bound by an election where the judgment is not satisfied (as occurred in *Priestly* v *Fernie*) would not accord with the intention of the parties, and might cause serious injustice to the third party. There are indications that the courts may be more willing today to recognise this state of affairs (cf. Diplock LJ in *Teheran-Europe Co. Ltd* v *S.T. Belton (Tractors) Ltd* [1968] 2 All ER 886 at 892-3).

15.3.1.2 Payment to the agent   The general rule is that where the principal is disclosed payment by either party to A does not discharge the liability of the party making payment to the other contracting party (*Butwick* v *Grant* [1924] 2 KB 483). This rule may be varied, however, by actual authority, by estoppel or by ratification. This exception to the general rule applies equally to payment by P (*Heald* v *Kenworthy* (1855) 10 Exch 739) and payment by the third party, although in this case the third party must comply with the exact authority given in order to discharge his liability to P (*The Netherholme, Glen Holme and Rydal Holme* (1895) 72 LT 79). In that case A was authorised to receive payments in cash, and it was found that payment to A by bill of exchange did not discharge the debt to P. The third party's authority to P to discharge his liability by payment to A most commonly arises by way of an estoppel based on the third party's conduct which has induced P to make payment to A (*Irvine & Co.* v *Watson & Sons* (1880) 5 QBD 414).

15.3.2 Undisclosed principal
In English law a contract may be established between P and a third party by virtue of agency even when the existence of P was not disclosed at the time of the negotiation of the contract between A and the third party. This rule is widely regarded as anomalous as a matter of legal theory, since it is almost impossible to reconcile it with the doctrine of privity (see *13.2*). It does not exist in most other legal systems, and especially not in those in which it is unnecessary since it is possible to contract for a benefit to be conferred on a third party. Herein lies the probable key to the doctrine: it is a necessary commercial expedient as a result of the privity doctrine. In *Keighley, Maxsted & Co.* v *Durant* [1901] AC 240 Lord Lindley said:

> [T]here is an anomaly in holding one person bound to another of whom he knows nothing and with whom he did not, in fact, intend to contract. But middlemen, through whom contracts are made, are common and useful in business transactions, and in the great mass of contracts it is a matter of indifference to either party whether there is an undisclosed principal or not. If he exists it is, to say the least, extremely convenient that he should be able to sue and be sued as principal . . ..

15.3.2.1 Limits on the doctrine   It is clear that in some circumstances to hold the third party bound to an undisclosed principal will be an unfair surprise, and certain limits exist upon the doctrine which are intended to prevent that. The first is that the third party will not be bound to an undisclosed P where from the terms of the contract it appears that A is the only possible principal. In some circumstances the impossibility of contracting as agent on behalf of P will be express. For example, in *UK Mutual SS Assurance Assoc v Nevill* (1887) 19 QBD 110

> the contract, which was constituted by the rules of a mutual insurance association, provided that only members of the association could be made liable for premiums. The defendant, a co-owner of a vessel insured by the association, was not liable for premiums unpaid by another co-owner since the defendant was not himself a member of the association.

In other circumstances the restriction on contracting as agent may be implied from the contract. For example, in *Humble* v *Hunter* (1848) 12 QB 310

> A entered into a contract in which he was described as 'owner' of a particular vessel. It was held that this description justified the inference that there was no true owner as principal behind A, so that P was unable to sue on the contract.

In subsequent cases the courts have been unwilling to make such inferences (e.g. *F. Drughorn Ltd* v *Rederiaktiebolaget Trans-Atlantic* [1919] AC 203: A described as 'charterer'), and it may be that the implied restrictions on the power to contract as agent are now restricted to the situation where A describes himself as owner, or otherwise asserts a full property right over the goods in question (cf. *The Astyanax* [1985] 2 Lloyd's Rep 109).

A further limit on the doctrine exists where the third party made the contract in the light of personal qualities of the person now alleged only to have been an agent. Where A has some personal skill (e.g. a portrait painter) P will not be entitled subsequently to perform the contract, just as rights under such a contract may not be assigned (see *14.4.3.1* and *14.5*). Equally, where A has some particular attribute in the eyes of the third party A may not contract on behalf of P. For example, in *Greer* v *Downs Supply Co.* [1927] 2 KB 28

> the third party contracted with A in order to obtain a set-off to which he was entitled on account of a debt owed to him by A. It was held that A could not in those circumstances make the contract on behalf of an undisclosed principal.

It may also be the case that personal qualities of P make it impossible for there to be a contract on his behalf where he is undisclosed at the time of contracting. The normal rule is that the fact that the third party is unwilling to contract with P does not prevent a contract coming into existence between them by virtue of the undisclosed principal doctrine of agency (*Dyster* v *Randall & Sons* [1926] Ch 932). If, however, A misrepresents the identity or existence of P, the third party will be able to resist any action on the contract by P (*Archer* v *Stone* (1898) 78 LT 34). Difficulty is caused by the case of *Said* v *Butt* [1920] 3 KB 497, in which P was found unable to sue on the contract despite the fact that A had made no representation as to his identity. In principle the case appears inconsistent with *Dyster* v *Randall & Sons*, but it is understandable why on the particular facts the case should have been decided as it was.

> P had attempted twice to enter the exact same contract with the third party, and had been refused, and so resorted to the subterfuge of an agent. In the circumstances (the sale of theatre tickets) it was impossible for the third party to ask every purchaser if they were acting for P.

Such a question is usually the only means of provoking the necessary misrepresentation. It does not seem on these facts that any injustice was done to P.

15.3.2.2 Legal effect The general rule is that while P remains undisclosed A can sue and be sued on the contract with the third party. A's right to sue is lost as soon as P intervenes (*Atkinson* v *Cotesworth* (1825) 3 B & C 647). The more important question concerns the effect of P's intervention on the third party's right to sue A.

The third party must elect whether to seek to make either A or P liable, and that election is binding on him so that once it has been made he cannot go back on it (*Scarf* v *Jardine* (1882) 7 App Cas 345). Election depends upon an act which unequivocally indicates that the third party is committed to the choice made. In *Priestly* v *Fernie* (1865) 3 H & C 977 (see *15.3.1.1*)

> the master of a ship signed a bill of lading, thus making himself personally liable. Goods covered by the bill of lading were both damaged and lost in transit. The plaintiff consignee of the goods obtained judgment against the master both in Australia and in the English High Court, but the judgment was not satisfied because of the master's bankruptcy. The plaintiff then sought to bring proceedings against the owners of the vessel.

The plaintiff was found to have chosen to make the master liable, and to be unable to go back on that decision. The courts may in some circumstances be reluctant to find that anything short of actually obtaining judgment amounts to an election and have, for example, found that the issue of a writ to commence proceedings against P did not prevent the third party abandoning those proceedings in order to seek payment from A (*Clarkson, Booker Ltd* v *Andjel* [1964] 2 QB 775). The facts of this case were, however, regarded by the court as exceptional, and the court indicated that in normal circumstances an election will occur when proceedings are commenced by issue of a writ against one or other potential defendant. In *Chestertons* v *Barone* (1987) 282 EG 87 the Court of Appeal suggested that in the case of an undisclosed principal, election requires evidence that the third party has abandoned any possible claim against the agent. The court then suggested that it would be difficult to imagine circumstances in which an election had been made without proceedings having been started, but that that would normally be the 'clearest evidence of an election'.

As in the case of assignment (see *14.4.1*), P is only able to take the benefit of A's contract with the third party to the extent that it may be encumbered with defences available against A. In particular, any set-off available to the third party against A will continue to operate against P (*Cooke v Eshelby* (1887) 12 App Cas 271). In that case the set-off against A was held not to prevail against P because the third party knew that A sometimes contracted on his own account and sometimes on the account of others, without disclosing which on any particular occasion. If the third party wished to rely on the set-off he should have enquired whether A was contracting on his own account for the contract in question. It must be doubted whether this sensible rule can really be said to rest on estoppel (as was suggested in *Cooke & Sons v Eshelby*), since until P is disclosed he cannot have made any representation.

Where the third party pays A before the existence of P is disclosed that payment is sufficient to discharge the third party's liability (*Coates v Lewes* (1808) 1 Camp 444). It would seem that where P pays A before P's existence is disclosed to the third party it would not be right for P's liability to be discharged by such payment, but such authority as exists is to the contrary (*Armstrong v Stokes* (1872) LR 7 QB 598). Although that decision has not yet been overruled, its validity has been doubted (*Irvine & Co. v Watson & Sons* (1880) 5 QBD 414). It is true that if A fails to pay the third party in this situation then hardship will result either for P or for the third party, but in those circumstances P should perhaps suffer the loss since he appears better placed to have avoided it.

15.3.3 Principal's liability for misrepresentation by the agent

In the law of tort generally, an employer is vicariously liable for torts committed by his employees in the course of their employment, but is not liable for torts committed by independent contractors who are doing work for him. It has already been noted that the distinction between employee and independent contractor is irrelevant in the law of agency (*15.1*): both may be constituted as agents. The question then arises in what circumstances the principal may be liable for misrepresentations made by an agent, for, as we have already seen, liability for misrepresentation is in most circumstances tortious (*9.4.2.4*). The merger of these different principles achieved by the law is to say that P is liable for misrepresentations made by A whether A is an employee or an independent contractor, provided the representations made were within A's actual or ostensible authority (*Uxbridge Permanent Benefit Building Society v Pickard* [1939] 2 KB 248). Moreover, it seems that the courts will regard an employee's course of employment as defined, for the purposes of those circumstances where he acts as agent, by the limits of his ostensible authority (*Armagas Ltd v Mundogas SA* [1985] 3 All ER 795; affirmed [1986] 2 All ER 385). This principle appears to be correct, since if the representation were not within A's ostensible authority there would be no ground on which the third party could claim reasonably to have relied on P, so that any reliance there was must have been restricted to A.

The above rule applies whether or not P knows of the falsity of the representation made on his behalf by A. It is not possible, however, to make a fraudulent representation out of a representation by A which, unknown to

A but within P's knowledge, is false if P did not authorise A to make the representation. In *Armstrong* v *Strain* [1952] 1 KB 232

> A represented that a house would be regarded as a safe investment by any building society, while P, who had not authorised A to make such statements, knew this not to be the case because of serious structural problems in the house.

The third party's action for fraud failed. It must be assumed that the representations were not within A's ostensible authority, but even then it may be questioned whether today A's representation would not have been regarded as negligent since A may well have had no ground to believe the statement made. The third party would then at least have been able to succeed against A in tort (see *9.3.2.1*).

15.3.4 Agent's unauthorised transfer of property
The purpose of a contract of sale of goods is the transfer of title in the goods between the seller and the buyer (see *4.5.1*). Many contracts of sale of goods are made by agents, and the question arises whether the agent may transfer the title to goods on behalf of his principal. The general rule is that where A has P's authority he can transfer title in goods on P's behalf, and that rule is enshrined in s.21(1) of the Sale of Goods Act 1979 (SoGA 1979). That section is usually said to incorporate the maxim *nemo dat quod non habet* ('no person may give that which they do not have'). The rule is subject to certain exceptions, of which the most important are stated here.

Where goods are sold by someone without the authority or consent of the owner title will not pass '. . . unless the owner of the goods is by his conduct precluded from denying the seller's authority to sell' (s.21(1) SoGA 1979). Where goods are sold by a 'mercantile agent' who had possession of the goods with the consent of the true owner, and who sold them in the ordinary course of his business as such an agent, then good title will also pass (s.2(1) Factors Act 1889). A mercantile agent is someone who has 'in the customary course of his business . . . authority . . . to sell goods . . .' (s.1(1) Factors Act 1889). Finally, where the goods are sold in 'market overt' good title will pass (s.22(1) SoGA 1979). The detailed operation of these rules, and other exceptions to the *nemo dat* principle, must be left to specialist works on the sale of goods (cf. P.S. Atiyah, *The Sale of Goods*, 8th ed., Pitman, 1990, Chapter 19).

15.4   RELATIONSHIP BETWEEN PRINCIPAL AND AGENT

15.4.1   Agent's obligations to the principal
The agent's obligations to his principal may derive from contract, or may be imposed by law in the form of tortious or fiduciary liability. The imposition of duties independently of contract is inevitable since in some circumstances there may be no contract between an admitted agent and his principal.

15.4.1.1   Duty to obey instructions   Where A has been authorised to act by means of a contract with P, and the contract sets out instructions which

A is to follow, A is under a contractual duty to follow those instructions and will be liable for breach of contract if he fails to do so. Failure to do that which was undertaken is clearly a breach of the duty to obey instructions, but it is equally a breach of that duty to act in excess of the authority given (cf. *Fray* v *Voules* (1859) 1 E & E 839). Where there is no contract between A and P there can be no duty to obey instructions as such, but there may still be a tortious duty to exercise due care and skill.

15.4.1.2 Duty to exercise due care and skill The duty to exercise due care and skill may arise out of a contract between A and P (cf. *10.6.3.2*), or may be imposed independently as tortious liability. In either case, the actual standard of care or skill demanded in the particular circumstances will be for the court to decide. It is sometimes said that the standard of care is greater in the case of agency made under contract than under a gratuitous agency where liability is based in tort. That statement is, however, potentially misleading. For example, it seems certain that the same standard of care and skill will be expected of a solicitor whether he is acting for remuneration or not, provided P knows A is a solicitor (see Stuart-Smith LJ in *Chaudhry* v *Prabhakar* [1988] 3 All ER 718, 721). Where the existence of a contract may make a difference, however, is that in some circumstances A promises by virtue of the contract that he possesses some special skill not possessed by everybody, and that he undertakes to exercise it on P's behalf. The contract may then result in the higher standard of care expected of a skilled person being expected of A, rather than the lower standard expected of an unskilled member of the general public (cf. *Esso Petroleum Co. Ltd* v *Mardon* [1976] 2 All ER 5: *10.1.2.2*). The same may result from a representation by an unpaid agent about the degree of skill he possesses (*Chaudhry* v *Prabhakar*). In *Chaudhry* v *Prabhakar* the Court of Appeal recognised that where the gratuitous agency arises between friends there may be no legal duty owed at all, and the relationship may give rise only to social obligations. May LJ in particular took the view that, in the light of the recent restrictive attitude to the existence of tortious duties of care, the defendant may have been unwise to concede that such a duty existed in the circumstances of this case (advice to a friend about the purchase of a second-hand car).

The remaining duties of A to P are 'fiduciary' duties, which is to say that they are duties originally developed by the Court of Chancery to protect a person, who has put his confidence in another, from abuse of that confidence. It is generally accepted that these duties impose high standards of conduct.

15.4.1.3 Duty to act personally The agent may not delegate his authority to act on behalf of P unless expressly or impliedly authorised so to do (*De Bussche* v *Alt* (1878) 8 ChD 286). The power to delegate may be implied if P knows at the time of creation of the agency that A intends to delegate and does not object (*Quebec & Richmond Railroad Co.* v *Quinn* (1858) 12 Moo PC 232). It may also be implied where it is the trade usage to allow such delegation. The courts will also allow delegation where the acts delegated are 'purely ministerial' and do not involve the confidence and discretion which

:ween P and A (*Allam & Co. Ltd* v *Europa Poster Services Ltd* [1968] ꞁ ʌıı ᴇʀ 826).

Where there is an authorised delegation there will not necessarily be a contractual relationship of privity between P and the sub-agent. In *Calico Printers' Association Ltd* v *Barclays Bank* (1931) 145 LT 51 Wright J said that in such circumstances P remained entitled to hold A liable for any failure of duty, and could not claim against the sub-agent. Privity would only be established between P and the sub-agent if it could be demonstrated that P authorised A to create a contract between the sub-agent and P. It must be questioned whether the statement that P cannot claim against the sub-agent applies equally in the case of a claim in tort. *Calico Printers' Association Ltd* v *Barclays Bank* was decided before the decision in *Donoghue* v *Stevenson* [1932] AC 562 (see *13.1*), which caused a great expansion of the duty of care in the tort of negligence; but courts today are reluctant to impose tortious duties into relationships which are, or potentially could be, governed by contracts (*13.4*).

15.4.1.4 Duty to act in good faith The characteristic duty of all fiduciary relationships is the duty to act in good faith, which may be subdivided into a duty to avoid any conflict of interest with P, and a duty not to make secret profits, including bribes, from the position of agent. There is inevitable overlap between these duties and the general rule against undue influence (see *8.6*).

The classic cases of conflict of interest are where A acts in his own right as principal as the other contracting party with P, as where A buys for himself goods he has been instructed to sell for P, or where A sells his own goods when he has been instructed to buy on behalf of P. The conflict of interest lies between A's duty to get the best possible deal for P and A's own interest in making a profit for himself. For example, in *De Bussche* v *Alt* (1878) 8 ChD 286

> the defendant was instructed to sell a ship for a minimum price of $90,000. Unable to find a buyer, the defendant finally bought it himself at the minimum price. Shortly afterwards he was able to sell it for $160,000. The defendant was forced by P to account for the profit made on this deal.

In addition, or as an alternative to recovering profits made by A, P may rescind the agency relationship. In *Logicrose Ltd* v *Southend United Football Club Ltd* [1988] 1 WLR 1256 Millett J ruled that recovery of the profit made did not imply affirmation of the contract by the principal, so as to bar him from rescinding the contract. He also ruled that the *restitutio in integrum* required as an ingredient of rescission does not include restitution of the illegal profit. It should be noted that P's remedy does not depend upon proof of any intentional wrongdoing by A; it is sufficient that there is the appearance of a potential conflict of interest. For example, in *Boardman* v *Phipps* [1967] 2 AC 46

> agents acting for trustees in relation to the shares in a company acquired extra shares in the company on their own account. It seems probable that the trustee principals

in this case suffered no loss, and may have benefited, from A's actions, but A was still obliged to account for profits made from the transaction.

It should also be noted that this duty may extend beyond the period of agency itself, if in all the circumstances A has acquired a standing in relation to P which itself endures (*Allinson* v *Clayhills* (1907) 97 LT 709).

A conflict of interest may arise where an agent has undertaken to act for more than one principal, although in such cases whether there is a conflict can only be determined by careful examination of the facts. So, in *Sears Investment Trust Ltd* v *The Lewis's Group Ltd, The Times,* 22 September 1992, an agent was not in breach of the duty of loyalty to his principal when the agency relationship had been terminated by agreement between them, and P had actively encouraged A to take instructions from the second principal in the affair. Harman J said that there could be no duty towards two principals without the clear agreement and knowledge of both. In *Kelly* v *Cooper* [1992] 3 WLR 936, in the particular context of estate agency where it is a matter of common knowledge that agents act concurrently for more than one principal, the Privy Council advised that a term should be implied into individual agency contracts permitting A to act for more than one P concurrently, and permitting A to withhold from P confidential information obtained through dealings with another principal.

A bribe is a commission paid to A without the knowledge of P. It is not necessary to show that A was influenced by it. For example, in *Boston Deep Sea Fishing & Ice Co.* v *Ansell* (1888) 39 ChD 339

a company director accepted bonuses from two other companies of which he was also a director paid on the strength of orders placed with those other companies by the first company. He was held liable to account for the bonuses.

The duty not to make secret profits extends further than the acceptance of bribes. It includes a prohibition on A's use of confidential information gained as a result of the relationship with P to make personal profit. For example, the acquisition of the shares in *Boardman* v *Phipps* was a secret profit made by exploiting information gained from the relationship of confidence. In either case, P's remedy is either to force A to account for the profit made, or to oblige A to pay damages for any loss sustained (*Mahesan* v *Malaysia Government Officers' Co-operative Housing Society Ltd* [1979] AC 374). In that case the argument that these remedies should be available cumulatively was rejected.

15.4.1.5 The duty to account It is essential to the idea of agency that where A receives money on behalf of P he must keep it separate from his own, and that A is in effect a trustee of P's money (*Foley* v *Hill* (1848) 2 HLC 28). A must keep proper accounts, which he may be required to produce for P's examination. Where A mixes P's money with his own in a single fund, P may be entitled to a tracing remedy to recover his property, provided it is still identifiable in the mixed fund (*Re Hallett's Estate* (1880) 13 ChD 696).

15.4.2 Agent's rights against the principal

15.4.2.1 Remuneration Where there is a contract providing for A to act on behalf of P, A is entitled to remuneration for the services he provides. Where A is a professional agent who usually provides his services for payment the courts will be willing to assume the existence of a contract even if concrete evidence is lacking (cf. the past consideration rule as applied to professionals: *6.3.3.2*).

In the case of an employee who, in the course of his employment, acts from time to time as agent for his employer, it may well be that remuneration is constituted by the salary he receives. His contract of employment may provide for additional payments of commission, but his entitlement to the salary will not depend upon the actual negotiation of any particular number of transactions on his employer's behalf. As far as any commission is concerned, however, an employee is in the same position as that usually occupied by an independent contractor who acts as agent; that is, the entitlement to remuneration depends upon the achievement of the tasks for which remuneration was promised. In technical terms, A's right to payment is subject to a promissory condition precedent (see *10.3.2.1*). A good example of this type of condition is provided by an estate agent's right to payment for negotiating the sale of a house. The usual situation is that the estate agent is not entitled to payment until there has been a completed sale. A claim to be entitled to commission where there has been no completed sale will only be allowed if the contract between the estate agent and the vendor provides for it in very clear language (*Luxor (Eastbourne) Ltd* v *Cooper* [1941] AC 108).

The entitlement to remuneration also depends upon A's performance being the cause of the transaction entered into by P (for a case with slightly unusual facts demonstrating this principle, see: *Bentleys Estate Agents Ltd* v *Granix Ltd* [1989] 27 EG 93). For example, in *Millar* v *Radford* (1903) 19 TLR 575

> A was instructed to find a purchaser or a tenant for P's property. A found a tenant, and was paid a commission. One year later the tenant purchased the property, and A claimed to be entitled to further commission on the sale. His claim was rejected because the second transaction did not result from A's efforts on behalf of P.

A vexed question in relation to A's right to remuneration is whether P is free to interfere with A's right to earn the commission. In the case of estate agents' contracts it seems that P is under no duty to refrain from preventing A earning his commission. In *Luxor (Eastbourne) Ltd* v *Cooper*

> P employed A, an estate agent, to find a purchaser for P's cinemas. A's fee was to be £10,000, payable if A introduced a purchaser who paid not less than £185,000 for the property. A introduced a purchaser who offered the stipulated amount 'subject to contract', but P withdrew from the sale. A claimed nevertheless to be entitled to the fee.

The House of Lords refused to imply a term into estate agents' contracts preventing vendors from depriving agents of the opportunity to earn their commission, so that A's action failed. It was once thought that this rule was of more general application, and it was said that P was not obliged to stay in business simply to allow A the opportunity to earn his commission (*Rhodes v Forwood* (1876) 1 App Cas 256). Nevertheless, that case has since been distinguished (*Turner v Goldsmith* [1891] 1 QB 544), and it seems that today the courts may be more willing to imply a term in general contracts of agency protecting A's right to earn the commission at least against P's breach of any contract upon which A's earning capacity rests (cf. *Alpha Trading Ltd v Dunnshaw-Patten* [1981] QB 290). The position would be quite different where the breach preventing A from earning the commission is committed by the third party (e.g. *Marcan Shipping (London) Ltd v Polish SS Co., The 'Manifest Lipkowy'* [1989] 2 Lloyd's Rep 138). It is most unlikely that a court should be willing to imply a term into the contract between P and A intended to prevent breach by the third party. In the final analysis, of course, such cases depend upon the particular facts as found by the court, but Bingham LJ (as he then was) made clear in *The 'Manifest Lipkowy'* that the usual tests for implication of a term as a matter of fact (ie, business efficacy and officious bystander: see generally *10.4*) would apply.

These principles have given rise to considerable litigation in the field of agents acting for vendors of real property. What the cases reveal, above all else, is that much turns upon the individual facts, and especially the precise words of the agency contract. In the absence of clear and precise wording, the courts appear to be reluctant to make vendor principals liable to estate agents unless the agent was the cause of a completed contract of sale.

15.4.2.2 Indemnity The agent is entitled to be indemnified by P for all liabilities reasonably incurred in A's performance of his duties on behalf of P (*Thacker v Hardy* (1878) 4 QBD 685). Expenses recoverable include any tortious liability incurred by A in performing P's explicit instructions (e.g. sale authorised by P of property belonging to a third party: *Adamson v Jarvis* (1827) 4 Bing 66). A is not entitled to an indemnity for liabilities incurred in the course of unauthorised acts (*Barron v Fitzgerald* (1840) 6 Bing NC 201). Nor is he entitled to an indemnity for liabilities which are incurred as a result of his own fault (*Lewis v Samuel* (1846) 8 QB 685), or which are illegal (*Re Parker* (1882) 21 ChD 408).

15.4.2.3 Lien An agent is entitled to a lien over P's property which is lawfully in his possession to secure debts arising out of the agency relationship. The lien does not entitle him to dispose of the goods in order to realise their value in satisfaction of the debt: it merely entitles him to keep the goods until payment is made (*West of England Bank v Batchelor* (1882) 51 LJ Ch 199). Since a lien is a possessory title only it is lost when the goods lawfully pass out of A's possession. The parties may contract to prevent the acquisition of such a lien (*Rolls Razor Ltd v Cox* [1967] 1 QB 552).

Unless the parties so contract, or there is a particular custom of the trade (as, for example, in the case of solicitors and bankers), the lien only operates in respect of debts arising out of the particular agency relationship, and does not cover other general debts owed by P to A.

15.5 RELATIONSHIP BETWEEN AGENT AND THIRD PARTY

In the usual circumstances of an agency created in order to effect a contract between P and the third party, once that contract comes into existence A drops out of the relationship, and need have no further dealings with the third party. In some circumstances, however, A may have incurred personal liabilities towards and rights from the third party.

15.5.1 Personal liability of agent

15.5.1.1 Undisclosed principal We have already seen (*15.3.2.2*) that if A contracts on behalf of an undisclosed principal, A is personally liable on the contract. Indeed, until the time P is disclosed, in the eyes of the third party A is the only person liable on the contract. At the point when P is disclosed the third party may elect whether to proceed against A or against P, so that A's personal liability may continue after P's existence becomes known.

15.5.1.2 Agent contracting in a personal capacity In a number of situations the agent will be held to have contracted in a personal capacity, and so will be liable on the contract made with the third party. The most obvious example of this rule is where it is the intention of all the parties that A should be a party to the contract in addition to P, and the contract therefore expressly so provides. Contracts of this kind only present difficulty where there is a question of construction of a written document as to whether this effect was in fact intended (see *15.5.1.3*, below).

A may also be held to have contracted in a personal capacity if he contracts on behalf of a non-existent principal. We have already seen that an agent's contracts cannot be ratified by a principal who did not exist at the time the contracts were made (*Kelner* v *Baxter* (1866) LR 2 CP 174: *15.2.5.1*). In the same case it was held that since the company had not been formed and so could not ratify the contracts purportedly made on its behalf, the promoters who had made the contracts were personally liable. Except in the case of companies (see s.36C Companies Act 1985), this personal liability of A who contracts for a non-existent P is not automatic, but depends upon the construction of the particular contract. In the absence of an intention that A be personally liable, A may still be liable for breach of warranty of authority (*15.5.1.5*).

Finally, A may be held to have contracted in a personal capacity if he contracts for an unnamed principal (see further *15.5.2*). The usual rule in this situation is that where A contracts *as agent* he does not make himself personally liable, but that rule may be varied as a matter of construction (*Hitchens, Harrison, Woolston & Co.* v *Jackson & Sons* [1943] AC 266).

15.5.1.3 Contracts in writing There may be an irresistible inference that A contracted to incur personal liability if he signed a written contract without qualifying that signature by words showing that he signed only on behalf of P, especially where there is no other reference to P in the contractual document (*Parker* v *Winlow* (1857) 7 E & B 942). The problem is that the word 'agent' on its own may be either a qualification or merely a description (*The Swan* [1968] 1 Lloyd's Rep 5 at 13). To avoid being held personally liable after signing a written contract A must show not only that he is employed as agent, but that he signed only in that capacity (*Universal Steam Navigation Co. Ltd* v *J. McKelvie & Co.* [1923] AC 492). In that case, after A's signature appeared the words 'as agents', and it is now generally accepted that that form will avoid personal liability on the part of A.

It is much more difficult for A to avoid personal liability after signing the contract without qualification if the only evidence to suggest his restricted status as agent is not intrinsic to the document. Such evidence will normally be excluded by the parol evidence rule (see *10.1.3*).

15.5.1.4 Other liability Where A puts his name to a contract made by deed he will be personally liable on it even when he has used qualifying words saying that he signed only as a representative (*Appleton* v *Binks* (1804) 5 East 148). This rule does not apply where A has been appointed under a power of attorney (s.7(1) Powers of Attorney Act 1971).

Where A puts his name to a negotiable instrument, to avoid being held liable on it he must indicate clearly that he is only acting on behalf of his principal (s.26(1) Bills of Exchange Act 1882). The generally accepted forms are 'for and on behalf of' and 'per pro'.

There was once a strong presumption that when A contracted on behalf of a foreign principal he incurred personal liability on the contract. That presumption appears no longer to be made (cf. *Teheran-Europe Co. Ltd* v *S.T. Belton (Tractors) Ltd* [1968] 2 All ER 886).

We have already seen that P is liable for false statements (amounting to torts) made within A's actual or ostensible authority (*15.3.3*). The question then arises whether A may be personally liable for such statements. Given the restrictive view of negligent misstatement now adopted by the House of Lords (in *Caparo Industries plc* v *Dickman* [1990] 1 All ER 568: see *9.3.2.1*), the assumption must be that such personal liability on A's part will not be lightly imposed. This conclusion is confirmed by Nicholls V-C in *Gran Gelato Ltd* v *Richcliff (Group) Ltd* [1992] 1 All ER 865 at 873), who says that good reason must be demonstrated before a duty may be imposed on A towards the third party directly, when P is already liable to that third party for failure on A's part. He went on to say that he did not believe P's insolvency, which might deny the third party a remedy, was a 'good reason' in this sense.

It should be noted that although the Property Misdescriptions Act 1991 imposes criminal liability on estate agents who make false or misleading statements in the course of their business, by s.1(4) no civil consequences flow from such criminal liability; the previous civil test of liability for such statements must still be satisfied.

15.5.1.5 Agent's unauthorised acts Where A lacked authority to make the contract with the third party on behalf of P which he purported to make then, unless the contract has subsequently been ratified by P, A will incur a personal liability to the third party on any one of three grounds. If A knew that he lacked authority he will be liable for deceit (*Polhill* v *Walter* (1832) 3 B & Ad 114). Alternatively, if A failed to act with due care in stating that he had authority to make the contract when in fact he had none, then he may be liable for negligent misstatement (see *9.3.2.1*).

The third party's most likely action against A who contracted without authority, however, is an action for breach of warranty of authority. It is said that there is a collateral contract between A and the third party in which A warrants that P exists and that A has authority from P to make the main contract in question. In *Collen* v *Wright* (1857) 8 E & B 647

> the defendant, in his capacity as land agent for one Gardner, had leased land belonging to Gardner to the plaintiff for a period of 12 years. Gardner was able to prove that the defendant lacked authority to grant such a long lease, so that the plaintiff's action against Gardner failed. The plaintiff then brought this action against the agent.

The defendant was found liable for breach of a collateral warranty of his authority. Consideration for this warranty lay in the third party entering the main contract. The advantage of the action for breach of warranty of authority is that it does not depend upon A's state of mind: A is liable even if he was entirely innocent in representing that he had P's authority (*Collen* v *Wright*).

15.5.2 Rights of the agent
It is axiomatic that if A has incurred personal liability on the main contract with the third party he will also acquire contractual rights against the third party. Where, therefore, in the circumstances outlined above A incurred a personal liability, he would also have acquired rights.

More difficult is the question whether A may purport to contract as agent, only later to reveal that he is in fact also principal. It is generally accepted that if A contracts on behalf of an unnamed principal he may acquire the contractual rights against the third party by revealing himself as principal, since if the third party was willing to contract without knowing who the principal was, it is highly unlikely that he should object to a contract with A (*Schmaltz* v *Avery* (1851) 16 QB 655). Even greater difficulty is presented when A claims to be entitled to take over a contract purportedly made on behalf of a named principal. If, after being informed that A contracted as principal, the third party affirms the contract A may then enforce it in his own name (*Rayner* v *Grote* (1846) 15 M & W 359). It will always be possible, however, for the third party to assert that the identity of the particular named principal was part of what induced him to make the contract, and on that ground to resist A's attempts to take over the contract rights. For example, in *The Remco* [1984] 2 Lloyd's Rep 205

> the plaintiff had represented that he was agent in chartering a ship from the defendants

on behalf of a named principal. He later sought to enforce the contract in his own name. The defendants were able to show that it was a matter of concern to them to know who was liable to make payment under the contract, and to show that they would not have entered a contract on these exact same terms had they known that the plaintiff was principal. For these reasons, the plaintiff's action failed.

15.6 TERMINATION OF THE RELATIONSHIPS OF AGENCY

Agency may be terminated by the voluntary act of one or both parties or by operation of law. In some circumstances agency may be irrevocable. The effect of termination is to bring A's actual authority to an immediate end. But P may nevertheless be bound by contracts made by A on his behalf after the moment of termination by virtue of an ostensible authority vested in A (*Trueman* v *Loder* (1840) 11 Ad & El 589). Rights to commission or to indemnity which vested in A before the time of termination remain recoverable, but no new rights may be created.

15.6.1 Voluntary termination
Where the agency was created by contract between P and A it may be terminated by agreement between them, just as any other contract may be rescinded by a fresh contract between the parties. More significantly, agency may be terminated unilaterally by P on giving notice, although in the case of agency created by contract P may be required to give a reasonable period of notice (*Martin-Baker Aircraft Co. Ltd* v *Canadian Flight Equipment Ltd* [1955] 2 QB 556). Nevertheless, it seems that although a revocation of authority may be a breach of contract entitling A to damages, the revocation will be effective since A's authority is not created by the contract but depends upon P's power to confer it (see *15.1*). P's power to terminate by notice may be affected by an implied term preventing P from interfering with A's ability to earn commission under the contract of agency (see *15.4.2.1*).

15.6.2 Termination by law

15.6.2.1 Death Since agency is regarded as a personal contract it is terminated automatically by the death of either party, even in the case where the other party has no knowledge of the death (*Campanari* v *Woodburn* (1854) 15 CB 400).

15.6.2.2 Insanity Insanity of either P or A results in the automatic termination of the agency (but see the Enduring Powers of Attorney Act 1985). It may still be possible for A to bind an insane principal by virtue of an ostensible authority (*Drew* v *Nunn* (1879) 4 QBD 661). It has been held in such a case that the agent was personally liable, but the case should probably be regarded as decided upon the special fact that A should have known of P's incapacity but did not, and so was effectively in breach of a warranty of authority (*Yonge* v *Toynbee* [1910] 1 KB 215).

15.6.2.3 Bankruptcy Bankruptcy of P imposes a legal incapacity, and so would automatically terminate the agency. Bankruptcy of A would not necessarily terminate the agency, but it would be likely to since it would probably make A unfit to perform his duties. Bankruptcy is a complex matter, requiring separate treatment beyond the scope of this book.

15.6.2.4 Frustration Where there is a contract of agency it is subject to the usual rules of frustration (see *11.4*).

15.6.3 Irrevocable agency

15.6.3.1 Authority coupled with an interest Agency is irrevocable if the authority granted to A is given for the purpose of protecting some interest of A's. For example, in *Gaussen* v *Morton* (1830) 10 B & C 731

> P owed A a large sum of money, and made A his agent by means of a power of attorney to sell certain land and to take the money owed to him out of the proceeds of sale. The agency was held to be irrevocable without A's agreement.

This rule only applies if the agency was specifically created to protect A's interest, and will not apply if A merely seeks incidentally to protect some interest of his own without that being P's intention (*Smart* v *Sandars* (1848) 5 CB 895).

15.6.3.2 Irrevocable power of attorney Where a power of attorney is expressed to be irrevocable and is given to secure some interest of the donee of the power (i.e. the agent), s.4 of the Powers of Attorney Act 1971 makes the power irrevocable for as long as the interest requires protection.

15.6.3.3 Agent already personally liable It is sometimes said that where, by performance on behalf of P, A has incurred a personal liability which was foreseeable at the time A's authority was created, the agency cannot be revoked without A's consent (*Read* v *Anderson* (1884) 13 QBD 779). This rule is clearly desirable, but is really only another way of stating the rule noted at the start of this section to the effect that termination of agency does not affect rights (such as the right to indemnity: *15.4.2.2*) which have accrued before termination.

Index